Instructors:
Your time is valuable. We're here for you!

SAGE COURSEPACKS: OUR CONTENT TAILORED TO YOUR LMS

We make it easy to import our quality instructor and student content into *your* school's learning management system (LMS).

- **NO NEW SYSTEM** to learn
- **INTUITIVE AND SIMPLE** to use
- Allows you to **CUSTOMIZE COURSE CONTENT** to meet your students' needs
- A variety of high-quality assessment questions and multimedia **ASSIGNMENTS TO SELECT FROM**
- **NO REQUIRED ACCESS CODES**

CONTACT YOUR SAGE SALES REPRESENTATIVE TO LEARN MORE:
sagepub.com/findmyrep

$SAGE coursepacks

For use in: Blackboard, Canvas, Brightspace by Desire2Learn (D2L), and Moodle

SAGE vantage

Course tools done right. Built to support your teaching. Designed to ignite learning.

SAGE vantage is an intuitive digital platform that blends trusted SAGE content with auto-graded assignments, all carefully designed to ignite student engagement and drive critical thinking. With evidence-based instructional design at the core, **SAGE vantage** creates more time for engaged learning and empowered teaching, keeping the classroom where it belongs—in your hands.

- **3-STEP COURSE SETUP** is so fast, you can complete it in minutes!
- Control over assignments, content selection, due dates, and grading **EMPOWERS** you to **TEACH YOUR WAY**.
- Dynamic content featuring applied-learning multimedia tools with built-in assessments, including video, knowledge checks, and chapter tests, helps **BUILD STUDENT CONFIDENCE**.
- eReading experience makes it easy to learn by presenting content in **EASY-TO-DIGEST** segments featuring note-taking, highlighting, definition look-up, and more.
- Quality content authored by the **EXPERTS YOU TRUST**.

SAGE Outcomes: Measure Results, Track Success

FOR STUDENTS, understanding the objectives for each chapter and the goals for the course is essential for getting the grade you deserve!

FOR INSTRUCTORS, being able to track your students' progress allows you to more easily pinpoint areas of improvement and report on success.

This title was crafted around specific chapter objectives and course outcomes, vetted by experts, and adapted from renowned syllabi. Tracking student progress can be challenging. Promoting and achieving success should never be. We are here for you.

COURSE OUTCOMES FOR INTRODUCTION TO CRIMINAL JUSTICE:

ARTICULATE the foundations of criminal justice, including definitions, theories, typologies, measurement issues, and the law.

EXAMINE the development of policing organizations and strategies and the challenges faced by the police.

EXPLAIN the structure and processes of the judiciary at the local, state, and federal levels.

EXPLAIN the goals, methods, and effectiveness of various forms of corrections.

ANALYZE important criminal justice issues and their impact on society.

Want to see how these outcomes tie in with this book's chapter-level objectives?
Visit us at **edge.sagepub.com/peak4e** for complete outcome-to-objective mapping.

Sara Miller McCune founded SAGE Publishing in 1965 to support the dissemination of usable knowledge and educate a global community. SAGE publishes more than 1000 journals and over 600 new books each year, spanning a wide range of subject areas. Our growing selection of library products includes archives, data, case studies and video. SAGE remains majority owned by our founder and after her lifetime will become owned by a charitable trust that secures the company's continued independence.

Los Angeles | London | New Delhi | Singapore | Washington DC | Melbourne

Introduction to Criminal Justice

Fourth Edition

A district judge once said, "When we pull back the layers of government services, the most fundamental and indispensable virtues are public safety and social order." This fourth edition is dedicated to those industrious students of today seeking to ensure that those virtues are upheld later in their chosen profession.

—K. J. P.

To Joel D. Lieberman, a great friend and colleague who has given me opportunities to live an extraordinary life.

—T. D. H.

Introduction to Criminal Justice

Practice and Process

Fourth Edition

Kenneth J. Peak
University of Nevada, Reno

Tamara D. Madensen-Herold
University of Nevada, Las Vegas

Los Angeles | London | New Delhi
Singapore | Washington DC | Melbourne

FOR INFORMATION:

SAGE Publications, Inc.
2455 Teller Road
Thousand Oaks, California 91320
E-mail: order@sagepub.com

SAGE Publications Ltd.
1 Oliver's Yard
55 City Road
London EC1Y 1SP
United Kingdom

SAGE Publications India Pvt. Ltd.
B 1/I 1 Mohan Cooperative Industrial Area
Mathura Road, New Delhi 110 044
India

SAGE Publications Asia-Pacific Pte. Ltd.
18 Cross Street #10–10/11/12
China Square Central
Singapore 048423

Copyright © 2021 by SAGE Publications, Inc.

All rights reserved. Except as permitted by U.S. copyright law, no part of this work may be reproduced or distributed in any form or by any means, or stored in a database or retrieval system, without permission in writing from the publisher.

All third party trademarks referenced or depicted herein are included solely for the purpose of illustration and are the property of their respective owners. Reference to these trademarks in no way indicates any relationship with, or endorsement by, the trademark owner.

Printed in Canada

Library of Congress Cataloging-in-Publication Data

Names: Peak, Kenneth J., 1947- author. | Madensen-Herold, Tamara, author.

Title: Introduction to criminal justice : practice and process / Kenneth J. Peak, Tamara D. Madensen-Herold.

Description: Fourth Edition. | Thousand Oaks : SAGE Publishing, 2020. | Revised edition of Introduction to criminal justice, [2019] | Includes bibliographical references and index.

Identifiers: LCCN 2019028968 | ISBN 9781544372938 (paperback) | ISBN 9781544372952 (epub) | ISBN 9781544372976 (pdf)

Subjects: LCSH: Criminal justice, Administration of—United States. | Crime—United States. | Criminal law—United States.

Classification: LCC HV9950 .P4293 2020 | DDC 364.973—dc23
LC record available at https://lccn.loc.gov/2019028968

Acquisitions Editor: Jessica Miller
Content Development Editor: Laura Kearns
Editorial Assistant: Sarah Manheim
Marketing Manager: Jillian Ragusa
Production Editor: Veronica Stapleton Hooper
Copy Editor: Amy Marks
Typesetter: C&M Digitals (P) Ltd.
Proofreader: Dennis W. Webb
Indexer: Sheila Bodell
Cover Designer: Scott Van Atta

This book is printed on acid-free paper.

19 20 21 22 23 10 9 8 7 6 5 4 3 2 1

/// BRIEF CONTENTS

PREFACE	xxi
ACKNOWLEDGMENTS	xxvii
ABOUT THE AUTHORS	xxix

PART I: CRIMINAL JUSTICE AS A SYSTEM: THE BASICS — 1

Chapter 1: Fundamentals of Criminal Justice: Essential Themes and Practices — 2

Chapter 2: Foundations of Law and Crime: Nature, Elements, and Measurement — 24

Chapter 3: Theories of Criminality and Crime — 54

Chapter 4: Ethical Essentials: Doing Right When No One Is Watching — 76

PART II: THE POLICE — 101

Chapter 5: Police Organization: Structure and Functions — 102

Chapter 6: Police at Work: Patrolling and Investigating — 128

Chapter 7: Policing Methods and Challenges: Issues of Force, Liability, and Technologies — 156

Chapter 8: Expounding the Constitution: Laws of Arrest, Search, and Seizure — 180

PART III: THE COURTS — 205

Chapter 9: Court Organization: Structure, Functions, and the Trial Process — 206

Chapter 10: The Bench and the Bar: Those Who Judge, Prosecute, and Defend — 238

Chapter 11: Court Methods and Challenges: Sentencing and Punishment — 262

PART IV: CORRECTIONS — 293

Chapter 12: Prisons and Jails: Structure and Function — 294

Chapter 13: The Inmates' World: The "Keepers" and the "Kept" — 318

Chapter 14: Corrections in the Community: Probation, Parole, and Other Alternatives to Incarceration — 342

PART V: SPANNING THE SYSTEM: METHODS AND ISSUES — 371

Chapter 15: Juvenile Justice: Philosophy, Law, and Practices — 372

Chapter 16: On the Crime Policy and Prevention Agenda: Drug Abuse, Sex Trafficking, Terrorism, and Immigration — 394

APPENDIX: BILL OF RIGHTS	**417**
ASSESS YOUR AWARENESS ANSWERS	**419**
GLOSSARY	**421**
NOTES	**431**
INDEX	**465**

/// DETAILED CONTENTS

PREFACE	xxi
ACKNOWLEDGMENTS	xxvii
ABOUT THE AUTHORS	xxix

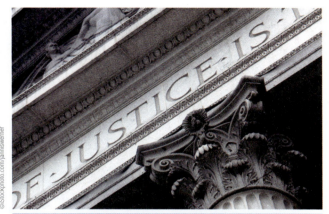

PART I: CRIMINAL JUSTICE AS A SYSTEM: THE BASICS

Chapter 1: Fundamentals of Criminal Justice: Essential Themes and Practices — 2

• Learning Objectives	3
• Assess Your Awareness	3
Introduction	4
Foundations of Criminal Justice: Legal and Historical Bases	4
The Criminal Law: How It Changes and How It Changes the System	5
The Consensus-Versus-Conflict Debate	6
Going Global: Marijuana Legalization Around the World	**9**
Crime Control and Due Process: Do Ends Justify Means?	10
You Be the . . . Legislator	**10**
Discretion: Making and Applying the Law	11
The Criminal Justice Process: An Overview of Flow and Functions	12
The Offender's Pathway Through the Process	14
Law Enforcement: Investigation/Arrest	14
Prosecution and Pretrial Activities	14
Practitioner's Perspective: Police Officer	**15**
Adjudication	16
Sentencing and Sanctions, Generally	17
Appellate Review	17
Corrections	18
The Juvenile Justice System	18
The Wedding Cake Model of Criminal Justice	18
Ethics Throughout the Criminal Justice System	20
You Be the . . . Judge	**21**
In a Nutshell	21
Key Terms & Concepts	22
Review Questions	22
Learn by Doing	22

Chapter 2: Foundations of Law and Crime: Nature, Elements, and Measurement — 24

• Learning Objectives	25
• Assess Your Awareness	25
Introduction	26
Common Law and Its Progeny	27
Modern-Day Sources and Hierarchy of Law	27
Federal Law	28
State Law	28
City/County Law	29
Criminal and Civil Law	29
Substantive and Procedural Law	31
Essential Elements: *Mens Rea* and *Actus Reus*	31
Mens Rea: *Intent Versus Motive to Commit Crime*	31
Investigating Further: Criminal and Civil Law— The O. J. Simpson Case	**32**
Actus Reus: *The Act*	33
Felonies and Misdemeanors	33
You Be the . . . Police Officer	**34**
Offense Definitions and Categories	34
Crimes Against Persons	34
Crimes Against Property	39
You Be the . . . Prosecutor	**39**
Public Order Crimes	40
White-Collar Crime	40
Organized Crime	42
Measuring Crime and Victimization	42
How Much Crime in the United States? Depends on Whom You Ask	42
The FBI's Uniform Crime Reports	43
Investigating Further: The Hierarchy Rule	**47**
The National Incident-Based Reporting System	47
The National Crime Victimization Survey	47
Going Global: Measuring Crime Victimization in England and Wales	**48**
Practitioner's Perspective: Criminal Justice Program Director, Former Law Enforcement Officer, and Drug Investigator	**49**

In a Nutshell 50
Key Terms & Concepts 50
Review Questions 51
Learn by Doing 51

Chapter 3: Theories of Criminality and Crime — 54

- Learning Objectives 55
- Assess Your Awareness 55

Introduction 56
   Criminology 56
Classical and Positivist Theories 56
   The Classical School 57
   Neoclassical Criminology 57
   Positivist Criminology 58
Biological, Trait, and Developmental Theories 58

Investigating Further: Ariel Castro—The Cleveland "Monster" 59

Social Structure Theories 60
   Social Disorganization Theory 61
   Strain Theory 61
Social Process Theories 62
   Learning Theory 62

You Be the . . . Crime Analyst 62

   Control Theory 63
   Labeling Theory 64

Practitioner's Perspective: Crime Analyst 65

Social Conflict Theories 65
Feminist Theories 66
Environmental Criminology Theories 69
   Routine Activity Theory 69
   Situational Crime Prevention 70

Going Global: International Environmental Criminologists 71

In Their Own Words: Offenders Speak . . . 71
   Armed Robbery 71
   Burglary 72

Investigating Further: Application of Crime Theories 72

You Be the . . . Criminologist 73
   Carjacking 73
In a Nutshell 74
Key Terms & Concepts 74
Review Questions 74
Learn by Doing 75

Chapter 4: Ethical Essentials: Doing Right When No One Is Watching — 76

- Learning Objectives 77
- Assess Your Awareness 77

Introduction 78
Good Examples of Bad Examples 78
Philosophical Foundations 79
   Types of Ethics 80
   Noble Cause Corruption 81
Ethics in Policing 81
   A Primer: The Oral Job Interview 81
   Police Corruption 82
   To Inform or Not to Inform: The Code of Silence 82
   The Law Enforcement Code of Ethics and Oath of Honor 83

Going Global: Mexico—Where an Entire Police Force May Be Corrupt 83

   Accepted and Deviant Lying 84

Investigating Further: Agency Policy Governing Police Conduct 85

   Accepting Gratuities 86

You Be the . . . Police Officer 87
   Greed and Temptation 87
   "Random Acts of Kindness": The Hidden Side of Police Work 87

Practitioner's Perspective: Police Internal Affairs Investigator 88

Investigating Further: A Hippocratic Oath for Police? 89

Ethics in the Courts 90
   Evolving Standards of Conduct 90
   The Judge 90
   Prosecutors 91

You Be the . . . Ethics Committee Member 92
   Defense Attorneys 92
   Other Court Employees 92
Ethical Conduct of Federal Employees . . . 93
   The Ethics Reform Act and the Whistleblower Protection Act 93
   The Federal Judiciary 93
Ethics in Corrections 94

You Be the . . . Correctional Officer 94

Ethics Tests for the Criminal Justice Student . . . 95
In a Nutshell 96
Key Terms & Concepts 97
Review Questions 97
Learn by Doing 98

PART II: THE POLICE

Chapter 5: Police Organization: Structure and Functions — 102
- Learning Objectives — 103
- Assess Your Awareness — 103

Introduction — 104
English and Colonial Roots: An Overview — 104
- *Sheriff* — 104
- *Constable* — 105
- *Coroner* — 105
- *Justice of the Peace* — 105

Practitioner's Perspective: Police Lieutenant — 106
- Police Reform in England, 1829 — 107

Policing Comes to the United States — 107
- *The Political Era, 1840s–1930s* — 107
- *The Reform Era, 1930s–1980s* — 107
- *The Community Era, 1980s–Present* — 109

Federal Law Enforcement — 110
- *Department of Homeland Security* — 110

Investigating Further: INTERPOL — 113
- *Department of Justice* — 113
- *Other Federal Agencies* — 116

State Agencies — 117
- *Patrol, Police, and Investigative Organizations* — 117

Going Global: Criminal Justice at Its Worst: Venezuela — 118
- *Other Special-Purpose State Agencies* — 119

Local Agencies: Municipal Police Departments and Sheriff's Offices — 119
- *Basic Operations* — 119
- *Organization* — 120

Interested in a Career? Some General Considerations — 122
- *A Comment on Immigration and Law Enforcement at All Levels* — 124

On Guard: The Private Police — 124
In a Nutshell — 126
Key Terms & Concepts — 126
Review Questions — 127
Learn by Doing — 127

Chapter 6: Police at Work: Patrolling and Investigating — 128
- Learning Objectives — 129
- Assess Your Awareness — 129

Introduction — 130
From Citizen to Patrol Officer — 130
- *Recruiting the Best* — 131
- *Does a College Degree Matter?* — 132
- *Recruit Training* — 133
- *Field Training Officer* — 134

Having the "Right Stuff": Defining the Role — 135
- *A Working Personality* — 135
- *Three Distinctive Styles of Policing* — 136
- *Four Basic Tasks* — 136
- *Perils of Patrol* — 137
- *A Study of Patrol Effectiveness* — 137

Stressors in Police Work — 138
- *Sources of Stress* — 138
- *Coping With Stress* — 139

Use of Discretion — 140
- *The Myth of Full Enforcement* — 140

Going Global: Saudi Arabia—Little to Do on Patrol — 140
- *Attempts to Define Discretion* — 141
- *Determinants of Discretionary Actions* — 141
- *Pros and Cons of Discretion* — 142

You Be the . . . Police Officer — 142

Community Policing and Problem Solving — 143
- *Evidence-Based Policing for Proactive Patrol* — 144

The Work of Forensics and Detectives — 145
- *Attributes of Detectives* — 146
- *Forensic Science and Criminalistics: Defining the Terms* — 146
- *Investigative Stages and Activities* — 147
- *A Word About Crime Scenes* — 148

Practitioner's Perspective: Crime Scene Investigator — 148

Uses of Informants and Interrogations	149
The Cyberthief Has Come: Be Prepared	149
Investigating Further: How "Cyber Detectives" Work	**150**
You Be the . . . Detective	**151**
A Major Challenge Today: People Getting Away With Murder	151
Using DNA Analysis	151
Investigating Further: A Cold Case Involving "The Boston Strangler"	**153**
In a Nutshell	153
Key Terms & Concepts	154
Review Questions	154
Learn by Doing	155

Chapter 7: Policing Methods and Challenges: Issues of Force, Liability, and Technologies — 156

• **Learning Objectives**	**157**
• **Assess Your Awareness**	**157**
Introduction	158
Use of Force: A Sacred Trust	158
From Harlem to Ferguson	159
Updates on Two Movements: Black Lives Matter and Blue Lives Matter	160
A Threshold Question: Police as "Guardians" or "Soldiers"?	161
Constitutional Policing and Legitimacy	161
Procedural Justice	162
You Be the . . . Police Officer	**163**
How to Develop Harmony, Justice, and Policy	163
Going Global: Police in India	**164**
Wielding a "Big Stick": Use of the Consent Decree	164
Another Item of Business: More Women and Minorities in Uniform	165
Police Brutality	165
Status of Police Body-Worn Cameras	166
When Failing the Public Trust: Civil Liability	166
A Process and a Personality	166
Torts and Negligence	168
Section 1983 Legislation	168
Practitioner's Perspective: Chief of Police	**169**
Potential Areas of Liability	170
You Be the . . . Judge	**171**

A Related Issue: How to Treat the Mentally Ill Population	172
Selected Technologies: Uses and Concerns	174
Facial Recognition	174
Preparing for a Future With Autonomous Vehicles	175
Addressing Texting While Driving	175
Handheld Drug-Testing Devices	176
In a Nutshell	176
Key Terms & Concepts	177
Review Questions	177
Learn by Doing	177

Chapter 8: Expounding the Constitution: Laws of Arrest, Search, and Seizure — 180

• **Learning Objectives**	**181**
• **Assess Your Awareness**	**181**
Introduction	182
Some Caveats	183
The Fourth Amendment	183
Probable Cause	183
The Exclusionary Rule	184
Investigating Further: Probable Cause	**184**
Arrests With and Without a Warrant	186
You Be the . . . Police Officer	**186**
Search and Seizure in General	187
Searches and Seizures With and Without a Warrant	188
Practitioner's Perspective: Special Agent	**191**
Investigating Further: NYPD—Stop and Frisk or Racial Profiling?	**193**
Going Global: Police Search and Seizure Around the World	**195**
Electronic Surveillance	197
The Fifth Amendment	197
Application	197
Decisions Eroding *Miranda*	199
You Be the . . . Judge	**199**
Lineups and Other Pretrial Identification Procedures	200
The Sixth Amendment	200
In a Nutshell	201
Key Terms & Concepts	202
Review Questions	202
Learn by Doing	202

PART III: THE COURTS

Chapter 9: Court Organization: Structure, Functions, and the Trial Process — 206
- Learning Objectives — 207
- Assess Your Awareness — 207

Introduction — 208
- Colonial Courts: An Overview — 208
- Our Adversarial System — 208
- The Influence of Courts in Policy Making — 209

Going Global: Adversarial Versus Inquisitorial Justice Systems — 209

Practitioner's Perspective: Attorney — 210

American Courts: A Dual Court System — 211

State Courts — 212
- Where Most Cases Begin: State Trial Courts — 212
- General Jurisdiction: Major Trial Courts — 213
- Appeals Courts — 214

You Be the . . . Judge — 215

Federal Courts — 216
- Federal Trial Courts: U.S. District Courts — 216
- U.S. Courts of Appeals: Circuit Courts — 217
- U.S. Supreme Court — 217

Investigating Further: Criminal Law From the U.S. Circuit Courts — 219

Making Preparations: Pretrial Processes — 220
- Booking, Initial Appearance, Bail, and Preliminary Hearing — 220
- Grand Juries — 222
- Arraignment — 223
- Plea Negotiation — 223
- Jury Trials — 225

You Be the . . . Defense Attorney — 226

- Pretrial Motions — 227
- Discovery — 227
- Diversion Programs/Problem-Solving Courts — 227

The Trial Process — 228
- Right to a Speedy Trial: "Justice Delayed . . ." — 228
- Trial Protocols — 230

Investigating Further: An Insider's View of a Lower Court — 232

Technologies in the Courts — 233
- Achieving Paper on Demand — 233
- Emerging Technologies — 233

In a Nutshell — 234
Key Terms & Concepts — 235
Review Questions — 235
Learn by Doing — 236

Chapter 10: The Bench and the Bar: Those Who Judge, Prosecute, and Defend — 238
- Learning Objectives — 239
- Assess Your Awareness — 239

Introduction — 240

Those Who Would Be Judges: Selection Methods and Issues — 241
- Methods of Selection in State Courts — 241
- Debating Judges and Politics — 242

You Be the . . . Judge — 243
- "Investing" in Judges? — 244

Judges' Benefits, Training, and Challenges — 244

The Art of Judging, Courtroom Civility, and Judicial Misconduct — 245
- "Good Judging" — 245
- Courtroom Civility — 246
- Judicial Misconduct — 246

Going Global: Studying Law — 247

The Attorneys — 248
- "Gatekeeper" of the Justice System: Prosecutor — 248

You Be the . . . Victim Advocate — 249
- Prosecutorial Immunity and Misconduct — 249
- "Guiding Hand of Counsel": Defense Attorney — 250

Practitioner's Perspective: Court Administrator — 252

Courtroom Work Group — 253
Defenses — 253
- Justification Defenses — 254
- Excuse Defenses — 255

Investigating Further: "Stand Your Ground" Laws — 255
Investigating Further: James Holmes—The "Batman" Shooter — 257
In a Nutshell — 258
Key Terms & Concepts — 259
Review Questions — 259
Learn by Doing — 259

Chapter 11: Court Methods and Challenges: Sentencing and Punishment — 262

- Learning Objectives — 263
- Assess Your Awareness — 263

Introduction — 266
Purposes of Punishment — 266
    Four Goals — 266
    Factors Influencing Punishment — 268
You Be the . . . Judge — 268
    Punishment Models, Methods, and Reforms — 269
    Making Punishment Fit the Crime — 272
Practitioner's Perspective: Criminal Defense Attorney — 273
You Be the . . . Legislator — 274
Types of Sentences to Be Served — 274
    Determinate and Indeterminate Sentences — 274
    Concurrent and Consecutive Sentences — 275
Sentencing Guidelines — 276
Going Global: Sentencing Guidelines in Australia — 276
    Background: Legislation and Court Decisions — 277
    Federal Sentencing Guidelines — 277
    State-Level Sentencing Guidelines — 279
Victim Impact Statements — 279
Investigating Further: Victim Impact Statements — 280
Capital Punishment — 281
    Arguments For and Against — 281
    Key Supreme Court Decisions — 283
    Methods of Execution — 284
Investigating Further: The Reality of Death by Lethal Injection — 285
    Wrongful Convictions: Rethinking the Death Penalty — 285
Investigating Further: DNA Exonerations — 286
    Recent Trends in Federal Executions — 287
Aggravating and Mitigating Circumstances — 287

Criminal Appeals — 287
In a Nutshell — 288
Key Terms & Concepts — 289
Review Questions — 289
Learn by Doing — 290

PART IV: CORRECTIONS

Chapter 12: Prisons and Jails: Structure and Function — 294

- Learning Objectives — 295
- Assess Your Awareness — 295

Introduction — 296
Correctional Facilities as Organizations — 297
    Distinguishing Jails and Prisons — 297
    Inmates, Employment, and Expenditures — 297
    Why the Decline in Correctional Populations? — 298
    Mass Incarceration in America: Time to Rethink and Reform? — 299
    General Mission and Features — 300
    Punishment for Some, a "Step Up" for Others — 300
Practitioner's Perspective: Jail Administrator — 301
    Classification of Inmates: A Cornerstone of Corrections — 302
State Prisons as Organizations — 303
    Do Prisons Rehabilitate? — 305
Federal Prisons — 305
    Prison Types and General Information — 305
    A Career With BOP — 306
    Community Corrections in the Federal System — 306
Supermax Prisons — 307
    Origin — 307
    Two Key Components: Operation and Design — 307

Effects on Inmates	307
Constitutionality	308
Going Global: The World's Worst Prisons	**308**
Private Prisons	309
Jails as Organizations	309
The New Generation/Direct Supervision Jail	311
Jail Treatment Programs	311
Making Jails Productive Through Labor	312
Technologies in Correctional Facilities: Going After Contraband	313
A Perilous Combination—Drones and Cell Phones	313
The Body Scanner	314
You Be the . . . Warden	**314**
Offender Programming and Management	315
"Virtual Visits" by Inmates and the Public	315
In a Nutshell	315
Key Terms & Concepts	316
Review Questions	316
Learn by Doing	317

Chapter 13: The Inmates' World: The "Keepers" and the "Kept" — 318

• Learning Objectives	319
• Assess Your Awareness	319
Introduction	320
The Nature of Incarceration	320
Deprivations and "Pains" of Imprisonment	321
Becoming "Prisonized"	322
Conditions of Confinement	322
Investigating Further: How a 7-Year Sentence Became 22 Years in Solitary Confinement	**323**
Practitioner's Perspective: Corrections Sergeant	**324**
Solitary Confinement: Use and Effects	325
Prison and Jail as Work	325
The Warden: Profile and Role	326
Correctional Officers	327
Jail Personnel	328
Issues of Prison Governance	329
Sexual Violence and Coercion	329
Drug Interdiction and Treatment	330
Women in Prison: Selected Rights and Challenges	330
You Be the . . . Judge	**331**
Mentally Ill Inmates	332
Geriatric Inmates	333
Prison Gangs	333
Coping With Riots	334
Prisoners' Constitutional Rights	335
Demise of the Hands-Off Doctrine	335
Selected Court Decisions	335
Going Global: One of the World's Most Congested, Wretched Prisons	**336**
You Be the . . . Criminal Justice Policy Maker	**338**
Preparation for Reentry and Aftercare	338
In a Nutshell	339
Key Terms & Concepts	339
Review Questions	339
Learn by Doing	340

Chapter 14: Corrections in the Community: Probation, Parole, and Other Alternatives to Incarceration — 342

• Learning Objectives	343
• Assess Your Awareness	343
Introduction	344
Why Alternatives to Incarceration?	344
Origins of Probation and Parole	345
Probation Begins: The Humble Shoe Cobbler	345
Parole Origins: Alexander Maconochie	346
Probation and Parole Today	347
Probation: Eligibility and Legal Rights	347
You Be the . . . Judge	**349**
Investigating Further: Terms and Conditions of Probation	**350**
Parole: Eligibility and Legal Rights	351
You Be the . . . Parole Board	**355**
Do Probation and Parole Work?	355
Functions of Probation and Parole Officers	356
Probation and "Front-End" Duties	356
Parole and "Back-End" Duties	357
Going Global: Probation Supervision	**358**
The Burden of Large Caseloads	358
To Arm or Not to Arm	359
Other Alternatives: Intermediate Sanctions	360
Intensive Supervision Probation and Parole	360
Practitioner's Perspective: Probation Officer	**361**
House Arrest	362
Electronic Monitoring	362
Shock Probation/Parole	363
Boot Camps/Shock Incarceration	363

Investigating Further: Success for the Waukesha County, Wisconsin, Day Report Center	**364**
Day Reporting Centers	364
Halfway Houses	365
Furloughs	365
Confronting Recidivists: The Risk-Need-Responsivity (RNR) Model	365
Restorative Justice	367
In a Nutshell	367
Key Terms & Concepts	368
Review Questions	368
Learn by Doing	368

PART V: SPANNING THE SYSTEM: METHODS AND ISSUES

Chapter 15: Juvenile Justice: Philosophy, Law, and Practices — 372

• Learning Objectives	373
• Assess Your Awareness	373
Introduction	374
History of Juvenile Justice	374
Early Treatment: Houses of Refuge, Reformatories	374
A Movement Begins: Illinois Legislation	375
Status Offenses	376
Unique Philosophy, Principles, and Goals	376
Parens Patriae and In Loco Parentis	376
Underlying Principles of the Juvenile Court	377
Goals of the Juvenile Justice System	378
More Legal Protection: The Juvenile Justice Reform Act of 2018	379
A Recent Shift in Policy, Principles, and Processes	379
Investigating Further: A Sampling of Recent Laws Enacted to Protect Juveniles	**380**
Juvenile Offending Today: Extent and Possible Causes	381
Practitioner's Perspective: Juvenile Court Counselor	**382**
Case Flow of the Juvenile Justice Process	383
You Be the . . . Police Officer	**385**
The Problem of Labeling	386
Is There a "School-to-Prison Pipeline"?	387
Youth Gangs: An Overview	388
What Defines a Youth Gang and Its Members?	388
Youth Gang Membership	388
Going Global: Juvenile Torture in Iraq	**388**
What Works With Youth Gangs?	389
Aftercare and Reentry	389
Significant Court Decisions	389
Right to Counsel	389
The Centerpiece: In Re Gault	390
Investigating Further: Forty-Five Years After *Gault*: The Experience of Corey Bauer	**390**
Burden of Proof Standard	391
Trial by Jury, Double Jeopardy, and Executions	391
Right to the Miranda Warning	391
In a Nutshell	392
Key Terms & Concepts	392
Review Questions	393
Learn by Doing	393

Chapter 16: On the Crime Policy and Prevention Agenda: Drug Abuse, Sex Trafficking, Terrorism, and Immigration — 394

• Learning Objectives	395
• Assess Your Awareness	395
Introduction	396
America's Drug Epidemic	396
Heroin, Cocaine, and Opioid "Pill Mills"	396
Investigating Further: Chasing "El Chapo"	**398**
What Can Be Done?	398
The Status of Medical and Recreational Marijuana Use	399
Sex Trafficking	399
Definition and Victimization	399
Investigating Further: How Some Sex Trafficking Victims Are Made	**400**
What Can Be Done?	400

The T Visa	401
Additional Efforts: The Diagnostic Center	401
Policing Terrorism	401
Definitions and Types	401
Right-Wing Extremists and Lone-Wolf Terrorists	403
Cyberterrorism: The Asian Threat	403
Investigating Further: The Radicalization of Zachary Chesser	**404**
Practitioner's Perspective: Director of IT and Electronic Security	**405**
Bioterrorism	406
What Can Be Done?	406
Related Issues: School Shootings and Gun Violence	407
Immigration: Who Should be Coming to America?	410
Many Questions, Few Answers	410
The Wall Conundrum	411
The Controversy Over Criminality	412
Those Who Would Seek Asylum	412
What Can Be Done?	413
You Be the . . . Police Officer	**413**
In a Nutshell	414
Key Terms & Concepts	414
Review Questions	414
Learn by Doing	415

APPENDIX: BILL OF RIGHTS	**417**
ASSESS YOUR AWARENESS ANSWERS	**419**
GLOSSARY	**421**
NOTES	**431**
INDEX	**465**

PREFACE

A Unique Approach

Famed educator John Dewey advocated the "learning by doing" approach to education, or problem-based learning. This book is written, from start to finish, with that philosophy in mind. Its approach also comports with the popular learning method espoused by Benjamin Bloom, known as Bloom's taxonomy, in which he called for "higher-order thinking skills"—critical and creative thinking that involves analysis, synthesis, and evaluation.

This book also benefits from the authors having many years of combined practitioners' and academic experience, including several positions in criminal justice administration, policing, corrections, and research and training for police agencies, major sports leagues, and private industries. Therefore, its chapters contain a palpable, real-world flavor that college and university criminal justice students typically find missing from their textbooks.

It is hoped that readers will put to use the several features of the book that are intended to help them accomplish the overall goal of learning by doing. In addition to chapter opening questions (which allow students to assess their knowledge of the chapter materials), learning objectives, and a chapter summary, each chapter contains a number of boxed features such as case studies, "Investigating Further," and "You Be the . . ." (Judge, Prosecutor, Defense Attorney, and so on, as the specific situation requires), as well as a list of key terms, review questions, and "Learn by Doing" activities at the end of each chapter. Also provided are "Practitioner's Perspectives" (in which people in the field describe their criminal justice occupations) as well as brief glimpses into comparative criminal justice systems, law, and practice in selected foreign venues ("Going Global"). Taken together, these supplemental materials should greatly enhance readers' critical analysis, problem-solving, and communication capabilities, allowing them to experience the kinds of decisions that must be made in the field.

In today's competitive job market, students who possess these kinds of knowledge, skills, and abilities will have better opportunities to obtain employment as a criminal justice practitioner and to succeed in the field. Although the book certainly delves into some theoretical, political, and sociological subject matter, it attempts to remain true to its *practical*, applied focus throughout and to the extent possible.

Distinctive Chapter Contents

This book also contains chapters devoted to topics not typically found in introductory criminal justice textbooks. For example, Chapter 4 is devoted to criminal justice ethics. Ethics is always a timely topic for our society and especially for today's criminal justice students and practitioners. Chapter 16 also describes four unique and contemporary issues on the U.S. criminal justice policy-making agenda: drug abuse, sex trafficking, terrorism, and immigration. Finally, several chapters also discuss the technologies employed in the system and the aforementioned global criminal justice practices.

In sum, this book introduces the student to the primary individuals, theorists, practitioners, processes, concepts, technologies, and terminologies as they work within or are applied to our criminal justice system. Furthermore, the concepts and terms learned in this introductory textbook will serve as the basis for more complex criminal justice studies of police, courts, and corrections in later course work.

Chapter Organization

To facilitate the book's goals, we first need to place the study of criminal justice within the big picture, which is accomplished in the four chapters in Part I. **Chapter 1** briefly examines why it is important to study criminal justice, foundations and politics of criminal justice, an overview of the criminal justice process and the offender's flow through the system, and how discretion and ethics apply to the field. **Chapter 2** considers the sources and nature of law (including substantive and procedural, and criminal and civil), the elements of criminal acts, felonies and misdemeanors, offense definitions and categories, and prevailing methods in use for trying to measure how many crimes are committed. **Chapter 3** examines some of the attempts to explain why people commit crimes (including the classical, positivist, biological, social structure, social process, social conflict, feminist, and environmental criminology theories), as well as field research that has uncovered offender motivation for committing specific crimes. **Chapter 4** concerns ethics and includes definitions and problems, with emphases on the kinds of ethical problems that confront the police, the courtroom work group, and corrections staff. Included are an ethical decision-making process; legislative enactments; and judicial decisions involving ethics at the federal, state, and local levels.

Part II consists of four chapters that address federal law enforcement and state and local policing in the United States. **Chapter 5** discusses the organization and operation of law enforcement agencies at the federal, state, and local (city and county) levels. Included are discussions of their English and colonial roots, the three eras of U.S. policing, and brief considerations of INTERPOL and the field of private security. **Chapter 6** focuses on the roles and tasks of policing, particularly with respect to the broad areas of training, patrolling, and investigating. After beginning with recruitment, training (including higher education for police), and stressors in policing, we consider patrol functions, use of discretion, community policing, and the work of criminal investigators (including crime scenes, use of informants, and cold cases). **Chapter 7** broadly examines several policing issues, especially those leading to changes in the aftermath of police shootings in a number of U.S. cities: the "guardian versus soldier" mindset, constitutional policing and legitimacy, and procedural justice. Also discussed are police corruption, civil liability, dealing with the mentally ill, and the use of and controversies surrounding selected technologies. **Chapter 8** examines the constitutional rights of the accused (as per U.S. Supreme Court decisions) as well as limitations placed on the police under the Fourth, Fifth, and Sixth Amendments; the focus is on arrest, search and seizure, the right to remain silent, and the right to counsel.

Part III consists of three chapters that generally examine the courts. **Chapter 9** examines court structure and functions at the federal, state, and trial court levels; included are discussions of pretrial preparations, the actual trial process, the jury system, and some court technologies. **Chapter 10** looks at the courtroom work group, including the judges, prosecutors, and defense attorneys, and legal defenses that are allowed under the law. Finally, **Chapter 11** discusses sentencing, punishment, and appeals. Included are the types and purposes of punishment, types of sentences convicted persons may receive, federal sentencing guidelines, victim impact statements, and capital punishment.

Part IV includes three chapters and examines many aspects of correctional organizations and operations. **Chapter 12** examines federal and state prisons and local jails in terms of their evolution and organization, inmate population trends (including mass incarceration) and classification, and some technologies. **Chapter 13** considers the "lives inside the walls" of both correctional personnel and inmates; included are selected court decisions concerning inmates' legal rights; administrative challenges with overseeing executions, inmate litigation, drugs, and gangs; and the work of personnel in local jails. **Chapter 14** reviews community corrections and alternatives to incarceration: probation, parole, and several other diversionary approaches. Included are discussions of the origins of probation and parole, functions of probation and parole officers, and several intermediate sanctions (e.g., house arrest, electronic monitoring).

Finally, Part V contains two chapters that consider methods and issues that span the criminal justice system. **Chapter 15** examines juvenile justice—an area in which the treatment of offenders is quite different in terms of its overall philosophy, legal bases, and judicial process. Included are the history and extent of juvenile crime, risk assessment (of offending), the case flow of juvenile courts, labeling, whether there is a school-to-prison pipeline, youth gangs, and juveniles' legal rights. **Chapter 16** provides an in-depth view of four particularly challenging problems and policy issues confronting society and the criminal justice system today: drug abuse, sex trafficking, terrorism, and immigration.

New Topics in the Fourth Edition

The following substantively new materials have been added to this revised fourth edition:

- New chapter-opening vignettes for each chapter that aim to increase student interest and engagement.
- Several new "Investigating Further" boxes explore current issues in criminal justice and help students dig deeper into the material.
- New "You Be the . . ." boxes offer a broader range of perspectives for students to take on, such as those of sentencing commissioners and policy makers.

Following are additional chapter-by-chapter additions:

Chapter 1: Updates on cannabis laws and gun legislation; new "Going Global" illustration on international marijuana legalization; new case studies for "You Be the . . ." boxes

Chapter 2: Coverage of crime measurement methods moved to this chapter; new case studies for "You Be the . . ." boxes; updates on recent white-collar crime offenses and crime statistics; new "Going Global" illustration of victimization measurement in England and Wales

Chapter 3: Chapter designed to focus strictly on theories of criminality and crime; new "You be the . . ." box focusing on crime analysis; updates to statistics involving female offenders; new "Going Global" illustration of international criminologists

Chapter 4: New police, courts, corrections case studies, and "Investigating Further" materials throughout; "Going Global" illustration; sample policy governing police conduct; "random acts of kindness" by police; "Hippocratic Oath for police" discussion

Chapter 5: Updates on federal agencies' activities; police organization chart; policing professionalization and laws; criminal justice in Venezuela; comment on immigration and law enforcement at all levels; new "Practitioner's Perspective" (police lieutenant)

Chapter 6: Golden State Killer case; patrol officers' use of evidence-based policing strategies; challenges posed to investigators by and investigating cybercriminals; case study involving a cybercrime/the dark web; low murder clearance rates; the use of DNA analysis

Chapter 7: New case studies; types of force; updates on Black Lives Matter and Blue Lives Matter movements; status of state laws concerning body-worn cameras; new "Practitioner's Perspective" (chief of police); dealing with mentally ill persons (moved from Chapter 16); uses of and potential problems with four selected technologies

Chapter 8: New summaries of *Mapp v. Ohio* and *Miranda v. Arizona* cases; new case studies; summaries of recent Supreme Court decisions governing Fourth Amendment issues; new "Going Global" illustration of search and seizure rights around the world

Chapter 9: New "Going Global" illustration of adversarial and inquisitorial justice systems; new case studies; updates to intermediate court of appeals and state court caseload statistics; new "You Be the . . ." box highlighting the role of defense attorneys; updates on courtroom technologies

Chapter 10: Updates on judicial campaign expenditures; new "Going Global" illustration of international law schools; new "You Be the . . ." box focusing on the role of a victim advocate; coverage of criminal defenses moved to this chapter

Chapter 11: Updates on national survey outcomes, exonerations and death penalty administration, and laws governing victim impact statements; new "You Be the . . ." box featuring the role of legislators regarding "chemical castration" laws; new "Going Global" illustration of sentencing guidelines in Australia

Chapter 12: Updates on correctional populations, employment, expenditures, Bureau of Prisons, and prison privatization; money bail reform; jail populations (contribution to mass incarceration); definition of recidivism; whether or not prisons rehabilitate; list of jail treatment programs and study results of their efficacy; contraband and use of drones and cell phones by inmates; technologies to combat same; new "You Be the . . ." box featuring the role of wardens

Chapter 13: Case study and data on solitary confinement; correctional officers' roles/similarities to public police; updates on prison sexual assaults, gangs, and the unique needs of female, elderly, or mentally ill inmates; case study on prison riots; case study of a highly overcrowded, wretched prison (in Haiti).

Chapter 14: Updates on probation, parole, and electronic monitoring statistics; new "Going Global" illustration of probation supervision throughout the world; updates to research on Risk-Need-Responsivity model effectiveness

Chapter 15: Explanation of the Juvenile Justice Reform Act of 2018; sampling of state laws recently enacted to protect juveniles; recent shift in policy, principles, and processes regarding juvenile offenders (including status of juvenile life-without-parole sentences); updated juvenile arrest rates and gang membership; case study of juvenile torture in Iraq; two case studies of incarcerated juveniles (one in solitary confinement)

Chapter 16: Material is nearly all new for this edition concerning drug abuse, sex trafficking, terrorism, and immigration; coverage of dealing with the mentally ill population was moved to Chapter 7

RESOURCES FOR INSTRUCTORS AND STUDENTS

edge.sagepub.com/peak4e

Many electronic features are also included with *Introduction to Criminal Justice: Practice and Process,* including the following:

SAGE COURSEPACKS FOR INSTRUCTORS makes it easy to import our quality content into your school's LMS. Intuitive and simple to use, it allows you to

Say NO to . . .

required access codes

learning a new system

Say YES to . . .

using only the content you want and need

high-quality assessment and multimedia exercises

For use in: Blackboard, Canvas, Brightspace by Desire2Learn (D2L), and Moodle

Don't use an LMS platform? No problem, you can still access many of the online resources for your text via SAGE edge.

SAGE coursepacks and SAGE edge include the following features:

- Our content delivered **directly into your LMS**
- An **intuitive, simple format** that makes it easy to integrate the material into your course with minimal effort
- Pedagogically robust **assessment tools** that foster review, practice, and critical thinking, and offer a more complete way to measure student engagement, including:
  - Diagnostic chapter **coursepack quizzes** that identify opportunities for improvement, track student progress, and ensure mastery of key learning objectives
  - **Test banks** built on Bloom's taxonomy that provide a diverse range of test items with ExamView test generation
  - **Instructions** on how to use and integrate the comprehensive assessments and resources provided
- A comprehensive, downloadable, easy-to-use *Media Guide in the Coursepack* **for every video resource**, listing the chapter to which the video content is tied, matching learning objective(s), a helpful description of the video content, and assessment questions
- **Sample course syllabi** for semester and quarter courses providing suggested models for structuring your courses
- Editable, chapter-specific **PowerPoint® slides** that offer complete flexibility for creating a multimedia presentation for your course
- **Lecture notes** that summarize key concepts by chapter to help you prepare for lectures and class discussions
- **Video resources** that bring concepts to life, are tied to learning objectives, and make learning easier
- **Chapter-specific discussion questions** to help launch engaging classroom interaction while reinforcing important content

SAGE vantage Version

The vantage version includes the following:

- **Assignable SAGE Premium Video** that is tied to learning objectives, and curated and produced exclusively for this text to bring concepts to life and appeal to different learning styles, featuring:
  - **Corresponding multimedia assessment options**
  - **Student on the Street videos, animated decision-making scenarios, and career insights from professionals in the field**
- Interactive **data literacy exercises** drawn from key figures in the book, which will help students not only to understand data but also to critically analyze and draw conclusions from it

Learn more at **edge.sagepub.com/peak4e**.

▶ Student on the Street Videos

Student on the Street Videos: Available only in the Interactive eBook, these videos feature student interviews highlighting misconceptions on key criminal justice concepts with author responses.

▶ Criminal Justice in Practice Videos

Criminal Justice in Practice Videos: Available only in Vantage, these animated decision-making scenarios challenge students to explore how they would respond to real-world situations faced by criminal justice professionals.

▶ Career Videos

Career Videos: Available only in Vantage, these videos feature interviews with criminal justice professionals discussing their day-to-day work and current issues related to technology, diversity, and cutting-edge developments in their field.

Study Tools for Students

SAGE edge for Students provides a personalized approach to helping students accomplish their coursework goals in an easy-to-use learning environment:

- Mobile-friendly **eFlashcards** strengthen understanding of key terms and concepts.
- Mobile-friendly practice **quizzes** allow for independent assessment by students of their mastery of course material.
- **Data literacy exercises** draw from the key figures in the book, helping students not only to understand data but also to critically analyze and draw conclusions from it.
- **Video resources** bring concepts to life, are tied to learning objectives, and enhance exploration of key topics.

ACKNOWLEDGMENTS

This fourth edition, like its predecessor, is the culmination of dedicated efforts on the part of several key individuals at SAGE Publications, Inc., and they should be recognized. First, this team effort was led by Jessica Miller, acquisitions editor; we greatly appreciate her ongoing commitment to this publishing effort and her astute experience and assistance toward that end. Also providing stellar performances in their roles were Laura Kearns and Adeline Grout, content development editors; Sarah Manheim, editorial assistant; Amy Marks, copy editor; and Veronica Stapleton Hooper, production editor.

—K. J. P. and T. D. H.

REVIEWERS OF THE FOURTH EDITION

Ross Allen
Rutgers University-Camden

Christopher Martinez
City University of New York

Jessica Noble
Lewis and Clark Community College

Lawrence A. Presley
Liberty University

R. D. Robertson
U.S. Drug Enforcement Administration

Tracey Woodard
University of South Carolina Upstate

/// ABOUT THE AUTHORS

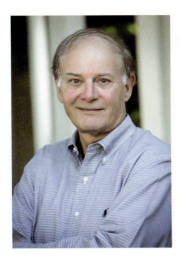

Kenneth J. Peak is emeritus professor and former chair of the Department of Criminal Justice, University of Nevada, Reno, where he was named "Teacher of the Year" by the university's Honor Society. Following four years as a municipal police officer in Kansas, he subsequently held positions as a nine-county criminal justice planner for southeast Kansas; director of a four-state technical assistance institute for the Law Enforcement Assistance Administration (based at Washburn University in Topeka); director of university police at Pittsburg State University (Kansas); acting director of public safety, University of Nevada, Reno; and assistant professor of criminal justice at Wichita State University. He has authored or coauthored 37 additional textbooks (relating to general policing, community policing, criminal justice administration, police supervision and management, and women in law enforcement), two historical books (on Kansas temperance and bootlegging), and more than 60 journal articles and invited book chapters. He is past chair of the Police Section of the Academy of Criminal Justice Sciences and past president of the Western Association of Criminal Justice. He received two gubernatorial appointments to statewide criminal justice committees while residing in Kansas and holds a doctorate from the University of Kansas.

Tamara D. Madensen-Herold is an associate professor of criminal justice and graduate director at the University of Nevada, Las Vegas (UNLV). She holds a doctorate from the University of Cincinnati. Her research interests include crime opportunity structures, place management, and crowd violence. She is the recipient of UNLV's Spanos Distinguished Teaching Award, Faculty Excellence Award, and Greenspun College of Urban Affairs Teaching Award. Her publications propose, extend, or test crime science theoretical models. They also help to translate research findings into practice and policy. Her work has appeared in various outlets, including *Criminology* and *Justice Quarterly*. She has published numerous practitioner-focused research papers, including two Problem-Oriented Policing Guides funded by the COPS Office and research monographs for which she received Herman Goldstein Excellence in Problem-Oriented Policing Awards. Her book *Preventing Crowd Violence* (coedited with Johannes Knutsson) has been translated into two foreign languages. Dr. Madensen-Herold serves as director of UNLV's Crowd Management Research Council and conducts research and training for police agencies, major sports leagues, and private industries.

CRIMINAL JUSTICE AS A SYSTEM
The Basics

PART 1

Chapter 1: Fundamentals of Criminal Justice: Essential Themes and Practices
Chapter 2: Foundations of Law and Crime: Nature, Elements, and Measurement
Chapter 3: Theories of Criminality and Crime
Chapter 4: Ethical Essentials: Doing Right When No One Is Watching

This part consists of four chapters. **Chapter 1** briefly examines why it is important to study criminal justice, the foundations and politics of criminal justice, an overview of the criminal justice process and the offender's flow through the system, and how discretion and ethics apply to the field.

Chapter 2 considers the sources and nature of law (including substantive and procedural, and criminal and civil), the elements of criminal acts, felonies and misdemeanors, offense definitions and categories, and prevailing methods in use for trying to measure how many crimes are committed.

Chapter 3 examines some of the attempts to explain why people commit crimes (including the classical, positivist, biological, social structure, social process, social conflict, feminist, and environmental criminology theories), as well as field research that has uncovered offender motivations for committing specific crimes.

Chapter 4 concerns ethics and includes definitions and problems, with emphases on the kinds of ethical problems that confront the police, the courtroom work group, and corrections staff. Included are an ethical decision-making process; legislative enactments; and judicial decisions involving ethics at the federal, state, and local levels.

CHAPTER 1

FUNDAMENTALS OF CRIMINAL JUSTICE
Essential Themes and Practices

The true administration of justice is the firmest pillar of good government.
—Inscription on the New York State Supreme Court, Foley Square, Manhattan, New York

When we pull back the layers of government services, the most fundamental and indispensable virtues are public safety and social order.
—Hon. David A. Hardy, Washoe County District Court, Reno, Nevada

LEARNING OBJECTIVES

As a result of reading this chapter, you will be able to

1. Explain the importance of studying and understanding our criminal justice system
2. Describe the foundations of our criminal justice system, including its legal and historical bases and the difference between the consensus and conflict theories of justice
3. Define the crime control and due process models of criminal justice
4. Describe the importance of discretion throughout the justice system
5. Describe the fundamentals of the criminal justice process—the offender's flow through the police, courts, and corrections components, and the functions of each component
6. Explain the wedding cake model of criminal justice
7. Discuss the importance of ethics and character in criminal justice

ASSESS YOUR AWARENESS

Test your knowledge of criminal justice fundamentals by responding to the following six true-false items; check your answers after reading this chapter.

1. Under the U.S. system of justice, people basically join together, form governments (thus surrendering their rights of self-protection), and receive governmental protection in return.
2. Very little, if any, political or discretionary behavior or authority exists in the field of criminal justice; its fixed laws and procedures prevent such influences.
3. All prosecutions for crimes begin with a grand jury indictment.
4. Police make the final decisions concerning the actual crimes with which a suspect will be charged.
5. *Parolee* is the term used to describe one who has been granted early release from prison.
6. The U.S. system of criminal justice is intended to function, and indeed does function in all respects, like a "well-oiled machine."

<< Answers can be found on page 419.

In 2015, Kalief Browder, a 22-year-old man from New York City, hanged himself in his parents' home. This suicide drew national attention because much had been publicized, just a year prior, about Mr. Browder and his time spent in detention at Rikers Island. He was arrested at the age of 16 after being accused of stealing a backpack. He was detained on Rikers Island for three years, despite never being tried or convicted for his alleged crime. While enduring repeated delays in the clogged Bronx court system, he was beaten by correctional officers and spent nearly two years in solitary confinement.[1] He was eventually released after the prosecutor determined that there wasn't enough evidence to try Mr. Browder for theft.

Many people claimed that Mr. Browder's suicide was the result of the mental and physical abuse he experienced in prison. His experience inspired New York City to end the use of solitary confinement for juveniles and influenced President Barack Obama's decision to ban juvenile solitary confinement in federal prisons. In 2019, New York City agreed to pay $3.3 million to settle a lawsuit brought on behalf of Mr. Browder's estate.[2]

Mr. Browder, like others with similar experiences of mistreatment, became a symbol of criminal justice system abuse in the United States. His experience, death, and subsequent calls for reform followed years of justice system policies and legislation that promoted a "tough-on-crime" approach to managing crime and criminals. This tough-on-crime approach resulted in backlogged courts and extreme prison overcrowding.

As you read this chapter, think about how the criminal law is influenced, and how new laws are made and ultimately changed, as society and its norms change. What types of laws help to keep residents safe

Master the content at edge.sagepub.com/peak4e

while also protecting taxpayers and prisoners from the costs associated with an unnecessarily punitive justice system? What political pressures would lawmakers feel in crafting such laws, and what risks do we face when our justice system does not function as intended?

INTRODUCTION

The U.S. criminal justice system as we know it has existed for more than a century and a half. Interest in crime and our justice system has generated thousands of television series and movies that examine how and why people commit crimes, how the justice system responds, the roles of people who work within our system, various punishments for criminal behavior, and our protections under the Bill of Rights. Some are fictional (*The Wire, CSI, Law & Order,* and *NCIS*), while others are based on true stories or follow real-life events (*The People v. O. J. Simpson: American Crime Story, The First 48, Unsolved Mysteries,* and *Cops*). These programs have contributed to society's general knowledge about our justice system, but fictional stories and dramatic editing can produce misleading or inaccurate information.

Kalief Browder, of the Bronx, New York, was sent to Rikers Island jail at the age of 16, accused of stealing a backpack. He would eventually spend three years at Rikers, two of which were in solitary confinement. Two years after his release, Browder hanged himself at his mother's home—the result, some say, of mental, physical and sexual abuse sustained while in custody.

The criminal justice system is a critical part of our free, democratic society, and for that reason alone, we need to study and understand it. It serves to define our culture and how we live. It also influences the way in which we interact with the rest of the world. The terrorist attacks that occurred on September 11, 2001, changed the way Americans felt about homeland safety and security. The events of 9/11 made people more aware that crime is an international problem. Crime regularly transcends national borders, and the manner in which our federal, state, and local criminal justice agencies must organize and plan in order to deal with crime has changed in many ways, as later chapters will show.

Another reason for carefully studying the criminal justice system is that, odds are, you and most Americans will be affected by crime during your lifetime. About 9 million serious criminal offenses are reported to the Federal Bureau of Investigation (FBI) each year, with about 1.3 million of them involving violence and 7.7 million involving damaged or stolen property.[3] Millions more offenses occur that are less serious in nature, and many crimes go unreported. Given the far-reaching and significant impact of criminal activity, Americans should understand how offenders are processed through the three major components of our system—police, courts, and corrections—and know their legal rights.

Finally, by studying the criminal justice system, you will understand how your tax dollars support criminal justice in federal, state, and local governments (which now spend about $284 billion annually and employ over 2.4 million persons).[4] A tremendous amount of resources are required to support our criminal justice system. But as the French novelist Alain-René Lesage stated several centuries ago, "Justice is such a fine thing that we cannot pay too dearly for it."[5] This chapter provides an overview of the foundations of the criminal justice system. You will learn about the legal and historical bases of the system, the crime control and due process models of crime, the stages of the criminal justice process, a four-tier model used to categorize and describe different types of criminal cases, and how discretion and ethics permeate the system.

FOUNDATIONS OF CRIMINAL JUSTICE: LEGAL AND HISTORICAL BASES

The foundation of our criminal justice system is the criminal law: laws that define criminal acts and how such acts will be punished. Indeed, enforcing these laws is what sets in motion the entire criminal justice process. But like most things in our dynamic society, the law is not static. Enactment of new criminal laws and changes to those laws are almost always triggered by social, political, and economic changes. New ways to commit crimes are discovered, new illegal drugs make their way to the marketplace, new weapons and technology (for criminals and police alike) come on the scene, and suddenly, lawmakers and law enforcement officials find themselves needing new tools to prevent and prosecute crimes. We turn first to how the law changes and the historical principles that still guide—and sometimes challenge—that process.

The Criminal Law: How It Changes and How It Changes the System

In the wake of news reports indicating abuses resulting from an overtaxed criminal justice system (such as the one outlined at the beginning of this chapter), many lawmakers and criminal justice officials have been exploring ways to divert offenders away from traditional system responses. Attempts to find alternatives to arrest, prosecution, and incarceration have included providing treatment to help offenders deal with underlying issues that cause criminal behavior (e.g., mental health or substance abuse issues), as well as decriminalizing nonviolent, low-level crimes (consider the discussion of cannabis law changes that follows later in this chapter). You will learn more about recent diversion laws and programs throughout this book.

The search for alternative approaches to crime and justice indicates a significant shift away from the many "tough-on-crime" laws that were enacted in the 1990s. Most politicians wanted to appear tough on crime, particularly following high-profile violent cases, like the kidnapping, sexual assault, and murder of 12-year-old Polly Klaas. Polly was abducted from her home in Petaluma, California, by Richard Allen Davis in 1993. California lawmakers responded just months after Davis confessed to his crimes by proposing the nation's first three-strikes law—a seemingly simple solution giving violent offenders only two chances to turn themselves around. If they did not, and they committed another crime, the third crime would be the final "strike" and the state could lock them up and throw away the key for 25 years to life.[6] California voters overwhelmingly approved the measure, and within two years more than 20 states and the federal government had done the same.[7]

Three-strikes law: a crime control strategy whereby an offender who commits three or more violent offenses will be sentenced to a lengthy term in prison, usually 25 years to life.

Supporters predicted the new law would curb crime and protect society by incapacitating the worst offenders for a long period of time, while opponents argued that offenders facing their third strike would demand trials (rather than plea bargain) and send prison populations skyrocketing.[8]

The law that was finally enacted in California was vastly different from what was originally intended—and with many negative and unanticipated repercussions.[9] According to the *New York Times,* the law was unfairly punitive and created a cruel and unfair criminal justice system that lost all sense of proportion, doling out life sentences disproportionately to black defendants. Under the statute, the third offense that could result in a life sentence could be any number of low-level felony convictions, like stealing a jack from the back of a tow truck, shoplifting a pair of work gloves from a department store, pilfering small change from a parked car, or passing a bad check.[10]

Three-strikes laws, while differing in content somewhat from state to state, all have a simple premise: making violent offenders with three qualifying convictions serve lengthy prison sentences.

John Locke, an English philosopher and physician and one of the most influential thinkers of his day, developed two influential theories concerning government and natural law: social contract and tacit consent.

Another English philosopher and social contract theorist, Thomas Hobbes, believed in individual rights and representative government.

Other studies of the California law found that prisoners added to the prison system in one decade's time would cost taxpayers an additional $8.1 billion in prison and jail expenditures.[11] Furthermore, three-strikes inmates sentenced for nonviolent offenses would serve 143,439 more years behind bars than if they had been convicted prior to the law's passage.[12] A nationwide study of three-strikes laws conducted about a decade after many states had adopted the law found no credible evidence to suggest that the law reduced crime.[13] Nearly 19 years after adoption of the three-strikes law, in November 2012, Californians voted to soften the sentencing law, to impose a life sentence only when the third felony offense is serious or violent, as defined in state law. The law also authorizes the courts to resentence thousands of people who were sent away for low-level third offenses and who present no danger to the public,[14] and it provides redress to mentally ill inmates—who were estimated to compose up to 40 percent of those inmates with life sentences under the three-strikes rule.[15]

As you will read throughout this book, the adoption of laws and the processing of cases through our justice system is heavily influenced by politics. Many lawmakers and other politicians want to do what is right for society, but their decisions can also be influenced by their desire to be reelected, made with limited or inaccurate information, or prompted by a "knee-jerk" response to a high-profile event, like Kalief Browder's detention experience or Polly Klaas's murder.

The Browder and Klaas cases provide excellent illustrations of the national impact of injustice and crime, the legislative process, and the democratic system of criminal justice that exists to deal with offenders. These cases also prompt us to consider questions about the interaction of government and the justice system: What is the source of legislative and law enforcement powers? How can governments presume to maintain a system of laws that effectively governs its people and, moreover, a legal and just system that exists to punish persons who willfully violate those laws? We now consider those questions.

The Consensus-Versus-Conflict Debate

The criminal justice system plays a central role in our democratic society. We enact criminal laws to maintain order and to punish those who violate the democratically decided rules. But is order maintained through consensus—agreement—or is it preserved through conflict, the exercise of power by certain groups over others? This debate is important because it forces us to look at how laws are created, to whom they are meant to apply, and the impact of our justice system in light of these competing perspectives.

Consensus Theory of Justice

Our society contains innumerable lawbreakers—many of whom are more violent than Richard Allen Davis. Most of them consent to police power in a cooperative manner, without challenging the legitimacy of the law if arrested and incarcerated. Nor do they challenge the system of government that enacts the laws or the justice agencies that carry them out. The stability of our government for more than 200 years is a testament to the existence of a fair degree of consensus as to its legitimacy.[16] Thomas Jefferson's statements in the Declaration of Independence are as true today as when he wrote them and are accepted as common sense:

> We hold these truths to be self-evident, that all men are created equal, that they are endowed by their Creator with certain inalienable Rights, that among these are Life, Liberty and the pursuit of Happiness—That to secure these rights, Governments are instituted among Men, deriving their just powers from the consent of the governed. That whenever any Form of Government becomes destructive of these ends, it is the Right of the People to alter or abolish it.

The principles of the Declaration are almost a paraphrase of John Locke's *Second Treatise on Civil Government*, which justifies the acts of government on the basis of Locke's social contract theory. In the state of nature, people, according to Locke, were created by God to be free, equal, and independent, and to have inherent inalienable rights to life, liberty, and property. Each person had the right of self-protection against those who would infringe on these liberties. In Locke's view, although most people were good, some would be likely to prey on others, who in turn would constantly have to be on guard against those who might harm them. To avoid this brutish existence, people joined together, forming governments to which they surrendered their rights of self-protection. In return, they received governmental protection of their lives, property, and liberty. As with any contract, each side has benefits and considerations; people give up their rights to protect themselves and receive protection in return. Governments give protection and receive loyalty and obedience in return.[17]

Jean-Jacques Rousseau, a Genevan conflict theorist, argued that while the coexistence of human beings in equality and freedom is possible, it is unlikely that humanity can escape alienation, oppression, and lack of freedom: "Everywhere he is in chains."

Maurice Quentin de La Tour

Locke believed that the chief purpose of government was the protection of property. Properties would be joined together to form a commonwealth. Once the people unite into a commonwealth, they cannot withdraw from it, nor can their lands be removed from it. Property holders become members of that commonwealth only with their express consent to submit to its government. This is Locke's famous theory of tacit consent: "Every Man . . . doth hereby give his tacit consent, and is as far forth obliged to Obedience to the Laws of the Government."[18] Locke's theory essentially describes an association of landowners.[19] Another theorist connected with the social contract theory is Thomas Hobbes, who argued that all people were essentially irrational and selfish. He maintained that people had just enough rationality to recognize their situation and to come together to form governments for self-protection, agreeing "amongst themselves to submit to some Man, or Assembly of men, voluntarily, on confidence to be protected by him against all others."[20] Therefore, they existed in a state of consensus with their governments.

Consensus theory of justice: explains how a society creates laws as a result of common interests and values, which develop largely because people experience similar socialization.

The consensus theory of justice assumes that most citizens in society share similar values and beliefs. It is based on the premise that even a diverse population of individuals hold the same morals or views concerning what should be labeled as "right" or "wrong" behavior. These views are reflected in the law. Society comes together to protect itself from those who threaten the well-being of others by passing laws that prohibit harmful behavior and outlining the punishments for engaging in these acts.

Consensus theory acknowledges that perspectives and values can change over time. Some behaviors that were previously illegal are legal today. For example, adultery, same-sex marriage, drinking alcohol, and conducting business on Sundays were all labeled as criminal activity in the past.[21] Further, what is illegal today might be deemed legal tomorrow. Public attitudes toward marijuana use are shifting. In 2000, only 31 percent of Americans supported the legalization of marijuana, but recent polls show that two-thirds (66 percent) now support it.[22] This shift in public opinion has resulted in the legalization of marijuana use in numerous states, as depicted in Figure 1.1.

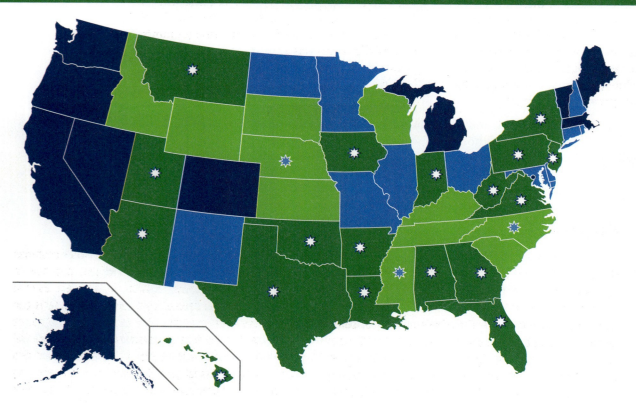

Figure 1.1 /// Cannabis Laws in the United States, as of 2019

Cannabis Laws in the United States
- Jurisdiction with legalized cannabis.
- Jurisdiction with both medical and decriminalization laws.
- Jurisdiction with legal psychoactive medical cannabis.
- ☆ Jurisdiction with no decriminalized cannabis possession laws.
- ✦ Jurisdiction with reduced decriminalized cannabis possession laws.
- Jurisdiction with cannabis prohibition.

Part 1: Criminal Justice as a System

Conflict Theory of Justice

Jean-Jacques Rousseau, a conflict theorist, differed substantively from both Hobbes and Locke, arguing that "man is born free, but everywhere he is in chains."[23] Like Plato, Rousseau associated the loss of freedom and the creation of conflict in modern societies with the development of private property and the unequal distribution of resources. Rousseau described conflict between the ruling group and the other groups in society, whereas Locke described consensus within the ruling group and the need to use force and other means to ensure the compliance of the other groups.[24]

The conflict theory of justice is based on the assumption that there will always be competing interests and viewpoints among members of society. People's beliefs can differ greatly and, as such, consensus is not possible. Women's right to abortion has been heavily debated since it was made legal across the country following the 1973 U.S. Supreme Court ruling in *Roe v. Wade*.[25] Yearly surveys reveal that opinions regarding abortion have remained relatively stable over time, and the country remains divided on this issue.[26]

Conflict theory of justice: explains how powerful groups create laws to protect their values and interests in diverse societies.

Since people do not share a common belief in what should or should not be legal, conflict theory maintains that laws reflect the interests of the most powerful people in society. Characteristics of certain groups make them more or less likely to be subjected to laws and criminal sanctions. These characteristics include age, class, race, and gender, as well as combinations of these attributes. The difference in laws governing crack cocaine and powder cocaine use is an example commonly used to support conflict theory. Prior to the Fair Sentencing Act of 2010, the penalty for possession of 5 grams of crack cocaine (commonly associated with poor, minority, and inner-city drug users) was a five-year mandatory prison sentence, but a person in possession of powder cocaine (commonly associated with wealthy, white drug users) would be subject to the same penalty only if the individual was carrying 500 grams of the drug.[27]

Going Global

Marijuana Legalization Around the World

In 2013, Uruguay (in South America) became the first country in the world to legalize cannabis for recreational use nationwide. Canada followed suit in 2018 and became the first major world economy to legalize recreational marijuana. Although British Columbia's minister of public safety noted that there are still many unknown health risks associated with the drug, there was broad public support across the country for marijuana legalization. News reporters shared stories of Canadians waiting in line for hours to buy the first state-approved marijuana cigarettes. Although medical marijuana had been legal in Canada since 2001, the new legislation allows adults to possess and carry up to 30 grams of dried cannabis, or enough to roll about 60 average joints. Most provinces also permit up to four home-grown marijuana plants per household.

Debates concerning legalization continue as more countries consider whether to decriminalize marijuana and how to regulate the drug's growth, distribution, and sale. Even in Canada, legalization debates continue. Dried cannabis can be purchased from government retailers in physical stores and online, but the federal government delayed approval of sales of cannabis edibles (marijuana infused food and liquid) for an additional year. The government is allowing the country's 13 provinces and territories to establish their own rules, creating discrepancies in regulations across the county. Physical and mental health risks, dangers of intoxication while driving, benefits of projected tax revenues, and the pardoning of previous drug offenders are among many issues being discussed as part of a larger national conversation.

Source: Adapted from Dan Bilefsky, "Legalizing Recreational Marijuana, Canada Begins a National Experiment," *New York Times*, October 17, 2018, https://www.nytimes.com/2018/10/17/world/canada/marijuana-pot-cannabis-legalization.html.

CRIME CONTROL AND DUE PROCESS: DO ENDS JUSTIFY MEANS?

Before learning about the specifics of the criminal justice process, it is important to consider how our system can serve the two seemingly competing goals of controlling crime and protecting the rights of persons accused of crime. How do we operate a system that is tough on crime and criminals while preserving the constitutional rights of those being accused? Crime control is an obvious and understandable goal for any society, but in a country founded on the ideals of freedom, liberty, and equality, we must be concerned about violating individual rights in our quest to achieve justice—we must ask whether the ends justify the means. For example, if the police illegally search a house and find clear evidence of several crimes, should the state be able to use that evidence to convict someone or should the evidence be excluded because the police violated the defendant's constitutional rights in the pursuit of crime control?

You will become familiar with these debates and conflicting objectives within the justice system as you learn more about the criminal justice process and the laws that govern police actions and ethics. By considering two different approaches to our criminal justice system, we can better understand how those accused of crimes move through the system and the different results—intended and otherwise—we might expect. In 1968, Herbert Packer described the two now-classic models of the criminal justice process in terms of two competing value systems: crime control and due process (see Table 1.1).[28]

You Be the . . .

Legislator

Gun violence is a major concern in the United States. In addition to recent school shootings and mass shootings at public events and workplaces, many communities (particularly disadvantaged communities) suffer from high numbers of gun-related violent crimes. We do not have a complete database of all U.S. gun violence incidents, but some estimates suggest that firearms are involved in more than 22,000 suicides, just under 13,000 homicides, and almost 500 unintentional deaths in America annually. Further, the average number of injuries per year involving guns is almost 100,000.

Concerns over gun violence must be balanced with the rights afforded by the Second Amendment of our U.S. Constitution, which reads, "A well regulated Militia, being necessary to the security of a free State, the right of the people to keep and bear Arms, shall not be infringed." While there is considerable debate regarding the amendment's intended scope, lawmakers across the county are considering whether to enhance citizens' rights to bear arms (e.g., by supporting laws that allow citizens to openly carry firearms) or to introduce legislation focused on enhancing gun control (e.g., by requiring background checks to purchase firearms).

1. Do laws that establish background check requirements, such as those proposed by the Bipartisan Background Checks Act of 2019, follow the consensus or conflict theory of justice?

2. What recent news stories might make lawmakers more likely to introduce gun rights or gun control legislation?

3. Does gun control legislation align more closely with the crime control model or the due process model?

Sources: Everytown for Gun Safety, "Gun Violence in America," https://everytownresearch.org/gun-violence-america/; H.R.8—Bipartisan Background Checks Act of 2019, 116th Congress (2019–2020), https://www.congress.gov/bill/116th-congress/house-bill/8.

Table 1.1 /// Packer's Crime Control and Due Process Models		
	Crime Control Model	Due Process Model
Views criminal justice system as an . . .	Assembly line	Obstacle course
Goal of criminal justice system	Controlling crime	Protecting rights of defendants
Values emphasized	Efficiency, speed, finality	Reliability
Process of adjudication	Informal screening by police and prosecutor	Formal, adversarial procedures
Focuses on . . .	Factual guilt	Legal guilt

The **crime control model** follows a highly traditional philosophy that Packer likened to an assembly line. The primary goal of this model is to deter criminal conduct and thus protect society. The accused is presumed guilty, police and prosecutors should have extensive freedom to exercise their own discretion (judgment) in the interest of crime control, legal loopholes should be eliminated, and offenders should be punished swiftly. This model views crime as a breakdown of individual responsibility; as such, only swift and certain punishment will deter and control crime.

In contrast, the **due process model**—likened to an obstacle course by some authors—focuses on fairness as its primary goal. In this model, criminal defendants should be presumed innocent, the courts' first priority is protecting the constitutional rights of the accused, and law enforcement officials—the police and prosecutors—must be held in check to preserve freedom and civil liberties for all Americans. As such, this model is designed to present "obstacles" for government actors at every stage, slowing down the process and affording an opportunity to uncover mistakes made in the pursuit of justice. This view also stresses that crime is not a result of individual moral failure but is driven by social influences (such as unemployment, racial discrimination, and other factors that disadvantage the poor); thus, courts that do not follow this philosophy are fundamentally unfair to these defendants. Furthermore, rehabilitation aimed at individual problems is embraced as a strategy to prevent future crime.

Packer indicated that neither of these models would be found to completely dominate national or local crime policy.[29] To argue that one of these models is superior to the other requires an individual to make a value judgment. How much leeway should be given to the police? Should they be allowed to "bend" the laws in order to get criminals off the streets? Do the ends justify the means? Or, should criminal justice officials be required to follow rules and be held to higher standards than criminals? Is it important that our system be seen as fair and impartial?

Crime control model: a model by Packer that emphasizes law and order and argues that every effort must be made to suppress crime and to try, convict, and incarcerate offenders.

Due process model: a model by Packer that advocates defendants' presumption of innocence, protection of suspects' rights, and limitations placed on police powers to avoid convicting innocent persons.

> **The Kalief Browder Case:** President Barack Obama signed an executive order to ban the solitary confinement of juveniles in federal prisons in 2016. Does this ban fall under the crime control model or the due process model, and what arguments would you make about why it falls under either category? What types of cases would make new laws—new laws focused on crime control or new laws focused on due process—more likely to be attractive to both the public and politicians?

DISCRETION: MAKING AND APPLYING THE LAW

After considering the two competing criminal justice models, you may wonder why the two models are even possible—in other words, how can criminal justice

Discretion: authority to make decisions in enforcing the law based on one's observations and judgment ("spirit of the law") rather than the letter of the law.

professionals follow different procedures in different situations when ours is a nation under the rule of law and due process? The answer is that players throughout the system exercise discretion, making decisions based on their own judgments in particular situations. As you consider the processes and cases presented throughout this book, you will see discretion at work in many different ways.

For example, lawmakers understand that they cannot anticipate the range of circumstances surrounding each crime or create laws that reflect all local attitudes and priorities concerning crime control. Further, they cannot possibly enact enough laws to cover all potentially harmful behavior, with exceptions described for every possible scenario where strict application of the law would result in injustice. The report of the President's Commission on Law Enforcement and Administration of Justice (published in 1967) made a pertinent comment in this regard:

> Crime does not look the same on the street as it does in a legislative chamber. How much noise or profanity makes conduct "disorderly" within the meaning of the law? When must a quarrel be treated as a criminal assault: at the first threat, or at the first shove, or at the first blow, or after blood is drawn, or when a serious injury is inflicted? How suspicious must conduct be before there is "probable cause," the constitutional basis for an arrest? Every [officer], however sketchy or incomplete his education, is an interpreter of the law.[30]

Accordingly, enacting laws is just a first step, and persons charged with the day-to-day response to crime must exercise their own judgment within the limits set by those laws. Basically, they must decide whether to take action, which official response is appropriate, and how the community's attitude toward specific types of criminal acts should influence decisions. For example:

- Police officers exercise extensive discretion in deciding whether to stop, search, or arrest someone (discussed in Chapter 6).
- Prosecuting attorneys decide whether to bring criminal charges against an arrestee, thus making one of the most important judgment calls in the system (discussed in Chapter 10).
- Judges exercise discretion in setting or denying bail, and in imposing sentences (even with sentencing guidelines, discussed in Chapter 11).
- Corrections officials decide key issues of where to house convicted criminals, how to discipline them for rules violations on the inside, and whether to grant them early release on parole (discussed in Chapters 12–14).

> **The Kalief Browder Case:** How does a law that bans the use of solitary confinement for juveniles affect a corrections official's discretion in managing inmate housing assignments? What might be the long-term impacts of solitary confinement bans on inmate mental health? Alternatively, how might limiting the discretion of corrections officials affect the overall safety of a correctional facility? When deciding when and under what conditions an inmate should be separated from other inmates, with whom should the discretion lie?

Criminal justice flow and process: the movement of defendants and cases through the criminal justice process, beginning with the commission of a crime, and including stages that involve actions of criminal justice actors working within police, courts, and correctional agencies.

THE CRIMINAL JUSTICE PROCESS: AN OVERVIEW OF FLOW AND FUNCTIONS

What follows is a brief description of the criminal justice flow and process in the United States. Figure 1.2 shows a flowchart of that system and summarizes the major stages of

Figure 1.2 /// The Sequence of Events in the Criminal Justice System

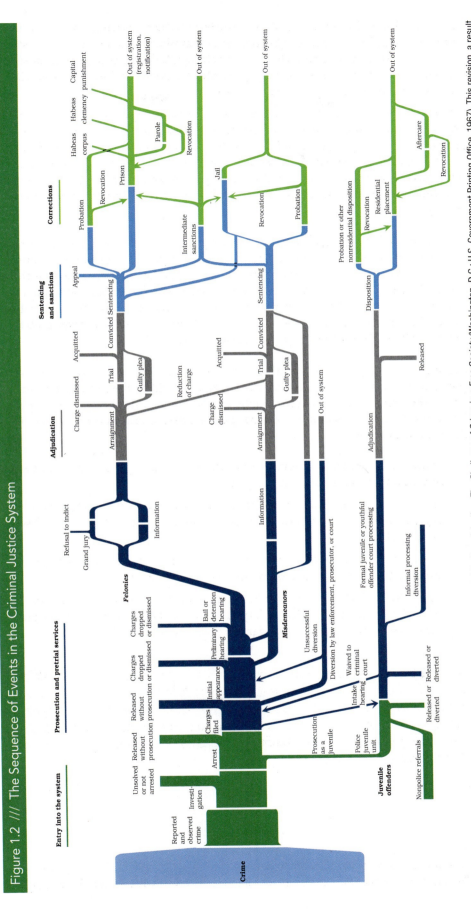

Source: Adapted from President's Commission on Law Enforcement and Administration of Justice, *The Challenge of Crime in a Free Society* (Washington, D.C.: U.S. Government Printing Office, 1967). This revision, a result of the Symposium on the 30th Anniversary of the President's Commission, was prepared by the Bureau of Justice Statistics in 1997.

Note: This chart gives a simplified view of case-flow through the criminal justice system. Procedures vary among jurisdictions. The weights of lines are not intended to show actual size of caseloads.

Scott Dekraai (L), sits next to his attorney, Assistant Public Defender Scott Sanders, at Orange County Superior Court in Santa Ana, California. The former tugboat worker pleaded guilty to first-degree murder for killing eight people in a Southern California hair salon where his ex-wife worked. Under the United States' system of justice, all criminal defendants prosecuted for serious crimes have the right to be represented by an attorney.

Arrest: the taking into custody or detaining of one who is suspected of committing a crime.

Prosecution: the bringing of charges against an individual, based on probable cause, so as to bring the matter before a court.

the process, including entry into the criminal justice system, prosecution and pretrial services, adjudication, sentencing and sanctions, and corrections. Note that *all* of the discussions in the following chapters of this book are based on the *people* and *processes* included in the depicted sequence of events.

The Offender's Pathway Through the Process

As we follow the path of the offender through the process, note that Figure 1.2 also depicts vertical pathways out of the criminal justice system. That is because many crimes fall out of the system for one of a variety of reasons: The crime is not discovered or reported to the police (the so-called dark figure of crime); no perpetrator is identified or apprehended; or, in some instances, a suspect is arrested, but the police later determine that no crime was committed, and the suspect is released from custody.

Law Enforcement: Investigation/Arrest

The flowchart in Figure 1.2 begins with "reported and observed crime." Police agencies learn about crime from the reports of victims or other citizens, from discovery by a police officer in the field, from informants, or from investigative and intelligence work. Once a law enforcement agency has established that a crime has been committed, the perpetrator must be identified and apprehended in order for the case to proceed through the system. Sometimes the offender is apprehended at the scene, but in other cases the police must conduct an investigation to find the perpetrator. Either way, the first formal step for most offenders in the criminal justice system is when the police take a suspect into custody for purposes of charging that person with a crime, known as an arrest.

Prosecution and Pretrial Activities

Next we enter the prosecution and pretrial services phase of the process—and the realm of the powerful individuals who "control the floodgates" of the courts process. After an arrest, police present information concerning the case and the accused (typically in the form of an official offense/arrest report) to the prosecutor, who will decide—at his or her discretion—if formal charges will be filed with the court. If no charges are filed, the accused must be released. The prosecutor can also elect, after initially filing charges, to drop charges (*nolle prosequi*) if he or she determines that the probable cause and/or evidence in the matter is weak. (Probable cause, discussed more fully in Chapter 8, is a legal term that basically refers to information that would lead a reasonable person to believe that a person has committed, is committing, or is about to commit a crime.) Furthermore, in some jurisdictions, defendants, often those without a prior criminal record, may be eligible for diversion from prosecution subject to the completion of specific conditions such as drug treatment. Successful completion of the conditions may result in charges being dropped or the record of the crime being expunged (meaning to legally strike or erase).

Initial Appearance

Persons charged with a crime must be taken for an initial appearance before a judge or magistrate without unnecessary delay (the amount of time is typically specified in the state's statutes or in municipal ordinances). There, the judge will inform the accused of the charges and decide whether there was probable cause for the police to make an arrest. If the offense is not very serious, the determination of guilt and assessment of a penalty may also occur at this stage.

Practitioner's Perspective

Police Officer

Kevin Wilmott
Police Officer in Southern California

Name: Kevin Wilmott
Position: Police Officer
Location: Southern California

What advice would you give to someone either wishing to study, or now studying, criminal justice and wanting to become a practitioner in this position? My biggest advice for students who are pursuing a career in law enforcement is to start looking into going on ride-alongs with agencies that they're interested in working for. A lot of times, agencies will offer civilian ride-alongs. Just call the department, and ask if you can go on a ride-along. Because that's the best way to really see if this is something that you're interested in. You can watch it on TV, you can read about it in a book, but until you actually go out in the field and shadow an officer and see what his or her "day in the life" is like, you don't really have a good idea. So I think the biggest thing is to go on ride-alongs and experience them first-hand.

Also, if you're not quite the age yet—typically the age is 21 for most agencies to be a police officer—a really good idea that I recommend is to look at civilian jobs in a police department. I started as a police dispatcher for two years. A lot of times there are positions for cadets, traffic enforcement or parking enforcement, dispatchers, records, whatever it may be. There are definitely civilian jobs where a lot of times the minimum age requirement is 18. So between 18 and 21 you can do that, and that actually gets you a foot in the door, as you get to see what it's like to work at a police department, and you can get to know the department and the community that you want to eventually work for as a police officer. It helps build your name and reputation with the department.

In general, what does a *typical* day look like for a practitioner in this position? Granted, our days are never quite routine, and every day is different. But, typically, a day in the life for me, for the most part, would start with going to briefing. In our briefing we go over what's going on in our community, what to look out for, if there have been any recent crimes or crime trends that we need to be aware of. We also get our assignments, which area of the city we'll be working, what car we're going to be in. After briefing, we get our vehicle ready, and that means putting all of our equipment in the patrol car, and then we go out and begin our shift. I currently work nights and weekends, so I personally am looking for impaired drivers. Some officers look out for drug users or traffic enforcement, and some are interested in working with quality-of-life issues with transciency, loitering, and things of that nature. But I personally am interested in DUI enforcement. So, a lot of times, when I'm not responding to a call for service, I'm out on the roads looking for people that may be impaired. And every so often we get dispatch for calls for service. Then at the conclusion of my shift, I gas up the vehicle, put it away, and take all the gear out of it. I also make sure I'm caught up on all my reports, because there's definitely a lot of report writing involved. The quieter hours are around three to five in the morning, so those are the times I try to catch up on all my reports.

To learn more about Kevin Wilmott's experiences as a police officer, watch the Practitioner's Perspective video in SAGE vantage.

Gary Leon Ridgway and his attorneys look over the plea agreement allowing him to escape the death penalty by pleading guilty to 48 counts of aggravated first-degree murder in the Green River serial killing cases.

Often, a defense attorney is also assigned at the initial appearance. All defendants who are prosecuted for serious crimes have a right to be represented by an attorney. If the court determines the defendant is indigent and cannot afford such representation, the court will assign counsel at the public's expense.

A decision about whether to release the defendant on bail or some other conditional release may also be made at the initial appearance. The court considers factors such as the seriousness of the charge; whether the defendant is a flight risk; and if he or she has a permanent residence, a job, and family ties. If the accused is likely to appear at trial, the court may decide that he or she should be released on recognizance (often termed "ROR," meaning that the defendant is released without having to provide bail, upon promising to appear and answer the criminal charge) or into the custody of a third party after the posting of a financial bond.

Preliminary Hearing or Grand Jury

The next step is to determine whether there is probable cause to believe the accused committed the crime and whether he or she should be tried. Depending on the jurisdiction and the case, this determination is made in one of two ways: through a preliminary hearing or through a grand jury. In a preliminary hearing, a judge determines if there is probable cause to believe that the accused committed the crime. If so, the case moves forward to trial, also known as "binding the defendant over" for trial. If the judge does not find probable cause, the case is dismissed.

In other jurisdictions and cases, the prosecutor presents evidence to a grand jury, which decides if there is sufficient evidence to bring the accused to trial. If the grand jury finds sufficient evidence, it submits to the court an indictment, a written statement of the essential facts of the offense charged against the accused. Misdemeanor cases and some felony cases proceed by the issuance of an "information," which is a formal, written accusation submitted to the court by a prosecutor (rather than an indictment from the grand jury). In some jurisdictions, indictments may be required in felony cases. Grand juries are discussed more in Chapter 9.

Adjudication

Adjudication: the legal resolution of a dispute—for example, when one is declared guilty or not guilty—by a judge or jury.

Next, in the middle of the flowchart shown in Figure 1.2, is the adjudication process. The adjudication process allows the defendant to respond to the charges brought against him or her, requires the government to prove its case (if the defendant claims that he or she is not guilty), and allows a judge or jury to decide whether the defendant is legally guilty or not guilty. Once an indictment or information has been filed with the trial court, the accused is scheduled for arraignment.

Arraignment

At the arraignment, the accused is informed of the charges, advised of the rights of criminal defendants, and asked to enter a plea to the charges. Generally, defendants enter a plea of guilty, not guilty, or *nolo contendere* (no contest).

If the accused pleads guilty or *nolo contendere* (accepts penalty without admitting guilt), the judge may accept or reject the plea. If the plea is accepted, the defendant has in effect given up his or her constitutional right to a trial, no trial is held, and sentencing occurs at this proceeding or at a later date. But contrary to popular media depictions, not guilty pleas and trials are very rare; approximately 95 percent of criminal defendants plead guilty as a result of plea bargaining between the prosecutor and the defendant.

Trial

If the accused pleads not guilty or not guilty by reason of insanity, he or she is basically forcing the government to prove its case—to prove the defendant's guilt beyond a reasonable doubt. A person accused of a serious crime is guaranteed a trial by jury but may request a bench trial where the judge alone, rather than a jury, will hear both sides of the case. In both instances the prosecution and the defense are permitted to present physical evidence and question witnesses, while the judge decides on issues of law. The trial results in an acquittal (not guilty) or a conviction (guilty) on the original charges or on lesser included offenses.

Sentencing and Sanctions, Generally

After a conviction, a sentence is imposed. With the exception of capital cases where the death penalty is being sought and the jury decides the punishment, the judge determines the sentence.

In arriving at an appropriate sentence, a sentencing hearing may be held at which time evidence of aggravating or mitigating circumstances is considered (aggravators are elements that tend to increase the offender's blame, such as use of torture; mitigators tend to reduce blame, such as youthfulness and lack of prior criminal record; these are discussed more in Chapter 11). Here the court may rely on presentence investigations by probation agencies and consider victim impact statements (a written or oral statement by the victim concerning the pain, anguish, and financial devastation the crime has caused).

The sentencing choices that may be available to judges and juries include one or more of the following:

- Death penalty (only in first-degree murder cases and only in certain states)
- Incarceration in a prison (for sentences of a year or longer), a jail (for sentences of up to a year), or another confinement facility
- Probation—allowing the convicted person to remain at liberty but subject to certain conditions and restrictions such as drug testing or drug treatment
- Fine—applied primarily as penalties in minor offenses
- Restitution—requiring the offender to pay compensation to the victim
- Intermediate sanction (used in some jurisdictions)—an alternative to incarceration that is considered more severe than straight probation but less severe than a prison term (e.g., boot camps, intense supervision often with drug treatment and testing, house arrest and electronic monitoring, and community service)

Sentences and punishment are discussed in Chapter 11, whereas intermediate sanctions, probation, and parole are examined in Chapter 14.

Appellate Review

Following trial and sentencing, a defendant may appeal his or her conviction or sentence by requesting that a higher court review the arrest and trial (a process known as appellate review). The appellate process provides checks on the criminal justice system by ensuring that errors at trial (except for those considered to be "harmless") did not

Acquittal: a court or jury's judgment or verdict of not guilty of the offenses charged.

Conviction: the legal finding, by a jury or judge, or through a guilty plea, that a criminal defendant is guilty.

Aggravating circumstances: elements of a crime that enhance its seriousness, such as the infliction of torture, killing of a police or corrections officer, and so on.

Mitigating circumstances: circumstances that would tend to lessen the severity of the sentence, such as one's youthfulness, mental instability, not having a prior criminal record, and so on.

Sanction: a penalty or punishment.

The U.S. Supreme Court has held that trial juries may hear and consider victim impact statements (concerning such factors as the pain, anguish, and suffering the defendant's crime has caused) when making sentencing decisions.

Indeterminate sentence: a scheme whereby one is sentenced for a flexible time period (e.g., 5–10 years) so as to be released when rehabilitated or when the opportunity for rehabilitation is presented.

Parole: early release from prison, with conditions attached and under supervision of a parole agency.

Determinate sentence: a specific, fixed-period sentence ordered by a court.

Wedding cake model of criminal justice: a model of the criminal justice process whereby a four-tiered hierarchy exists, with a few celebrated cases at the top, and lower tiers increasing in size as the seriousness of cases declines and informal processes (use of discretion) become more likely to occur.

adversely affect the fairness of trial processes and the defendant's constitutional rights. In death penalty cases, appeals of convictions are automatic. In other cases, the appellate court has sole discretion over whether to review the case.

Corrections

The next phase into which the offender enters is corrections, as shown in Figure 1.2. Offenders sentenced to incarceration usually serve time in a local jail or a state prison. Offenders sentenced to less than one year generally go to jail; those sentenced to more than one year go to prison.

A prisoner may become eligible for parole after serving a portion of his or her indeterminate sentence (a range, such as 5–10 years). Parole is the conditional release of a prisoner before the prisoner's full sentence has been served. The decision to grant parole is made by an authority such as a parole board, which has power to grant or revoke parole (i.e., return the parolee to prison) or to discharge a parolee altogether. In some jurisdictions, offenders serving what is called a determinate sentence—a fixed number of years in prison—will not come before a paroling authority, because each offender is required to serve out the full sentence prior to release, less any earned "good time credits" (a reduction in the time served in jail or prison due to good behavior, participation in programs, and other activities).

If released by a parole board or through mandatory release, the parolee will be under the supervision of a parole officer in the community for the balance of his or her unexpired sentence. This supervision is governed by specific conditions of release, and the parolee may be returned to prison ("parole revocation") for violations of such conditions.

Once a person who is suspected of committing a crime is released from the jurisdiction of a criminal justice agency, he or she may commit a new crime (recidivate) and thus need to be processed again through the criminal justice system. Studies show that individuals with prior criminal histories are more likely to be rearrested than those without a prior history.

The Juvenile Justice System

Juvenile courts usually have jurisdiction over matters concerning children, including delinquency, neglect, and adoption. They also handle "status offenses" such as truancy and running away, which are not applicable to adults. State statutes define which persons are under the original jurisdiction of the juvenile court. The maximum age of original juvenile court jurisdiction in delinquency matters is 17 in most states.[31] Chapter 15 examines the juvenile justice system.

THE WEDDING CAKE MODEL OF CRIMINAL JUSTICE

The criminal justice system flowchart shown in Figure 1.2 makes it easy to see the steps through which the offender moves through the process horizontally. It is also helpful to see how the system treats cases differently by viewing it vertically, as shown in the wedding cake model of criminal justice, developed by Samuel Walker (see Figure 1.3).[32]

18 ■ Part 1: Criminal Justice as a System

Figure 1.3 /// The Wedding Cake Model of Criminal Justice

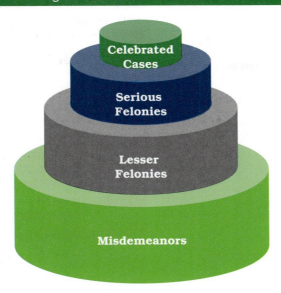

This approach begins with the premise that not all criminal cases are viewed or handled in the same manner—by either the police or the judiciary. The type of treatment given to a particular case, including its outcome, is determined mostly by factors such as the seriousness of the charge, current policies and political influences, and the defendant's status and resources. Some cases are run-of-the-mill and are treated as such, but some involve high-profile crimes and/or criminals and command much more attention.

As shown in Figure 1.3, the wedding cake model divides criminal justice system proceedings into four different categories: celebrated cases, serious felonies, lesser felonies, and misdemeanors. This partitioning of cases allows for a closer analysis of how the criminal justice system deals with them.

Layer 1: Celebrated Cases

The top layer of the wedding cake model includes the "celebrated cases." These cases command a great deal of media attention because the crimes are unusual (such as when James Holmes killed 12 people and injured 70 others in a mass shooting at a movie theater in Aurora, Colorado; or when Dzhokhar Tsarnaev, along with his brother, detonated two bombs at the Boston Marathon, killed a police officer, kidnapped a man, and engaged in a shootout with police) or because the defendants are celebrities or high-ranking officials (consider singer R. Kelly's criminal sexual abuse trial; O. J. Simpson, the celebrated athlete and actor whose "trial of the century" has been the topic of numerous books and documentaries; and Aaron Hernandez, the former NFL player who was convicted of murder). The legal process for these types of cases is not different from that of the "usual" case, but because of their complexity or high-profile nature, many more resources are devoted in the form of forensic tests, use of expert witnesses, jury sequestering (seclusion), cameras in the courtroom, and crowd control. At the same time, due to the widespread media and public attention given to the cases, extra care is taken to ensure that defendants' rights are protected and that the accused are not given preferential treatment based on their status.

Layer 2: Serious Felonies

The second layer of the wedding cake includes serious felonies, which are violent crimes committed by people with lengthy criminal records and who often prey on people they do not know. These are viewed by the police and prosecutors as the cases that are most

Convicted offenders who are to be incarcerated will serve time in either a local jail (typically for misdemeanants serving less than one year) or a federal or state prison (for felons, and usually for more than one year).

deserving of "heavy" treatment and punishment, and there is not as great a chance that the defendant will be allowed to enter into a plea agreement before trial.

Layer 3: Lesser Felonies

On the third layer of the wedding cake are the lesser felonies, which tend to be nonviolent and typically viewed as less important than the felonies in Layer 2. These offenders might have no criminal record; might have had a prior relationship with the victim; and might be charged with drug-related, financial, or other such crimes. A good portion of these cases will be filtered out of the system prior to trial and end in plea agreements.

Layer 4: Misdemeanors

Layer 4 consists of misdemeanor cases, which make up about 90 percent of all criminal matters. They include less serious and public order crimes: public drunkenness, minor theft, disturbing the peace, and so on. Police are more likely to deal with these cases informally and use their discretion to determine whether an arrest is necessary. When arrests are made, they will be handled by the lower courts—where the large number of cases handled by these courts require quick case processing, making trials rare. Many misdemeanor cases are resolved with plea agreements and penalties that involve fines, probation, or short-term jail sentences.[33]

ETHICS THROUGHOUT THE CRIMINAL JUSTICE SYSTEM

Robert F. Kennedy, in his 1960 book, *The Enemy Within: The McClellan Committee's Crusade Against Jimmy Hoffa and Corrupt Labor Unions*, stated that

> in the fall of 1959 I spoke at one of the country's most respected law schools. The professor in charge of teaching ethics told me the big question up for discussion among his students was whether, as a lawyer, you could lie to a judge. I told the professor . . . that I thought we had all been taught the answer to that question when we were six years old.[34]

As Kennedy, the late U.S. attorney general and U.S. senator, implied, by the time people reach the point of being college or university students, it is hoped that everyone—in particular, those studying the field of criminal justice—will have had deeply ingrained in them the need to practice exemplary and ethical behavior. Ethical behavior is often reemphasized in postsecondary education when instructors explain the need for academic honesty. The importance of ethics is often reinforced in other social settings, for example, in work environments (employees are entrusted with property and other responsibilities), at home (parents and other caregivers explain the importance of treating others with respect), in sports (coaches emphasize the importance of fair play), and at church (treating others as you want to be treated is often taught as a guiding principle).

Character in the criminal justice arena is of utmost importance. Without it, nothing else matters. Character, it might be said, is who we are when no one is watching. Having character means that people do not betray their fellow human beings or violate oaths of office or public trust. Unfortunately, character of mind and actions cannot be taught solely in a

You Be the . . .

Judge

Four male juveniles were burglarizing a home when Baltimore County Police Officer Amy Caprio was called to the scene. Officer Caprio approached a stolen vehicle the teens drove to the neighborhood. When she reached the vehicle, she encountered one of the juveniles behind the wheel. She drew her weapon and fired once after the vehicle accelerated toward her. The juvenile struck her with the vehicle and fled the scene. Officer Caprio, who had served on the department for 3 years and 10 months, was rushed to the hospital where she was pronounced dead. Further investigation revealed that the juvenile who killed the officer was waiting in the driver's seat of the stolen vehicle while his three associates carried out the burglary. All four teens were eventually charged with felony murder.

1. The juveniles were tried as adults for this crime. Does this decision by the prosecutor mostly closely align with the crime control or due process model of justice?
2. Should the prosecutor have had the discretion to try these juveniles as adults? Would it change your mind if they had been 12-year-olds rather than 17-year-olds?
3. Do you believe politics played a part in the decision to charge all four with murder?
4. What aggravating or mitigating circumstances of this case might be discussed at trial?
5. Where would this type of case fit on the wedding cake model of criminal justice?

Source: For more information, see Jessica Anderson, "Jury Sees Video Showing Moments Before Baltimore County Officer Amy Caprio's Death," *Baltimore Sun,* April 23, 2019, https://www.baltimoresun.com/news/crime/bs-md-co-caprio-trial-openings-20190422-story.html.

college or university classroom, nor can it be implanted in a doctor's office, administered intravenously, or ingested as a pill.

Prior to commencing your journey into the field of criminal justice (and, later, reading Chapter 4, concerning ethics), you might do well to first ask yourself these questions: Should police officers receive free coffee from restaurants and quick-stop establishments? Free or half-priced meals? What about judges? Prison wardens? If judges, wardens, or other criminal justice professionals are not "rewarded" with such "freebies," then should police officers be able to accept such "gifts" while on- or off-duty? On what grounds do many police officers expect such favored treatment? And can this lead to ethical problems with respect to their work?

At its root, the field of criminal justice is about people and their activities; and in the end, the primary responsibilities of people engaged in this field is to ensure that they be of the highest ethical character and treat everyone with dignity and respect. Therefore, as indicated earlier, this textbook, unlike most or all others of its kind, devotes an entire chapter to the subject of ethics—or what essentially constitutes "correct" behavior in criminal justice.

Ethics: a set of rules or values that spells out appropriate human conduct.

/// IN A NUTSHELL

- It is important to study the criminal justice system because it serves to shape our government and culture, and because all of us are potential victims, witnesses, and taxpaying supporters of our justice system. Furthermore, we need to understand the rights afforded to us by our Constitution.

- The consensus theory of justice argues that laws reflect the values and beliefs shared by most people in society, whereas the conflict theory of justice maintains that laws are created to protect the interests of the most powerful people in society.

- The due process model of criminal justice holds that criminal defendants should be presumed innocent and constitutional rights of the accused should be emphasized over conviction of the guilty. Conversely, the crime control model, likened to an assembly line, emphasizes deterring criminal conduct and protecting society; eliminating legal loopholes, swiftly punishing offenders, and granting a high degree of discretion to police and prosecutors. Neither of these models, however, completely dominates national or local crime policy.
- Discretion is exercised throughout the criminal justice system, because violations of laws vary in their seriousness, and there are not enough human and financial resources to enforce all laws equally. Therefore, persons charged with enforcing laws, adjudicating cases, and punishing offenders exercise considerable judgment in terms of deciding whether to take action, which official response is appropriate, and to what extent the community's attitude toward specific types of criminal acts should affect such decisions.
- Although the offender's path through the criminal justice process may be viewed as horizontal in nature, there are many points through which an offender can take a vertical pathway out of the system.
- The wedding cake model of criminal justice argues that not all criminal cases are viewed or handled in the same manner by either the police or the courts—some are treated with more discretion, while others are subjected to more formal processes. The processing of cases by the criminal justice system is divided into four categories: celebrated cases, serious felonies, lesser felonies, and misdemeanors. The type of treatment given to a particular case is determined by factors such as the seriousness of the charge, current policies and political influences, and the defendant's status and resources.
- Criminal justice officials must behave ethically. People engaged in this field must be of the highest ethical character and treat everyone with dignity and respect.

/// KEY TERMS & CONCEPTS

Review key terms with eFlashcards at **edge.sagepub.com/peak4e**.

Acquittal   17
Adjudication   16
Aggravating circumstances   17
Arrest   14
Conflict theory of justice   9
Consensus theory of justice   8
Conviction   17
Crime control model   11
Criminal justice flow and process   12
Determinate sentence   18
Discretion   12
Due process model   11
Ethics   21
Indeterminate sentence   18
Mitigating circumstances   17
Parole   18
Prosecution   14
Sanction   17
Three-strikes law   5
Wedding cake model of criminal justice   18

/// REVIEW QUESTIONS

Test your understanding of chapter content at **edge.sagepub.com/peak4e**.

1. Having read the chapter, do you believe it is important for you to study the structure and function of our criminal justice system? Why or why not?
2. How and why are laws created according to the consensus model of criminal justice? According to the conflict model of criminal justice?
3. How would you describe the crime control and due process models of criminal justice? What indicators might be present in your local community that would help you determine the most dominant model?
4. What are the major points at which an offender is dealt with in the criminal justice process, as he or she moves through the police, courts, and corrections components?
5. What are the four tiers of the wedding cake model of criminal justice, and how is discretion by criminal justice officials used differently at each stage?
6. How would you characterize the importance of discretion and ethics throughout the justice system?

/// LEARN BY DOING

As indicated in this textbook's preface, this "Learn by Doing" section, as well as those at the end of subsequent chapters, is an outgrowth of teachings by famed educator John Dewey, who advocated the "learning by doing" or problem-based approach to education. It also follows the popular learning method espoused by Benjamin Bloom in 1956, known as Bloom's taxonomy, in which he called for "higher-order thinking skills"—critical and creative thinking that involves analysis, synthesis, and evaluation.[35]

The following scenarios and activities will shift your attention from textbook-centered instruction and move the emphasis to student-centered projects. By being placed in these hypothetical situations, you can thus learn—and apply—some of the concepts covered in this chapter, develop skills in communication and self-management, at times become a problem solver, and learn about and address current community issues.

1. Assume that you are an officer in your campus criminal justice honor society and are invited to speak at the society's monthly meeting concerning your view of how crime is perceived and dealt with in your community. You opt to approach the question from Packer's crime control and due process perspectives. Given what you know about crime and criminal justice in your community, what will you say in your presentation?

2. As a member of your campus criminal justice honor society, you are asked to speak at a meeting of your local police department's Citizens' Police Academy, focusing on the general need for citizens to "become involved" in addressing crime. What will you say?

3. Your criminal justice professor asks you to prepare your own succinct diagram of the criminal justice process, including brief descriptions of each of the major stages (arrest, initial appearance, and so on) as a case flows through the process. What will your final product look like?

4. As part of a class group project concerning the nature of crime and punishment, you are asked by your fellow group members to develop a 10-minute presentation on the wedding cake model of criminal justice. How will you describe it?

/// STUDY SITE

Get the tools you need to sharpen your study skills. SAGE edge offers a robust online environment featuring an impressive array of free tools and resources.

Access practice quizzes, eFlashcards, video, and multimedia at **edge.sagepub.com/peak4e**.

CHAPTER 2

FOUNDATIONS OF LAW AND CRIME
Nature, Elements, and Measurement

The Constitution of the United States was made not merely for the generation that then existed, but for posterity—unlimited, undefined, endless, perpetual posterity.

—Henry Clay

LEARNING OBJECTIVES

As a result of reading this chapter, you will be able to

1. Explain how modern-day law evolved from English common law
2. Describe the three sources of law in the U.S. legal system
3. Identify the differences between criminal and civil law
4. Explain the difference between substantive and procedural law
5. Review two critical elements of the criminal law—criminal intent (*mens rea*) and the physical commission of the criminal act (*actus reus*)
6. Describe how felonies and misdemeanors are placed into two separate broad categories
7. Delineate the definitions of, and distinctions between, crimes against persons and property; the different degrees of homicide; and offenses classified as public order, white-collar, and organized crime
8. Explain the three primary methods for measuring crime and advantages and disadvantages of each

ASSESS YOUR AWARENESS

Test your knowledge of the foundations of law and crime by responding to the following nine true-false items; check your answers after reading this chapter.

1. The U.S. legal system is based on English common law.
2. A person who, upon returning home, discovers that her premises have been illegally entered and valuables removed, will correctly tell police, "I've been robbed."
3. Under current U.S. law, one can be charged only for those criminal acts that he or she actually performs, and not for failure to act or perform in some manner.
4. As opposed to the situation under English common law, today one may use force, even deadly force, if he or she reasonably believes that an attack against him or her is imminent.
5. No particular amount of time is necessary for one to legally premeditate a murder.
6. Rape and theft are often referred to as public order or victimless crimes.
7. The term *white-collar crime* was introduced in 1939, when a researcher discovered that many crimes were committed by persons of respectability and high social status in the course of their occupations.
8. If a burglar enters a premise and also commits a rape and a murder while inside, the hierarchy rule requires police to report to the FBI only the crime of murder.
9. Carjacking is now one of the FBI's eight Part I crimes.

<< Answers can be found on page 419.

As stated in this chapter, one's intent while committing a crime is not always easy to prove. For example, in a crime of homicide, there are a variety of possible outcomes, and the prosecutor will "look behind the act" to determine the killer's state of mind, the elements of the crime that were present, and so on. For example, in 2017, a 10-month-old girl in Methuen, Massachusetts, suffered cardiac arrest and was revived twice. While police worked to revive the child, the mother, who was a former drug addict, shuffled back and forth between her bedroom and bathroom. Police wondered whether this was nervous behavior, or whether she was flushing evidence of the drug that had harmed her baby. With no obvious signs of child endangerment in the residence, criminal justice officials found it difficult to identify the responsible party or determine intent. A prosecutor who reviews this case must ask and attempt to answer several questions:

- Was this a crime or an unfortunate accident?
- Did someone purposefully expose this child to a lethal dose of fentanyl?
- If not purposeful, did someone recklessly expose the child to this substance, or did the child ingest residue unintentionally left on an object?

As you will learn in this chapter, different crimes contain different elements and correspond with various levels of punishment. Think about why different facts should lead to a different criminal charge and punishment. What facts are important in defining crimes and why? Why should these facts matter? What other facts might help you to decide more easily what really happened and what type of crime might have been committed against this infant?

The answers to these questions are at the very heart of the criminal law and of our system of justice, which holds people criminally responsible only when the state can prove beyond a reasonable doubt that the accused committed each and every element of a crime without a valid defense.

INTRODUCTION

John Adams famously said we have a "government of laws and not of men," meaning that our democracy is not ruled at the whim of kings or rulers or demagogues. As explained in Chapter 1, Americans willingly give up some of their rights to their elected governments to create laws and to receive protection for their persons and property. It thus becomes important that Americans possess fundamental knowledge of our laws: how they are created and to what types of behaviors they apply.

Confusion sometimes surrounds the definition of specific crimes and criminal justice system responses. We might hear someone screaming, "I've been robbed!" on television or in the movies after returning home and discovering that his house has been entered and ransacked (he was not robbed; he was burglarized). Or, someone discovers a dead body and exclaims, "He's been murdered!" A person may have indeed been killed, but many killings are not criminal in nature; only a judge or jury can decide if a murder has taken place. News reporters commonly mistake jail for prison and might erroneously state, "John Jones, a convicted murderer, was sentenced to 10 years in jail today" (if sentenced to 10 years, Jones will serve his time in a prison, not a jail). As French philosopher Voltaire wrote, "If you wish to converse with me, define your terms." That statement represents the major purpose of this chapter.

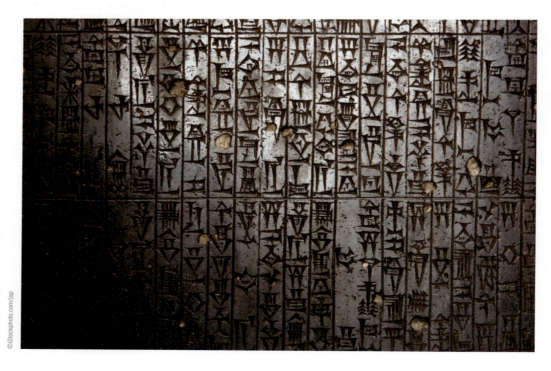

The Code of Hammurabi, written in about 1780 B.C.E., set out crimes and punishments based on *lex talionis*—"an eye for an eye, a tooth for a tooth." It is the earliest-known example of a ruler's setting forth a body of laws arranged in orderly groupings.

The reader should bear in mind, however, that several important components of the rule of law are not discussed here, primarily because they go beyond the reach of an introductory textbook. Persons wishing to inquire more deeply into the law—for example, in such areas as conspiracies, attempted crimes, omissions, and causation—would be wise to enroll in criminal law and procedure courses.

COMMON LAW AND ITS PROGENY

Rules were laid out in ancient societies. The use of societal laws can be traced back to the reign of Hammurabi (1792–1750 B.C.E.), the sixth king of the ancient empire of Babylon. The Code of Hammurabi set out crimes and punishments based on lex talionis—"an eye for an eye, a tooth for a tooth." A more recent source of law is found in the Mosaic Code of the Israelites (1200 B.C.E.), in which, according to tradition, Moses—acting as an intermediary for God—passed on the law to the tribes of Israel. The Mosaic Code includes the Bible's Ten Commandments and contains descriptions of forbidden behaviors that are still defined as criminal acts in modern society (e.g., thou shall not kill nor steal).

Lex talionis: Latin for "an eye for an eye, a tooth for a tooth"; retaliation or revenge that dates back to the Bible and the Middle Ages.

But the system of law as we know it today (except for Louisiana's, which is based on the French civil code) is based on common law: collections of rules, customs, and traditions of medieval England, created during the reign of Henry II (1154–1189 C.E.), who began the process of unifying the law. Henry established a permanent body of professional judges who traveled a "circuit" and sat on tribunals in shires throughout the Crown's realm. These judges eventually gave the Crown jurisdiction over all major crimes and sowed the seeds of the trial by jury and the doctrine of *stare decisis*.[1]

The *stare decisis* (Latin for "to stand by things settled") doctrine is perhaps the most distinctive aspect of Anglo-American common law. According to *Black's Law Dictionary*, *stare decisis* is the doctrine stating that, when a court has once laid down a principle of law as applicable to a certain state of facts, it will adhere to that principle—and apply it in the same manner to all future cases where the facts are substantially the same.[2] This doctrine binds courts of equal or lower status or levels in a given jurisdiction to the principles established by the higher appellate courts within the same jurisdiction.

Stare decisis: Latin for "to stand by a decision"—a doctrine referring to court precedent, whereby lower courts must follow (and render the same) decisions of higher courts when the same legal issues and questions come before them, thereby not disturbing settled points of law.

For example, the federal courts have a three-tier structure (see Figure 2.1). According to the *stare decisis* doctrine, a federal district court in Maryland is required to follow the decisions of the Fourth Circuit Court of Appeals, of which it is a part, as well as those of the U.S. Supreme Court. However, it is not bound by the decisions of other district courts.[3] Note, however, that our system of law still must remain flexible and capable of change, and thus courts can also revisit earlier decisions and set new precedents.

MODERN-DAY SOURCES AND HIERARCHY OF LAW

In addition to the two primary types of law—criminal and civil (discussed in the next section)—the U.S. legal system features different sources of law and jurisdictions where those laws are enforced and administered. Our system of government is based on the concept of federalism, which divides government powers between the federal government and other government entities, including state and local governments. We have federal and state laws with corresponding federal and state courts to preside over such cases. Within those two legal arenas, laws—criminal and civil—are organized hierarchically, with different priorities and legal effects depending on their source and application.

Federalism: a type of government that divides powers between a national (federal) government and governments of smaller geographic territories, including states, counties, and cities.

Again, terminology is critical to understanding law. Generally speaking, a *statute* is a law enacted by Congress (a federal law) or by a state legislature (a state law). Statutes are also known as *statutory law*. A *code* or *ordinance* typically refers to a law enacted by a local

Chapter 2: Foundations of Law and Crime

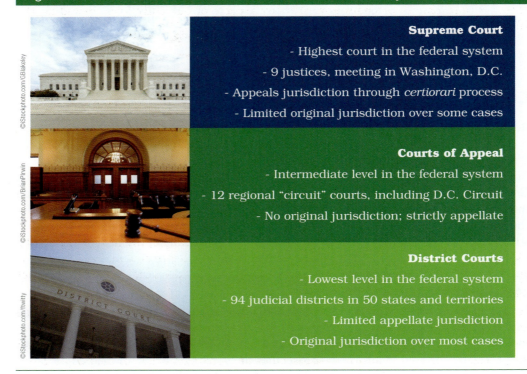

Figure 2.1 /// Three-Tier Structure of the U.S. Federal Court System

Supreme Court
- Highest court in the federal system
- 9 justices, meeting in Washington, D.C.
- Appeals jurisdiction through *certiorari* process
- Limited original jurisdiction over some cases

Courts of Appeal
- Intermediate level in the federal system
- 12 regional "circuit" courts, including D.C. Circuit
- No original jurisdiction; strictly appellate

District Courts
- Lowest level in the federal system
- 94 judicial districts in 50 states and territories
- Limited appellate jurisdiction
- Original jurisdiction over most cases

lawmaking body—a county board or a city council, for example (municipal laws). These and other types of laws are prioritized as follows:

Federal Law

1. The U.S. Constitution—"the supreme law of the land," which takes precedence over state constitutions and law even if they conflict
2. Federal statutes—civil and criminal laws enacted by Congress
3. Administrative laws—orders, directives, and regulations for federal agencies, such as workplace laws promulgated by the Occupational Safety and Health Administration (OSHA)
4. Federal common law—published decisions from the U.S. Supreme Court and the U.S. Circuit Courts of Appeal, which, like the common law from England (discussed earlier), establish legal "precedence" and must be followed by lower courts in the federal and state systems (Chapter 9 describes how the Supreme Court decides to hear cases and render its decisions.)

State Law

1. State constitutional law—state constitutional rulings (from a state's highest court) that may give greater protection or rights than the federal constitution but may not give less, and that contain protections similar to the U.S. Constitution—civil rights and liberties, separation of powers, and checks and balances[4]
2. State statutes—laws enacted by state legislatures, including criminal laws like statutes prohibiting murder or robbery
3. State common law—precedent established in published opinions by state appellate judges when deciding civil or criminal cases

City/County Law

Municipal ordinances or codes govern many aspects of our daily lives, including the following:

- Building and construction standards
- Rent control
- Noise and nuisance regulations
- Public health and safety
- Business licenses
- Civil rights and antidiscrimination

CRIMINAL AND CIVIL LAW

Simply put, criminal law applies to criminal matters, for example, when someone breaks a law prohibiting the commission of a robbery. Civil law applies to civil matters, for example, when two parties have a property dispute or want to get divorced. These two distinct types of law differ in several critical ways.

First, each type involves different parties. Criminal law represents what we as a people have decided is criminal behavior, and crimes are considered harmful to all of us in society. As such, when someone commits a crime, the state or government—through the prosecutor or district attorney—prosecutes the person on behalf of the people. Since the title of a case always first references the party that brought suit against the other (i.e., the government entity responsible for prosecution in a criminal case), a typical criminal case name is something like *U.S. v. Jones* or *State of Maine v. Smith*. In a civil matter, two individuals (or business entities like a corporation) are on either side. In a property dispute, such as when A erects a fence over the property line of B, one neighbor brings a lawsuit against the other so that the court can referee their dispute. Or, if a person is injured using a product like a hairdryer, that person can bring a civil case against the manufacturer, probably a corporation. A typical civil law case name is something like *Jones v. Smith* or *Jones v. ABC Corporation*. In the former example, Jones is the party bringing the suit—the plaintiff—and Smith is the party defending against the suit—the defendant. Not surprisingly, these two types of cases are heard in different courts, and most courthouses have separate criminal and civil "divisions," where judges are more experienced in either of these particular types of cases.

Another important difference involves how these cases are decided. In a criminal case, the prosecutor or the state has the burden of proving—the burden of proof—the defendant's guilt "beyond a reasonable doubt." This sometimes-heavy burden is designed to force the government—the prosecutor—to prove its case with the strongest possible evidence to avoid wrongful convictions of innocent persons. Underlying our rule of law in the United States is the all-important concept that one is innocent until proven guilty. Sometimes the burden shifts to the defense to prove something, as with self-defense claims (discussed in Chapter 9). In a civil case, the burden on the party seeking damages or a remedy is less than in a criminal matter—those representing this party must prove their case by a "preponderance of the evidence." The precise difference between the legal standards of "beyond a reasonable doubt" and "preponderance of the evidence" can be hard to distinguish, even for experienced lawyers.

Criminal law: the body of law that defines criminal offenses and prescribes punishments for their infractions.

Civil law: a generic term for all noncriminal law, usually related to settling disputes between private citizens, governmental, and/or business entities.

Plaintiff: the party bringing a lawsuit or initiating a legal action against someone else.

Defendant: a person against whom a criminal charge is pending; one charged with a crime.

Burden of proof: the requirement that the state must meet to introduce evidence or establish facts.

Sources of federal law include the U.S. Constitution, the U.S. Supreme Court, and those laws enacted by Congress.

Reasonable doubt: the standard used by jurors to arrive at a verdict—whether or not the government (prosecutor) has established guilt beyond a reasonable doubt.

Reasonable doubt can be difficult to explain; in fact, several courts prefer not to attempt to give the jury any explanation at all. However, in most cases reasonable doubt means that, after hearing all of the evidence, jurors do not possess an abiding conviction—to a moral certainty—that the charges brought against the defendant are true. This does not necessarily mean absolute certainty—there can still be some doubt, but only to the extent that it would *not* affect a "reasonable person's" belief that the defendant is guilty. By contrast, if such doubt *does* affect a reasonable person's belief that the defendant is guilty, then the prosecution has not met its burden of proof, and the judge or jury must acquit—find the defendant not guilty.

The civil standard of a preponderance of the evidence is a much less difficult burden to meet and is often referred to as the "50 percent plus a feather" test. It asks jurors to decide which way the evidence causes the scales of justice to tip, toward guilt or innocence, and to decide the case on that basis.

The major difference between civil and criminal matters is the penalty. In a criminal case, the state or prosecutor seeks to punish a defendant with prison or jail time, a monetary fine, or both (or perhaps a community-based punishment such as probation, discussed in Chapter 14). In a civil matter, one party is seeking "damages" (money or some legal remedy) from the other party rather than trying to send him or her to jail or prison. In the property dispute example, A would be required to tear down or move the fence and perhaps pay for the legal fees B incurred in bringing the suit. And in the hairdryer example, the corporation could be ordered to pay the consumer's medical expenses and legal fees.

Some conduct can give rise to both a criminal and a civil matter, as the case of O. J. Simpson illustrates (see "Investigating Further"). A few examples might serve to explain the difference—and how the two types of cases can cause problems for the police and misunderstanding by the public.

Assume that Jane calls the police to her home and tells the officer that she and her husband, Bill, recently separated and he went to their home and removed some furniture and other goods that she does not believe he should have taken. The officer must inform Jane that there is nothing he can do—at this point, this is a *civil*, not a criminal, matter. Jane may be upset with the officer, but legally the police have no jurisdiction in such disputes. Assume, however, that Bill goes to the home and makes serious threats of injury toward Jane, and she then goes to court and obtains a temporary protection order (TPO) commanding Bill to avoid any form of contact with her; Bill then disregards the TPO and stalks Jane at her place of employment. Because he violated the court's order, this has now become a *criminal* matter, and the police may arrest Bill.

Table 2.1 /// Differences Between Civil and Criminal Law

	Civil	Criminal
Burden of proof	"Preponderance of evidence"	"Beyond a reasonable doubt"
Nature of crime	A private wrong	A public wrong
Parties	Case is filed by an individual party	Some level of government files charges against the individual
Punishment	Usually in the form of monetary compensation for damages caused; no incarceration	Jail, fine, prison, probation, possibly death
Examples	Landlord/tenant dispute, divorce proceeding, child custody proceeding, property dispute, auto accident	Person accused of committing some crime (or, perhaps, neglecting a duty to act)

Or, look again at the example of someone erecting a fence that cuts across his neighbor's property. The neighbor refuses to move or tear down the fence, so the matter is taken to court. This is a civil cause of action. Both sides have a dispute that the courts will resolve if the parties cannot reach an agreement. Assume further that the neighbors cannot resolve the fence matter, and one day while one of them is working in his yard the other attacks him with a club. Now the attacking neighbor could face a criminal charge from the state (assault with a deadly weapon) and a civil lawsuit by the injured neighbor (for medical expenses and emotional trauma).

Table 2.1 shows the primary differences between civil and criminal law.

SUBSTANTIVE AND PROCEDURAL LAW

Substantive law is the written law that defines criminal acts—the very "substance" of the criminal law. Examples are laws that define and prohibit murder and robbery. Procedural law (discussed in detail in Chapter 8) sets forth the procedures and mechanisms for processing criminal cases. The following examples of procedural law stem from constitutional amendments: Police officers are required to obtain search and arrest warrants, except in certain situations (Fourth Amendment), officers must give the *Miranda* warning before a suspect is interrogated while in custody (Fifth Amendment), and defendants have the right to an attorney at key junctures during criminal justice system processing (Sixth Amendment). Note that these laws govern how police officers, lawyers, judges, corrections officers, and a host of others do their work in the justice system. Procedural law also prescribes rules concerning legal jurisdiction, jury selection, appeal, evidence presented to a jury, order of conducting a trial, and representation of counsel.

Substantive law: the body of law that spells out the elements of criminal acts.

Procedural law: rules that set forth how substantive laws are to be enforced, such as those covering arrest, search, and seizure.

Legal jurisdiction: the authority to make legal decisions and judgments, often based on geographic area (territory) or the type of case in question.

ESSENTIAL ELEMENTS: *MENS REA* AND *ACTUS REUS*

The Latin term for criminal intent is *mens rea*, or "guilty mind," and its importance cannot be overstated. Our entire legal system and criminal laws are designed to punish only those actors who *intend* to commit their acts. As will be seen later in the discussion of homicide, acts that are clearly intentional and premeditated (e.g., murder in the first degree) are punished most severely, while those acts that are less intentional and/or accidental are punished less harshly. For example, assume that Bill, while hunting deer, shoots another hunter while out in the woods. If the prosecutor has evidence to show the shooting was purely accidental in nature (the other hunter was out of position, or Bill's gun malfunctioned), the prosecutor will not charge Bill with unlawful killing. If, by contrast, the evidence shows that Bill intended to shoot the other hunter (again, considering evidence of the position of the two men, the number of shots, or proof of Bill's planning), the prosecutor will charge Bill with homicide.

Mens Rea: Intent Versus Motive to Commit Crime

There is an important distinction to be made between *intent* and *motive*. One's specific intent concerns what he or she is seeking to do and is connected to a purpose or goal; motive refers to one's reason for doing something. For example, when a poverty-stricken woman steals milk for her child, her intention is to steal, but her motive is to provide for her child. Therefore, motive (the "why" someone is stirred to perform an action) is grounded primarily in psychology; intent, conversely, is the result of one's motive, is grounded in law, and carries a higher degree of blameworthiness because a harmful act was committed. Crime movies often focus a great deal on offenders' possible motives for committing particular crimes. However, as one law professor put it, "As any first year law student will tell you, motive is irrelevant in determining criminal liability. Unlike in the television show . . . in the perceived

Intent, specific: a purposeful act or state of mind to commit a crime.

Motive: the reason for committing a crime.

Investigating Further

Criminal and Civil Law—The O. J. Simpson Case

O. J. Simpson was once a wealthy and admired college and professional football player as well as a movie and television personality. But in 1994 he was charged with stabbing to death his estranged wife, Nicole, and her friend, Ron Goldman. The media covered the trial live as California prosecutors presented evidence of Simpson's history of domestic abuse and damning DNA evidence from the crime scene, while Simpson's "Dream Team" of high-caliber defense attorneys cross-examined the state's witnesses and dissected their evidence in hopes of creating reasonable doubt about Simpson's guilt. After the nearly yearlong trial, the jury deliberated only four hours before returning not-guilty verdicts on all charges. One year later, the victims' parents filed a civil suit against Simpson, alleging that he caused the victims' wrongful deaths and seeking millions of dollars in damages for those deaths. Many people wondered how the families could hope to win when Simpson had been found not guilty in the criminal trial. The answer lies in the differences between the criminal and civil cases. In the civil case, the burden of proof on the families to establish guilt was less than the burden on the prosecutors in the criminal case. The families needed to show only by a preponderance of the evidence—rather than beyond a reasonable doubt—that Simpson killed the victims. The civil jurors needed to decide only which way the scales of justice tipped, toward guilt or innocence, not whether the state had proven Simpson's guilt beyond a reasonable doubt. Indeed, the civil jury found Simpson responsible for the deaths and awarded the families $33.5 million in damages. So although Simpson was acquitted in the criminal trial and did not serve any prison time, he was adjudged responsible in the civil trial and ordered to pay money damages for his conduct.

[*Authors' note:* In an unrelated case, in October 2008 Simpson was convicted on 12 criminal charges and received a 33-year prison sentence stemming from a robbery at a Las Vegas casino hotel room in 2007 in which he and several cohorts attempted to retrieve memorabilia and personal items from two sports collectibles dealers. Becoming eligible for parole after serving 9 years of his sentence in a medium-security prison in Lovelock, Nevada, Simpson was granted parole in July 2017.]

Sources: For a complete analysis of the Simpson case, see, for example, Jeffrey Toobin, *The Run of His Life: The People v. O. J. Simpson* (New York: Random House, 1998); Lawrence Schiller and James Willwerth, *American Tragedy: The Uncensored Story of the O. J. Simpson Defense* (New York: Random House, 1996); Joseph Bosco, *A Problem of Evidence: How the Prosecution Freed O. J. Simpson* (New York: William Morrow, 1996); CNN.com, O. J. Simpson Main Page, http://www.cnn.com/US/OJ/; Eric Levenson, "O. J. Simpson Granted Parole After 9 Years in Prison," CNN, July 20, 2017, http://www.cnn.com/2017/07/20/us/oj-simpson-parole-hearing/index.html.

---

real world of criminal liability, motive is just a bit player, appearing only in limited circumstances, usually as a consideration in certain defenses. Ordinarily, the only real questions at trial are (1) did the defendant commit the illegal act and (2) did she have the necessary mental state (*mens rea*, or intent)?"[5]

To determine the requisite *mens rea* for a specific crime, we look to the criminal statute that defines the offense. But you will not find the term "*mens rea*" as part of any criminal law. Instead, this element is expressed through a variety of terms that differ from state to state. For example, an intentional crime might be defined as an act committed "intentionally," "willfully," or "maliciously," while a less serious crime—an accidental crime—can be expressed as an act committed "negligently," "recklessly," or "without due caution." The terms used to express *mens rea* are not uniform, so criminal justice professionals must learn to identify these terms and understand how they operate within a criminal statute (see the discussion of homicide and related exercises later in this chapter).

One's intent while committing a crime is not always easy to prove. As is discussed later, regarding the crime of homicide, when A shoots B, there are a variety of possible outcomes, and the prosecutor will "look behind the act" to determine what was going on in the mind

One's criminal intent is a major consideration in our legal system; for example, one who intentionally kills someone during a robbery may well be charged with premeditated murder.

A hunter who accidentally (without intent) shoots and kills another typically would not be charged with premeditated murder.

of the killer, and whether to reduce what appears to be a charge of murder in the first degree (an intentional killing) to one of manslaughter (an accidental killing).

Actus Reus: The Act

Another critical feature of the U.S. criminal justice system is that we do not punish people for merely thinking about committing criminal acts; rather, the law generally requires a voluntary, overt act—killing, injuring, threatening, or breaking and entering, for example. The intentional *failure* to act (an "omission") can also be criminal but only when there is a legal duty to do something, such as when a person willfully fails to pay income tax owed or a parent fails to feed a child or give him or her medical attention.

The rule for establishing criminal liability is to prove that the defendant committed the *actus reus* element (the criminal act) with the *mens rea* ("guilty mind") set forth in the particular criminal law. When these two critical elements are present, it is known as "concurrence." For example, a man in a ski mask breaking into a locked home might seem to be committing the *actus reus* element for burglary (see "Crimes Against Property," below). But what if he is doing so to save himself from a terrible snowstorm after his car broke down? The all-important *mens rea* element is missing, and there is no concurrence. Accordingly, the prosecutor must prove both elements beyond a reasonable doubt—a question of fact for the jury to decide.

Actus reus: Latin for "guilty deed"—an act that accompanies one's intent to commit a crime, such as pulling out a knife and then stabbing someone.

Mens rea: Latin for "guilty mind"—the purposeful intention to commit a criminal act.

FELONIES AND MISDEMEANORS

Crimes are also classified into two broad categories based on the severity of the criminal act and the corresponding punishment. Felonies are offenses punishable by death or that have a possible sentence of more than one year of incarceration in prison. Many states further divide their felonies into different classes; for example, under Arizona's laws, first-degree murder is a Class 1 felony and is punishable by death or life imprisonment; sexual assault is a Class 2 felony (the number of years for which one may be sentenced to prison for this and other offenses will differ, depending on an offender's prior record); aggravated robbery (the offender has an accomplice) is a Class 3 felony; and forgery is generally a Class 4 felony.[6]

A misdemeanor is a less serious offense and is typically punishable by fines or incarceration for less than one year in a local jail. Like felonies, misdemeanors are often classified under state laws. In Arizona, shoplifting is a Class 1 misdemeanor (if the value of items taken is less than $1,000 and the item is not a firearm); reckless driving is a Class 2 misdemeanor; a vehicle driver who dumps trash on a highway or road is guilty of a Class 3 misdemeanor.[7]

Felony: a serious offense with a possible sentence of more than a year in prison.

Misdemeanor: a lesser offense, typically punishable by a fine or up to one year in a local jail.

Chapter 2: Foundations of Law and Crime

You Be the . . .

Police Officer

The Nevada Revised Statutes[8] set forth the following statutory provisions related to driving. Read them carefully and then respond to the questions posed.

> NRS 484B.657. Vehicular manslaughter.
>
> A person who, while driving or in actual physical control of any vehicle, proximately causes the death of another person through an act or omission that constitutes simple negligence is guilty of vehicular manslaughter.
>
> NRS 484B.653. Reckless driving.
>
> It is unlawful for a person to: (a) Drive a vehicle in willful or wanton disregard of the safety of persons or property, (b) Drive a vehicle in an unauthorized speed contest on a public highway, or (c) Organize an unauthorized speed contest on a public highway.
>
> NRS 484B.165. Using handheld wireless communications device.
>
> Except as otherwise provided in this section, a person shall not, while operating a motor vehicle on a highway in this State: (a) Manually type or enter text into a cellular telephone or other handheld wireless communications device, or send or read data using any such device to access or search the Internet or to engage in nonvoice communications with another person, including, without limitation, texting, electronic messaging and instant messaging, or (b) Use a cellular telephone or other handheld wireless communications device to engage in voice communications with another person, unless the device is used with an accessory which allows the person to communicate without using his or her hands, other than to activate, deactivate or initiate a feature or function on the device.

1. What is the *mens rea* element under the vehicular manslaughter statute? What is the *actus reus* element?
2. Provide an example of what would qualify as reckless driving under section (a).
3. A woman who is texting while driving strikes and kills a pedestrian who is crossing the street. The woman was not speeding. Can she be charged for a violation of NRS 484B.165—Using handheld wireless communications device? Why or why not?

OFFENSE DEFINITIONS AND CATEGORIES

Crimes Against Persons

Crimes against persons: violent crimes, to include homicide, sexual assault, robbery, and aggravated assault.

Crimes against persons are what most people consider "violent crime" or "street crime," such as certain homicides, sexual assaults, robberies, and aggravated assaults. As you will learn later in this chapter, the Federal Bureau of Investigation (FBI) defines these crimes as offenses that involve force or threat of force.

Homicide

The taking of a human life—homicide—is obviously the most serious act that one can perpetrate against another person. But not every killing is criminal in nature, as the following examples demonstrate:

- Justifiable homicide—self-defense, legal state or federal executions, acts of war, or when a police officer uses lawful lethal force
- Excusable homicide—killings that are wholly accidental, such as when a person who is driving the speed limit and paying full attention hits a small child who darts into the street from behind a large RV, where no reasonable person could have known that such a risk was possible or preventable

Table 2.2 /// The "Ladder" of Homicide Crimes and the Required *Mens Rea*

Charge	Mens Rea	Example
Murder (Intentional Killings)		
First-Degree Murder	Premeditated, with malice aforethought	Planning to kill your wife's boyfriend by waiting at his home one evening and killing him when he arrives
Second-Degree Murder	Intentional but not premeditated	Unexpectedly seeing your wife's boyfriend several days after you discover their affair, then quickly grabbing a gun you keep in your car and killing him
Manslaughter (Accidental Killings)		
Voluntary Manslaughter	Committed in the "heat of passion"; being adequately provoked and not having time to "cool off" before the act	Arriving home and finding your wife and her boyfriend together, immediately grabbing a nearby weapon, and killing one or both of them in a blind rage
Involuntary Manslaughter	Unintentional/accidental; causing a death while breaking the law (typically a misdemeanor criminal law) or while being negligent	Texting while driving and then accidentally hitting a child who darts out into the street
Felony Murder (Strict Liability)		
Felony/First-Degree Murder	Unintentionally causing a death while intentionally committing a dangerous felony; no *mens rea* required = strict liability	While burglarizing your boss's office to steal from the petty cash fund, she arrives unexpectedly, discovers you there, has a heart attack, and dies

Criminal homicides fall into two categories: murder (intentional killings) and manslaughter (accidental killings). Within these two categories, offenses are ranked in seriousness by degrees. As mentioned earlier, under our system of justice, the premise underlying homicide is that "when A shoots B, there are a variety of possible outcomes." The prosecutor must attempt to determine the shooter's intent, which can result in criminal charges ranging from murder in the first degree to involuntary manslaughter. A useful way to think of the universe of possible homicide charges is as a "ladder of offenses," going from the least serious up to the most serious (see Table 2.2).

Murder. The term *murder* includes only intentional killings, which are categorized by degrees:

- *Murder in the first degree* (sometimes termed "murder one") is the unlawful, intentional killing of a human being with *premeditation and deliberation* (often termed "P&D") and *malice aforethought*. Federal and state statutes define murder and its elements differently, but generally they all require the elements of intent, P&D, and malice aforethought.

    P&D means the defendant thought about committing the act before doing so. Courts generally look at the following factors to determine P&D: evidence of planning, the manner of killing, and the prior relationship between the defendant and the victim.[9] Courts also look at the *time* the defendant may have spent contemplating or planning in order to determine whether premeditation existed, but courts differ on this issue. The federal courts have held that *no* minimum time period is necessary, and a jury can determine from the facts whether or not a defendant premeditated murder.[10] Malice aforethought is often said to be shown when someone acts with "a depraved heart," evidenced by one's

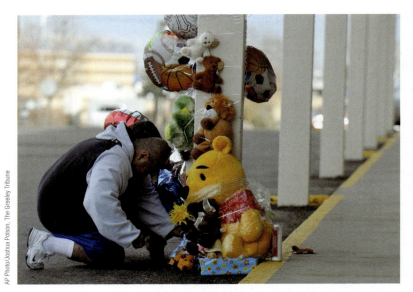

Excusable killings include those that are accidental in nature, such as when a driver strikes and kills a toddler who darts out into the street; in such cases the driver will not be deemed culpable (blameworthy).

Felony-murder rule: the legal doctrine that says that, if a death occurs during the commission of a felony, the perpetrator of the crime may be charged with murder in the first degree, regardless of the absence of intent, premeditation and deliberation, or malice aforethought.

conscious intent to shoot another person with a gun or stab someone with a knife.

Dangerous conduct can also be prosecuted as first-degree murder under the **felony-murder rule**, which provides that if a death occurs during the commission of a felony, the defendant will be charged with murder in the first degree, regardless of his or her intent (a crime that does not require a *mens rea* element is known as a "strict liability" crime—see also the discussion of statutory rape, later). The classic example involves multiple defendants robbing a bank and during the robbery the bank security guard dies from a heart attack. In that case, all the defendants may be charged with first-degree murder under the felony-murder rule. Likewise, if one of the bank robbers panics and shoots a security guard, all of the defendants will be charged with first-degree murder even though the robbers intended only to rob, not to kill anyone. The felony-murder rule is designed to deter those who might otherwise commit dangerous felonies. If a would-be bank robber knows the penalty for an accidental death during his or her crime might be a charge of first-degree murder, perhaps the robber will think twice about committing the crime.

- *Murder in the second degree* ("murder two") is distinguished from first-degree murder in that it is also intentional—with malice—yet *impulsive*, without P&D. An example would be when two men get into an argument at a bar, and one pulls a knife and stabs the other to death. He intended to stab the other man, but the killing did not involve premeditation. Furthermore, although the intent to kill is an essential element of both first- and second-degree murder, a defendant can also be found guilty of second-degree murder if his or her actions show gross recklessness and a high disregard for human life, and there is extreme risk of death. Although it will depend on the jury's views, acts such as allowing a dangerous dog to run free and bite a child, intentionally shooting a gun into a crowd of people, throwing a heavy object off a roof onto a crowded street below, and playing Russian roulette (loading a gun and intentionally firing it at another person) have led to conviction for second-degree murder. As you will see later, these actions could also qualify as involuntary manslaughter.[11]

Manslaughter. The term *manslaughter* refers to accidental killings, categorized as voluntary (intentional but without malice) and involuntary (unintentional):

- *Voluntary manslaughter* is an intentional killing, but it involves (at least in the eyes of the law) no malice. Instead, there is "heat of passion" to a degree that a "reasonable person" might have been provoked into killing someone. The best example is when a person comes home early in the day and finds his or her significant other in the arms of another person, becomes enraged, grabs a gun, and kills one or both of them. The killer acted in the heat of passion rather than intentionally. A killing can be downgraded on the homicide ladder, from murder to voluntary manslaughter, only if the actor was adequately provoked (generally, words alone—as in an argument—are not enough to provoke, but seeing something like a cheating spouse is), and the actor must not have had time to "cool off." The person discovering his cheating spouse cannot leave, go to a bar

Part 1: Criminal Justice as a System

and drink a few beers, and then return to the scene and kill the offending couple (this would be first-degree murder, as explained earlier). The "passion" that aroused the person to kill must have arisen contemporaneously—at the time of the provocation—and continued until the time of the criminal act.

The circumstances of a killing might cause a prosecutor to look at both second-degree murder and voluntary manslaughter as possible charges. When a perpetrator clearly killed with intent but without P&D (e.g., two people fighting with weapons), a second-degree murder charge is appropriate. But when that same actor is fighting with weapons because the victim provoked her and she did not have time to "cool off" after that provocation, the charge could be downgraded to voluntary manslaughter. A prosecutor will consider all of the evidence to determine the right homicide charge, up or down the "ladder."

- *Involuntary manslaughter* is typically established in one of two ways: (1) through acts of negligence, such as when one is driving too fast on a slick road and kills a pedestrian, or (2) via the misdemeanor-manslaughter rule—similar to the felony-murder rule, but the crime involved is a misdemeanor. For example, a man enters a convenience store and shoplifts a six-pack of beer; the clerk chases him out the door but slips and falls, striking his head on the sidewalk and dying from the force of the impact. The shoplifter may be charged with involuntary manslaughter, as his actions caused the clerk's death.

> **The Methuen Fentanyl Case:** Now that you have learned the different types of homicide and how the critical element of *mens rea* determines the degree and punishment, consider the scenario (from the beginning of the chapter) under which the jury could have convicted the mother from Methuen, Massachusetts, and how *mens rea* plays a part in each of the following:
>
> - *First-degree murder:* The mother intentionally gave fentanyl to her child, and she planned the child's death.
> - *Second-degree murder:* The mother gave fentanyl to her child intentionally but did not plan for the child to die.
> - *Voluntary manslaughter:* The mother held her child while consuming fentanyl while experiencing severe withdrawal symptoms, knowing that the child would likely be exposed and harmed by the drug.
> - *Involuntary manslaughter:* The mother used fentanyl but never anticipated that the child would accidentally and unintentional be exposed to the drug.
>
> Further, consider the fact that drug paraphernalia was found in the mother's car during the subsequent investigation. But the police noted that the mother, father, and grandparents were highly cooperative during the investigation. How might those facts affect a case for homicide?

Sexual Assault

Sexual assault, referred to as "rape" or "forcible rape" under some older state laws, was historically defined as the carnal knowledge of a female forcibly and against her will, and most criminal laws did not recognize rape of men, same-sex rape, or rape between spouses. Today, most states have adopted the modern definition of sexual assault—sexual contact without the victim's consent, but with no limitations on gender or relationship of perpetrator and victim. Most states have also recognized that sexual assault occurs when someone has sexual contact with a person who is incapable of consenting (someone who is

Robbery involves taking, or attempting to take, anything of value from another person by force or threat of force or violence, where the victim is in fear of injury or death.

intoxicated, under anesthesia, or mentally challenged). In such cases, the perpetrator knows or should know that the victim cannot consent to the act. Beginning in 2013, the FBI removed the term *forcible* from the agency's definition of rape and it is now defined as "penetration, no matter how slight, of the vagina or anus with any body part or object, or oral penetration by a sex organ of another person, without the consent of the victim." About 134,000 rapes are reported to the police annually in the United States.[12]

Like other crimes, sexual assault is categorized by degrees depending on the type of contact, from sexual penetration without the consent of the victim (first degree, the most serious) to unwanted sexual contact that does not result in physical injury (often third degree). Like homicide, sexual assault includes a "strict liability" crime with no *mens rea* element, also known as "statutory rape." This crime is defined as sexual contact between a "victim" of a certain age, typically between ages 12 and 16, and a "perpetrator" who is older, typically 19 and above.

Robbery

Robbery is the taking of or attempt to take anything of value from the care, custody, or control of a person or persons by force or threat of force or violence and/or by putting the victim in fear. About 319,000 robberies are reported to the police annually in the United States.[13] As stated earlier in this chapter, many times people who come home to find their houses have been broken into claim they have been "robbed" when they obviously have not been (they have been burglarized), given that robbery requires a face-to-face taking—a combination of theft and assault.

Aggravated Assault

Aggravated assault is an unlawful attack upon another for the purpose of inflicting severe or aggravated bodily injury. This offense is usually accompanied by the use of a weapon or by other means likely to produce death or great bodily harm. When aggravated assault (or even regular assault, as long as there is a threat) and larceny-theft (described in the next section) occur together, the offense falls under the category of robbery. Each year about 811,000 aggravated assaults are reported in the United States.[14]

As is the case with homicide crimes, criminal justice students often have difficulty understanding the "ladder" of assault crimes. A few examples will help to clarify the differences:

- First, the mere placing of someone in fear for his or her safety is an assault. If Joe yells at Jack threateningly, "I'm going to beat your brains out," this is an assault. An *assault*, then, occurs when one person makes threatening gestures that alarm someone and makes that person feel under attack; actual physical contact is not necessary.

- But if Joe intentionally strikes Jack on his cheek, the intentional physical contact intended to harm raises this conduct to the crime of *assault and battery*.

- Finally, if Joe gets a tire iron out of his car and strikes Jack with it several times, inflicting severe injury, Joe has now committed an *aggravated assault*.

Crimes Against Property

Crimes against property are offenses where no violence is involved, only the taking of property—crimes such as burglary, larceny-theft, motor vehicle theft, and arson.

Burglary

Burglary is the unlawful entry of a structure to commit a felony or theft. To classify an offense as a burglary, the use of force to gain entry need not have occurred, nor does anything of value have to have been stolen. The FBI, in its *Uniform Crime Reports* (detailed later in this chapter), defines "structure" as an apartment, barn, house trailer or houseboat when used as a permanent dwelling, office, railroad car (but not an automobile), stable, or vessel (i.e., ship). About 1.4 million burglaries are reported annually in the United States.[15]

Larceny-Theft

Larceny-theft is the unlawful taking, carrying, leading, or riding away of property from the possession of another; it includes attempted thefts as well as thefts of bicycles, motor vehicle parts and accessories, shoplifting, pocket-picking, or the stealing of any property or article that is not taken by force and violence or by fraud. The value of the item stolen is significant, and in all states the monetary worth will determine whether the larceny-theft is a felony or a misdemeanor; each state's statutes will set forth its limits. For example, according to Massachusetts statutes, if the item is worth more than $250, it is a felony; Iowa, however, has several classifications: It is a "serious misdemeanor" if the item stolen is valued between $200 and $500, an "aggravated misdemeanor" if worth between $500 and $1,000, and a felony if worth more than $1,000.[16] Each year about 5.5 million larceny-thefts are reported to the police in the United States.[17]

> **Crimes against property:** crimes during which no violence is perpetrated against a person, such as burglary, theft, and arson.

You Be the . . .

Prosecutor

A mother in New York asks her sister to babysit her infant son for two days while she goes to a job interview. The mother asks that either her sister or her sister's 17-year-old daughter give the boy a teaspoonful of medicine two times per day, but she fails to inform them of the proper dosages. The sister becomes distracted and forgets to medicate the infant. Later, realizing that the medicine has not yet been administered, the 17-year-old daughter gives the infant what turns out to be an overdose of the medicine, and the infant dies. A potentially relevant law in New York is as follows:

New York Penal Law § 125.25: A person is guilty of *murder in the second degree* when . . . under circumstances evincing a depraved indifference to human life, and being eighteen years old or more the defendant recklessly engages in conduct which creates a grave risk of serious physical injury or death to another person less than eleven years old and thereby causes the death of such person (penalty: 15 to 25-year prison term).

As the prosecutor reviewing this case, you must ask and attempt to answer several questions:

1. What crime, if any, was committed here?
2. If there was a crime committed, who bears responsibility (culpability) for it?
3. If any of the involved parties is charged, would you have enough evidence to prove the *actus reus* and *mens rea* elements for second-degree murder?

Note: See The New York State Senate, The Laws of New York, Section 125.25, Murder in the Second Degree, https://www.nysenate.gov/legislation/laws/PEN/125.25.

Motor Vehicle Theft

Motor vehicle theft involves the theft or attempted theft of a land-based, self-propelled vehicle that does not run on rails and is not classified as farm equipment. Examples of motor vehicles include cars, buses, motorcycles, trucks, snowmobiles, and scooters. Approximately 773,000 motor vehicle thefts are reported annually in the United States. The estimated loss associated with these events is approximately $6 billion.[18]

Arson

Arson is any willful or malicious burning of or attempting to burn, with or without intent to defraud, a dwelling house, a public building, a motor vehicle or aircraft, personal property of another, and so forth. There are different types of arsonists, with very different motives for setting fires. Each year about 41,000 arsons are reported to police, with an average loss per event of about $15,600. About half (45 percent) of all arsons involve structures (residential, storage, public, and so on).[19]

Public Order Crimes

Public order crimes: offenses that violate a society's shared norms.

Public order crimes are offenses that violate general public values or the norms shared among most members of society. They are sometimes called "victimless" crimes, since many people argue that these crimes harm only the offenders. Public order crimes are also sometimes called "complaintless" crimes, since many involve consensual activities or do not involve clearly identifiable victims. Offenses classified as public order crimes include drug-related crimes, prostitution, public drunkenness, gambling, and various forms of disorderly conduct. Although public order crimes often involve consensual activities between offenders (e.g., a drug dealer and a drug user, a prostitute and a "John" who pays for sex), violence and other serious criminal offenses often accompany these activities. For example, shootings and homicides are commonplace in open-air drug markets when dealers fight over market territory. Further, human trafficking is closely tied to prostitution. The United Nations Office on Drugs and Crime reports that sexual exploitation accounts for up to almost half of all human trafficking in North, Central, and South America.[20]

White-Collar Crime

White-collar crime: crimes committed by wealthy or powerful individuals in the course of their professions or occupations.

The concept of white-collar crime, sometimes called occupational or corporate crime, was introduced in 1939 in an address to the American Sociological Association by Edwin Sutherland, who defined it as "a crime committed by a person of respectability and high social status in the course of his occupation."[21] White-collar crime challenges many of the traditional assumptions concerning criminality—that it occurs in the streets and is mostly committed by criminals who are lower class and uneducated. Sutherland, after examining 40 years of records held by regulatory agencies, courts, and commissions, reported that of the 70 largest industrial and mercantile corporations, each had violated at least one law, averaged eight violations apiece, and had an adverse decision related to false advertising, patent abuse, wartime trade violations, price fixing, fraud, or intended manufacturing and sale of faulty goods.[22]

Although we frequently hear of white-collar criminals, the extent of white-collar crime is difficult to measure for several reasons. First, collecting accurate data is difficult since official statistics and victim surveys generally do not include much information concerning this type of crime. And, for obvious reasons, corporations zealously guard their public image and thus prefer to regulate themselves and maintain a code of silence. In addition, the police, social scientists, and members of the media are often inexperienced in the ways of corporate crime, much of which involves insider corporation- and industry-specific knowledge. Furthermore, although the Sherman Antitrust Act (1890) and hundreds of laws and regulatory agencies exist to keep white-collar crime in check and to police corporations—through recalls, warnings, consent agreements, injunctions, fines, and criminal proceedings—guilty companies often maintain legions of attorneys and accountants who possess considerable expertise in seeing that their bosses are seldom if ever punished.[23] We do know, however, that white-collar crime is the largest and most costly type of crime in the United States. As criminologist Frank Hagan put it, "All the other forms of criminal behavior together do not equal the costs of occupational and organizational (corporate) crime."[24]

Several celebrity white-collar crime cases have made national news. Most people have heard of Bernie Madoff's $50 billion fraudulent Ponzi scheme (where one basically uses new investors' funds to pay early investors, rather than using profits earned by the individual or organization running the operation); Madoff was sentenced to 150 years in prison for his crimes.[25] Or they know that businesswoman/author/television personality Martha Stewart was convicted of committing and lying about insider trading, in which she sold stock that she knew was likely to plunge in price.[26] These celebrated cases are well known, but white-collar crime can take many more forms, including the following:

- A 2019 college admissions bribery scandal, called Operation Varsity Blues, exposed parents and university staff involved in bribery and other forms of fraud to facilitate applicant admissions to top American colleges and universities.

- A Swiss pharmaceutical company pleaded guilty and paid a record $500 million in fines for price fixing on vitamins.

- Medical quackery and unnecessary surgical procedures victimize more than two million Americans, cost $4 billion, and result in 12,000 deaths per year. Fee splitting and "ping-ponging" (in which doctors refer patients to other doctors in the same office) also occur.

- A major auto manufacturing company, aware that a defect (which would cost $11 to repair) in one of its vehicles could result in a fiery explosion during a rear-end collision (even at low speeds), decided it would be cheaper not to recall the vehicles and make repairs but, instead, to pay drivers' injury and death claims.[27] Lawyers engage in "ambulance-chasing," file unnecessary lawsuits, and falsify evidence.

- Corporations dump or release toxic chemicals and hazardous materials into the environment to cut costs and avoid regulatory laws.

- Companies steal secrets and patents from one another and thus commit corporate espionage.

- Individuals steal the identities of others, with nearly 18 million persons in the United States being victimized by identity thieves in any given year.[28] Offenders may target victims of natural disasters or other types of victims in phony fund-raising schemes.

- Nigerian letter scams often involve emailed pleas to help transfer money from Nigeria or some other part of the world, with false promises of financial compensation if victims agree to provide their banking information.

An often-cited crime typology, developed by Herbert Edelhertz, distinguishes between two types of white-collar crime.[29] The first type involves crimes committed in the course of offenders' occupations by those operating inside business, government, or other establishments in violation of their duty of loyalty and fidelity to employer or client. These crimes could include commercial bribery and kickbacks, embezzlement, insider trading, expense account fraud, or any other offense committed by an offender in the course of carrying out his or her work duties. The second type of white-collar crime involves crimes incidental to and in furtherance of business operations (but not the central purpose of the business). For example, producing false company financial statements, using deceptive advertising, or committing antitrust violations can indirectly benefit the offender by benefiting his or her employment company.

Organized Crime

Organized crime is a term used to describe illegal acts committed by individuals involved in illegal organizations. White-collar criminals commit crimes as part of larger organizations, using their association or relationship with legitimate businesses and organizations to carry out their offenses. Organized crime offenders differ in that they use their association or relationship with illegal entities to carry out criminal activities. These illegal groups commonly engage in behaviors known as racketeering activities. The FBI defines these activities under the Racketeer Influenced and Corrupt Organizations (RICO) statute,[30] and they include the following: bribery (including sports), counterfeiting, embezzlement of union funds, mail and wire fraud, money laundering, obstruction of justice, murder for hire, drug trafficking, prostitution and sexual exploitation of children, alien smuggling, trafficking in counterfeit goods, theft from interstate shipment, and interstate transportation of stolen property. Organized crime may also include the following state crimes: murder, kidnapping, gambling, arson, robbery, bribery, extortion, and various drug offenses.

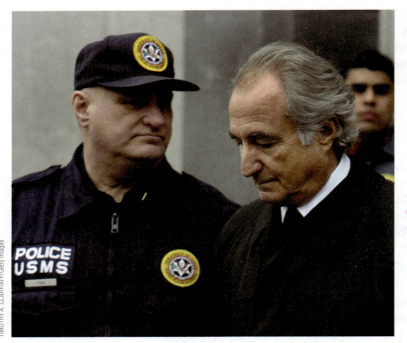

Bernie Madoff, a former stockbroker and financial advisor, was convicted of operating a Ponzi scheme that is considered to be the largest of its kind in U.S. history.

Organized crime: crimes committed by members of illegal organizations.

MEASURING CRIME AND VICTIMIZATION

Data about actual crime rates—incidents, offenders, location, and so on—help us more fully understand after the fact just how prevalent crime and offenders are. This information can then guide scholars and researchers to seek explanations for rates that are spiking or falling (see the criminological theories covered in Chapter 3). Crime measurement attempts to answer the question of "how much" with respect to crime in the United States, arming both criminal justice professionals and policy makers with critically important information to run this complex, human system.

How Much Crime in the United States? Depends on Whom You Ask

Mark Twain once said, rather famously, that there are "lies, damn lies, and statistics."[31] Unfortunately, that assessment of statistics is somewhat (if not significantly) accurate with respect to U.S. reported crime figures. One example that will make the point is two different data sets reporting hate crimes. Specifically, in a recent year, the Federal Bureau of Investigation's (FBI's) *Uniform Crime Reports* (discussed in the next section) reported a total of 7,175 hate crimes (with 8,493 victims).[32] However, the National Crime Victimization Survey (NCVS, also discussed later in this chapter) reported an annual average of *250,000* violent hate crime victimizations. This significant discrepancy is largely due to the fact that more than half (54 percent) of victims in the NCVS did not report their crimes to the police. Furthermore, in the NCVS, hate-related victimizations are based on victims' *suspicion* of the offenders' motivation, rather than on the police's suspicion.[33] Thus, crime figures must be viewed with caution and with an understanding of the limitations associated with each data source.

Errors and variations notwithstanding, to comprehend the impact of crime on our society, criminologists, victimologists, sociologists, psychologists, and members of other related disciplines need such information for their research and for making planning and policy recommendations. Knowing the nature and extent of crime also helps us understand the social forces that are driving those offenses and aggregated trends. Furthermore, measuring crime is one of the best ways to determine the effectiveness of our criminal justice agencies and policies. We can better examine the structure and functions of the police (by looking at reported crimes and the proportion of crimes solved by arrest or other means), the courts (to determine the types of punishment and treatment that offenders are receiving), and corrections organizations (to ascertain, among other things, whether or not offenders are being returned to prisons and jails).

Having crime data also allows for calculations of a national *crime rate* (discussed later), which in turn provides us with a "victim risk rate"—the odds that we (or relatives and friends) will become a victim of a serious crime.

Discussed first is the FBI's *Uniform Crime Reports*, followed by a review of a more in-depth method of capturing and analyzing reported crimes: the National Incident-Based Reporting System; finally, the National Crime Victimization Survey is examined. As you will learn, these three sources of crime information are very different in their approaches and findings.

Uniform Crime Reports: published annually by the FBI, each report describes the nature of crime as reported by law enforcement agencies; includes analyses of Part I crimes.

The FBI's *Uniform Crime Reports*

The Uniform Crime Reporting (UCR) Program was conceived in 1929 by the International Association of Chiefs of Police to meet a need for reliable, uniform crime statistics for the nation. In 1930, the FBI was tasked with collecting, publishing, and archiving those statistics. Today, several annual statistical publications, such as the comprehensive *Crime in the*

FBI: UCR

Uniform Crime Reporting

The Uniform Crime Reporting (UCR) Program has been the starting place for law enforcement executives, students of criminal justice, researchers, members of the media, and the public at large seeking information on crime in the nation. The program was conceived in 1929 by the International Association of Chiefs of Police to meet the need for reliable uniform crime statistics for the nation. In 1930, the FBI was tasked with collecting, publishing, and archiving those statistics.

Today, four annual publications, *Crime in the United States*, *National Incident-Based Reporting System*, *Law Enforcement Officers Killed and Assaulted*, and *Hate Crime Statistics* are produced from data received from over 18,000 city, university/college, county, state, tribal, and federal law enforcement agencies voluntarily participating in the program. The crime data are submitted either through a state UCR Program or directly to the FBI's UCR Program.

In addition to these reports, information is available on the Law Enforcement Officers Killed and Assaulted (LEOKA) Program and the Hate Crime Statistics Program, as well as the traditional Summary Reporting System (SRS) and the National Incident-Based Reporting System (NIBRS).

The FBI is undertaking a redesign of the system that has supported the FBI's UCR Program for more than 30 years. In support of this initiative, the FBI is currently managing the UCR Technical Refresh. Details

Explore Our Services
Publications
- Crime in the United States
- Law Enforcement Officers Killed and Assaulted (LEOKA)
- Hate Crime Statistics
- National Incident-Based Reporting System (NIBRS)
- Cargo Theft 2014 (pdf) | Cargo Theft 2013 (pdf)
- Human Trafficking (pdf)

NIBRS Resources
- NIBRS Overview

Recent Program Updates
- National Use-of-Force Data Collection
- Historical Rape Definition Retired (pdf)
- New Rape Definition (pdf)
- New Rape Definition Frequently Asked Questions (pdf)
- New Rape Fact Sheet (pdf)

Latest Releases

Law Enforcement Officers Killed and Assaulted 2016
The latest edition of Law Enforcement Officers Killed and Assaulted provides national statistics on lives lost in 2016. Details

Crime Stats for 2016
Violent crime increased and property crimes decreased during 2016 when compared to 2015 data. Details

The Federal Bureau of Investigation's Uniform Crime Reporting Program publishes annual crime data for selected crimes as reported to the police in the United States.

United States, are produced from data provided by more than 18,000 law enforcement agencies across the United States.

Other ancillary annual publications, such as *Hate Crime Statistics* and *Law Enforcement Officers Killed and Assaulted*, address specialized facets of crime such as hate crime or the murder and assault of law enforcement officers.[34] Special studies, reports, and monographs prepared using data mined from the UCR Program's large database are published each year as well. In addition to these reports, information about the National Incident-Based Reporting System (discussed later in this chapter), answers to general UCR questions, and answers to specific UCR questions are available on the program's website.

For the purposes of the *Uniform Crime Reports*, the FBI divides offenses into two groups, Part I and Part II crimes. Each month, contributing agencies voluntarily submit information to the FBI concerning the number of Part I offenses reported to them, as well as those offenses that were cleared by arrest, and the age, sex, and race of persons arrested for each of the offenses.

Crime Rate

A fundamental aspect of calculating and understanding crime concerns how the FBI calculates the crime rate. The formula used is not complicated in nature. It is as follows: number of crimes reported, divided by the population of the jurisdiction in question, then multiplied by 100,000; this renders the number of crimes reported for each 100,000 population. It is depicted as follows:

$$\frac{\text{Number of offenses}}{\text{Population of the jurisdiction}} \times 100{,}000$$

Crime rate: the number of reported crimes divided by the population of the jurisdiction, and multiplied by 100,000 persons; developed and used by the FBI *Uniform Crime Reports*.

As an example, assume, as in a recent year, that about 1,247,321 violent crimes were reported to the police in the United States; also, for that year the nation's reported population was 325,719,178. According to this formula, the resulting crime rate for that year was 382.9 violent crimes per 100,000 population.[35]

The crime rate formula can also be considered a "victim risk rate," or the chances of one's becoming a victim; therefore, the chances of one's being a victim of a violent Part I offense for that recent year were about 383 in 100,000.

Part I Offenses

Part I or "index" crimes are composed of eight serious felonies—murder, rape, robbery, aggravated assault, burglary, larceny-theft, motor vehicle theft, and arson. About 9 million such crimes are reported each year (about 1.3 million being violent and 7.7 million, property).[36] The first four of these eight offenses are deemed crimes against *persons* and are defined in the UCR Program as offenses that involve force or threat of force.

As seen in Table 2.3, crimes of murder had declined each year between 2012 and 2014. However, murders increased between 2014 and 2015 by about 12.1 percent and increased again by about 9.6 percent in 2016. Between 2016 and 2017 the number of homicides reported to the police in the United States remained relatively stable (less than a 1 percent decline).[37]

The FBI's annual *Uniform Crime Reports* contain a "Crime Clock" that depicts the average time intervals between Part I crimes; a sample Crime Clock is shown in Figure 2.2.

Part II Offenses

In addition to information concerning the eight Part I offenses, the FBI provides arrest-only data for about 20 Part II offenses—simple assaults, forgery, embezzlement, prostitution, vandalism, drug violations, and so forth.[38]

Part 1: Criminal Justice as a System

Table 2.3 /// Rates of Murder Committed in the United States

Year	Population	Murder and Nonnegligent Manslaughter	Murder and Nonnegligent Manslaughter Rate
2010	309,330,219	14,722	4.8
2011	311,587,816	14,661	4.7
2012	313,873,685	14,856	4.7
2013	316,497,531	14,319	4.5
2014	318,907,401	14,164	4.4
2015	320,896,618	15,883	4.9
2016	323,405,935	17,413	5.4
2017	325,719,178	17,284	5.3

Source: Adapted from Federal Bureau of Investigation, "Table 1. Volume and Rate per 100,000 Inhabitants, 1998–2017," *Crime in the United States—2017* (Washington, D.C.: Uniform Crime Reporting Program).

Figure 2.2 /// FBI's UCR "Crime Clock"

Source: Federal Bureau of Investigation.

Cautions and Criticisms of UCR Data

Each year when the FBI's *Crime in the United States* is published, many people and groups with an interest in crime rush to use the crime figures in attempts to rank and compare crimes in cities and counties. The FBI is quick to point out each year in its *Uniform Crime Reports* that making such comparisons is ill advised, due to the variety of characteristics of different states, counties, and communities.

Many variables can contribute to the amount of crime occurring in a specific jurisdiction. First, it is important to understand a jurisdiction's industrial/economic base, its dependence on neighboring jurisdictions, its transportation system, its reliance on tourism and conventions, its proximity to military installations and correctional facilities, and so forth. Indeed, the strength and aggressiveness of the local police are also key factors in understanding the nature and extent of crime occurring in an area.

In addition to the crime theories discussed earlier, other factors known to affect the volume and type of crime are largely outside the control of the criminal justice system:

- Population density and degree of urbanization
- Variations in composition of the population, particularly youth concentration
- Stability of the population with respect to residents' mobility, commuting patterns, and transient factors
- Modes of transportation and highway system
- Economic conditions, including median income, poverty level, and job availability
- Cultural factors and educational, recreational, and religious characteristics[39]

Critics of UCR data—who include any person engaged in serious research into crime, criminology, victimology, and so on—commonly note the shortcomings of these data (see Table 2.4).[40]

The Hierarchy Rule: Definition and Application

In tabulating how many crimes occur each year, law enforcement agencies are instructed by the FBI to use what is known as the hierarchy rule, which basically says that when more than one Part I offense is committed during a criminal event, the law enforcement agency must identify and report only the offense that is highest on the hierarchy list.[41]

Put another way, the hierarchy rule requires counting only the most serious offense and ignoring all others. Note, however, that this rule applies only to the crime reporting process; it does *not* affect the number of charges for which the defendant may be prosecuted in the courts.

Hierarchy rule: in the FBI *Uniform Crime Reports* reporting scheme, the practice whereby only the most serious offense of several that are committed during a criminal act is reported by the police.

Table 2.4 /// Limitations of the Uniform Crime Reports

Although the FBI's *Uniform Crime Reports* include several unique publications such as special reports providing statistics on hate crimes and law enforcement officers killed and assaulted, the data have some limitations.

UCR LIMITATIONS

- Offense data are available only for a small number (eight) of all crimes committed in the United States.
- The UCR data list only crimes reported to law enforcement agencies (not all crimes that occur are known to the police).
- Reporting of citizens' reports of crime by the police is voluntary; therefore, police may choose not to report or might report inaccurately (thus UCR data may be affected by the reporting practices of local law enforcement).
- The hierarchy rule (discussed in the text) is used, meaning that when a number of crimes are committed as part of a single criminal act, only the most serious offense of all of them is reported to the UCR.
- Attempted crimes are combined with completed crimes.
- When computing crime rates, the UCR counts incidents involving all kinds of targets (e.g., crimes of burglary are against businesses and residents, not against "populations").
- The UCR includes very little information concerning crime victims.

Note: A complete UCR handbook may be viewed at https://ucr.fbi.gov/additional-ucr-publications/ucr_handbook.pdf.

Source: Federal Bureau of Investigation's Uniform Crime Reports

Investigating Further

The Hierarchy Rule

To better understand the hierarchy rule in these exercises, you may wish to first revisit the Part I offenses listed earlier in this chapter, ranked in terms of their severity.

1. Assume that Doe, during the daytime hours, enters Smith's home through an unlocked back door and removes furniture that is valued at about $10,000. If Doe is apprehended, under the hierarchy rule the *only* crime that the police will report to the FBI is

   a. burglary   c. robbery
   b. theft   d. felony-theft

2. Further assume that Smith returns home and finds Doe inside; after scuffling briefly, Doe strikes Smith sharply with a candlestick holder, rendering Smith unconscious and near death. Then Doe, fearing he will be caught and returned to prison if Smith testifies against him, picks up a nearby vase and strikes enough blows to end Smith's life. What crime(s) has Doe committed? Under the UCR Program's hierarchy rule, which crime(s) will be reported by the police to the FBI?

The National Incident-Based Reporting System

Being aware of the criticisms leveled over time against the UCR Program, the U.S. Department of Justice in 1988 launched the National Incident-Based Reporting System (NIBRS). Although the UCR Program collects and analyzes data for eight Part I offenses, the NIBRS furnishes crime data provided by more than 5,900 participating federal, state, and local law enforcement agencies for 49 specific crimes (called Group A offenses) grouped into 23 crime categories.[42] The FBI posts an interactive map, which depicts the locations of participating agencies and the number of offenses reported for each of the major crime categories. This map can be accessed at https://nibrs.fbi.gov/.

With NIBRS, legislators, municipal planners/administrators, academicians, sociologists, and the public have access to more comprehensive, detailed, accurate, and meaningful crime information than the traditional UCR system can provide. With such information, law enforcement can better make a case to acquire the resources needed to fight crime. The NIBRS also enables agencies to locate similarities in crime-fighting problems so that agencies can work together to develop solutions or discover strategies for addressing the issues. Several NIBRS manuals, studies, and papers are available on the UCR Program's website at https://www.fbi.gov/services/cjis/ucr.

There are important differences between the UCR and the NIBRS data sets. For example, the NIBRS does not apply the UCR's "hierarchy rule" (discussed earlier). If more than one crime was committed by the same person or group of persons during the same event, then all of the crimes would be reported in the NIBRS database. Further, in addition to having the UCR Program's two crime categories—crimes against persons (e.g., murder, rape, and aggravated assault) and crimes against property (e.g., robbery, burglary, and larceny-theft), the NIBRS includes a third crime category, crimes against society, to represent society's prohibitions against certain types of activities (e.g., drug or narcotic offenses). The more detailed NIBRS data are scheduled to become the national crime data standard by January 1, 2021.[43]

National Incident-Based Reporting System: a crime reporting system in which police describe each offense that occurs during a crime event as well as characteristics of the offender.

The National Crime Victimization Survey

The National Crime Victimization Survey (NCVS), created to address some of the shortcomings of the UCR Program, has been collecting data on personal and household victimization

National Crime Victimization Survey: a random survey of U.S. households that measures crimes committed against victims; includes crimes not reported to police.

> ### Going Global
>
> **Measuring Crime Victimization in England and Wales**
>
> The Crime Survey for England and Wales (CSEW), known as the British Crime Survey (BCS) until 2012, is a victimization survey conducted in England and Wales. The CSEW, like the National Crime Victimization Survey (NCVS) conducted in the United States, measures crime levels in England and Wales by asking residents directly whether they have experienced crime in the previous year. In addition to victimization experiences, the CSEW asks respondents in a random sample of households about their opinions regarding different crime-related issues. Respondents are asked about their perceptions of the police, the criminal justice system, and crime and antisocial behavior. Whereas the NCVS collects data on residents age 12 and older, the CSEW collects information from residents age 10 and older.
>
> Like the NCVS, the CSEW provides a rich source of data about crime victimization and victim characteristics. Both surveys are used to help track crime trends and estimate the amount of crime that goes unreported to the police. Both surveys are used by crime and victimization policy makers and researchers who wish to know more about why some people are more likely to be victimized than others. The CSEW and the NCVS have been particularly useful sources of information for crime scientists (also known as environmental criminologists, see Chapter 3) who find that a large proportion of victimization is experienced by a small proportion of victims. For example, one estimate finds that 1 to 2 percent of potential targets account for about half of all crime. Understanding why some people are targeted more often than others has helped crime scientists to develop strategies to reduce crime by preventing repeat victimization.
>
> *Sources:* U.S. Census Bureau, National Crime Victimization Survey, https://www.census.gov/programs-surveys/ncvs.html; Office for National Statistics, Crime Survey for England and Wales, https://www.ons.gov.uk/surveys/informationforhouseholdsandindividuals/householdandindividualsurveys/crimesurveyforenglandandwales; Graham Farrell and Ken Pease, "Repeat Victimization," in Gerben Bruinsma and David Weisburd (Eds.), *Encyclopedia of Criminology and Criminal Justice* (New York: Springer, 2014), pp. 4371–4381.

since 1973. The NCVS claims on its website to be "the nation's primary source of information on criminal victimization." Each year, data are obtained from a nationally representative sample of about 95,000 households comprising nearly 240,000 persons on the frequency, characteristics, and consequences of criminal victimization in the United States. Each household is interviewed twice during the year. The survey enables the Bureau of Justice Statistics to estimate the likelihood of victimization by rape, sexual assault, robbery, assault, theft, household burglary, and motor vehicle theft for the population as a whole as well as for segments of the population such as women, the elderly, members of various racial groups, city dwellers, or other groups. The NCVS provides the largest national forum for victims to describe the impact of crime and characteristics of violent offenders.[44]

The survey—which asks respondents to report crime experiences occurring in the past six months—is administered by the U.S. Census Bureau (under the U.S. Department of Commerce) on behalf of the Bureau of Justice Statistics (under the U.S. Department of Justice).

The four primary objectives of the NCVS are to

- Develop detailed information about the victims and consequences of crime
- Estimate the number and types of crimes not reported to the police
- Provide uniform measures of selected types of crimes
- Permit comparisons over time and types of areas[45]

Practitioner's Perspective

Criminal Justice Program Director, Former Law Enforcement Officer, and Drug Investigator

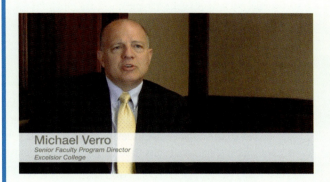

Name: Michael Verro
Position: Criminal Justice Program Director; Former Law Enforcement Officer and Drug Investigator
Location: Excelsior College, Albany, New York

What is your career story? Prior to working for Excelsior College, I was in law enforcement, starting when I was 18 years old. I started doing seasonal work as a peace officer, which is like private security, but they have police authority. When I got out of college, I realized that law enforcement was an area I wanted to go into as a profession. So for the next couple of years, I started like most people do in private security. I was a private investigator, a bodyguard, and worked my way up. At about age 27, I was hired as a police officer and I did that for 25 years. For 15 of those years, I worked as both a police officer and a detective. I was subsequently recruited to the DEA drug task force, and I worked for them for about three years.

I eventually went back to work as a police officer and then came back to New York and worked again as a peace officer. That really led into my world of academia; and now, I'm the program director for criminal justice at Excelsior.

What characteristics and skills are most helpful to succeed in this position? To me, skills are trainable. And there's a big distinction between training and education. That's one thing I think a lot of people have a misconception about. For education, you go to college. You learn theory, application, and critical thinking. Whereas training and some of the other skills are usually taught at an academy, things like driving, shooting, and defensive tactics.

But there are some psychological and mental skills people should possess for this career. And I consider those to be traits or characteristics of their broader personality. Things such as maturity, intelligence, wanting to help other people, and being level headed. Those are very important characteristics and skills, and some they should possess if they're going to go into this field.

Do you see any common trends in this position? When I went on the job almost 30 years ago, there wasn't a lot of technology. We carried a radio around on our hip that we used to call the brick, because it was about the size of a red building brick. It was very heavy and unreliable. Years ago, you had to call for dispatch and then wait and hope that they could go through their information, their databases or make phone calls as quickly as possible to obtain the information you wanted. Nowadays, every patrol car has a laptop with immediate access to information at your fingertips. Police officers wear body cameras, everything is digitally recorded, and they're using drones for surveillance and intelligence gathering. It used to be, again, when we looked to get a warrant—let's say a search warrant—it was basically searching a house. Now, there are digital search warrants if you want to ascertain information off computers or servers. So technology is growing—not only from the criminal justice perspective but also from the crime perspective. Every 90 days, there's some new form of digital crime being perpetrated, and the criminal justice system has to keep up with that.

What are some challenges and misconceptions you face in this position? One of the hardest things that we have to deal with is the fact that criminal justice education is often seen as more of a trainable thing, that it's not really taken seriously in academia as an actual degree, or not considered one of the real sciences. That's a misconception. It's kind of like psychology in that it wasn't really seen as a science until the late 1800s.

To learn more about Michael Verro's experiences as a criminal justice program director, law enforcement officer, and drug investigator, watch the Practitioner's Perspective video in SAGE vantage.

The NCVS categorizes crimes as "personal" or "property." Personal crimes cover rape and sexual attack, robbery, aggravated and simple assault, and purse-snatching/pocket-picking, whereas property crimes cover burglary, theft, motor vehicle theft, and vandalism.

A potential problem with the NCVS is that it estimates crime based on a representative sample; it would be too costly and time consuming to try to survey all U.S. residents. Also, since in relies on victim reports, there is the possibility that respondents might forget crimes, be unable to recall crime details, or provide inaccurate information to surveyors.[46]

/// IN A NUTSHELL

- Our legal system is based on the English common law: collections of rules, customs, and traditions. At its core is the doctrine of *stare decisis*, meaning that when a court has decided a case based on a set of facts, it will adhere to that principle, and other courts will apply that decision in the same manner to all future cases where facts are substantially the same.

- There are three sources of law in the U.S. legal system: federal law, state law, and city/county law.

- There are both civil and criminal laws at the federal, state, and local levels. Many more laws are enacted each year by the U.S. Congress, state legislatures, and city councils.

- Substantive law is the written law that defines or regulates our rights and duties. Procedural law sets forth the procedures and mechanisms for processing criminal cases.

- Two essential elements that underlie our system of law are *mens rea* (criminal intent) and *actus reus* (a criminal act or a failure to act where there is a legal duty).

- Criminal laws define crimes by specifying the *actus reus* (such as killing for homicide and the taking of property for robbery) and the *mens rea* (intentionally, recklessly, by force, unintentionally, etc.). Most crimes are categorized by degrees depending on the seriousness of the physical contact or threat (threatening versus physical contact) and the perpetrator's *mens rea* (intentional versus accidental), or based on the value of items stolen or damaged in crimes against property.

- Common crime categories include crimes against persons, crimes against property, public order crimes, white-collar crime, and organized crime.

- Crimes in the United States are measured and reported in three primary ways: the FBI's *Uniform Crime Reports*, the National Incident-Based Reporting System, and the National Crime Victimization Survey. Each has its unique approaches as well as advantages and disadvantages.

/// KEY TERMS & CONCEPTS

Review key terms with eFlashcards at **edge.sagepub.com/peak4e**.

Actus reus 33	Felony 33	National Incident-Based Reporting System 47
Burden of proof 29	Felony-murder rule 36	Organized crime 42
Civil law 29	Hierarchy rule 46	Plaintiff 29
Crime rate 44	Intent, specific 31	Procedural law 31
Crimes against persons 34	Legal jurisdiction 31	Public order crimes 40
Crimes against property 39	*Lex talionis* 27	Reasonable doubt 30
Criminal law 29	*Mens rea* 33	*Stare decisis* 27
Defendant 29	Misdemeanor 33	Substantive law 31
Federalism 27	Motive 31	*Uniform Crime Reports* 43
	National Crime Victimization Survey 47	White-collar crime 40

/// REVIEW QUESTIONS

Test your understanding of chapter content at **edge.sagepub.com/peak4e**.

1. What are the differences between criminal law and civil law?
2. How would you define and explain the importance and contributions of *mens rea* and *actus rea* as they operate in our legal system?
3. What is the difference between one's motive and one's intent to commit a crime, and which is the most important in our legal system?
4. A Nebraska law states the following: "Any person who knowingly or intentionally causes or permits a child or vulnerable adult to ingest methamphetamine, a chemical substance used in manufacturing methamphetamine, or paraphernalia is guilty of a Class I misdemeanor." The *mens rea* for this crime is _____; the *actus reus* element of this crime is _____.
5. What is the difference between white-collar crime and organized crime?
6. What are the three primary methods of measuring the extent of crime, and what have been offered as disadvantages for some of them?

/// LEARN BY DOING

Below are two additional case studies, each of which is grounded in actual case facts and chapter materials (concerning sexual assault and homicide, respectively). While studying each scenario, first assume that you are the *prosecuting* attorney and decide which charge(s), if any, should be brought against the accused on the basis of the facts. Next, assume the role of the *defense* attorney and explain, given the facts, what defenses should legitimately be made against the crime(s) charged. Remember that the Sixth Amendment entitles every defendant to the "guiding hand" of effective counsel, whose job it is to ensure that all legal protections are afforded. Answers and/or outcomes for each case are provided in the Notes section. For purposes of discussion, however, approach all of them as if there are no absolute, totally correct answers.

A high school principal threatens a graduating senior that if she does not have sex with him, he will prevent her from graduating. She submits against her will and then reports the incident to police after she is able to graduate. The state prosecutes the man under a first-degree sexual assault statute that reads as follows:

> A person who knowingly has sexual intercourse without consent with a person of the opposite sex commits the offense of sexual intercourse without consent. "Without consent" shall mean the victim is compelled to submit by force or by threat of force.

1. What is the prosecution's best argument that this is precisely the type of situation the law seeks to prevent and that the defendant is guilty of first-degree sexual assault? What facts would you want to know in your capacity as a prosecutor to bolster your case?
2. What is the defense attorney's best argument that this statute does not apply in this case? What other facts would you want to know to strengthen your argument?
3. You are a state lawmaker—how would you revise this statute to better address this case and ones like it? Be specific and rewrite the law as necessary.[47]

Peterson is relaxing at home when he hears noises in the alley behind his house; he looks in that direction and sees three men who are removing parts from his parked vehicle. Peterson approaches the men and tells them to stop what they are doing; he then runs inside his home, obtains a pistol, and returns to the alley. By now the three men are back in their vehicle and preparing to drive away. Peterson approaches them and tells them not to move, or he will shoot. The driver exits the car and, with a wrench in his hand, begins advancing toward Peterson. Peterson then warns the driver not to come any closer. Still carrying the wrench, the man continues to move toward Peterson, who then shoots and kills him.

4. What is the *primary* legal issue here?
5. Also consider the following questions:
   - What charge should the prosecutor bring against Peterson: Murder in the first degree? Murder in the second degree? Manslaughter?
   - Did Peterson act in self-defense?
   - What other options might have been available to Peterson, aside from obtaining a gun and returning to the alley? Besides shooting the driver?[48]

The following two activities will allow you to explore and discuss several of the crime data sources discussed in this chapter:

6. As part of a criminal justice honor society paper to be presented at a local conference, you are asked to use the Internet and determine how many crimes were reported for your city, your county, your state, and the United States during the past calendar year. How will you proceed?

7. Your criminal justice professor is working on a journal article concerning the dangers of police work, and she asks you to obtain some information on police deaths and assaults. Using the FBI's UCR website and its supplemental report, *Law Enforcement Officers Killed and Assaulted* (at https://ucr.fbi.gov/ucr-publications), what would you report?

/// STUDY SITE

Get the tools you need to sharpen your study skills. SAGE edge offers a robust online environment featuring an impressive array of free tools and resources.

Access practice quizzes, eFlashcards, video, and multimedia at **edge.sagepub.com/peak4e**.

Introducing...

SAGE vantage™

Course tools done right.
Built to support teaching. Designed to ignite learning.

SAGE vantage is an intuitive digital platform that blends trusted SAGE content with auto-graded assignments, all carefully designed to ignite student engagement and drive critical thinking. Built with you and your students in mind, it offers easy course set-up and enables students to better prepare for class.

SAGE vantage enables students to **engage** with the material you choose, **learn** by applying knowledge, and **soar** with confidence by performing better in your course.

PEDAGOGICAL SCAFFOLDING
Builds on core concepts, moving students from basic understanding to mastery.

CONFIDENCE BUILDER
Offers frequent knowledge checks, applied-learning multimedia tools, and chapter tests with focused feedback.

TIME-SAVING FLEXIBILITY
Feeds auto-graded assignments to your gradebook, with real-time insight into student and class performance.

QUALITY CONTENT
Written by expert authors and teachers, content is not sacrificed for technical features.

HONEST VALUE
Affordable access to easy-to-use, quality learning tools students will appreciate.

 To learn more about **SAGE vantage**, hover over this QR code with your smartphone camera or visit **sagepub.com/vantage**

CHAPTER 3

THEORIES OF CRIMINALITY AND CRIME

Children will watch anything, and when a broadcaster uses crime and violence and other shoddy devices to monopolize a child's attention, it's worse than taking candy from a baby.

—Newton N. Minow, Chair, Federal Communications Commission

Crimes are not to be measured by the issue of events, but by the bad intentions of men.

—Marcus Tullius Cicero

LEARNING OBJECTIVES

As a result of reading this chapter, you will be able to

1. Explain the importance of criminology and how research contributes to public policy
2. Distinguish between the classical and positivist schools of criminology and their explanations for criminality
3. Explain how biological and physical traits have been used to explain criminality
4. Describe how social structures in society—characteristics of urban environments and access to legitimate opportunities—create conditions conducive to crime
5. Distinguish between three types of theories—learning, control, and labeling—that represent social process explanations of crime
6. Explain why social conflict theorists believe that crime is a product of powerful groups who dominate less powerful groups to protect their interests
7. Summarize the assumptions of feminist theories and how rates of female offending have changed over time
8. Describe environmental criminology theories that explain why crime occurs
9. Discuss offender motives behind specific crime types

ASSESS YOUR AWARENESS

Test your knowledge of theories of criminality and crime by responding to the following seven true-false items; check your answers after reading this chapter.

1. The classical school of criminology maintains that people have free will and choose whether or not to engage in crime.
2. Research shows that most men carry an extra Y chromosome—the "criminal" chromosome—which makes them more likely to commit crime.
3. According to social disorganization theory, specific characteristics of neighborhoods, not people, are linked to higher rates of criminal behavior.
4. Labeling theorists believe that by labeling people as offenders, we can stop people from committing crimes.
5. Environmental criminologists argue that opportunities play a major role in causing crime.
6. Statistics show that arrests of female offenders for property crimes have increased dramatically over the past several years.
7. Interviews with known burglars reveal that these offenders are motivated strictly by financial gain.

<< Answers can be found on page 419.

Clarisa Figueroa, a 46-year-old woman from the Chicago area, announced in October 2018 that she was pregnant. This baffled those who knew Figueroa, including her family, since she had previously had her fallopian tubes tied. Still, over the next several months, Figueroa appeared to plan for the delivery of a baby. She posted photos on Facebook of a decorated nursery and ultrasound photos of a fetus. She told people that she planned to name the child after her 20-year-old son who had died recently.

As time grew closer to her anticipated due date, Figueroa and her 24-year-old daughter plotted to kill a pregnant woman and steal the woman's baby. On her way home from high school, 19-year-old Marlen Ochoa-Lopez, who was nine months pregnant, drove to Figueora's home. Ochoa-Lopez had met Figueroa through a Facebook group for mothers. Figueora told her that she had baby items, including clothes and a stroller, that Ochoa-Lopez was looking for. When Ochoa-Lopez arrived at the house, prosecutors say that Figueroa strangled the expecting mother for almost five minutes before cutting the baby from her womb and dumping her body in a garbage can outside the home with the cable still around her neck.

SAGE edge™
Master the content at edge.sagepub.com/peak4e

Figueora called 911 when the baby experienced breathing problems and turned "pale and blue." After arriving at the hospital, the baby boy was placed on life support but was pronounced brain-dead. Figueora subsequently set up a GoFundMe page for the baby and posted pictures of an infant in the hospital before she, and members of her family, were arrested. The baby died almost two months after being cut from his murdered mother's body.

This type of crime, also known as fetal abduction, is particularly gruesome. Prosecutors in Chicago now face the task of proving in court the "facts" recounted here. It is easy to see why many people, including those who sit on juries involving fetal abduction cases, struggle to understand why a person would be motivated to engage in such behavior. The facts of the case have yet to be proved in court, but understanding the motivation behind particular types of crime can be useful to those tasked with prosecuting criminal cases.

Criminologists look for answers concerning why people commit crime and why crime occurs, and their work is a critical part of criminal justice study. As you consider the criminological theories discussed in this chapter, try to answer these questions: Why would someone engage in a crime like fetal abduction? And how can we prevent this type of crime from happening in the future?

INTRODUCTION

What causes some people to devote much or most of their lives to preying on and harming others? Is it their "nature" or how they were "nurtured"? How could someone enter an elementary school and kill 26 children and teachers? Or shoot up a movie theater, leaving 12 dead and more than 70 wounded?[1] Are such people just base and cruel? Is crime a product of poverty and need? Congenital defects? Greed? Vengeance?

We humans have always sought to better understand the world around us, and so we seek answers to such questions. We have long sought to unravel the mysteries of human behavior and nature, and the authors of many books have attempted to explain these mysteries. This chapter briefly addresses some of these explanations.

The chapter looks first at the two major, original schools of criminological thought: classical and positivist. It then provides an overview of six major **theoretical paradigms** used by criminologists to explain criminal behavior and crime. Within each of these paradigms, you will be introduced to specific theories that propose different causes of criminal activity. After looking at theorists' efforts over the past two and a half centuries to explain crime, the chapter ends with a brief review of offenders' motivations (in their own words) for selected crimes—armed robbery, burglary, and carjacking.

Theoretical paradigm: a framework consisting of a group of theories that propose similar explanations for a particular type of behavior or event (e.g., crime).

Criminology

Before delving into the world of criminology, students should ask why this field of study—and its findings—are important to the criminal justice system. An obvious answer is that, by understanding why crime occurs, we can perhaps learn how to better deter and stop crime from happening in the first place. Although our understanding has improved, crime continues to occur and, given human nature, probably always will. So, studies in criminology can provide useful findings to policy makers all along the criminal justice spectrum—from juvenile courts seeking to stop would-be criminals early in life; to lawmakers and judges deciding on appropriate sentencing schemes; to corrections officials seeking to manage probationers, inmates, and parolees in hopes of reducing recidivism.

CLASSICAL AND POSITIVIST THEORIES

Until the 18th century, criminal behavior was explained by most Europeans in supernatural or quasi-religious terms. Criminal behavior was caused by forces outside the individual, and people who committed criminal acts were deemed "possessed" by the devil. In an effort to rid society of such evil, the accused was not allowed to put forth a defense, confessions could be obtained through the use of torture, and the penalty for most offenses was some form of physical punishment or death.

This response to crime changed in the mid-18th century, when the classical school of criminology emerged and focused criminal responsibility away from outside evil forces and onto the individual. Criminality was attributed to an individual's free will—criminals made a rational choice to commit crimes. Then in the 19th century, new theorists, the positivists, would argue that crime is caused by factors that individuals cannot control, pointing instead to scientific explanations—biological, psychological, and sociological—as forces that affect free will and decision making.

The Classical School

Cesare Beccaria published his classic *Essays on Crime and Punishments* in 1764, in which he bemoaned that potential criminals had no way of anticipating the unpredictable nature of the criminal law; attempted to expose the injustices in, and arbitrariness of, the administration of law and punishment; and encouraged reform in the way law was enforced to be more consistent and rational. The **classical school** of criminology evolved from this movement, the main principles of which were as follows:

- Criminal behavior is rational, and most people have the potential to engage in such behavior.
- People may choose to commit a crime after weighing the costs and benefits of their actions.
- Fear of punishment is what keeps most people law-abiding; therefore, the severity, certainty, and speed of punishment affect the crime rate.
- The punishment should fit the crime rather than the offender.
- The criminal justice system must be predictable, with laws and punishments known to the public.

Beccaria and his contemporary, Jeremy Bentham, who argued that the laws should provide "the greatest good for the greatest number," saw the purpose of punishment to be deterrence, rather than vengeance, and emphasized the certainty of punishment over its severity.[2] In other words, these early criminologists argued that it was most important that people be caught and punished. Creating more severe sanctions was less important; in fact, overly harsh punishments could be detrimental to achieving justice and deterrence. They argued that punishments should "fit the crime" and be proportionate to the harm caused by the offense.

Although classical criminology laid the cornerstone of modern western criminal law as it was formulated from 1770 to 1812,[3] its influence began to decline in the 19th century, largely because of the rise of science and in part because its principles did not take into account differences among individuals or the manner in which crimes were committed.[4]

Cesare Beccaria, an Italian jurist, philosopher, and politician who is best known for his essays on crime and punishment, believed that punishment should be proportional to the crime, that it is better to prevent crimes than to punish them, and that crimes are prevented more effectively by the *certainty* rather than the *severity* of punishment.

Classical school (of criminology): a perspective indicating that people have free will to choose between criminal and lawful behavior, and that crime can be controlled by sanctions and should be proportionate to the offense.

Neoclassical Criminology

Classical ideas began to take on new life in the 1980s, when scholars again began arguing that crimes may result from the rational choice of people who have weighed the benefits to be gained from the crime against the costs of being caught and punished (**neoclassical criminology**). They also argued that the criminal law must take into account the differences

Neoclassical criminology: an approach to crime that is grounded in the concept of rational choice but that views the accused as exempted from conviction if circumstances prevented the exercise of free will.

Chapter 3: Theories of Criminality and Crime ■ 57

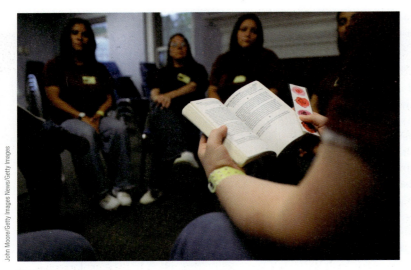

Positivists seek to find the basic cause of one's crimes and believe in rehabilitating offenders rather than punishing them. Prison therapy groups represent one method of rehabilitation.

Positivist school: a school of thought that argues science can be used to discover the true causes of crime, which include factors outside of offenders' control.

among individuals. To a large extent, sentencing reform, criticisms of rehabilitation, and greater use of incarceration sprung from this renewed interest in classical ideas. However, the positivist school of thought (positivist criminology) has dominated U.S. criminology since the beginning of the 20th century.

Positivist Criminology

By the middle of the 19th century, the classical school seemed to be out of date, in large part because of the expansion of science. In its place emerged positivist criminology—a philosophical approach proposed by French sociologist Auguste Comte—emphasizing the criminal actor rather than the criminal act,[5] and using science to study the offender's body, mind, and environment. Positivists seek to uncover the basic cause of crime, relying heavily on scientific experts, and believing in rehabilitating "sick" offenders rather than punishing them.[6] Following are some of the tenets of this viewpoint:

- Human behavior is controlled by physical, mental, and social factors, not by free will.
- Criminals are different from noncriminals.
- Science can be used to discover the true causes of crime and to treat offenders.[7]

One of the earliest and most famous positivists was Italian criminologist Cesare Lombroso. Working as a physician in the 19th century, he believed that offenders were a product of their abnormal physical features. He referred to offenders as "atavistic," throwbacks to some earlier stage in human evolution or to an apelike ancestor, and thought they were "born criminal." Having been influenced by the evolutionary doctrines of Charles Darwin, Lombroso saw in criminals some of the same characteristics that were found in "savages" or "prehuman people": a slanting forehead, abnormal teeth, excessively long arms and dimensions of the jaw and cheekbones, ears of unusual size, a sparse beard, a twisted nose, woolly hair, recessed eyes (and pronounced supraorbital ridges, or bony structures surrounding the eye sockets), fleshy and swollen lips, excessive vanity, or the presence of tattoos.[8]

Lombroso's theories, however, failed to explain crime fully—obviously, many offenders did not possess any, much less all, of these "born criminal" characteristics—so over time these "revelations" fell out of favor. Nonetheless, for his groundbreaking work that forced people to consider the makeup of the criminal in addition to his or her offense, Lombroso is today known as "the father of criminology."[9]

In the sections that follow, you will learn more about how criminologists have attempted to explain crime and criminal behavior. Six major theoretical paradigms are presented. It is important to note that this is only a brief and partial introduction to criminological theory. Still, you will become familiar with many of our discipline's most influential theories and theorists, and be able to apply these theories to explain specific criminal events.

BIOLOGICAL, TRAIT, AND DEVELOPMENTAL THEORIES

Biological and trait theories explain that criminal behavior is the outcome of physical or psychological differences between offenders and nonoffenders. Biological explanations

Investigating Further

Ariel Castro—The Cleveland "Monster"

Some people are thought to be purely evil, such as Ariel Castro, who abducted three young women—Amanda Berry, Michelle Knight, and Gina DeJesus—over the course of several years and then imprisoned them in his home in urban Cleveland, Ohio, for more than a decade. He raped, abused, and starved them, while depriving them of simple needs like sunlight, a working bathroom, regular showers, and the ability to see the outside (windows were boarded). He fathered a child with Berry, and he threatened to kill Knight if she didn't deliver the baby safely. Berry was able to escape one day when Castro made the uncharacteristic mistake of leaving an interior door unlocked and going out, allowing Berry to go to the front door to bang and scream for help. Castro pleaded guilty to 937 criminal counts including kidnapping, sexual assault, and aggravated murder (for killing at least one unborn child by beating Knight when she was pregnant with Castro's child).

At his sentencing, Castro told the courtroom he was not a monster, but he was "sick" because he was addicted to pornography. Castro's view of his own behavior follows the tenets of positivist criminology. He argued that he was different from noncriminals due to social factors (in this case, pornography) that influenced his behavior. However, Judge Michael Russo responded with a classic statement of *mens rea* by observing, "You were acquainted with the kidnap victims and that was a factor in your abduction strategy. You had an outwardly normal relationship with your girlfriend—it's clear you are able to choose who you wished to victimize." Judge Russo clearly believed that Castro's behavior could best be explained by classical school criminologists who argue that people choose whether or not to commit crime, based on their own free will.

In August 2013, Castro was sentenced to life plus 1,000 years, but within a month of his sentencing, he committed suicide by hanging himself in his prison cell. His "house of horrors" was demolished shortly after his sentencing.

Source: Eliott C. McLaughlin and Pamela Brown, "Judge Sentences Cleveland Kidnapper Ariel Castro to Life, Plus 1,000 Years," CNN, August 1, 2013, http://www.cnn.com/2013/08/01/justice/ohio-castro/.

---

of crime became unpopular when Lombroso's research was discredited by later scholars. However, these explanations and others that focus on the link between physical attributes and criminal behavior have regained popularity over time. Biological and trait theories focus on the impact that physical traits (including brain structure and chemistry) and genetics have on a person's propensity to engage in crime.

Like Lombroso, scholars in the first half of the 20th century examined physical differences between criminals and noncriminals. William Sheldon studied 200 juvenile delinquents in Boston and concluded that criminal behavior could be linked to different body types, or somatotypes.[10] He argued that more serious offenders tend to be athletically built ("mesomorphic" body type), whereas nondelinquents possess less muscular physical structures. Although later research found at least partial support for this theory,[11] theorists began to acknowledge that other factors, including psychological (e.g., temperament) and social (e.g., gang-involved lifestyles or parental treatment) influences, were also important in explaining criminal behavior and could be used to explain the physical differences observed between offenders and nonoffenders.

During the second half of the 20th century, advances in the field of molecular biology led to the belief that a link might exist between chromosomal abnormality and criminal behavior. For example, most females have two X chromosomes, and the majority of males have an XY set. Some males carry an extra Y chromosome (**XYY chromosome**), and scientists have hypothesized that this "criminal" chromosome produces tall men, generally with below-average intelligence, who behave aggressively or antisocially.

XYY chromosome: the so-called criminal chromosome; criminal behavior is thought to be caused, in some offenders, by an extra Y chromosome—believed to cause agitation, aggression, and greater criminal tendencies.

Italian criminologist Cesare Lombroso saw in criminals a pattern of physical characteristics that were found in "savages" or "prehuman people."

Adoption studies: criminological research that looks at whether adopted children share criminal tendencies with their biological or adoptive parents.

Dual hazard prediction: the argument that people are most likely to engage in criminal behavior if they (1) have traits associated with crime and (2) are raised in environments conducive to criminal behavior.

Like Lombroso's early theory, studies failed to find conclusive evidence to support the XYY theory.[12] Still, recent research has shown a direct association between a wide variety of traits and criminal activity. These characteristics include deficits in frontal, temporal, and subcortical brain regions; lower IQ scores; hormone imbalances; and outcomes related to birth complications (e.g., low birth weight and forceps delivery).[13]

It is difficult to determine whether criminal behavior is caused by biology or individual traits (nature), or whether it is caused by socialization practices (nurture)—including how children are raised. In response, researchers have conducted studies of identical twins who share the same genetic makeup. Many identical twins are raised together, which could mean that they are more likely to spend time together, be treated alike by families and friends, and share more of a common identity than do fraternal twins or other types of siblings.[14] Therefore, researchers have relied on adoption studies of identical twins to determine if crime is inherited. Although the evidence is mixed, one large study in Denmark found that only 13.5 percent of adopted boys had criminal convictions if neither their biological nor adoptive parents had criminal histories. However, 20 percent of adopted boys had criminal convictions if their biological parents engaged in crime, even though their adoptive parents did not.[15]

Almost all scholars now agree that individual traits likely influence criminal behavior. Developmental theories, often referred to as life-course criminology, explicitly acknowledge the impact of traits on human behavior. Most developmental theorists argue that traits are important, but that a person's social environment also matters. When people who are biologically predisposed to crime are raised in environments conducive to crime (e.g., with abusive parents or in high-crime communities), they are most likely to engage in crime. For example, the identical twin study discussed previously found that adopted boys were most likely to commit crime if their biological parents *and* their adoptive parents had criminal histories. The outcome of this combination of criminogenic factors (nature and nurture) is called the dual hazard prediction.[16] Developmental theorists attempt to explain the role of traits, in different environments, over the course of a person's life.[17]

FROM THEORY TO POLICY TO PRACTICE

If biological and trait explanations for crime are true, what public policy decisions should lawmakers and criminal justice professionals make in response? For example, when scientists identified certain hereditary patterns of criminality, lawmakers in Oklahoma required that repeat offenders be sterilized to stop the chain of criminality. These laws were constitutional in the United States until 1942.[18] How would you respond to the following findings? Consider all the potential risks and benefits.[19]

- Children with a criminal biological father will have criminal tendencies.
- Childhood attention-deficit/hyperactivity disorder (ADHD) may be linked to criminality.[20]

SOCIAL STRUCTURE THEORIES

Social structure theories explain that criminal behavior is caused by the ways in which societies are organized. Social structure theorists maintain that criminal behavior is the product of factors associated with culture and social class—such as poverty, race, family structure, and challenges related to immigration. They argue that these external social factors, not individual biological traits, cause criminality. Two of the most prominent social structure theories are social disorganization theory and strain theory.

Social Disorganization Theory

Social disorganization theory was developed by scholars at the University of Chicago who studied the organization of cities. In the 1930s and 1940s, Clifford Shaw and Henry McKay mapped the home addresses of juveniles who had engaged in delinquent activities. They found that the vast majority of delinquent youths lived in neighborhoods with high rates of poverty, diversity (e.g., places where new immigrant groups were likely to reside), and population turnover (i.e., people continually moving in and out). They argued that these community characteristics weakened core social institutions—including schools, churches, and families—and caused *social disorganization*. Children who live in socially disorganized neighborhoods are less likely to be supervised by adults and more likely to associate with other unsupervised youths, who are exposed to or involved in criminal organizations on the streets (e.g., gangs). The values they learn from established criminals, in the absence of parents or other supervising adults, lead them to engage in delinquent rather than prosocial behaviors.[21]

In their analysis, Shaw and McKay found that levels of delinquency remained remarkably stable in neighborhoods over time, despite the fact that different ethnic groups moved in and out of these areas. They concluded that neighborhood characteristics, not the characteristics of individuals, were the cause of delinquent behavior and crime.[22] Later theorists and researchers, including Robert Sampson and colleagues in the 1990s, expanded on social disorganization theory and found further evidence to suggest that Shaw and McKay's initial assumption was correct; neighborhood characteristics cause conditions that increase levels of crime.[23]

William H. Sheldon believed that human beings can be separated into three distinct body types, and that more serious offenders tended to be athletically built, or mesomorphic.

Social disorganization theory: a theory maintaining that neighborhood characteristics, including poverty, racial heterogeneity, and resident transiency, break down social controls and lead to criminal behavior.

Strain Theory

Building on the work of Émile Durkheim, the famed French sociologist of late 19th century, Robert Merton argued that high-crime societies suffer from *anomie*—a state of normlessness, in which people ignore the existing rules and values of society. Merton argued that social change can cause anomie if rules about appropriate conduct become unclear or if the change makes it more difficult for people to achieve their goals.[24] **Strain theory** explains that crime occurs when people living in disadvantaged, dysfunctional, and generally normless families or communities feel as though legitimate opportunities for success and prosperity are out of reach. Merton argued that when society places extreme emphasis on the accumulation of wealth as a symbol of success, but does not provide or emphasize legitimate means for achieving wealth (e.g., jobs or education), people feel strain. Some individuals will turn to crime as a means to reach their goals and alleviate feelings of strain.[25]

Robert Agnew later expanded on Merton's theory and argued that people could experience strain vicariously (i.e., be affected by strain felt by others close to them) and that people could suffer from anticipating future feelings of strain (e.g., worrying about losing a job). Agnew also identified the specific types of strain that are most likely to cause crime, including parental rejection, child abuse and neglect, chronic unemployment, marital problems, homelessness, and criminal victimization, among others.[26] Numerous

Strain theory: a theory that argues criminal behavior is caused by feelings of strain, which occur when people believe that legitimate means of achieving success are not accessible to them.

researchers, including Agnew, have found evidence that suggests these strains are linked to criminal behavior.[27]

FROM THEORY TO POLICY TO PRACTICE

Policy makers are finding that policies grounded in social structure explanations for crime reduce criminal activity. For example, providing housing vouchers to move families from disadvantaged areas to more affluent areas has reduced juvenile arrests for violent crime.[28]

- What other types of policies would reduce levels of social disorganization in specific communities?
- What can be done to reduce strain among people in society? ■

SOCIAL PROCESS THEORIES

Many criminologists believe that social structure theories place too much emphasis on crime committed by poor and disadvantaged members of society. Subsequently, they do not believe that social structure theory adequately explains crime that is committed by more affluent, middle- or upper-class people. Therefore, social process theories argue that any person—regardless of social class, education, or nature of the family, neighborhood, or community—can become a criminal. Three key social process theories are learning theory, control theory, and labeling theory.

Learning Theory

Learning theory: a theory asserting that criminal behaviors are learned from associating with others and from social interactions and social experiences.

The basis of learning theory is simple: People learn how to become criminal. Edwin Sutherland was the first learning theorist. He studied at the University of Chicago (where social disorganization theory was developed) and developed his learning theory,

You Be the . . .

Crime Analyst

You were recently hired as a crime analyst for a major metropolitan police department. The department's police chief is particularly concerned about violent crime in her jurisdiction, so you produce a map of all gun violence incidents across the city. As expected, you find that these violent incidents cluster in particular places. Some neighborhoods have significantly more violence than others, some street segments within those neighborhoods have significantly more violence than other segments, and some specific addresses on those segments have more violence than other addresses. You believe that these maps will be particularly useful for developing new crime-prevention policing strategies.

Having completed an introduction to criminal justice course as part of your undergraduate education, you are familiar with social structure theories of crime. Drawing from your knowledge of these theories, how would you answer the following questions from the police chief?

1. What is more important to understand: the characteristics of offenders or the characteristics of high-crime places?
2. What factors are causing crime to cluster in particular neighborhoods?
3. Why do youths in these areas become involved in violent crime?
4. What could the police do to try and prevent violent crime, based on the findings of your analysis?

specifically referred to as differential association theory, while trying to explain why characteristics of disorganized areas caused crime. Sutherland also studied white-collar crime and affluent criminals, and so he questioned the assumption that neighborhood and individual factors—including poverty, race, age, and mental disorders—caused criminal behavior.

Sutherland's research led him to believe that that there were social learning processes that could turn anyone into a criminal, anytime or anywhere. He argued that criminal behavior is learned while interacting with others, whether on the streets or in a corporate boardroom. This learning occurs within primary groups (family; friends; peers; one's most intimate, personal companions) and involves learning techniques, motives, drives, rationalizations, and attitudes associated with crime. When a person is exposed to more definitions *favorable* to violation of law than definitions *unfavorable* to violation of law, they will engage in criminal behavior.[29]

Conducting research to test learning theory is difficult. One of the problems with such research is determining which comes first, the delinquency or the delinquent friends. It might be that nondelinquents are corrupted by hanging out with delinquent friends. Or, it might be that "birds of a feather flock together," and delinquent juveniles are more likely to pick friends who will engage in similar behaviors. Still, studies find that delinquents tend to hang out with other delinquents and others who share positive views of criminal behavior, providing at least partial support for learning theory.[30]

Strain theorists argue that crime is caused by frustration, hopelessness, and anger resulting from living in disadvantaged and dysfunctional families and/or communities, where opportunities for success and prosperity are largely nonexistent.

The Figueroa Fetal Abduction Case: Before someone can engage in a horrific criminal act like fetal abduction, they must first know how to commit the act. Sutherland argued that people are most likely to learn the techniques to commit specific crimes while interacting in small intimate groups. However, Sutherland's theory was developed in the 1930s and 1940s, long before media played a prominent role in humans' daily lives. Media stories now regularly highlight the details of criminal acts. The Internet is filled with descriptions and videos that provide "how-to" guides for committing crimes. How do you think Figueroa "learned" to commit her crime? Do you think her close friends or family played a role? Could she have "learned" this crime through media reports or websites?

Control Theory

Unlike learning theory, which starts with the assumption that people are born "good" and learn to be "bad," control theory assumes that people are born "bad" and must be controlled or learn to control themselves in order to be "good." Control theorists argue that all people naturally pursue their self-interests and seek pleasure while trying to avoid harm.

In the 1960s, Travis Hirschi proposed a control theory: social bond theory. He argued that instead of asking, "Why do people commit crime?" criminologists should ask, "Why don't people commit crime?" According to Hirschi, people do not commit crime when they have strong bonds to society. These bonds consist of four elements: (1) attachment to family and prosocial others, (2) commitment to social norms and institutions (e.g., school, work, church), (3) involvement in conventional activities that leave little time to think

Control theory: a theory that describes criminal behavior as a natural outcome of people's desire to seek pleasure in the absence of effective social controls.

about or engage in crime, and (4) belief in shared social values and norms. People with weak societal bonds are "free" to follow their natural instinct to seek pleasure, and this might involve engaging in criminal conduct.[31]

About two decades later, Hirschi collaborated with Michael Gottfredson and developed a second control theory. Gottfredson and Hirschi's "general theory of crime" maintains that criminal behavior occurs when parents fail to instill self-control in their children. If children are not taught to resist their natural impulses, they will be unable to control their desire for immediate gratification. Gottfredson and Hirschi explain that low levels of self-control lead to criminal behavior, and it also causes many criminals to engage in other dangerous or risky activities, such as excessive drinking, smoking, fast driving, and unprotected sex.[32]

Hirschi's social bond theory is one of the most influential and tested theories of juvenile delinquency. Gottfredson and Hirschi's theory of self-control has also been the focus of extensive research. Over the past several decades, studies have supported the basic tenets of control theory. In reviewing the literature, some researchers argue that control theory has received more empirical support than any other theory of crime.[33]

Labeling Theory

Why is the possession of cocaine labeled a criminal act, while possession and even home manufacturing of alcohol is not? Why is it that one who shoots a bald eagle is guilty of committing a felony federal offense (with maximum penalties of up to $100,000 and/or one year in federal prison)[34] while the same man who, the day before, killed a large elk might well be labeled a skilled "sportsman" and praised for his marksmanship? Such questions underscore labeling theory. This theory encourages us to consider why particular acts are labeled as criminal and how labels can affect future criminal behavior.

Labeling theory: a theory contending that labeling a person as a deviant or criminal makes that person more likely to engage in future criminal behavior.

Labeling theorists believe that no criminal act is deviant in and of itself; rather, behavior is considered deviant—and labeled as a crime—only because some group has determined that certain behavior should be criminalized. Labeling theorist Edwin Lemert claimed that people who experience stigmatizing social reactions to their behaviors will begin to identify themselves as deviant. Once their identify is affected and they accept the label as truth, people will engage in crime simply because they see themselves as criminals (a reaction that Lemert called "secondary deviance").[35] Howard Becker argued that once rule-breakers accept the deviant label as their "master status" (e.g., "I am a gang member" or "I am a thief"), a self-fulfilling prophecy begins, and they are more likely to engage in future criminal behavior.[36]

Tests of labeling theory have found that criminal justice interventions are often associated with negative outcomes. For example, research suggests that juveniles who are subjected to formal criminal sanctions are more likely to become involved in street gangs and with deviant peers and subsequently engage in serious delinquency.[37] In general, there is considerable evidence to suggest that people who are subjected to criminal sanctions are more likely to commit crime in the future, a finding that is used to support labeling theory.[38]

FROM THEORY TO POLICY TO PRACTICE

If the explanations for crime offered by social process theories are true, what public policy decisions should lawmakers and criminal justice professionals make in response?

- How would you apply social process theories to gangs, and what public policies might help prevent gang membership and proliferation?[39]
- How can the criminal justice system avoid labeling of both adults and juveniles? ■

Practitioner's Perspective

Crime Analyst

Name: DJ Rogers
Position: Crime Analyst
Location: Colorado

What is your career story? I've been a crime analyst in four different law enforcement agencies in Colorado for about 28 years. I started with the first department I worked with right after I graduated with my undergraduate degree.

I was an economics and history major, and I think that at the time the department was looking for an outside perspective. So when I applied, I think they thought it was interesting that I was coming from a different background, and I had some thoughts coming from those areas of study about how my backgrounds cross-applied to criminal justice and to the operation of law enforcement. So they kind of took a chance on me, and I thought I'd do a few years and then go to graduate school. And 28 years later, I'm still here.

Crime analysis is probably unusual in law enforcement settings in that I don't know what it looks like right now, but traditionally it's probably actually been a field that's been more open and friendly to females than males. You've seen it for a variety of reasons. I don't go to those meetings as much as I used to, but I would bet you there's still more women serving as analysts now than there are guys.

What are some challenges and misconceptions you face in this position? If you talked to a broad cross-section, the challenges that most folks are going to see facing crime analysis is how the whole function of analysis is being defined and integrated in the operation of the department. We're still trying to figure where it fits best, so a lot of analysts in the field struggle with the issue. Another big issue is the information itself. The data you use to do your job is both less than pristine and not consistently documented. Exchanging that information in a meaningful sense between agencies is still a challenge. A lot of work being done in the last few years is focused largely on those issues, though, so they will probably improve.

One of the key myths is that people think what they see in the media is similar or typical to what actually happens in police departments. What the media tend to draw on are actually atypical in real life. The media creates this impression, especially in analysis, that we're always working serial homicides or serial sex assaults, when in fact your average analyst in your average department is going to be largely focused on burglary or motor vehicle theft, among other things. Essentially, we are focused on the other more mundane, but more pervasive pattern crimes that are more amenable to analysis. Violent crime is more difficult in those regards.

What directions do you envision your department going in the future? I think that as far as looking at the future of crime analysis, it seems like what we've all struggled with is the concept of actionable intelligence. At the moment, unfortunately, it takes us a week to pull the data together, get the reports, do our analysis, and get the analytical product out there, and by the time that happens we're three days late. So, we're seeing that a lot of agencies are starting their own real-time analytical pods (or real-time working groups), in which they do a better job of culling that data from our dispatch systems and turning that around into real-time actionable intelligence.

To learn more about DJ Rogers' experiences as a crime analyst, watch the Practitioner's Perspective video in SAGE vantage.

SOCIAL CONFLICT THEORIES

Some criminologists in the 1960s challenged the theoretical paradigms mentioned previously on the grounds that these theories did not do enough to highlight the effects of economic and racial inequality. **Social conflict theory**, sometimes also called radical or critical

Social conflict theory: a theory that explains crime as an outcome of conflicting interests between groups in society and the dominant group's attempts to control and exploit groups with less power.

theory, maintains that the criminal justice system serves the interests of the dominant groups and classes of a society, and that the police can do nothing more than act repressively against those who challenge the established order.[40] The working class, women (particularly those who are single heads of household and are socially isolated), and ethnic minorities (those from non-English-speaking backgrounds and refugees, in particular) are the most likely to suffer oppressive treatment based on class division, sexism, and racism. Criminal laws are designed by those who are in power, and the laws are intended to oppress those who are not in power. These theorists argue that affluent and high-status people commit as many crimes as do the oppressed, but the latter groups are more likely to be apprehended and punished.

One of the earliest conflict theorists was George B. Vold, who believed that many behaviors are defined as crimes because it is in the best interest of the dominant groups to do so.[41] According to Vold and other conflict theorists, crime is a product of group struggle. Humans are by nature social beings, forming groups out of shared interests and needs. The criminal law serves the goals of the dominant group, which controls the legislative process. When the behaviors of subordinate groups come into conflict with the dominant group's interests, they are punished by the criminal justice system.[42]

More recently, conflict theorists have argued that capitalism causes criminal behavior. For example, Elliott Currie draws attention to violent crime in the United States to provide evidence that capitalism (a form of social conflict with "winners" and "losers" engaged in economic competition) is linked to crime. Elliott argues that if governments in capitalist societies do not take steps to limit inequality or provide a "safety net" for those who are unsuccessful at accumulating wealth, then the capitalist system will produce high rates of serious violent crime.[43]

FROM THEORY TO POLICY TO PRACTICE

If the social conflict theory explanations for crime are true, what public policy decisions should lawmakers and criminal justice professionals make in response?

- How might government funding for prosecutors' offices in comparison to public defenders' offices contribute to crime, and how can lawmakers fix the disparity?[44]
- How would critical theorists explain the historical differences between sentences for possession of crack cocaine and powder cocaine, and how would you recommend reforming other sentencing differences?[45]

FEMINIST THEORIES

It has been said that "crime is a young man's game."[46] Women commit far fewer crimes (especially violent crimes) than their male counterparts, but women represent one of the fastest growing populations of incarcerated people in the United States. Feminist theory, sometimes classified as part of the aforementioned social conflict theories, attempts to explain why women do not offend at the same rate as men, why they are more likely to commit different types of offenses than men, and why their rates of offending continue to increase over time. Freda Adler, criminologist and author of *Sisters in Crime*, wrote the following in 1975:

> Women are no longer indentured to the kitchens, baby carriages, or bedrooms of America. There will be no turning back to the days when women found it necessary to justify their existence by producing babies or cleaning houses. Women have chosen to desert those kitchens and plunge exuberantly into the formerly all-male quarters of the working world.[47]

Feminist theory: a theory that explains how gender inequality affects female offending and justice system responses to crimes committed by females.

At about the time Adler wrote those words, women were entering the labor force in large numbers. With passage of the Equal Employment Opportunity Act in 1972,[48] women were given the right to compete with men for jobs and promotions, and to receive the same compensation upon being hired. Later, the Pregnancy Discrimination Act of 1978,[49] which required employers to treat pregnancy, childbirth, and related medical conditions in the same manner as any other temporary disability, and the Family and Medical Leave Act of 1993,[50] which allowed employees to take 12 weeks of unpaid leave for the birth or adoption of a child, helped women to participate in the labor force. By extension, these increases in labor force participation of women would become related to their significantly higher crime rates.[51]

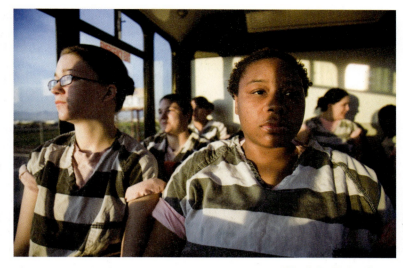

The study of crime has historically focused on male offenders, but the recent extent and nature of female criminality—more predatory and violent—has brought them more attention from criminologists as well.

Adler's work, as well as Rita Simon's *Women and Crime*,[52] proposed that the emancipation of women and increased economic opportunities for women allowed women to be as crime-prone as men. Some scholars argue that absolutely no empirical evidence supports these claims.[53] These theories have also invited much criticism from other feminist writers, who argue instead that feminism has made female crime more visible through increased reporting, policing, and sentencing of female offenders.[54]

Table 3.1 shows five-year arrest trends for women. The table shows that, as with the nation at large, arrests of women have declined overall—but mostly due to large decreases in

Table 3.1 /// Five-Year Arrest Trends for Women			
Offense Charged	2013	2017	Percent Change
TOTAL[1]	2,071,394	1,938,561	−6.4
Violent crime[2]	66,925	69,868	+4.4
Property crime[2]	410,700	308,495	−24.9
Murder and nonnegligent manslaughter	823	984	+19.6
Rape	276	437	+58.3
Robbery	8,626	8,781	+1.8
Aggravated assault	57,200	59,666	+4.3
Burglary	31,158	25,815	−17.1
Larceny-theft	369,459	268,505	−27.3
Motor vehicle theft	8,814	13,007	+47.6
Arson	1,269	1,168	−8.0
Other assaults	210,675	207,429	−1.5
Forgery and counterfeiting	15,885	13,186	−17.0
Fraud	38,472	31,830	−17.3

(Continued)

Table 3.1 /// (Continued)			
Offense Charged	2013	2017	Percent Change
Embezzlement	5,388	5,524	+2.5
Stolen property; buying, receiving, possessing	14,439	15,070	+4.4
Vandalism	27,643	29,013	+5.0
Weapons; carrying, possessing, etc.	8,205	10,301	+25.5
Prostitution and commercialized vice	19,199	12,682	−33.9
Sex offenses (except rape and prostitution)	3,111	2,523	−18.9
Drug abuse violations	221,227	276,015	+24.7
Gambling	588	459	−21.9
Offenses against the family and children	17,832	18,424	+3.3
Driving under the influence	201,187	176,059	−12.5
Liquor laws	70,348	43,749	−37.8
Drunkenness	61,328	50,334	−17.9
Disorderly conduct	89,647	70,710	−21.1
Vagrancy	3,667	3,802	+3.7
All other offenses (except traffic)	575,817	587,580	+2.0
Suspicion	95	40	−57.9
Curfew and loitering law violations	9,061	5,508	−39.2

1. Does not include suspicion.
2. Violent crimes in this table are offenses of murder and nonnegligent manslaughter, rape, robbery, and aggravated assault. Property crimes are offenses of burglary, larceny-theft, motor vehicle theft, and arson.

Source: Federal Bureau of Investigation, "Table 35. Five-Year Arrest Trends, by Sex, 2013–2017," *Crime in the United States—2017* (Washington, D.C.: Uniform Crime Reporting Program), https://ucr.fbi.gov/crime-in-the.u.s/2017/crime-in-the.u.s.-2017/tables/table-35.

property crimes (largely as a result of decreased arrests related to larceny-theft and disorder-related crimes). Arrests of women for violent crime have increased by more than 4 percent, with large percentage increases in arrests for murder/nonnegligent manslaughter and rape. Fluctuations in crime and arrest numbers are always subject to error due to reporting issues, but these general trends are worth examining and interpreting within our theoretical explanations.

FROM THEORY TO POLICY TO PRACTICE

Feminist theorists note that girls who run away from home to escape physical or sexual abuse can face further victimization—by the system, if they are labeled as an offender (e.g., if they engaged in prostitution to survive on the streets)—and by their families, if they are forced to return home.[55]

- If the feminist theory explanations for crime are true, what public policy decisions should lawmakers and criminal justice professionals make in response?
- How can the justice system "level the playing field" and reduce gender inequalities that lead to female criminality?

ENVIRONMENTAL CRIMINOLOGY THEORIES

Environmental criminology, also called crime science, is one of the newest theoretical paradigms within our discipline. Rather than trying to explain criminal behavior, environmental criminology theorists attempt to explain patterns of crime events and focus on how offenders find and choose their crime targets. These theories assume that opportunity is a root cause of crime; people cannot commit crime if opportunities for such behavior are restricted or blocked. Two of the most prominent environmental criminology theories are routine activity theory and situational crime prevention.

Routine Activity Theory

In the 1960s and 1970s, violent crime began to increase dramatically. From a traditional criminological perspective, this was unexpected. In general, social conditions were improving. Unemployment rates were dropping, graduation rates improved, college enrollments were increasing, and the average family income was on the rise. Lawrence Cohen and Marcus Felson suggested that the increase in crime could be explained by changes in people's daily routine activities.[56] Following World War II, people were more likely to spend time away from home. For example, women were entering the workforce, more people had jobs or attended college, and more people spent time away traveling and on vacation with their families.

Cohen and Felson's research demonstrated that changes in routine activities were associated with higher rates of crime (e.g., burglaries). They used this finding to support their proposed **routine activity theory**. The original version of this theory argued that three elements must converge in time and space in order for a crime to occur: A motivated offender must find a suitable target in the absence of a capable guardian. Since the theory was first proposed in 1979, Felson and John Eck introduced additional elements that influence crime, and the entire theory is represented by the crime triangle, also called the problem analysis triangle, presented in Figure 3.1.[57] Guardians can protect targets, handlers can control offenders, and managers are responsible for creating safe places.

Routine activity theory: a theory that explains the elements necessary for a crime to occur, as well as the types of controllers who can block criminal opportunities.

Many studies, subsequent to Cohen and Felson's initial analysis, report findings consistent with routine activity theory. Recent studies have found support for the theory in a variety of contexts. For example, one study found that routine activities on the Internet could be used to predict who was most likely to be a target of Internet fraud.[58]

Figure 3.1 /// Problem Analysis Triangle

Source: The Problem Analysis Triangle is reprinted by permission of the authors and The Center for Problem Oriented Policing.

Figure 3.2 /// Twenty-Five Techniques of Situational Crime Prevention	
Increase the Effort	1. Harden target 2. Control access to facilities 3. Screen exits 4. Deflect offenders 5. Control tools/weapons
Increase the Risks	6. Extend guardianship 7. Assist natural surveillance 8. Reduce anonymity 9. Use place managers 10. Strengthen formal surveillance
Reduce the Rewards	11. Conceal targets 12. Remove targets 13. Identify property 14. Disrupt markets 15. Deny benefits
Reduce Provocations	16. Reduce frustrations and stress 17. Avoid disputes 18. Reduce arousal and temptation 19. Neutralize peer pressure 20. Discourage imitation
Remove Excuses	21. Set rules 22. Post instructions 23. Alert conscience 24. Assist compliance 25. Control drugs and alcohol

Source: Adapted from Center for Problem-Oriented Policing, "25 Techniques of Crime Prevention," www.popcenter.org/25techniques.

Situational Crime Prevention

Situational crime prevention: a theory maintaining that crimes will occur if they are easy to commit, carry low risk, provide large rewards, provoke people, and are excusable, as judged by a wide range of potential offenders.

Ronald Clarke argues that crime opportunities can be blocked by manipulating features of physical and social environments. In his theory, called **situational crime prevention**, he focuses attention away from criminal dispositions, or the characteristics of people that might make them more likely to engage in crime. Instead, Clarke argues all people have the potential to commit crimes. According to this theory, crimes occur when they are easy to commit, carry low risks of detection, provide large rewards, provoke people into action (e.g., committing a violent act), and involve behaviors that can be easily justified (e.g., "I only stole something; I didn't hurt anyone").

For each of the five dimensions of criminal opportunity—effort, risk, reward, provocations, and excuses—situational crime prevention offers five prevention techniques. Figure 3.2 highlights these dimensions and associated techniques. Police and others interested in preventing a specific crime in a particular place can use this figure to consider possible interventions that would block criminal opportunity or make crime less attractive to potential offenders.

Evidence to support situational crime prevention usually comes in the form of case studies. Case studies typically involve detailed descriptions of a particular crime problem and the types of activities used to address the problem. These studies reveal that certain situational crime prevention techniques have been effective in reducing a wide variety of crimes, including robberies, burglaries, auto thefts, obscene phone calls, welfare and refund frauds, graffiti, and assaults.[59]

Going Global

International Environmental Criminologists

One of the most recently proposed environmental criminology theories was developed by Swedish criminologist Per-Olof H. Wikström. Wikström holds many positions, including professor of ecological and developmental criminology at the University of Cambridge and professorial fellow of Girton College. His theoretical ideas have been shaped largely by his involvement in longitudinal research (in this case, research that follows the same group of people over a long period of time). He has studied the development of young people in the United Kingdom to better understand what causes crime and how we can prevent it.

Wikström's *situational action theory* builds on the dual hazard prediction argument (discussed earlier in this chapter) and suggests that whether or not a person engages in crime depends on the settings he or she encounters (the types of opportunities discovered) and how the individual perceives these settings (whether his or her moral beliefs allow the person to consider crime as an option). This is only a small piece of Wikström's larger theory, but it should help to illustrate how he draws together several different theories of crime, including learning, control, and routine activities theories.

Among his many other prestigious awards, Wikström received the 2016 Stockholm Prize in Criminology for his outstanding achievements in criminological theory and research.

Source: For a more comprehensive overview of situational action theory, see Per-Olof H. Wikström, "Character, Circumstances, and the Causes of Crime," in A. Liebling, S. Maruna, and L. McAra (Eds.), *The Oxford Handbook of Criminology* (Oxford, U.K.: Oxford University Press, 2017), pp. 415–444.

IN THEIR OWN WORDS: OFFENDERS SPEAK

With a background in some of the major criminological theories for why people commit crimes, this is a good opportunity to consider the motives and methods that offenders themselves offer to explain their criminal behavior. Using a variety of field-research methods (including interviews with active offenders, incarcerated individuals, and probationers and parolees), researchers have allowed us to learn from actual criminals—armed robbers, burglars, and carjackers—and thus narrow the "distance" between students and their criminal subjects.

Armed Robbery

The motive underlying the crime of armed robbery is clear: financial gain (and another long-standing dynamic—temptation; discussed in Chapter 4). Unlike perpetrators of most forms of street crime, armed robbers are never secret or ambiguous. And, like the crime of carjacking, discussed later, the crime of robbery bridges property and violent crimes.[60] The armed robber must also create the illusion of impending death or serious injury in the victim's mind.

By announcing their intentions to rob, armed robbers believe they are committing themselves irrevocably to the offense; that is the "make or break" moment, and they must establish dominance over the victims and convince them they are not in a position to resist, and displaying a weapon usually precludes the need to do much talking.[61] The most difficult aspect of armed robberies, according to those who commit them, is the transfer of goods. Here, robbers must keep their victims under strict control while attempting to make sure they have obtained everything of value; it must be done quickly, lest the police or a passerby discover the act.[62] Finally, robbers must escape—another difficult stage of the robbery. Armed robbers must maintain their control over their victims while increasing their distance from them. Robbers can either flee—possibly bringing attention to themselves or allowing their victims to raise an alarm—or force their victims to flee. The latter allows offenders to leave the scene in a leisurely manner.⁶³

Burglary

Burglars, like armed robbers, are motivated primarily by money in order to maintain their "high-living" lifestyle; however, they may also be motivated by noneconomic reasons, including the "thrill" of the act, as well as by revenge.⁶⁴ Burglars, then, while usually being prompted by a perceived need for cash, may also derive psychic rewards as a secondary benefit, finding the crime to be exciting. Some also commit residential burglaries to get even with someone for a real or imagined wrong—an attack on one's status, identity, or self-esteem. For example, a burglar can have an argument over a traffic or parking matter, and then follow the victim home; later, after learning the victim's

Investigating Further

Application of Crime Theories

For each of the following scenarios, determine which of the theories described in this chapter might be applied in order to understand the person's motivation for engaging in criminal behavior:

- An employee in a county treasurer's office has developed a means of "juggling the books" and circumventing expenditure controls in such a way as to embezzle county funds. She examines the risks of doing so (i.e., engaging in unethical behavior, getting arrested) against the benefits that would be derived from committing the crimes (i.e., converting to her possession perhaps hundreds of thousands of dollars in a very short period of time). She has also determined that punishment for such crimes is not "swift and certain" because her methods would be difficult to detect (and, to her knowledge, embezzlers receive relatively light punishments). She also perceives that she lives in a society that values people who are financially successful and that the legal means for attaining such success are otherwise unavailable to her. She thus embezzles the funds.

- A young woman attending college desires to complete her education and enter into a successful career. With financial obstacles in the way, she weighs the benefits and drawbacks of employment with a local "dating service," which she has learned is actually a cover for women to engage in acts of prostitution. One deterrent, however, is that if arrested, she would be deemed a less-than-acceptable member of society; however, she also perceives that degrees of punishment in such cases are typically light. At the same time, she is aware that society reveres those who become educated, obtain a good position, and live comfortably. To do so, however, she must somehow find the means to afford her tuition and living expenses. In the end, she opts to take the position with the dating service, thus risking being arrested and labeled as an outcast, in order to achieve her goals.

- A 16-year-old boy is contemplating whether or not to drop out of school and join a local gang. He knows that to do so he will have to suffer painful initiation rites and that the lifestyle poses considerable dangers. Conversely, he is also aware that his city's policing of gangs is relatively lax, punishment is not certain, and financial rewards are promising. His legal options for obtaining lucrative employment and financial comfort are limited if not altogether blocked, given his likewise limited (i.e., below-average) education and training. After considering his options and looking at both the benefits and the potential disadvantages, he decides the benefits outweigh the deterrents, and he joins the gang.

You Be the . . .

Criminologist

Richard R. is a 24-year-old, white male convicted of the murder and sexual assault of a young woman; he is currently on death row. Richard's childhood includes sexual abuse by an uncle and lengthy exposure to substance abuse by his parents. He relates that these experiences contributed to his own sexual deviance and substance abuse, and prevented him from developing the social skills necessary to sustain a normal, healthy adult relationship with any family members or peers. As a result, his teenager years were marked with such deviant acts, including violence against family members and male and female acquaintances. Over time, "acting out" physically evolved into full-blown, felonious victimization, which led to his current crimes, incarceration, and sentencing. He had long fantasized about violence and killing others, usually by strangulation or with a knife; over time, these fantasies became so prevalent that he eventually lacked the ability to distinguish between reality and fantasy, often misperceiving others' words and actions. He has been in and out of mental health care facilities since his early teens, at which time he was diagnosed as suffering from acute depression, suicidal thoughts, long-term substance abuse, and interpersonal problems. When medicated, Richard has appeared able to control his behaviors; however, when not medicated, he would typically revert to his destructive, antisocial behaviors.

During his time on death row, Richard has demonstrated only one episodic break with reality and acute depression—when told a state court had denied his appeal. He presents as very docile and now appears to embrace religion, which seemingly gives him a much more calm demeanor and an acceptance of others and his situation. He comprehends why he is on death row, has been able to assist in his legal appeals, and demonstrates a low level of depression (beyond that which is normal for such inmates). He indicates remorse for his past victims, the murdered woman in particular, and seems convinced that if he is in fact executed, his spiritual body will live on in a peaceful afterlife.

1. How would a classical criminologist's explanation differ from a positivist criminologist's explanation of Richard's behavior?
2. Which social process theory—learning, control, or labeling—do you believe best explains why Richard committed sexual assault and murder?
3. How could these crimes have been prevented, according to environmental criminology theories?
4. In sum: Is Richard a criminal in every sense, morally and legally deserving of capital punishment?

routine, he or she may burglarize the person's home to settle the "grudge"—possibly even destroying more goods than are removed.[65]

Carjacking

According to one study,[66] with the exception of homicide, "probably no offense is more symbolic of contemporary urban violence than carjacking." Indeed, following the 1992 murder of a woman when two men commandeered her car in Washington, D.C., carjacking was made a federal crime punishable by up to 25 years in prison.[67] Unlike most robberies, carjacking is directed at an object rather than a person; still, weapons are used in two-thirds to three-fourths of carjackings.[68]

Carjackers are motivated by two primary objectives: opportunity (i.e., weighing potential risks and rewards) and situational inducements (peer pressure, need for cash or drugs, or revenge). They typically have a precarious day-to-day existence, exacerbated by "boom or bust" cycles, and are always under some degree of financial pressure. The sale of stolen vehicles and parts can be very lucrative, with carjackers either selling the car parts or delivering the car to a "chop shop," where it will be stripped; items of value include tire rims, hubcaps, and stereos—for which the average carjacker will be paid about $1,750 per car.[69]

/// IN A NUTSHELL

- Criminology offers explanations for crime. Research grounded in criminological theory provides evidence for policy makers (e.g., lawmakers, police, judges) who develop interventions to reduce crime.

- The classical school of criminology was the first attempt to explain crime in rational terms. Theorists postulated that criminal behavior is rational; people have free will to choose whether or not they will commit crime; punishments should fit the crime; and justice must be predictable. The more recent reemergence of the classical school (in the form of neoclassical criminology) encouraged sentencing reform, criticisms of rehabilitation, and greater use of incarceration.

- The positivist school of thought, which has dominated U.S. criminology since the beginning of the 20th century, uses science to study the body, mind, and environment of offenders to determine how they could be rehabilitated. It is believed that human behavior is controlled by biological traits and social factors, not by free will.

- Biological and trait theories of crime offer that the causes of crime are found in the biological makeup of offenders and are the result of some biological element or defect; criminals are *born* and not *made* by their home or social environment. People are most likely to engage in crime if they possess criminogenic traits and are raised in environments that promote criminal behaviors.

- Social structure theories of crime suggest that criminal behavior is influenced by the ways in which societies are structured. For example, communities that are socially disorganized have weak social institutions, and these areas are more likely to experience high rates of crime. Individuals who live in societies with weak social norms are less likely to pursue goals through legitimate means and more likely to commit crime if blocked or restricted access to legitimate means produces feelings of strain.

- Social process theories of crime argue that criminal behavior is the product of interactions with others. Crime can occur as a result of learned behavior, lack of controls or bonds with others, or negative societal reactions that label offenders and ultimately affect their identities and future behaviors.

- Social conflict theories of crime explain that factors such as economic and racial inequality generate crime. Behaviors that threaten the interests of powerful groups are labeled as crimes. Less powerful groups are subjected to criminal sanctions when their actions threaten the established order.

- Feminist crime theories explain why women commit fewer and different crimes than men, and why they might be subjected to criminal justice sanctions for different reasons than men.

- Environmental crime theories maintain that opportunity is a necessary condition for crime. Crime occurs based on the routine activities of groups and individuals and attractiveness (or unattractiveness) of specific crime opportunities.

- In their own words, criminals explain and rationalize their acts in a variety of ways, including financial gain, the need to maintain street status and a partying lifestyle, revenge, and "thrill seeking."

/// KEY TERMS & CONCEPTS

Review key terms with eFlashcards at **edge.sagepub.com/peak4e**.

Adoption studies   60
Classical school (of criminology)   57
Control theory   63
Dual hazard prediction   60
Feminist theory   66
Labeling theory   64
Learning theory   62
Neoclassical criminology   57
Positivist school   58
Routine activity theory   69
Situational crime prevention   70
Social conflict theory   65
Social disorganization theory   61
Strain theory   61
Theoretical paradigm   56
XYY chromosome   59

/// REVIEW QUESTIONS

Test your understanding of chapter content at **edge.sagepub.com/peak4e**.

1. What were the prevailing beliefs concerning the causes of crime prior to the mid-1700s?

2. How did Cesare Beccaria and the classical school form the foundation for explaining crime in more rational terms?

3. What were the major contributions of the positivist school of criminology in attempting to explain criminality?

4. How would you describe the link between biology and crime?
5. How do social structures influence criminal behavior?
6. What is the difference between the three major social process theories: learning, control, and labeling?
7. Why are less powerful groups more likely than dominant groups to be subjected to criminal sanctions, according to social conflict theories?
8. Why did early feminist theorists believe that women would eventually engage in the same amount of crime as men?
9. Why do environmental criminologists argue that opportunity is an important cause of crime?
10. What is one difference and one similarity between the motives of robbers and the motives of burglars?

/// LEARN BY DOING

1. Assume that our legal system is neoclassical: People make a rational choice to commit crimes after weighing the benefits to be gained against the costs of being caught and punished, but the criminal law must take into account differences among individuals. You are engaged in a class debate concerning the following resolution: "Our legal system has struck an excellent balance between holding people responsible for their crimes and allowing them to be excused for their crimes." Choose a side, and stake out your argument.

2. Your criminal justice professor hands out the following scenario: John, age 14, is on an errand for his parents (who are in a lower socioeconomic class) when he decides to stop at a crafts shop and look at model cars and airplanes—a hobby he greatly enjoys. While in the store, he puts two small bottles of model paint in his pockets and leaves, but he is quickly stopped by a clerk as he attempts his escape. Explain the possible reasons for John's actions in view of the biological, social process, and environmental criminology theories of crime discussed in this chapter.

3. The legalization of marijuana continues to be a highly controversial issue. Describe how the social conflict theories of crime might be used to explain illegal marijuana use.

/// STUDY SITE

Get the tools you need to sharpen your study skills. SAGE edge offers a robust online environment featuring an impressive array of free tools and resources.

Access practice quizzes, eFlashcards, video, and multimedia at **edge.sagepub.com/peak4e**.

Associated Press/J. Scott Applewhite

CHAPTER 4

ETHICAL ESSENTIALS
Doing Right When No One Is Watching

Ethics is knowing the difference between what you have a right to do and what is right to do.

—Justice Potter Stewart[1]

LEARNING OBJECTIVES

As a result of reading this chapter, you will be able to

1. Articulate legitimate ethical dilemmas that arise with police, courts, and corrections practitioners
2. Explain the philosophical foundations that underlie and mold modern ethical behavior
3. Discuss the need for, and application of, ethical standards as they concern police
4. Explain the importance of ethics in the court system
5. Delineate the unique ethical considerations and obligations that exist with federal employees
6. Explain the interplay of ethics with the subculture and job-related stress in corrections practitioners
7. Understand what ethical tests can help criminal justice students and practitioners decide how to address ethical dilemmas

ASSESS YOUR AWARENESS

Test your knowledge of ethics by responding to the following seven true-false items; check your answers after reading this chapter.

1. The term *ethics* is rooted in the ancient Greek idea of "character."
2. The "ends justify the means" philosophy is typically a good, safe philosophy for the police and judges to follow.
3. Communities sometimes seem to tolerate questionable police behavior, if it is carried out to benefit the greater public good (such as dealing with violent gang members).
4. During an oral interview, applicants for policing jobs should *never* indicate a willingness to "snitch" on another officer whom they observe doing something wrong.
5. The receipt of gratuities by criminal justice personnel is a universally accepted practice.
6. Whistleblowers who expose improper acts of their coworkers now have no legal protection.
7. Because of their constitutional obligations, prosecutors and defense attorneys are not bound to the same ethical standards as other criminal justice employees.

<< Answers can be found on page 419.

In July 2017, a suspect attempting to flee from Utah state troopers ran his pickup truck head-on into a truck driven by 43-year-old William Gray. The suspect died in the crash. At the hospital, police attempted to obtain a blood sample from the unconscious, severely burned Gray. Nurse Alex Wubbels refused the police request for a blood draw, pointing out that Gray was not under arrest, that police did not have a warrant to obtain the blood, and that police could not obtain consent because the man was unconscious. The police believed they had implied consent by virtue of Gray's commercial driver's license (CDL). (This point soon became a legal controversy, as some attorneys argued that federal regulations regarding Gray's CDL allowed police to obtain the sample; other attorneys disagreed.) Video shows the officer saying, "I either go away with blood in vials or body in tow," then placing Wubbels under arrest, grabbing her, pulling her arms behind her back, handcuffing her, and dragging her out of the hospital as she screams. An internal investigation found the officer and his supervisor violated several department policies during Wubbels's arrest; a review by the city's civilian review board also found that both officers violated department policies. The arresting officer was terminated and his supervisor demoted; both appealed their punishments. Wubbels agreed to a $500,000 payment to settle the dispute.[2]

As you read this chapter, consider whether or not Wubbels should have been arrested and if there were other means available to police to address the situation. Also, consider how tenuous the relationship can be between police and citizens, how quickly matters can get out of hand, and how police use of force can easily be viewed as "crossing the line" and be deemed unethical in nature. Perhaps a good "test" in this particular case (per the Supreme Court in *Graham v. Connor*, discussed in Chapter 7) is whether or not the officer's actions were reasonable in light of the facts and circumstances facing him, without regard to his underlying intent or motivation.

INTRODUCTION

As regular practice is essential to being a renowned musician, and a perfect cake is essential to having a beautiful wedding, so too is ethics essential to being a criminal justice practitioner. A Latin term that might be used to describe this relationship is *sine qua non*—"without which, nothing." A fundamental knowledge of ethics, as well as some guideposts concerning what constitutes unethical behavior, is an important topic in today's society and for all criminal justice students—not only to guide their own behavior but also because unethical behavior at times appears to permeate contemporary U.S. politics/government, business, and sports.

What specific behaviors are clearly unethical for criminal justice employees? What criteria should guide these employees in their work? To what extent, if any, should the public allow criminal justice employees to violate citizens' rights in order to maintain public order?

This chapter attempts to address these questions and examines many types of ethical problems that can and do arise in police departments, courts, and corrections agencies. The focus is necessarily on the police, who find themselves in many more situations where corruption and brutality can occur than do judges and corrections personnel.

This is not a black-and-white area of study; in fact, there are definitely "shades of gray" for many people where ethics is called into question. Also problematic is that some people who are hired into criminal justice positions simply are not of good character. Furthermore, as addressed in Chapter 1, we cannot *train* people to have high ethical standards, nor can we infuse ethics intravenously. In sum, character and ethics are largely things that people either have or don't have.

GOOD EXAMPLES OF BAD EXAMPLES

To frame the concept of ethics and demonstrate how one's value system can easily be challenged in criminal justice work, consider the following scenarios, all of which are based on true events, and what you might deem to be an appropriate response and punishment (if any) for each:

- *Police:* A Chicago police officer was reprimanded for violating rules that prohibit officers from making political statements while on duty. Specifically, he had posted on social media a picture of himself, in uniform, holding an American flag and a homemade sign that read, "I stand for the anthem. I love the American flag. I support my president and the 2nd Amendment." But the reprimand only seemed to intensify his rhetoric, as he began posting inflammatory material about women, welfare recipients, and those who disagree with his politics. He also tangled with social media users, saying, "Keep listening for that knock on the door," and often boasted that he would continue to avoid serious punishment. His superiors twice tried to fire him, though he appealed those efforts and won. "The police dept didn't and CAN'T fire me," he wrote. The officer is one of the most disciplined officers in the department, having been suspended seven times for a total of 111 days.[3]

- *Courts:* For several weeks, a wealthy divorcée receives menacing telephone calls that demand social dates and sexual favors. The caller's voice is electronically disguised. The suspect also begins stalking the woman. After working several clues and surveillances at the victim's home, you, a federal agent, finally make contact with a suspect and determine that he is the chief judge of the state's supreme court. Upon confronting him, you are told by the judge to "forget about it, or you'll be checking passports in a remote embassy."[4]

- *Corrections:* Following a number of high-profile deaths and cases of abuse, several civil rights organizations and advocates for the mentally ill demanded an investigation of a southern state's prison system where more than 12,000 inmates were alleged as being held in solitary confinement. Cases cited included an inmate who died after being gassed three times in a solitary confinement cell and one who was scalded to death while locked by corrections officers in a prison shower. It was also alleged that inmates were beaten and sexually assaulted, and that racial disparity exists: Black inmates made up 44 percent of the prison population but represented 57 percent of the inmates in solitary confinement. In addition, it was believed that nearly a quarter of all inmates with mental illnesses were housed in solitary confinement.[5]

PHILOSOPHICAL FOUNDATIONS

The term *ethics* is rooted in the ancient Greek idea of "character." Ethics involves doing what is right or correct, and the term is generally used to refer to how people should behave in a professional capacity. Many people would argue, however, that no difference should exist between one's professional and personal behavior. In other words, ethical rules of conduct should apply to everything a person does.

A central problem with understanding ethics concerns the questions of "whose ethics" and "which right." This becomes evident when one examines controversial issues such as the death penalty, abortion, use of deadly force, and gun control. How individuals view a particular controversy depends largely on their values, character, or ethics. Both sides of controversies such as these believe they are morally right. These issues demonstrate that to understand behavior, the most basic values must be examined and understood.

Another area for examination is **deontological ethics**, which does not consider consequences but instead examines one's duty to act. The word *deontology* comes from two Greek roots, *deos*, meaning "duty," and *logos*, meaning "study." Thus, deontology means the study of duty. When police officers observe a violation of law, they have a duty to act. Officers frequently use this duty as an excuse when they issue traffic citations that appear to have little utility and do not produce any great benefit for the rest of society. For example, when an officer writes a traffic citation for a prohibited left turn made at two o'clock in the morning when no traffic is around, the officer is fulfilling a departmental duty to enforce the law. From a utilitarian standpoint (where we judge an action by its consequences), however, little if any good was served. Here, duty, and not good consequences, was the primary motivator.

Deontological ethics: one's duty to act.

One of the ethical responsibilities of police officers is to testify truthfully in court concerning what they saw, heard, and did during the performance of their duties.

Immanuel Kant, an 18th-century philosopher, expanded the ethics of duty by including the idea of "good will."[6] People's actions must be guided by good intent. In the previous example, the officer who wrote the traffic citation for an improper left turn would be acting unethically if the ticket was a response to a quota or some irrelevant motive. However, if the citation was issued because the officer truly believed that it would result in some good outcome, it would have been an ethical action.

Some people have expanded this argument even further. Richard Kania argued that police officers should be allowed to freely accept gratuities because such actions would constitute the building blocks of positive social relationships between the police and the public.[7] In this case, duty is used to justify what under normal circumstances would be considered unethical. Conversely, if officers take gratuities for self-gratification rather than to form positive community relationships, then the action would be considered unethical by many.

Types of Ethics

Ethics usually involves standards of fair and honest conduct; what we call conscience, the ability to recognize right from wrong; and actions that are good and proper. There are absolute ethics and relative ethics. **Absolute ethics** has only two sides—something is either good or bad, black or white. Some examples in police ethics would be unethical behaviors such as bribery, extortion, excessive force, and perjury, which nearly everyone would agree are unacceptable behaviors by the police.

Relative ethics is more complicated and can have a multitude of sides with varying shades of gray. What one person considers to be ethical behavior may be deemed highly unethical by someone else. Not all ethical issues are clear-cut, however, and communities *do* seem willing at times to tolerate extralegal behavior if there is a greater public good, especially in dealing with problems such as gangs and the homeless. This willingness on the part of the community can be conveyed to the police. Ethical relativism can be said to form an essential part of the community policing movement, discussed more fully in Chapter 6.

A community's acceptance of relative ethics as part of criminal justice may send the wrong message: that few boundaries are placed on justice system employee behaviors and that, at times, "anything goes" in their fight against crime. As John Kleinig pointed out, giving false testimony to ensure that a public menace is "put away" or illegally wiretapping an organized crime figure's telephone might sometimes be viewed as "necessary" and "justified," though illegal.[8]

This is the essence of the crime control model of criminal justice (discussed in Chapter 1). Another example is that many police believe they are compelled to skirt along the edges of the law—or even violate it—in order to arrest drug traffickers. The ethical problem here is that even if the action could be justified as morally proper, it remains illegal. For many persons, however, the protection of society overrides other concerns.

This viewpoint—the "principle of double effect"—holds that when one commits an act to achieve a good end and an inevitable but intended effect is negative, then the act might be justified. A long-standing debate has occurred about balancing the rights of individuals against the community's interest in calm and order.

These special areas of ethics can become problematic and controversial when police officers use deadly force or lie and deceive others in their work. Police could justify a whole range of activities that others may deem unethical simply because the consequences resulted in the greatest good for the greatest number—the *utilitarian* approach (or **utilitarianism**). If the ends justified the means, perjury would be ethical when committed to prevent a serial killer from being set free to prey on society. In our democratic society, however, the means are just as important as, if not more important than, the desired end.

As examples, citizens in some jurisdictions may not object to the police "hassling" suspected gang members—pulling them over in their cars, say, and doing a field interview—or telling homeless people who are loitering in front of a heavy tourism area or public park to "move along."

It is no less important today than in the past for criminal justice employees to appreciate and come to grips with ethical essentials. Indeed, ethical issues in policing have been affected by three critical factors:[9] (1) the growing level of temptation stemming from the illicit drug trade; (2) the potentially compromising nature of the organizational

---

Absolute ethics: the type of ethics where there are only two sides—good or bad, black or white; some examples would be unethical behaviors such as bribery, extortion, excessive force, and perjury, which nearly everyone would agree are unacceptable for criminal justice personnel.

Relative ethics: the gray area of ethics that is not so clear-cut, such as releasing a serious offender in order to use him later as an informant.

Utilitarianism: in ethics, as articulated by John Stuart Mill, a belief that the proper course of action is that which maximizes utility—usually defined as that which maximizes happiness and minimizes suffering.

culture—a culture that can exalt loyalty over integrity, with a "code of silence" that protects unethical employees; and (3) the challenges posed by decentralization (flattening the organization and pushing officers' decision making downward) through the advent of community-oriented policing and problem solving (the community era of policing is discussed in Chapter 6).

Noble Cause Corruption

When the police practice relative ethics and the principle of double effect, described earlier, it is known as noble cause corruption—what Thomas Martinelli, perhaps gratuitously, defined as "corruption committed in the name of good ends, corruption that happens when police officers care too much about their work."[10] It basically holds that when an act is committed to achieve a good end (such as an illegal search) but its outcome is negative (the person who is searched eventually goes to prison), the act might still be justified.

Although noble cause corruption can occur anywhere in the criminal justice system, we might look at the police for examples. Officers might bend the rules, such as not reading a drunk person his rights or performing a field sobriety test; planting evidence; issuing "sewer" tickets—writing a person a ticket but not giving it to her, resulting in a warrant issued for failure to appear in court; "testilying," or "using the magic pencil," whereby police officers write up an incident in a way that criminalizes a suspect—this is a powerful tool for punishment. Noble cause corruption carries with it a different way of thinking about the police relationship with the law. Here, officers operate on a standard that places personal morality above the law, becoming legislators *of* the law and acting as if they *are* the law.[11] Some officers rationalize such activities; as a Philadelphia police officer put it, "When you're shoveling society's garbage, you gotta be indulged a little bit."[12] Obviously the kinds of noble cause behaviors mentioned here often involve arrogance on the part of the police and ignore the basic constitutional guidelines the occupation demands. Administrators and middle managers must be careful to take a hardline view that their subordinates always tell the truth and follow the law. A supervisory philosophy of discipline based on due process, fairness, and equity, combined with intelligent, informed, and comprehensive decision making, is best for the department, its employees, and the community.[13]

Noble cause corruption: a situation in which one commits an unethical act but for the greater good; for example, a police officer violates the Constitution in order to capture a serious offender.

ETHICS IN POLICING

Having defined the types of ethics and some dilemmas, next we discuss in greater detail some of the ethical issues faced by police leaders and their subordinates.

A Primer: The Oral Job Interview

During oral interviews for a position in policing, applicants are often placed in a hypothetical situation that tests their ethical beliefs and character. For example, they may be asked to assume the role of Officer Brown, who is checking on foot an office supplies retail store that was found to have an unlocked door during early morning hours. On leaving the building, Brown observes another officer, Smith, removing a $200 writing pen from a display case and placing it in his uniform pocket. What should Officer Brown do?

This kind of question commonly befuddles the applicant: "Should I rat on my fellow officer? Overlook the matter? Merely tell Smith never to do that again?" Unfortunately, applicants may do a lot of "how am I *supposed* to respond" soul searching and second-guessing with these kinds of questions.

Bear in mind that criminal justice agencies do not wish to hire someone who possesses ethical shortcomings; it is simply too potentially dangerous and expensive, from both legal

Police executives typically address the public during critical incidents or investigations. Here, Chicago Police Chief Eddie Johnson comments on the allegation by actor and singer Jussie Smollett that he was the victim of a hate crime assault in February 2019. (Smollett was later indicted for paying two men to stage the crime against him.)

and moral standpoints, to take the chance of bringing into an agency someone who is corrupt. That is the reason for such questioning and a thorough background investigation of applicants.

Before responding to a scenario like the one concerning Officers Brown and Smith, the applicant should consider the following issues: Is this likely to be the first time that Smith has stolen something? Don't the police arrest and jail people for this same kind of behavior?

In short, police administrators should *never* want an applicant to respond that it is acceptable for an officer to steal. Furthermore, it would be incorrect for an applicant to believe that police do not want an officer to "rat out" another officer. Applicants should never acknowledge that stealing or other such activities are to be overlooked.

Police Corruption

"For as long as there have been police, there has been police corruption."[14] Thus observed police expert Lawrence Sherman about one of the oldest problems in U.S. policing. Indeed, the Knapp Commission investigated police corruption in the early 1970s, finding that there are two primary types of corrupt police officers: the "meat-eaters" and the "grass-eaters." Meat-eaters spend a good deal of their working hours aggressively seeking out situations that they can exploit for financial gain, including gambling, narcotics, and other lucrative enterprises.

Grass-eaters, the commission noted, constitute the overwhelming majority of those officers who accept payoffs; they are not aggressive but will accept gratuities from contractors, tow-truck operators, gamblers, and the like. Although such officers probably constitute a small percentage of the field, any such activity is to be identified and dealt with sternly.

Police corruption: misconduct by police officers that can involve but is not limited to illegal activities for economic gain, gratuities, favors, and so on.

Police corruption can be defined broadly, from major forms of police wrongdoing to the pettiest forms of improper behavior. Another definition is "the misuse of authority by a police officer in a manner designed to produce personal gain for the officer or for others."[15] Police corruption is not limited to monetary gain, however. Gains may be made through the acceptance of services received, status, influence, prestige, or future support for the officer or someone else.[16]

To Inform or Not to Inform: The Code of Silence

Let's continue with the earlier scenario. Remember that Officer Brown witnessed Officer Smith putting an expensive ink pen in his pocket after they found an unlocked office supplies retail business on the graveyard shift. If reported, the misconduct will ruin Smith, but if not reported, the behavior could eventually cause enormous harm. To outsiders, this is not a moral dilemma for Brown at all; the only proper path is for her to report the misconduct. However, arguments exist both for and against Brown's informing on her partner. Reasons for informing include the fact that the harm caused by a scandal would be outweighed by the public's knowing that the police department is free of corruption; also, individual episodes of corruption would be brought to a halt. Brown, moreover, has a sworn duty to uphold the law. Reasons against informing include the facts that, at least in Brown's mind, the other officer is a member of the "family" and a skilled police officer is a valuable asset whose social value far outweighs the damage done by moderate corruption.[17]

A person who is in charge of investigating police corruption would no doubt take a punitive view, because police are not supposed to steal, and they arrest people for the same kinds of acts every day. Still, the issue—and a common question during an oral interview when citizens are being tested for police positions—is whether or not Brown would come forth and inform on her fellow officer.

It is necessary to train police recruits on the need for a corruption-free department. The creation and maintenance of an internal affairs unit and the vigorous prosecution of law-breaking police officers are also critical to maintaining the integrity of officers.

The Law Enforcement Code of Ethics and Oath of Honor

The Law Enforcement Code of Ethics (LECE) was adopted by the International Association of Chiefs of Police (IACP) in 1957 and has been revised several times since then. It is a powerful proclamation, and tens of thousands of police officers across the nation have sworn to uphold this code upon graduating from their academies. Unfortunately, the LECE is also quite lengthy, covering rather broadly the following topics as they relate to police officers: primary responsibilities, performance of one's duties, discretion, use of force, confidentiality, integrity, cooperation with other officers and agencies, personal/professional capabilities, and private life.

The IACP adopted a separate, shorter code that would be mutually supportive of the LECE but also easier for officers to remember and call to mind when they come face-to-face with an ethical dilemma. It is the Law Enforcement Oath of Honor, and the IACP is hoping the

Going Global

Mexico—Where an Entire Police Force May Be Corrupt

Mexican police have long been known to engage in crime, graft, and corruption. Recently, relatives of 43 missing students demanded justice in Mexico City. Officials believe the students were abducted by corrupt police officers and handed over to a local drug gang.

An entire municipal police force in central Mexico was terminated in late 2018 following suspicions of corruption and ties to organized crime. State and military personnel took control of security in Tehuacán, disarming 205 police officers on the force; another 113 officers, including the agency's director, were unaccounted for and believed to have fled the city. The terminations followed increases in violent crimes, after which the officers underwent evaluations to determine if they were fit for duty and their weapons used to commit crimes. Authorities also determined that a majority of the police did not receive adequate screening for being hired and should not have been working on the force.

The wholesale termination demonstrated the level to which organized crime and corruption have penetrated the local police, who are particularly vulnerable to such behavior as they are overworked, underpaid, and understaffed. The math is not complicated: If a police officer is paid the U.S. equivalent of $200 per month, and organized crime offers $1,000 a month, there is little doubt they will choose the latter. There is evidence that organized crime groups even secure positions for their own people within the police force and that some police units operate kidnapping rings.

Source: Parker Asmann, "Suspension of Entire Local Police Force Shows Depth of Mexico Corruption," Insight Crime, August 28, 2018, https://www.insightcrime.org/news/brief/suspension-entire-local-police-force-shows-depth-mexico-corruption/.

oath will be implemented in all police agencies and by all individual officers. It may be used at swearing-in ceremonies, graduation ceremonies, promotion ceremonies, beginnings of training sessions, police meetings and conferences, and so forth.[18] The Law Enforcement Oath of Honor is as follows:

> On my honor, I will never
>
> betray my badge, my integrity,
>
> my character or the public trust.
>
> I will always have the courage to hold
>
> myself and others accountable for our actions.
>
> I will always uphold
>
> the constitution, my community and the
>
> agency I serve.[19]

Slippery slope: the idea that a small first step can lead to more serious behaviors, such as the receipt of minor gratuities by police officers believed to eventually cause them to desire or demand receipt of items of greater value.

Accepted lying: police activities intended to apprehend or entrap suspects. This type of lying is generally considered to be trickery.

Deviant lying: occasions when officers commit perjury to convict suspects or are deceptive about some activity that is illegal or unacceptable to the department or public in general.

Accepted and Deviant Lying

In many cases, no clear line separates acceptable from unacceptable behavior in policing. The two are separated by an expansive gray area that comes under relative ethics. Some observers have referred to such illegal behavior as a "slippery slope," meaning that people tread on solid or legal ground but at some point slip beyond the acceptable into illegal or unacceptable behavior.

Criminal justice employees lie or deceive for different purposes and under varying circumstances. In some cases, their misrepresentations are accepted as an essential part of a criminal investigation, whereas in other cases they are viewed as violations of law. David Carter examined police lying and perjury and found a distinction between accepted lying and deviant lying.[20] Accepted lying includes police activities intended to apprehend or entrap suspects. This type of lying is generally considered to be trickery. Deviant lying, by contrast, refers to occasions when officers commit perjury to convict suspects or are deceptive about some activity that is illegal or unacceptable to the department or public in general.

Lying and deception have long been used by the police to identify and arrest criminals; this undercover DEA agent is posing as a student as part of a drug investigation.

Deception has long been practiced by the police to ensnare violators and suspects. For many years, it was the principal method used by detectives and police officers to secure confessions and convictions. Accepted lying is allowed by law, and to a great extent it is expected by the public. Gary Marx identified three methods police use to trick a suspect: (1) performing the illegal action as part of a larger, socially acceptable, and legal goal; (2) disguising the illegal action so that the suspect does not know it is illegal; and (3) morally weakening the suspect so that the suspect voluntarily becomes involved.[21] The courts have long accepted deception as an investigative tool. For example, the U.S. Supreme Court ruled in *Illinois v. Perkins* that, when investigating crimes, police undercover agents are not required to administer the *Miranda* warning to incarcerated inmates.[22] Lying, although

84 ■ Part 1: Criminal Justice as a System

acceptable by the courts and the public in certain circumstances, does result in an ethical dilemma. It is a dirty means to accomplishing a good end—the police using untruths to gain the truth relative to some event.

In their examination of lying, Thomas Barker and David Carter identified two types of deviant lying: lying that serves legitimate purposes and lying that conceals or promotes crimes or illegitimate ends.[23] Lying that serves legitimate goals occurs when officers lie to secure a conviction, obtain a search warrant, or conceal omissions during an investigation. Barker found that police officers believe that almost one-fourth of their agency would

Investigating Further

Agency Policy Governing Police Conduct

Following is a sample departmental policy pertaining to officers' conduct; read it and respond to the questions below:

A. **General Conduct: Obedience to Laws and Regulations**

  a. Officers shall obey the constitutional, civil, and criminal laws of the city, its state, and the federal government.

  b. Officers shall obey all lawful orders.

  c. Violations include, but are not limited to
   - Committing a willful violation of constitutional civil rights that demonstrates reckless disregard.
   - Committing infractions of policy concerning traffic codes (e.g., driving over the speed limit, parking in unauthorized locations, failing to wear seat belts).
   - Inflicting punishment or mistreatment (both physical and/or mental) upon a prisoner or person in custody or detention or a citizen.
   - Violating any local, state, or federal criminal or civil codes or ordinances.
   - Refusing or failing to protect a prisoner's civil rights.
   - Making slanderous or libelous statements intending to harm the reputation of another member of this agency or any person in general.
   - Using excessive force to hold, arrest, or detain any person, or using prohibited devices, procedures, tactics, or techniques to do so.

B. **Conduct Unbecoming an Officer**

  a. Honesty, efficiency, and integrity are the guideposts for a police officer's conduct. All officers are employed to serve the citizens of this jurisdiction, who are entitled to courteous, efficient response to requests for police services.

  b. All officers, whether on or off duty, shall be governed by ordinary and reasonable rules of good conduct and behavior and shall not commit any act which could adversely reflect on this department.

  c. Officers shall not reveal any information of which they have knowledge unless it is given to a person entitled to have the information.

  d. All officers when off duty, but in uniform, shall conduct themselves as though they were on duty.

  e. Members shall conduct themselves (on duty as well as off duty) in a manner that does not damage or might likely damage or bring the public image, integrity, or reputation of the Police Department into discredit, disrepute, or impair its efficient and effective operation.

  1. Based on what you've read above, is this policy adequate for governing all improper acts of commission or omission by the officers in this agency?

  2. If not, which policy or policies might be added? Which of the above might be amended?

commit perjury to secure a conviction or to obtain a search warrant.[24] Lying becomes an effective, routine way to sidestep legal impediments. When left unchecked by supervisors, managers, and administrators, lying can become organizationally accepted as an effective means of nullifying legal entanglements and removing obstacles that stand in the way of convictions. Examples include using the services of nonexistent confidential informants to secure search warrants, concealing that an interrogator went too far, coercing a confession, or perjuring oneself to gain a conviction.

Lying to conceal or promote criminality is the most distressing form of deception. Examples range from when the police lie to conceal their use of excessive force when arresting a suspect to obscuring the commission of a criminal act.

Accepting Gratuities

Gratuities: the receipt of some benefit (a meal, gift, or some other favor) either for free or for a reduced price.

Many police officers commonly accept gratuities as a part of their job. Restaurants frequently give officers free or half-price meals and drinks, and other businesses routinely give officers discounts for services or merchandise. While some officers and their departments accept the receipt of such gratuities as a legitimate part of their job, other agencies prohibit such gifts and discounts but seldom attempt to enforce any relevant policy or regulation. Finally, some departments attempt to ensure that officers do not accept free or discounted services or merchandise and routinely enforce policies or regulations against such behavior.[25]

There are two basic arguments *against* police acceptance of gratuities. First is the slippery slope argument, discussed earlier, which proposes that gratuities are the first step in police corruption. This argument holds that once gratuities are received, police officers' ethics are subverted and they are open to additional breaches of their integrity. In addition, officers who accept minor gifts or gratuities are then obligated to provide the donors with some special service or accommodation. Furthermore, some critics propose that receiving a gratuity is wrong because officers are receiving rewards for services that they are obligated to provide as part of their employment. That is, officers have no legitimate right to accept compensation in the form of a gratuity. If the police ever hope to be accepted as members of a full-fledged profession, they must address whether the acceptance of gratuities is professional behavior.

Former New York police commissioner Patrick V. Murphy was one of those who believed that "except for your pay check, there is no such thing as a clean buck."[26] He also noted that judges, teachers, doctors, and other professionals do not accept special consideration from restaurants, convenience stores, movie theaters, and so on.

Here is an example of a policy developed by a sheriff's office concerning gratuities:

1. Without the express permission of the Sheriff, members shall not solicit or accept any gift, gratuity, loan, present, or fee where there is any direct or indirect connection between this solicitation or acceptance of such gift and their employment by this office.

2. Members shall not accept, either directly or indirectly, any gift, gratuity, loan, fee, or thing of value, the acceptance of which might tend to improperly influence their actions, or that of any other member, in any matter of police business, or which might tend to cast an adverse reflection on the Sheriff's Office.

3. Any unauthorized gift, gratuity, loan, fee, reward, or other thing falling into any of these categories coming into the possession of any member shall be forwarded to the member's commander, together with a written report explaining the circumstances connected therewith. The commander will decide the disposition of the gift.[27]

You Be the...

Police Officer

One of the authors was directly involved in the following case study: Assume that you are a small-town police officer and it is summertime. You are driving your patrol car one evening when a vehicle suddenly pulls up beside you, and the woman driver yells, "Officer, my baby's dying!" You have her drive her car to the curb, and she then carries the child to your patrol car. You note that the infant is about eight months of age, her face has a blue tinge to it, her eyes are rolled back, and she does not appear to be breathing. You quickly check her airway, resolve the situation (the baby's airway had become obstructed by her tongue during a seizure) and convey them to the hospital. Two months later, learning from a friend where you live, the same woman comes to your home. Sobbing, she says, "Officer, my husband is in jail for disorderly conduct, I'm broke, and my kids have no food or milk. I need money to bail him out of jail so he can get back to work and buy groceries. You gave me help once—can you help me now?" Her husband, well known to your police agency for past crimes, does not enjoy a good reputation in town.

1. Will you do something to assist the woman financially? If not, explain.
2. If yes, will you loan her grocery money only, or enough so that she can also bail her husband out of jail?
3. Assume you recently received a large income tax refund and thus decide to give her enough money to bail her husband out of jail so that he can return to his job. Is this ethical? Why or why not? If you do, how might the other officers react if learning of your conduct?

Greed and Temptation

Edward Tully underscored the vast amount of temptation that confronts today's police officers and what police leaders must do to combat it:

> Socrates, Mother Teresa, or other revered individuals in our society never had to face the constant stream of ethical problems of a busy cop on the beat. One of the roles of [police leaders] is to create an environment that will help the officer resist the temptations that may lead to misconduct, corruption, or abuse of power. The executive cannot construct a work environment that will completely insulate the officers from the forces which lead to misconduct. The ultimate responsibility for an officer's ethical and moral welfare rests squarely with the officer.[28]

Most citizens have no way of comprehending the amount of temptation that confronts today's police officers. They frequently find themselves alone inside retail businesses after normal business hours, clearing the building after finding an open door or window. A swing or graveyard shift officer could easily obtain considerable plunder during these occasions, acquiring everything from clothing to tires for a personal vehicle. At the other end of the spectrum is the potential for huge payoffs from drug traffickers or other big-money offenders who will gladly pay the officer to look away from their crimes. Some officers, like the general public, find this temptation impossible to overcome.

"Random Acts of Kindness": The Hidden Side of Police Work

This chapter section has focused on efforts to evaluate, constrain, and discipline different forms of police behavior. Perhaps it is appropriate, therefore, to balance the issue by pointing out another, often overlooked side of the issue: police behaviors that are laudable and reveal a completely different face from that which the public perceives.

Practitioner's Perspective

Police Internal Affairs Investigator

Name: Zack Thew
Position: Police Internal Affairs Investigator
Location: Reno, Nevada

What is your career story? I got a bachelor's degree in criminal justice. Shortly after that, I was employed by the Reno Police Department. I had the opportunity to work various assignments as an officer. I was a training officer, a lead negotiator, and a part of our mentoring program. After several years of doing that, I went into the detective division, where I worked in the fraud unit, the sex crimes unit, the robbery homicide unit, and the computer crimes unit before promoting to sergeant.

What misconceptions do you often hear about this position? A misconception for internal affairs is that investigators are on a witch hunt or that they're trying to discipline employees for the sake of discipline. Certainly, accountability is at the heart of what we do, but good internal affairs investigators are conscious of employees' rights. They work very closely with employees and the association, and they work to protect the rights of those employees and ensure that all the investigations are fact-based and fair, and that the conclusions are reasonable.

Another misconception held by some members of the public is that the unit exists to cover up or protect substandard or criminal activity by the officers. And that's simply not true. I think how you address both of those misconceptions is to be as transparent, fair, and consistent as possible.

What role does diversity play in this position? Diversity plays a major role in internal affairs. Unfortunately, police often find themselves in situations that are grayer more than they are black-and-white. To be able to adapt to those situations and hold ourselves accountable under those circumstances, we need to understand the situation from as many perspectives as possible. We do that with a diverse approach. We look at it from the perspective of the involved citizens, the officers, the supervisors, the administrators, the media, the politicians, the community, and understand those perspectives so we can have an idea of the big picture with the course of action we ultimately take.

Do you see any common trends in this position? The current trend in internal affairs is a push for transparency. The public at large is very inquisitive, and the media and politicians are discerning. They want to know what's happening with their police department and how their organization is serving them. The fact of the matter is, we do not have as big of a segment of the population that blindly trusts the police as they existed before. So again, it's fostering that relationship, and holding our people accountable, and being transparent.

What advice would you give to someone either wishing to study, or now studying, criminal justice and wanting to become a practitioner in this position? My advice for students who want to pursue this career is to spend some time in internal affairs to understand the demands of the job. Be as varied as you possibly can be in your work and personal experience, and understand current events, both inside and outside of your organization. That's going to help you know what you need to do to make your organization successful and what the expectations are from the public. Set high standards and hold yourself accountable above all else.

To learn more about Zach Thew's experiences as a police internal affairs investigator, watch the Practitioner's Perspective video in SAGE vantage.

Each day police officers perform countless "random acts of kindness" that seldom come to the public's attention. Yet, as one of this book's authors can attest from personal experience, many are the times that officers do act in unique and unexpected ways in order to help someone in distress, such as passing the hat (literally) to collect funds to buy food

Investigating Further

A Hippocratic Oath for Police?

The 2015 President's Task Force on 21st Century Policing heard from 140 witnesses who described many different ways of creating a positive culture of policing. One such witness, distinguished police researcher David Kennedy of the John Jay College of Criminal Justice in New York, suggested there should be a Hippocratic Oath for policing. The Oath, existing as early as 275 A.D. and historically taken by physicians, directs the physician to "prescribe only beneficial treatments, according to his abilities and judgment, to refrain from causing harm or hurt, and to live an exemplary personal and professional life." As society's "doctors" (both often seeing people at their worst, when they are most in need of assistance), Kennedy argued that law enforcement officers' goal should be likewise, to avoid use of force if at all possible, even when it is allowed by law and by policy. Certainly concepts discussed in Chapter 6 (community policing and problem solving) as well as constitutional policing and legitimacy (Chapter 7), appear to speak to this culture of policing.

According to Kennedy, "Respectful language; thoughtful and intentional dialogue about the perception and reality of profiling and the mass incarceration of minorities; and consistent involvement, both formal and informal, in community events all help ensure that relationships of trust between police and community will be built. The vision of policing in the 21st century should be that of officers as guardians of human and constitutional rights."

1. Should such an oath exist for policing?
2. If so, should it be implemented nationally or on an agency-by-agency basis as part of the individual department's policies and procedures?
3. Which federal official or agency might create and oversee its practical application?
4. Would such an oath be enforceable? If so, which agency would enforce it, and what penalties might exist for violations?

---

for a group of hungry undocumented immigrants while they are being detained; giving a hard-core alcoholic enough whiskey (from a bottle of bourbon confiscated long before) that he might sleep in his cell, keeping the hallucinations of the delirium tremens (DTs) at bay; lying on their bellies during a downpour to retrieve cash from a storm sewer so that an elderly couple (who, shortly before, had been bound, gagged, beaten, and robbed) might have at least some of their money returned (while fleeing their home, the robber had dropped a considerable number of bills in the yard and gutter); or giving a woman money to feed herself and her baby while her husband is in the local jail.

The following deeds, however, *were* reported by the media:

- A Miami, Florida, officer caught a struggling single mother shoplifting food from a grocery store for her family. Rather than take her to jail, the officer purchased the food for the mother and showed her the local food banks and churches where she could get assistance until she got back on her feet.[29]
- Officers in New York City and Palatka, Florida, noticing that homeless men were virtually walking barefoot, purchased new shoes for them.[30]
- After a 20-year-old wheelchair-bound man was robbed of $4,000 he was saving for a new wheelchair, officers not only caught the robber and returned his money but also created a fund so that he could purchase the very best of wheelchairs (his other one at times got stuck in the snow).[31]
- Officers in Benicia, California, and Phoenix, Arizona, learning that teens were walking long distances each day (one going nine miles to and from work, the

other, two miles to school), purchased bicycles for them and arranged for them to obtain helmets and other necessities.

- When a Nicoma, Oklahoma, police officer learned that a bike had been stolen at knifepoint from a boy on his beat who had autism, he collected money from his department and his second job to buy the boy a new bike.[32]

ETHICS IN THE COURTS

Although the public tends to think of criminal justice ethics primarily in terms of the police, certainly other criminal justice professionals—including the court work group—have expectations in this regard as well. The ethical standards and expectations—and some examples of failings—of those individuals are discussed next.

Evolving Standards of Conduct

The first call during the 20th century for formalized standards of conduct in the legal profession came in 1906, with Roscoe Pound's speech "The Causes of Popular Dissatisfaction With the Administration of Justice."[33] However, the first canons of judicial ethics probably grew out of a professional baseball scandal in 1919, in which the World Series was "thrown" to the Chicago White Sox by the Cincinnati Reds. Baseball officials turned to the judiciary for leadership and hired U.S. District Court Judge Kenesaw Mountain Landis as baseball commissioner—a position for which Landis was paid $42,500, compared to his $7,500 earnings per year as a judge. This affair prompted the 1921 American Bar Association (ABA) convention to pass a resolution of censure against the judge and appoint a committee to propose standards of judicial ethics.[34]

In 1924, the ABA approved the Canons of Judicial Ethics under the leadership of Chief Justice William Howard Taft, and in 1972, the ABA approved a new **Model Code of Judicial Conduct**; in 1990, the same body adopted a revised model code. Nearly all states and the District of Columbia have promulgated standards based on the code. In 1974, the United States Judicial Conference adopted a Code of Conduct for United States Judges, and Congress over the years enacted legislation regulating judicial conduct, including the Ethics Reform Act of 1989.

Model Code of Judicial Conduct: adopted by the House of Delegates of the American Bar Association in 1990, it provides a set of ethical principles and guidelines for judges.

The Judge

Judges are discussed generally in Chapter 10; however, here the focus is on their ethical responsibilities. Ideally, our judges are flawless, not allowing emotion or personal biases to creep into their work, treating all cases and individual litigants with an even hand, and employing "justice tempered with mercy." The perfect judge has been described as follows:

> The good judge takes equal pains with every case no matter how humble; he knows that important cases and unimportant cases do not exist, for injustice is not one of those poisons which . . . when taken in small doses may produce a salutary effect. Injustice is a dangerous poison even in doses of homeopathic proportions.[35]

Not all judges, of course, can attain this lofty status and find themselves succumbing to temptation and human faults and foibles. Judges can become embroiled in improper conduct or overstep their bounds in many ways: abuse of judicial power (against attorneys or litigants); inappropriate sanctions and dispositions (including showing favoritism or bias); not meeting the standards of impartiality and competence (discourteous behavior, gender bias and harassment, incompetence); conflict of interest (bias; conflicting financial interests or business, social, or family relationships); and personal conduct (criminal or sexual misconduct, prejudice, statements of opinion).[36]

Following are examples of some true-to-life ethical dilemmas involving the courts:[37]

- A judge persuades jailers to release his son on a nonbondable offense.
- A judge is indicted on charges that he used his office for a racketeering enterprise.
- Two judges attend the governor's $500-per-person inaugural ball.
- A judge is accused of acting with bias in giving a convicted murderer a less severe sentence because the victims were homosexual.
- A judge whose car bears the bumper sticker "I am a pro-life Democrat" acquits six pro-life demonstrators of trespassing at an abortion clinic on the grounds of necessity to protect human life.

Such incidents certainly do little to bolster public confidence in the justice system. People expect more from judges, who are "the most highly visible symbol of justice."[38]

Unfortunately, codes of ethical conduct have not eradicated these problems or allayed concerns about judges' behavior. Indeed, one judge who teaches judicial ethics at the National Judicial College in Reno, Nevada, stated that most judges attending the college admit never having read the Model Code of Judicial Conduct before seeking judicial office.[39]

According to the American Judicature Society, during one year 25 judges were suspended from office, and more than 80 judges resigned or retired either before or after formal charges were filed against them; 120 judges also received private censure, admonition, or reprimand.[40]

The key to judicial ethics is to identify the troublesome issues and to create an "ethical alarm system" that responds.[41] Perhaps the most important tenet in the code and the one that is most difficult to apply is that judges should avoid the *appearance* of impropriety—in other words, it is not enough that judges *do* what is just; they must also avoid conduct that would create in the public's mind a perception that their ability to carry out responsibilities with integrity, impartiality, and competence is impaired.

Ethical requirements for the federal judiciary and other federal employees are discussed later in this chapter.

Prosecutors

Given their power and authority to decide which cases are to be prosecuted, prosecuting attorneys must closely guard their ethical behavior. It was decided in 1935 (in *Berger v. United States*) that the primary duty of a prosecutor is "not that he shall win a case, but that justice shall be done."[42]

Instances of prosecutorial misconduct were reported as early as 1897[43] and are still reported today. One of the leading examples of unethical conduct by a prosecutor is *Miller v. Pate* (1967), in which the prosecutor concealed from the jury in a murder trial the fact that a pair of undershorts with red stains contained not blood but red paint.[44]

According to Elliot Cohen, misconduct works: Oral advocacy is important in the courtroom and can have a powerful effect. Another significant reason for such conduct is the harmless error doctrine, in which an appellate court can affirm a conviction despite the presence of serious misconduct during the trial. Only when appellate courts take a stricter, more consistent approach to this problem will it end.[45]

You Be the...

Ethics Committee Member

A U.S. district court judge in Alabama was controversial even before he was arrested on allegations of beating his wife. He was criticized for hearing government cases while his aviation company was getting hundreds of thousands of dollars in government business. He was also infamous for having an extramarital affair with his courtroom assistant, as well as for his messy public divorce.

In May 2015, Judge Mark Fuller resigned because of a fight he had with the same former courtroom assistant—now his wife—who is heard yelling, "He's beating on me! Please help me!" to a police dispatcher.

A five-judge review panel investigated Fuller's behavior, and a U.S. House of Representatives committee considered conducting impeachment hearings against him.

However, because of his lifetime appointment to the bench, the judge could not be forced off the bench; he could only be reprimanded and asked to resign, and the congressional committee could have recommended impeachment.

1. Should judges with lifetime appointments receive such protections while sitting on the bench?
2. If not, what would kind of system would you propose?

Source: See Brad Freeman, "Wife-Beating Judge Loses It: Why Mark Fuller's New Defense Is Beyond the Pale," *Salon*, March 31, 2015, http://www.salon.com/2015/03/31/wife_beating_judge_loses_it_why_mark_fullers_new_defense_is_beyond_the_pale/.

Defense Attorneys

Defense attorneys, too, must be legally and morally bound to ethical principles as agents of the courts. Cohen suggested the following moral principles for defense attorneys:[46]

- Treat others as ends in themselves and not as mere means to winning cases.
- Treat clients and other professional relations in a similar fashion.
- Do not deliberately engage in behavior apt to deceive the court as to truth.
- Be willing, if necessary, to make reasonable personal sacrifices of time, money, and popularity for what you believe to be a morally good cause.
- Do not give money to, or accept money from, clients for wrongful purposes or in wrongful amounts.
- Avoid harming others in the course of representing your client.
- Be loyal to your client, and do not betray his or her confidence.

Other Court Employees

Other court employees have ethical responsibilities as well. For example, an appellate court judge's secretary is asked by a good friend who is a lawyer whether the judge will be writing the opinion in a certain case. The lawyer may be wishing to attempt to influence the judge through his secretary, renegotiate with an opposing party, or engage in some other improper activity designed to alter the case outcome.[47] Bailiffs, court administrators, court reporters, courtroom clerks, and law clerks all fit into this category. It would be improper, say, for a bailiff who is accompanying jurors back from a break in a criminal trial to mention that the judge "sure seems annoyed at the defense attorney" or for a law clerk to tell an attorney friend that the judge she works for prefers reading short bench memos.[48]

ETHICAL CONDUCT OF FEDERAL EMPLOYEES

The laws governing the ethical conduct of federal employees are contained in a variety of statutes, the two major sources of which are Title 18 of the U.S. Code and the Ethics in Government Act of 1978 (enacted following the Watergate scandal of the early 1970s to promote public confidence in government). The latter act has been amended a number of times, with its most significant revision occurring in the Ethics Reform Act of 1989 (Public Law 101-194). A brief general description of that law, as well as expectations of the federal judiciary, is provided next.

The Ethics Reform Act and the Whistleblower Protection Act

The Ethics Reform Act addresses a number of areas of ethical concern, including the receipt of gifts, financial conflicts involving employees' positions, personal conflicts that may affect their impartiality, misuse of position (for private gain), and outside activities or employment that conflicts with their federal duties (such as serving as an expert witness or receiving payment for speaking, writing, and teaching).

In 1989, the Whistleblower Protection Act (Public Law 101-12) strengthened the protections provided in the Ethics Reform Act. These whistleblower protection laws prohibit reprisal against federal employees who reasonably believe that their disclosures show "a violation of law, rule, or regulation, gross mismanagement, a gross waste of funds, an abuse of authority, or a specific and substantial danger to public health and safety."

Whistleblower Protection Act: a federal law prohibiting reprisal against employees who reveal information concerning a violation of law, rules, or regulations; gross mismanagement or waste of funds; an abuse of authority; and so on.

The Federal Judiciary

The Code of Conduct for United States Judges was initially adopted by the Judicial Conference on April 5, 1973. This code applies to U.S. circuit judges, district judges, Court of International Trade judges, Court of Federal Claims judges, bankruptcy judges, and magistrate judges. Following are the code's canons of ethical behavior:[49]

Canon 1: A judge should uphold the integrity and independence of the judiciary.

Canon 2: A judge should avoid impropriety and the appearance of impropriety in all activities.

Canon 3: A judge should perform the duties of the office impartially and diligently.

Canon 4: A judge may engage in extrajudicial activities that are consistent with the obligations of judicial office.

Canon 5: A judge should refrain from political activity.

Implicit in these canons are restrictions on judges' soliciting or accepting gifts; outside employment; and payment for appearances, speeches, or written articles.

Federal judges have the authority to resolve significant public and private disputes. Occasionally, however, a matter assigned to them may involve them or their families personally, or affect individuals or organizations with which they have associations outside of their official duties. In these situations, if their impartiality might be compromised, they must disqualify (or recuse) themselves from the proceeding.

Disqualification is required under Canon 3C(1) of the ABA's Code of Conduct for United States Judges, if the judge

- Has personal knowledge of disputed facts
- Was employed in a law firm that handled the same matter while he or she was there

- Has a close relative who is a party or an attorney
- Personally owns, or has an immediate family member who owns, a financial interest in a party
- As a government official, served as a counsel in the case

ETHICS IN CORRECTIONS

Most correctional officers—like police officers and judges—who work in jails and prisons are dedicated, honest, and law abiding in nature. Occasionally, however, correctional officers are found to have engaged in inappropriate behaviors. Some of those behaviors involve a variety of inappropriate relationships that can develop between inmates and staff members, to include such activities as bringing in contraband (such as drugs or tobacco) or physical or sexual abuse (generally involving male officers and female inmates).[50]

The strength of the corrections subculture can also contribute to ethical problems in correctional facilities; it correlates with the security level of a correctional facility and is strongest in maximum-security institutions. Powerful forces within the correctional system have a stronger influence over the behavior of correctional officers than do the administrators of the institution, legislative decrees, or agency policies.[51] Indeed, it has been known for several decades that the exposure to external danger in the workplace creates a remarkable increase in group solidarity.[52] Some of the job-related stressors for correctional officers are similar to those the police face: the ever-present potential for physical danger, hostility directed at officers by inmates and even by the public, unreasonable role demands, a tedious and unrewarding work environment, and dependence on one another to effectively and safely work in their environment.[53] For these reasons, several norms of corrections work have been identified: Always go to the aid of an officer in distress, do

You Be the . . .

Correctional Officer

Correctional Officer Ben Jones has worked for one year in a medium-security housing unit in a state prison and has gotten on friendly terms with an inmate, Stevens. Known to have been violent, manipulative, and associating with a similarly rough crowd while on the outside, now Stevens appears to be a model inmate; in fact, Officer Jones relies heavily on Stevens to keep him informed of the goings-on in the unit as well as to maintain its overall cleanliness and general appearance. Over time, the two address each other on a first-name basis and increasingly discuss personal matters; Jones occasionally allows Stevens to get by with minor infractions of prison rules (e.g., being in an unauthorized area or entering another inmate's cell). Today Stevens mentions that he is having problems with his fiancée—specifically, that he has received a "Dear John" letter from her, stating that she is dating other men and is "moving on." Upon arriving home from work that evening, Jones finds a case of wine on his porch. No card was left with the case of wine, but at work the next morning Stevens winks at Jones and asks if he "ventured into the vineyard last night."

1. Should Officer Jones report the incident?
2. Has Jones's behavior thus far violated any standards of ethics for correctional officers? If so, what form of punishment (if any) would be appropriate?
3. What should be the relationship between Jones and Stevens in the future?
4. What could Jones have done differently, if anything?

not "rat," never make another officer look bad in front of inmates, always support an officer in a dispute with an inmate, always support officer sanctions against inmates, and do not wear a "white hat" (participate in behavior that suggests sympathy or identification with inmates).[54] Security issues and the way in which individual correctional officers have to rely on each other for their safety make loyalty to one another a key norm.

The proscription against ratting out a colleague is strong. Cases have been documented in which officers who reported inappropriate activities were labeled by colleagues as "rats" and "no-goods" and sometimes received death threats; even though they were transferred to other institutions, the labels traveled with them. In this regard, the American Correctional Association (ACA) Code of Ethics states that "[m]embers shall report to appropriate authorities any corrupt or unethical behaviors in which there is sufficient evidence to justify review."[55]

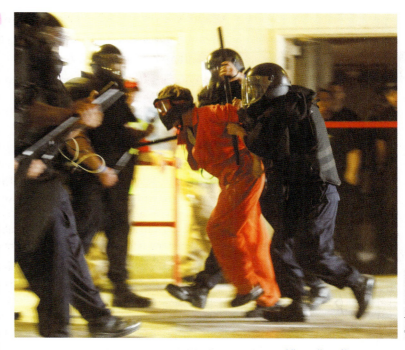

Like police officers, correctional officers in jails and prisons at times must exercise force—which raises ethical considerations and concerns for them as well.

In another case, a female correctional officer at a medium-security institution reported some of her colleagues for sleeping on the night shift. She had first approached them and expressed concern for her safety when they were asleep and told them that if they did not refrain from sleeping, she would have to report them to the superintendent. They continued sleeping, and she reported them. The consequences were severe: Graffiti was written about her on the walls, she received harassing phone calls and letters, her car was vandalized, and some bricks were thrown through the windows of her home.[56] Obviously, she deserved better, both in terms of protection during these acts and with the investigation and prosecution of the parties involved.

It would be grossly unfair to suggest that the kinds of behaviors depicted here reflect the behavior of correctional officers in all places and at all times. The case studies do demonstrate, however, the power and loyalty of the group, and correctional administrators must be cognizant of that power. It is also noteworthy that the corrections subculture, like its police counterpart, provides several positive qualities, particularly in crisis situations, including mutual support and protection, which is essential to the emotional and psychological health of officers involved; there is always the "family" to support you.

ETHICS TESTS FOR THE CRIMINAL JUSTICE STUDENT

Following are some tests to help guide you, the criminal justice student, to decide what is and is not ethical behavior:[57]

- *Test of common sense:* Does the act make sense, or would someone look askance at it?
- *Test of publicity:* Would you be willing to see what you did highlighted on the front page of the local newspaper?
- *Test of one's best self:* Will the act fit the concept of oneself at one's best?

- *Test of one's most admired personality*: What would one's parents or minister do in this situation?
- *Test of hurting someone else*: Will it cause pain for someone?
- *Test of foresight*: What is the long-term likely result?

Other questions that a criminal justice practitioner might ask are "Is it worth my job and career?" and "Is my decision legal?"

Another tool is that of "the bell, the book, and the candle." Ask yourself these questions: Do bells or warning buzzers go off as I consider my choice of actions? Does it violate any laws or codes in the statute or ordinance books? Will my decision withstand the light of day or spotlight of publicity (the candle)?[58] In sum, all we can do is seek to make the best decisions we can and be a good person and a good justice system employee, one who is consistent and fair. We need to apply the law, the policy, the guidelines, or whatever it is we dispense in our occupation without bias or fear and to the best of our ability, being mindful along the way that others around us may have lost their moral compass and attempt to drag us down with them. To paraphrase Franklin Delano Roosevelt, "Be the best you can, wherever you are, with what you have."

"The bell, the book, and the candle" test can be used as a guide against making unethical decisions.

In closing, it might be good to mention that ethics is important to all criminal justice students and practitioners, not only because of the moral/ethical issues and dilemmas they confront each day but also because they have a lot of discretion with the people with whom they are involved—such as the discretion to arrest or not arrest, to charge or not charge, to punish or not punish, and even to shoot or not shoot.

/// IN A NUTSHELL

- Ethics involves doing what is right or correct in a professional capacity. Deontological ethics considers one's duty to act. Immanuel Kant expanded the ethics of duty by including the idea of "good will." People's actions must be guided by good intent.

- There are two types of ethics: absolute and relative. Absolute ethics has only two sides—something is either good or bad. Relative ethics is more complicated and can have varying shades of gray. What is considered ethical behavior by one person may be deemed highly unethical by someone else.

- The "principle of double effect"—also known as noble cause—refers to the commission of an unethical act in order to achieve a good outcome.

- The Knapp Commission identified two types of corrupt police officers: the "meat-eaters" and the "grass-eaters." The branch of the department and the type of assignment affect opportunities for corruption. Officers' code of silence can interfere with the efforts of police leadership to uncover police corruption.

- The Law Enforcement Code of Ethics (LECE) was adopted in 1957; more recently a separate, shorter code was adopted, which is easier for officers to remember when they come face-to-face with an ethical dilemma; it is the Law Enforcement Oath of Honor.

- Accepted lying includes police activities intended to apprehend or entrap suspects. This type of lying is generally considered to be trickery. Deviant lying occurs when officers commit perjury to convict suspects or are deceptive about some activity that is illegal or unacceptable.

- There are two basic arguments *against* police acceptance of gratuities. First is the slippery slope argument, which proposes that gratuities are the first step in police corruption. In addition, when officers accept minor gifts or gratuities, they may then be obligated to provide the donors with some special service or accommodation.

- The first call for formalized standards of conduct in the legal profession came in 1906, with Roscoe Pound's speech "The Causes of Popular Dissatisfaction with the Administration of Justice." In 1924, the ABA approved the Canons of Judicial Ethics, and in 1972, the ABA approved a new Model Code of Judicial Conduct; in 1990, the same body adopted a revised model code. Nearly all states and the District of Columbia have established standards based on the code.

- In 1974, the United States Judicial Conference adopted a Code of Conduct for federal judges, and Congress over the years has enacted legislation regulating judicial conduct.

- Judges can engage in several types of abuses of judicial power, such as showing favoritism or bias, not being impartial, engaging in conflicts of interest, and being unethical in their personal conduct.

- Prosecutors and defense attorneys, too, must be legally and morally bound to ethical principles as agents of the courts.

- Federal employees are governed by the Ethics Reform Act of 1989, which addresses the receipt of gifts, financial and personal conflicts, and outside activities or employment that conflicts with their federal duties.

- Corrections personnel confront many of the same ethical dilemmas as police personnel.

- The strength of the corrections subculture correlates with the security level of a correctional facility and is strongest in maximum-security institutions.

- Some simple ethical tests can guide criminal justice students and practitioners in working through ethical quandaries.

/// KEY TERMS & CONCEPTS

Review key terms with eFlashcards at **edge.sagepub.com/peak4e**.

Absolute ethics 80	Gratuities 86	Relative ethics 80
Accepted lying 84	Model Code of Judicial Conduct 90	Slippery slope 84
Deontological ethics 79	Noble cause corruption 81	Utilitarianism 80
Deviant lying 84	Police corruption 82	Whistleblower Protection Act 93

/// REVIEW QUESTIONS

Test your understanding of chapter content at **edge.sagepub.com/peak4e**.

1. How would you define *ethics*?
2. What are examples of relative and absolute ethics?
3. What specific examples of legitimate ethical dilemmas arise with police, courts, and corrections practitioners in the course of their work?
4. How would you describe the codes and canons of ethics that exist in police departments, courts, and corrections agencies? What elements do they have in common?
5. How does the principle of double effect pose problems for criminal justice and society?
6. Why was the Law Enforcement Oath of Honor developed, and how does it differ from the Code of Ethics?
7. What constitutes police corruption? What are its types, and what are the most difficult ethical dilemmas presented in this chapter? Consider the issues presented in each dilemma.
8. Do you believe criminal justice employees should be allowed to accept minor gratuities? Explain your response as well as pros and cons for doing so.
9. In what ways can judges, defense attorneys, and prosecutors engage in unethical behaviors?
10. What forms of behavior by correctional officers in prisons or jails may be unethical?
11. What are some of the ethics "tests" for criminal justice students?

/// LEARN BY DOING

Following are several brief case studies (*based on actual occurrences*) involving criminal justice employees. Having read this chapter's materials, determine for each case the ethical dilemmas involved and what you believe is the appropriate outcome.

1. You are sitting next to a police officer in a restaurant. When the officer attempts to pay for the meal, the waiter says, "Your money is no good here. An officer just visited my son's school and made quite an impression. Plus, I feel safer having cops around." The officer again offers to pay, but the waiter refuses to accept payment. The police department has a policy prohibiting the acceptance of free meals or gifts.

2. A judge often makes inappropriate sidebar comments and uses sexist remarks or jokes in court. For example, a woman was assaulted by her husband who beat her with a telephone; from the bench the judge said, "What's wrong with that? You've got to keep her in line once in a while." He begins to address female lawyers in a demeaning manner, using such terms as *sweetie*, *little lady lawyer*, and *pretty eyes*.[59]

3. (a) An associate warden and "rising star" in the local prison system has just been stopped and arrested for driving while intoxicated in his personal vehicle and while off duty. There are no damages or injuries involved, he is very remorseful, and he has just been released from jail. His wife calls you, the warden, pleading for you to allow him to keep his job. (b) One week later, this same associate warden stops at a local convenience store after work; as he leaves the store, a clerk stops him and summons the police—the individual has just been caught shoplifting a package of cigarettes. You have just been informed of this latest arrest.

/// STUDY SITE

Get the tools you need to sharpen your study skills. SAGE edge offers a robust online environment featuring an impressive array of free tools and resources.

Access practice quizzes, eFlashcards, video, and multimedia at **edge.sagepub.com/peak4e**.

Introducing...

SAGE vantage™

Course tools done right.
Built to support teaching. Designed to ignite learning.

SAGE vantage is an intuitive digital platform that blends trusted SAGE content with auto-graded assignments, all carefully designed to ignite student engagement and drive critical thinking. Built with you and your students in mind, it offers easy course set-up and enables students to better prepare for class.

SAGE vantage enables students to **engage** with the material you choose, **learn** by applying knowledge, and **soar** with confidence by performing better in your course.

PEDAGOGICAL SCAFFOLDING	**CONFIDENCE BUILDER**	**TIME-SAVING FLEXIBILITY**	**QUALITY CONTENT**	**HONEST VALUE**
Builds on core concepts, moving students from basic understanding to mastery.	Offers frequent knowledge checks, applied-learning multimedia tools, and chapter tests with focused feedback.	Feeds auto-graded assignments to your gradebook, with real-time insight into student and class performance.	Written by expert authors and teachers, content is not sacrificed for technical features.	Affordable access to easy-to-use, quality learning tools students will appreciate.

To learn more about **SAGE vantage**, hover over this QR code with your smartphone camera or visit **sagepub.com/vantage**

THE POLICE

PART 2

Chapter 5: Police Organization: Structure and Functions
Chapter 6: Police at Work: Patrolling and Investigating
Chapter 7: Policing Methods and Challenges: Issues of Force, Liability, and Technologies
Chapter 8: Expounding the Constitution: Laws of Arrest, Search, and Seizure

This part consists of four chapters. **Chapter 5** discusses the organization and operation of selected federal law enforcement agencies as well as the roles and operations of state and local (municipal police and county sheriffs) agencies. Included are discussions of the English and colonial roots of policing, the three eras of policing after arrival in the United States, and brief considerations of INTERPOL and private police (security).

Chapter 6 focuses on the roles and tasks of policing, particularly with respect to the broad areas of training, patrolling, and investigating. After beginning with recruitment, training (including higher education for police), and stressors in policing, we consider patrol functions, use of discretion, community policing, and the work of criminal investigators (including crime scenes, use of informants, and cold cases).

Chapter 7 broadly examines several policing issues, especially those leading to changes in the aftermath of police shootings in a number of U.S. cities: the "guardians" versus "soldiers" mindset, constitutional policing and legitimacy, and procedural justice. Also discussed are police corruption, civil liability, dealing with the mentally ill, and the use of and controversies surrounding selected technologies.

Chapter 8 examines the constitutional rights of the accused as well as limitations placed on the police under the Fourth, Fifth, and Sixth Amendments; the focus is on arrest, search and seizure, the right to remain silent, and the right to counsel.

CHAPTER 5

POLICE ORGANIZATION
Structure and Functions

We are born in organizations, educated by organizations, and most of us spend much of our lives working for organizations. We spend much of our leisure time paying, playing, and praying in organizations. Most of us will die in an organization, and when the time comes for burial, the largest organization of all—the state—must grant official permission.

—Amitai Etzioni

LEARNING OBJECTIVES

As a result of reading this chapter, you will be able to

1. Describe how policing began in England, to include the four major police-related offices that evolved and came to America
2. Discuss the three eras of policing and August Vollmer's major contributions to advancing early policing
3. Explain the duties and functions of selected federal law enforcement agencies and the departments into which they are organized
4. Delineate the various types of specialized functions that are found in state law enforcement agencies
5. Distinguish between the functions of municipal police and county sheriff's agencies
6. Describe the basic qualifications and attributes for one to obtain a career in a law enforcement agency
7. Explain how and why private policing was developed, and the contemporary purposes and issues of the private police

ASSESS YOUR AWARENESS

Test your knowledge of police structure and functions by responding to the following nine true-false items; check your answers after reading this chapter's materials.

1. The four primary criminal justice officials of early England—sheriff, constable, coroner, and justice of the peace—remain in existence today.
2. The "architect" and "crib" of policing—the person and agency where most initial practices were developed—were J. Edgar Hoover, in the Philadelphia Police Department.
3. The creation of the Department of Homeland Security in 2002 (and the concurrent reorganization of several major federal law enforcement departments and agencies) was the most significant transformation of the U.S. government in over a half century.
4. Full-time professional policing, as it is generally known today, began in the early 1900s in New York City.
5. The patrol function may be said to represent the backbone of policing.
6. State law enforcement agencies typically perform only one function: patrolling state highways.
7. INTERPOL is the oldest, best-known, and probably only truly international crime-fighting organization.
8. Private police (security officers) greatly outnumber the public police, and while some of their duties are similar, the overall powers of private police are entirely different.
9. For many good reasons, there is a strong likelihood that, within the next 10 years, all municipal and county police agencies will be absorbed and consolidated into a single, national, centralized force.

<< Answers can be found on page 419.

Most European and many Asian countries have police organizations that are centralized into one national police force. In the United States, however—where the citizens have always been much more fearful and mistrusting of a strong, centralized government—there has always been a tradition of utilizing a fragmented, localized approach to policing. This view has resulted in the decentralized system of policing that is seen today in its more than 18,000 individual municipal and county police agencies, in addition to those at the federal and state levels. Police jurisdictions are guarded zealously; this means that federal law enforcement agencies in the United States have virtually no authority over local police departments or their investigations unless a federal offense is involved. This fragmented policing model is favored by many or most people for several reasons.

First and foremost, they argue that local policing allows greater knowledge of and solutions to local problems and that it provides local accountability, with officers being answerable to the citizens of that locality rather than to some remote federal or state authority (indeed, municipal police chiefs typically serve at the pleasure of the governing boards and county sheriffs are generally elected by the citizens at large).

This model is also felt to spur innovation: Almost all of the recent advances in community policing, problem solving, smart policing, and crime prevention were initiated at the local level. Those who favor partial or total consolidation of police services, however, point to its potential advantages, including likely cost savings achieved by combining expensive services (e.g., jail, communications, equipment) and economies of scale in purchasing larger quantities of vehicles, uniforms, radios, and other equipment; consistency across the jurisdiction in terms of standards for recruitment and training; uniformity of policies and procedures; direct lines of communication; possibly better training, investigative, and other functions; coordination of efforts; and ease of information and data sharing.[1]

As you read this chapter and, in particular, study our federal system of law enforcement, consider whether or not there should be a single, national police force as is found in many other countries. Would such a system work in the United States? Would there be political obstacles to its creation? Other impediments?

INTRODUCTION

How did the police come into being? How are they "designed" and organized to accomplish their mission? These are legitimate questions.

This chapter's primary aims are (1) to look at the early development of policing and (2) to inform the reader about the role and functions of contemporary federal, state, and local agencies, as well as the private police.

The chapter begins with a brief history of the evolution of four primary criminal justice officers—sheriff, constable, coroner, and justice of the peace—from their roots in early England to their coming to America. Following is an overview of the three eras of policing in the United States, and the events and shortcomings that were a part of the first two eras, thus leading to today's *community era*. Discussed next are the structures and functions of selected major federal law enforcement agencies and **organizations** that compose the Department of Homeland Security and Department of Justice. After a discussion of the primary duties of state-level law enforcement organizations, next is a review of local law enforcement—municipal police and county sheriff's agencies. The world's premier international crime-fighting organization, INTERPOL, is described briefly in an "Investigating Further" box. The chapter concludes with general discussions of how to pursue a law enforcement career as well as the field of private policing.

Note that this chapter's descriptions of federal law enforcement agencies' roles, composition, and organization may be modified by the time of this textbook's publication, particularly if the Trump administration opts to revise some agencies' policies, priorities, and practices.

Organization: an entity of two or more people who cooperate to achieve one or more objectives.

ENGLISH AND COLONIAL ROOTS: AN OVERVIEW

All four of the primary criminal justice officials of early England—sheriff, constable, coroner, and justice of the peace—either still exist or existed until recently in the United States. Accordingly, it is important to grasp a basic understanding of these offices, including their early functions in England and, later, in America.

Sheriff

The word *sheriff* is derived from *shire-reeve*—*shire* meaning "county" and *reeve* meaning "agent of the king." The shire-reeve appeared in England before the Norman Conquest of 1066. His job was to maintain law and order in the tithings (groupings of ten households). At the present time in England, a sheriff's only duties are to act as an officer of the court, to summon juries, and to enforce civil judgments.[2]

Sheriff: the chief law enforcement officer of a county, typically elected and frequently operating the jail as well as law enforcement functions.

The first sheriffs in America appeared in the early colonial period. Today, the American sheriff remains the basic source of rural crime control. Sheriff's offices are discussed more later.

Constable

Like the sheriff, the constable can be traced back to Anglo-Saxon times. The office began during the reign of Edward I, when every parish or township had a constable. As the county militia turned more and more to matters of defense, only the constable pursued felons. Hence the ancient custom of citizens raising a loud "hue and cry" and joining in pursuit of criminals lapsed into disuse. The constable had a variety of duties, including collecting taxes, supervising highways, and serving as magistrate. The office soon became subject to election and was conferred upon local men of prominence. The creation of the office of justice of the peace around 1200 quickly changed this trend forever; soon the constable was limited to making arrests only with warrants issued by a justice of the peace. As a result, the office, deprived of social and civic prestige, was no longer attractive. It carried no salary, and the duties were often dangerous.[3] In the American colonies, the position fell into disfavor largely because most constables were untrained and believed to be wholly inadequate as officials of the law.[4]

Constable: in England, favored noblemen who were forerunners of modern-day U.S. criminal justice functionaries; largely disappeared in the United States by the 1970s.

Coroner

The office of coroner has been used to fulfill many different roles throughout its history and has changed steadily over the centuries since it began functioning by the end of the 12th century. From the beginning, the coroner was elected; his duties included oversight of the interests of the Crown, including criminal matters. In felony cases, the coroner could conduct a preliminary hearing, and the sheriff often came to the coroner's court to preside over the coroner's jury. This "coroner's inquest" determined the cause of death and the party responsible for it. Initially, coroners were given no compensation, yet they were elected for life. Soon, however, they were given the right to charge fees for their work.[5] The office was slow in gaining recognition in America, as many of the coroners' duties were already being performed by the sheriffs and justices of the peace. By 1933, the coroner was recognized as a separate office in two-thirds of the states. By then, however, the office had been stripped of many of its original functions. Today, in many states, the coroner legally serves as sheriff when the elected sheriff is disabled or disqualified. However, since the early part of the 21st century, the coroner has basically performed a single function: determining the causes of all deaths by violence or under suspicious circumstances.[6]

Coroner: an early English court officer; today one (usually a physician) in the United States whose duty it is to determine cause of death.

Justice of the Peace

The justice of the peace (JP) can be traced back as far as 1195 in England. Early JPs were wealthy landholders. The duties of JPs eventually included the granting of bail to felons, which led to corruption and criticism as the justices bailed out people who clearly should not have been released into the community. By the 16th century, the office came under criticism again because of the caliber of the people holding it (wealthy landowners who bought their way into office).[7] By the early 20th century, England had abolished the property-holding requirement, and many of the medieval functions of the JP's office were removed. Thereafter, the office possessed strictly extensive criminal jurisdiction but no civil jurisdiction whatsoever. This contrasts with the American system, which gives JPs limited jurisdiction in both criminal and civil cases. By 1930, the office had constitutional status in all of the states. JPs have long been allowed to collect fees for their services. As in England, it is typically not necessary to hold a law degree or to have pursued legal studies in order to be a JP in the United States.[8]

Justice of the peace (JP): a minor justice official who oversees lesser criminal trials; one of the early English judicial functionaries.

Practitioner's Perspective

Police Lieutenant

Name: Brian D. Fitch, Ph.D.
Position: Police Lieutenant (retired), Los Angeles County Sheriff's Department
Location: Los Angeles, California

What are the primary duties and responsibilities of a practitioner in this position? In most law enforcement agencies, particularly municipal agency sheriff departments, the core function of what we do is patrol—what we call field operations. That's the officer or the deputy on the street, driving around in a marked vehicle, interacting with the public, enforcing the law, writing traffic citations, taking police reports, investigating crimes. That is, by far, the bulk of what we do. The public expects us to staff our shift with enough people to respond to their calls in a timely manner. They expect us to investigate a crime as soon as it's occurred. So the bulk of what officers do is devoted to the first responder kind of fieldwork.

Law enforcement officers can be involved in anything from—for example, where I'm currently assigned, we're constantly dealing with all kinds of things, from homicide, to a body dump, to investigating a traffic citation, to arresting a drunk driver. But most of those functions are what we call line functions. Only a small percentage of a given agency is assigned to do detective work or to follow-up work. And that percentage becomes even smaller when you look at specialties with the detective work, like homicide. Some cities have relatively small populations, or have a particularly small rate of crimes, and those cities may not have any homicides in a given year. So that doesn't lend itself towards having a whole team of homicide investigators.

Many smaller agencies will employ the resources of a larger agency here within Los Angeles County. The Los Angeles County Sheriff's Department homicide unit investigates homicides for a number of smaller municipal police agencies, some of whom have 80, 90, or 100 officers. They still defer to the sheriff's department because of the amount of time and resources involved. And some of these investigations get very lengthy. If you look at the idea of becoming a profiler, which has become popular on TV, you'll see that the LA County Sheriff's Department, an agency of 10,000 sworn people, has one profiler assigned. At the LAPD, we have one profiler assigned. So within the whole Southern California basin of about 10 million people, we have about two profilers. So landing a job like that is as much luck and timing as is anything else.

What are some challenges you face in this position? Going back historically, police officers were familiar with people on their beat, like shop owners, residents, they got to talk with people on a daily basis. They were able to develop relationships, and that was important because when people felt they needed to report a crime, they knew exactly where to go. So now, when we put our officers in cars, we're able to cover a lot of geographic area and we increase our overall visibility, but we lose that relationship with the community. Law enforcement can't do its job without the community. I believe it was Sir Robert Peel who said, "The police are the public and the public are the police." In order for us to do our job effectively, law enforcement can't be everywhere and we can't be all-knowing and all-doing. Law enforcement needs and must have both the support and involvement of the community. So this move toward community policing is a move toward involving the community in improving quality of life, helping law enforcement officers solve crimes, and just generally trying to rekindle that relationship between law enforcement and the people who we are sworn to serve and protect.

To learn more about Brian Fitch's experiences as a police lieutenant, watch the Practitioner's Perspective video in SAGE vantage.

Police Reform in England, 1829

In England, after the end of the Napoleonic Wars in 1815, workers protested against new machines, food riots, and an ongoing increase in crime. The British army, traditionally used to disperse rioters, was becoming less effective as people began resisting its commands. In 1822, England's ruling party, the Tories, moved to consider new alternatives. The prime minister appointed Sir Robert Peel to establish a police force to combat the problems. Peel, a wealthy member of Parliament,[9] finally succeeded in 1829 when Parliament passed the Metropolitan Police Act. The London police are nicknamed "bobbies" after Sir Robert Peel.[10] Peel's remark that "the police are the public, and the public are the police" emphasized his belief that the police are first and foremost members of the larger society.[11]

POLICING COMES TO THE UNITED STATES

This section provides an overview of the three eras of U.S. policing—political, reform, and community—that were shaped and defined by the varying goals and philosophies of each over time.

Sir Robert Peel's "bobbies" were established in London in 1829.

The Political Era, 1840s–1930s

In 1844, the New York state legislature passed a law establishing a full-time preventive police force for New York City. However, this new body came into being in a very different form than in Europe. The American version, as begun in New York City, was deliberately placed under the control of the city government and city politicians. The American plan required that each ward in the city be a separate patrol district, unlike the European model, which divided the districts along the lines of criminal activity. The process for selecting officers was also different. The mayor chose the recruits from a list of names submitted by the aldermen and tax assessors of each ward; the mayor then submitted his choices to the city council for approval. This system resulted in most of the power over the police going to the ward aldermen, who were seldom concerned about selecting the best people for the job. Instead, the system allowed and even encouraged political patronage and rewards for friends.[12]

This was the political era of policing, from the 1840s to the 1930s. Politics were played to such an extent that even nonranking patrol officers used political backers to obtain promotions, desired assignments, and transfers.

Police corruption also surfaced at this time. Corrupt officers wanted beats close to the gamblers, saloonkeepers, madams, and pimps—people who could not operate if the officers were "untouchable" or "100 percent coppers."[13] Political pull for corrupt officers could work for or against them; the officer who incurred the wrath of his superiors could be transferred to the outposts, where he would have no chance for financial advancement.

Still, it did not take long for other cities to adopt the general model of the New York City police force. New Orleans and Cincinnati adopted plans for a new police force in 1852, Boston and Philadelphia followed in 1854, Chicago in 1855, and Baltimore and Newark in 1857.[14] By 1880, virtually every major American city had a police force based on Peel's model.

Political era: from the 1840s to the 1930s, the period of time when police were tied closely to politics and politicians, dependent on them for being hired and promoted, and for assignments—all of which raised the potential for corruption.

The Reform Era, 1930s–1980s

During the early 20th century, reformers sought to reject political involvement by the police, and civil service systems were created to eliminate patronage and ward

Reform era: also the professional era, from the 1930s to 1980s, when police sought to extricate themselves from the shackles of politicians, and leading to the crime-fighter era—with greater emphases being placed on *numbers*—arrests, citations, response times, and so on.

influences in hiring and firing police officers. In some cities, officers were not permitted to live in the same beat they patrolled in order to isolate them as completely as possible from political influences.[15] However, policing also became a matter viewed as best left to the discretion of police executives. Any noncrime activities required of police were considered "social work." The reform era (also termed the professional era) of policing would soon be in full bloom.

The policing career of August Vollmer has been established as a major factor in the shaping and development of police professionalism, or the reform era (see Figure 5.1). In April 1905,

Figure 5.1 /// The Crib of Modern Law Enforcement: August Vollmer and the Berkeley Police Department

1905 — Vollmer is elected Berkeley town marshal.

1906 — Trustees create detective rank. Vollmer initiates a red light signal system to reach beat officers from headquarters; telephones are installed in boxes. A police records system is created.

1908 — Two motorcycles are added to the department. Vollmer begins a police school.

Hulton-Deutsch/Corbis Historical/Getty Images

1909 — Trustees approve the appointment of a Bertillon expert and the purchase of fingerprinting equipment. A modus operandi file is created, modeled on the British system.

1911 — All patrol officers are using bicycles.

1914 — Three privately owned autos are authorized for patrol use.

1915 — A central office is established for police reports.

1916 — Vollmer urges Congress to establish a national fingerprint bureau (later created by the FBI in Washington, D.C.), begins annual lectures on police procedures, and persuades a biochemist to install and direct a crime laboratory at police headquarters.

1917 — Vollmer guides the development of the first lie detector and begins developing radio communications between patrol cars, handwriting analysis, and use of business machine equipment (a Hollerith tabulator).

Vintage Images/Alamy

1918 — Entrance examinations are initiated to measure the mental, physical, and emotional fitness of recruits; a part-time police psychiatrist is employed.

AP Photos/Uncredited

1919 — Vollmer begins testing delinquents and using psychology to anticipate criminal behavior. He implements a juvenile program to reduce child delinquency.

1921 — Vollmer has the first completely motorized force; officers furnish their own automobiles. Vollmer recruits college students for part-time police jobs.

at age 29, Vollmer became the town marshal in Berkeley, California; as indicated earlier, this was a time when police departments were notorious for their corruption and politics.

Vollmer commanded a force of only 3 deputies; his first act as town marshal was to request an increase in his force from 3 to 12 deputies in order to form day and night patrols.[16] Obtaining that, he soon won national publicity for being the first chief to order his men to patrol on bicycles (his research demonstrated that officers on bicycles would be able to respond three times more quickly to calls for service than men on foot). Vollmer then persuaded the Berkeley City Council to purchase a system of red lights. The lights, hung at each street intersection, served as an emergency notification system for police officers—the first such signal system in the country.[17]

In 1906, Vollmer began to question the suspects he arrested, finding that nearly all criminals used their own peculiar method of operation, or modus operandi. In 1907, he sought the advice of a professor of biology at the University of California, becoming convinced of the value of scientific knowledge in criminal investigation.[18] Vollmer's most daring innovation, however, came in 1908 with the idea of a formal police school that drew on the expertise of university professors and included courses on police methods and procedures, fingerprinting, first aid, criminal law, anthropometry, photography, and public health. In 1916, he persuaded a professor of pharmacology and bacteriology to become a full-time criminalist supervising the department's criminal investigation laboratory. By 1917, Vollmer had his entire patrol force operating out of automobiles; it was the first completely mobile patrol force in the country.[19] In 1918, to improve the quality of police recruits in his department, Vollmer began to hire college students as part-time officers and to administer a set of intelligence, psychiatric, and neurological tests to all applicants (out of this group of "college cops" came several outstanding and influential police leaders across the United States). Finally, in 1921, in addition to experimenting with the lie detector, two of Vollmer's officers installed a crystal set and earphones in a Model T touring car, thus creating the first radio car.[20]

Chief August Vollmer developed many "firsts" in the Berkeley, California, police department during the professional (reform) era of policing.

The crime-fighter image gained popularity under the reform model of policing, when officers were to remain in their "rolling fortresses," going from one call to the next with all due haste. Much police work was driven by *numbers*—numbers of arrests and calls for service, response time to calls for service, numbers of tickets written and miles driven by a patrol officer during a duty shift, and so on. For many people, like Los Angeles chief of police William Parker, the police were the "thin blue line," protecting society from barbarism. Parker viewed urban society as a jungle, needing the restraining hand of the police; the police had to enforce the law without fear or favor. Parker opposed any restrictions on police methods. The law, he believed, should give the police wide latitude to use wiretaps and to conduct search and seizure.[21]

The Community Era, 1980s–Present

Today, policing is in the community era, practicing community policing and problem solving. This strategy was born because of the problems that overwhelmed the reform era, beginning in the 1960s. During the reform era, officers had little long-term effect in dealing with crime and disorder; they were neither trained nor encouraged to consider the underlying causes of problems on their beats.[22]

In addition, several studies struck at the very heart of traditional police methods. For example, it was learned that response time had very little to do with whether or not an arrest was made at the scene; detectives were greatly overrated in their ability to solve

Community era: beginning in about 1980, a time when the police retrained to work with the community to solve problems by looking at their underlying causes and developing tailored responses to them.

crimes;[23] less than 50 percent of an officer's time was committed to calls for service; and of those calls handled, more than 80 percent were noncriminal incidents.[24] As a result, a new "common wisdom" of policing came into being. The police were trained to work with the community to solve problems by looking at their underlying causes and developing tailored responses to them. Community policing and problem solving are discussed more thoroughly in Chapter 6.

FEDERAL LAW ENFORCEMENT

Federal law enforcement agency personnel make more than 150,000 arrests per year. More than half (46 percent) are for immigration crimes, most of which are in the five judicial districts along the U.S.-Mexican border. About one in seven (15 percent) of all federal arrests are for drug offenses, and another 15 percent are for supervision violations (failure to appear, probation, and so on).[25]

Federal law enforcement agencies: federal organizations that, for example, are charged with protecting the homeland (DHS); investigating crimes (FBI) and enforcing particular laws, such as those pertaining to drugs (DEA) or alcohol/tobacco/firearms/explosives (ATF); and guarding the courts and transporting prisoners (USMS).

Most federal law enforcement agencies are found within the Department of Homeland Security (DHS) and the Department of Justice (see Table 5.1), both of which are discussed in this section (note that the Central Intelligence Agency, or CIA, works as an independent agency).

Department of Homeland Security

Within one month of the terrorist attack on U.S. soil on September 11, 2001, President George W. Bush issued a proposal to create a new Department of Homeland Security (DHS)—which was established in November 2002 and became the most significant transformation of the U.S. government in over a half century. All or parts of 22 different federal departments and agencies were combined, beginning in January 2003, and 80,000 new federal employees were immediately put to work.[26] Congress committed $32 billion toward safeguarding the nation, developing vaccines to protect against biological or chemical threats, training and equipping first responders (local police, firefighters, and medical personnel), and funding science and technology projects to counter the use of biological weapons and assess vulnerabilities. In the 10 years after 9/11, more than $635 billion was appropriated by the federal government to support homeland security efforts.[27] Figure 5.2 shows the current organizational structure of the DHS.

Table 5.1 /// Selected Federal Law Enforcement Agencies
Department of Homeland Security
Citizenship and Immigration Services
Customs and Border Protection (CBP)
Immigration and Customs Enforcement (ICE)
Secret Service
Transportation Security Administration
Coast Guard
Department of Justice
Federal Bureau of Investigation (FBI)
Bureau of Alcohol, Tobacco, Firearms and Explosives (ATF)
United States Marshals Service (USMS)
Drug Enforcement Administration (DEA)
Bureau of Prisons (BOP)

Figure 5.2 /// Department of Homeland Security Organizational Structure

U.S. Department of Homeland Security

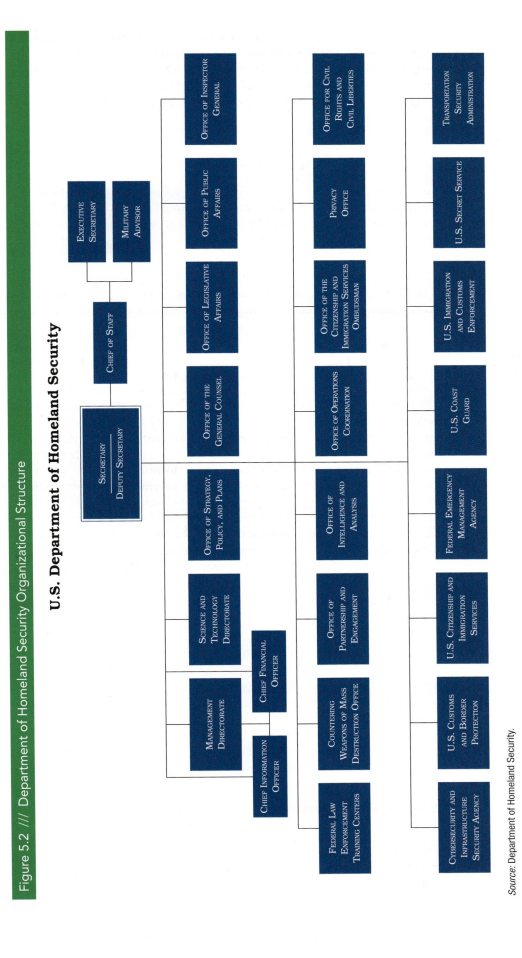

Source: Department of Homeland Security.

Following are brief descriptions of the major law enforcement agencies organizationally located within the DHS; all of them have full law enforcement authority. (*Note:* A number of additional federal agencies have law enforcement authority and are not discussed here, including the Federal Bureau of Prisons, U.S. Forest Service, U.S. Fish and Wildlife Service, U.S. Capitol Police, U.S. Mint Police, and the Bureau of Indian Affairs.)

- *Customs and Border Protection (CBP)* is one of the largest federal law enforcement agencies, with more than 60,000 agents. CBP is responsible for preventing terrorists and terrorist weapons from entering the United States while facilitating the flow of legitimate trade and travel. CBP protects nearly 7,000 miles of border with Canada and Mexico and 95,000 miles of shoreline.[28] On a typical day, CBP processes more than 1.1 million passengers and pedestrians, apprehends more than 1,100 criminal suspects at ports of entry, and seizes more than 9,000 pounds of narcotics.[29]

- *Immigration and Customs Enforcement (ICE)* is the largest investigative arm of the DHS, with about 20,000 sworn employees in more than 400 offices in the United States and 46 foreign countries.[30] ICE is responsible for identifying and shutting down vulnerabilities both in the nation's borders and in economic, transportation, and infrastructure security.[31] In 2010, a Homeland Security Investigations agency was formed within ICE to investigate financial crimes, money laundering and smuggling, intellectual property theft, cybercrimes, human trafficking and other rights violations, narcotics and weapons smuggling/trafficking, international gang activity, and international art and antiquity theft.[32]

- The *Transportation Security Administration (TSA)* protects the nation's transportation systems. TSA employs about 50,000 personnel at more than 450 airports and field offices. With the U.S. economy improving and air travel increasing, agents are screening approximately two million people each day. TSA's organization includes federal air marshals, who are armed federal law enforcement officers deployed on passenger flights worldwide to protect airline passengers and crew against the risk of criminal and terrorist violence.[33] With the exception of its air marshals, TSA personnel hold the title of "officer" in name only; they neither carry guns nor have law enforcement powers.[34]

- The *Coast Guard* is the nation's leading maritime law enforcement agency; it has broad police power to enforce, or assist in enforcing, federal laws and treaties on waters under U.S. jurisdiction and other international agreements on the high seas. Its officers possess the civil authority to board any vessel subject to U.S. jurisdiction; once aboard, they can inspect, search, inquire, and arrest.[35]

- The *Secret Service* employs about 6,500 personnel worldwide (3,200 special agents, 1,300 uniformed officers, 2,000 specialized/technical support personnel).[36] Its agents protect the president and other high-level officials and investigate counterfeiting and other financial crimes, including financial institution fraud, identity theft, computer fraud, and computer-based attacks on our nation's financial, banking, and telecommunications infrastructure. The Secret Service's domestic Uniformed Division protects the White House complex and the vice president's residence as well as foreign embassies and missions in the Washington, D.C., area. The Secret Service has agents assigned to approximately 125 offices located in cities throughout the United States and in select foreign cities.[37]

- The *Federal Protective Service* within the DHS employs about 1,000 law enforcement police officers, criminal investigators, security officers, and support personnel (as well as more than 10,000 contract security personnel); they focus on federal facilities (e.g., buildings, dams, power plants) and identify and assess threats, conduct surveillance, monitor suspicious activity, undertake deterrence patrols, engage in community policing activities, and oversee screening operations for 9,500 federal facilities worldwide.[38]

INTERPOL: the only international crime-fighting organization; it collects intelligence information, issues alerts, and assists in capturing world criminals, and it has nearly 200 member countries.

Investigating Further

INTERPOL

The International Criminal Police Organization, better known as INTERPOL, is the oldest, the best-known, and probably the only truly international crime-fighting organization for crimes committed on an international scale, such as drug trafficking, bank fraud, money laundering, and counterfeiting. INTERPOL agents do not patrol the globe, nor do they make arrests or engage in shootouts. They are basically intelligence gatherers who have helped many nations work together in attacking international crime since 1923.

Lyon, France, serves as the headquarters for INTERPOL's crime-fighting tasks and its 194 member countries. INTERPOL focuses on a number of crime areas that have transnational dimensions, including cybercrime, corruption, drugs, financial and high-tech crime, fugitives, maritime piracy, organized crime, terrorism (including bioterrorism), and trafficking in human beings. It also manages a range of databases with information on names and photographs of known criminals, wanted persons, fingerprints, DNA profiles, stolen or lost travel documents, stolen motor vehicles, child sex abuse images, and stolen works of art. INTERPOL also disseminates critical crime-related data through its system of international notices. There are eight kinds of notices, of which the most well known is the Red Notice, an international request for an individual's arrest.

INTERPOL has one cardinal rule: It deals only with common criminals; it does not become involved with political, racial, or religious matters. It has a basic three-step formula for offenses that all nations must follow for success: (1) Pass laws specifying the offense is a crime, (2) prosecute offenders and cooperate in other countries' prosecutions, and (3) furnish INTERPOL with and exchange information about crime and its perpetrators. This formula could reverse the trend that is forecast for the world at present: criminals' increasing capability for violence and destruction. The following crimes, because they are recognized as crimes by other countries, are covered by almost all U.S. treaties of extradition: murder, rape, bigamy, arson, robbery, burglary, forgery, counterfeiting, embezzlement, larceny, fraud, perjury, and kidnapping.

Sources: INTERPOL, "About INTERPOL," https://www.interpol.int/en/Who-we-are/What-is-INTERPOL; also see Michael Fooner, *Interpol: Issues in World Crime and International Criminal Justice* (New York: Plenum Press, 1989), p. 179.

Because its roles and purpose are closely related to the protection of the United States against terrorism and other crimes, a discussion of INTERPOL is provided in the "Investigating Further" box above.

Department of Justice

The Department of Justice (DOJ) is headed by the attorney general, who is appointed by the U.S. president and confirmed by the Senate. The president also appoints the attorney general's assistants and the U.S. attorneys for each of the judicial districts. The U.S. attorneys in each judicial district control and supervise all federal criminal prosecutions and represent the government in legal suits in which it is a party. These attorneys may appoint committees to investigate other governmental agencies or offices when questions of wrongdoing are raised or when possible violations of federal law are suspected or detected.

The DOJ is the official legal arm of the U.S. government. Within the Justice Department are several law enforcement organizations that investigate violations of federal laws; we discuss the Federal Bureau of Investigation; Bureau of Alcohol, Tobacco, Firearms and Explosives; Drug Enforcement Administration; and U.S. Marshals Service in the sections that follow. Figure 5.3 shows the organizational chart for the Department of Justice.

Homeland Security comprises multiple law enforcement agencies, including officers performing both customs and border protection duties.

Chapter 5: Police Organization

Figure 5.3 /// Department of Justice Organizational Chart

Source: US Department of Justice.

Federal Bureau of Investigation

The Federal Bureau of Investigation (FBI) was created and funded through the Department of Justice Appropriation Act of 1908. A new era was begun for the FBI in 1924 with the appointment of J. Edgar Hoover, who was determined to professionalize the organization, as director. Special agents were college graduates, preferably with degrees in law or accounting. During Hoover's tenure in office, many notorious criminals, such as Bonnie Parker, Clyde Barrow, and John Dillinger, were tracked and captured or killed.[39]

The bureau's top four priority areas are to protect the United States:

1. From terrorist attacks
2. Against foreign intelligence operations and espionage
3. Against cyberattacks and high-tech crimes
4. Against public corruption at all levels

Other priorities are to protect civil rights, combat transnational/national criminal organizations and enterprises, combat major white-collar crime, and combat significant violent crime.[40]

Today the FBI has 56 field offices, approximately 350 resident agencies, and more than 60 foreign liaison posts called legal attachés. About 30,000 agents, analysts, and support employees perform professional, administrative, technical, and other functions.[41]

To combat terrorism, the bureau can now monitor Internet sites, libraries, churches, and political organizations. In addition, under revamped guidelines, agents can attend public meetings for the purpose of preventing terrorism.[42] The FBI's laboratory examines blood, hair, firearms, paint, handwriting, typewriters, and other types of evidence—at no charge to state police and local police agencies. The FBI also operates the National Crime Information Center (NCIC), through which millions of records—including wanted persons as well as stolen vehicles and all kinds of property items or any object with an identifying number—are entered. The FBI also publishes the annual *Uniform Crime Reports*, discussed in Chapter 2.

The FBI's Special Agent Selection System is described at https://www.fbijobs.gov/sites/default/files/how-to-apply.pdf (also see FBI job postings by clicking on the "Search Jobs" tab from the main https://www.fbijobs.gov page). Although simplistic in its appearance, the process involves a number of individual activities by applicants and FBI personnel at each phase and typically requires one year or longer to complete.

Bureau of Alcohol, Tobacco, Firearms and Explosives

The Bureau of Alcohol, Tobacco, Firearms and Explosives (ATF) originated as a unit within the Internal Revenue Service in 1862, when certain alcohol and tobacco tax statutes were created. Like the FBI and several other federal agencies, ATF has a rich and colorful history, much of which has involved capturing bootleggers and disposing of illegal whiskey stills during Prohibition. ATF administers the U.S. criminal code provisions concerning alcohol and tobacco smuggling and diversion. ATF also maintains a U.S. Bomb Data Center (to collect information on arson- and explosives-related incidents) and a Bomb and Arson Tracking System, which allows local, state, and other federal agencies to share information about bomb and arson cases.[43]

J. Edgar Hoover was the first director of the Federal Bureau of Investigation and served in that capacity from 1924 until his death in 1972, at age 77.

Today ATF has about 5,100 full-time employees, 2,600 of whom are special agents in 25 field divisions; agents work nearly 38,000 cases per year (approximately 93 percent of which are firearms cases, 4 percent are arson cases, 2 percent are explosives cases, and less than 1 percent are alcohol and tobacco cases).[44]

Drug Enforcement Administration

Today's Drug Enforcement Administration (DEA) had its origin with the passage of the Harrison Narcotics Tax Act, signed into law on December 17, 1914, by President Woodrow Wilson.[45] It was created as the DEA by President Richard Nixon in July 1973 in order to create a single federal agency to coordinate and enforce the federal drug laws. In 1982, the organization was given primary responsibility for drug and narcotics enforcement, sharing this jurisdiction with the FBI. Briefly, major responsibilities of the more than 5,000 DEA agents, under the U.S. Code, include the following: investigation of, and coordination with, major violators of controlled substance laws in domestic and international venues; management of a national drug intelligence program in cooperation with federal, state, local, and foreign officials; and seizure and forfeiture of assets derived from, traceable to, or intended to be used for illicit drug trafficking.[46] The DEA makes about 30,000 arrests per year, and recently its number of arrests for opioids has increased by 154 percent.[47]

Some agencies operate mobile forensic crime laboratories in addition to those that are fixed.

U.S. Marshals Service

The U.S. Marshals Service (USMS) is one of the oldest federal law enforcement agencies, established under the Judiciary Act of 1789. Today, the USMS has 94 U.S. marshals, one for each federal court district. The USMS employs about 3,600 deputy U.S. marshals and criminal investigators, who arrest about 84,000 fugitives per year, transport federal prisoners, and protect about 2,600 federal judges and provide security for prosecutors and witnesses; they also conduct courthouse threat analyses and investigations (about 3,000 threats are received each year), and perform security, rescue, and recovery activities for natural disasters and civil disturbances.[48] Each district headquarters office is managed by a politically appointed U.S. marshal and a chief deputy U.S. marshal, who direct a staff of supervisors, investigators, deputy marshals, and administrative personnel. The USMS also operates the Witness Security Program. Federal witnesses are sometimes threatened by defendants or their associates; if certain criteria are met, the USMS will provide a complete change of identity for witnesses and their families, including new Social Security numbers, residences, and employment. In 1971, the USMS created the Special Operations Group (SOG), consisting of a well-trained elite group of deputy marshals that could respond to priority or dangerous missions anywhere within the United States within a few hours.[49]

Other Federal Agencies

Two other significant federal agencies outside of the Department of Justice with unique missions and contributions to the enforcement of the U.S. Code are the Central Intelligence Agency and the Internal Revenue Service.

Central Intelligence Agency

Although not a law enforcement agency, the Central Intelligence Agency (CIA) is of significance at the federal level to the nation's security and warrants a brief discussion. The National Security Act of 1947 established the National Security Council, which in 1949 created a subordinate organization, the CIA. Considered the most clandestine government service, the CIA participates in undercover and covert operations around the world for the purposes of managing crises and providing intelligence.⁵⁰ The agency offers career opportunities in five broad areas (analysis, clandestine, STEM, enterprise & support, and foreign language) as well as undergraduate student scholarship and internship opportunities.⁵¹ Persons who are interested may also take a "Job Fit" test on the CIA website, at https://www.cia.gov/careers/opportunities/job-fit-tool.

Internal Revenue Service

The Internal Revenue Service (IRS) has as its main function the monitoring and collection of federal income taxes from American individuals and businesses. Since 1919, the IRS has had a Criminal Investigation (CI) division employing "accountants with a badge." While other federal agencies also have investigative jurisdiction for money laundering and some Bank Secrecy Act violations, the IRS is the only federal agency that can investigate potential criminal violations of the Internal Revenue Code.⁵² The CI branch of the IRS comprises approximately 3,500 employees worldwide, about 2,500 of whom are special agents whose investigative jurisdiction includes tax, money laundering, and Bank Secrecy Act laws.⁵³

STATE AGENCIES

As with federal law enforcement organizations, a variety of organizations, duties, and specializations can be found in the 50 states—although, generally, state troopers and highway patrol officers perform a lot of the same functions as their county and municipal counterparts: enforcing state statutes, investigating criminal and traffic offenses (and, by virtue of those roles, knowing and applying laws of arrest, search, and seizure), making arrests, testifying in court, communicating effectively in both oral and written contexts, using firearms and self-defense tactics proficiently, and effectively performing pursuit driving, self-defense, and lifesaving techniques until a patient can be transported to a hospital. Such agencies also maintain a wide array of special functions, including special weapons and tactics (SWAT) teams, drug units and task forces, marine and horse patrol, and so on.⁵⁴

State police: a state agency responsible for highway patrol and other duties as delineated in the state's statutes; some states require their police to investigate crimes against persons and property.

Patrol, Police, and Investigative Organizations

Perhaps the first distinction that might be made at the state level is between state police or highway patrol organizations and the state bureaus of investigation. Each state's statutes—and, often, the agency's name—will indicate the types of functions their agencies are authorized to perform. For example, a state's *highway patrol* division typically patrols and investigates crashes on the state highway system, while an agency that is officially named a state police organization typically performs a broader array of law enforcement functions in addition to those related to traffic. As an example, although the Missouri State Highway Patrol states on its website that its troopers provide assistance to motorists and "investigate highway traffic crashes and other roadway emergencies," it also states that "other responsibilities include assisting local peace officers upon request, investigating crimes, and enforcing criminal laws."⁵⁵

While many state troopers are, by statute, authorized to provide traffic control on their state's highways, others can conduct criminal investigations. Here, Georgia troopers investigate a shooting.

Some agencies are even designated as *public safety* organizations and often encompass several agencies or divisions. For example, the Hawaii Department of Public Safety, by statute, includes a law enforcement division (with general arrest duties, a narcotics division, a sheriff division, and an executive protection unit), a corrections division (handling inmate intake, incarceration, paroling authority, and industries), and a victim compensation commission.[56] **State bureaus of investigation** (SBIs), as their name implies, are investigative in nature and might be considered a state's equivalent to the FBI; they investigate all manner of cases assigned to them according to their state's laws and usually report to the state's attorney general. SBI investigators are plainclothes agents who usually investigate both criminal and civil cases involving the state and/or multiple jurisdictions. They also provide technical support to local agencies in the form of laboratory or record services and may be asked by city and county agencies to assist in investigating more serious crimes (e.g., homicide).

State bureau of investigation: a state agency that is responsible for investigating crimes involving state statutes; they may also be called in to assist police agencies in serious criminal matters, and often publish state crime reports.

Going Global

Criminal Justice at Its Worst: Venezuela

Persons living anywhere in the world except Venezuela may want to consider themselves fortunate, given that criminal justice and the rule of law are virtually nonexistent there. Indeed, Venezuela is officially rated by the World Justice Project at the bottom of the Rule of Law Index. As crime continues to grow, inflation can rise as much as 2,000 percent per year, and the country has the highest homicide rate in Latin American and the Caribbean (73 people per day are murdered). It is also the most corrupt country in Latin America, with military leaders using their control over food imports to skim millions in public funds; state jobs and benefits doled out only to those who vote in favor of President Nicolas Maduro; police who are poorly paid, trained, equipped, and often corrupt; an inefficient and politicized judicial system; and a system of violent and largely overcrowded prisons that are under the control of prison gang leaders.

Caracas, the nation's capital, with about two million people, suffers from waves of crime and violence largely attributable to mobile street gangs and organized crime groups. The city is notorious for brazen, violent crimes (murder, robbery, kidnapping) perpetrated in neighborhoods across the city. Armed criminals target pedestrians and motorists. Robberies and scams occur at public ATMs, even those inside hotels and banks (which suggests complicit bank employees). Hundreds of police officers are killed across the country each year, many of whom are victims of targeted assassination and for the purpose of obtaining the victims' weapons and ammunition. Caracas has also been given a medium-threat level for terrorist activity directed at or affecting official U.S. government interests.

Antigovernment protests against corruption, poverty, and crime often occur, frequently devolving into violent clashes with riot police. The prevailing culture of violence and corruption only foments the erosion of human rights, constraints on press freedoms, arbitrary arrest/detention of antigovernment protestors, and the presence of significant government corruption.

Border security at ports of entry remains vulnerable and susceptible to corruption, cross-border violence, kidnapping, drug trafficking, and smuggling. Criminal activity at the country's three airports is significant, as arriving and departing travelers have been robbed or even murdered. Individuals wearing official uniforms and presenting fake credentials often commit crimes. Use of airport taxis is strongly discouraged, as the number of travelers in airport taxis who are robbed or kidnapped by taxi drivers is so high that the U.S. Embassy requires its employees to travel to and from the airport in armored vehicles.

Sources: Will Bordell and Jon Robins, "'A Crisis for Human Rights': New Index Reveals Global Fall in Basic Justice," *The Guardian*, January 31, 2018, https://www.theguardian.com/inequality/2018/jan/31/human-rights-new-rule-of-law-index-reveals-global-fall-basic-justice; World Justice Project, "WJP Rule of Law Index 2017–2018," https://worldjusticeproject.org/our-work/research-and-data/wjp-rule-law-index-2017–2018; U.S. Department of State, Overseas Security Advisory Council, "Venezuela 2018 Crime & Safety Report," https://www.osac.gov/Pages/ContentReportDetails.aspx?cid=23791.

Other Special-Purpose State Agencies

In addition to the traffic, investigative, and other units mentioned earlier, several other special-purpose state agencies, including police and other law enforcement organizations, have developed over time to meet particular needs. For example, many state attorney general's offices have units and investigators that investigate white-collar crimes; fraud against or by consumers, Medicare providers, and food stamp recipients; and crimes against children and seniors.[57]

States may also have limited-purpose units devoted to enforcing the following:

- Alcoholic beverage laws (regarding the distribution and sale of such beverages, monitoring bars and liquor stores, and so on)
- Fish and game laws (relating to hunting and fishing, to ensure that persons who engage in these activities have proper licenses and do not poach, hunt, or fish out of season, exceed their limit, and so on)
- State statutes and local ordinances on college and university campuses
- Agricultural laws, to include cattle brand inspection and enforcement
- Commercial vehicle laws, such as those federal and state laws pertaining to weights and permits of interstate carriers (i.e., tractor-trailer rigs) and ordinances applying to taxicabs
- Airport laws—in addition to TSA employees (discussed earlier), airport police provide support for the local city/county police by enforcing statutes and ordinances; patrolling (foot and vehicle); monitoring threats to people, property, and aircraft; and generally providing information and service to the traveling public

Special-purpose state agencies: specially trained units for particular investigative needs, such as those for violations of alcoholic beverage laws, fish and game laws, organized crime, and so on.

LOCAL AGENCIES: MUNICIPAL POLICE DEPARTMENTS AND SHERIFF'S OFFICES

Today, Sir Robert Peel (discussed earlier in this chapter) would be amazed because, according to the federal Bureau of Justice Statistics, there are now about 18,000 federal, state, county, and municipal police agencies in the United States.[58] The municipal agencies comprise about 477,000 sworn full-time police officers,[59] and sheriff's offices employ about 190,000 sworn full-time deputies.[60] Next we focus on the organization and functions of these local agencies.

Basic Operations

Following is a brief overview of their employee composition, educational requirements, starting salaries, and some authorized equipment. Municipal police departments provide a range of enforcement, investigative, and order-maintenance functions; they employ an average of 2.1 full-time officers per 1,000 population; about one in eight of these sworn employees is a woman, and one in four is a member of a racial or ethnic minority. About 15 percent of local police agencies require new officers to have some college experience, with 11 percent requiring at least a two-year college degree. The average starting salary for an entry-level local officer is about $44,000. Significantly, about half of local police agencies employ fewer than 10 sworn personnel. Almost three-fourths of these agencies require their officers to wear protective body armor at all times while on duty; 68 percent use video cameras in patrol cars, more than 80 percent authorize the use of electronic control devices (such as a Taser), and more than 90 percent of agencies serving 25,000 or more residents use in-car computers. More information concerning municipal police agencies may be obtained from the Bureau of Justice Statistics.[61]

Municipal police department: a police force that enforces laws and maintains peace within a specified city or municipality.

County sheriff's office: a unit of county government with a sheriff (normally elected) and deputies whose duties vary but typically include policing unincorporated areas, maintaining county jails, providing security to courts in the county, and serving warrants and court papers.

In county sheriff's offices, about one in eight sworn employees is a woman, and 19 percent are members of a racial or ethnic minority. About 10 percent of sheriff's offices require new deputies to have some college experience, with 7 percent requiring at least a two-year college degree. The average starting salary for an entry-level deputy is about $31,000. About three-fifths of sheriff's departments employ fewer than 25 sworn personnel. Fifty-seven percent of these agencies require their officers to wear protective body armor at all times while on duty; two-thirds use video cameras in patrol cars, 66 percent authorize the use of electronic control devices, and more than 85 percent of agencies serving 100,000 or more residents use in-car computers.[62]

Because of the diversity of sheriff's offices throughout the country, it is difficult to describe a "typical" office.[63] In addition to the aforementioned investigative, enforcement, and order-maintenance duties found in municipal police agencies, sheriff's offices are found to

- Maintain and operate county correctional institutions
- Serve civil processes (protective orders, liens, evictions, garnishments, and attachments) and perform other civil duties, such as extradition and transportation of prisoners
- Collect certain taxes and conduct real estate sales (usually for nonpayment of taxes) for the county
- Serve as bailiff of the courts

In Chapter 6 we will consider the kinds of screening methods used in hiring new officers (see Figure 6.1), as well as typical topics covered in basic recruit academies (see Table 6.1). For more related discussion, see the "Interested in a Career?" section later in this chapter.

Organization

Organizational structure or chart: a diagram of the vertical and horizontal parts of an organization, showing its chain of command, lines of communication, division of labor, and so on.

Every police agency, no matter what its size, has an organizational structure or chart, even though it may not be prominently displayed for all to see in the agency's facility—or it may not even be written down at all. Even a community with only a town marshal has an organizational structure, although the structure will be very horizontal, with the marshal performing all of the functions displayed in Figure 5.4, the basic organizational chart for a small agency.

In Figure 5.4, agency operations, or line-element, personnel are engaged in active police functions in the field. They may be subdivided into primary and secondary operations elements. The patrol function—often called the backbone of policing—is the primary operational element because of its major responsibility for policing. (The patrol function

Figure 5.4 /// A Basic Police Organizational Structure

Figure 5.5 /// Portland Police Bureau Organizational Chart

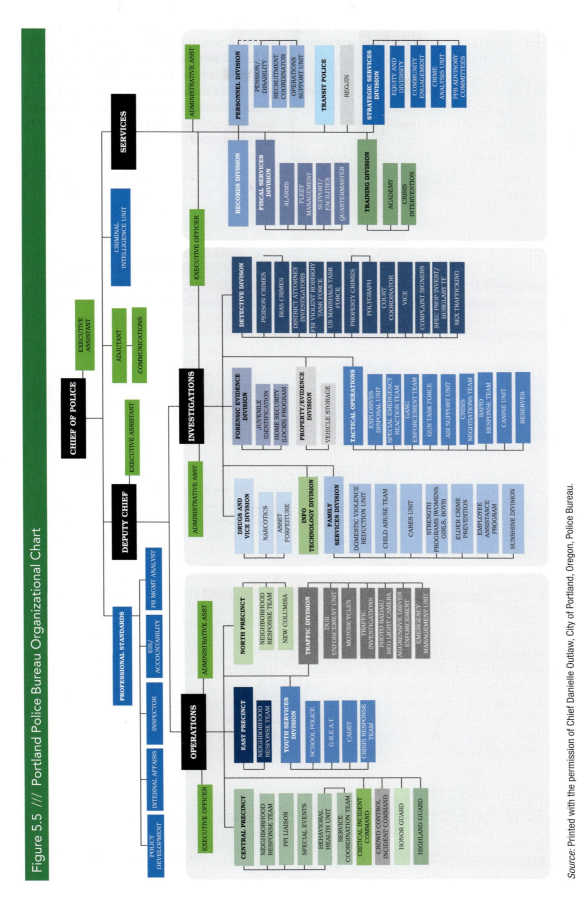

Source: Printed with the permission of Chief Danielle Outlaw, City of Portland, Oregon, Police Bureau.

Note: REGJIN = Regional Justice Information Network; DUII = driving under the influence of intoxicants; PPI = Portland Patrol Inc.; G.R.E.A.T. = Gang Resistance Education and Training; Sunshine Division is a program providing emergency food and clothing relief to families and individuals in need; https://www.portlandoregon.gov/police/article/250329.

An example of a police organization's auxiliary services is the work done by crime laboratory services.

is examined in Chapter 6.) In most small police agencies, patrol forces are responsible for all operational activities: providing routine patrols, conducting traffic and criminal investigations, making arrests, and functioning as generalists. The investigative and youth functions are the secondary operations elements. (The investigative function is discussed in Chapter 6, and juvenile rights in Chapter 15.) The support (or nonline) functions and activities can become quite numerous, especially in a large agency. These functions fall within two broad categories: staff (or administrative) services and auxiliary (or technical) services. The staff services usually involve personnel and include such matters as recruitment, training, promotion, planning and research, community relations, and public information services. Auxiliary services are the kinds of functions that civilians rarely see. They include jail management, property and evidence, crime laboratory services, communications, and records and identification. Many career opportunities exist for those who are interested in police-related work but who cannot or do not want to be a field officer.

Greater specialization and variety of assignments may be seen in the organizational structure of a larger police organization, such as the Portland, Oregon, Police Bureau (PPB), shown in Figure 5.5. This structure not only shows the various components of the organization but also does the following:

- Apportions the workload among members and units according to a logical plan
- Ensures that lines of authority and responsibility are as definite and direct as possible
- Places responsibility and authority and, if responsibility is delegated, holds the delegator responsible
- Coordinates the efforts of members so that all will work harmoniously to accomplish the mission

Chain of command: vertical and horizontal power relations within an organization, showing how one position relates to others.

In sum, this structure establishes the chain of command and determines lines of communication and responsibility.

Obviously, the larger the agency, the greater the need for specialization and the more vertical the organizational chart will become. With greater specialization comes the need and opportunity for officers to be assigned to different tasks, often rotating from one assignment to another after a fixed interval. For example, in a medium-sized department serving a community of 100,000 or more, it would be possible for a police officer with 10 years of police experience to have been a dog handler, a motorcycle officer, a detective, and a traffic officer while simultaneously holding a slot on the special-weapons or hostage-negotiation team.

INTERESTED IN A CAREER? SOME GENERAL CONSIDERATIONS

Generally speaking, there are a number of common elements—often termed KSAs (for knowledge, skills, and abilities)—of employment in many federal, state, and local law enforcement positions, such as the following:

- U.S. citizenship and possession of a valid driver's license
- Age requirement (at the federal level, applicants must be less than 37 years of age)
- Written test
- Structured oral interview (typically consisting of situational questions posed by an oral board)
- Memory recall assessment (e.g., applicants might be provided with a person's photograph and identifying characteristics and then asked to recall as many details as possible)
- Medical exam (to test for any chronic disease or condition that could impair full performance of the job duties)
- Drug testing (typically, satisfactory completion of a drug test is a condition for placement)
- Background investigation[64]

Furthermore, the following minimum qualifications may be in effect prior to an offer of employment, depending on the agency:

- A basic training program (typically of 4–6 months' duration) must be completed successfully.
- A person convicted of a crime of domestic violence cannot lawfully possess a firearm or ammunition (see 18 U.S.C. Section 1001).
- Persons required to carry a firearm while performing their duties must satisfactorily complete firearms training.
- Positions (particularly federal and state) may require mobility and relocation, including travel relating to the duties of the job and in terms of assignment to a duty station; applicants must also sign a mobility agreement.[65] At the federal level, a law enforcement availability pay bonus is provided to agents that is an additional 25 percent of their annual base pay.

Several websites are invaluable for persons seeking law enforcement careers. The following websites include information on qualifications, physical fitness and health standards, and pretraining requirements:

- USAJOBS, jobsearch.usajobs.gov (search for "Law Enforcement")
- Federallawenforcement.org, "Careers with Federal Law Enforcement Agencies," https://www.federallawenforcement.org/careers/
- The Balance, "Federal Criminal Justice and Law Enforcement Careers," https://www.thebalancecareers.com/federal-law-enforcement-jobs-974533
- Federal Government Jobs, "FBI, CIA, & Homeland Security Jobs," http://www.federaljobs.net/law.htm
- Police Employment, The Police Job Board, "Federal Police Jobs," http://www.policeemployment.com/federal-police

More general information concerning federal employment may be obtained from the federal government's human resources office, the Office of Personnel Management, at www.opm.gov.

Although some agencies require a high school diploma, others require at least a bachelor's degree. Grade-point-average (GPA) requirements can vary; in some federal agencies, a superior academic achievement pay bonus is available to those applicants with higher GPAs; some agencies also provide a Foreign Language Award Program, which provides cash awards for persons qualifying. Some agencies prohibit employees from having visible body markings (tattoos, body art, branding) on the head, face, neck, and extremities.[66] Again, websites should be consulted for such requirements and proscriptions.

A Comment on Immigration and Law Enforcement at All Levels

Chapter 16 discusses immigration in detail as a national challenge and policy issue. This is an area in which law enforcement at all levels (federal, state, and local) is sometimes used as a political tool and may be caught in the middle as emotions and sometimes outright violence flare. Immigration has become a national talking point and political lightning rod. Some states have passed laws that undermine federal law, and some cities and even individual police agencies have passed laws and enacted policies dictating whether to limit their cooperation with federal law enforcement agencies. Sanctuary cities and protests have cropped up and are a source of governmental clashes, immigrant children have been separated from their parents at the U.S.-Mexican border, governments debate aid to undocumented immigrants, the federal government has issued threats to those jurisdictions violating federal laws, our nation squabbles with other nations, and so on. Meanwhile, detention centers have sprung up nationwide to hold undocumented immigrants (a number of whom have died), thousands of people have walked across the southern border seeking asylum, and a national debate is ongoing over the building of a border wall.[67] Again, law enforcement agencies at all levels are caught up in these political skirmishes and policy matters, while political entities debate and vacillate on matters such as whether or not to investigate, arrest, deport, detain, and house these individuals under a vast array of immigration laws.

ON GUARD: THE PRIVATE POLICE

Much has changed in society and the private security industry since 1851, when Allan Pinkerton initiated the Pinkerton National Detective Agency, specializing in railroad security. Pinkerton established the first private security contract operation in the United States. His motto was "We Never Sleep," and his logo, an open eye, was probably the genesis of the term "private eye."

Today, according to the late loss-prevention expert Saul Astor, "We are a nation of thieves"[68]—and, it might be added, a nation that needs to be protected against would-be active shooters, terrorists, rapists, robbers, and other dangerous people. According to the federal Bureau of Justice Statistics, there are about 3.1 million violent-crime victimizations and 13.3 million property-crime victimizations each year in the United States.[69]

As a result, and especially given the recent spate of mass shootings (discussed in Chapter 16), the United States has become highly security minded concerning its computers, lotteries, celebrities, college campuses, casinos, nuclear plants, airports, shopping centers, mass transit systems, hospitals, and railroads. Such businesses, industries, and institutions have recognized the need to conscientiously protect their assets against threats of crime and other disasters—as well as the limited capabilities of the nation's full-time sworn officers and agents to protect them—and have increasingly turned to the "other police"—those of the private police or security—for protection. As examples, in Oakland, California, several neighborhoods have hired private security patrols, with each household paying $20 per month for unarmed patrols to operate 12 hours per day; Beverly Hills Public Schools contracts with a firm to provide armed safety personnel at a cost of about $1 million per year; and many retailers have created a Business Improvement District where each pays an additional "tax" for projects, some of which include security services. Closely related are the numerous police agencies and sheriff's offices using civilians to take reports (both in person and on the phone), enforce parking regulations, respond to some calls, and all manner of other duties that free sworn officers for higher priority calls.

According to the federal Bureau of Labor Statistics, today about 1.1 million **private police/security officers** provide such services (compared with 807,000 police officers and detectives); their median salary is about $27,000 per year.[70] Indeed, *Forbes* estimates there are now about 20 million private security officers working worldwide, in an industry worth about $180 billion—and growing.[71] In-house security services, directly hired and controlled by the company or organization, are called **proprietary services**. **Contract services** are those outside firms or individuals hired by the individual or company to provide security services for a fee. The most common security services provided include contract guards, alarm services, private investigators, locksmith services, armored-car services, and security consultants.

Private police/security officers: all nonpublic officers, including guards, watchmen, private detectives, and investigators; they have limited powers and only the same arrest powers as regular citizens.

Proprietary services: in-house security services whose personnel are hired, trained, and supervised by the company or organization.

Contract services: a for-profit firm or individuals hired by an individual or company to provide security services.

Although some of the duties of the security officer are similar to those of the public police officer, their overall arrest powers are entirely different. First, because security officers are not police officers, court decisions have stated that the security officer is not bound by the *Miranda* decision concerning suspects' rights. Furthermore, security officers generally possess only the same authority to effect an arrest as does the common citizen (the extent of a citizen's arrest power varies, however, depending on the type of crime, the jurisdiction, and the status of the citizen). In most states, warrantless arrests by private citizens are allowed when a felony has been committed and reasonable grounds exist for believing that the person arrested committed it. Most states also allow citizen's arrests for misdemeanors committed in the arrester's presence.

The tasks of the private police are similar to those of their public counterparts: protecting executives and employees, tracking and forecasting security threats, monitoring alarms, preventing and detecting fraud, conducting investigations, providing crisis management and prevention, and responding to substance abuse.[72] Still, there are concerns about the field. First, studies have shown that security officer recruits often have minimal education and training; because the pay is usually quite low, the jobs often attract only those people who cannot find other jobs or who are seeking temporary work. Thus, much of the work is done by the young and the retired.[73]

Fortunately, over the past two decades, the private security field has seen

- Gains in certification, standards, and academic programs in colleges and universities
- Encouragement for greater professionalism through conferences, research and publications, and associations such as ASIS International, the International Association of Chiefs of Police, and the National Sheriffs' Association
- Improved background screening for hiring security personnel (mandated by the Private Security Officer Employment Authorization Act of 2004, which authorized

Our society has increasingly turned to the "other police"—those of the private sector—for protection.

a fingerprint-based criminal history check of state and national criminal history records to screen prospective and current private security officers)

- Improved training of security practitioners (22 states require basic training for licensed security personnel)[74]

Another long-standing issue—prompted by many shootings involving private security personnel—concerns whether or not private police should be armed. These concerns are prompted by training requirements that should be met (in 15 states, security officers can carry weapons on the job without any firearms training at all) as well as the balance that must be struck between providing a safe environment for the officers and their clients, while ensuring that their workspace does not devolve into one in which, as two authors put it, the officers "themselves pose the greatest threat."[75]

/// IN A NUTSHELL

- All four of the primary criminal justice officials of early England—sheriff, constable, coroner, and justice of the peace—either still exist or existed until recently in the United States.
- In 1829, Sir Robert Peel established professional policing as it is known today, under the Metropolitan Police Act of 1829. Later, in 1844, the New York state legislature passed a law establishing a full-time preventive police force for New York City. However, this new body took a very different form than in Europe. The U.S. version was placed under the control of the city government and city politicians, thus launching the first era of policing: the political era, from the 1840s to the 1930s.
- The reform (also known as the professional) era of policing, from the 1930s to the 1980s, sought to remove police from political control. August Vollmer was a major contributor to this era, being the architect of many developments in policing that paved the way for today's practices. Civil service systems were created, and soon the crime-fighter image was projected; much police work was driven by *numbers*—arrests, calls for service, response time to calls for service, number of tickets written, and so on. The police were the "thin blue line," but crimes continued to increase, and the police were becoming increasingly removed from their communities.
- The community era of policing, 1980s to the present, was born because of the problems that overwhelmed the reform era. The police were trained to work with the community to solve problems by looking at their underlying causes and developing tailored responses to them.
- At the federal level, agencies of the Department of Homeland Security were formed in 2003 to combat terrorism; agencies of the Department of Justice and other federal agencies support that and other efforts as well.
- State law enforcement agencies are of two primary types: general law enforcement agencies engaged in patrol and related functions, and state bureaus of investigation.
- Today there are approximately 18,000 police agencies, each with an organizational structure divided into a number of operations and support functions.
- Although there are some advantages to a nation's having a single, national police force, municipal and county policing in the United States has always been primarily decentralized, fragmented, and localized.
- INTERPOL is the oldest, the best-known, and probably the only truly international crime-fighting organization for crimes committed on an international scale; its agents do not patrol the globe, nor do they make arrests or engage in shootouts. They are basically intelligence gatherers who have helped many nations work together in attacking international crime since 1923.
- There are a number of common elements—often termed KSAs (for knowledge, skills, and abilities)—of employment in many federal, state, and local law enforcement positions; many such positions (particularly at the federal level) now involve the enforcement of immigration laws.
- The field of private policing or security is much larger than public policing; it is divided into in-house security services, called *proprietary services*, and *contract services*, where outside firms or individuals are hired by the individual or company to provide security services for a fee. Private security officers are not bound by court decisions that govern the public police, and generally they possess the same authority to make an arrest as a private citizen.

/// KEY TERMS & CONCEPTS

Review key terms with eFlashcards at edge.sagepub.com/peak4e.

Chain of command   122
Community era   109

Constable   105
Contract services   125

Coroner   105
County sheriff's office   120

Federal law enforcement agencies 110
INTERPOL 113
Justice of the peace (JP) 105
Municipal police department 119
Organization 104
Organizational structure or chart 120
Political era 107
Private police/security officers 125
Proprietary services 125
Reform era 108
Sheriff 104
Special-purpose state agencies 119
State bureau of investigation 118
State police 117

/// REVIEW QUESTIONS

Test your understanding of chapter content at **edge.sagepub.com/peak4e**.

1. What were the four major police-related offices and their functions during the early English and colonial periods?
2. What are the three eras of local policing, what were August Vollmer's contributions to policing's reform era, and what primary problems of the two initial eras led to the development of the current community era?
3. What are the major agencies within the Department of Homeland Security and the Department of Justice, and what are their primary functions?
4. What general qualifications, job requirements, and benefits are involved in careers in federal law enforcement agencies?
5. How would you describe the primary differences between federal and state law enforcement agencies?
6. What functions do the Central Intelligence Agency and the Internal Revenue Service perform?
7. How does INTERPOL function, and what are its primary contributions to crime fighting?
8. What are some advantages and disadvantages of a nation's having a single, national, centralized police force?
9. What are some of the differences between municipal police agencies and county sheriff's departments?
10. Using a simple organizational structure that you have drawn, how would you describe the major functions of a local (i.e., municipal or county) police agency?
11. Why were the private police organizations developed, and what are their contemporary purposes and issues?

/// LEARN BY DOING

1. Assume that you are part of a group that is studying the feasibility of a single, national police force in the United States, such as those found in many countries around the world. All state, county, and municipal police organizations would be abolished and absorbed into this single centralized agency, with one governing board, one set of laws to enforce and agency policies to uphold, and standardized training and pay/benefits. Develop arguments both for and against this proposal, perhaps including the history of policing, all possible positive and negative consequences that might occur from this single entity, its political pitfalls and favor with the general public, and whether or not you would support this proposal.
2. Do an Internet search to determine the extent to which the following four police-related offices are still authorized and used in the United States and in your state: sheriff, constable, justice of the peace, and coroner.
3. You have been assigned to describe your state's special-purpose law enforcement agencies for a class presentation. Prepare a lecture outline covering those agencies and the services they provide.

/// STUDY SITE

Get the tools you need to sharpen your study skills. SAGE edge offers a robust online environment featuring an impressive array of free tools and resources.

Access practice quizzes, eFlashcards, video, and multimedia at **edge.sagepub.com/peak4e**.

CHAPTER 6

POLICE AT WORK
Patrolling and Investigating

Down these mean streets a man must go who is not himself mean, who is neither tarnished nor afraid. He is the hero, he is everything. He must be . . . a man of honor.

—Raymond Chandler, *The Simple Art of Murder* (1950)

Murder, though it have no tongue, will speak.

—Shakespeare, *Hamlet*, Act II, Scene 2

LEARNING OBJECTIVES

As a result of reading this chapter, you will be able to

1. Explain the kinds of topics that are taught in the recruit academy and overall methods for preparing recruits for a career in policing
2. Explain what is meant by a working personality, roles, styles, and four basic tasks of policing
3. Identify potential stressors and perils in policing
4. Define police discretion, how and why it is allowed to function, and some of its advantages and disadvantages
5. Explain the current era of policing, the community era, and the prevailing philosophy and strategies of community policing and problem solving
6. Define forensics and criminalistics, describe the investigative process, and review how crime scenes and criminal interrogations should be handled
7. Describe the challenges posed to criminal investigators by today's cybercrimes as well as cold cases, and what must be done to address them

ASSESS YOUR AWARENESS

Test your current knowledge of police patrol and investigations by responding to the following seven true-false items; check your answers after reading this chapter.

1. Normally there are only three types of tests one has to pass in order to become a police officer: a background check, a criminal record check, and a polygraph exam.
2. Studies show that a police officer who has a college degree is no better in terms of overall performance than one who is without a degree.
3. As typically shown in movie and television portrayals, detective work is primarily action packed and involves a successful search for offenders.
4. The four basic tasks of policing that involve the public are patrolling, tracking, arresting, and appearing in court.
5. DNA is the most sophisticated and reliable type of physical evidence.
6. Police officers, being governed by laws and procedure manuals, actually have very little discretion in how they perform their jobs.
7. The chances of a murderer being caught is now about 8 in 10.

<< Answers can be found on page 419.

The Golden State Killer terrorized all of California in the 1970s and 1980s—a period of time when there were no extensive DNA, mapping, automated fingerprinting, or other databases and forensic technologies and investigative tools that are taken for granted today. The murderer was clever and sadistic, staying one step ahead of police while killing at least 12 people, raping more than 50 (many in very cruel fashion), and committing some 100 burglaries over a 10-county area between 1974 and 1986. But one persistent investigator and DNA expert, Paul Holes, created a road map to the killer through his genetics.

Holes used DNA recovered from a 1980 rape/murder crime scene to begin the investigation: an evidence kit from a rape and murder of a couple that had been placed in a freezer in 1980. A lab converted the sample into a format that could be read by a website that allows users to upload their genetic information for family history searches and analyzes hundreds of thousands of DNA data points to determine relatedness. Holes found 10 to 20 distant relatives of the killer; he knew that if he traced back the lineages of distant cousins far enough, he could find a common ancestor they shared with the killer.

Holes and his team used census data, old newspaper clippings and a gravesite locator for finding the deceased relatives. The family trees were created using a tool on Ancestry.com. After four months of work examining family trees, they had pieced together about 25 distinct family trees from the great-great-great grandparents; the trees composed roughly 1,000 family members and would include the suspect. The team began scouring the trees for men about the killer's age who had connections to Sacramento and other locations of the crimes. They found two. One was eventually eliminated by a DNA test of a relative; the other was Joseph James DeAngelo, a 72-year-old retired police officer who was quietly living near Sacramento. Deputies surveilled DeAngelo, and in April 2018 they pounced on an item discarded by DeAngelo that contained his DNA, producing a match. More than four decades after he commenced his horrible crime spree, DeAngelo was arrested in Citrus Heights on April 24. He now faces eight counts of murder.[1] (In the aftermath of the DeAngelo case, several genealogical database firms changed their terms of service, allowing users to deny law enforcement from accessing their genetic information.)

As you read this chapter, consider the essential traits that one must possess, the knowledge that must be obtained, and the skills one must have in order to be a successful police officer as well as criminal investigator.

INTRODUCTION

How do I become a police officer? What would I do as one? Could I be a detective? A criminal profiler? How do I qualify to work in forensics? Do police have to arrest everyone they see breaking the law?

These are all legitimate, often-heard questions as posed by university students. Unfortunately, owing in large measure to Hollywood's portrayals of police work and investigations, there are many misperceptions about the field. First, the odds of one's becoming a criminal profiler are virtually nil—as are the odds of some federal agent academy trainee being brought out to help investigate a serial killer case (as was the plot in the movie *The Silence of the Lambs*). Second, one who wishes to work in a forensics lab must have a background in chemistry, biology, or a related natural science field (e.g., biochemistry or microbiology). Finally, to become a detective, one must typically begin as a regular officer; then, with years of training, experience, and often testing or at least an oral examination, one might be deemed worthy of being an investigator. This chapter hopes to remedy those misperceptions, at least in part, by looking at some of the primary roles and functions of the individuals who work in police organizations. Beginning with the kinds of knowledge, skills, and abilities sought at the point of their recruitment, we then consider how they are trained and eventually begin working either as officers on patrol or as criminal investigators.

First is a review of the types of persons who are sought for and hired into policing, as well as their initial training at the academy; included is a consideration of the benefits of higher education for police and the subculture of the "cop's world"—the roles, styles, and tasks of the police; included are some stressors of the policing occupation, discretionary use of authority by police in enforcing the law, and the community era of policing (and its new methods of patrolling for officers). Then we examine those who investigate crimes, the detectives; included is a review of the investigative process, crime scene handling, attributes of detectives, unique challenges posed by high-tech cybercrimes, and how DNA analyses are performed (including their use in handling cold cases).

FROM CITIZEN TO PATROL OFFICER

The idea of a police subculture was first proposed by William Westley in his 1950 study of the Gary, Indiana, Police Department, where he found, among many other things, a high degree of secrecy and violence.[2] The police develop traditions, skills, and attitudes that are unique to their occupation because of their duties and responsibilities. In this section, we consider how citizens are brought into, and socialized within, the police world.

Recruiting the Best

Recruiting an adequate pool of applicants is an extremely important facet of the police hiring process. August Vollmer, the renowned Berkeley, California, police innovator and administrator, discussed in Chapter 5, said that law enforcement candidates should

> have the wisdom of Solomon, the courage of David, the patience of Job and leadership of Moses, the kindness of the Good Samaritan, the diplomacy of Lincoln, the tolerance of the Carpenter of Nazareth, and, finally, an intimate knowledge of every branch of the natural, biological and social sciences.[3]

Police officers are solitary workers, spending most of their time on the job unsupervised. At all times they must be able to make sound decisions and adjust quickly to changing situations during periods that are unpredictable and unstable, chaotic, or high stress—all the while acting ethically and in keeping with the U.S. Constitution, their state statutes, and their agency's policy and procedures manual. For these reasons, police agencies must attempt to attract the best individuals possible.

Figure 6.1 shows the general kinds of screening and testing methods used with new police recruits in the United States. Even after a person meets the minimum qualifications for being a police officer (age, education, no disqualifying criminal record), and is recruited into the testing process, much work and testing remain before he or she is ready to be sent to the streets as a police officer. This so-called hurdle process is shown in Figure 6.2. Not all types of tests shown in the figure are employed by all of the 18,000 federal, state, county, and municipal law enforcement agencies in America, nor are these tests necessarily given in the sequence shown. Furthermore, this gamut of testing can easily require several months to complete, depending on the number and types of tests used and the ease of scheduling and performing them.

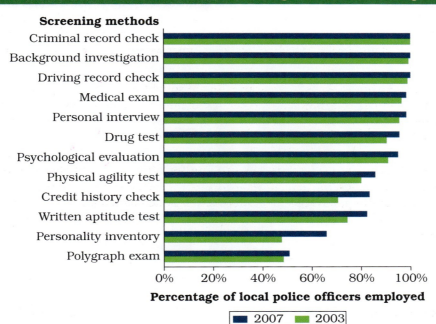

Figure 6.1 /// Local Police Officers' Selected Screening Methods in the Hiring Process

Source: Brian A. Reaves, *Hiring and Retention of State and Local Law Enforcement Officers* (Washington, D.C.: U.S. Department of Justice, Bureau of Justice Statistics, October 2012), p. 14, https://www.bjs.gov/content/pub/pdf/hrslleo08st.pdf.

Note: Most current data available.

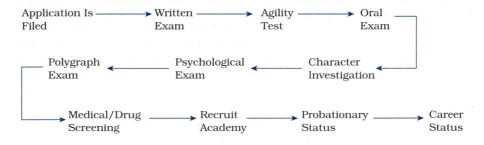

Figure 6.2 /// Major Elements of the Police Hiring Process

Application Is Filed → Written Exam → Agility Test → Oral Exam → Character Investigation → Psychological Exam → Polygraph Exam → Medical/Drug Screening → Recruit Academy → Probationary Status → Career Status

Does a College Degree Matter?

To interact with an educated public, enforce the rule of law, investigate crimes, testify in court, write cogent and accurate reports, and perform the myriad other duties for which we call upon the police, one would assume that all officers must obtain a two- or four-year college degree prior to assuming the role. Such, however, is not even close to being the case. Indeed, only 15 percent of all police agencies have some college requirement, with 1 percent requiring a four-year degree for new officers, and fewer than one-fourth (23 percent) requiring a two-year degree.[4]

In 1973, the National Advisory Commission on Criminal Justice Standards and Goals, recognizing the need for higher education (i.e., education beyond high school, at a college or university in particular) among police officers, recommended that all police officers have a four-year college education by 1982.[5] Indeed, from 1967 to 1986, every national commission that studied crime, violence, and police in America maintained that a college education could help the police do their jobs better.[6] Obviously, the recommendations of those commissions have not been followed.

Higher education (for police): education beyond high school, at a college or university, in particular).

Abundant empirical evidence indicates that college-educated police officers are better officers. For example, compared to non-college-educated officers, college-educated officers have significantly fewer founded citizen complaints;[7] have better peer relationships;[8] are likelier to take a leadership role in the organization;[9] tend to be more flexible;[10] are less dogmatic and less authoritarian;[11] take fewer leave days, receive fewer injuries, have less injury time, have lower rates of absenteeism, use fewer sick days, and are involved in fewer traffic accidents;[12] have greater ability to analyze situations and make judicious decisions; and have a more desirable system of personal values.[13] Furthermore, college graduates are accused of negligent use of a firearm significantly less often than are officers who lack a college degree.[14]

Many studies have indicated that college-educated persons make better officers, yet relatively few agencies require a college degree for hiring.

A strong endorsement for police higher education came in 1985, when a lawsuit challenged the Dallas, Texas, Police Department's requirement that all applicants for police officer positions possess 45 credit hours and at least a C average at an accredited college or university. The Fifth Circuit Court of Appeals and, eventually, the U.S. Supreme Court upheld the educational requirement. According to the circuit court,

A significant part of a police officer's function involves his ability to function effectively as a crisis intervenor, in family fights, teen-age rumbles, bar brawls, street corner altercations, racial disturbances, riots and similar situations. Few professionals are so peculiarly charged with individual responsibilities as police officers. Mistakes of judgment could cause irreparable harm to citizens or even to the community. The educational requirement bears a manifest relationship to the position of police officer. We conclude that the district court's findings . . . are not erroneous.[15]

Finally, Norm Stamper, former police chief in Seattle, Washington, observed that not only do the degree and college credits matter, but so does

> getting up in the morning for classes or attending at night after work, reading dense texts, writing term papers, questioning professors, associating with people and ideas that force you to think, [and] taking midterms and finals. The politics of higher education, the discipline of learning *how* to learn—that was the most useful thing about higher ed.[16]

Recruit Training

Once hired into an agency, police recruits are taught a variety of subjects in academy training (see Table 6.1). They are taught to nurture a "sixth sense": suspicion. A suspicious nature is as important to the street officer as a fine touch is to a surgeon. The officer should be able to visually recognize when something is wrong or out of the ordinary.

Academy training: where police and corrections personnel are trained in the basic functions, laws, and skills required for their positions

Sixth sense: in policing, the notion that an officer can "sense" or feel when something is not right, as in the way a person acts, talks, and so on.

Table 6.1 /// Major Subject Areas Included in Basic Training Programs in State and Local Law Enforcement Training Academies

Training Area	Percentage of Academies With Training	Average Number of Hours of Instruction Required per Recruit*
Operations		
Report writing	99%	25 hrs.
Patrol procedures	98	52
Investigations	98	42
Traffic accident investigations	98	23
Emergency vehicle operations	97	38
Basic first aid/CPR	97	24
Computers/information systems	61	9
Weapons/defensive tactics/use of force		
Defensive tactics	99%	60 hrs.
Firearms skills	98	71
Use of force	98	21
Nonlethal weapons	88	16

(Continued)

Table 6.1 /// (Continued)		
Training Area	Percentage of Academies With Training	Average Number of Hours of Instruction Required per Recruit*
Self-improvement		
Ethics and integrity	98%	8 hrs.
Health and fitness	96	49
Communications	91	15
Professionalism	85	11
Stress prevention/management	81	6
Legal education		
Criminal/constitutional law	98%	53 hrs.
Traffic law	97	23
Juvenile justice law/procedures	97	10

*Excludes academies that did not provide this type of instruction.

Source: Brian A. Reaves, *State and Local Law Enforcement Training Academies, 2013* (Washington, D.C.: U.S. Department of Justice, Bureau of Justice Statistics, February 2016), p. 5, https://www.bjs.gov/content/pub/pdf/slleta13.pdf.

Police recruits undergo training in a variety of subjects during their many weeks in the academy.

Field training officer (FTO): one who is to oversee and evaluate the new police officer's performance as he or she transitions from the training academy to patrolling the streets.

Table 6.1 displays the predominant subjects included in academy training of new officers and the average length of time devoted to each. The table shows that large blocks of time are devoted to defensive tactics/weapons skills, criminal/constitutional law, patrol procedures, and health and fitness.

Field Training Officer

Once the recruits leave the academy, they are not merely thrown to the streets to fend for themselves in terms of upholding the law and maintaining order. Another important part of this acquisition process involves being assigned to a veteran officer for initial field instruction and observation. This veteran is sometimes called a **field training officer (FTO)**.[17] This training program provides recruits with an opportunity to make the transition from the academy to the streets under the protective arm of a veteran officer. Recruits are on probationary status, typically ranging from six months to one year; their employment may be terminated immediately if their overall performance is unsatisfactory during that period.

Most FTO programs consist of three identifiable phases:

1. Introductory phase (the recruit learns agency policies and local laws)
2. Training and evaluation phase (the recruit is introduced to more complicated tasks that patrol officers confront)
3. Final phase (the FTO acts strictly as an observer and evaluator while the recruit performs all the functions of a patrol officer)[18]

The length of time rookies are assigned to FTOs will vary. A formal FTO program might require close supervision for a range of 1–12 weeks.

Most police officers also receive in-service training throughout their careers, because their states require a minimum number of hours of such training. News items, court decisions, and other relevant information can also be covered at roll call before the beginning of each shift. Short courses ranging from a few hours to several weeks are available for in-service officers through several means such as videos and nationally televised training programs.

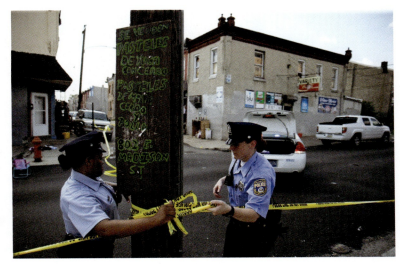

To assist in their transition from the training academy to the street, new officers are typically assigned to work with a veteran field training officer for a period of time before being released to act on their own.

HAVING THE "RIGHT STUFF": DEFINING THE ROLE

In addition to possessing the "bare essentials" mentioned earlier—a high degree of ethics/integrity (determined via polygraph, record check, and other means), knowledge of applicable laws and procedures (obtained at the basic academy), communication skills, physical fitness, and so on—who are the police and what are they supposed to do? Although a seemingly straightforward question, the policing role is far more complex than merely saying they "enforce the law" or "serve and protect."

Policing role: the function of the police in contemporary society.

One of the greatest obstacles to understanding the American police is the crime-fighter image. Because of film and media portrayals, many people believe that the role of the police is confined to the apprehension of criminals.[19] However, only about 20 percent of the police officer's typical day is devoted to fighting crime per se.[20] And, as Jerome Skolnick and David Bayley point out, the crimes that terrify Americans the most—robbery, rape, burglary, and homicide—are rarely encountered by police on patrol. In their words:

> Only "Dirty Harry" has his lunch disturbed by a bank robbery in progress. Patrol officers individually make few important arrests. The "good collar" is a rare event. Cops spend most of their time passively patrolling and providing emergency services.[21]

Also, many individuals enter police work expecting it to be exciting and rewarding, as depicted on television and in the movies. Later they discover that much of their time is spent with boring, mundane, and trivial tasks—and that paperwork is seldom stimulating.

A Working Personality

Since the publication of Westley's examination of police subculture in 1950, the notion of a police personality has become a popular area of study. In 1966, Jerome Skolnick described what he termed the working personality of the police.[22] He determined that the police role contained two important variables: danger and authority. Danger is a constant feature of police work. Police officers, constantly facing potential violence, are warned at the academy to be cautious. They are told many war stories of officers shot and killed at domestic disturbances or traffic stops. Consequently, they develop "perceptual shorthand," Skolnick said, that they use to identify certain kinds of people as "symbolic assailants"—individuals whom the officer has come to recognize as potentially violent based on their gestures, language, and attire.

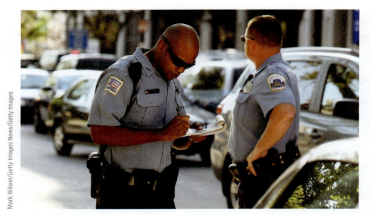

As opposed to Hollywood's portrayals, very little police work is action packed. Here, Washington, D.C., police cite people who are talking on cell phones while driving.

Policing styles: James Q. Wilson argued that there are three styles of policing: watchman, legalistic, and service.

Three Distinctive Styles of Policing

James Q. Wilson also attempted to clarify what it is that the police are supposed to do; Wilson maintained that there are three distinctive policing styles:[23]

- The *watchman* style involves the officer as a "neighbor." Here, officers act as if order maintenance (rather than law enforcement) is their primary function. The emphasis is on using the law as a means of maintaining order rather than regulating conduct through arrests. Police ignore many common minor violations, such as traffic and juvenile offenses. These violations and so-called victimless crimes, such as gambling and prostitution, are tolerated; they will often be handled informally. Thus the individual officer has wide latitude concerning whether to enforce the letter or the spirit of the law; the emphasis is on using the law to give people what they "deserve."

- The *legalistic* style casts the officer as a "soldier." This style takes a much harsher view of law violations. Police officers issue large numbers of traffic citations, detain a high volume of juvenile offenders, and act vigorously against illicit activities. Large numbers of other kinds of arrests occur as well. Chief administrators want high arrest and ticketing rates not only because violators should be punished but also because it reduces the opportunity for their officers to engage in corrupt behavior. This style of policing assumes that the purpose of the law is to punish.

- The *service* style views the officer as a "teacher." This style falls in between the watchman and legalistic styles. The police take seriously all requests for either law enforcement or order maintenance (unlike in the watchman-style department) but are less likely to respond by making an arrest or otherwise imposing formal sanctions. Police officers see their primary responsibility as protecting public order against the minor and occasional threats posed by unruly teenagers and "outsiders" (tramps, derelicts, out-of-town visitors). The citizenry expects its service-style officers to display the same qualities as its department store salespeople: They should be courteous, neat, and deferential. The police will frequently use informal sanctions instead of making arrests.

Four Basic Tasks

Tasks of policing (four basic): enforce the law, perform welfare tasks, prevent crime, and protect the innocent.

Patrol officers may be said to perform four basic tasks of policing:

1. *Enforce the laws:* Although this is a primary function of the police, as we saw earlier, they actually devote a very small portion of their time to "chasing bad guys."

2. *Perform welfare tasks:* Throughout history, the police have probably done much more of this type of work than the public (or the police themselves) realize; following are some of them:

   - "Check the welfare of" kinds of calls, where someone has not been seen or heard from for some time and may be deceased, ill, missing, or in distress
   - "Be on the lookout" (BOLO) calls, where someone has wandered away from a nursing home or an assisted living home, is a juvenile runaway, and so forth

- Delivering death notifications/messages
- Delivering blood to hospitals (particularly in more rural areas where blood banks are not available)
- Assisting firefighters and animal control units
- Reporting burned-out street lights or damaged traffic signs
- Performing all manner of errands simply because they are available—locking and unlocking municipal parking lots, collecting receipts from municipal entities such as golf courses, delivering agendas to city/county commissioners, and so forth

3. *Prevent crime:* This function of police involves engaging in random patrol and providing the public with crime prevention information.
4. *Protect the innocent:* By investigating crimes, police are systematically removing innocent people from consideration as crime suspects.

Perils of Patrol

Although workers die at much higher rates in several occupations other than policing—commercial fishing, logging, piloting airplanes, roofing, and recycling materials, in particular[24]—police officers' lives are still rife with occupational hazards. Each year, an average of about 150 police officers die while on duty, and about 25 to 50 of them will be killed through felonious means; another 49,500 will be assaulted.[25] On average, the slain officer was in his or her late 30s, and he or she had worked in law enforcement about a dozen years.[26]

Officers seldom know for certain whether a citizen whom they are about to confront is armed, high on drugs or alcohol, or perhaps even planning to die at the hands of the police using a technique known as "suicide by cop." This danger is heightened during the hours of darkness, when patrol officers encounter burglars looking to invade homes and businesses, people who are intoxicated from a night of partying, and so on.

A Study of Patrol Effectiveness

The best-known study of patrol effectiveness, the **Kansas City Preventive Patrol Experiment**, was conducted in Kansas City, Missouri, in 1973. Researchers—wanting to know if random patrol had any significant effect on crime, police response rates to crime, or citizen fear of crime—divided the city into 15 beats, which were then categorized into five groups of three matched beats each. Each group consisted of neighborhoods that were similar in terms of population, crime characteristics, and calls for police services. In one beat area, there was no preventive patrol (police responded only to calls for service); another beat area had increased patrol activity (two or three times the usual amount of patrolling); and in the third beat there was the usual level of patrol service. Citizens were interviewed and crime rates were measured during the year the experiment was conducted.

The study found that the deterrent effect of policing was not reduced by the elimination of routine patrolling; nor were citizens' fear of crime, their attitudes toward the police, or the ability of the police to respond to calls reduced. The Kansas City Preventive Patrol Experiment (depicted in Figure 6.3) indicated that the traditional assumption of "Give me more cars and more money, and we'll get there faster and fight crime" was probably not a viable argument.[27]

Kansas City Preventive Patrol Experiment: in the early 1970s, a study of the effects of different types of patrolling on crime—patrolling as usual in one area, saturated patrol in another, and very limited patrol in a third area; the results showed no significant differences.

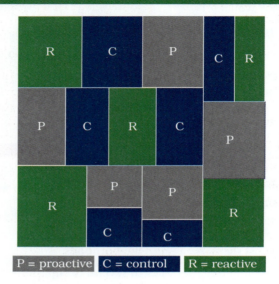

Figure 6.3 /// Schematic Representation of the Kansas City Preventive Patrol Experiment

Source: George L. Kelling, Tony Pate, Duane Dieckman, and Charles E. Brown, *The Kansas City Preventive Patrol Experiment: A Summary Report* (Washington, D.C.: Police Foundation, 1974). Reprinted with permission of the Police Foundation.

STRESSORS IN POLICE WORK

There is an aspect of police work that officers would prefer to ignore but that must be acknowledged: the stress induced by the job. Indeed, Sir W. S. Gilbert observed, "When constabulary duty's to be done, the policeman's lot is not a happy one."[28] Therefore, those persons either working in the field or contemplating doing so must know of the challenges of stress and how to cope with them. The job of policing has never been easy, as many of the people they confront are armed and dangerous; but the dangers of the job have increased as a result of today's drug problems, gangs, mass shootings, critical incidents, threats of terrorism, weaponry, and other issues, as well as the "fishbowl" effect of the work, given the close scrutiny, videotaping, and calls for accountability of today's police.

Stress: discomfort and distress caused by situations that officers face on the job.

Sources of Stress

Stress can come from a number of directions, so police officers can experience discomfort and distress as a result of a wide range of problems and situations. The four general sources of stress are (1) organizational and administrative practices, (2) the criminal justice system, (3) the public, and (4) stress intrinsic to police work itself.

Organizational and Administrative Practices

A primary source of stress is the police organization itself. Police departments typically are highly bureaucratic and possibly authoritarian in nature, which creates stress for individual officers in at least two ways. First, police departments follow strict policies and procedures, general orders, and rules and regulations that are dictated by top management. Street officers and first-line supervisors seldom have direct input into their formulation, resulting in officers feeling powerless and alienated about the decisions that directly affect their jobs. Second, these rules dictate how officers specifically perform many of their duties and responsibilities. They are created to provide officers with guidance and direction. Police officers, however, sometimes view these rules as mechanisms used by management to restrict their freedom and discretion or to justify punishing them when they make incorrect decisions or errors.

Female and minority police officers also face unique problems. Because policing has traditionally been a male- and white-dominated occupation, in many agencies female and minority officers do not always have the same standing or career options as their counterparts. In addition, female officers might confront sexual harassment,[29] whereas minority officers might feel they are ostracized by people of their own race for being "traitors" against them and their neighborhoods.

By its nature, policing carries a high potential for danger. This funeral procession escorts an officer who was shot dead while answering a report of a traffic accident in February 2017.

The Criminal Justice System

Each component of the criminal justice system affects the other components. For example, judges have openly displayed hostile attitudes toward the police, or prosecutors have not displayed proper respect to officers, arbitrarily dismissing cases, having them appear in court during regularly scheduled days off, and advocating rulings restricting police procedures. Another example occurs when parole officers and probation officers do an inadequate job of supervising parolees, which results in their being involved in an inordinate amount of crime. The courts have the most direct impact on police officers and probably are the greatest source of stress from the criminal justice system.

The Public

When police officers perform community services, they also become involved in conflicts or negative situations. They arrest citizens, they write tickets, and they give citizens orders when intervening in domestic violence or disorder situations. Often, to resolve problems, they make half of the participants happy, but the other half are unhappy. The problem is that police officers develop unrealistic or inaccurate ideas about citizens as a result of their negative encounters. Officers must keep their relationship with citizens in proper perspective. This is achieved by open, straightforward discussions of public attitudes and encounters with citizens. It also means that managers must emphasize the importance of good relations between the police and the public and of the majority of citizens supporting and respecting the police.

Stressors Intrinsic to Police Work

Police work is fraught with situations that pose physical danger to officers. Domestic violence, felonies in progress, and fight calls often require officers to physically confront suspects. It would seem that the work itself, since it includes dealing with dangerous police activities and people, would be the most stressful part of police work. Traumatic incidents can require long-term follow-up support for law enforcement personnel.

Coping With Stress

If officers do not relieve the pressure of the job, they eventually may suffer heart attacks, nervous breakdowns, back problems, headaches, psychosomatic illnesses, or alcoholism. They may also experience excessive weight gain or loss; combativeness or irritability;

excessive use of sick leave; excessive use of alcohol, tobacco, or drugs; marital or family disorders; inability to complete an assignment; loss of interest in work, hobbies, and people in general; more than the usual number of "accidents," including vehicular and other types; and shooting incidents. It is imperative that officers learn to manage their stress before it causes deep physical and/or emotional harm. One means is to engage in hobbies or activities that provide legitimate means of relaxing and venting. Exercise, proper nutrition, and positive lifestyle choices (such as not smoking and using alcohol only in moderation) are also essential for good health.

USE OF DISCRETION

Chapter 1 discussed how discretionary use of authority permeates the entire U.S. criminal justice system; here we focus on how discretion is employed in policing. The power to use discretion in performing one's role is at the very core of policing. However, as is discussed in this section, this power can be controversial—and used for both good and bad.

The Myth of Full Enforcement

The law is written in black and white; however, the manner in which most laws are enforced by the police can be said to be colored gray. Noted police scholar Herman Goldstein wrote in 1963 that the police should be "Enforcing the law without fear or favor."[30] However, the truth is anything but (except for laws or policies related to domestic violence and driving under the influence, for example, where the police are given no discretion but to arrest).

Consider this scenario: The municipal police chief or county sheriff is asked during a civic club luncheon speech which laws are and are not enforced by his or her agency. The official

Going Global

Saudi Arabia—Little to Do on Patrol

The police in Saudi Arabia assist with enforcing the very cruel (by Western standards) Islamic law, which is governed by the Koran and can include amputations of limbs, which are conducted in many cities and with some frequency on the Justice Square in Riyadh. Believing that public beheadings and amputations deter other prospective offenders, the police encourage people in the vicinity of the square to witness these events. When a thief's right hand is cut off in public, it may be hung from a hook high on a streetlight pole on Justice Square for all to see. Because there is a near total absence on Saudi Arabian streets of gangs, drive-by shootings, purse snatchings, and contraband, the police patrol the streets in Chevrolets, BMWs, and Volvos, looking for minor infractions of the law.

Owing to the aforementioned harsh criminal code, there is little for the Saudi police to do in terms of crime prevention or investigation. The religious police—the *Mutaween*—patrol and stroll in their white cotton robes and sandals and look, as one writer observed, like "desert nomads who have stumbled unexpectedly into this century." They look for people who are improperly dressed or women who have a loose strand of hair falling across their face or who need to adjust their *tarhas* (head coverings). Around-the-clock patrols ensure that shops are closed in time for daily prayers and that only married couples are sitting in family sections of restaurants. The patrols often follow persons suspected of being involved in what is deemed immoral behavior, such as drug use, homosexuality, gambling, and begging. Teams of religious police will also destroy home satellite dishes, which bring uncensored Western television broadcasts into Saudi homes.

Sources: U.S. citizen living in Saudi Arabia, personal communication, September 12, 1994; Chris Hedges, "Everywhere in Saudi Arabia, Islam Is Watching," *New York Times*, January 6, 1993, p. A4(N), col. 3.

response will inevitably be that *all* of the laws are enforced equally, all of the time. Yet the chief or sheriff knows that full enforcement of the laws is a myth—that there are neither the resources nor the desire to enforce them all, nor are all laws enforced impartially. There are legal concerns as well. For example, releasing some offenders (to get information about other crimes, because of a good excuse, etc.) cannot be the official policy of the agency (and letting an offender go is a form of discretion as well); however, the chief or sheriff cannot broadcast that fact to the public. Indeed, it has been stated that "the single most astonishing fact of police behavior is the extent to which police do *not* enforce the law when they have every legal right to do so."[31]

Attempts to Define Discretion

The way police make arrest decisions is largely unknown (see possible determining factors, described in the next section). What *is* known, however, is that when police observe something of a suspicious or an illegal nature, two important decisions must be made: (1) whether to intervene in the situation and (2) how to intervene. The kinds, number, and possible combinations of interventions are virtually limitless. What kinds of decisions are available for an officer who makes a routine traffic stop? David Bayley and Egon Bittner observed long ago that officers have as many as 10 actions to select from at the initial stop (e.g., order the driver out of the car), 7 strategies appropriate during the stop (such as a roadside sobriety test), and 11 exit strategies (including releasing the driver with a warning), representing a total of *770* different combinations of actions that might be taken![32]

Criminal law has two sides—the formality and the reality. The formality is found in the statute books and opinions of appellate courts. The reality is found in the practices of enforcement officers. In some circumstances, the choice of action to be taken is relatively easy, such as arresting a bank robbery suspect. In other situations, such as quelling a dispute between neighbors or determining how much party noise is too much, the choice is more difficult.[33] Our system tends to treat people as individuals. One person who commits a robbery is not the same as another person who commits a robbery. Our system also takes into account why and how a person committed a crime (his or her intent, or *mens rea*, discussed in Chapter 2). The most important decisions take place on the streets, day or night, generally without the opportunity for the officer to consult with others or to carefully consider all the facts.

Determinants of Discretionary Actions

The power of discretionary policing can be awe-inspiring. Kenneth Culp Davis, an authority on police discretion, writes, "The police are among the most important policy makers of our entire society. And they make far more discretionary determinations in individual cases than does any other class of administrators; I know of no close second."[34]

What determines whether the officer will take a stern approach (enforcing the letter of the law with an arrest) or will be lenient (issuing a verbal warning or some other outcome short of arrest)? Several variables enter into the officer's decision:

1. The *law* is indeed a factor. For example, many state statutes and local ordinances now mandate that the police arrest for certain suspected offenses, such as driving under the influence or domestic violence.
2. The *officer's attitude* can also be a factor. First, some officers are more willing to empathize with offenders who feel they deserve a break than others. Furthermore, police, being human, can bring to work either a happy or an unhappy disposition. Personal viewpoints can also play a role, such as when, for example, the officer is fed up with juvenile crimes that have been occurring of late and thus will not give any leniency to youths that he or she encounters. Also, as Carl Klockars and Stephen

Mastrofski observed, although violators frequently offer what they feel are very good reasons for the officer to overlook their offense, "every police officer knows that, if doing so will allow them to escape punishment, most people are prepared to lie through their teeth."35

3. Another major consideration in the officer's choice among options is the citizen's attitude. If the offender is rude and condescending, denies having done anything wrong, or uses some of the standard clichés that are almost guaranteed to rankle the officer—such as "You don't know who I am" (someone who is obviously very important in the community), "I'll have your job," "I know the chief of police," or "I'm a taxpayer, and I pay your salary"—the probable outcome is obvious. By contrast, the person who is honest with the officer, avoids attempts at intimidation and sarcasm, and does not try to "beat the rap" may fare better.

In addition to these considerations, other factors that an officer may take into account when deciding whether or not to arrest might include injury to and preference of the victim; prior criminal record of the offender; amount and strength of evidence; peer and agency pressure regarding certain kinds of crimes; media coverage of this and other related crimes; and availability and credibility of witnesses. The officer's specific assignment may also come into play. For example, homicide investigators would care little about a driver's tendency to disobey traffic laws, whereas one who is an assigned and dedicated traffic officer will likely treat such offenses much more seriously.

Pros and Cons of Discretion

Having discretionary authority carries several advantages for the police officer: First, because the law cannot (and should not) cover every sort of situation the officer encounters, discretion allows the officer to have the flexibility to treat different situations in accordance with humanitarian and practical goals. For example, assume an officer pulls over a speeding motorist, only to learn that the car is en route to the hospital with a woman who is about to deliver a baby. While the agitated driver is endangering everyone in the vehicle as well as other motorists on the roadway, discretion allows the officer to be compassionate and empathetic, giving the car a safe escort to the hospital rather than issuing a citation for speeding. In short, discretionary use of authority allows the police to employ a philosophy of "justice tempered with mercy."

You Be the . . .

Police Officer

Assume a police officer pulls over a vehicle for swerving across the center line. The driver, a 17-year-old college student who is an elementary education major, admits she's been drinking at a party. The breathalyzer test reveals a .07 blood alcohol concentration. In this state .07 can result in a charge of either "driving after having consumed alcohol" or a more serious "driving while ability is impaired." There are two others in the car: One young woman has a badly swollen jaw after having fallen at the party; the driver is attempting to get her to the urgent care facility. The injured passenger, an older sister of the driver, is visibly pregnant.

1. What discretionary issues are presented?
2. Given all of the facts at hand, how do you believe the officer should deal with the driver?

One disadvantage of discretionary authority is that those officers who are the least trained and experienced have the greatest amount of discretion to exercise. In other words, as the rank of the officer *increases*, the amount of discretion that he or she can employ typically *decreases*. The patrol officer or deputy, being loosely supervised on the streets, makes many discretionary decisions about whether or not to arrest, search, frisk, and so forth. Conversely, the chief of police or sheriff will be highly constrained by department policies and procedures, union agreements, affirmative action laws, and/or governing board guidelines and policies. Another disadvantage is that allowing police to exercise such discretion belies their need to appear impartial—treating people differently for committing essentially the same offense. Critics of discretion also argue that such wide latitude in decision making may serve as a breeding ground for police corruption; for example, an officer may be offered a bribe to overlook an offense.

As part of their community-policing and problem-solving efforts, many agencies use bicycle patrols to focus on crime prevention and greater interaction with the community. But community policing involves much more than merely having bike patrols or creating a "Community Relations Unit."

See the case study in the accompanying "You Be the . . . Police Officer" box and respond to the questions posed.

COMMUNITY POLICING AND PROBLEM SOLVING

Chapter 5 discussed the three eras of policing, including today's "community era." Following is a brief description of policing in terms of how it moved from the political and reform eras—both of which experienced problems in terms of recognizing and working with the community. The seeds of community policing and problem solving were sown in London in 1829 when, as stated in Chapter 4, Sir Robert Peel offered that "the police are the public and . . . the public are the police," and that by establishing patrol beats, officers could get to know citizens and thus be better able to gather information about neighborhood crime and disorder. As you saw in Chapter 5, however, in the United States that close police-public association over time often led to powerful political influences and corruption in terms of who was hired, who was promoted, and who could bring elected officials the most votes. This led to the onset of the reform era in the 1930s. Reforms included the removal of police from the influence of the community and politics through the creation of civil service systems. The community era of policing recognized that the public has a vested interest in addressing—as well as vital information concerning—neighborhood crime and disorder, and thus a return to Peel's principles was needed, and the two entities should work hand in glove to resolve problems.

Community policing and problem solving: a proactive management philosophy that involves police-community collaboration and a four-step process (scanning, analyzing, response, and assessment) to focus police activities and thus enable officers to respond more effectively to crime and disorder with arrests or other appropriate actions.

Problem-oriented policing, which began to develop in the mid-1980s, was grounded in principles different from, but complementary to, those of community-oriented policing. Problem-oriented policing is a strategy that puts the community policing philosophy into practice. It advocates that police examine the underlying causes of recurring incidents of crime and disorder. The problem-solving process helps officers identify problems, analyze them completely, develop response strategies, and assess the results. Police must be equipped to define more clearly and to understand more fully the problems they are expected to handle. They must recognize the relationships between and among incidents—for example, incidents involving the same behavior, the same address, or the same people. The police must therefore develop a commitment to analyzing problems—gathering information from police files, the minds of experienced officers, other agencies of government, and private sources as well. It can also require conducting house-to-house surveys and talking with victims, complainants, and offenders. It includes an uninhibited search for the most effective response to each problem, looking beyond just the criminal justice system to a wide range of alternatives; in sum, police must try to design a customized response that holds the greatest potential for dealing effectively with a specific problem in a specific place under specific conditions.

Thousands of police agencies have thus broken away from their reactive, incident-driven methods that characterized the reform era—where police would race from call to call, take an offense report, and leave the scene without seeking any resolution to problems or achieving any long-term benefits. This change in philosophy and strategies goes far beyond merely creating a "crime prevention specialist" position, a "community relations unit," a foot or bicycle patrol, or a neighborhood mini-station.

Finally, as mentioned in Chapter 3, what every criminal justice employee knows is that three elements must exist in order for a crime to occur: an offender, a victim, and a location, as shown in Figure 6.4. The problem analysis triangle helps officers visualize the problem and understand the relationships among these three elements. Additionally, it helps officers analyze problems, it suggests where more information is needed, and it assists with crime control and prevention. Simply put, if there is a victim and he or she is in a place where crimes occur but there is no offender, no crime occurs. If there is an offender and he or she is in a place where crimes occur but there is nothing or no one to be victimized, then no crime will occur. If an offender and a victim are not in the same place, there will be no crime. Part of the analysis phase involves finding out as much as possible about the victims, offenders, and locations where problems exist in order to understand what is prompting the problem and what can be done about it.

Evidence-Based Policing for Proactive Patrol

Noted police researcher Lawrence Sherman of Cambridge University (and former research director of the Police Foundation) once began a scholarly monograph by stating, "Of all the ideas in policing, one stands out as the most powerful force for change: police practices should be based on scientific evidence about what works best."[36]

Several analogies can be drawn from the field of medicine, where, for many decades, use of the simple tourniquet[37] and doctors washing their hands prior to delivering babies[38] were generally disregarded as unimportant or even dangerous; however, once rigorous evaluations of these practices were conducted, they became standard procedures for saving lives.

Figure 6.4 /// Problem Analysis Triangle

Source: *Theory for Practice in Situational Crime Prevention*, edited by Martha J. Smith and Derek B. Cornish. Copyright © 2003 by Lynne Rienner Publishers, Inc. Used with permission of the publisher.

A relatively new concept known as evidence-based policing pushes patrol in this direction and holds important implications for the field. This approach and tactical decision-making process emphasizes statistical analysis, empirical research, and controlled field experiments (i.e., in this context, *evidence* refers to scientific research, not investigative forms of evidence). Evidence-based policing has its roots in problem-oriented and community-oriented policing and is grounded in the notions that policies and practices should be supported by evidence and analytics, and that research should not be ignored.[39]

Evidence-based policing: an approach and tactical decision-making process that emphasizes statistical analysis, empirical research, and controlled field experiments.

In practice, then, what are some activities officers can perform while on patrol to be more evidence based and effective? First, officers should determine where in their beats or sectors crimes are concentrated (known as hot spots) and then patrol them more heavily when not answering calls for service. Also, while answering calls for service, officers can use crime prevention principles: Does this crime give you any clues about whether a similar crime will occur here in the future? Can this event give you a clue about the deeper problems at this place? Can this victim or witness give you any further information about crime in the area, besides just information about the crime at hand?

It is also important to engage with the public while patrolling a hot spot. Officers can leave their vehicles, approach people in the street, talk to residents and business owners, and show good visibility. They can also increase visibility by parking in high crime neighborhoods to write reports, talk to crime analysts, use their computer-aided dispatch, look at crime maps, or other use such systems to identify problem locations. Crime prevention through environmental design (CPTED) principles can be used to address specific problems (such as making proper requests to install more lighting in a dark alley where crimes are rife). Finding out "what works" in other jurisdictions in addressing certain problems will also help to determine how to be more proactive, tailored, focused, or place based with the officer's own crime problems.[40]

THE WORK OF FORENSICS AND DETECTIVES

Policies concerning time on the job, qualifications (knowledge, skills, abilities), and testing/interviewing will vary from agency to agency, but at some point the police officer may wish to be laterally assigned to a detective assignment (or to SWAT, K-9, gangs, drugs, motorcycle/bicycle patrol, or other specialty assignments). Aside from the status that a detective assignment might bring, it also often carries a raise in salary, a civilian clothing allowance, on-call pay, day-shift work, the ability to generally manage one's own time and activities (as opposed to being closely supervised), and other perquisites. But not everyone is destined to be good in this role because, as will be seen in the next section, the successful investigator must possess several personal attributes.[41]

The challenges involved with investigating crimes may well be characterized by a quote from Ludwig Wittgenstein: "How hard I find it to see what is right in front of my eyes!"[42] The art of sleuthing has long fascinated the American public, and news reports on the expanding uses of DNA and television series such as *CSI: Crime Scene Investigation* have done much to capture the public's fascination with criminal investigation and forensic science in the 21st century. This interest in "sleuthing" is not a recent phenomenon. For decades, Americans have feasted on the exploits of dozens of fictional masterminds, like Sherlock Holmes, Agatha Christie's Hercule Poirot and Miss Marple, Clint Eastwood's portrayal of Detective "Dirty Harry" Callahan, and Peter Falk's Columbo, to name a few.

As discussed in the sections that follow, in reality, investigative work is largely misunderstood, often boring, and generally overrated; it results in arrests only a fraction of the time, and it relies strongly on the assistance of witnesses and even some luck.

Attributes of Detectives

Detective/criminal investigator: a police officer who is assigned to investigate reported crimes, to include gathering evidence, completing case reports, testifying in court, and so on.

To begin to understand the role of detectives/criminal investigators, one must first understand that these individuals typically begin their careers as police officers before being promoted to detective. In other words, unless hired by a state or federal agency, such as a state bureau of investigation or the Federal Bureau of Investigation and specifically to be trained as an investigator, one must go through the traditional hurdle process outlined previously and be hired as a patrol officer. Then, having distinguishing himself or herself in that role and (as is commonly done) having worked for a specified number of years and obtained enough experience, one may then test and interview for "the gold badge." To be effective, detectives must also be trained in general areas such as the laws of arrest, search, and seizure; investigative principles and practices (to include forensics and criminalistics); judicial proceedings; and oral and written communications. More specialized training will often be required if individuals are specializing in areas such as sex crimes, family crimes, homicide investigation, and gang and drug enforcement.

In sum, to be successful, the investigator must possess four personal attributes to enhance the detection of crime: an unusual capability for observation and recall; extensive knowledge of the law, rules of evidence, scientific aids, and laboratory services; power of imagination; and a working knowledge of social psychology.[43]

Forensic Science and Criminalistics: Defining the Terms

Forensic science: the study of causes of crimes, deaths, and crime scenes.

The terms *forensic science* and *criminalistics* are often used interchangeably. Forensic science is the broader term; it is that part of science used to answer legal questions. It is the examination, evaluation, and explanation of physical evidence in law. Forensic science encompasses pathology, toxicology, physical anthropology, odontology (development of dental structure and dental diseases), psychiatry, questioned documents, ballistics, tool work comparison, and serology (the reactions and properties of serums), among other fields.[44]

Criminalistics: the interdisciplinary study of physical evidence related to crime; drawing on mathematics, physics, chemistry, biology, anthropology, and many other scientific fields.

Criminalistics is one branch of forensic science; it deals with the study of physical evidence related to crime. From such a study, a crime may be reconstructed. Criminalistics is interdisciplinary, drawing on mathematics, physics, chemistry, biology, anthropology, and many other scientific fields.[45] Basically, the analysis of physical evidence is concerned with identifying traces of evidence, reconstructing criminal acts, and establishing a common origin of samples of evidence. The types of information that physical evidence can provide are as follows:[46]

- Information on the *corpus delicti* (or "body of the crime") is physical evidence showing that a crime was committed, such as tool marks, a broken door or window, a ransacked home, and missing valuables in a burglary, or a victim's blood, a weapon, and torn clothing in an assault.

- Information on the *modus operandi* (or method of operation) is physical evidence showing means used by the criminal to gain entry, tools that were used, types of items taken, and other signs—items left at the scene, an accelerant used at an arson scene, the way crimes are committed, and so forth.

- *Linking a suspect with a victim* is one of the most important linkages, particularly with violent crimes. It includes hair, blood, clothing fibers, and cosmetics that may be transferred from victim to perpetrator. Items found in a suspect's possession can also be linked to a victim.

- *Linking a person to a crime scene* is also a common and significant linkage. It includes fingerprints, glove prints, blood, semen, hairs, fibers, soil, bullets, cartridge cases, tool marks, footprints or shoeprints, tire tracks, and objects that belonged to the criminal. Stolen property is the most obvious example.

- In terms of *disproving or supporting a witness's testimony,* evidence can indicate whether or not a person's version of events is true. An example is a driver whose car matches the description of a hit-and-run vehicle. If blood is found on the underside of the car and the driver claims that he hit a dog, tests on the blood can determine whether the blood is from an animal or from a human.
- One of the best forms of evidence for *identification of a suspect* is DNA evidence, which proves "individualization." It can prove, without a doubt, that the person whose DNA was found was at the crime scene (discussed later in this chapter).

Forensic scientists examine of all kinds of articles and substances in their search for physical evidence that will link persons to their crimes.

Locard's exchange principle: the notion that offenders both leave something at the crime scene and take something from it; the crime scene analyst or investigator's job is to locate that evidence and use it in the investigation.

Investigative Stages and Activities

Detectives operate under an age-old theory that there is no such thing as a perfect crime; criminals either leave a bit of themselves or take something away from the crime scene. This is termed **Locard's exchange principle**, which asserts that when any person comes into contact with an object or another person, a cross-transfer of evidence—in the form of fingerprints, hairs, fibers, and all manner of residue or other materials—will occur.[47] An example is when a victim is strangled to death (by an assailant who is not wearing gloves); the suspect may well have the victim's skin cells under his nails, the victim's hair on his clothing, and other such residual material on his person.[48]

Cases not solved in the initial phase of the apprehension process are assigned either to an investigative specialist or, in smaller police agencies, to an experienced uniformed officer who functions as a part-time investigator.

Following are brief descriptions of the basic investigative stages:[49]

- *The preliminary investigation:* Duties include establishing whether a crime has been committed; securing from any witnesses a description of the perpetrator and his or her vehicle; locating and interviewing the victim and all witnesses; protecting the crime scene (and searching for and collecting all items of possible physical evidence); determining how the crime was committed and what the resulting injuries were, as well as the nature of property taken; recording in field notes and sketches all data about the crime; and arranging for photographs of the crime scene.

- *The continuing investigation:* This stage includes follow-up interviews; developing a theory of the crime; analyzing the significance of information and evidence; continuing the search for witnesses; beginning to contact crime lab technicians and assessing their analyses of the evidence; conducting surveillances, interrogations, and polygraph tests, as appropriate; and preparing the case for the prosecutor.

- *Reconstructing the crime:* At this stage, the investigator seeks a rational theory of the crime. Most often, inductive reasoning is used: The collected information and evidence are analyzed carefully to develop a theory. One of the major traits of criminals is vanity; their belief in their own cleverness, not chance, is the key factor in their leaving a vital clue. Investigators look for mistakes.

- *Focusing the investigation:* When this stage is reached, all investigative efforts are directed toward proving that one suspect (perhaps with accomplices) is guilty of the crime. This decision is based on the investigator's analysis of the relationships among the crime, the investigation, and the habits and attitudes of the suspect.

A Word About Crime Scenes

Crime scene: any location where a crime occurred and that may contain forensic evidence relating to and supporting a criminal investigation.

On the subject of the **crime scene**, we will not go into detail concerning the roles of patrol officers, crime-scene technicians, and investigators; however, it should be emphasized that the protection of the crime scene and all evidence contained therein is of utmost importance for these personnel if the scene is to be properly preserved and evidence properly collected and analyzed. It is critical that at the moment they arrive, responding personnel are trained to (1) describe vehicles (make, model, color, condition, license plate number) and individuals (height, weight, race, age, clothing, sex, distinguishing features), including their direction of travel from first observation; (2) assess the scene for officer safety (downed power lines, animals, biohazards, chemicals, weapons); (3) watch for violent

Practitioner's Perspective

Crime Scene Investigator

Name: Angela Benford
Position: Crime Scene Investigator
Location: Aurora, Colorado

What is your career story? I started as an Explorer with the Arapahoe County Sheriff's Department, which is a program for the Boy Scouts. I started there at 15. There, I got to work with police officers and the Crime Prevention Unit and the crime lab, and I was exposed to all of the different criminal justice programs. When I started that, I was going to be a police officer, so I went to college and majored in criminal justice. But then, I took the science class that they have designed for the criminal justice students, Intro to Criminalistics, and I got hooked. We had a person come in and talk to us about blood spatter interpretation, and we did shoe print castings. And I decided that's what I wanted to do. So I added another major and took a bunch of chemistry and double majored in criminal justice and chemistry.

What are some challenges and misconceptions you face in this position? Some of the biggest myths are perpetuated by the media, with TV shows like *CSI* and *NCIS*, and others on reality TV. In these shows, if you're a crime scene investigator, you show up on the scene, you collect all the evidence, you process all the evidence, and you arrest the suspect. But in reality, there are multiple jobs for each of those actions. The crime scene investigators are the ones that go out to the scenes and document the evidence. Then we bring it back to a lab specialist, and depending on what type of evidence it is, it could go to a latent print examiner or a question document examiner, so there are multiple jobs in that. And then it's a detective's job to go out and interview suspects and arrest them. In some police departments the roles are more merged, but the larger the police department, the more individuated the roles are.

What directions do you envision your department going in the future? What I see changing in the future of crime scene investigation is that technology is going to keep growing and growing. Already we have a 3-D scanner that we take out to a scene, and it documents the measurements and takes photographs, and we can then create a model of the scene back at the lab. These technologies are going to get even better. To the point where you might be a jury member in court and they bring in a computer, and you can walk through the crime scene as they're talking about it.

To learn more about Angela Benford's experiences as a crime scene investigator, watch the Practitioner's Perspective video in SAGE vantage.

persons and attend to any emergency medical needs; and (4) prevent any unauthorized persons from entering the scene. A good resource for crime-scene investigation, published by the National Institute of Justice, is titled *Crime Scene Investigation: A Reference for Law Enforcement Training*.[50]

Uses of Informants and Interrogations

No discussion of police involvement in criminal investigations would be complete without consideration of police use of informants as well as interrogations, both of which occupy a central role in this arena. Sometimes common citizens act as informants concerning crime and disorder (which is the lifeblood of community policing and problem solving, discussed earlier), contacting the police to report suspicious or criminal activity—perhaps when observing suspicious people coming and going at all hours and in high volume at a house in their neighborhood. A more controversial use of informants occurs when the person providing information is a criminal himself or herself. The police must often rely heavily on such persons to obtain information about crimes, arrest offenders, and obtain probable cause for arrest and search warrants. Prosecutors also must become involved with such persons; in exchange for providing information, the informant expects some benefits from the state in return, such as monetary payments, immunity from prosecution, sentence reductions, dropped charges, and even the freedom to continue criminal activity. This situation becomes problematic when such informants engage in outright lying or exaggeration, which can contribute significantly to wrongful convictions; therefore, controversy has developed over time concerning the use of confidential informants, with their testimony often challenged in court.[51]

Informant: a person who covertly provides information about criminal activity to police, with some expectation of benefit in exchange—money, dropped or reduced charges, and so on. However, because such persons are often criminals themselves, their credibility and use are often questioned.

Prior to discussing the use of interrogations, it is first necessary to explain how they differ from police interviews. An interview involves merely questioning an individual in order to obtain superficial information; for example, a field interview by a patrol officer would include obtaining an individual's name, address, place of employment, and so on. These questions might be said to be *inquisitory*.

Interrogations, by contrast, are more purposeful—even accusatory—focusing on a specific crime and thus involving the formal questioning of a suspect in order to obtain incriminating information and/or a confession. Accordingly, persons being interrogated may well be reluctant, uncooperative, and even hostile toward such questioning—and may warrant being given the *Miranda* warning, discussed in Chapter 8.

Interrogation: in criminal law, the process whereby police question a person who is suspected of having knowledge of or having committed a crime; it typically involves informing the suspect of his or her rights under *Miranda*.

Experienced investigators often adhere to the following "articles of faith" during interrogations: Take your time; keep a written record of information gleaned; avoid asking yes/no questions; and observe any changes in the suspect's behavior and visual cues (e.g., lack of eye contact, foot or finger tapping, short breaths, tightly clenched or wringing hands, clearing of the throat, fidgeting in the chair).[52]

As with the discussion of crime scenes, this description is very simplistic. Any serious—and successful—attempt at interrogating suspects must typically involve considerable training and experience.

The Cyberthief Has Come: Be Prepared

If Americans weren't afraid of the cybercriminal element before now, they should be. This nation has witnessed a sea change in how criminals use technology to invent new types of crimes and to commit traditional ones. Attempting to pull off a bank robbery in front of dozens of cameras and security guards is "old school" for even moderately intelligent criminals, who can now act in the privacy of their homes with the click of a mouse. The police need to make significant changes in order to detect, investigate, and solve these cybercrimes, but most agencies have yet to begin this process.

Investigating Further

How "Cyber Detectives" Work

In early 2017, an 18-year-old woman was found dead in her Portland, Oregon, apartment from an overdose of a synthetic opioid. At the scene, detectives found indications that the drug had been shipped through the mail, an envelope with a fictitious return address, and a distinctive brand of pregnancy kit that was sold only at one retail outlet and was likely used to conceal the drugs during shipment. They also found a notepad with an alphanumeric code. Turning to a federal agent who was regarded as an expert in dark web marketplaces, they learned that the code was the dead girl's encryption program key designed to increase the security of email communications on the web. Using the key, detectives determined that she had purchased the opioid five days before her death on a marketplace known as AlphaBay. Detectives then purchased the drug from the site, which arrived wrapped in the same pregnancy kit with the same shipping labels found in the apartment; the labels originated from an online company that accepted only Bitcoin digital currency and was tied to two email addresses. Detectives then subpoenaed all records connected to those email addresses, which led them to a person of interest—who they learned was in a relationship with a woman who worked in the same store that sold many units of the pregnancy kits. After surveillance of the couple revealed their shipping large numbers of parcels, they were arrested on drug charges in two states but were suspected of being connected to more than a dozen drug overdose deaths across the United States. This case illustrates the important role that technologies and training can play in investigations.

Some agencies have turned to civilian specialists for these functions, where expertise is best found outside the agency. They would all do well to follow the advice of Jim Collins, author of a popular book entitled *Good to Great*, who said that the leader's role is to get the right people on the bus (and the wrong people off the bus) and then figure out where to drive it.

Sources: Adapted from Police Executive Research Forum, *The Changing Nature of Crime and Criminal Investigations*, January 2018, p. 48, https://www.policeforum.org/assets/ChangingNatureofCrime.pdf; Jim Collins, *Good to Great: Why Some Companies Make the Leap . . . And Others Don't* (New York: HarperCollins, 2001), p. 41.

Drug overdoses and fatalities, such as those involving fentanyl (discussed in Chapter 16), are often the result of traffickers ordering their drugs on the Internet and then dispersing them via the U.S. mail. The use of ransomware, a type of online attack that blocks victims' access to their computers until they pay a ransom, has become a billion-dollar-a-year enterprise. Even some police agencies have been hacked and forced to pay a ransom. Electronic chips in cars have made it difficult for thieves to start the engine and steal a vehicle, so instead they use a key-fob jamming device that tricks the car owner into thinking the car is locked when it is not. Once inside the vehicle, the thief can likely access registration and insurance information and perhaps more personal information that can be used for identity theft.

Small devices are inserted into ATMs and gas pumps to skim credit card and debit card information, and "sextortion" has taken on a life of its own, with offenders coercing or blackmailing victims into providing sexually explicit images of themselves (often with a threat to post embarrassing information about them if they do not). Harassment, stalking, and child exploitation also occur on the Internet. The so-called dark web (a largely hidden part of the Internet that is encrypted, untraceable, and anonymous) provides hackers with a means to engage in these activities as well as a marketplace through which to buy and sell an array of illegal goods.

All of these methods leave no doubt that criminal investigations must be retooled so that detectives can quickly secure and access smartphones and other communications devices; review social media of victims, suspects, and acquaintances; review area camera feeds and gunshot detection systems; know how to "crack" into virtual assistants (e.g., Amazon's Alexa) and other such devices; and develop expertise in working with the dark web.

You Be the . . .

Detective

As the coach opened the door to the locker room, the only light that shone was from the players' large shower area. Upon flipping the light switch, he saw the body of his once-"ace" pitcher, Hines, lying on the floor in the shower. In his pale left hand he held a gun. There was a bullet wound in his left temple. Under his tanned right hand was a note saying, "My pitching days are gone, my debts and humiliation more than I can bear. Sorry." His nearby locker contained a half-empty bottle of beer, his uniform, an uneaten stadium hot dog, a picture of his two children, and his Acme-brand ball glove with "RH" stamped in the webbing. Wet footprints were observed walking in and out of the shower. Upon surveying the scene, the responding detective said, "I do not believe this was a suicide."

1. Was this a suicide or a murder?
2. What fact(s) led you to this conclusion?

A Major Challenge Today: People Getting Away With Murder

There was a time, several decades ago, when the odds of solving ("clearing" in police parlance) a murder by an arrest or other means was more than 90 percent. That was because murder was generally a crime of passion and committed by a relative or close acquaintance, so it really wasn't too challenging to learn who had motive and opportunity. Now, although there is little research on clearance rates,[53] we know that the nature of murder has changed, with the advent of anonymous, drive-by shootings and other gang activities, growing distrust of the police (particularly in the inner cities), and witnesses who are too afraid to talk to police. All of this amounts to today's national murder clearance rate of about 60 percent.[54]

Clearance rate: the percentage of crimes that either resulted in an arrest or were cleared by some other means.

DNA: deoxyribonucleic acid, which is found in all cells; used in forensics to match evidence (hair, semen) left at a crime scene with a particular perpetrator.

This problem is especially acute in larger U.S. cities such as Chicago, which has been clearing only about one-fourth of its murders and has had to confront fear, politics, no-snitching mentality, gangs, diminishing resources for police, and discontent with policing in minority communities. Similar situations exist in Baltimore and New Orleans. Memphis, Tennessee, which used to see a 99 percent clearance rate, recently saw a rate as low as 38 percent.[55] Weekends bring multiple murders and many wounded, and few arrests. And, when murders are not solved and killers are left to roam the streets, the problem is only made worse.

Today, the power of what can be done with DNA, as well as its variety of uses, is incredible.

Using DNA Analysis

As discussed later in this chapter, today DNA is the most sophisticated and reliable type of physical evidence (see Figure 6.5). Police are now able to submit to laboratories evidence that until recently was not even possible to examine. For example, "touch" DNA evidence

Figure 6.5 /// What Is DNA?

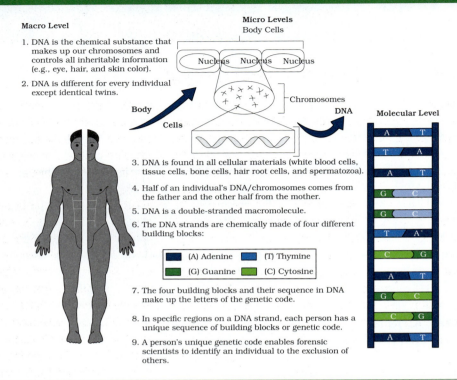

can now be examined and requires very small amounts of skin cells left on an object after it has been touched or handled; it can be used to determine whether a defendant merely touched a weapon or whose hand threw drugs to the floor of a room.[56]

A testimonial to DNA's promise in investigations is offered by a former supervising criminalist of the Los Angeles County Sheriff's Department:

> The power of what we can look for and analyze now is incredible. It's like magic. Every day we discover evidence where we never thought it would be. You almost can't do anything without leaving some DNA around. DNA takes longer than fingerprints to analyze, but you get a really big bang for your buck.[57]

Furthermore, DNA has allowed investigative personnel to exonerate people who were convicted in the past for crimes they did not commit. Indeed, the National Registry of Exonerations at the University of Michigan Law School lists more than 2,400 exonerations since 1989 with the help of DNA evidence.[58]

Also see the accompanying "Investigating Further" feature concerning how DNA is used to solve cold cases. These are cases selected for investigation that are usually at least a year old and cannot be addressed by the original investigative personnel because of workload, time constraints, or the lack of viable leads. Cases are prioritized on the basis of the likelihood of an eventual solution, with the highest priority cases being those in which there is an identified homicide victim, suspects were previously named or identified through forensic methods, an arrest warrant was previously issued, significant physical evidence can be reprocessed, newly documented leads have arisen, and critical witnesses are available and willing to cooperate.

Cold case: no standard time-related definition of a "cold case" exists regarding when an investigation goes "cold"; rather, it is generally the point when all viable leads in an investigation have been exhausted and detectives cease their investigative efforts—to be reopened if further information or evidence becomes available.

Investigating Further

A Cold Case Involving "The Boston Strangler"

A serial murderer was loose in the city of Boston and its suburbs during the early 1960s. All 13 victims were women ranging in age from 19 to 85; often they were found alone, strangled with their own nylon stockings, and sexually assaulted. Detectives had few solid leads, but in 1964 one Albert DeSalvo—a Massachusetts man with a long history of breaking and entering—was arrested and eventually sentenced to life in prison after being linked to numerous other sexual assaults throughout New England. While in custody for those offenses, DeSalvo confessed to the Boston Strangler murders. DeSalvo never went to trial for the murders, however, and he was killed in 1973 by a fellow inmate while serving his sentence for sexual assault. Despite his confession, uncertainty lingered in terms of whether DeSalvo was actually the Boston Strangler because of inconsistencies with his statements, psychiatric examinations suggesting that he was not being truthful, and the lack of physical evidence connecting him to the crime scenes. Furthermore, many of the details he gave about the murders could have been obtained from their related press coverage. Indeed, the true identity of the Boston Strangler remained unknown for nearly a half century, while the murders inspired books, movies, and numerous documentaries.

In 2012, the Boston Police Department revisited the Strangler murders as a cold case. Scientists were able to match DNA provided from Albert DeSalvo's nephew to seminal fluid that was collected at the scene of the Strangler's last murder. Given that the test was unable to identify a specific individual, investigators now had enough evidence, however, to exhume DeSalvo's body for a more thorough examination. It was subsequently determined that DNA from DeSalvo's teeth and bones were a match to the seminal fluid gathered at the scene of the murder. Therefore, nearly 50 years after the discovery of the final victim, the evidence was conclusive: Albert DeSalvo was indeed the Boston Strangler.

Sources: Jack Thomas, "Victims of the Boston Strangler," *Boston Globe*, June 13, 2002, https://www.bostonglobe.com/metro/2013/07/11/victims-boston-strangler/CwbsZlSNcfwmhSetpqNlhL/story.html; "He's Not the Boston Strangler. He Didn't Kill My Aunt," *Guardian*, September 21, 2000, http://www.theguardian.com/g2/story/0,3604,371006,00.html; Philip Bulman, "Solving Cold Cases With DNA: The Boston Strangler Case," *NIJ Journal* 273 (2014): 48–51, http://www.nij.gov/journals/273/Pages/boston-strangler.aspx. For further information concerning this and other such cases, see Eric W. Hickey, *Serial Murderers and Their Victims*, 5th ed. (Belmont, Calif.: Wadsworth, Cengage Learning).

/// IN A NUTSHELL

- The idea of a police subculture was first proposed in 1950 by William Westley, who found a high degree of secrecy and violence.

- Recruit academy training covers a variety of subjects; neophyte officers learn how to use lethal and less lethal weapons, and how to deal with criminal suspects, offenders, victims, and witnesses; hands-on training and simulated situations are also employed.

- Studies show that higher education is important for police officers, in order to interact with an educated public, enforce the rule of law, investigate crimes, testify in court, write cogent and accurate reports, and perform myriad other duties. From 1967 to 1986, every national commission that studied crime, violence, and police in America maintained that a college education could help the police to do their jobs better.

- After leaving the academy, new officers are assigned to a veteran officer—a field training officer—for initial field instruction and observation; this phase of training helps recruits make the transition from the academy to the streets under the protective arm of a veteran officer, while on probationary status.

- Jerome Skolnick said officers develop a working personality, and that the police role contains two important variables: danger and authority. Consequently, they develop a "perceptual shorthand" to identify certain kinds of people as "symbolic assailants"—those who pose a physical threat to them.

- Police have four basic tasks: enforcing the laws, performing welfare tasks, preventing crimes, and protecting the innocent.
- James Q. Wilson maintained that there are three distinctive policing styles: the watchman style, the legalistic style, and the service style.
- Although workers in several other occupations die at much higher rates than those in policing, this occupation still has many occupational hazards.
- There are several stressors for police, both within and outside of their employing agency. It is important that officers take appropriate measures to reduce or eliminate stress.
- Full enforcement of the laws by police is a myth; they typically have considerable discretion in whether or not to arrest someone. Determining factors include the law (e.g., some ordinances mandate arrest for certain offenses, such as domestic violence), the officer's attitude (concerning the law that is violated, as well as toward the offender), and the citizen's attitude toward the officer.
- Today, under the community-policing philosophy, officers are trained to examine the underlying causes of problems in the neighborhoods on their beats and to involve citizens in the long-term resolution of neighborhood problems.
- The fields of forensic science and criminalistics are the most rapidly developing areas in policing—and probably in all of criminal justice.
- There are a number of key factors in how police officers and detectives must treat crime scenes and conduct suspect interrogations.
- DNA is the most sophisticated and reliable type of physical evidence, used to obtain convictions in hundreds of cases as well as to exonerate many arrestees. It has also been used to solve dozens of cold cases.
- It is imperative that criminal investigators become trained—or that agencies hire specially trained civilians—for the task of investigating increasingly more complicated cybercrimes. They must also do whatever is possible to increase clearance rates for murders.
- DNA continues to have tremendous value in solving cold cases.

/// KEY TERMS & CONCEPTS

Review key terms with eFlashcards at **edge.sagepub.com/peak4e**.

Academy training   133
Clearance rate   151
Cold case   152
Community policing and problem solving   143
Crime scene   148
Criminalistics   146
Detective/criminal investigator   146
DNA   151
Evidence-based policing   145
Field training officer (FTO)   134
Forensic science   146
Higher education (for police)   132
Informant   149
Interrogation   149
Kansas City Preventive Patrol Experiment   137
Locard's exchange principle   147
Policing role   135
Policing styles   136
Sixth sense   133
Stress   138
Tasks of policing (four basic)   136

/// REVIEW QUESTIONS

Test your understanding of chapter content at **edge.sagepub.com/peak4e**.

1. What ideal traits are sought among those persons wishing to enter policing?
2. How are police recruits socialized into the police subculture while in academy training, and what are some topics that trainees study while attending the academy?
3. What are the methods and purposes of the FTO concept?
4. What is meant by the working personality, how was the concept developed, and how does it function?
5. What are the four basic tasks of the police?
6. What are the primary styles of policing?
7. What are the primary causes of stress among police officers?
8. What examples can you provide of police use of discretion? What are some pros and cons of police use of discretionary authority?
9. How should a crime scene be handled, and why?
10. What primary difference is there between a detective's interviewing and interrogating someone, and what are some tips for how the latter should be performed?

11. What is a cold case, and what criteria are used to treat a criminal case as such?

12. What are the attributes, myths, and methods that tend to revolve around investigative personnel?

13. What successes do today's criminal investigators seem to be having with cybercrime investigations? Cold cases? Murder investigations?

/// LEARN BY DOING

1. You are a patrol sergeant lecturing to your agency's Citizens' Police Academy about the patrol function. Someone asks, "Sergeant, your officers obviously can't enforce all of the laws all of the time. Which laws are always enforced, and which ones are not?" How do you respond to her (without saying something absurd like "We enforce all of the laws, all of the time," which of course would be untrue)? How would you fully explain police discretion to the group?

2. You have been assigned to develop an examination for persons seeking a detective assignment in your agency. What will be the content of your exam? (For guidance, you may wish to begin by reviewing the study guide for the investigator's exam used by the Los Angeles County District Attorney's Office, Examination Unit, at http://da.co.la.ca.us/sites/default/files/invstudyguide.pdf.)

3. For a practical view of "what works" in terms of addressing all kinds of criminal matters, visit the website of the Center for Problem-Oriented Policing at http://www.popcenter.org/problems/. The center has published more than 70 POP guides, which summarize how a variety of problems of crime and disorder can be examined and addressed.

/// STUDY SITE

Get the tools you need to sharpen your study skills. SAGE edge offers a robust online environment featuring an impressive array of free tools and resources.

Access practice quizzes, eFlashcards, video, and multimedia at **edge.sagepub.com/peak4e**.

CHAPTER 7

POLICING METHODS AND CHALLENGES
Issues of Force, Liability, and Technologies

Paramount among the policies of law enforcement organizations are those controlling use of force.

—The President's Task Force on 21st Century Policing, 2015

LEARNING OBJECTIVES

As a result of reading this chapter, you will be able to

1. Describe the test used for determining whether police use of force was reasonable or unreasonable

2. Assess police use of force in terms of the current state of police-community (particularly minority group) relations resulting from a number of widely publicized, fatal police shootings and the Black Lives Matter and Blue Lives Matter movements

3. Define constitutional policing, legitimacy, procedural justice, and consent decrees as they apply to police efforts to bring harmony to their whole approach—and to achieve a "guardian" rather than "soldier" mindset

4. Review what is meant by the term *police brutality* and, in that connection, the current status of officers' body-worn cameras

5. Explain civil liability, the types of police actions (or inaction) that are vulnerable to lawsuits and how police officers—including their supervisors—might be held criminally liable for their misconduct

6. Delineate several types of technologies that are assisting police in their duties but that might also raise privacy and use concerns

ASSESS YOUR AWARENESS

Check your current knowledge of police methods and challenges by responding to the following eight true-false items; check your answers after reading this chapter.

1. Recent deaths involving police and minority citizens in the United States, and the ensuing unrest, demonstrate that the public wants less police militarization and more body-worn cameras to be employed.

2. Police behavior can be described as "brutal" in only one way: when they use physical violence toward a citizen.

3. Constitutional policing, legitimacy, and procedural justice should form the foundation of policing, rather than police having a "soldier" mindset.

4. Several studies have shown that hiring women and minorities as police officers is, practically speaking, a futile effort, as they are less effective in this type of work.

5. Although the police can be sued, the fear of civil liability is of minor concern to those who administer or perform police work.

6. Currently the only legal means of being compensated when police violate someone's rights is to take the matter to a criminal trial.

7. The decision by a police officer to pursue a citizen in a motor vehicle is among the most critical that can be made.

8. Because of its widespread, long-standing use by police, software that provides facial recognition and the ability to detect texting while driving may be used without concern for legal or privacy issues.

<< Answers can be found on page 419.

The March 2018 fatal police shooting in Sacramento, California, of Stephon Clark—a 22-year-old unarmed black man shot eight times, mostly in his back—raised questions about the degree to which he posed a threat to officers at the time he was hit. Within one month of the shooting, California legislators proposed a bill that would limit firearm use by police officers. The bill, the Police Accountability and Community Protection Act (AB 931), was introduced in the state assembly to change the existing guidelines covering police violence from "reasonable force" to "necessary force." This change in statutory language would permit officers to discharge their weapons only when there are no clear alternatives—or, as a member of the assembly put it, to ensure that "the use of deadly force stresses the sanctity of human life and is only used when necessary." In addition to spirited legislative debate, five California police unions quickly opposed the bill, generally arguing that the bill's provisions would have negative effects on officers' safety, carry high cost to redesign training programs, and exacerbate an already persistent hiring problem. Conversely, the bill was endorsed by the American Civil Liberties Union (ACLU), which stated that "[t]he killing of Michael Brown in Ferguson [Missouri, in August 2014], and so many others since, have laid bare this truth: our country's laws protect the police, not the people."[1]

As you read this chapter, consider which side's arguments should prevail, whether or not such laws are needed in all states, and if there are enough limitations (state laws, court decisions, agency policies) on when police may use of deadly force.[2]

INTRODUCTION

This chapter focuses on two topics that are involved in several of the cases discussed in this book: police use of force and civil liability. Few chapters in this textbook discuss matters as grave as these. It concerns concepts that all police practitioners must understand and behaviors they must attempt to demonstrate: possessing a culture of ethical behavior and integrity, and minimizing or eliminating serious police transgressions and other violations of public trust—as well as the results of failing to do so. Police leaders, being responsible for the manner in which their subordinates wield their power and authority, are heavily implicated in these areas. The responsibility for ensuring that subordinates act correctly relative to their position in a lawful and effective manner lies squarely with their leaders.

This chapter begins by looking at how and why many members of society feel betrayed by recent events in which police have used (at times lethal) force, the chasm that exists as a result, and how changes in the police mindset and adoption of different police methods and philosophies (e.g., constitutional policing, procedural justice) are needed to bridge that gap. Also included is a look at measures that already exist to do so, including new databases and the use of consent decrees and body-worn cameras, as well as a discussion of the kinds of inappropriate police behaviors that can lead to civil liability. Continuing with its overall theme of policing methods, the chapter concludes with a brief examination of selected police technologies in terms of concerns about their legal, moral, and practical uses.

USE OF FORCE: A SACRED TRUST

The police must use force at times to protect themselves or others; such force can include verbal directives, empty-hand control (grabs, holds), less lethal means (e.g., chemical sprays, baton, electrical device), and lethal means; the great majority of the time, such force is justified and applied appropriate to the circumstances. The issue that is often raised in a given situation is whether or not the type of force employed was reasonable under the circumstances—considering the severity of the crime, whether the suspect posed a threat, and whether the suspect was resisting or attempting to flee. At the present time, the application of force in a given situation is frequently challenged—and recorded on video.

American society vests a tremendous amount of authority in its police officers. Indeed, the police are the only element of our society (except for military units, under certain circumstances) that is permitted to use force—up to and including that which is lethal in nature—against its citizens. Balancing the scales, however, is the understanding that the police will use this tool judiciously, only when necessary, and as a last resort.

The U.S. Supreme Court ruled that the **use of force** must be

Use of force: the type and amount of effort required to compel compliance by an unwilling suspect.

[o]bjectively reasonable in view of all the facts and circumstances of each particular case, including the severity of the crime at issue, whether the suspect poses an immediate threat to the safety of the officers or others, and whether he is actively resisting arrest or attempting to evade arrest by flight.[3]

However, determining what constitutes "objectively reasonable" is not always an easy task. Perhaps a good "test" (as provided by the Supreme Court in *Graham v. Connor*, 1989) is whether or not an officer's actions were reasonable in light of the facts and circumstances confronting him or her, without regard to the officer's underlying intent or motivation.

Given the unusually high number of police shootings—often involving unarmed minorities—that came to light in the United States beginning in 2014, an unusual measure was taken in late 2014 to examine the potential use-of-force problem: the creation of the President's Task Force on 21st Century Policing. The task force noted that "recent events . . . have exposed rifts in the relationships between local police and the communities they protect and serve." Its mission was to determine "how to foster strong, collaborative relationships between local law enforcement and the communities they protect and to make recommendations to the President on how policing practices can promote effective crime reduction while building public trust."[4]

The sections that follow discuss some of the problems that exist between the police and citizens they serve, as well as some ideas for bridging the rifts in police-community relations.

From Harlem to Ferguson

Britain's Benjamin Disraeli observed more than a century ago, "No man will treat with indifference the principle of race. It is the key of history." That is an excellent viewpoint from which to begin considering police-minority relations in the United States since the country's establishment—and especially since the 1950s.

Even before the race riots and civil unrest of the civil rights movement and Vietnam War began in earnest, James Baldwin, the African American sociologist, was moved to write in 1960 about police in Harlem:

> None of the Police Commissioner's men, even with the best will in the world, have any way of understanding the lives led by the people they swagger about in twos and threes controlling. Their very presence is an insult, and it would be, even if they spent their entire day feeding gumdrops to children.[5]

Indeed, for many minorities, the four words inscribed over the entrance to the U.S. Supreme Court building in Washington, D.C.—Equal Justice Under Law—have long been hollow; for them, justice is perceived as neither equal nor blind. In the aftermath of the 2014 police shooting death of Michael Brown in the city of Ferguson, Missouri, angry protesters raged for a week

Problems of police-minority relations are long-standing in nature. Here, a 17-year-old civil rights demonstrator is attacked by a police dog in Birmingham, Alabama, in May 1963.

as gas and rubber bullets were used, the National Guard was deployed, a police officer was shot, and the U.S. Department of Justice was compelled to issue a scathing report about the widespread racially biased abuses by police, who routinely targeted African Americans for arrests and ticketing. Much controversy also ensued concerning the use of the state's National Guard and military equipment and tactics.

Subsequent police shootings of minorities in other cities fostered many more thousands of demonstrations and "die-ins" across the country (as well as federal lawsuits against some officers' employing agencies). "Black Lives Matter" (discussed below) became their rallying cry, and even new university courses of that nature were launched at the University of Miami School of Law, San Diego University, Dartmouth College, and other institutions of higher education.[6]

Incidents that involve minority group members will often heighten the tension and lead to charges of racism against the entire police agency. One columnist offered that "it is the police culture, more than race . . . that is at the crux of the problem . . . a mentality of brutality."[7] In response to excessive use of force by police, Human Rights Watch stated in a report that

> [p]olice abuse remains one of the most serious and divisive human rights violations in the United States. The excessive use of force by police officers, including unjustified shootings, severe beatings, fatal chokings, and rough treatment, persists because overwhelming barriers to accountability make it possible for officers who commit human rights violations to escape due punishment and often to repeat their offenses.[8]

Human Rights Watch also noted in the report that officers who repeatedly commit human rights violations tend to be a small minority but that they are protected, routinely, by the silence of their fellow officers and by flawed systems of reporting, oversight, and accountability; by the scarcity of meaningful information about trends in abuse; by the lack of data regarding police departments' responses to those incidents; and by the lack of departmental plans or actions to prevent brutality.

Black Lives Matter: a movement that initiated national scrutiny of police shootings after an unarmed black teenager, Michael Brown, was shot by police and died in St. Louis in August 2014.

Blue Lives Matter: a movement formed in New York City after the killings of two officers, to publicize that dozens of police officers are murdered each year and that police work is increasingly dangerous.

Updates on Two Movements: Black Lives Matter and Blue Lives Matter

As a result of the succession of fatal police shootings, two movements have sprung up in an attempt to protect certain groups. First, the previously mentioned Black Lives Matter (BLM) movement initiated national scrutiny of police shootings after an unarmed black teenager, Michael Brown, was killed by police in St. Louis in August 2014. Brown's death led to widespread protests, prompted a White House commission to call for reforms, and galvanized this movement and national attention on police use of deadly force. The BLM movement's website states that its mission is "to build local power and to intervene in violence inflicted on Black communities by the state and vigilantes."[9] BLM maintains an active voice and claims that it has "initiated broader conversation about racism in the U.S.," its "influence on American politics is growing," and it has "popularized civil disobedience and the need to put our bodies on the line."[10]

A response to Black Lives Matter has been the Blue Lives Matter movement by police, which was formed in New York City after the killings of two officers, to publicize that

Black Lives Matter protesters gather in New York City in July 2016, on the second anniversary of the death of Eric Garner, to demand justice for Garner and many other black victims of police brutality in recent years.

160 ■ Part 2: The Police

dozens of police officers are murdered each year and that police work is increasingly dangerous. Indeed, the U.S. Senate and at least 14 states have introduced bills that would classify violent attacks on police as hate crimes (most such bills either have died or are sitting in a legislative committee for review, however).[11]

A Threshold Question: Police as "Guardians" or "Soldiers"?

The contemporary chasm between police and minorities, and many people in society-at-large, often revolves around how the police are now too often being seen as "soldiers" or "warriors." The previously mentioned killings of young African American men and others have caused many people to ask whether or not there exists within the police culture a "warrior mindset." The President's Task Force stated that

> [l]aw enforcement culture should embrace a guardian mindset to build public trust and legitimacy. Toward that end, police and sheriffs' departments should adopt procedural justice [discussed below] as the guiding principle for internal and external policies and practices to guide their interactions with the citizens they serve.[12]

A significant distinction exists between the two roles. Former Shoreline, Washington, police chief Susan Rahr questioned this distinction:

> Why are we training police officers like soldiers? Although police officers wear uniforms and carry weapons, the similarity ends there. The missions and rules of engagement are completely different. The soldier's mission is that of a warrior: to conquer. The rules of engagement are decided before the battle. The police officer's mission is that of a guardian: to protect. The rules of engagement evolve as the incident unfolds. Soldiers must follow orders. Police officers must make independent decisions. Soldiers come into communities as an outside, occupying force. Guardians are members of the community, protecting from within.[13]

Added Boston police commissioner William Evans, "In Boston, we don't train our recruits to be a military force. I want my officers to come out as problem-solvers, not an occupying force." And, as Kansas City, Missouri, chief Terry Zeigler put it, "For a long time, the police academy has been based on a military boot camp type of philosophy. That is missing the point. Policing is mostly about manners and courtesy."[14]

Constitutional policing: policing practices that emphasize the protection of civilians' civil rights and equal protection under the law.

A crowd of protesters faces Alabama state troopers during one of three Selma-to-Montgomery marches in 1965.

Constitutional Policing and Legitimacy

Several of the aforementioned race-related incidents have led to a careful review of police practices and calls for reform. At the heart of this review are the many police leaders who are looking at their agency's culture in a new light—raising questions about disparate treatment with respect to the use of deadly force.

Police chief executives are now becoming much more heavily involved in what is termed constitutional policing—a cornerstone of community policing and problem-solving efforts. When a police agency develops policies and practices that advance the constitutional goals of protecting citizens' rights and provides equal protection under the law, then, as New Haven, Connecticut, police chief Dean Esserman put it, "The Constitution is our boss. We are not warriors, we are guardians. The [police] oath is to the Constitution."[15]

Constitutional policing, then, forms the foundation of community policing. Police agencies cannot form positive and productive relationships with the citizens they serve if those communities do not trust the police or believe that the police see their mission as protecting civil rights as well as public safety. Too often, concerns with constitutional aspects of policing occur only after the fact—when police officials, community members, and the courts look at an officer's actions to determine whether or not laws, ordinances, or agency policies were violated. Now there is a growing recognition among police leaders that constitutional policing should be on the minds of all agency members on an everyday basis.

A related concept is that of **police legitimacy**: the extent to which the community believes that police actions are appropriate, proper, and just, and its willingness to recognize police authority. If the police have a high level of perceived legitimacy, community members tend to be more willing to cooperate with the police and to accept the outcome of their interactions with the police. Public confidence involves the belief that the police are honest, are trying to do their jobs well, and are striving to protect the community against crime and violence. Moreover, legitimacy reflects the willingness of residents to defer to the law and to police authority, that is, their sense of obligation and responsibility to accept police authority. Finally, legitimacy involves the belief that police actions are morally justified and appropriate to the circumstances.[16]

Clearly this relationship with the citizenry is what Sir Robert Peel had in mind when he said, "The police are the public, and the public are the police."

Procedural Justice

Procedural justice and police legitimacy both relate to the creation of a culture of integrity. Adopting procedural justice as the guiding principle for policies and practices can be the underpinning of a change in culture, and should also contribute to building trust and confidence in the community. Succinctly put, **procedural justice** revolves around four central principles or pillars:

- The first pillar of procedural justice is the perception of *fairness to all*. This is not just about outcomes. In determining whether or not their treatment by police was fair, citizens will consider the process by which the officer's decision was made as much as the outcome of a decision. Often, the outcome of an interaction is less important than the interaction itself—whether the involved parties experienced respectful treatment. If, say, a person deems he or she was treated fairly and with respect in receiving a traffic ticket, he or she is much less likely to lodge a complaint against the officer.

- The second pillar concerns *voice*. All people want to be heard and feel as though they have a measure of control over their fate; this helps them feel that their opinions matter and that someone is listening to their side of the story and giving some consideration to their concerns.

- The third pillar, *transparency and openness of process*, means that the processes by which decisions are made do not rely on secrecy or deception. Here, key decisions are made out in the open as much as possible, as opposed to behind closed doors or on a whim. When officers are as transparent as possible, community members are more likely to accept the outcome, even if unfavorable.

- The fourth pillar, *impartiality and unbiased decision making*, means decisions are made based on relevant evidence or data rather than on personal opinion, speculation, or guesswork. People want the facts. When people take the extra few minutes to make apparent to others the data used to make decisions, understanding and acceptance are generally the outcome.[17]

Legitimacy (of police): the extent to which the community believes that police actions are appropriate, proper, and just, and its willingness to recognize police authority.

Procedural justice: a philosophy meaning that the manner in which an individual regards the criminal justice system is tied closely to the perceived fairness of the *process* and how he or she was treated rather than to the perceived fairness of the *outcome*.

You Be the...

Police Officer

Fair, Procedural Policing—or Not?

As you read the following scenario, consider the "guardian versus soldier" distinction as well as the concept of constitutional policing:

> A police officer gave a woman a ticket for making an illegal turn. When the woman protested that there was no sign prohibiting the turn, the officer pointed to one that was bent out of shape, leaning over, and barely visible from the road. Furious and feeling the officer hadn't listened to her, the woman decided to appeal the ticket by going to court. On the day of her hearing, she was anxious to tell her side of the story. However, when she began to speak, the judge (being familiar with the location and the stop sign issue) interrupted her and summarily ruled in her favor, dismissing the case.

How do you believe the woman felt? Vindicated? Victorious? Satisfied? How would the officer feel? Was justice served in this case?

How to Develop Harmony, Justice, and Policy

What is the solution for cities that recently experienced fatal police shootings and severe racial unrest in their aftermath—cities that are vastly different in their demographics but quite similar in attitudes and emotions? If someone had the perfect answer to that question, he or she would probably become very wealthy. Although it takes years if not decades for the many underlying social problems in such communities to reach a boiling point, a priority is to seriously examine these cities' relationships with and understanding of their minority communities. In a community such as Ferguson—where 67 percent of the population but only 5 percent of police officers were African American—and in a nation where many people see discrimination and prejudice when blacks are arrested at nearly three times the rate of people of other races, a good starting point is to diversify the agency, thus giving people a greater sense of representation and voice. As one witness told the President's Task Force concerning youth in poor communities:

> By the time you are 17 you have been stopped and frisked a dozen times. That does not make that 17-year-old want to become a police officer. The challenge is to transform the idea of policing in communities among young people into something they see as honorable. They have to see people at local events, as the person who lives across the street, not someone who comes in and knows nothing about my community.[18]

Other reform ideas include stopping the **militarization of the police** (their aforementioned use of military tactics and equipment); mandating the use of body-worn cameras; having the U.S. Department of Justice investigate such shootings to determine whether any civil rights violations occurred; and implementing training on racial profiling, dehumanization, and stereotyping.

A final note: coming to light in the wake of the aforementioned police shooting deaths of the mid-2010s was the near total lack of data concerning such shootings. Measures were then put in place to initiate a national database tracking such shootings in the United States. The U.S. Senate passed the Death in Custody Reporting Act in December 2014, mandating that all states do so or risk losing millions of dollars in federal grants.[19]

Militarization (of the police): the idea that the increasing use (since 9/11) of military equipment and tactics by the police has made them pattern themselves around and adopt the military model.

Going Global

Police in India

As many problems as there might appear to exist in American police systems, they pale in comparison to the methods and problems of the police in India, where the police have long been known as corrupt, brutal, and in need of reform. According to Human Rights Watch, a lengthy succession of governments has failed to rein in police abuses and compel the police to become more professionalized.

Human rights violations are rampant; indeed, while the country is modernizing rapidly, the police continue to use extralegal methods of abuse and threats. Police routinely employ arbitrary arrest, detention, and torture in order to get confessions, and even murder people who are detained (one even being hanged from a tree inside a police station). People are badly beaten with batons and water boarded, and officers report being ordered to commit such acts or be jailed or fired from their jobs. Receiving little or no encouragement to collect forensic evidence and witness statements, they instead hold suspects illegally and frequently subject them to torture in order to extract a confession.

Human Rights Watch reports that, while not excusing abuses, abysmal conditions for police officers contribute to violations. Officers are required to be on call 24 hours a day, work long hours, and sometimes live in tents or filthy barracks at the police station. Many are separated from their families for long periods of time, and they often lack essential vehicles, mobile phones, and investigative tools. Groups that are most vulnerable include the traditionally marginalized people in India, including the poor, women, Dalits (the so-called untouchables), and religious and sexual minorities. Police often fail to investigate crimes against them because of discrimination, the victims' inability to pay bribes, or their lack of social status or political connections.

A Human Rights Watch spokesperson says India's status as the world's largest democracy is undermined by a police force that thinks it is above the law; Indians thus avoid contact with the police out of fear, leading to crimes going unreported and unpunished.

Sources: See "The Shortcomings of India's Police Are Not Entirely Their Fault," *The Economist*, August 18, 2018, https://www.economist.com/asia/2018/08/18/the-shortcomings-of-indias-police-are-not-entirely-their-fault; also see Human Rights Watch, "India: Overhaul Abusive, Failing Police System," August 4, 2009, https://www.hrw.org/news/2009/08/04/india-overhaul-abusive-failing-police-system; Human Rights Watch, *Broken System Dysfunction, Abuse, and Impunity in the Indian Police*, August 2009, https://www.hrw.org/sites/default/files/reports/india0809web.pdf.

Wielding a "Big Stick": Use of the Consent Decree

How does a police agency that has serious problems involving improper use of force and other inappropriate behaviors alter its entire culture and foster an environment of constitutional policing and legitimacy? One of the ways to foster such meaningful change was made possible by the 1994 Violent Crime Control and Law Enforcement Act, which gave the U.S. Department of Justice Civil Rights Division authority to investigate state and local law enforcement agencies that it believes have unconstitutional policies or engage in unconstitutional patterns or practices of conduct.[20] This law also allows the Department of Justice to sue any police agency if it has exhibited a "pattern and practice" of using excessive force and/or violating people's civil rights. Furthermore, such agencies can be compelled to change those practices through what is known as a consent decree (also known as a memorandum of agreement).[21]

Consent decree: where police officers have violated citizens' civil rights, a tool used by the courts to compel an agency to generally perform within the dictates of the Constitution and make specific reforms.

Dozens of cities have found themselves placed under consent decree by a court and compelled to change in such areas as policies and training, collecting and analyzing data, obtaining the necessary technology to effectively monitor officer behaviors, and even developing community-policing strategies. If unwilling to comply, the agency can be sued by the Department of Justice and possibly even be placed under a receiver who has total control over its operations.[22] In short, consent decrees can provide an essential blueprint for policing constitutionally, providing detailed goals to be met. This is typically accomplished under the watchful eye of an outside federal monitor (usually a team) and a federal judge, in order to measure whether the purposes of the agreement are being achieved.²³

Another Item of Business: More Women and Minorities in Uniform

Another desirable goal for today's police agencies is for them to be represented by more women and minorities. Only about one in eight, or 12 percent, of local (city and county) police officers are female, and one in ten is a first-line supervisor. Obviously, unless and until recruiting and retention efforts are improved and the field is generally made to appear more attractive to women (including having more women in police executive positions to serve as role models), what has long been the status quo is unlikely to change. Members of racial and ethnic groups are more visible in police ranks, however; they represent more than a quarter (27 percent) of full-time local police officers—about 130,000 officers—or an increase of about 150 percent since 1987.²⁴

According to research by the National Center for Women and Policing, female officers

- Are as competent as their male counterparts
- Are less likely than male officers to use excessive force
- Use a less authoritarian style that relies less on physical force—and communication skills that allow them to defuse situations
- Implement community-oriented policing and problem solving, which emphasizes communication and cooperation
- Are more effective in responding to crimes against women than are male officers
- Can help reduce problems of sex discrimination and harassment within their agencies²⁵

One of the challenges facing police agencies today is how to achieve greater representation by female and minority police officers.

Police Brutality

Throughout U.S. history, police agencies have faced allegations of brutality and corruption. In the late 19th century, New York police sergeant Alexander "Clubber" Williams epitomized police brutality, speaking openly of using his nightstick to knock people unconscious, batter them to pieces, or even kill them. Williams openly sought opportunities for graft in an area in downtown New York that was the heart of vice and nightlife, often termed Satan's Circus. This was Williams's beat, where his reputation for using force and brutality became legendary.

Many people contend that there are actually three means by which the police can be "brutal." There is the literal sense of the term, which involves the physical abuse of others. There is the verbal abuse of citizens, exemplified by slurs or epithets. Finally, for many people who feel downtrodden, the police symbolize brutality because the officers represent the majority group's law, which serves to keep the minority groups in their place. It is perhaps this last form of police brutality that is of the greatest concern for anyone who is interested in improving community relations. Why? Because it is a philosophy or frame of mind. And it is probably the most difficult to overcome.

Police brutality: unnecessary use of force by police against citizens, resulting in injury.

Citizen use of the term **police brutality** encompasses a wide range of practices, from the use of profane and abusive language to the actual use of physical force or violence.[26] Although no one can deny that some police officers use brutal practices, it is impossible to know with any degree of accuracy how often and to what extent these incidents occur. They are low-visibility acts, and many victims decline to report them. It is doubtful that police brutality will ever disappear forever. There are always going to be, in the words of A. C. Germann, Frank Day, and Robert Gallati, "Neanderthals" who enjoy their absolute control over others and become tyrannical in their arbitrary application of power.[27]

Status of Police Body-Worn Cameras

Another outgrowth of the aforementioned police shootings and the emphasis on greater police transparency has been a call for officers to use **body-worn cameras**. With cell phones recording what appear to be a number of questionable if not criminal cases of police use of force—and what also appears for many people to be misrepresentation or cover-up of facts by police in the aftermath—many politicians and activists argue that all officers should be compelled to do so.

Body-worn camera: an audio, video, or photographic recording system worn by police to record their interactions with the public or to gather video evidence at crime scenes.

Nearly all states have enacted legislation or have pending legislation governing how their cities will use body-worn cameras, although these laws will differ in terms of when, where, and how cameras may be used; public access to footage; public records requests; storage time; and the like.[28] These statutes are intended to address two compelling issues: (1) When, specifically, should the cameras be used; and (2) who should be allowed to view which kinds of footage?

Another concern, one that applies to the individual agencies themselves, is that body-worn cameras can carry tremendous costs—not from the equipment itself (ranging from a few hundred to a few thousand dollars per camera), but from the time required to store and edit the videos, as well as from the impact of public disclosure or open-records requests under the Freedom of Information Act (FOIA). It could be extremely challenging, if not impossible, for police to dedicate personnel and equipment to store, redact, and provide videos for all open-records requests (to include those by defense attorneys).[29]

WHEN FAILING THE PUBLIC TRUST: CIVIL LIABILITY

A Process and a Personality

According to one observer, the sequence of events has become all too familiar: In the aftermath of a fatal police shooting, there come angry calls by the family and sympathetic groups for a criminal investigation and conviction of the responsible officer. The local prosecutor or grand jury typically decides not to bring charges against the officer—or, if tried, the officer is acquitted. Then the community protests ensue (if not already occurring). Next, the Department of Justice is called upon to conduct a federal civil rights probe, which may or may not occur (but also tends to produce no criminal charges). Finally, the family of the victim files a wrongful death lawsuit against the city or police department behind the incident.[30]

To understand how such a series of events might occur, we must first revisit a few fundamental tenets of policing as an occupation. As mentioned in Chapter 6, in 1966 Jerome Skolnick described what he termed the *working personality* of the police as consisting of two important variables—danger and authority—and including a "perceptual shorthand" that includes a "symbolic assailant," wherein police often rely on certain cues such as demeanor, language, and attire, to determine whether an individual they confront is a threat to their safety.[31] A number of authors have argued that, for police, young black males can satisfy this mental shorthand.[32]

Witness the following cases, each of which involved the shooting death of an African American man, a debate concerning whether or not the police used excessive force, the police arguing that they acted appropriately in the circumstances, and a large financial settlement sought by (and often awarded) the surviving family members:

- The family of a South Carolina man reached a $6.5 million settlement in 2018 in his fatal shooting death. He was struck in the back by a bullet while running away from a police officer, who reportedly pulled him over for a broken brake light; the officer was later charged with murder in the case. A state circuit judge refused to release the officer on bail, saying that doing so "would constitute an unreasonable danger to the community."[33]

- In New Jersey, a grand jury declined bringing charges against two officers after a struggle with a 32-year-old man in their custody who was acting in a "bizarre" fashion; a police dog was unleashed on him, resulting in the man's death. Lawyers for police say they acted appropriately and were physically threatened. The family later filed a $10 million civil suit.[34]

- A police officer in South Carolina was charged with a felony firearms offense after discharging his firearm into a vehicle, killing its 68-year-old occupant in his driveway. The officer had tried to pull him over on suspicion of driving under the influence and claimed the man had grabbed for his gun, while his family argued that a video showed he never tried to do so. The officer pleaded guilty to a misdemeanor "misconduct in office" charge in a plea arrangement. In an ensuing civil suit, the family settled for $1.2 million.[35]

- A 25-year-old Florida man who family members say had paranoid schizophrenia died after police shot him. The family's lawyer said video of the shooting made clear that police used excessive lethal force. A video showed the man running toward a police car with a broomstick in his hand. Prosecutors declined to bring charges against the officers; the family filed a $20 million civil lawsuit against the city, its former police chief, and two officers.[36]

Civil liability: in tort law, the basis for which a cause of action (e.g., fine) is made to recover damages; in criminal justice, where a police or corrections officer, for example, violates someone's civil rights.

Not all of the above or other persons who have been fatally shot by the police were young black males, of course, but when such incidents happen, close scrutiny of the incident will be brought to bear to determine the facts surrounding the matter and if prejudice might have been at its core.

With the possible exception of professionals working in the medical field (and possibly in prisons), no group of workers is arguably more susceptible to litigation and civil liability than police employees. Frequently cast into confrontational situations, and given the complex nature of their work and its requisite training needs, they will from time to time act in a manner that evokes public scrutiny, complaints, and calls for financial remuneration to persons who have suffered as a result (see next section). As we will see, the price of failure among public servants can be quite high, in both human and financial terms.

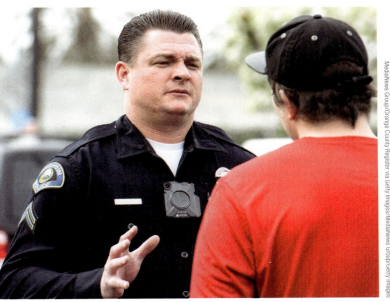

An outgrowth of recent officer-involved shootings across the United States is an emphasis on greater police transparency—and calls for officers to use body-worn cameras.

American citizens (and legal counsel) have long known how to seek redress from the courts. As examples, in Baltimore the family of Freddie Gray (whose death led to murder and/or assault charges against six police officers in 2015) received $6.4 million,[37] and in Cleveland the estate of 12-year-old Tamir Rice was awarded $6 million.[38] Larger cities now spend hundreds of millions of dollars per year on such cases.[39]

Torts and Negligence

A **tort** is the infliction of some injury on one person by another. Three categories of torts generally cover most of the lawsuits filed against criminal justice practitioners: negligence, intentional torts, and constitutional torts.

Negligence can arise when a criminal justice employee's conduct creates a danger to others. In other words, the employee did not conduct his or her affairs in a manner so as to avoid subjecting others to a risk of harm and may be held liable for the injuries caused to others.[40] Intentional torts occur when an employee engages in a voluntary act that has a substantial likelihood of resulting in injury to another; examples are assault and battery, false arrest and imprisonment, malicious prosecution, and abuse of process. Constitutional torts involve employees' duty to recognize and uphold the constitutional rights, privileges, and immunities of others; violations of these guarantees may subject the employee to a civil suit, most frequently brought in federal court under 42 U.S. Code Section 1983, discussed in the next section.[41]

Assault, battery, false imprisonment, false arrest, invasion of privacy, negligence, defamation, and malicious prosecution are examples of torts that are commonly brought against police officers. **False arrest** is the arrest of a person without probable cause. False imprisonment is the intentional illegal detention of a person; this can occur not only in jail but also whenever someone is confined to a specified area. For example, the police may fail to release an arrested person after a proper bail or bond has been posted, they can delay the arraignment of an arrested person unreasonably, or authorities can fail to release a prisoner after they no longer have authority to hold him or her.

A single act may be a crime as well as a tort. For example, if Officer Smith, in an unprovoked attack, injures Jones, the state will attempt to punish Smith in a criminal action by sending him to jail or prison, fining him, or both. The state would have the burden of proof at criminal trial, having to prove Smith guilty "beyond a reasonable doubt." Furthermore, Jones may sue Smith for money damages in a civil action for the personal injury he suffered. In this civil suit, Jones would have the burden of proving Smith's acts were tortious by a "preponderance of the evidence"—a lower standard than that in a criminal court and thus easier to satisfy.

Section 1983 Legislation

The primary civil instrument that can be used against the police is **Section 1983**. Following the Civil War and in reaction to the activities of the Ku Klux Klan, Congress enacted the Ku Klux Klan Act of 1871, later codified as U.S. Code, Title 42, Section 1983. It states that

> [e]very person who, under color of any statute, ordinance, regulation, custom, or usage of any State or Territory, subjects, or causes to be subjected, any citizen of the United States or any other person within the jurisdiction thereof to the deprivation of any rights, privileges, or immunities secured by the Constitution and laws, shall be liable to the party injured in an action at law, suit in equity, or other proper proceeding for redress.

A trend is for such litigants to cast a wide net in their lawsuits, suing not only the principal actors in the incident, but agency administrators and supervisors as well. This breadth of suing represents the notion of *vicarious liability*, or the doctrine of *respondeat superior*, an old legal

---

Tort: a civil wrong or infraction; the remedy will be damages awarded in civil trial.

Negligence: failure to perform a duty owed.

False arrest: unlawful physical restraint by a police officer, for no valid reason.

Section 1983: a portion of the U.S. Code that allows a legal action to be brought against a police officer or other person in position of authority who, it is believed, used his or her position ("acted under color of law") to violate one's civil rights.

Vicarious liability: a legal doctrine whereby a person is responsible for the actions of another and is to exercise reasonable and prudent care in supervising that person.

Respondeat superior: Latin for "let the master answer"—a doctrine in liability that establishes a duty of supervisors to control their employees and be considered liable for their actions.

maxim meaning "let the master answer." In sum, an employer can be found liable in certain instances for wrongful acts of the employee.

Police supervisors have also been found liable for injuries arising out of an official policy or custom of their department. Injuries resulting from a chief's verbal or written support of heavy-handed behavior resulting in the use of excessive force by officers have resulted in such liability.[42]

Practitioner's Perspective

Chief of Police

Jeri Williams
Chief of Police with the Oxnard Police Department

Name: Jeri Williams
Position: Chief of Police
Location: Oxnard, California

What do you find to be the most enjoyable aspects of policing? It's the kind of job where I didn't have to do the same thing every day. It was different every single day. I got to help people every single day. What I couldn't believe was that people were paying me money to put bad guys in jail. That blew my mind—who wouldn't want to do this all the time? When it came to promotion, I had some male supervisors who used to say some crazy things about women and females, and they used to tell me that I couldn't do things because I was black and female. I got promoted anyway. Sometimes the demotivators can be a great motivation.

What advice would you give to someone either wishing to study, or now studying, criminal justice and wanting to become a practitioner in this position? Research your agencies very well, and don't just apply any place. You really have to make sure you're a good fit for that agency. We are looking for people who are honest and have integrity, people who are problem solvers, and people who can properly and actively communicate with people. We've found tremendous success lately hiring people from our own community, which is a double bonus for us because they understand the culture of the city, but can also rise to the occasion and pass through all the hoops we have to becoming a police officer. When you're interviewing for a position, be honest and forthright. You have to be able to portray honor and integrity, and command presence. We're looking for people who are physically fit and maintain the stamina of being a police officer. We want to see that you want to be a community servant, to do right by people every day that you go out there.

What directions do you envision your department going in the future? Regardless of what is going on in the national agenda with law enforcement, we as police officers remain steadfast in what we've been doing for one hundred years, and that's treating people with integrity and respect, really taking the time to listen to people, providing a service that's the platinum standard, as well as taking the bad guys to jail. You can't have one without the other. There are some officers who believe that if they're focused on customer service, then they won't be able to arrest people. We have to be able to walk in tandem and make our arrests and still provide customer service. I think when we as law enforcement believe that and embody that, regardless of what's going on in other places, people will still feel safe and security in their homes and communities. I know it sounds altruistic to think that, but quite frankly, I think that's why I'm in this profession. I know for a fact that there are 330 other police chiefs in the state of California who think the same way. I would love for the noise going on nationally to diminish. I would love for other police officers to recognize that I don't wear a badge just for the Oxnard Police Department, I wear it for everyone else who has taken an oath to be a peace officer, and that regardless of what's going on, that I stand true to my honor and integrity as a police officer. That's where I'd love for us to be years down the road.

To learn more about Jeri Williams' experiences as a chief of police, watch the Practitioner's Perspective video in SAGE vantage.

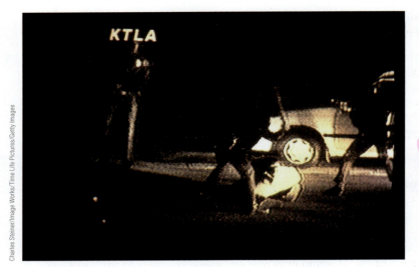

The 1991 beating of Rodney King by Los Angeles police officers resulted in King's being awarded $3.8 million for his injuries.

Proximate cause: a factor that contributed heavily to an event, such as an auto crash or death.

Duty of care: a legal obligation imposed on someone; in the case of the police, they have a legal responsibility to see that persons in their custody are free from harm, given necessary medical assistance when necessary, and treated humanely.

Failure to protect: a situation in which police place someone in jeopardy, such as by giving out the location of a battered spouse or names of victims or witnesses.

Potential Areas of Liability

To help readers to conceptualize what is meant by police civil liability, the following sections discuss some general areas in which police liability may be found.

Proximate Cause

Proximate cause is basically something that causes an event, particularly an injury due to negligence or an intentional wrongful act. In other words, the injury caused would not have occurred but for the cause. As an example, it is established by asking, "But for the officer's conduct, would someone have been injured or killed?" If the answer to this question is no, then proximate cause is established, and the officer can be held liable for the damage or injury. An example is where an officer is inappropriately and negligently involved in a high-speed chase and the fleeing driver strikes an innocent third party.[43] Proximate cause also may be found when an officer who leaves the scene of an accident is aware of dangerous conditions (e.g., spilled oil, smoke, vehicle debris, stray animals) and does not give proper warning to motorists.[44]

Persons in Custody and Safe Facilities

Courts generally rule that police officers have a duty of care to persons in their custody, including a legal responsibility to take reasonable precautions to keep detainees free from harm, to render medical assistance when necessary, and to treat detainees humanely.[45] This duty, however, typically does not include self-inflicted injury or suicide, because these acts are generally considered to result from the detainee's own intentional conduct.[46] However, if a prisoner's suicide is "reasonably foreseeable" from his or her actions or statements, then the jailer has a duty of care to help prevent that suicide.

Police also need to provide safe facilities. For example, the construction of a Detroit jail's holding cell did not allow officers to observe detainees' movements; there were no electronic monitoring devices for observing detainees, and there was an absence of detoxification cells required under state department of corrections rules. Therefore, following a suicide in this facility, the court held that these building defects contributed to the detainee's death.[47]

Failure to Protect

This form of negligence may occur if a police officer fails to protect a person from a known and foreseeable danger. Claims of failure to protect most often involve battered women. However, police informants, witnesses, and other people dependent on the police can be a source of police liability if an officer fails to take reasonable action to prevent them from being victimized. (See the accompanying "You Be the . . . Judge" box.)

Vehicle Pursuits

Vehicle pursuits are of great concern because they involve tremendous potential for injury, property damage, and liability. As one police manual describes it, "The decision by a police officer to pursue a citizen in a motor vehicle is among the most critical that can be made,"[48] putting innocent third parties—other drivers and bystanders—at risk. Police policy and procedure manuals are very thorough where pursuits are concerned, and they typically order the supervisor to shut down the pursuit unless there is probable cause to believe the suspect presents a clear and immediate threat to the safety of others, or has committed or is attempting to commit a violent felony.

Two cases explain the law of high-speed pursuits. The first involves two Sacramento County, California, deputies who pursued a motorcyclist for a traffic violation at speeds greater than 100 miles per hour; the motorcycle crashed, and the deputies' vehicle could not stop in time, striking and killing the motorcycle's passenger. The passenger's family claimed in a civil suit that the pursuit violated the crash victim's due process rights under the Fourteenth Amendment. The U.S. Supreme Court, in *County of Sacramento v. Lewis* (1998),[49] held that the proper standard in such cases is whether the officer's conduct "shocks the conscience." That is, was the conduct offensive to a reasonable person's sense of moral goodness? The Court felt that, in this case, deputies had no intent to harm the suspects and thus their behavior did not "shock the conscience." In 2007, the Supreme Court heard another case involving the level of force used by police in such pursuits. A deputy's pursuit of a 19-year-old Georgia youth, driving at speeds up to 90 miles per hour for 9 miles, ended in a violent crash that left the youth a quadriplegic. His lawyers argued that the Fourth Amendment protects against the use of excessive force—and that when high-speed drivers have their cars stopped in pursuits, a "seizure" occurs for Fourth Amendment purposes. The Supreme Court held that an officer's attempt to terminate a dangerous high-speed car chase that threatens the lives of innocent bystanders "does not violate the Fourth Amendment, even when it places the fleeing motorist at risk of serious injury or death."[50] Still, it is important to remember that a police pursuit is justified only when the necessity of apprehension outweighs the degree of danger created by the pursuit.

You Be the . . .

Judge

What, if any, legal obligation is held by the police to protect someone from his or her estranged spouse who has been served with a legal restraining order? That question was at the crux of a lawsuit from Castle Rock, Colorado, which was ultimately heard by the U.S. Supreme Court. Jessica Gonzales's restraining order required her husband to remain at least 100 yards from her and their three daughters except during specified visitation times. One evening the husband took possession of the three children in violation of the order; Mrs. Gonzales repeatedly urged the police to search for and arrest her husband, but they took no immediate action (due to her having allowed her husband to take the children at various hours). At approximately 3:20 a.m., the husband appeared at the city police station and instigated a shoot-out with the police (he died). A search of his vehicle revealed the corpses of the three daughters, whom the husband had killed prior to his arrival. U.S. cities are generally immune from lawsuits, so in this case the Supreme Court was asked to decide whether Jessica Gonzales could sue the city because of inaction by its police officers.

1. Were the police *morally* responsible for the deaths of the three girls?
2. Were the police *legally* responsible for their deaths?
3. If you believe Gonzales should be allowed to sue the city, and the police were liable, how much financial compensation should she receive?

See the Notes section at the end of the book for the outcome and whether or not the city was deemed as liable for its police department's actions.[51]

A Related Issue: How to Treat the Mentally Ill Population

Richard Lee Quintero's 911 call in North Carolina in March 2018 went viral because many viewed it as a humorous sound bite for entertainment. In the call, Quintero reported that he was Jesus Christ and then turned himself in for burglarizing a pizza business. Later, however, matters turned far worse. Suffering from chronic paranoid schizophrenia and confined to jail for three weeks, Quintero later amputated his own tongue. From there, he was sent to a week in a hospital and then to a maximum-security prison. After being deemed incapable of standing trial, the charges were later dropped.

The State of Our Mental Health

According to the National Alliance on Mental Illness, the state of our mental health as a nation is not good; approximately one in five adults in the United States—43.8 million or 18.5 percent—experience mental illness in a given year; moreover, one in five youths aged 13–18 experience a severe mental disorder at some point in their lifetime, 18.1 percent of adults experience an anxiety disorder such as posttraumatic stress disorder, and 26 percent of adults staying in a homeless shelter live with serious mental illness (see Figure 7.1). Unfortunately, many—40 percent or more—of these people do not realize they are mentally ill—a condition known as anosognosia—so outpatient treatment is critical.

Given the ubiquitous nature of mental illness, police everywhere and at all levels will inevitably come into contact with persons suffering from it; in the sections that follow we discuss those contacts and what police can do in dealing with such individuals.

Front-End, Back-End Issues

At the front end of the problem, an estimated 20 to 40 percent of police calls for service involve mentally ill persons, while an estimated 7 percent of police contacts in jurisdictions with 100,000 or more people involve the mentally ill. One survey found that about 9 in 10 (92 percent) of patrol officers have at least one encounter with a mentally ill person in crisis each month, and officers average about six such encounters per month. On the back end, America's jails and prisons have been termed by the Treatment Advocacy Center as the "new asylums" because they house more mentally ill persons than any psychiatric hospital in the country. Researchers have found that more than half the inmates in jails and state prisons are mentally ill, particularly with depressive disorder, schizophrenia, and bipolar disorder.

What Can Police Do?

There are several recommendations for police interactions with the mentally ill, as espoused by psychiatrists, including responding with more than one officer (e.g., preferably in uniform and without using red lights or sirens); remaining with the individual until help arrives; moving slowly and reassuring the person; trying to obtain help from friends, relatives, and others known to the individual; using a weapon only when necessary to save a life; not arguing with a person who is delusional, instead trying to bring him or her back to reality; taking all suicidal behavior seriously; ensuring the individual is not physically ill or injured; and trying to get the person to a treatment facility.

Thousands of agencies across the United States have adopted crisis intervention training or team (CIT) approaches, which involve training officers for 40 hours or more about mental illness issues, signs and symptoms, practical ways to deescalate a situation, and how to let a person in crisis vent. CIT employs role-play scenarios that emphasize how to avoid the use of weapons if the person is posing a danger only to themselves. Officers are also trained to know the various diversionary options in their jurisdictions (e.g., mental health or medical facilities) so that they can help the person involved rather than taking the individual to jail. CIT programs are critical for modern officers. As an example, the Seattle, Washington, Police Department website provides a short video of police partnering with mental health experts at https://www.king5.com/video/news/

Figure 7.1 /// Mental Health Facts in the United States

PREVALENCE OF MENTAL ILLNESS

1 in 5 U.S. adults (47.6 million people) experience mental illness each year

1 in 25 U.S. adults (11.4 million people) experience serious mental illness each year

1 in 6 U.S. youth aged 6-17 (7.7 million people) experience a mental health disorder each year

LIVING WITH MENTAL ILLNESS

19.3% of U.S. adults with mental illness also experience a substance use disorder

13.4% of U.S. adults with serious mental illness have no insurance coverage

60% of U.S. counties do not have a single practicing psychiatrist

IMPACT OF MENTAL ILLNESS

People with depression have a **40%** higher risk of developing cardiovascular and metabolic diseases than the general population.

Across the U.S. economy, serious mental illness causes **$193.2 billion** in lost earnings each year

The rate of unemployment is higher among U.S. adults who have mental illness **(5.8%)** compared to those who do not **(3.6%)**

37% of adults incarcerated in the state and federal prison system have a diagnosed mental illness

Source: Data courtesy of the National Alliance on Mental Illness, the Substance Abuse and Mental Health Services Administration, and the National Institute of Mental Health.

local/seattle-police-on-patrol-with-mental-health-experts/281-8097045, and the department's crisis response team is discussed at https://www.seattle.gov/police/about-us/crisis-response-team.

SELECTED TECHNOLOGIES: USES AND CONCERNS

Any discussion of policing methods (and related challenges) must include their use of technologies, which have had a tremendous impact on the field and greatly expand and change the work of patrol officers, criminal investigators, forensics, and other specialized assignments (e.g., bomb disposal). With those technologies—now including the use of video cameras on light poles, satellites and drones to observe from the skies, smartphones that relay all sorts of information to sentinel towers, and license plate readers tracking people's movements—come a number of concerns, however. For example, in January 2015, the U.S. Senate Judiciary Committee indicated "privacy concerns of the highest order." Civil rights organizations and even several federal judges have expressed strong concerns about using the devices without a search warrant.[52]

Next is a sampling of several police technologies either in use or in development that have raised some of these concerns.

Facial Recognition

In January 2018, Google launched a new app that allowed users to take a selfie to determine whether or not their face matched any of those in historical paintings. This new app was instantly popular and became a source of amusement—except for people living in Texas and Illinois; those two states' privacy laws restrict the use of facial recognition technology.[53]

But advances in biometrics—measurements of a person's physical or behavioral characteristics, even including one's unique heartbeat—have brought applications that can often be used for good. For example, when police had difficulty identifying the man who opened fire on a newsroom in Maryland, killing five people, the department sent a picture of the suspect to the Maryland Coordination and Analysis Center, which combed through one of the nation's largest databases of mug shots and driver's license photos in search of a match (and one was made). It can also provide a more efficient means of searching for missing persons, using software that can detect faces in the real-time video feed of officers' body-worn cameras (the software sends facial images to a secure artificial intelligence service, which checks the face against a missing persons database in real time as an officer is patrolling an area; if an officer's camera picks up a face that is in the missing persons database, it triggers a voice alert).[54]

Using computerized crime mapping, police can obtain a wide perspective on crime. (FIR stands for field information reports.)

The Maryland databases, as well as others, have become the source of some debate, as questions arise as to whether or not these mug shot databases are updated to eliminate images of people who were never charged, had charges dropped or dismissed, or who were found not guilty; some states want legislation mandating auditing to ensure that facial

174 ■ Part 2: The Police

recognition is used only for legitimate law enforcement purposes and could only be used with a court order.⁵⁵

Undoubtedly such technology will continue to advance; police agencies will continue to seek means of quickly matching names or images of suspects against their databases of arrested individuals. Clearly, however, civil rights groups will continue to monitor the progress of biometrics as well as its potentially unconstitutional uses.

Preparing for a Future With Autonomous Vehicles

Some experts predict that autonomous—driverless—vehicle (AV) technology could be here very soon, even within 15 to 20 years. As with the rest of society, police agencies have much to do to prepare for this coming technology, as it is going to have a number of profound and probably unforeseen consequences.⁵⁶

First, the good news: AVs will likely bring a world in which drivers do not commit traffic violations or cause traffic crashes. Traffic congestion could be reduced or eliminated, mobility will be enhanced, and motorists (particularly long-distance commuters) will have countless hours of free time to devote to work or pleasurable activities (such as shopping on the Internet) while being transported safely. For their part, the police might equip AVs with cameras, license plate readers, radar, and gunshot detection systems.⁵⁷

AVs, though, are also associated with a number of critical issues. First, how will police prepare for the inevitable use of AVs by terrorists, hackers, and other criminals? Such persons could attempt to utilize AVs to transport illicit drugs, pack the vehicles with bombs and drive into public buildings, tamper with the vehicle control systems, and transport undocumented aliens or victims of sex trafficking. The criminal element must be considered, and steps taken, to prevent these types of occurrences.⁵⁸

Another issue related to the advent of AVs is the role of police as determiners of liability. Traditionally, the officer makes the determination of fault at a traffic crash scene; if an AV malfunctions, or becomes involved in a serious traffic collision, who is liable and should be ticketed—the AV manufacturer or the vehicle owner/operator? Police officers will be tasked with assigning this liability, and questions may arise as to whether or not the vehicle was built to operate safely or if the operator was negligent (e.g., in not obtaining required maintenance and software updates for the vehicle).⁵⁹

States must therefore enact regulations regarding the implementation and operation of AV technology on their roads. For their part, law enforcement agencies must begin to work with AV manufacturers and lawmakers to ensure law enforcement's needs and concerns are considered in the development of these vehicles and the related regulations—for example, giving the police the ability to take control of AVs in certain circumstances.⁶⁰

Addressing Texting While Driving

A prototype has been developed, although it is not yet legally available to or used by police, that can determine at a traffic crash scene whether a driver was texting on his or her smartphone. The device displays a log with the driver's every move leading up to the time of the crash. Such a device would be beneficial for the police as well as society: Each day an average of nine people are killed and 1,000 more are injured in crashes involving distracted driving.⁶¹

Opponents are already arguing that getting a phone's history ought to require a warrant, as the Fourth Amendment's protections are lost with such devices. However, proponents note that this technology does not provide information on the content of the user's text or email or social media post, but only whether or not the phone was in use. They add that texting laws alone do not work, and that such a device would merely be a tool for police to use to catch these people, to deter texting while driving, and to save lives.⁶²

As a New York bill is currently written, the driver involved in a crash would be asked to hand over his or her cell phone to the officer, who would then plug the Textalyzer into it; and, as with a Breathalyzer, drivers who refuse to hand over their phones could lose their driver's licenses.[63] This and similar bills might be challenged before the U.S. Supreme Court, however. Although the Court held in 2014 that police officers need a warrant to search cell phones, it could be argued that the Textalyzer is not unconstitutional because phone records can already be made available to police through warrants from phone carriers.[64]

Handheld Drug-Testing Devices

In Chapter 16 we will discuss contemporary drug problems and enforcement in greater detail; here we discuss briefly a means of quickly and easily identifying drugs that are encountered by officers on patrol.

Today, with so many illicit drugs on the streets, it is no longer a simple task to identify them on sight or to perform lab testing. Synthetic cathinones (bath salts), cannabinoids (K2, spice), and opioids (fentanyl, W-18) can all look like white powders and be visually indistinguishable from one another.[65]

To address this problem, police agencies are now using handheld narcotics analysis technology that not only cuts drug testing costs but also assists officers in improving the safety of themselves and their communities. These handheld instruments are smaller, faster, more affordable, and easier to use than traditional chemistry kits, and they can test for many more illegal substances. The officer simply aims a laser beam at the substance and scans for hundreds of suspected illicit substances, precursors, and cutting agents in a single, definitive, presumptive evidence scan.[66] Drug samples can be prioritized in mere minutes so that key cases can be investigated and evidence handed over to prosecutors in a few days. Evidence from handheld narcotics analyzers can also be used to offer suspects plea deals; if a suspect refuses the offer, the case will proceed to trial.[67]

This device also addresses other drug-related issues: First, some drugs, such as fentanyl, can hurt, injure, or even kill officers who come in direct contact with them; these analyzers allow illegal drugs, precursors, and cutting agents to be tested without removing them from their containers, thus preventing exposure to potentially dangerous chemicals.[68]

Second, with respect to protecting the chain of custody in drug cases, these devices maintain its integrity by documenting pertinent information and storing it in a way that precludes tampering; they also automatically record data such as the time, date, and analysis. Additional information—such as the arresting officer, case ID number, description, and defendant—can also be entered manually within the application.[69]

Of course, the uses of DNA continue to expand and be of major importance to criminal justice functions, as seen in Chapter 6 with the discussion of the Golden State Killer case.

/// IN A NUTSHELL

- The exceptionally high—and well-publicized—number of police shootings involving unarmed minorities in recent years resulted in a national task force study, demands for better recordkeeping of such shootings, the use of body-worn cameras by police, and greater demands for transparency and less militarization of police.
- The current state of police-minority relations may be dire, but several approaches—including constitutional policing, procedural justice, and greater transparency—if adopted, can serve to change the mindset of police and bridge the gap with the community.
- Although women and minority representation in policing has grown over the past two decades, these groups are still underrepresented overall; for reasons relating to representation, community relations, effectiveness and diversity, greater numbers of both women and minorities are needed.

- Historically, three forms of police brutality have been recognized: the physical abuse of others, the verbal abuse of citizens, and officers representing the majority group's law.
- There are several principles of police interactions with the mentally ill; thousands of agencies across the United States have adopted Crisis Intervention Training/Teams (CIT).
- The specter of civil liability looms large over police work. Often being in confrontational situations, police officers may from time to time act in a manner that evokes public scrutiny and complaints. They and their superiors may be sued for a variety of reasons if a citizen believes his or her rights were violated; the primary civil instrument that can be used against the police is Section 1983.
- High-speed vehicle pursuits by police are legally permissible but are to be used only when certain conditions are met.
- Technology has improved the capabilities of nearly every aspect of police patrol and investigations—bringing with it some concerns about citizens' right to privacy.

/// KEY TERMS & CONCEPTS

Review key terms with eFlashcards at **edge.sagepub.com/peak4e**.

Black Lives Matter 160
Blue Lives Matter 160
Body-worn camera 166
Civil liability 167
Consent decree 164
Constitutional policing 161
Duty of care 170
Failure to protect 170
False arrest 168
Legitimacy (of police) 162
Militarization (of the police) 163
Negligence 168
Police brutality 166
Procedural justice 162
Proximate cause 170
Respondeat superior 168
Section 1983 168
Tort 168
Use of force 158
Vicarious liability 168

/// REVIEW QUESTIONS

Test your understanding of chapter content at **edge.sagepub.com/peak4e**.

1. How would you describe the "sacred trust" that is given the police in terms of the use of force?
2. What kinds of problems have arisen in recent years regarding police use of force, and what approaches and philosophies might police adopt in order to bridge the chasm that now exists in many communities as a result of that use of force?
3. To what purposes might consent decrees and body-worn cameras be applied to improve policing today?
4. Why is it desirable to bring more women and minorities into the field of policing?
5. What are the types of police brutality? Which one is most problematic for the police?
6. How would you define U.S. Code, Title 42, Section 1983? How is it applied?
7. What is meant by duty of care and failure to protect, and what are some examples as these concepts apply to police supervisors and officers?
8. How might the police be deemed liable if they are involved in vehicle pursuits?
9. How would you explain the overall state of mental health in the United States, problems afflicting our mentally ill population, and the approaches police can use to assist those who are so afflicted?
10. How have technologies assisted police functions, and what tools involve some privacy issues concerning their use?

/// LEARN BY DOING

1. In the past six months, there has been a spike in the number of citizen complaints in your community alleging inappropriate use of force by police against minorities. Local interest groups and churches are demanding data concerning police use of force as well as a review of policies regarding same. As your police department's community liaison, you are asked to respond to these demands. What approaches will you take?

2. Your police chief assigns you the task of developing a new method for recruiting both women and minority police officers. Money is no object, because the mayor has made agency diversity a top priority for the coming year. What will you recommend in terms of how to reach individuals in markets from which officers are not typically recruited?

3. Your criminal justice professor assigns your class a group project wherein you are to argue which technologies are the most useful in crime fighting. How will you respond, and why?

/// STUDY SITE

Get the tools you need to sharpen your study skills. SAGE edge offers a robust online environment featuring an impressive array of free tools and resources.

Access practice quizzes, eFlashcards, video, and multimedia at **edge.sagepub.com/peak4e**.

Introducing...

SAGE vantage™

Course tools done right.

Built to support teaching. Designed to ignite learning.

SAGE vantage is an intuitive digital platform that blends trusted SAGE content with auto-graded assignments, all carefully designed to ignite student engagement and drive critical thinking. Built with you and your students in mind, it offers easy course set-up and enables students to better prepare for class.

SAGE vantage enables students to **engage** with the material you choose, **learn** by applying knowledge, and **soar** with confidence by performing better in your course.

PEDAGOGICAL SCAFFOLDING

Builds on core concepts, moving students from basic understanding to mastery.

CONFIDENCE BUILDER

Offers frequent knowledge checks, applied-learning multimedia tools, and chapter tests with focused feedback.

TIME-SAVING FLEXIBILITY

Feeds auto-graded assignments to your gradebook, with real-time insight into student and class performance.

QUALITY CONTENT

Written by expert authors and teachers, content is not sacrificed for technical features.

HONEST VALUE

Affordable access to easy-to-use, quality learning tools students will appreciate.

To learn more about **SAGE vantage**, hover over this QR code with your smartphone camera or visit **sagepub.com/vantage**

CHAPTER 8

EXPOUNDING THE CONSTITUTION
Laws of Arrest, Search, and Seizure

We must never forget that it is a constitution we are expounding.
—John Marshall, *McCulloch v. Maryland* (1819)[1]

LEARNING OBJECTIVES

As a result of reading this chapter, you will be able to

1. Define and provide examples of probable cause
2. Explain the rationale for, ramifications of, and exceptions to the exclusionary rule
3. Distinguish between arrests and searches and seizures with and without a warrant
4. Review what is meant by "stop and frisk"
5. Explain generally to what extent the police may use electronic devices in order to obtain information from members of the public
6. Discuss some significant ways in which the *Miranda* decision has been eroded
7. Describe what rights are held by criminal defendants regarding the right to counsel, for both felony and misdemeanor arrests

ASSESS YOUR AWARENESS

Test your knowledge of your constitutional rights regarding arrest, search, and seizure by responding to the following seven true-false items; check your answers after reading this chapter.

1. The standard for a legal arrest, search, and seizure is probable cause.
2. The exclusionary rule requires that evidence obtained by police in violation of the Fourth Amendment must *not* be used against the defendant in a criminal trial.
3. There are essentially two ways for the police to make an arrest: with a warrant and without a warrant.
4. The courts grant police greater latitude in searching automobiles, which can be used to help make a getaway and to hide evidence.
5. The *Miranda* warning remains intact from its original version; no deviations in its explanation or practice by police are permitted.
6. Generally, police do not have to "search" for things they see in plain view.
7. The Sixth Amendment guarantees the right to a speedy and public trial, as well as the assistance of counsel to those accused of crimes by our justice system.

<< Answers can be found on page 419.

A group of armed robbers targeted Radio Shack and T-Mobile stores in Michigan and Ohio between late 2010 and early 2011. The offenders forced employees to the back of the stores and filled their bags with new smartphones. A few of the robbers were eventually arrested; one confessed to the crimes and turned his cell phone over to police. Investigators reviewed the calls made from his phone around the time of the robberies and identified the cell phone numbers of other individuals they believed participated in the crimes. Although the evidence was not strong enough to obtain a warrant, police gained access to the cell phone records through the Stored Communications Act. Through these records, they determined that Timothy Carpenter was within a two-mile radius of the stores at the time of the crimes. Carpenter was arrested and charged with armed robbery.

Just a few years prior, in August 2009, a San Diego police officer pulled over David Riley for expired registration tags. The officer then found that Riley's driver's license was suspended, and, following department policy for such cases, he searched the car before having it towed and impounded. He found two illegal handguns under the hood and arrested Riley. As is standard practice during a lawful arrest, the officer searched Riley and found his cell phone in a pocket. The phone contained evidence—pictures, cell phone contacts, texts messages, and video clips—indicating Riley's membership in a local gang. The cell phone also included a picture of a different vehicle that Riley owned and that had been involved in a gang shooting a few days earlier. Ballistics tests would later show that the handguns found in Riley's car were linked

Cell phones have changed everything, including the law that governs police officers when they arrest someone.

to the earlier shooting. Based in part on the evidence recovered from his cell phone, Riley was charged in connection with a gang shooting.

Like most people around the world today, Timothy Carpenter and David Riley used their cell phones in such a way that the phones contained many private details about their lives—pictures, contacts, communications with other people, videos, and even records of their physical locations. Some of those details were evidence of criminal activity, but surely other "evidence" on these phones was simply the typical private, personal information we all carry with us wherever we go.

The Fourth Amendment to the U.S. Constitution protects us from unreasonable police searches and seizures, and the long line of U.S. Supreme Court cases interpreting the Fourth Amendment repeatedly recognize that we have reasonable expectations of privacy in certain circumstances. Sometimes, that expectation of privacy requires police to get a warrant before they can search people and places.

Did Timothy Carpenter have an expectation of privacy concerning the places in which his phone was used, even if the phone produced a record of his movements? Did David Riley have an expectation of privacy in the contents of his cell phone? Did Carpenter's and Riley's crimes change those expectations? Did the police have a legitimate, overriding interest in seizing evidence from these phones? Should the government be able to use personal cell phone evidence against suspects in criminal trials?

Think about these questions and about the contents on your own cell phone as you read further and learn about the critically important area of constitutional law in the criminal justice system.

INTRODUCTION

What constitutional rights do Americans possess regarding arrest, search, and seizure? How are the police constrained by those rights? If the police have a search warrant for a friend you are accompanying, may they search you as well? If the police knock on your apartment door, must you allow them to enter if you do not see a search warrant in their possession? And if they arrest you, should they be able to search your person, your car, your apartment—your cell phone? These are challenging questions if someone is not familiar with the Bill of Rights. After you read this chapter, however, the answers should be clear.

Most college and university students probably have few opportunities to witness police actions that concern the U.S. Constitution. Although they may become directly and innocently involved with arrest, search, and seizure by being present at parties, in friends' vehicles, or at their places of employment, most Americans' knowledge of the Bill of Rights probably comes from movies and television crime shows—which are questionable at best in terms of how they portray police conduct. This chapter will clarify any such confusion.

We focus in this chapter on three of the ten amendments that constitute the Bill of Rights: the Fourth Amendment (probable cause, the exclusionary rule, arrest, search and seizure, electronic surveillance, and lineups), the Fifth Amendment (confessions and interrogations), and the Sixth Amendment (right to counsel and interrogation). Chapter 9 covers the Eighth Amendment, prohibiting cruel and unusual punishment; furthermore, Chapter 1 covers the concept of due process, which is guaranteed by the Fourteenth Amendment. As such, these two amendments are not examined in detail in this chapter. Also note that the law as it pertains to juvenile offenders is quite different from that for adults; juvenile law is covered in Chapter 15.

Some Caveats

Students of criminal justice might do well to remember the classic words of John Adams, who said in 1774 that a republic is "a government of laws, and not of men."[2] The Bill of Rights was enacted largely to protect all citizens from excessive governmental power.

As was seen in previous chapters of this book, criminal justice practitioners have far-reaching powers. Furthermore, agencies of criminal justice have the added benefit of using expert witnesses, forensic crime laboratories, undercover agents, informants, and so forth. Therefore, the Bill of Rights serves as an important means of "balancing the scales"—controlling the police and others so that they conduct themselves in a manner suited to a democratic society. Criminal justice professionals must conform their behavior to the rule of law as set forth not only in the U.S. Constitution but also in the state constitutions, statutes enacted by state legislatures, municipal ordinances, and the precedent of prior interpretations by the courts.

Remember also that the law is *dynamic*—that is, constantly changing—by virtue of acts by federal and state courts as well as their legislative bodies. Therefore, criminal justice practitioners must stay abreast of such changes and have formal mechanisms for imparting these legal changes to their employees. In the best case, agencies will have an in-house assistant district attorney—or, at the least, one who is on call—to render advice concerning legal matters.

A final note: Anyone who believes our legal system to be unduly harsh and restrictive might wish to read the brief discussion of Saudi Arabia police tactics in the Chapter 6 "Going Global" feature. Remember that governments—through their criminal justice systems (and, too often, their military forces)—may employ many methods to maintain order and attempt to maintain "justice." In Saudi Arabia or China, however, the methods used would be far different from those in the United States. But would "justice" really result? And would many Americans want to *live* in one of those venues?

THE FOURTH AMENDMENT

> The right of the people to be secure in their persons, papers, and effects, against unreasonable searches and seizures, shall not be violated, and no Warrants shall issue, but upon probable cause, supported by Oath or affirmation, and particularly describing the place to be searched, and the persons or things to be seized.

The **Fourth Amendment** is intended to limit overzealous behavior by the police. Its primary protection is the requirement that a neutral, detached magistrate, rather than a police officer, issue warrants for arrest and search. The all-important principle of separation of powers in our American government demands that the legal right to search be decided by someone other than an agent for the police, because the police are not expected to be neutral or objective with respect to police matters. Instead, a neutral judicial officer oversees this important police function—the judicial branch oversees the executive branch to ensure law enforcement actions are constitutional.[3]

Probable Cause

The standard for a legal arrest, as well as for **search and seizure**, is **probable cause**. This important concept is elusive at best; it is often quite difficult for professors to explain and even more difficult for students to understand. One way to define probable cause is to say that for an officer to make an arrest or conduct a search of someone's person or effects, he or she must have a reasonable basis to believe that a crime has been or is about to be committed by that individual (which, in the case of a search, can include the individual's mere possession of some form of illegal contraband).

Fourth Amendment: in the Bill of Rights, it contains the protection against unreasonable searches and seizures and protects people's homes, property, and effects.

Warrant, arrest: a document issued by a judge directing police to immediately arrest a person accused of a crime.

Warrant, search: a document issued by a judge, based on probable cause, directing police to immediately search a person, a premises, an automobile, or a building for the purpose of finding illegal contraband felt to be located therein and as stated in the warrant.

Search and seizure: in the Fourth Amendment, the term refers to an officer's searching for and taking away evidence of a crime.

Probable cause: a reasonable basis to believe that a crime has been, or is about to be, committed by a particular person.

That definition still may not help much to explain this concept. However, if you read carefully the example provided in the accompanying "Investigating Further" box (which is based on an actual case), you should have a better understanding of this concept—and how it is applied in the field.

Of course, the facts and probable cause indicators of each case are different. The court will examine the type and amount of probable cause that the police officer had, but the officer cannot add to the probable cause used to make an arrest *after* making the arrest. The judge will then determine whether or not sufficient probable cause existed to arrest the individual based on the officer's knowledge of the facts *at the time of* the arrest.

The U.S. Supreme Court has upheld convictions when probable cause was provided by a reliable informant,[4] when it came in an anonymous letter,[5] and when a suspect fit a Drug Enforcement Administration profile of a drug courier.[6]

The Exclusionary Rule

As mentioned above, the Fourth Amendment protects people's right to be secure against unreasonable searches and seizures in their houses, papers, and effects. However, simple as that may sound, the manner in which the amendment is applied on the street is more complicated. First of all, not *all* searches are prohibited—only those that are unreasonable. Another issue has to do with how to handle evidence obtained illegally. Should murderers be released, Justice Benjamin Cardozo asked, simply because "the constable blundered"?[7] The Fourth Amendment says nothing about how it is to be enforced; this is a problem that has stirred a good amount of debate for a number of years. Most of this debate has focused on the constitutional necessity for the exclusionary rule, which basically requires that all evidence obtained in violation of the Fourth Amendment must be excluded from government use in a criminal trial.

Exclusionary rule: the rule (see *Mapp v. Ohio*, 1961) providing that evidence obtained improperly cannot be used against the accused at trial.

Investigating Further

Probable Cause

At midnight, a 55-year-old woman, having spent several hours at a city bar, wished to leave the bar and go to a nightclub in a rural part of the county. A man offered her a ride, but rather than driving directly to the nightclub, he drove to a remote place and parked the car. There he raped the woman and forced her to sodomize him. She fought him and later told the police she thought she had broken the stems (side pieces) of his black glasses. After the assault, he drove her back to town; when she got out of the car, she saw the license plate number and thought that the hood of the car was colored red. Her account of the crime and her physical description of the rapist led the officers to have a suspect in mind, so they immediately conducted a photograph lineup with the victim. A known rape/sodomy suspect's picture was shown to her (along with those of several other men who were of similar physical description) in a photo lineup. She tentatively identified the suspect in the mug shot, but she was not absolutely certain (the suspect's mug shot had been taken several years earlier).

With this information and without an arrest or search warrant, two police officers hurried to the suspect's home to question him. Upon entering the suspect's driveway, the officers observed a beige car—but it had a red hood; next the officers noted that the vehicle's license number matched the one given by the victim; finally, as the suspect came out of the home, the officers observed that the front of his eyeglasses frame was black plastic, but the side pieces (temples) were gold-colored metal.

1. Upon entering the suspect's driveway, what observations did the officers make that might lead "a reasonable person" to believe that the suspect had committed the offenses?
2. Do the officers have enough probable cause to make a warrantless arrest of the individual?
3. Is there anything else they could legally do to further establish the suspect's guilt (such as a live, in-person lineup, as discussed later in the chapter)?

The exclusionary rule first appeared in the federal criminal justice system when the U.S. Supreme Court ruled in *Weeks v. United States* (1914) that all illegally obtained evidence was barred from use in federal prosecutions.[8] Then, in *Mapp v. Ohio* (1961), the Court applied the doctrine to the states' courts.[9] In May 1957, three Cleveland police officers went to the home of Dollree Mapp to investigate intelligence that suggested the owner was hiding a recent bombing suspect and engaged in an illegal gambling operation. Mapp, after telephoning her lawyer, refused the police entry without a search warrant. Mapp refused entry again three hours later, but police forcibly entered the home. Mapp demanded to see a search warrant; an officer waved a piece of paper at her, which she grabbed and placed down her shirt. The officers struggled with Mapp to retrieve the piece of paper, at which time Mapp's attorney arrived at the scene. The attorney was not allowed to enter the house or to see his client. One officer searched her upstairs bedroom found a brown paper bag containing books that he deemed to be obscene. A jury convicted Mapp of possession of obscene, lewd, or lascivious materials, and she was sentenced to an indefinite term in prison. In June 1961, the U.S. Supreme Court overturned the conviction, holding that the Fourth Amendment's prohibition against unreasonable search and seizure had been violated and that as

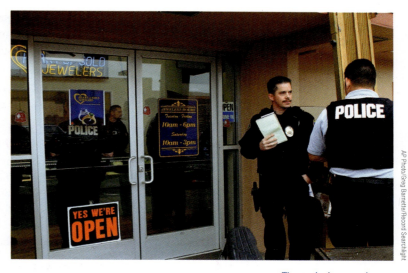

The exclusionary rule requires that evidence obtained improperly by the police must not be used in a criminal trial. These two officers wait outside a jewelry store for a search warrant to be signed by a judge so that they may then search the property for stolen goods.

> the right to be secure against rude invasions of privacy by state officer is . . . constitutional in origin, we can no longer permit that right to remain an empty promise. We can no longer permit it to be revocable at the whim of any police officer who, in the name of law enforcement itself, chooses to suspend its enjoyment.[10]

Although the exclusionary rule continues to safeguard citizens against unreasonable search and seizure, a 2016 U.S. Supreme Court decision limited the scope of this protection, particularly for those who have outstanding arrest warrants. Acting on an anonymous tip, Utah detective Douglas Fackrell observed Edward Joseph Strieff Jr. leaving a residence where drug sales were suspected. Without sufficient evidence, Detective Fackrell illegally stopped Strieff for questioning. During the stop, Fackrell discovered that Strieff had an outstanding warrant and arrested him. Fackrell conducted a lawful search following the arrest and found that Strieff was carrying a drug pipe and methamphetamine. In a 5–3 decision,[11] the U.S. Supreme Court ruled that, even though the initial investigatory stop was unconstitutional, exclusion of the evidence obtained during the search incident to arrest was not justified and the items found during the search could be lawfully considered as evidence for trial since the defendant had an outstanding warrant, which led directly to the subsequent arrest and search.

The Timothy Carpenter and David Riley Cases: Now that you understand the Fourth Amendment, expectations of privacy, and the landmark *Mapp* case, reconsider the two cell phone cases that opened this chapter and how police obtained "evidence" from these phones. Was the police action an invasion of privacy in either case? Did officers have time or a legal obligation to obtain warrants first? The defendants' attorneys argued that the cell phone evidence was obtained illegally and that, under the exclusionary rule established in the *Mapp* case, the government should not have been able to use it in court. How do you think the U.S. Supreme Court ruled in these cases? We revisit both cases later in this chapter.

Chapter 8: Expounding the Constitution

Arrests With and Without a Warrant

It is always best for a police officer to arrest someone with a warrant, because that means a neutral magistrate—rather than a police officer—has examined the facts and determined that the individual should be arrested in order to make an accounting of the charge(s). An arrest made with a valid warrant will be presumed constitutional or legal, so an officer will always opt to act with a warrant when possible.

Affidavit: any written document in which the signer swears under oath that the statements in the document are true.

To obtain an arrest warrant, the officer or a citizen swears in an affidavit (as an "affiant") that he or she possesses certain knowledge that a particular person has committed an offense. This person might be, as an example, a private citizen who informs police or the district attorney that he or she attended a party at a residence where drugs or stolen articles were present. Or, as is often the case, a detective gathers physical evidence or interviews witnesses or victims and determines that probable cause exists to believe that a particular person committed a specific crime. In either case, the affidavit is presented to a judge, and if the judge finds that probable cause exists, he or she will issue the arrest warrant. Officers will execute the warrant, taking the suspect into custody to answer the charges.

Exigent circumstance: an instance in which quick, emergency action is required to save lives, protect against serious property damage, or prevent suspect escape or evidence destruction; in such cases, officers can enter a structure without a search warrant.

Furthermore, the Supreme Court has held that police may not make "a warrantless and nonconsensual entry into a suspect's home in order to make a routine felony arrest" except where there are exigent circumstances.[12] Exceptions made based on exigent circumstances apply only when the officer possesses probable cause and immediate action is required—to prevent danger to life or serious damage to property, the escape of a suspect, the destruction of evidence,

You Be the . . .

Police Officer

One spring afternoon a police officer was dispatched to the residence of several university students, who were hosting a keg party for about 20 guests. They reported that three unknown men (two white, one African American) entered the home, had a few beers, and quickly left. Soon thereafter, a party guest also left and discovered that the stereo had been taken from his car, parked in the back yard. A description of the men and their vehicle was given to the officer, who soon (within 20 minutes and a mile from the crime scene) observed a vehicle and three men, all of whom matched the description that was given. The officer stopped the vehicle, informed the dispatcher of the stop and location, and approached the vehicle.

1. Are exigent circumstances and probable cause sufficient for the officer to search the vehicle without a warrant or the men's consent? If you believe not, how do you propose the three men be handled while a warrant is sought from a judge?

2. Assume the officer asks the vehicle's driver for permission to search the vehicle, and consent is given; what is the officer's next move? Instead, assume the driver of the vehicle refuses to give the officer permission to search the vehicle; what action(s) do you believe the officer can then legally take?

3. Assume the officer, with or without a warrant, locates the stolen stereo equipment inside the vehicle under the driver's seat. Can the officer then arrest only the vehicle's driver, or should all other occupants be arrested as well?

4. Following the arrest of one or more of the occupants, can they then be searched (if necessary, see the "Searches Incident to Lawful Arrest" section, later in this chapter)?

5. What other issues arise for the officer (e.g., his or her safety) once an arrest is made of one or more of the occupants?

or some other such action.[13] Patrol officers, unlike detectives, rarely have the time or opportunity to perform an arrest with a warrant in hand because the suspect is generally trying to escape, dispose of evidence, and so on. Although the situation described in the accompanying "You Be the... Police Officer" box involves consent to search, it serves as a good example.

Police may not randomly stop a vehicle to spot-check the driver's license and registration; to do so they must at a minimum possess articulable, reasonable suspicion (e.g., that a motorist is unlicensed, the automobile is not registered, or the vehicle or an occupant is subject to arrest for violation of law).[14] However, the Supreme Court ruled in 1990 that the stopping of all vehicles passing through sobriety checkpoints—a form of seizure—did not violate the Constitution, although singling out individual vehicles for random stops without probable cause is not authorized.[15] Several days later, it ruled that police were not required to give drunk-driving suspects a *Miranda* warning and could videotape their responses.[16] The Supreme Court held also that police may arrest *everyone* in a vehicle in which drugs are found,[17] and that police may set up roadblocks to collect information from motorists about crime. Short stops, "a very few minutes at most," are not too intrusive, considering the value in crime solving, the Court noted.[18]

Police officers may perform warrantless arrests and searches under certain circumstances if they have probable cause to do so.

Search and Seizure in General

An old saying holds that "a person's home is his castle," and the police are held to a high Fourth Amendment standard when wanting to enter and search someone's domicile. Regarding what have become known as "knock and announce" cases, the U.S. Supreme Court has determined that the Fourth Amendment requires the police to first knock and announce their presence before entering a person's home for the purpose of executing a warrant; the Court allows exceptions, however, if knocking and announcing would be likely to endanger the officers or lead to the destruction of evidence. In mid-2011, the Supreme Court expanded the ability of police to enter a home without a warrant—but under exigent circumstances. In *Kentucky v. King*, police in Lexington were pursuing a drug suspect and banged on the door of an apartment where they thought they smelled marijuana.[19] After identifying themselves, the officers heard movement inside the apartment and, suspecting that evidence was being destroyed, kicked in the door and found King smoking marijuana. King, convicted of multiple drug crimes, appealed, and Kentucky's highest court ruled there were no "emergency circumstances" present and thus the drugs were inadmissible because police should have sought a search warrant. The Supreme Court disagreed, saying that the police acted reasonably: When police knock on a door and there is no response, and then hear movement inside that suggests evidence is being destroyed, they are justified in breaking in.

In other Fourth Amendment cases, the Court has upheld a warrantless search and seizure of garbage in bags outside the defendant's home,[20] as well as approaching seated bus passengers and asking permission to search their luggage for drugs (because, they reasoned, such persons should feel free to refuse the officer's request).[21] The Court also decided that no "seizure" occurs (and therefore the Fourth Amendment does not apply) when a police officer is in a foot pursuit (here, a juvenile being chased by an officer threw down an object, later determined to be crack cocaine).[22]

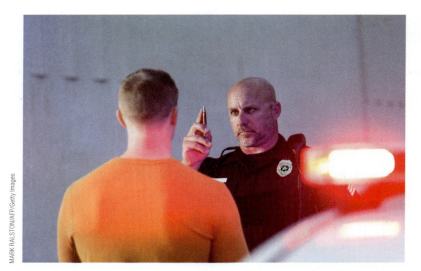

The U.S. Supreme Court has ruled that the stopping of all vehicles passing through sobriety checkpoints—a form of seizure—does not violate the Constitution.

Searches and Seizures With and Without a Warrant

As with arrests, the best means by which the police can search a person or premises is with a search warrant that has been issued by a neutral magistrate. A warrant will be issued only if a judge finds, after reviewing a police officer's sworn affidavit, that there is probable cause to believe the named person possesses sought-after evidence (e.g., a weapon or stolen goods), or that the evidence is present at a particular location. Again, as with an arrest with a warrant, typically it is the detectives who have the "luxury" of searching and seizing with a warrant after interviewing victims and witnesses, perhaps obtaining analyses at a forensics laboratory, and gathering enough available evidence to request a search warrant. Figure 8.1 shows the pertinent parts of a search and seizure warrant form for persons or property that is used by the U.S. district courts, for execution by agents of the federal government.

Patrol officers rarely have the opportunity to perform a search with a warrant, as the flow of events typically requires quick action to prevent escape and to prevent evidence from being destroyed or hidden. Five types of searches may be conducted without a warrant: (1) searches incident to lawful arrest, (2) searches during field interrogation (stop-and-frisk searches), (3) searches of automobiles under special conditions, (4) seizures of evidence that is in "plain view," and (5) searches when consent is given.

Searches Incident to Lawful Arrest

In *Chimel v. California* (1969), officers arrested Chimel without a warrant in one room of his house and then searched his entire three-bedroom house, including the garage, attic, and workshop. The U.S. Supreme Court said that searches incident to a lawful arrest are limited to the area within the arrestee's immediate control or that area from which he or she might obtain a weapon, emphasizing that such searches are justified in large part to ensure officer safety. Therefore, if the police are holding a person in one room of the house, they cannot search and seize property in another part of the house, away from the arrestee's immediate physical presence.[23]

Another advantage given the police was the Court's allowing a warrantless, in-home "protective sweep" of the area in which a suspect is arrested to reveal the presence of anyone else who might pose a danger. Such a search, if justified by the circumstances, is not a full search of the premises and may include only a cursory inspection of those spaces where a person could be hiding.[24] In April 2009, the Supreme Court held in *Arizona v. Gant* that, when an individual has been arrested and is in police custody away from his or her vehicle, unable to access the vehicle, officers may not then search the vehicle without a warrant. Here, the officers did so, and discovered a handgun and a plastic bag of cocaine; the Court overturned nearly three decades of such a police practice, saying it is a violation of the Fourth Amendment's protection against unreasonable searches and seizures.[25] In essence, the Court is saying that police may search the passenger compartment of a vehicle incident to a recent occupant's arrest only if it is reasonable to believe that the arrestee might access the vehicle at the time of the search or that the vehicle contains evidence of the offense of arrest.

Finally, in mid-2013, in a decision that Justice Samuel Alito described as "the most important criminal procedure case this court has heard in decades," the Supreme Court held in

Figure 8.1 /// Federal Court Search and Seizure Warrant Form, U.S. District Courts

AO 93 (Rev. 11/13) Search and Seizure Warrant

UNITED STATES DISTRICT COURT
for the

In the Matter of the Search of)
(Briefly describe the property to be searched)
or identify the person by name and address)) Case No.
)
)
)

SEARCH AND SEIZURE WARRANT

To: Any authorized law enforcement officer

An application by a federal law enforcement officer or an attorney for the government requests the search of the following person or property located in the _____ District of _____
(identify the person or describe the property to be searched and give its location):

I find that the affidavit(s), or any recorded testimony, establish probable cause to search and seize the person or property described above, and that such search will reveal *(identify the person or describe the property to be seized)*:

YOU ARE COMMANDED to execute this warrant on or before _____ *(not to exceed 14 days)*
❐ in the daytime 6:00 a.m. to 10:00 p.m. ❐ at any time in the day or night because good cause has been established.

Unless delayed notice is authorized below, you must give a copy of the warrant and a receipt for the property taken to the person from whom, or from whose premises, the property was taken, or leave the copy and receipt at the place where the property was taken.

The officer executing this warrant, or an officer present during the execution of the warrant, must prepare an inventory as required by law and promptly return this warrant and inventory to _____.
(United States Magistrate Judge)

❐ Pursuant to 18 U.S.C. § 3103a(b), I find that immediate notification may have an adverse result listed in 18 U.S.C. § 2705 (except for delay of trial), and authorize the officer executing this warrant to delay notice to the person who, or whose property, will be searched or seized *(check the appropriate box)*
❐ for _____ days *(not to exceed 30)* ❐ until, the facts justifying, the later specific date of _____.

Date and time issued: _____

_____
Judge's signature

City and state: _____

_____
Printed name and title

(Continued)

(Continued)

AO 93 (Rev. 11/13) Search and Seizure Warrant (Page 2)

Return		
Case No.:	Date and time warrant executed:	Copy of warrant and inventory left with:

Inventory made in the presence of :

Inventory of the property taken and name of any person(s) seized:

Certification

    I declare under penalty of perjury that this inventory is correct and was returned along with the original warrant to the designated judge.

Date: _____

_____
Executing officer's signature

_____
Printed name and title

[Print] [Save As...] [Reset]

Source: United States Courts, Form Number: AO 93

Practitioner's Perspective

Special Agent

Name: Dan Burke
Position: Special Agent, Food and Drug Administration's Office of Criminal Investigations

What is your career story? I started off doing internships. That's the best advice I can give college students: get in there, get internships, and get to know someone. I was lucky in that I got the job right out of college, but I did a co-op. That's when the government gives you a paid internship, and after you graduate, they agree to hire you as an agent. I came on as an agent in the Treasury Department, and from there I worked my way up.

What are some challenges and misconceptions you face in this position? There are a lot of challenges when it comes to law enforcement, and particularly federal law enforcement. You're dealing with crimes that are national, and oftentimes international in scope, and when you're dealing with that, you have to deal with a lot of different jurisdictions and laws, so it takes a while to understand the nuances of the jurisdictions that you're working in. The investigations also tend to take a lot longer.

The Internet is also a big challenge. It's the digital, cyber Wild West and it takes a lot of training and experience to understand how to investigate in that environment. But at the end of the day, it's satisfying when the long arm of the law can reach beyond your borders and reach through your screen. I've had cases where I never really had to get up from my desk; I was able to do almost entire cases sitting in front of the computer.

Some of the myths definitely do come from television. Cases are not made in hour- or half-hour-long segments. I've spent days and weeks on surveillance. Wire taps are not easy to get, contrary to popular belief, and they're very expensive. In general, managers don't like you spending a lot of money to pursue an investigation. It's difficult to write up a search warrant. You have to spend time on that, and you can't just go kicking in doors.

What role does diversity play in this position? In my career in federal law enforcement, I've arrested doctors, lawyers, even a CEO of a major corporation. So those cases can be quite interesting and challenging. You just never know how someone of that high status who's put a lot of their life into their career is going to react when it all comes tumbling down when I come through the door with an arrest warrant or search warrant. I've also been party to arrests involving religious people, and those are very sensitive circumstances. One thing I have learned is that it really runs the gamut in terms of the diversity of people who chooses to commit crimes.

What directions do you envision your department going in the future? I think there definitely is a future in law enforcement. It's a frustrating job, and students need to know that going into it. You're not always going to be thought of as the good guy. What you do are controversial things; you serve subpoenas and search warrants, you arrest people. That's sometimes difficult to understand and get your head around. There will always be positions because there will always be crime. So job security—wise, you're going to be okay. But you have to understand what you're going to be doing. You're putting yourself out there as the tip of the spear, if you will. You're that line between the good guys and the bad guys, and you have to make sure you stay on the good side of that line. You have to try to do the right thing at all times, even if that means losing a case, even if that means the bad guy is going to walk.

To learn more about Dan Burke's experiences as a special agent, watch the Practitioner's Perspective video in SAGE vantage.

Maryland v. King that police can collect DNA from people arrested but not yet convicted. The majority compared taking a DNA swab to fingerprinting, viewing it as a reasonable search that can be considered a routine part of a booking procedure.[26]

> **The David Riley Case:** The San Diego police officer searched Riley's cell phone "incident to a lawful arrest," almost as an extension of Riley's person—like his wallet or a bag he may have been carrying. Was the search as invasive as taking a cheek swab for DNA? Or is it more like looking for weapons or contraband on an arrestee?
>
> In 2014, the U.S. Supreme Court agreed with Riley's attorneys that the police search of Riley's cell phone was illegal. Speaking for the majority, Chief Justice John Roberts wrote:
>
>> Digital data stored on a cell phone cannot itself be used as a weapon to harm an arresting officer or to effectuate the arrestee's escape. Law enforcement officers remain free to examine the physical aspects of a phone to ensure that it will not be used as a weapon—say, to determine whether there is a razor blade hidden between the phone and its case. Once an officer has secured a phone and eliminated any potential physical threats, however, data on the phone can endanger no one.[27]
>
> Roberts also confirmed the realities of our modern digital lives and how the Court must interpret the Constitution with contemporary issues in mind, especially when reviewing police power:
>
>> Modern cell phones are not just another technological convenience. With all they contain and all they may reveal, they hold for many Americans "the privacies of life." The fact that technology now allows an individual to carry such information in his hand does not make the information any less worthy of the protection for which the Founders fought.

Reasonable suspicion: suspicion that is less than probable cause but more than a mere hunch that a person may be involved in criminal activity.

Stop and Frisk

In 1963, Cleveland detective McFadden, a veteran of 19 years of police service, first noticed Terry and another man who appeared to be "casing" a retail store. McFadden observed the suspects making several trips down the street, stopping at a store window, walking about a half-block, turning around and walking back again, pausing to look inside the same store window. At one point they were joined by a third party, who spoke with them and then moved on. McFadden claimed that he followed them because he believed it was his duty as a police officer to investigate the matter further.

Soon the two rejoined the third man; at that point McFadden decided the situation demanded direct action. The officer approached the subjects and identified himself, then requested that the men identify themselves as well. When Terry said something inaudible, McFadden "spun him around so that they were facing the other two, with Terry between McFadden and the others, and patted down the outside of his clothing." In a breast pocket of Terry's overcoat, the officer felt a pistol. McFadden found another pistol on one of the other men. The two men were arrested and ultimately convicted for concealing deadly weapons. Terry appealed on the grounds that the search was illegal and that the evidence should have been suppressed at trial.

The U.S. Supreme Court disagreed with Terry, holding in *Terry v. Ohio* that the police have the authority to detain a person briefly for questioning even without probable cause if they have "reasonable suspicion" that the person has committed a crime or is about to

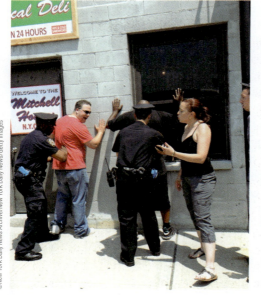

Despite officers being trained in mock scenarios, as seen here in the Bronx, the NYPD's aggressive stop-and-frisk program was abandoned after being deemed unconstitutional.

commit a crime. Reasonable suspicion is a lower standard than probable cause but more than a mere hunch that someone may be involved in criminal activity. Officers must be able to articulate a reasonable factual basis for a stop. Such detention—known as a **Terry Stop**—does not constitute an arrest, and a person may be frisked for a weapon if an officer reasonably suspects the person is carrying one and fears for his or her life. The *Terry* decision ushered in a new era for police officers, allowing them to stop and frisk suspects based only on reasonable suspicion, and not the higher threshold of suspicion required under a probable cause standard.[28]

An important extension of the *Terry* doctrine—known as the "plain feel" doctrine—was handed down in 1993 in *Minnesota v. Dickerson*, in which a police officer observed a man leave a notorious crack house and then try to evade the officer.[29] The man was eventually stopped and patted down, or frisked, during which time the officer felt a small lump in the man's front pocket that was suspected to be drugs. The officer removed the object—crack cocaine wrapped in a cellophane container—from the man's pocket. Although the arrest and conviction were later thrown out as not being allowed under *Terry*, the Court also allowed such seizures in the future when officers' probable cause is established by the sense of touch.

Another important Supreme Court decision in February 1997 took officer safety into account. In *Maryland v. Wilson*, the Court held that police may order passengers out of vehicles they stop, regardless of any suspicion of wrongdoing or threat to the officer's safety.[30] Citing statistics showing officer assaults and murders during traffic stops, the

Terry Stop: also known as a "stop and frisk"; when a police officer briefly detains a person for questioning and then frisks ("pats down") the person if the officer reasonably believes he or she is carrying a weapon.

Investigating Further

NYPD—Stop and Frisk or Racial Profiling?

In the early 1990s, the New York Police Department (NYPD), like most large, metropolitan forces, began taking a proactive approach to fighting crime. A centerpiece of the department's approach was an aggressive stop-and-frisk policy by which officers targeted high-crime areas and the people in them, often developing suspicion from the mere fact that a person was in such an area. Officers focused on persons who, for example, made "furtive movements," such as a hand going for something in a waistband or someone who seemed nervous. Others targeted people who appeared to be coming and going from certain buildings associated with illegal activity. The result of this approach was an unprecedented number of stops: 175,000 during a 15-month period in 1998 and 1999. But the demographic breakdown of those stops was troubling to many: blacks (26 percent of the city's population) accounted for 51 percent of the total, Hispanics (24 percent of the population) accounted for 33 percent, and whites (43 percent of the population) accounted for only 13 percent. Civil libertarians claimed the NYPD was engaged in illegal racial profiling. The NYPD responded by touting significantly lower rates for index crimes during the stop-and-frisk era.

Ultimately, the U.S. District Court for the Southern District of New York ruled in August 2013 that NYPD's stop-and-frisk practices were unconstitutional, violating the civil rights of racial minorities. The law enforcement community responded that the decision would dramatically change policing—and likely crime rates. In a move that seemed to signal the beginning of the end of stop-and-frisk, the NYPD in March 2015 issued new stop-and-frisk guidelines, requiring officers to be able to articulate facts establishing an objective justification for making the stop. Officers can no longer stop and frisk simply because suspects are making furtive movements in a high-crime area or because they fit a generalized description of a suspect, such as an African American male in a certain age group.

Source: Daniel Bergner, "Is Stop and Frisk Worth It?" *Atlantic Monthly* (April 2014), http://www.theatlantic.com/features/archive/2014/03/is-stop-and-frisk-worth-it/358644/; see also "The Hunted and the Hated," *Nation*, https://www.youtube.com/watch?v=7rWtDMPaRD8 (originally posted October 9, 2012).

The courts have held that motorists have no expectation of privacy during a traffic stop if contraband hidden in a vehicle is detected by a drug-sniffing dog.

Court noted that the "weighty interest" in officer safety is present whether a vehicle occupant is a driver or a passenger.

In January 2013, the Supreme Court heard arguments in a landmark Fourth Amendment case involving nearly 50 years of uncertainty over whether or not police securing blood tests (for people who might be driving under the influence) without a suspect's consent is constitutional. Tyler McNeely, of Cape Girardeau, Missouri, was pulled over for speeding. McNeely refused an on-scene breath test, so the trooper took him to a hospital, where McNeely again refused a test. The trooper told the lab technician to take a blood sample anyway, without a warrant. McNeely's blood-alcohol level was almost double the legal limit. However, the Supreme Court ruled in *Missouri v. McNeely* (2013) that police must obtain a warrant in order to subject a drunk-driving suspect to a blood test.[31] The Court found that the natural metabolism of alcohol in the bloodstream did not constitute an exigency that would justify a warrantless blood test. Further in 2016, the Supreme Court held in *Birchfield v. North Dakota* that, while the Fourth Amendment permits states to require warrantless breath tests prior to an arrest for drunk driving, it does not permit states to criminalize the refusal of warrantless blood tests by suspected drunk drivers.[32]

Searches of Automobiles

The third general circumstance allowing a warrantless search is when an officer has probable cause to believe that an automobile contains criminal evidence. The U.S. Supreme Court gives the police greater latitude in searching automobiles, because a vehicle can be used to effect a getaway and to hide evidence. In *Carroll v. United States* (1925), officers searched the vehicle of a known bootlegger without a warrant but with probable cause, finding 68 bottles of illegal booze. On appeal, the Court ruled that the seizure was justified. *Carroll* established two rules, however: First, to invoke the *Carroll* doctrine, the police must have enough probable cause that if there had been enough time, a search warrant would have been issued; second, urgent circumstances must exist that require immediate action.[33]

The Court also allows the police to enter an impounded vehicle following a lawful arrest in order to inventory its contents,[34] and has stated that a person's general consent to a search of the interior of an automobile also justifies a search of any closed container found inside the car that might reasonably hold the object of the search.[35] And, when an officer has probable cause to search a vehicle, the officer may search objects belonging to a passenger in the vehicle, provided the item the officer is looking for could reasonably be in the passenger's belongings[36] (such as finding drugs in a passenger's purse). Finally, motorists have no expectation of privacy during a traffic stop if contraband is hidden in a vehicle and detected by a drug-sniffing dog,[37] although police cannot extend the length of a routine traffic stop to allow a drug-sniffing dog to arrive on scene if the original purpose of the stop has been addressed (e.g., a ticket has been issued), unless the officer can demonstrate reasonable suspicion of additional criminal drug activity.[38]

In 2012, the Supreme Court ruled in *U.S. v. Jones* that police violated the Constitution when they attached a global positioning system (GPS) device to a suspect's vehicle without a search warrant.³⁹ Police had followed a drug trafficking suspect for a month and eventually found nearly 100 kilograms of cocaine and $1 million in cash when raiding the suspect's home in Maryland. Justice Antonin Scalia noted that the Fourth Amendment's protection of "persons, houses, papers, and effects, against unreasonable searches and seizures" extends to automobiles as well, and that even a small trespass, if committed in "an attempt to find something or to obtain information," constitutes a "search" under the Fourth Amendment. More recently, the Supreme Court in *Byrd v. United States* (2018) ruled that police violated Terrence Byrd's Fourth Amendment rights when they searched his car and found heroin and body armor in the trunk.⁴⁰ The police conducted a warrantless search, noting that Byrd was driving a rental car (with the renter's permission) but was not listed on the rental agreement. The Supreme Court ruled unanimously that Byrd, even though not listed on the rental agreement, had a reasonable expectation of privacy against a warrantless government vehicle search.

Going Global

Police Search and Seizure Around the World

In the United States, the Fourth Amendment protects people against unreasonable government searches and seizures. It is our Constitution that affords us these protections. People in other countries are also protected from unreasonable and overly intrusive actions by the government and other private parties. An individual's right to privacy is articulated in more than 180 national constitutions.⁴¹ Consider the following examples:

Article 14 of Italy's Constitution

> Home inspections, searches, or seizures shall not be admissible save in the cases and manners complying with measures to safeguard personal liberty. Controls and inspections for reason of public health and safety, or for economic and fiscal purposes, shall be regulated by appropriate laws.

Article 99 of Honduras's Constitution

> No entrance or search may be made without the consent of the occupant or without order from a competent authority. Nevertheless, it [the home] may be searched, in case of urgency, to prevent the commission of or impunity from crimes, or to avoid grave injury to persons or damage to property. Except in cases of urgency, search of the home may not take place between six o'clock in the evening and six o'clock in the morning, without incurring responsibility. The law shall determine the requirements and formalities regarding the manner in which the entrance, inspection or search may be carried out, as well as the responsibilities that may be incurred by the authority carrying it out.

Section 72 of Denmark's Constitution

> House searching, seizure, and examination of letters and other papers as well as any breach of the secrecy to be observed in postal, telegraph, and telephone matters shall take place only under a judicial order unless particular exception is warranted by Statute.

Chapter 2, Section 14 of South Africa's Constitution:

> Everyone has the right to privacy, which includes the right not to have—
> a. their person or home searched;
> b. their property searched;
> c. their possessions seized; or
> d. the privacy of their communications infringed.

Source: Constitute, *Search*, https://www.constituteproject.org.

Plain-View and Open-Field Searches

Essentially, police do not have to search for items that are seen in plain view. If police are lawfully on the premises and the plain-view discovery is inadvertent, then they may seize the contraband. For example, if an officer has been admitted into a home with an arrest or search warrant and sees drugs and paraphernalia on a living room table, he or she may arrest the occupants on drug charges as well as the ones related to the warrant. Or, if an officer during a lawful traffic stop observes drugs in the backseat of the car, he or she may arrest for that as well. When an officer found a gun under a car seat while looking for the vehicle identification number, the Court upheld the search and the resulting arrest as being a plain-view discovery.[42] Furthermore, fences and the posting of "No Trespassing" signs afford no expectation of privacy and do not prevent officers from viewing open fields without a search warrant.[43] Nor are police prevented from making a naked-eye aerial observation of a suspect's backyard or other curtilage (the grounds around a house or building).[44]

However, in *Collins v. Virginia* (2018), the Supreme Court ruled that police may not make a warrantless entry of curtilage in order to conduct a search, even if it involves a vehicle search.[45] Officer David Rhodes, while investigating two traffic incidents, observed a motorcycle under a tarp on a residential property. Suspecting that this was the motorcycle involved in the traffic incidents, Rhodes entered the property without a warrant, lifted the tarp, and confirmed that the vehicle identification number (VIN) matched the VIN of a stolen motorcycle. When Ryan Austin Collins returned to the property, he was arrested and the key to the motorcycle was found in his possession. While lower courts ruled that the warrantless search was justified under the Fourth Amendment's automobile exception, the Supreme Court ruled that this exception does not permit the warrantless entry of a home *or its curtilage* in order to search a vehicle.

Looking at the plain-view doctrine, assume police officers are lawfully inside a home to execute an arrest warrant on a suspected bank robber. If, by chance, they happen to observe this illegal marijuana operation, the officers could then also arrest the occupant on drug charges.

The Supreme Court has ruled that residential porches are also considered part of the home itself and cannot be searched without a warrant. Officers from the Miami-Dade Police Department received a tip that marijuana was being grown in a house. The officers approached the front door (porch) with a drug dog. The Labrador retriever alerted officers to the presence of marijuana in the house; subsequently, officers obtained a search warrant and discovered the plants inside. The Supreme Court ruled, in *Florida v. Jardines* (2013), that the police can use residential porches to communicate with occupants, but a search that involves more intrusive measures (in this case, the use of a drug dog) constitutes an illegal search.[46] Thus, searches conducted from porches (and that go beyond the basic senses of a police officer) are not subject to the plain-view or open-field search exception.

Consent to Search

Another permissible warrantless search involves situations in which citizens consent to a search of their persons or effects—provided that the defendant's consent is given voluntarily. However, police cannot deceive people into believing they have a search warrant when they in fact do not.[47] Nor can a hotel clerk give a valid consent to a warrantless search of the room of one of the occupants; hotel guests have a reasonable expectation of privacy, and that right cannot be waived by hotel management.[48] Further, absent consent from hotel operators, police must have a warrant or administrative subpoena to inspect hotel guest records.[49]

What if one occupant of a home consents to a search while the other occupant refuses? In a recent case, a wife gave police permission to search for her husband's drugs, but the husband refused to give such permission; the officers went ahead and searched and found cocaine. The Supreme Court reversed the husband's conviction, saying the Constitution does not ignore the privacy rights of an individual who is present and asserting his rights.[50] However, in a feature of the law that should be important to college students with roommates, an occupant may still give police permission to search when the other resident is absent or does not protest. In fact, in 2014, the Supreme Court expanded police powers to seek consent from a co-occupant, ruling that even after an occupant has refused consent to search and the police then legally arrest that occupant for some other reason, the police may return and seek consent from a co-occupant who then has the right to voluntarily consent to a search of the entire premises.[51]

Electronic Surveillance

Katz v. United States (1967) held that any form of electronic surveillance, including wiretapping, is a search and violates a reasonable expectation of privacy.[52] The case involved a public telephone booth, deemed by the Court to be a constitutionally protected area where the user has a reasonable expectation of privacy. This decision expressed the view that the Constitution protects people, not places. Thus, the Court has required that warrants for electronic surveillance be based on probable cause, describe the conversations that are to be overheard, be for a limited period of time, name subjects to be overheard, and be terminated when the desired information is obtained.[53] However, the Court has also held that electronic eavesdropping (i.e., when an informant wears a "bug," or hidden microphone) does not violate the Fourth Amendment.[54]

THE FIFTH AMENDMENT

No person shall be held to answer for a capital, or otherwise infamous crime, unless on a presentment or indictment of a Grand Jury, except in cases arising in the land or naval forces, or in the Militia, when in actual service in time of war or public danger; nor shall any person be subject for the same offense to be twice put in jeopardy of life or limb; nor shall be compelled in any criminal case to be a witness against himself, nor be deprived of life, liberty, or property, without due process of law; nor shall private property be taken for public use, without just compensation.

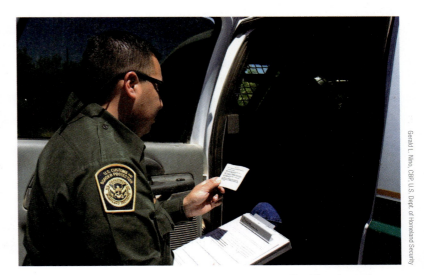

Fifth Amendment: in the Bill of Rights, among other protections, it guards against self-incrimination and double jeopardy.

The *Miranda* warning must be given after a suspect is in custody and before interrogation begins; otherwise, any statements might be thrown out in court.

Application

Today, the Fifth Amendment applies not only to criminal defendants but also to any witness in a civil or criminal case and anyone testifying before an administrative body, a grand jury, or a congressional committee. However, the privilege does not extend to blood samples, handwriting exemplars, and other such items not considered as testimony.[55]

The right against self-incrimination is one of the most significant provisions in the Bill of Rights. Basically it states that no criminal defendant shall be compelled to take the witness stand and/or give evidence against himself or herself. This right is expressed in the so-called *Miranda* warning (also known as "Mirandizing" someone), which requires police, at the point of having someone in custody and before questioning him or her about a crime or criminal activity, to inform the suspect "you have the right to remain silent. Anything you say can and will be used against you in a court of law. You have the right to an attorney. If you cannot afford an attorney, one will be provided for you."

The *Miranda* warning stems from a case involving a 23-year-old man, Ernesto Miranda, who raped 18-year-old Barbara Ann Johnson. Johnson was walking to a Phoenix, Arizona, bus stop on the night of March 2, 1963, when Miranda shoved her into his car, tied her hands and ankles, and drove her to the edge of the city, where he raped her. He then drove Johnson to a street near her home, letting her out of the car and asking that she pray for him. The police subsequently picked up Miranda and included him in a police station lineup. Miranda was identified by several women; one identified him as the man who had robbed her at knifepoint a few months earlier, and Johnson thought he was the rapist.

Miranda was a 23-year-old eighth-grade dropout with a police record dating back to age 14, and he had also served time in prison for driving a stolen car across a state line. During questioning, the police told Miranda that he had been identified by the women; Miranda then made a statement in writing that described the rape incident. He also noted that he was making the confession voluntarily and with full knowledge of his legal rights. He was soon charged with rape, kidnapping, and robbery.

At trial, officers admitted that during the interrogation the defendant was not informed of his right to have counsel present and that no counsel was present. Nonetheless, Miranda's confession was admitted into evidence. He was convicted and sentenced to serve 20–30 years for kidnapping and rape.

On appeal, the U.S. Supreme Court overturned Miranda's conviction, stating that the current practice of incommunicado interrogation is at odds with one of our Nation's most cherished principles—that the individual may not be compelled to incriminate himself. Unless adequate protective devices are employed to dispel the compulsion inherent in custodial surroundings, no statement obtained from the defendant can truly be the product of free choice.[56]

There are two legal triggers for the *Miranda* warning: custody and interrogation. Once a suspect has been placed under arrest, the police must give the suspect the *Miranda* warning before an interrogation (discussed in Chapter 6) is conducted for a suspected offense, whether a felony or a misdemeanor. If an officer does not give the warning when required, a defense attorney may ask the court to exclude the suspect's confession or statements. Once a Mirandized suspect invokes his or her right to silence, however, interrogation must cease. The police also may not readminister *Miranda* and interrogate the suspect later unless the suspect's attorney is present. If, however, the suspect initiates further conversation, any confession he or she provides is admissible.[57] Moreover, after an accused has invoked the right to counsel, the police may not interrogate the same suspect about a different crime.[58]

An exception to the *Miranda* requirement is the brief, routine traffic stop, but a custodial interrogation of a DUI (driving under the influence) suspect requires the *Miranda* warning.[59] And the police may question a suspect who poses a public-safety threat—known as the "public-safety exception." For example, when a clearly armed suspect runs into a public place and hides the gun, officers can legally ask the suspect about the location of the gun without violating *Miranda*.⁶⁰ In a more extreme example under the same exception, police were able to question Boston Marathon bomber Dzhokhar Tsarnaev for 16 hours without a *Miranda* warning because of the potential threat of co-conspirators and more planned bombings.⁶¹

Decisions Eroding *Miranda*

It has been held that a second interrogation session held after the suspect had initially refused to make a statement did not violate *Miranda*.⁶² The Court also decided that when a suspect waived his or her *Miranda* rights, believing the interrogation would focus on minor crimes, but the police shifted their questioning to a more serious crime, the confession was valid; there was no police deception or misrepresentation.⁶³ And when a suspect invoked his or her right to assistance of counsel and refused to make written statements, then voluntarily gave oral statements to police, the statements were admissible.⁶⁴ Finally, a suspect need not be given the *Miranda* warning in the exact form as it was outlined in *Miranda v. Arizona*. In one case, the waiver form said the suspect would have an attorney appointed "if and when you go to court." The Court held that as long as the warnings on the form reasonably convey the suspect's rights, they need not be given verbatim.⁶⁵ Further, a suspect must clearly invoke the *Miranda* right. The Supreme Court has ruled that even when a suspect remained silent during three continuous hours of police questioning, the suspect had not invoked his rights under *Miranda*—suspects must specifically say that they are choosing to remain silent.⁶⁶

Photo lineups, known as a "six-pack," are considered more likely to lead to misidentifications than live lineups.

You Be the . . .

Judge

In 2013, the U.S. Supreme Court reviewed a case that focused on issues related to the Fifth Amendment, *Miranda* rights, and refusal to answer law enforcement questioning. *Salinas v. Texas* involved the questioning of Genovevo Salinas, who investigators suspected might have information pertaining to a double homicide. The investigators interviewed Salinas at his parents' home, and Salinas's father voluntarily gave the police his son's shotgun. Salinas voluntarily answered questions later at the police station for about an hour until an officer asked him if ballistics analysis would show that his shotgun was used in the killings; at that point Salinas remained silent and began behaving in a suspicious manner (e.g., staring at the floor, biting his lip, clenching his hands, shuffling his feet).

Salinas was later arrested and found guilty of murder. During his trial, the prosecutor told the jury that Salinas refused to answer the ballistics question and argued that this was proof of his guilt. His lawyers appealed and argued that he was punished for exercising his Fifth Amendment right against self-incrimination.

1. Does *Miranda* apply during voluntary police interviews (outside of a custodial interrogation)?
2. Can prosecutors use a suspect's silence during police interviews to infer guilt during a criminal trial, or do Fifth Amendment protections apply?

The Supreme Court's decision for this case is provided in the Notes section at the end of the book.⁶⁷

Lineups and Other Pretrial Identification Procedures

Lineup: a procedure in which police ask suspects to submit to a viewing by witnesses to determine the guilty party, based on personal and physical characteristics; information obtained may be used later in court.

A police **lineup** or other face-to-face confrontation after the accused has been arrested is considered a critical stage of criminal proceedings; therefore, the accused has a right to have an attorney present. If counsel is not present, the evidence obtained is inadmissible.[68] However, the suspect is not entitled to the presence and advice of a lawyer before being formally charged, or when the police are using the more typical modern technique of a photo lineup, by showing a witness individual photos or a group of several photos typically referred to as a "six-pack."[69]

Faulty eyewitness identifications are the leading cause of wrongful convictions, and as a result, the law regarding their use has changed significantly in recent years (see Chapter 11 for more on wrongful convictions). Lineups—whether in person or through photos—must be fair and cannot be unreasonably suggestive, for example, by the suspect's being much taller than the others in the lineup or being the only person wearing a leather jacket similar to that worn by the perpetrator.[70] If identification procedures violate a suspect's due process rights to fairness, police risk having identifications made during these procedures excluded from evidence at trial. Further, in light of extensive social science research on faulty eyewitness identifications, many law enforcement agencies have changed their identification practices to include safeguards such as informing the witness that the suspect may or may not be in the lineup or photo set, preventing detectives working the case from being present to avoid giving inadvertent supportive or other cues to witnesses, and having witnesses record their level of certainty at the time of identification.[71] Some courts have instituted much stricter legal standards for admitting eyewitness evidence.[72]

Sixth Amendment: in the Bill of Rights, it guarantees the right to a speedy and public trial by an impartial jury, the right to effective counsel at trial, and other protections.

Poole

Cotton

Explore the case of Ronald Cotton (right), who served 11 years in prison for a sexual assault he did not commit. Despite studying her attacker closely, the victim misidentified Cotton in live and photo lineups, mistaking him for the real perpetrator, Bobby Poole (left).

THE SIXTH AMENDMENT

In all criminal prosecutions the accused shall enjoy the right to a speedy and public trial, by an impartial jury of the State and district wherein the crime shall have been committed, which district shall have been previously ascertained by law, and to be informed of the nature and cause of the accusation; to be confronted with the witnesses against him; to have compulsory process for obtaining witnesses in his favor, and to have the assistance of counsel for his defense.

Many people believe that the **Sixth Amendment** right of the accused to have the assistance of counsel before and during trial is the greatest right we enjoy in a democracy.

Powell v. Alabama (1932) established that in a capital case, when the accused is poor and illiterate, he or she enjoys the right to assistance of counsel for his or her defense and due process.[73] In *Gideon v. Wainwright* (1963), the Supreme Court mandated that all indigent people charged with felonies in state courts be provided counsel.[74] *Gideon* applied only to felony defendants, but *Argersinger v. Hamlin* (1973) extended the right to counsel to indigent people charged with *misdemeanor* crimes if they face the possibility of incarceration (however short the incarceration may be).75

For defendants with resources, who represents them in court is a matter of their own choice. In 2012, a home health care agency owner, Sila Luis, was indicted on Medicare fraud charges. Prosecutors alleged that Luis paid illegal kickbacks to patients and billed the federal government for services not rendered by her companies. Following existing federal law, the courts decided to freeze all her assets, including the $45 million she was accused of fraudulently procuring, as well as another $2 million contained within her accounts. In 2016, the U.S. Supreme Court ruled in *Luis v. United States* that the defendant's Sixth Amendment right to retain her counsel of choice was violated since she was unable to hire an attorney using her own assets.76 As a result, pretrial restraint of assets unrelated to the crime(s) in which a defendant is charged is now deemed unconstitutional.

Another landmark decision concerning the right to counsel is *Escobedo v. Illinois* (1964).77 Danny Escobedo's brother-in-law was fatally shot in 1960; Escobedo was arrested and questioned at police headquarters; and his request to confer with his lawyer was denied, even after the lawyer arrived and asked to see his client. The questioning of Escobedo lasted several hours, during which time he was handcuffed and forced to remain standing. Eventually, he admitted being an accomplice to murder. At no point was Escobedo advised of his rights to remain silent or to confer with his attorney. Escobedo's conviction was ultimately reversed by the U.S. Supreme Court, based on a violation of his right to counsel. However, the real thrust of the decision was his Fifth Amendment right not to incriminate himself and to be informed of his rights; when a defendant is scared, flustered, ignorant, alone, and bewildered, he or she is often unable to effectively make use of protections granted under the Fifth Amendment without the advice of an attorney. Note that *Miranda*, decided two years later, simply established the guidelines for the police to inform suspects of all of these rights.

The Sixth Amendment's provision for a speedy and public trial is discussed in Chapter 9.

/// IN A NUTSHELL

- The Fourth Amendment protects the right of the people to be secure in their persons, papers, and effects, against unreasonable searches and seizures; and no search or arrest warrants shall be issued without probable cause, describing the place to be searched and disclosing the persons or things to be seized.

- The standard for a legal arrest, search, and seizure is probable cause, meaning that for an officer to make an arrest or conduct a search of someone's person or effects, he or she must have a reasonable suspicion that a crime has been or is about to be committed by that individual (which, in the case of a search, can include the person's merely possessing some form of illegal contraband).

- The exclusionary rule forbids evidence obtained in violation of the Fourth Amendment from being used against the defendant in a criminal trial.

- There are two ways for the police to make an arrest: with a warrant, and without a warrant. It is always best for a police officer to arrest someone with a warrant, because a warrant means that a neutral magistrate has examined the facts and determined that the individual should be arrested in order to make an accounting of the charge(s).

- Police officers must obtain a warrant when making a felony arrest, unless exigent circumstances are present (immediate action being required) and the officer possesses probable cause to make the arrest.

- As with arrests, the best means by which the police can search a person or premises is with a search warrant issued by a neutral magistrate. The process for obtaining a search warrant is the same as for an arrest warrant; in this case, a determination is made after the magistrate hears evidence from an affiant about whether probable cause exists to believe a person possesses evidence of a crime, such as stolen property or a weapon believed to have been used in committing the crime.

- The police may detain a person briefly for questioning, even without probable cause, if they believe that the person has committed a crime or is about to commit a crime, and the person may be frisked for a weapon if an officer reasonably suspects the person is carrying one and fears for his or her life. An extension of that rule involves the "plain feel" doctrine, according to which police, having reasonable cause to believe a person possesses drugs and feeling what resembles such an object on his or her person, may remove the object and make an arrest.
- The police have greater latitude in searching automobiles, because they can be used to conduct a getaway and to hide evidence.
- The police may search incident to lawful arrest and do not need a search warrant for items that are seen in plain view or when citizens give police consent. The police must, however, obtain a search warrant to search a suspect's cell phone or conduct a blood test.
- Police may use drug-sniffing dogs at traffic stops but not near homes without a warrant; they may also collect DNA swabs from arrestees as part of a routine booking procedure.
- The right against self-incrimination, under the Fifth Amendment, states that no criminal defendant shall be compelled to take the witness stand and give evidence against himself or herself. Once a suspect is arrested, the *Miranda* warning must be given before he or she is interrogated for any offense, be it a felony or a misdemeanor.
- The Sixth Amendment guarantees the accused the right to have the assistance of counsel during custodial interrogation and during trial.

/// KEY TERMS & CONCEPTS

Review key terms with eFlashcards at **edge.sagepub.com/peak4e**.

Affidavit   186
Exclusionary rule   184
Exigent circumstance   186
Fifth Amendment   197
Fourth Amendment   183
Lineup   200
Probable cause   183
Reasonable suspicion   192
Search and seizure   183
Sixth Amendment   200
Terry Stop   193
Warrant, arrest   183
Warrant, search   183

/// REVIEW QUESTIONS

Test your understanding of chapter content at **edge.sagepub.com/peak4e**.

1. What protections are afforded citizens by the Fourth, Fifth, and Sixth Amendments?
2. What is an example of probable cause?
3. What, from both police and community perspectives, are the ramifications of having or not having the exclusionary rule?
4. How would you distinguish between arrests and searches and seizures with and without a warrant? Which method for arresting or searching is always best and why?
5. In what significant ways has the *Miranda* decision been eroded, and what future challenges might arise given the continuing tension between law enforcement powers and individual civil rights?
6. What limitations are placed on the police in their ability to use high-tech electronic equipment in order to listen in on conversations? Search for drugs?
7. What are two major court decisions concerning right to counsel, and how do they apply in everyday life?

/// LEARN BY DOING

1. Your criminal justice professor has assigned a class project wherein class members are to determine which amendment in the Bill of Rights—the Fourth, Fifth, or Sixth—contains the most important rights that are protected under a democracy. You are to analyze the three amendments and present your findings as to which one is the most important.
2. As part of a criminal justice honor society exercise, you are debating which period of legal history was the most important: the so-called due process revolution of the Warren Court (when the Supreme Court granted many additional rights to the accused through *Gideon, Miranda, Escobedo,* and so forth), or the more conservative era that followed under the Rehnquist

Court (during which time many Warren Court decisions were eroded, and more rights were given to the police). Choose a side, and defend your opinion.

3. From the time of his confirmation in 1969, Chief Justice Warren Burger viewed the exclusionary rule as an unnecessary and unreasonable intrusion on law enforcement. Assume that as part of a group project, you are to prepare a pro-con paper that examines why there should or should not be an exclusionary rule as a part of our system of justice. What will be your arguments, pro and con?

/// STUDY SITE

Get the tools you need to sharpen your study skills. SAGE edge offers a robust online environment featuring an impressive array of free tools and resources.

Access practice quizzes, eFlashcards, video, and multimedia at **edge.sagepub.com/peak4e**.

THE COURTS

PART 3

Chapter 9: Court Organization: Structure, Functions, and the Trial Process
Chapter 10: The Bench and the Bar: Those Who Judge, Prosecute, and Defend
Chapter 11: Court Methods and Challenges: Sentencing and Punishment

This part consists of three chapters. **Chapter 9** examines court structure and functions at the federal, state, and trial court levels; included are discussions of pretrial preparations, the actual trial process, the jury system, and some court technologies.

Chapter 10 looks at the courtroom work group, including the judges, prosecutors, and defense attorneys, and legal defenses that are allowed under the law.

Chapter 11 discusses sentencing, punishment, and appeals. Included are the types and purposes of punishment, types of sentences convicted persons may receive, federal sentencing guidelines, victim impact statements, and capital punishment.

CHAPTER 9

COURT ORGANIZATION
Structure, Functions, and the Trial Process

The place of justice is a hallowed place.

—Francis Bacon

Courts are at the center of life's important moments.

—Howard Conyers, former Washoe County, Nevada, district court administrator

LEARNING OBJECTIVES

As a result of reading this chapter, you will be able to

1. Explain the methods and purposes of the adversarial court system
2. Explain court jurisdiction and how it is determined
3. Identify the purpose and process of state appeals courts
4. List the functions of the various tiers of the federal court system, including appeals courts
5. Relate the activities that occur during the pretrial process as attorneys prepare for trial
6. Delineate the trial process, from opening statements through conviction and appeal
7. Discuss the impact of new technologies on the courts

ASSESS YOUR AWARENESS

Test your knowledge of court structure and functions as well as the trial process and jury system by responding to the following six true-false items; check your answers after reading this chapter.

1. America's court system relies on the adversarial system, which includes, among other things, the cross-examination of witnesses.
2. America's court system consists of a national system of federal courts as well as 50 state court systems, plus those in the District of Columbia and U.S. territories.
3. Federal judges are nominated by the president and confirmed by the Senate, and they have a lifetime appointment.
4. All courts generally have unlimited jurisdiction to hear civil and criminal trials as well as appeals.
5. The Sixth Amendment gives the accused the right to a trial by an impartial jury of peers—meaning 12 people who are "similar in nearly all regards" to the defendant.
6. A convicted person may quickly and easily—and at any time—leave the state court appellate system and appeal in a federal court.

<< Answers can be found on page 419.

In Orlando, Florida, 25-year-old Casey Anthony was charged with the murder of her 2-year-old daughter Caylee. It was Anthony's mother who called to report Caylee missing after she learned her granddaughter had been gone for 31 days. Anthony told police that Caylee was with a babysitter and that she worked at Universal Studios; both of these claims (and other statements she made) were found to be untrue. Police and hundreds of volunteers looked for Caylee before her decomposed body was found 6 months later in a wooded area not far from Anthony's home. Prosecutors alleged that Anthony used chloroform (traces were found in the trunk of her car) and suffocated her daughter by placing duct tape over the girl's mouth and nose. Before, during, and after the trial, the case captivated the nation.

Judges who preside over these types of trials must determine whether they believe that jurors can impartially weigh evidence presented in trial. Given the extent of media coverage surrounding Anthony's case, Judge Belvin Perry Jr., faced the difficult task of finding jurors who could set aside their preformed judgments about Anthony's guilt or innocence. Motions for a change of venue (which are discussed as part of the pretrial motions that you will learn about in this chapter) are often filed by defense attorneys in high-profile cases. Yet Judge Perry decided to hold the trial where Anthony was charged (in Orlando) and import a jury from Clearwater, Florida, 100 miles away. This decision was costly and caused many hardships for jurors, who were sequestered for two months in a hotel far away from home. Jurors were not permitted to use personal computers or cell phones, and they were unable to watch news media channels.

Do you agree with critics that a traditional change of venue would have been a better course of action for this trial? Do you believe that these jurors were more impartial than jurors who might have been selected from the jurisdiction in which the murder took place?

As you read this chapter, consider these questions and the role of our nation's courts, which deal not only with high-profile cases like Anthony's but also with the much more minor and numerous cases that overload our state trial courts.

INTRODUCTION

Courts have existed in some form for thousands of years. The court system has survived the dark eras of the Inquisition and the Star Chamber (which enforced unpopular political policies in England during the 1500s and 1600s and, without a jury or public view, meted out severe punishment, including whipping, branding, and mutilation). The U.S. court system developed rapidly after the American Revolution and led to the establishment of law and justice on the western frontier.

In this chapter, we first consider the adversarial system the courts employ and how the courts influence our lives as policy-making bodies. Then the focus shifts to the several levels of courts found in the United States. Your attention is drawn to the case of Barry Kibbe, presented near the beginning of the section on federal courts; this case provides a rare look at the entire criminal trial and appeals process, all the way to the U.S. Supreme Court.

Colonial Courts: An Overview

Our nation's colonial courts began modestly. Thomas Olive, deputy governor of West Jersey in 1684, described the prevailing court system when he wrote that he was "in the habit of dispensing justice sitting in his meadow."[1] As the population of the colonies grew, however, formal courts of law appeared in Virginia, Massachusetts, Maryland, Rhode Island, and Connecticut, among other venues. The colonies drew on the example set by the English Parliament in that the colonial legislatures became the highest courts.[2]

Beneath the legislatures (those who make and change laws) were the superior courts, which heard both civil and criminal cases. Over time, some colonies established trial courts headed by a chief justice and several associate justices. Appeals from the trial courts were heard by the governor and his council in what were often called "courts of appeals."[3] Courts established at the county level played a key role in both the government and the social life of the colonies. In addition to having jurisdiction in both civil and criminal cases, county courts fulfilled many administrative duties, including setting and collecting taxes, supervising the building of roads, and licensing taverns.

Dual court system: the state and federal court systems of the United States.

State court system: civil or criminal courts in which cases are decided through an adversarial process; typically including a court of last resort, an appellate court, trial courts, and lower courts.

Federal court system: the four-tiered federal system that includes the Supreme Court, circuit courts of appeal, district courts, and magistrate courts.

Eventually, however, the founders of the new republic had profound concerns about the distribution of power between courts and legislatures, and between the states and the federal government. Coming from the experience of living under English rule, they feared the tyranny that could flow from the concentration of governmental power. At the same time, they were living with the problems associated with a weak centralized government. This conflict prompted the delegates to the Constitutional Convention of 1787 to create a federal judiciary that was separate from the legislative branch of government. As a result, today we have the **dual court system**—one implemented by the **state court system** (inherited directly from the Crown of England) and the other created by Congress and entrusted to the **federal court system**.[4]

Our Adversarial System

Ralph Waldo Emerson stated that "every violation of truth ... is a stab at the health of human society."[5] Certainly, most people would agree that the traditional, primary purpose of our courts is to provide a forum for seeking and obtaining the truth. Indeed, the

U.S. Supreme Court declared in 1966 in *Tehan v. U.S. ex rel. Shott* that "the basic purpose of a trial is the determination of truth."⁶

Our American court system relies on the **adversarial system**, which uses several means to get at the truth. First, evidence is tested under this approach through cross-examination of witnesses. Second, power is lodged with several different people; each courtroom actor is granted limited powers to counteract those of the others. If, for example, the judge is biased or unfair, the jury can disregard the judge and reach a fair verdict. If the judge believes the jury has acted improperly, he or she can set aside the jury's verdict and order a new trial. Furthermore, both the prosecuting and defense attorneys have certain rights and authority under each state's constitution. This series of checks and balances is aimed at curbing misuse of the criminal courts.

Adversarial system: a legal system wherein there is a contest between two opposing sides, with a judge (and possibly a jury) sitting as an impartial arbiter, seeking truth.

The Influence of Courts in Policy Making

Determining what the law says and providing a public forum involve the courts in policy making. **Policy making** can be defined as choosing among alternative choices of action. The policy decisions of the courts affect virtually all of us in our daily living. In recent decades, the courts have been asked to deal with issues that previously were within the purview of the legislative and executive branches. Because many of the Constitution's limitations on government are couched in vague language, the judicial branch must help

Policy making: the act of creating laws or setting standards to govern the activities of government; the U.S. Supreme Court, for example, has engaged in policy making in several areas, such as affirmative action, voting, and freedom of communication and expression.

Going Global

Adversarial Versus Inquisitorial Justice Systems

As noted in this chapter, courts in the United States rely on the adversarial system of justice, particularly for our most serious cases. Each courtroom actor is granted powers to counteract the power of others. Under this model, defendants are judged by peers (a jury) and evidence is presented orally. Because the adversarial model allows lay decision makers to determine guilt, careful attention is given to the development of rules of evidence that will be presented to jurors. Judges serve as the gatekeepers who determine what evidence is and is not admissible for jurors to consider.

Inquisitorial justice systems (such as those we use in the United States to judge minor crimes, like misdemeanors) represent the primary justice system used by other countries, including Japan, Germany, China, and Scotland. Inquisitorial systems share some common characteristics with adversarial systems. For example, both systems differ only slightly in their standards of proof, have a presumption of innocence, provide the right to counsel, and provide (to varying degrees) the right to confrontation by the accused.

However, the primary function of the courts operating within an inquisitorial system is to take responsibility for finding the truth. Documentation is preferred over oral evidence presentation, and plea bargaining (which interferes with the ultimate discovery of "truth") is generally not permitted in the strict sense. Rather than offering rules of evidence, the judge is relied upon to determine the reliability and significance of evidence.

Most criminal law systems are not considered to be purely adversarial or purely inquisitorial, since most fall somewhere between these two ideological systems. However, experts have argued that the Netherlands employs the most inquisitorial justice system, while the justice system in England/Wales employs the most adversarial system in Western Europe. Consider the strength and weaknesses of each system and which system you believe is best situated to achieve justice.

Source: Peter J. Van Koppen and Steven D. Penrod. (2003). "Adversarial or Inquisitorial: Comparing Systems," in Peter J. Van Koppen and Steven D. Penrod (Eds.), *Adversarial Versus Inquisitorial Justice: Psychological Perspectives on Criminal Justice Systems*, pp. 2–20. New York: Plenum.

Practitioner's Perspective

Attorney

Name: Jeff Mason
Position: Attorney
Location: Colorado

What is your career story? I became interested in the law at an early age. My dad was a cop growing up, so I grew up on cop stories and probably still get my fair share of them. That's what interested me in getting my bachelor's degree in criminal justice and criminology. I also went on to get a master's degree. And it was really during my undergraduate studies that I developed an interest in writing and, specifically, in persuasive writing. I really found that I enjoyed and began to excel at writing and trying to persuade an audience to adopt my viewpoints. So I'm not entirely sure how it happened, but I decided that based on those interests that I might do well in a legal career.

What are some challenges and misconceptions you face in this position? I think there are a number of challenges from the legal side. The law is a big thing, it's always changing and no two cases are the same. How the law applies to a particular case is always different from that of the previous case. It's also a sensitive area, dealing with the criminal system. It can be a very emotionally challenging field. It's an area ripe with challenges and a lot of that has to do with the nature of the work itself.

I'm the first to appreciate a good crime drama or movie, but it certainly does create a challenge as far as the public perception of the judicial process. Everything isn't exactly how it's portrayed, and I often find myself watching these shows and saying, well, this is incorrect. There's a public perception that the judicial process is more action packed than it might really be at trial.

What role does diversity play in this position? Diversity is something I see all the time. There is a diverse body of lawyers these days. I even notice that in law school, that there are men and women of every background. The same is true of the parties as well; the courts are unique in that they deal with cases of every type, civil and criminal. So you see corporations, individuals, men and women of a variety of ethnic backgrounds.

What are some challenges you face in this position? Technology has become the biggest challenge. The Constitution and laws are evolving as technology evolves and changes, so that is a battle that legislatures and judges have to deal with on a daily basis. These laws have been around for some time now, and we have to find ways to apply them, given the different and unique circumstances in which these crimes and offenses are committed. I know that, for example, technological advancements such as GPS, cell phones, even night vision goggles, interplay with constitutional rights against unreasonable searches and seizures. These are things that courts have to wrestle with and address on a daily basis as law enforcement tactics also advance.

To learn more about Jeff Mason's experiences as an attorney, watch the Practitioner's Perspective video in SAGE vantage.

interpret the law and deal with potentially volatile social issues, such as those involving prisons, abortion, and schools.[7]

U.S. Supreme Court decisions have dramatically changed race relations, resulted in the overhaul of juvenile courts, increased the rights of the accused, prohibited prayer and segregation in public schools, legalized abortion, and allowed for destruction of the U.S. flag. State and federal courts have together overturned minimum residency requirements for welfare recipients, equalized school expenditures, and prevented road and highway construction from damaging the environment. They have eliminated the requirement of a high school diploma for a firefighter's job and ordered increased property taxes to desegregate public schools. More recently, the federal courts blocked travel bans that sought to keep foreign nationals from Middle Eastern nations from entering the United States. Cases in which courts make policy determinations usually involve government, the Fourteenth Amendment, and the need for equity—the remedy most often used against governmental violations of law. Recent policy-making decisions by the judicial branch have been based not on the Constitution but, rather, on federal statutes concerning the rights of the disadvantaged and consumers and the environment.[8]

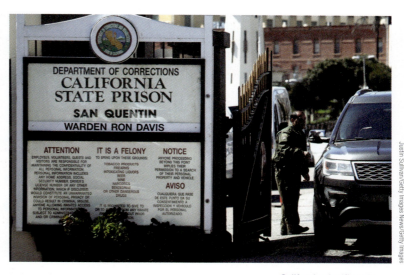

California significantly reduced prison populations by nearly 30,000 inmates over the course of 15 months following the U.S. Supreme Court ruling in *Brown v. Plata*.

Perhaps nowhere have the nation's courts had more of an impact than in the prisons—from which tens of thousands prisoner petitions are filed each year in the U.S. district courts (approximately 80 percent of them filed by state prisoners).[9] Judicial intervention has extended to prisoners the recognition of the constitutional rights of free speech, religion, and due process; abolished the South's plantation model of prisons; accelerated the professionalization of U.S. correctional managers; encouraged a new generation of correctional administrators more amenable to reform; reinforced the adoption of national standards for prisons; and promoted increased accountability and efficiency of prisons. And while judicial intervention previously failed to prevent the explosion in prison populations and costs,[10] recent judicial decisions have ordered reductions in the numbers of inmates housed in correctional facilities. In 2011, the U.S. Supreme Court ruled that court-mandated inmate population limits are necessary to protect prisoners' constitutional rights and prevent **Eighth Amendment** violations involving cruel and unusual punishments.[11]

Eighth Amendment: in the Bill of Rights, it contains the protection against excessive bail and fines, as well as cruel and unusual punishment.

It may appear that the courts are overbroad in their review of issues. However, judges "cannot impose their views . . . until someone brings a case to court, often as a last resort after complaints to unresponsive legislators and executives."[12] Plaintiffs must be truly aggrieved and have a legal right to bring their case to court. The independence of the judicial branch, particularly at the federal court level, where judges enjoy lifetime appointments, allows the courts to champion the causes of the underclasses: those with fewer financial resources or votes (by virtue of, say, being a minority group) or without a positive public profile.[13] Also, the judiciary is considered to be the "least dangerous branch," having no enforcement powers. Moreover, the decisions of the courts can be overturned by legislative action. Thus, the judicial branch depends on a perception of legitimacy surrounding its decisions.[14]

AMERICAN COURTS: A DUAL COURT SYSTEM

To better understand the U.S. court system, it is first important to know that this country has a dual court system: both a national system of federal courts and 50 state court systems. Although often sharing similar names, they operate under different constitutions and laws, as outlined in the sections that follow.

Before exploring these different courts, we take up the critical issue of **jurisdiction**, which is best defined as a court's legal authority to hear and decide a particular type of case. Jurisdiction is set forth in state and federal law, and it is typically based on geography (i.e., where the case is physically located) and subject matter (what the case is about: criminal, civil, juvenile, etc.). Courts hear only cases that fall under their jurisdiction and authority;

Jurisdiction, court: the authority of a court to hear a particular type of case, based on geography (city, state, or federal) and subject matter (e.g., criminal, civil, probate).

Chapter 9: Court Organization ■ 211

Table 9.1 /// State and Federal Courts	
State Courts	**Federal Courts**
Appellate Jurisdiction—Courts of Last Resort	
State supreme court	U.S. Supreme Court
Appellate Jurisdiction—Intermediate Courts of Appeals	
State courts of appeals	Circuit courts of appeals
Trial Courts	
State trial courts	U.S. district courts
Limited Jurisdiction Trial Courts	
Traffic, juvenile, justice of the peace (for example)	Tax, admiralty, bankruptcy (for example)

our courts are organized along state and federal lines and then further along subject matter lines (see Table 9.1). At the lower end are the limited-jurisdiction state trial courts, handling traffic cases, misdemeanors, and juvenile matters, for example. At the highest level is the U.S. Supreme Court, which hears a limited number of appeals on federal and constitutional legal issues. The great majority of the nation's judicial business occurs at the state—not the federal—level, and our discussion begins there.

STATE COURTS

Where Most Cases Begin: State Trial Courts

Major court complexes, like this one in San Diego, California, are common in bigger cities where a variety of courts—state and federal—handle sometimes overwhelming caseloads.

At the lowest level of state courts are trial courts of limited jurisdiction, also known as inferior courts or lower courts. There are more than 13,500 trial courts of limited jurisdiction in the United States, staffed by about 18,000 judicial officers. The lower courts constitute 85 percent of all judicial bodies in the United States.[15]

Variously called district, justice, justice of the peace, city, magistrate, or municipal courts, the lower courts decide a restricted range of cases. These courts are created and maintained by city or county governments and therefore are not part of the state judiciary. The caseload of the lower courts is staggering—more than 84 million cases a year, an overwhelming number of which are traffic cases (more than 45 million).[16]

The workload of the lower courts can be divided into felony criminal cases, nonfelony criminal cases, and civil cases. In the felony arena, lower court jurisdiction typically includes the preliminary stages of felony cases. Therefore, after an arrest, a judge in a trial court of limited jurisdiction will hold the initial appearance, appoint counsel for indigents, and conduct the preliminary hearing. Later, the case will be transferred to a trial court of general jurisdiction for trial (or plea) and sentencing.[17]

General Jurisdiction: Major Trial Courts

State trial courts of general jurisdiction are usually referred to as the major trial courts. There are an estimated 2,000 major state trial courts, staffed by more than 11,000 judges.

Each court has its own support staff consisting of a clerk of the court, a bailiff, and others. In most states, the trial courts of general jurisdiction are also grouped into judicial districts or circuits. In rural areas, these districts or circuits encompass several adjoining counties, and the judges are true generalists who hear a variety of cases and literally ride the circuit; conversely, larger counties have only one circuit or district for the area, and the judges are often specialists assigned to hear only certain types of cases.[18] The term *general jurisdiction* means that these courts have the legal authority to decide all matters not specifically delegated by state law to the lower courts of limited jurisdiction. The most common names for these courts are district, circuit, and superior.[19] On the criminal justice front, most serious criminal violations, including many drug-related offenses, are heard in these trial courts of general jurisdiction. Although the courts are overburdened with heavy case filings, most criminal cases do not go to trial, and the dominant issue in the courts of general jurisdiction is not guilt or innocence, but what penalty to apply to someone who has entered a guilty plea through plea bargaining (described later in this chapter). Figure 9.1 shows an organizational structure for a county district court serving a population of 300,000. Note the variety of functions and programs that exist, in addition to the basic court role of hearing trials and rendering dispositions.

Within the state trial court system, a number of specialty courts or problem-solving courts, such as drug, family, mental health, veterans, and domestic violence courts, have become more common. They are used to divert criminal defendants into treatment programs rather than jail or prison (see "Diversion Programs/Problem-Solving Courts," later in this chapter).

Figure 9.2 shows the caseload trends for state criminal trial courts in the United States. As with crime in general, caseloads are declining in the trial courts.

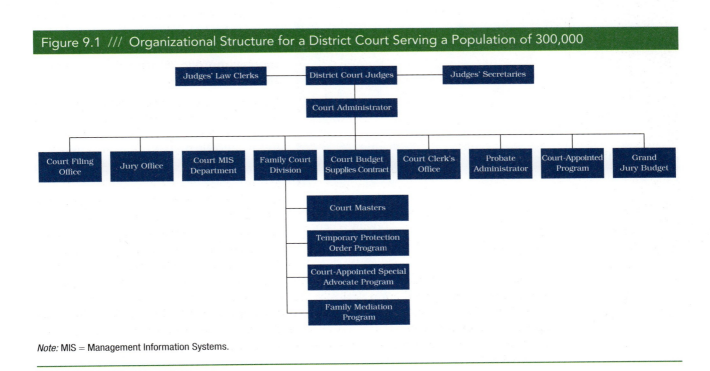

Figure 9.1 /// Organizational Structure for a District Court Serving a Population of 300,000

Note: MIS = Management Information Systems.

Figure 9.2 /// State Court Incoming Caseloads, 2007–2016

Total incoming caseloads in state courts reached an apex of just over 106.1 million cases at the onset of the Great Recession in 2008. Between 2009 and 2015, aggregate caseloads declined at an average annual rate of nearly 3.5 percent. However, in 2016, that rate fell to a 2.5 percent decrease overall.

Source: www.courtstatistics.org.

Intermediate court of appeals: a state court that stands between a trial court and a court of last resort; it typically has appellate jurisdiction only.

Appeals Courts

After a conviction in a criminal case or a judgment in a civil case, the first stop for an appeal in the state courts is known as an **intermediate court of appeals** (ICA). These courts stand between trial courts and courts of last resort (state supreme courts), and they typically have appellate jurisdiction only; that is, they hear only appeals.

State courts have experienced a significant growth in appellate cases that would overwhelm a single appellate court such as a state's supreme court. To alleviate the caseload burden on courts of last resort, state officials have responded by creating ICAs, which must hear all properly filed appeals. As of 2019, 41 states had established permanent ICAs. The only states not having an ICA are sparsely populated with low volumes of appeals: Delaware, Maine, Montana, New Hampshire, Rhode Island, South Dakota, Vermont, West Virginia and Wyoming (also, the District of Columbia does not have ICAs). Nevada's population and caseloads grew in recent years, prompting voters in 2014 to approve the creation of an ICA, which began hearing its first cases in early 2015.[20] The structure of the ICAs varies. In most states these bodies hear both civil and criminal appeals, and these courts typically use rotating three-judge panels. Also, the state ICAs' workload is demanding: According to the National Center for State Courts, state ICAs report that more than 185,000 cases are filed annually.[21] ICAs engage primarily in error corrections; they review trials to make sure that the law was followed and the overall standard is one of fairness. The ICAs represent the final stage of the process for most litigants. Very few cases make it to the appellate court in the first place, and of those cases, only a small portion will be heard by the state's court of last resort.[22]

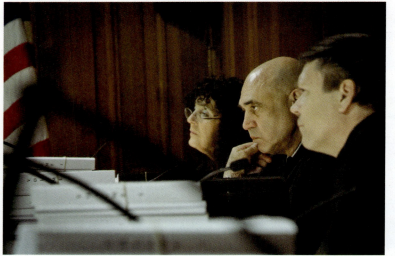

Appellate court judges Sandra Sgroi, left, John Leventhal, center, and Mark Dillon, right, three members of a four-judge panel, listen to oral arguments from attorneys appealing for the public release of records from the grand jury in the videotaped chokehold death of Eric Garner, Tuesday, June 16, 2015, in New York.

The state's **court of last resort** is usually referred to as the state supreme court. The specific names differ from state to state, as do the number of judges (from a low of five to as many as nine). Unlike the ICAs, these courts do not use panels in making decisions; rather, the entire court sits to decide each case. All state supreme courts have a limited amount of original jurisdiction in dealing with matters such as disciplining lawyers and judges.[23] Nowhere is the policy-making role of state supreme courts more apparent than in deciding death penalty cases—which, in most states, are appealed automatically to the state's highest court, thus bypassing the ICAs. The state supreme courts are also the ultimate review board for matters involving interpretation of state law.[24] In states not having ICAs, the state supreme court has no power to choose which cases will be placed on its docket. However, the ability of most state supreme courts to choose which cases to hear makes them important policy-making bodies. Whereas ICAs review thousands of cases each year, looking for errors, state supreme courts handle a hundred or so cases that present the most challenging legal issues arising in that state.

Court of last resort: the last court that may hear a case at the state or federal level.

Causation: a link between one's act and the injurious act or crime, such as one tossing a match in a forest and igniting a deadly fire.

You Be the . . .

Judge

On a very cold night in Rochester, New York, Barry Kibbe and a friend met Stafford at a bar. Stafford had been drinking so heavily that the bartender refused to serve him more alcohol, so Kibbe offered to take him barhopping elsewhere. They visited other bars, and at about 9:30 p.m., Kibbe and his friend drove Stafford to a remote point on a highway and demanded his money. They also forced Stafford to lower his trousers and remove his boots to show he had no money hidden. Stafford was then abandoned on the highway, in the cold. A half-hour later, a man driving his truck down the highway saw Stafford standing in the highway, waving his arms for him to stop. The driver didn't see Stafford soon enough to stop, and Stafford was struck and killed. Even though the driver of the truck killed Stafford, Kibbe was arrested and charged with robbery and second-degree murder, raising a challenging question of **causation**—a necessary element in holding someone criminally responsible for a death.

State Court Actions: In *State v. Kibbe*, Kibbe was tried and convicted of robbery and murder in the second degree. At trial, the judge did not instruct the jury on the subject of causation (e.g., that the government had to prove Kibbe had actually caused Stafford's death). On appeal to New York's appeals court, in *Kibbe v. Henderson*, Kibbe argued that the judge should have given the jury such an instruction so that they would have to determine whether the state had proved this element beyond a reasonable doubt, but the appellate court affirmed his conviction. Then, on appeal to New York's supreme court, the conviction was also affirmed. Both courts found that the judge did not err in failing to instruct the jury about causation.

Federal Court Actions: Having exhausted all possible state remedies, Kibbe then sought redress in the federal court, filing a writ of *habeas corpus* with the U.S. district court having jurisdiction and arguing that the trial judge had violated his due process rights by not giving the jury instructions regarding causation. The district court denied the habeas petition, saying that no constitutional question had been raised.

Next, Kibbe appealed to the Second U.S. Circuit Court of Appeals, making the same argument. This court, however, reversed his conviction, saying that Kibbe had been deprived of due process because of the trial judge's failure to instruct the jury on causation. Next, the government appealed, this time to the U.S. Supreme Court; in *Henderson v. Kibbe*, the Supreme Court, issuing a writ of certiorari (defined later in this chapter) to the lower court, decided to hear the case.

1. How do you believe the U.S. Supreme Court should rule—for or against Kibbe? Why?
2. Who was Henderson (Kibbe's adversary) in this case?
3. What is meant by "exhausting all possible state remedies"?
4. What is meant by *habeas corpus*?

Answers to these questions are provided in the Notes section at the end of the book.[25]

FEDERAL COURTS

The accompanying "You Be the . . . Judge" box describes a case that uniquely demonstrates the entire appellate process through the dual state and federal court systems, going through the state courts and all the way to the U.S. Supreme Court.

Federal Trial Courts: U.S. District Courts

District courts: trial courts at the county, state, or federal level with general and original jurisdiction.

The U.S. district courts, like their counterparts in the state court system, may be fairly described as the "workhorses" of the federal judiciary, because nearly all civil or criminal cases heard in the federal courts are initiated at the district court level. Indeed, there are about 359,000 annual combined filings for civil cases and criminal defendants in the U.S. district courts.[26]

The locations of the U.S. district courts are outlined in Figure 9.3 (sometimes designated by region—"northern" or "eastern," for example). Congress created 94 U.S. district courts, 89 of which are located within the 50 states. There is at least one district court in each state (some states have more, such as California, New York, and Texas, each of which has four). Congress has created 678 district court judgeships for the 94 districts. The president nominates district judges, who must then be confirmed by the Senate; they then serve for life unless removed for cause. In the federal system, the U.S. district courts are the federal trial courts of original jurisdiction for all major violations of federal criminal law (some 500 full-time magistrate judges hear minor violations).[27] They can also hear appeals from state supreme courts (involving constitutional questions) and lower federal courts.

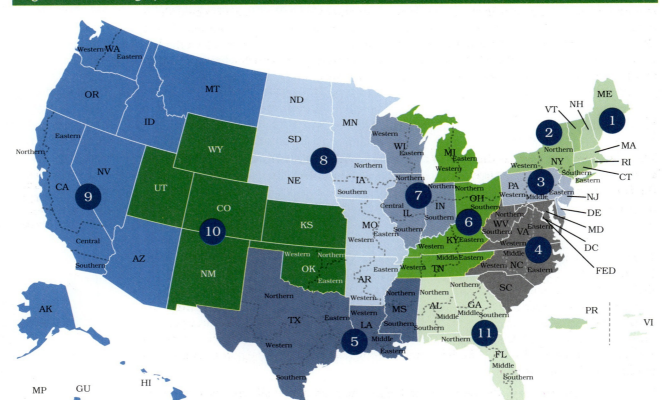

Figure 9.3 /// Geographic Boundaries of U.S. Courts of Appeals and District Courts

216 ■ Part 3: The Courts

District court judges are assisted by an elaborate supporting cast of clerks, secretaries, law clerks, court reporters, probations officers, pretrial services officers, and U.S. marshals. The larger districts also have a public defender. Another important actor at the district court level is the U.S. attorney—the federal prosecutor. There is one U.S. attorney in each district. The work of district judges is significantly assisted by 352 bankruptcy judges, who are appointed for 14-year terms by the court of appeals in which the district is located.

U.S. Courts of Appeals: Circuit Courts

Much like the state court system, the federal system provides intermediate courts of appeals—intermediate between U.S. district courts and the U.S. Supreme Court. These courts are known as the circuit courts of appeals, referring to the 13 geographic areas—or circuits—where these courts are seated and over which they exercise jurisdiction. Eleven of the circuits are identified by number, and two others are called the D.C. Circuit and the Federal Circuit (see Figure 9.3). A court of appeals hears appeals from the U.S. district courts located within its circuit, as well as appeals from decisions of federal administrative agencies. These courts, receiving about 28,000 appellate filings per year, are the last stop for an appeal before it reaches the U.S. Supreme Court.[28]

The judges who sit on the circuit courts of appeals are nominated by the president and confirmed by the Senate. As with the U.S. district courts, the number of judges in each circuit varies, from 6 in the First Circuit to 28 in the Ninth, depending on the volume and complexity of the caseload. Each circuit has a chief judge (chosen by seniority or on a rotating basis) who has supervisory responsibilities. Several staff positions aid the judges in conducting the work of the courts of appeals. A circuit executive assists the chief judge in administering the circuit. The clerk's office maintains the records. Each judge is also allowed to hire three law clerks. In deciding cases, the courts of appeals may use rotating three-judge panels. Or, by majority vote, all the judges in the circuit may sit together to decide a case or reconsider a panel's decision. Such *en banc* hearings are rare, however.[29] Because the U.S. Supreme Court hears so few cases (see next section), the U.S. circuit court decisions are very often the last word on legal issues and, as such, their decisions have great impact in setting legal precedent and in shaping the law for the many people who live within a circuit court's geographic jurisdiction.

Circuit courts: originally courts wherein judges traveled a circuit to hear appeals, now courts with several counties or districts in their jurisdiction; the federal court system contains 11 circuit courts of appeals (plus the District of Columbia and territories), which hear appeals from district courts.

U.S. Supreme Court

The U.S. Supreme Court, as the highest court in the nation, has ultimate jurisdiction over all federal courts, as well as over state courts in cases involving issues of federal law; it is the final interpreter of federal constitutional law. In the sections that follow, we briefly discuss its jurisdiction, practices, workload, and administration.

U.S. Supreme Court: the court of last resort in the United States, also the highest appellate court; it consists of nine justices who are appointed for life.

Judges and Advocacy

The Supreme Court, formed in 1790, and other federal courts have their basis in Article III, Section 1, of the Constitution, which provides that "the judicial Power of the United States, shall be vested in one supreme Court, and in such inferior Courts as the Congress may from time to time ordain and establish."[30] The Supreme Court is composed of nine justices: one chief justice and eight associate justices. As with other federal judges appointed under Article III, they are nominated to their post by the president and confirmed by the Senate, and they serve for life.[31] Each new term of the Supreme Court begins, by statute, on the first Monday in October.

Not just any lawyer may advocate a cause before the high court; all who wish to do so must first secure admission to the Supreme Court bar. Applicants must submit an application form that requires applicants to have been admitted to practice in the highest court

The front page of this grand jury indictment against former NFL star Michael Vick shows that Vick was prosecuted in U.S. District Court—federal court—for multiple violations of federal criminal laws. An indictment is one method by which a criminal case can move forward to trial or a plea deal.

of their state for a period of at least three years (during which time they must not have been the subject of any adverse disciplinary action), and they must appear to the Court to be of good moral and professional character. Applicants must also swear or affirm to act "uprightly and according to law, and . . . support the Constitution of the United States."³²

Conferences and Workload

The Supreme Court does not meet continuously in formal sessions during its nine-month term. Instead, the Court divides its time into four separate but related activities. First, some amount of time is allocated to reading through the thousands of petitions for review of cases that come annually to the Court—usually during the summer and when the Court is not sitting to hear cases. Second, the Court allocates blocks of time for oral arguments—the live discussion in which lawyers for both sides present their clients' positions to the justices. During the weeks of oral arguments, the Court sets aside its third allotment of time, for private discussions of how each justice will vote on the cases they have just heard. Time is also allowed for the justices to discuss which additional cases to hear. These private discussions are usually held on Wednesday afternoons and Fridays during the weeks of oral arguments. The justices set aside a fourth block of time to work on writing their opinions.[33]

The Court has complete discretion to control the nature and number of the cases it reviews by means of the *writ* (order) *of certiorari*—an order from a higher court directing a lower court to send the record of a case for review. The Court considers requests for *writs of certiorari* according to the *rule of four*. If four justices decide to review a case—to "grant cert," the Court will hear the case. Several criteria are used to decide if a case requires action: First, does the case concern an issue of constitutional or legal importance? Does it fall within the Court's jurisdiction (the Court can hear only cases that are mandated by Congress or the

The U.S. Supreme Court, in Washington, D.C., is where the court's nine justices meet, deliberate, and render the law of the land.

Investigating Further

Criminal Law From the U.S. Circuit Courts

In 2010, the U.S. Court of Appeals for the Ninth Circuit (the largest circuit in the country, which includes the heavily populated state of California) heard an appeal from a criminal defendant who was convicted based on evidence the police obtained after placing a GPS tracking device on his car without first obtaining a search warrant. The police placed the device by going to the defendant's house in the early morning hours and sneaking up the defendant's rather long driveway to his car parked just outside his garage. They then tracked his vehicular movements, which provided evidence of his marijuana-growing activities. He was convicted and later appealed, claiming the police action was a violation of his Fourth Amendment protections. The Ninth Circuit justices disagreed and ruled the police action was constitutional, enabling law enforcement agencies in similar cases to use GPS tracking without a warrant.

That same year, on the other side of the country, the U.S. Court of Appeals for the D.C. Circuit ruled in a similar case that the use of a GPS tracking device was a search under the Fourth Amendment. The ruling stemmed from a case in which, in 2005, federal officers obtained a search warrant to attach a GPS tracking device to the car of a Washington, D.C., nightclub owner and suspected drug dealer, Antoine Jones. But officers attached the device a day later than the warrant required and they did so in Maryland, rather than in the D.C. jurisdiction the warrant specified. Nonetheless, they tracked Jones for nearly a month and ultimately brought criminal charges against him based on the GPS evidence. Jones was tried in the U.S. District Court for the D.C. Circuit, where his attorneys argued that the GPS tracking violated Jones's Fourth Amendment protections because the GPS tracking was a "search" and the device was installed in violation of the warrant's requirements. The court disagreed with respect to Jones's movements tracked on public streets and areas outside his driveway and home. The GPS evidence was admitted, and Jones was convicted. But the D.C. Circuit reversed, and the effect was a new rule that governed law enforcement in the D.C. Circuit's jurisdiction: Get a warrant before using GPS tracking, or risk having tracking evidence thrown out at trial.

After these decisions, the "law of the land" in the Ninth Circuit governed police actions in the states within that circuit, and officers were able to use GPS tracking devices without first obtaining a warrant, whereas in the D.C. Circuit, officers were required to get a warrant. The U.S. Supreme Court then heard the Jones case and ruled in 2012 that law enforcement must first obtain a warrant to use GPS tracking devices on vehicles. But until that ruling was issued, the circuit court decisions differentially affected millions of people and law enforcement officers in their respective jurisdictions.

Sources: See U.S. v. Jones, 565 U.S. 400, 132 S.Ct. 945 (2012) and *U.S. v. Pineda-Moreno*, 617 F.3d 1120 (9th Cir. 2010).

Standing: a legal doctrine requiring that one must not be a party to a lawsuit unless he or she has a personal stake in its outcome.

Constitution)? Does the party bringing a case have standing—a strong vested interest in the issues raised in the case and in its outcome?[34] The Court hears only a tiny fraction of the thousands of petitions that come before it. When it declines to hear a case, the decision of the lower court stands as the final word on it. The Court's caseload has increased over time; today the Court has 7,000–8,000 cases on the docket per term, and formal written opinions are delivered in about 70–80 cases.[35]

Administration

The chief justice orders the business of the Supreme Court (a description of the chief justice's role is provided in Chapter 10) and administers the oath of office to the president and vice president upon their inauguration. According to Article I, Section 3, of the Constitution of the United States, the chief justice is also empowered to preside over the Senate in the event that it sits as a court to try an impeachment of the president.

The clerk of the Court serves as the Supreme Court's chief administrative officer, supervising a staff of 30 under the guidance of the chief justice. The marshal of the Court supervises all building operations. The reporter of decisions oversees the printing and publication of the Court's decisions. Other key personnel are the librarian and the public information officer. In addition, each justice is entitled to hire four law clerks, almost always recent top graduates of law schools, many of whom have served clerkships in a lower court the previous year.[36]

MAKING PREPARATIONS: PRETRIAL PROCESSES

In Chapter 1, we briefly discussed the sequence of major events that compose the U.S. criminal justice system, from the point of entry of the offender into the system and through the related police, courts, and corrections components. Here, we focus on the pretrial process, the events that occur prior to the trial itself. (We discuss judges as well as the roles and strategies of prosecution and defense attorneys in Chapter 10.)

Booking, Initial Appearance, Bail, and Preliminary Hearing

As stated in Chapter 1, the criminal justice process is engaged when one is arrested. Following that, the accused will then proceed through the steps detailed in the sections that follow.

Booking

Booking: the clerical procedure that occurs after an arrestee is taken to jail, during which a record is made of his or her name, address, charge(s), arresting officers, and time and place of arrest.

Basically a clerical function, booking usually involves taking the suspect to a police station or sheriff's office, where he or she may be fingerprinted, photographed, questioned, read his or her rights, and possibly be given a bail amount that must be paid in order to gain release until the next stage in the process. Meanwhile, the prosecutor will be sent a copy of the offense report written by the police, and will be considering whether or not enough probable cause (discussed in Chapter 8) exists to believe the suspect committed the offense.

Initial Appearance

Initial appearance: a formal proceeding during which the accused is read his or her rights and informed of the charges and the amount of bail required to secure pretrial release.

Within a reasonable time after arrest, the suspect has his or her initial appearance in court, where the judge gives the defendant formal notice of the charge(s), advises the suspect of his or her rights—including the right to a government-provided attorney if the defendant cannot afford one, and sets bail in appropriate cases. The judge also performs a cursory review of the evidence, and if he or she does not believe such evidence establishes probable cause that the defendant may have committed the crime charged, the case will be dismissed. Notice that defendants typically do not enter a plea at this stage because they have not yet been appointed an attorney, so they have not yet had a chance to consult anyone about their case.

Bail

Bail is also known as "pretrial release," allowing defendants to remain out of jail while awaiting trial and affording them time to help with their defense and to maintain ties with family and their job. But bail is not a right, nor is it guaranteed under the U.S. Constitution. In fact, most state laws provide that bail cannot be granted in cases involving certain violent felonies. If a judge does grant bail, however, the Constitution's Eighth Amendment prohibits the bail amount from being "excessive." To ensure a fair decision-making process, a bail hearing is conducted (usually as part of the initial appearance), and the judge must consider a variety of factors, including

- The risk that the defendant will flee before trial
- The defendant's criminal record
- The seriousness of the charges
- The safety of the community

Bail: surety (e.g., cash or paper bond) provided by a defendant to guarantee his or her return to court to answer to criminal charges.

There are several ways to make bail, all of which attempt to ensure that the accused will later appear in court and most of which require a financial commitment from defendants or their family or friends. The court typically requires either cash or a bond, the latter of which is basically an insurance policy the defendant buys insuring his or her appearance. Defendants can "make bail" directly with some courts, but in other jurisdictions the defendant will have to get a bond through a bail bond company, which typically requires a nonrefundable payment of 10 percent of the bail amount. Either way, if the defendant fails to appear in court, the court issues a warrant for the defendant's arrest, and he or she loses any money posted with the court.

The bail decision can be critical for criminal defendants. Again, pretrial release affords defendants the chance to keep their jobs and maintain family and community ties, and to assist with their defense. Being denied bail—pretrial detention—can be devastating on all of these fronts, and it can provide prosecutors and police better access to the defendant for continued questioning and investigation (subject to certain *Miranda* limitations). So it is important to consider what types of defendants are detained and whether the process is truly fair. In 2015, researchers released findings showing that the bail decision is unfairly affecting the poor and racial minorities, with African American defendants being detained four times more often than whites.[37] The same study concluded that 75 percent of people held in pretrial detention are there for nonviolent offenses, but they simply cannot afford bail and so they are incarcerated in county jails until their cases are resolved. Indeed, 65 percent of jail populations are unconvicted defendants awaiting trial.[38] Therefore, the bail decision affects not only defendants but

Bail bonds operations are commonly located near county jails to serve criminal defendants seeking freedom on bail while their cases are pending. Judges and bail bond agents use similar criteria in making decisions about bail.

also our already-overcrowded jails and the criminal justice professionals tasked with keeping those populations secure.

Preliminary Hearing

Preliminary hearing: a stage in the criminal process conducted by a magistrate to determine whether a person charged with a crime should be held for trial based on probable cause; does not determine guilt or innocence.

The preliminary hearing (which the defendant may choose to waive in some jurisdictions) allows a judge (no jury is present) to decide whether or not probable cause is sufficient against the person charged to proceed to trial. The prosecutor will offer physical evidence and testimony to try to get the accused "bound over" for trial while the defense offers counter-evidence. If the judge finds enough probable cause, he or she will order the accused to appear at trial to answer the state's formal charges, which the prosecutor will file in the form of an "information" (versus an "indictment," discussed in the next section). The preliminary hearing can help the accused and his or her counsel to prepare for trial, because they are able to hear much of the state's case. But as discussed in the next section, in some states, the prosecutor avoids this effect by presenting the case before a secretive grand jury.

Grand Juries

Grand jury: a body that hears evidence and determines probable cause regarding crimes and can return formal charges against suspects; use, size, and functions vary among the states.

The primary function of the modern grand jury is to review the evidence presented by the prosecutor and to determine whether there is probable cause to return an indictment. Although all states have some form of the grand jury, only about half of all states use grand juries routinely to bring formal charges, rather than relying solely on a prosecutor's decision (or after a preliminary hearing).³⁹ The prosecutor presents evidence to the grand jury, and, much like the judge in a preliminary hearing, the grand jury must find probable cause to charge the defendant with a crime. If that happens, the grand jury issues an "indictment"—a formal charge—and trial (or plea bargaining) will ensue.

The importance of the grand jury function cannot be overstated because, without an indictment, the state cannot move forward with criminal charges against a defendant. Consider the 2014 case from Ferguson, Missouri, where a white Ferguson police officer, Darren Wilson, shot and killed unarmed, 18-year-old Michael Brown during an encounter in the street. The case sparked intense media coverage and debate over police-citizen race relations and the appropriate use of police force in encounters with unarmed suspects, with many people assuming Wilson had acted criminally because Brown was unarmed. The case against Wilson went to a St. Louis County grand jury, which—after 25 days of hearing testimony and reviewing evidence—determined there was not enough probable cause to conclude that Wilson acted criminally. But the Brown-Wilson proceedings were different from a typical grand jury review in several ways: The prosecutor did not recommend charges against Wilson, more than 60 witnesses testified (versus the typical three or four), and Officer Wilson himself testified for more than four hours.⁴⁰ Some observers believe that, in cases like Wilson's, the state effectively "tries" the case but without the public oversight of a typical criminal trial, and, in that way, the grand jury role can be significant.

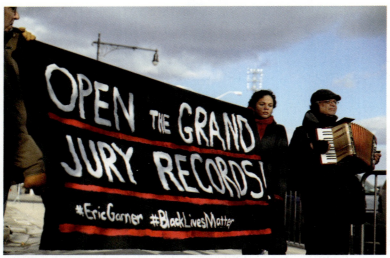

Grand jury testimony transcripts are not made public in an effort to encourage honest witness testimony and promote impartial juror decisions.

Although the use of grand juries and their roles vary across states, the Fifth Amendment to the U.S. Constitution requires a grand jury indictment for *all* federal criminal charges.

For federal cases involving complex and long-term investigations (such as those involving organized crime, drug conspiracies, or political corruption), "long-term" grand juries will be impaneled. In most jurisdictions, grand jurors are drawn from the same pool of potential jurors as are any other jury panels, and in the same manner. But unlike potential jurors in regular trials, grand jurors are not screened for biases or other improper factors.

The Federal Rules of Criminal Procedure provide that the prosecutor, grand jurors, and the grand jury stenographer are prohibited from disclosing what happened before the grand jury, unless ordered to do so in a judicial proceeding. Secrecy prevents the escape of people whose indictment may be contemplated, ensures that the grand jury can deliberate without outside pressure, prevents witness tampering prior to trial, and encourages people with information about a crime to speak freely.

A prosecutor can obtain a subpoena to compel anyone to testify before a grand jury, without showing probable cause and, in most jurisdictions, without even showing that the person subpoenaed is likely to have relevant information.

In the federal system, a witness cannot have his or her lawyer present in the grand jury room, although witnesses may interrupt their testimony and leave the grand jury room to consult with their lawyer. A few states do allow a lawyer to accompany the witness. A witness who refuses to appear before the grand jury risks being held in contempt of the court.

If the grand jury refuses to return an indictment, the prosecutor can try again; double jeopardy does not apply to a grand jury proceeding. No judge is present in the grand jury room when testimony is being taken.[41]

> **The Casey Anthony Case:** Florida uses grand juries to bring formal charges against a suspect and issue indictments in first-degree murder cases. In the case against Anthony, 19 grand jurors—10 women and 9 men—heard testimony from a variety of witnesses, including police officers, an FBI agent, a cadaver dog handler, and Anthony's father. At the time of the grand jury hearing, Anthony's daughter was still missing; her body had not yet been found. Still, the grand jury deliberated for only about 30 minutes before issuing a criminal indictment for first-degree murder.

Arraignment

After being formally charged, the accused will again be advised of his or her rights, and is asked to enter a formal plea. A defendant may plead "not guilty," "guilty," or "no contest" (also known as *nolo contendere*). A "not guilty" plea means the defendant claims innocence and is forcing the state to prove its case at trial, whereas a "guilty" plea relieves the state of that burden and the defendant is convicted without trial. The *nolo* plea is unique in that it allows a defendant to plead guilty for purposes of avoiding trial, but the plea cannot be used against him or her later in a civil case (because technically he has not admitted guilt). The court must always approve a plea of *nolo contendere*.

If the plea at arraignment is "not guilty," a trial must occur (unless plea bargaining takes place).

Arraignment: a criminal court proceeding during which a formally charged defendant is informed of the charges and asked to enter a plea of guilty or not guilty.

Plea Negotiation

When defendants enter a "guilty" or "no contest" plea, they often do so through a **plea negotiation**, or **plea bargaining**. In fact, the great majority of criminal convictions—typically more than 90 percent—are obtained through plea deals, without any courtroom fact-finding. In essence, in exchange for the defendant's plea of guilty, the government is willing to give the defendant certain concessions.

There are several forms of plea bargaining. The accused can engage in *charge bargaining* (offering to plead guilty to a lesser offense than the one charged, thus hoping for a

Plea negotiation (or bargaining): a preconviction process between the prosecutor and the accused in which a plea of guilty is given by the defendant, with certain specified considerations in return—for example, having several charges or counts tossed out, and a plea by the prosecutor to the court for leniency or shorter sentence.

lighter sentence), *count bargaining* (pleading guilty to, say, three of the charged counts and having the remaining six counts thrown out), or negotiating how he or she will serve an imposed sentence (e.g., two five-year terms to be served concurrently, as opposed to consecutively).

As the defendant benefits from plea bargaining, so does the government. First, criminal court dockets in most jurisdictions are seriously overburdened and the state simply cannot take every case to trial, so there is great pressure to resolve cases out of court. Further, the prosecutor "wins" a conviction while reducing the time, money, and uncertainty involved in taking the case to trial, whereas a jury may acquit because the defense produces unanticipated evidence or witnesses. The process also eases the burden on witnesses and prospective jurors, and can reduce the overcrowding of jails by more quickly funneling offenders out of pretrial detention and into prison or some form of community corrections (discussed in Chapter 14).

Certainly, there are many reasons why a high percentage of cases are bargained out of the system, and one can only imagine the havoc that would be caused in the court system if 9 of 10 cases that are plea bargained had to be tried. However, by signing the deal and pleading guilty, the defendant waives a number of constitutional protections. But consider the realities of a typical barroom killing. There might be evidence of premeditation and malice that is sufficient to justify a jury verdict of murder in the first degree. Or, the defendant's longtime status as an alcoholic might convince the jury that he was unable to form the necessary intent to be heavily punished. Perhaps the defendant may indicate that he acted in the "heat of passion," pointing to a verdict of manslaughter, or even that he acted in self-defense. When such cases are given to the jury to decide, a variety of outcomes are possible. Therefore, plea negotiations allow the prosecutor and the defense to arrive at some middle ground of what experience has shown to be "justice," without the defense running the risk of heavy punishment for the defendant, and the government not having to devote many days to trial—with the risk of the defendant's being acquitted.[42]

Michael Brown was fatally shot by Officer Darren Wilson on August 9, 2014, in Ferguson, Missouri. On November 24, 2014, the St. Louis County grand jury decided not to indict Wilson, finding that he acted within the limits of the lethal-force law.

Some authors believe plea bargaining reduces the courthouse to something akin to a Turkish bazaar, where people barter over the price of copper jugs. They see it as justice on the cheap. Others believe that plea bargaining works to make the job of the judge, the prosecutor, and the defense attorney much easier, while sparing the criminal justice system the expense and time needed to conduct many more trials.

No matter where one stands on the issue, however, it is ironic that, in general, both police and civil libertarians oppose plea bargaining. Police and others in the crime control camp view plea bargaining as undesirable because defendants can avoid conviction and responsibility for crimes they committed when allowed to plead guilty to (and be sentenced for) lesser and/or fewer charges; police, in the crime control camp, would prefer to see the defendant convicted for the crime committed.

Civil libertarians and other supporters of the due process model also oppose plea bargaining, but for different reasons: When agreeing to negotiate a plea, the accused forfeits a long list of legal protections afforded under the Bill of Rights: the presumption of innocence; the government's burden of proof (beyond a reasonable doubt); and the right to face one's accuser, testify, and present witnesses in one's defense, the right to have an attorney and a trial by jury (except for lesser offenses), and the right to an appeal if convicted. Another concern is that an innocent defendant might be forced to enter a plea of guilty because of the threat of trial or police and prosecutorial coercion.

It is important to consider both positions. In our quest for justice, we must ask whether plea bargaining sacrifices too many of the defendant's rights. We must also ask if plea bargaining impedes justice by giving too many benefits to guilty persons.

Jury Trials

Most civilizations—even the most primitive in nature—have used some means to get at the truth: to tell right from wrong, guilt from innocence, and so forth. In Burma, each suspected party to a crime had to light a candle, and the person whose candle burned the longest was not punished.[43] In Borneo, suspects poured lime juice on a shellfish; whoever's shellfish squirmed first was the guilty party.[44] The "trial by ordeal" method was also used around the world, with people's guilt or innocence determined by subjecting them to a painful task (often using fire and water); the idea was that God would intercede and help the innocent by performing a miracle on their behalf.[45]

The Sixth Amendment to the U.S. Constitution ensures that our method is more civilized, guaranteeing the defendant a trial by an impartial jury of his or her peers. Many people view the jury as the most sacred aspect of our criminal justice system, because it is where common citizens determine the truth and assess punishment. Not all criminal defendants are guaranteed a right to trial by jury (i.e., if charged with a *lesser misdemeanor*—one that has a penalty of less than six months in jail); furthermore, the defendant may waive the right to a jury trial and be tried by a judge alone (known as a *bench trial*). There are advantages and disadvantages to each, and a wise defendant will want to discuss them with an attorney.

The method of selecting citizen *peers* to hear the evidence is important. First, in most states a questionnaire is mailed to people (whose names were obtained from voter, taxpayer, driver, or other lists) to determine who is qualified to serve, with certain exemptions given to specific groups. Those who are qualified to serve are then sent a *summons* to appear and form a jury pool, from which a smaller number of prospective jurors is selected for a process known as *voir dire* ("to speak the truth"), where the prosecutor and defense attorney question and screen pool members to determine whether they can be fair and impartial and decide the case based on the evidence presented. With the judge overseeing the selection process, both the prosecution and the defense can challenge and have removed an unlimited number of jurors *for cause*, meaning for some reason one is prejudiced against their side. But both the prosecution and the defense also receive a limited number of *peremptory challenges* (usually set by statute), which allow them to remove jurors without any reason or explanation.

Criminal trials in the United States often involve a jury of one's peers to hear the evidence; then, if rendering a conviction, the same jury may be used to determine the proper form and extent of punishment.

Generally, 12 jurors and 2 alternates are selected for a criminal trial, but that number is not required by the Constitution. In *Williams v. Florida*, the U.S. Supreme Court observed that the decision to fix the size of a jury at 12 "appears to have been a historical accident" and that a 6-member jury satisfied the constitutional requirement.[46] Nor is a unanimous verdict by the jury required by either the U.S. Constitution or the U.S. Supreme Court, so in some states a majority of "votes" from the jurors will support a verdict.[47] Figure 9.4 shows

Figure 9.4 /// Jury Trials and Service in United States

Percentage of Trials by Case Type

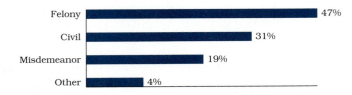

- Felony: 47%
- Civil: 31%
- Misdemeanor: 19%
- Other: 4%

Estimated Number of Adults Involved in Jury Selection Annually

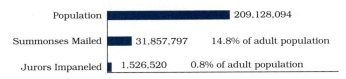

- Population: 209,128,094
- Summonses Mailed: 31,857,797 — 14.8% of adult population
- Jurors Impaneled: 1,526,520 — 0.8% of adult population

Note: This estimate was extrapolated using survey results for 1,546 counties representing 70 percent of the U.S. population.

Source: Reprinted with permission from The National Center for State Courts, Center for Jury Studies.

You Be the . . .

Defense Attorney

In 2001, Michael Vick rose to national fame as a star quarterback with the NFL's Atlanta Falcons—the first African American player to be selected in the first round of the NFL draft. Vick then had six successful seasons with the Falcons, going to the playoffs twice and being selected to three Pro Bowls. But in 2007, Vick was implicated in an illegal dog-fighting operation in his home state of Virginia. Federal and state law enforcement authorities found evidence of an extensive dog-fighting venue at Vick's sprawling rural compound, along with evidence of illegal interstate activities, including dog trafficking, online betting, and drug sales. Authorities also found evidence of dog torture and killings, and Vick was soon charged with breaking a host of both Virginia state laws and federal laws.

With his NFL career in shambles, Vick faced prosecution in both venues of our dual court system, and many observers asked where Vick would first answer for his alleged crimes and would he—could he—be brought to justice twice, raising questions of double jeopardy under the Fifth Amendment to the U.S. Constitution. The U.S. government took the lead in prosecuting Vick first. He was granted bail with certain conditions, including drug testing. He was indicted by a federal grand jury, meaning the government could proceed with formal charges against him. Facing such charges and the prospect of extensive evidence of his illegal activities and brutality against the dogs used in his fighting operations, what would you have recommended as Vick's defense attorney?

1. Would you have recommended that he seek a plea deal (meaning, a plea negotiation) rather than take the case before a jury? Why?
2. What would have been the pros and cons of pursuing a jury trial, given the facts of this case?
3. More about the outcome of this case is provided in the Notes section at the end of the book.[48]

Source: CNN Library, *Michael Vick Fast Facts*, November 10, 2014, http://www.cnn.com/2013/06/24/us/michael-vick-fast-facts/.

several aspects of jury service and trials in the United States as reported by the Center for Jury Studies: the estimated number of jury trials, the percentage of actual trials by case type, and the estimated number of adults involved in jury service each year.

Pretrial Motions

Prior to the trial, either the defendant or the prosecutor may file pretrial motions/processes with the court in order to be better positioned for trial. Defense motions include requests to suppress evidence (e.g., the defense believes that a police search, physical evidence, or a confession was obtained illegally), to reduce bail (if the accused is still in jail awaiting trial), to conduct discovery (discussed in the next section), to change venue (to move the trial to another city, if a highly publicized or emotional crime is charged), and to delay trial (known as a "continuance").

Discovery

No member of the court work group—including judges, prosecutors, and defense attorneys—likes major surprises or "bombshell" evidence coming to light in the courtroom. Discovery is simply the exchange of information between prosecution and defense, in order to promote a fair adversarial contest between the two sides and help the truth come to light. Essentially, each side is entitled to learn the other's strengths and weaknesses as well as the evidence and theories on which each will rely.

Discovery has become quite controversial in recent years, with prosecutors often being accused of withholding evidence that should have been provided to the defense, to the point that many jurisdictions have individuals—typically attorneys, skilled in the laws of evidence—serving as "discovery masters" to ensure fair exchange of information by both sides. Generally, the prosecution has a higher burden of providing "exculpatory" evidence (that which tends to support the defendant's innocence).[49] However, because the U.S. Supreme Court has required the prosecution to disclose only evidence that is both material and exculpatory, this has become a confusing area of law and formal/informal policy—with some states adopting conservative, others liberal, and still others "middle ground" rules of discovery[50]—so that the question of what is to be exchanged is not always clear-cut.

Ray Tensing, a white University of Cincinnati police officer, shot and killed Samuel DuBose, an unarmed black motorist, after DuBose tried to drive away during a traffic stop. Tensing was wearing this shirt under his uniform. The county judge agreed with Tensing's defense attorneys that the shirt was prejudicial and would not allow prosecutors to admit the shirt into evidence.

Pretrial motions/processes: any number of motions filed by prosecutors and defense attorneys prior to trial, for instance, to quash evidence, change venue, conduct discovery, challenge a search or seizure, raise doubts about expert witnesses, or exclude a defendant's confession.

Discovery: a procedure wherein both the prosecution and the defense exchange and share information as to witnesses to be used, results of tests, recorded statements by defendants, or psychiatric reports, so that there are no major surprises at trial.

Diversion program: a sentencing alternative that removes a case from the criminal justice system, typically to move a defendant into another treatment program or modality.

Diversion Programs/Problem-Solving Courts

The increasing number of criminal cases in our already-overburdened courts, together with the high recidivism (reoffending) rate, has spawned a number of alternative courts and diversion programs around the country, including drug courts, mental health courts, veterans courts, and even some courts dedicated to offenders with gambling addictions. By 2015, more than 3,000 drug courts were operating in every U.S. state and territory,[51] and today more than 300 mental health courts operate in most U.S. jurisdictions.[52] A 2016 report by the National Drug Court Institute suggests that many more adult drug courts,

Amanda Nagel hugs her 9-month-old daughter, Alexis, while waiting to appear in drug court in Placer County, California. Nagel, who had been arrested on a methamphetamine charge, told the judge she wants to go straight and stay out of jail to take care of her daughter. Drug courts, mental health courts, and veterans courts are just a few of the specialty courts operating across the country to divert low-risk offenders out of the criminal justice system.

veterans treatment courts, family drug courts, and hybrid drug/DUI courts will be established over the next few years.[53] These "problem-solving" courts allow eligible defendants—typically first-time, nonviolent offenders—to move their cases to a court where specialized court professionals (prosecutors, defense attorneys, judges, social workers, physicians, and treatment professionals) can better address the unique features of these defendants and their cases.

The model for these specialty courts is fairly similar across jurisdictions, utilizing either a pre-plea or post-plea process. In the former instance, a defendant demonstrates eligibility for the court's services and is not required to plead guilty but is diverted to the specialty court's program. In the latter instance, the defendant is diverted to the court's program after an initial guilty plea. In both models, defendants are then given the opportunity to complete a program to treat the problems that landed them in criminal trouble in the first place: drug rehabilitation for the drug offender; mental health counseling/medication for the mentally ill offender; and specialized debriefing/counseling for military veterans, most of whom are suffering from posttraumatic stress disorder (PTSD) and other postcombat issues. If the defendant successfully completes the court-ordered "program," the charges are dropped (for a pre-plea case) or the guilty plea is vacated (in a post-plea case). If the defendant fails to carry out his or her end of the court agreement, the state can pursue the original criminal charges and the defendant will risk a conviction and a possible jail or prison sentence.

Research indicates that many of these courts, drug courts in particular, are succeeding in providing treatment and reducing recidivism. Many drug courts report an average of 8 to 14 percent lower recidivism rates than other justice system responses, with some of the best courts yielding a 35 to 80 percent lower rate. The long-term effects of such programs appear to be promising as well, with positive effects (nonrecidivism, or remaining "clean") lasting from 3 years to 14 years in some cases.[54]

THE TRIAL PROCESS

After all pretrial processes have been addressed, the next challenge is to get the case into the courtroom in a timely manner and then see that certain rules are followed and defendants' rights protected. This trial process is described in the sections that follow.

Trial process: all of the steps in the adjudicatory process, from indictment or charge to conviction or acquittal.

Right to a Speedy Trial: "Justice Delayed . . ."

Swift justice is a term that is fairly well emblazoned in our collective psyche—and has even been the title for a number of books, movies, and even some television series. Bringing offenders to justice in a timely manner is felt to be essential to sending a meaningful message to offenders, to convey a message of deterrence to the general public, to maintain public confidence in the judicial process, and generally to help the criminal justice system better do its job.

Similarly, the adage that "justice delayed is justice denied" says much about the long-standing goal of processing court cases with due deliberate speed. Charles Dickens condemned the practice of slow litigation in 19th-century England.[55] Dickens was considerably harsh toward England's Chancery Courts in his novel *Bleak House*,[56] and Shakespeare mentioned "the law's delay" in *Hamlet*.[57] Most important, even our founding fathers saw fit to hasten the movement of criminal matters into the courtroom: The Sixth Amendment to the Constitution states in part, "In all criminal prosecutions, the accused shall enjoy the right to a speedy and public trial." As a result, the consequences of delay to society are potentially severe. The U.S. Supreme Court has ruled that if the defendant's right to a speedy trial has been violated, then the indictment must be dismissed and/or the conviction overturned.[58] Certainly some criminal defendants want their trial dates delayed (or "continued") as long as possible—giving time for the community's emotions surrounding the crime to subside, the memories of its victims and witnesses to fade, and the defense to uncover further evidence. Others, however—particularly those who cannot post bail and are awaiting trial in a jail, and/or have jobs and family to return to—want their "day in court" to arrive as soon as possible.

But what does a "speedy trial" mean in practice, and how does an appellate court know if the right has been denied? Those questions have been addressed at the *federal* level, with Congress enacting the Speedy Trial Act of 1974.[59] This act mandates a 30-day limit from the point of arrest to indictment and 70 days from indictment to trial. Thus, federal prosecutors have a total of 100 days from the time of arrest until trial.

However, there is very little in the way of fixed, enforced time limits at the *state* level, and the U.S. Supreme Court has refused to give the concept of a "speedy trial" any precise time frame.[60] Also, where they exist, most state laws fail to provide the courts with adequate and effective enforcement mechanisms; furthermore, if a prosecutor has clearly taken an excessively long amount of time to bring a case to trial, existing time limits may be waived due to the court's own congested dockets. As a result, there are no "teeth" in state statutes concerning time limits, so state-level speedy trial laws are often not followed in practice.

The concern, then, is with *unnecessary* delay. Where a court must determine whether or not the defendant's right to a speedy trial was violated, the Supreme Court in *Barker v. Wingo* established the following test:[61]

- *Length of delay*: A delay of a year or more from the date of arrest or indictment, whichever occurs first, was termed "presumptively prejudicial"; however, as noted earlier, the Supreme Court has never explicitly ruled that any absolute time limit applies.

- *Reason for the delay*: The prosecution may not excessively delay the trial for its own advantage; however, a trial may be delayed for good reason, such as to secure the presence of a key witness.

- *Time and manner in which the defendant has asserted his right*: If a defendant agrees to the delay when it works to his own benefit, he cannot later claim that he has been unduly delayed.

- *Degree of prejudice to the defendant that the delay has caused*: Delays can affect evidence and impair the defense; for example, witnesses might die, move away, or their memories fade; records or evidence can be lost or destroyed.[62]

Delay (trial): an attempt (usually by defense counsel) to have a criminal trial continued until a later date.

Speedy Trial Act of 1974: later amended, a law originally enacted to ensure compliance with the Sixth Amendment's provision for a speedy trial by requiring that a federal case be brought to trial no more than 100 days following the arrest.

> **The Casey Anthony Case:** Anthony was arrested for her daughter's murder on July 16, 2008, and was officially charged (by a grand jury) with first-degree murder on October 14, 2008. Jury selection for Anthony's trial didn't begin until May 8, 2011. On July 3, 2011, the trial's closing arguments began. On July 5, 2011, nearly three years after she was first arrested, Anthony was found not guilty of murdering her daughter.[63]

Trial Protocols

After the judge has given the jury its preliminary instructions—emphasizing that the defendant is presumed innocent until proven guilty—and other pretrial issues have been settled, typically the pattern of the trial process is as follows:

1. *Opening statements:* The prosecutor goes first, as he or she has the burden of proof (and must prove every element of the crimes charged—beyond a reasonable doubt), followed by the defense (although in many jurisdictions the defense can opt to defer making its opening statements until later, when it presents its main case, or waive it altogether). The purpose of this step is to succinctly outline the facts they will try to prove during the trial—and it is *not* a time to argue with the other side.

2. *Prosecution's case:* The prosecution will present its side of the case, presenting and questioning its witnesses and admitting relevant evidence. The defense may cross-examine these prosecution witnesses. A "redirect" allows the prosecution to reexamine its witnesses. Once the prosecution has finished presenting its evidence, it will rest its case.

3. *Motion to dismiss:* As a formality, at this point during a criminal trial the defense will often make a motion to dismiss all charges, arguing that the state has not proved its case and, that being so, there is no need for the defense to put on its case. This request is generally denied by the judge, opening the way for the defense case.

4. *Defense's case:* Next, the defense presents its main case through direct examination of its chosen witnesses. The prosecution is then given an opportunity to cross-examine the defense witnesses, and, during redirect, the defense may reexamine its witnesses. The defendant cannot be compelled to testify against himself or herself but has the right to testify in his or her own defense if so desired. The defense then rests. Because a defendant is presumed innocent until proven guilty, the defense is not required to put on a case at all. If the defense does not have good evidence or bases for cross-examination of the state's witnesses, the defense can simply rest, and the jury or judge will have to decide if the state has proven its case beyond a reasonable doubt.

5. *Prosecution rebuttal:* The prosecution may offer evidence to refute the arguments made by the defense.

6. *Closing arguments:* This is a time for both sides to review the evidence so that it is clear to the jury before they begin their deliberations. The order of closing arguments varies by jurisdiction. In some jurisdictions, the state always argues first, but in others the defense does.[64] The prosecution will offer reasons why the evidence proves the defendant's guilt, and the defense will explain why the defendant should be acquitted. This is *not* the time for the prosecutor to offer personal opinion, make inflammatory or discriminatory remarks, or comment on the defendant's failure to testify. Such misconduct may result in a reversal of a conviction on appeal.

7. *Jury instructions:* The judge's instructions to the jury are important and, if improper, may later be grounds for a reversal and new trial. Also known as "charging the jury," the judge will explain the law that is applicable to that particular criminal case and the possible verdicts, and will typically include general comments concerning the presumption of the defendant's innocence, that guilt be proved beyond a reasonable doubt, and that the jury may not draw inferences from the fact that the defendant did not testify in his or her own behalf.

8. *Jury deliberations and verdict:* The jury will deliberate for as long as it takes to reach a verdict. In most states, unanimous agreement must be met for a verdict

to be reached (however, as noted earlier, a unanimous verdict is not required by the Constitution). Once the jury has determined its verdict, either guilty or not guilty for each crime in question, the verdict will be read to the court. Then, either side, or the judge, may "poll the jury," asking all jurors individually if the verdict as read is theirs; if not unanimous, the jury may be returned to its room to deliberate again, or be discharged. If the jury acquits the defendant, the case is over. The prosecutor cannot appeal an acquittal because of the Fifth Amendment protection against double jeopardy. The jury may, instead, convict the defendant of some charges while acquitting him or her of others.

9. *Posttrial motions*: If the jury delivers a guilty verdict, the defense will usually ask the judge to override the jury's decision and acquit the defendant or grant him or her a new trial. This motion is almost always denied.

   - *Sentencing*: If the defendant was convicted of the crime(s), sentencing will be determined by the judge immediately after the verdict is read or at a later court date. In arriving at a sentence, the judge generally orders a presentence investigation report (PSI) by probation or court services personnel, to look at the history of the person convicted, any extenuating circumstances, a review of his or her criminal record, and a review of the specific facts of the crime. The person or agency preparing the PSI makes a recommendation to the court about the type and severity of the sentence. The judge may, however, be limited by federal and state sentencing guidelines (discussed in Chapter 11); some crimes carry a mandatory minimum sentencing requirement, while other sentences may be based largely on the discretion of the judge.

   - *Punishments*: After a conviction, and upon receiving the PSI or using sentencing guidelines, the judge may opt for one of the following punishments:
     - Incarceration
     - Probation
     - Fines
     - Restitution
     - Community service

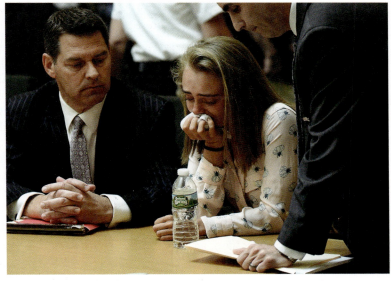

10. *Appeal*: After conviction, the defendant may challenge the outcome. Potential grounds for appeal in a criminal case include legal error (e.g., improperly admitted evidence, improper jury instructions), juror misconduct, ineffective counsel, or lack of sufficient evidence to support a guilty verdict. If this error affected the outcome of the case, the appeal is granted—the conviction is overturned—and, in some instances, the case is remanded back to the trial court and a retrial is ordered (the prosecutor may choose to drop charges if facing a retrial without key evidence, for example). If the appeals court finds that the error(s) would not have affected the outcome, then the errors are considered harmless, and the appeal is denied.[65] Note also that, for the *first* appeal, the U.S. Supreme Court has said that if the person convicted is indigent, then free, appointed counsel must be provided.[66] However, the Court ruled later that, after losing the initial appeal, the convicted person is *not* entitled to free appointed counsel for any subsequent appeals.[67]

Michelle Carter, 20, encouraged her boyfriend through text messages and phone calls to kill himself, which he did. At trial, Carter's defense team argued for acquittal, as there were no laws against encouraging suicide. Carter was convicted of involuntary manslaughter in June 2017. After Massachusetts's highest court upheld her conviction, Carter's attorneys filed a final appeal with the U.S. Supreme Court in July 2019.

The Casey Anthony Case: Following Anthony's trial, the five women and seven men on the jury took less than 11 hours to decide that Anthony was not guilty of murdering her 2-year-old daughter (they did not convict her of either first-degree murder or manslaughter). The jury did find Anthony guilty of four misdemeanors related to providing false information to police.

Investigating Further

An Insider's View of a Lower Court

The Honorable Kevin Higgins, a lower court judge in Nevada, provided compelling realism and insight—as well as a bit of humor—in describing the workings and proper decorum of people and lawyers who are about to litigate cases in his courtroom:

> We tend to be the fast-food operators of the court system—high volumes of traffic for short visits with a base of loyal repeat customers. Don't plan on having a private conversation with your client or a witness amidst the throngs of other people trying to do the same thing. Prepared attorneys can be in and out in short order. Meeting your client for the first time after calling out his name in the lobby can take longer.
>
> Patience is a virtue and communication with the bailiffs and court staff will keep everyone happy. We coordinate the court's calendar, your calendar, and opposing counsel's calendar with the availability of the witnesses.
>
> Here are a few other "do's" and "don'ts" for successfully navigating this Court:
>
> - Everyone goes through the metal detector. Having to go back to your car to stow your Leatherman [a pocket knife/multi-tool], linoleum cutting knife, stun gun, giant padlock or sword-cane (all items caught by security) can be annoying.
>
> - I once ruled against a very sweet elderly lady who reminded me of my own grandmother. She simply didn't have a case and I thought I had ruled fairly and gently. As she slowly walked by the front of the bench on the way out of the courtroom, she looked up and said, "Aw, go ____ yourself," and walked out the door. My mouth was hanging open; I just didn't know what to do. I'm fairly sure that this is the first and last time someone will get away with this, so even if the judge rules against you, smile on the way out. You can mutter to yourself all you want on the way back to the office rather than the holding cell in the back of the courthouse.
>
> - I once watched a gentleman in the back row feed his parrot peanuts while it was sitting on his shoulder. I assumed I had a parrot case in the pile somewhere, but after the last case was called, the parrot left without testifying. I asked the security officer why he let the man with the parrot come into court. I was told that the man had been there to watch a friend's case and that his sick parrot needed to be fed every 15 minutes. While admiring the logic of his decision, I have advised our new court security officers that unless an animal is actually a service animal, various beasts, fish, and fowl are not allowed in simply to watch court.
>
> - Expect the unexpected. Recent interesting events include a live pipe bomb being left at the front door by a concerned citizen; a gentleman dancing on top of his motor home in the parking lot while his laundry hung from the trees and his morning coffee perked on the propane stove he had set up in the next space; and the occasional ammonia discharges into the holding cell by one of the neighboring businesses.

Are you surprised by Judge Higgins's comments concerning the manner in which some people conduct themselves in a court of law?

Source: Adapted from Hon. Kevin Higgins, "An Insider's View of Justice Court," *Nevada Lawyer* 16, no. 8 (August 2008), p. 21. Reprinted with permission from Judge Kevin G. Higgins.

TECHNOLOGIES IN THE COURTS

Like the police (particularly in the forensics area, described in Chapter 4), the courts are unveiling new technologies that it is hoped will provide more efficient and effective operations. Some of those technologies are described in the sections that follow.

Achieving Paper on Demand

A major goal for all courts in the United States is to go "paper on demand" (POD)—denoting an environment in which the routine use of paper no longer exists in general. Rather, paper documents may be used for court business only rarely, and as a last resort. The ultimate goal is that there be no more lost files, all receipts be issued electronically, all police citations be issued electronically, all filing formats and forms be standardized, all judges use POD, and there be no more folders in the courtroom.

Toward that end, electronic case filing has been possible for many years and allows courts to realize dramatic increases in efficiency and reductions in related costs—in clerical staff alone. Electronic filing also enables some court services—such as the payment of fines and fees, collection of fines and penalties, provision of case information and documents to the public, and jury management—to be centralized or regionalized for improved efficiency and service. In addition, an electronic case file enables a court to better distribute its workload across the system.

Raymond Dargan, 20, of New Brunswick, New Jersey, is arraigned on burglary and robbery charges at the Hunterdon County Jail via videoconference. Conducting initial appearances and arraignments via videoconference is increasingly common, especially in metropolitan areas where the courts and jails process record numbers of offenders.

Emerging Technologies

Following are five other areas in which court technologies are emerging or have already been put in place:

- *Digital recording:* Significant savings can be realized by replacing court stenographers with digital audio- or video-recording equipment. Many states have used digital recording extensively, and some states have used digital recording exclusively for many years without experiencing significant issues.

- *Conducting hearings via videoconferencing:* Videoconferencing has improved rapidly in both cost and quality over the past few years. Prices for basic capabilities have been reduced considerably, and the quality of the networks has improved steadily.

- *Use of tablets and apps to present evidence:* The Federal Judicial Center[68] highlights the Chambers Online Automation Training (COAT) program. This program provides online training modules to teach judges and other court staff how to use court technology effectively. Currently available training includes information on connecting to chambers from remote locations, computer security, courtroom technology, and the use of tablet devices (e.g., iPads).[69] The proliferation and relatively low cost of tablet devices are changing the way in which attorneys present evidence in the courtroom. For example, prosecutors in the San Diego County District Attorney's Office use TrialPad, an iPad application, that allows jurors to examine photos, videos, audio files, and transcripts on large courtroom screens and replaces expensive, single-use exhibit boards.[70]

- *Annotation monitors:* In addition to widely adopted large, flat-screen, high-definition monitors that attorneys use to display images to jurors (instead of using traditional projectors and screens), annotation monitors allow witnesses to mark an exhibit with notations. These marked exhibits can be preserved for later viewing during jury deliberations. More recently, these systems are being replaced by tablet devices with annotation capabilities.

- *Evidence cameras:* During in-court proceedings, an evidence camera can instantaneously convert a paper document or physical exhibit to an electronic image for monitor display. An evidence camera can enlarge small physical items (e.g., a four-inch-by-six-inch photograph or wristwatch face) for all courtroom participants to see.[71]

Educational institutions are helping to introduce new courtroom technologies. The National Judicial College in Reno, Nevada, offers its students access to its "Model Courtroom," which offers hands-on experience with some of the latest courtroom technologies. Persons can plug in their laptops to refer to notes; retrieve documents, charts, and photographs; and forward evidentiary material digitally to the presiding judge's monitor. Evidence can be shown on the LCD displays where court participants are sitting: the jury box/room, the attorneys' lectern, or the witness stand. Video/audio feeds may also be relayed to the media room for reporters covering the trial, the attorney conference room (where a victim may choose to view the trial away from the defendant), and a remote-site language interpreter. During trials, attorneys and witnesses may employ the LCD's touch screen technology to provide annotations on evidence. Cameras, evidence presentation tools, monitors, and computer hardware and software serve to introduce students to new technologies in a dynamic learning center. Instructional sessions can be viewed in real time by registrants with a computer and Internet capability, and mock trials can be streamed. The National Judicial College fields questions from court personnel across the country seeking input about incorporating technology into their own courtrooms.[72]

/// IN A NUTSHELL

- As the population of the U.S. colonies grew, formal courts of law appeared based on the English system; however, fearing tyranny from this concentration of governmental power, a federal judiciary was created that was separate from the legislative branch of government. We now have the dual court system—one implemented by the state courts, the other created by Congress and entrusted to the federal courts.

- The policy decisions of the courts affect virtually all of us in our daily living. Perhaps nowhere have the nation's courts had more of an impact than in the prisons.

- The courts must appear to do justice—and provide rights that are embodied in the due process clause. Our court system relies on the adversarial system, using several means to get at the truth: Evidence is tested through cross-examination of witnesses, and power is lodged with several different people. This series of checks and balances is aimed at curbing misuse of the criminal courts.

- Each state has a court of last resort, all but 11 states have an appellate court, and there are trial courts of general jurisdiction that decide all matters not specifically delegated to lower courts.

- Lower state trial courts have limited jurisdiction, but after an arrest, the judge conducts the initial appearance, appoints counsel for indigents, and conducts the preliminary hearing.

- There are 94 U.S. district courts, which are trial courts of original jurisdiction for all major violations of federal criminal law.

- Federal judges are nominated by the president and confirmed by the Senate, and they serve for life. The U.S. Supreme Court has complete discretion to control the nature and number of the cases it reviews, and it hears only a tiny fraction of the thousands of petitions that come before it. The chief justice orders the business of the U.S. Supreme Court.

- There are 11 circuit courts of appeals plus the D.C. Circuit and the Federal Circuit; they hear appeals from the federal district courts located within their circuits, as well as appeals from decisions of federal administrative agencies.

- The criminal justice process is engaged when one is arrested. Following that, the accused will then proceed through a series of steps; at some point, the prosecutor will prepare an information setting forth the charge against the defendant; some jurisdictions use a grand jury to bring formal charges, rather than the prosecutor's doing so unilaterally.

- Discovery is the pretrial exchange of information between prosecution and defense, in order to promote a fair adversarial contest between the two sides and help the truth come to light.

- The Sixth Amendment gives defendants the right to a trial by an impartial jury of his or her peers. The jury system is felt by many to be the most sacred aspect of our criminal justice system, because it is where common citizens sit as a forum to determine the truth and assess the punishment to be meted out.

- The Sixth Amendment guarantees the accused the right to a speedy and public trial. Although there are fixed, enforced time limits at the federal level, the Supreme Court has never defined a "speedy trial" with precise time frames at the state level. Rather, courts must use a test to determine whether or not the defendant's right to a speedy trial was violated.

- The courts are unveiling new technologies that it is hoped will provide more efficient and effective operations. These include paper on demand, digital recording, videoconferencing, use of tablets and apps, annotation monitors, and evidence cameras in the courtroom.

/// KEY TERMS & CONCEPTS

Review key terms with eFlashcards at **edge.sagepub.com/peak4e**.

Adversarial system 209
Arraignment 223
Bail 221
Booking 220
Causation 215
Circuit courts 217
Court of last resort 215
Delay (trial) 229
Discovery 227
District courts 216
Diversion program 227
Dual court system 208
Eighth Amendment 211
Federal court system 208
Grand jury 222
Initial appearance 220
Intermediate court of appeals 214
Jurisdiction, court 211
Plea negotiation (or bargaining) 223
Policy making 209
Preliminary hearing 222
Pretrial motions/processes 227
Speedy Trial Act of 1974 229
Standing 220
State court system 208
Trial process 228
U.S. Supreme Court 217

/// REVIEW QUESTIONS

Test your understanding of chapter content at **edge.sagepub.com/peak4e**.

1. How is the adversarial system of justice related to the truth-seeking function of the courts?
2. How do the courts influence public policy making?
3. What are the types of, and reasons for, courts having specific types of jurisdiction?
4. What are the roles of the state court systems?
5. What is the structure and function of the trial courts of general and limited jurisdiction?
6. How does the U.S. Supreme Court decide to hear an appeal, and approximately how many cases does the Court hear per term?
7. What are some of the pretrial activities that occur?
8. Why does our jury system exist, and how is a jury formed?
9. What is meant by a right to a "speedy" trial? What are the ramifications of a defendant's being denied this right?
10. What are the major points of the trial process, from opening statements through appeal?

/// LEARN BY DOING

1. Your local League of Women Voters is establishing a new study group to better understand the court system as it relates to political affairs. You are asked to explain the dual (federal and state) court system. You opt to use *Kibbe v. Henderson* as a good—and rare—example of a convicted offender's flow through both systems. Prepare your presentation.

2. Some countries do not subscribe to the adversarial process as part of their court system, believing that it is too combative, slow, and cumbersome, and can lead to a "win at all cost" mentality among the lawyers. Rather, they use a nonadversarial or inquisitorial system, in which the court or a part of the court is actively involved in determining the facts of the case (as opposed to the court's being primarily an impartial referee, as in the adversarial system). Your instructor asks you to participate in a pro-con group project concerning the adversarial process. Choose a side and make your defense.

3. Your criminal justice professor has assigned the class to debate the pros and cons of plea negotiation. What do you believe will be the prominent arguments presented by each side?

4. Assume you are a court administrator and your chief judge has tasked you to "bring the courtrooms into the new decade" by making recommendations concerning technologies that should be acquired. Using information and descriptions of the technologies presented in this chapter, select and prioritize which new technologies you would recommend be obtained, and why.

/// STUDY SITE

Get the tools you need to sharpen your study skills. SAGE edge offers a robust online environment featuring an impressive array of free tools and resources.

Access practice quizzes, eFlashcards, video, and multimedia at **edge.sagepub.com/peak4e**.

Introducing...

$SAGE vantage^{TM}$

Course tools done right.
Built to support teaching. Designed to ignite learning.

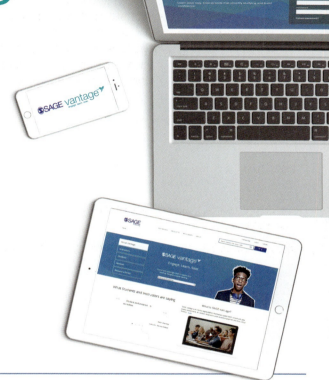

SAGE vantage is an intuitive digital platform that blends trusted SAGE content with auto-graded assignments, all carefully designed to ignite student engagement and drive critical thinking. Built with you and your students in mind, it offers easy course set-up and enables students to better prepare for class.

SAGE vantage enables students to **engage** with the material you choose, **learn** by applying knowledge, and **soar** with confidence by performing better in your course.

PEDAGOGICAL SCAFFOLDING	CONFIDENCE BUILDER	TIME-SAVING FLEXIBILITY	QUALITY CONTENT	HONEST VALUE
Builds on core concepts, moving students from basic understanding to mastery.	Offers frequent knowledge checks, applied-learning multimedia tools, and chapter tests with focused feedback.	Feeds auto-graded assignments to your gradebook, with real-time insight into student and class performance.	Written by expert authors and teachers, content is not sacrificed for technical features.	Affordable access to easy-to-use, quality learning tools students will appreciate.

To learn more about **SAGE vantage**, hover over this QR code with your smartphone camera or visit **sagepub.com/vantage**

CHAPTER 10

THE BENCH AND THE BAR
Those Who Judge, Prosecute, and Defend

Fiat justitia ruat coelum [Let justice be done, though heaven should fall].
—Emperor Ferdinand I, 1563

Four things belong to a Judge:

To hear courteously,

To answer wisely,

To consider soberly, and

To decide impartially.

—Socrates

LEARNING OBJECTIVES

As a result of reading this chapter, you will be able to

1. Explain the five methods of judicial selection, and why the subject of judicial selection has come under scrutiny
2. List some of the benefits, training, and challenges of judges
3. Describe why courtroom civility is important, as well as the meaning of "good judging"
4. Relate the major duties of prosecutors and defense attorneys (to include their roles in plea negotiation)
5. List the six main actors who participate in the courtroom work group and describe the courtroom subculture
6. Discuss the various defenses that defendants may use in criminal cases to reduce or eliminate their criminal liability

ASSESS YOUR AWARENESS

Test your knowledge of the duties of judges, prosecutors, and defense attorneys by responding to the following seven true-false items; check your answers after reading this chapter.

1. Studies indicate that there is no difference in terms of how judges are selected; in all states, they are simply elected.
2. In recent years, people involved with courtroom matters have become much less friendly and less well-behaved.
3. The prosecutor may be fairly said to be the single most powerful person in the American criminal justice system.
4. A criminal defense attorney's primary role is to help the defendant escape punishment, even if the defendant is indeed guilty as charged.
5. A prosecutor's primary duty is not to convict, but to see that justice is done.
6. One's transition from public or private attorney to the role of judge can involve a number of psychological problems and issues.
7. An individual can use one of only two defenses against being charged with a crime: "I didn't know it was a crime" or "I was too intoxicated to know what I was doing."

<< Answers can be found on page 419.

In early 2019, Tracie Hunter, former Hamilton County (Ohio) juvenile court judge, was waiting for a federal judge to decide whether she would serve a six-month sentence imposed for a judicial misconduct conviction. A grand jury initially indicted Hunter in 2014 on nine felony charges: two counts of tampering

Master the content at edge.sagepub.com/peak4e

with evidence, two counts of forgery, two counts of theft in office, two counts of having unlawful interest in a public contract, and one count of misuse of credit cards. She was eventually convicted on only one charge related to using her judicial position to give her brother, a juvenile court employee, confidential documents.[1] She was allowed to remain free while pursuing appeals.

The judge who initially sentenced Hunter, Judge Norbert Nadel (now retired), stated that jail time was warranted in this case because Hunter breached the public's trust. After the jury's verdict, Nadel remarked, "The evidence showed that the conduct of Judge Hunter dealt a serious blow to public confidence in our judicial system, and could very well justify a jail sentence for Judge Hunter."[2]

After the federal judge who reviewed the case rejected her appeal, Common Pleas Judge Patrick Dinkelacker imposed the original six-month sentence in July 2019. At the hearing, Scott Croswell, a special prosecutor during Hunter's original trial remarked, "What she wants to do is play by her own set of rules. That's the very attitude and the very conduct that put her in the predicament that she's in and, frankly, has caused all this pain to her and caused all this turmoil to the community."[3] Upon being sentenced, Hunter refused to walk and a bailiff dragged her out of the courtroom.

Judicial misconduct represents a serious threat to public confidence in those we trust to carry out justice. High-profile cases include instances in which judges have been removed from office for the following:[4]

- Posting comments considered sexist, racist, perverse, and homophobic
- Having an affair (including having sex in judicial chambers) with a party involved in a case over which the judge was presiding
- Initiating a fistfight with a public defender just outside the courtroom
- Campaign misconduct
- Domestic violence

We often think of judges as all-powerful players in the criminal justice system. As you read this chapter, think about the role of each of the courtroom actors. How much power and discretion should each of the actors have? What ethical standards should these actors be held to, both in the courtroom and in their personal lives?

INTRODUCTION

In Chapter 9, we looked at the general nature of courts and judges; this chapter expands that discussion, focusing more on judges and other key personnel who are involved in the courts and their operation.

It is a part of our human nature that we hate losing. Therefore, even though in theory attorneys in a criminal courtroom are engaged in a truth-seeking process, make no mistake: They are *competing* from beginning to end—trying to persuade the judge to include or exclude evidence or witnesses, to persuade the judge or jury of the guilt or innocence of the defendant, to sway the judge or jury that the convicted person should or should not be severely punished, and so on. This adversarial legal process is what drives our criminal justice system. Indeed, renowned defense attorney Percy Foreman is said to have remarked, "The best defense in a murder case is that the deceased should have been killed."[5] In a murder case where a woman was charged with shooting her husband, Foreman so slandered the victim that "the jury was ready to dig up the deceased and shoot him all over again."[6] As will be seen in this chapter, the challenges (and criticisms) facing today's judges are several. They must successfully serve many masters and occupy many roles. As criminologist Abraham Blumberg noted:

The "grand tradition" judge, the aloof brooding charismatic figure in the Old Testament tradition, is hardly a real figure. The reality is the working judge who must be politician, administrator, bureaucrat, and lawyer in order to cope with a crushing calendar of cases.[7]

The chapter opens by considering the means by which judges ascend to the bench. This once-simple task has come under intense scrutiny—particularly in relation to the partisan election of judges, for which they must often solicit campaign contributions. Then we discuss the benefits and problems that occur when one becomes a judge; following that is an examination of the need for courtroom civility and a look at judicial misconduct. The roles and strategies of two other very important court figures—prosecutors and defense attorneys—are also reviewed.

THOSE WHO WOULD BE JUDGES: SELECTION METHODS AND ISSUES

The manner in which state and local court judges assume the bench matters—and it differs widely from state to state. The method used to select judges is important for at least four reasons: The type of judicial selection system affects judges' experience level; it determines the ability of qualified, but less politically connected, individuals to serve; it affects the gender and racial diversity of the judiciary; and it affects the public's perception of judicial impartiality and independence.[8] Across the United States at least five methods of judicial selection are used, but no two states use exactly the same selection method. In many states, more than one method of selection is used—for judges at different levels of the court system and even among judges serving at the same level. And when the same method is used, there are still variations in how the process works in practice.

Judicial selection (methods of): means by which judges are selected for the bench, to include election, a nominating commission, or a hybrid of these methods.

Methods of Selection in State Courts

As noted in Chapter 9, all federal judges are nominated by the president and confirmed by the Senate, and they serve for life (unless they resign or are impeached). When a vacancy (due to death, retirement, or resignation of a judge)[9] occurs at the state level, however, candidates are as likely as not to face an election as part of their selection process. This becomes particularly important given that 97 percent of the cases heard in the United States are handled by state judges. Furthermore, every year, millions of Americans find themselves in state courts, whether called for jury service, to address a minor traffic offense, as a crime victim, or in a small claims case.[10]

The following five methods of selection used in state courts[11] are also depicted in Figure 10.1:

- *Commission-based appointment* (also known as merit selection or the Missouri Plan): Judicial applicants are evaluated by a nominating commission, which then sends the names of the best-qualified candidates to the governor, who appoints one of those nominees. In most commission-based appointment systems, judges run unopposed in periodic retention elections, where voters are asked whether the judge should remain on the bench.

- *Partisan election*: In a partisan election, multiple candidates may seek the same judicial position. Voters cast ballots for judicial candidates as they do for other public officials, and candidates run with the official endorsement of a political party. The candidate's party affiliation is listed on the ballot.

Merit selection: a means of selecting judges whereby names of interested candidates are considered by a committee and recommendations are then made to the governor, who then makes the appointment; known also as the Missouri Plan.

Figure 10.1 /// Initial Selection of State Judges (Trial Courts of General Jurisdiction)

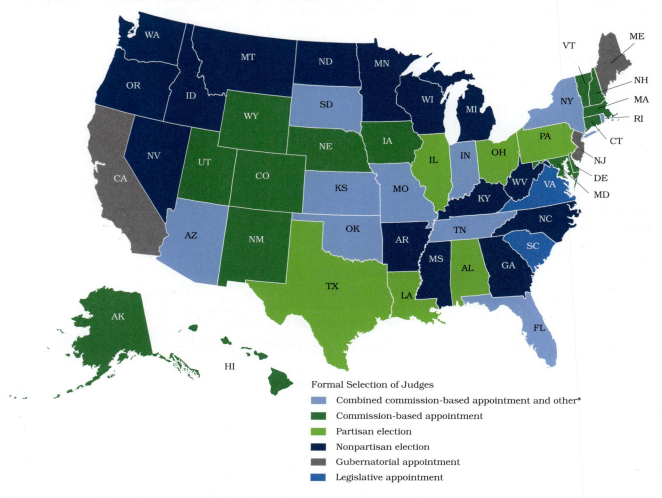

Formal Selection of Judges
- Combined commission-based appointment and other*
- Commission-based appointment
- Partisan election
- Nonpartisan election
- Gubernatorial appointment
- Legislative appointment

*In these states, appellate court judges are chosen through commission-based appointment, and trial court judges are chosen through commission-based appointment or in partisan or nonpartisan elections.

Source: Reprinted with permission from Institute for the Advancement of the American Legal System and American Judicature Society.

- *Nonpartisan election:* In a nonpartisan election, a judicial candidate's party affiliation, if any, is not designated on the ballot.
- *Gubernatorial appointment:* A judge is appointed by the governor (without a judicial nominating commission). The appointment may require confirmation by the legislature or an executive council.
- *Legislative appointment/election:* This is the process by which judges are nominated and appointed or elected by legislative vote only.

Debating Judges and Politics

"They're awful. I hate them." Thus spoke former U.S. Supreme Court justice Sandra Day O'Connor (the first female appointed to the U.S. Supreme Court) concerning her views of judicial elections in May 2009 at an American Bar Association summit.[12]

242 ■ Part 3: The Courts

O'Connor added that the public is growing increasingly skeptical of elected judges in particular, with surveys showing that more than 70 percent of the public are considerably more distrustful of judges than they have been in the past. At risk, O'Connor said, is the public perception that judges are "just politicians in robes."[13] O'Connor also said in November 2007 that "if I could wave a magic wand, I would wave it to secure some kind of merit selection of judges across the country."[14]

Our courts make decisions every day that affect nearly every aspect of our lives. Therefore, to a large extent, the quality of justice Americans receive depends on the quality of the judges who dispense it. The debate over how America chooses its judges has escalated in the 21st century. Consider this: In March 2009, the U.S. Supreme Court considered a case concerning a newly elected West Virginia Supreme Court of Appeals justice, Brent Benjamin, who voted on a mining company dispute; the mining company contributed $3 million in an election campaign to help Benjamin get elected. Instead of removing himself from the vote (known in the courts as recusal), Benjamin instead possibly cast the deciding vote in the 3–2 case—in favor of the mining company. There was no law in West Virginia saying a judge can't hear a case involving someone who financed his or her campaign. During oral arguments in the case, former justice David Souter said, "The system . . . is not working well."[15] The U.S. Supreme Court ruled in June 2009 that Benjamin's failure to recuse himself violated the Fourteenth Amendment's due process clause.[16]

Several states are now evaluating their judicial selection systems with a view to altering their current processes. And, by ruling in the West Virginia case, the Supreme Court certainly put a spotlight on this issue—one that has already been settled in about two dozen states by eliminating political fund-raising by their judicial candidates through the use of various merit selection systems.[17]

You Be the . . .

Judge

In 1984, 18-year-old Terrance Williams was convicted of murdering 56-year-old Amos Norwood in Philadelphia. The trial prosecutor sought the death penalty in this case and, upon conviction, Williams was indeed sentenced to death.

In 2012, Williams filed an appeal, his attorneys claiming that the trial prosecutor had engaged in misconduct by obtaining false testimony and suppressing exculpatory evidence (i.e., evidence favorable to the defendant). The appeals court found that the trial prosecutor committed these violations and stayed Williams's execution, while also ordering a new sentencing hearing. However, on further appeal the Pennsylvania Supreme Court reinstated Williams's death sentence.

In 2015, the U.S. Supreme Court agreed to review the state supreme court's ruling. At issue was the fact that the chief justice of Pennsylvania Supreme Court was former district attorney Ronald Castille, the person who earlier in his career had approved the trial prosecutor's request to seek the death penalty for Williams in the first place. Although Williams had filed a motion asking Chief Justice Castille to recuse himself (to avoid a conflict of interest), Castille denied the motion and voted in this case.

1. Under what circumstances should judges recuse themselves from a case?
2. Did Castille act inappropriately when he denied Williams's motion for recusal?

The U.S. Supreme Court's ruling in this case is provided in the Notes section at the end of the book.[18]

"Investing" in Judges?

Adding fuel to the fire over judicial selection is the amount of money now being spent to fund judges' elections. Expenditures on state supreme court elections has skyrocketed since the 1990s. For example, whereas 7 states had at least one sitting justice who had been involved in a race costing $1 million or more during his or her tenure in 1999, this number jumped to more than 20 states by the start of 2017.[19] Furthermore, special interest groups have ramped up their efforts to influence the composition of state courts, making contributions to candidates, funding television ads, and pressuring candidates to speak publicly about their political views. In state supreme court elections in 2015–2016, special interest group spending represented 40 percent of the total dollars spent in such races.[20]

JUDGES' BENEFITS, TRAINING, AND CHALLENGES

Judges enjoy several distinct benefits of office, including life terms for federal positions and in some states. Ascending to the bench can be the capstone of a successful legal career for a lawyer, even though a judge's salary can be less than that of a lawyer in private practice. Judges warrant a high degree of respect and prestige as well; from arrest to final disposition, the accused face judges at every juncture involving important decisions about their future: bail, pretrial motions, evidence presentation, trial, and punishment.

Although it would seem that judges are the primary decision makers in the courts, such is not always the case. Judges often accept recommendations from others who are more familiar with the case—for example, bail recommendations from prosecutors, plea negotiations struck by prosecuting and defense counsels, and sentence recommendations from probation officers. Judges frequently accept such input in the kind of informal courtroom network that exists. Although judges run the court, if they deviate from the consensus of the courtroom work group, they may be sanctioned: Attorneys can make court dockets go awry by requesting continuances or by not having witnesses appear on time.

Newly elected judges are not simply "thrown to the wolves" and expected to immediately begin to conduct trials, listen to arguments, understand rules of evidence, render verdicts and sentences, and possibly write opinions, without the benefit of training or education. Many states mandate judicial education for new judges, sometimes even prior to assuming the role, as well as mandatory in-service or continuing education thereafter.

Judges are elected in many U.S. jurisdictions, but their campaigns and the money used to fund them are under increasing scrutiny amid questions of how judges can possibly remain objective and resist influence on the bench.

Other challenges can await a new jurist-elect or appointee. Judges who are new to the bench commonly face three general problems:

- *Mastering the breadth of law they must know and apply.* New judges would be wise, at least early in their careers, to depend on other court staff, lawyers who appear before them, and experienced judges for invaluable information on procedural and substantive aspects of the law and local court procedures. Through informal discussions and formal meetings, judges learn how to deal with common problems. Judicial training schools and seminars have also been developed to ease the transition into the judiciary.

- *Administering the court and the docket while supervising court staff.* One of the most frustrating aspects of being a presiding judge is the heavy caseload and corresponding administrative problems. Instead of having time to reflect on challenging legal questions or to consider the proper sentence for a convicted felon, trial judges must move cases. They can seldom act like a judge in the "grand tradition."[21] Judges are required to be competent administrators, a fact of judicial life that comes as a surprise to many new judges. One survey of 30 federal judges found that three-fourths had major administrative difficulties on first assuming the bench, while half complained of heavy caseloads. One judge maintained that it takes about four years to "get a full feel of a docket."[22]

- *Coping with the psychological discomfort* that accompanies the new position. Most trial judges experience psychological discomfort on assuming the bench. Three-fourths of new federal judges acknowledged having psychological problems in at least one of five areas: maintaining a judicial bearing both on and off the bench, dealing with the loneliness of the judicial office, sentencing criminals, forgetting the adversary role, and handling local pressure. One judge remembers his first day in court: "I'll never forget going into my courtroom for the first time with the robes and all, and the crier tells everyone to rise. You sit down and realize that it's all different, that everyone is looking at you and you're supposed to do something."[23] Like police officers and probation and parole workers, judges complain that they "can't go to the places you used to. You always have to be careful about what you talk about. When you go to a party, you have to be careful not to drink too much so you won't make a fool of yourself."[24] And the position can be a lonely one:

    > After you become a . . . judge some people tend to avoid you. For instance, you lose all your lawyer friends and generally have to begin to make new friends. I guess the lawyers are afraid that they will someday have a case before you and it would be awkward for them if they were on too close terms with you.[25]

Judges frequently describe sentencing criminals as the most difficult aspect of their job: "This is the hardest part of being a judge. You see so many pathetic people and you're never sure of what is a right or a fair sentence."[26]

THE ART OF JUDGING, COURTROOM CIVILITY, AND JUDICIAL MISCONDUCT

To fully understand judges' role in the criminal justice system, we must consider some of the less obvious facets of their work on and off the bench: the art and craft of judging, maintaining civility among the many courtroom players, and the critical issue of judicial misconduct.

"Good Judging"

What traits make for "good judging"? Obviously, judges should treat each case and all parties before them in court with absolute impartiality and dignity while providing leadership for court operations. But judging requires more than just those activities and roles. For example, a retired jurist with 20 years on the Wisconsin Supreme Court stated that the following qualities define the art and craft of judging:

- Judges are keenly aware that they occupy a special place in a democratic society. They exercise their power in the most undemocratic of institutions with great restraint.
- They are aware of the necessity for intellectual humility—an awareness that what we think we know might well be incorrect.
- They do not allow the law to become their entire life; they get out of the courtroom, mingle with the public, and remain knowledgeable of current events.[27]
- Other writers believe that judges should remember that the robe does not confer omniscience or omnipotence; as one trial attorney put it, "Your name is now 'Your Honor,' but you are still the same person you used to be, warts and all."[28]

Courtroom Civility

As if it weren't difficult enough to strive for and maintain humility, civility, and balance in their personal lives, judges must also enforce courtroom civility. Many persons have observed that we are becoming an increasingly uncivil society; the courts are not immune to acts involving misconduct.

Personal character attacks by lawyers, directed at judges, attorneys, interested parties, clerks, jurors, and witnesses, both inside and outside the courtroom, in criminal and civil actions have increased at an alarming rate.[29] For example, an attorney stated that opposing and other attorneys were "a bunch of starving slobs," "incompetents," and "stooges."[30] Such behavior clearly does not enhance the dignity or appearance of justice and propriety that is so important to the courts' public image and function. The Model Code of Judicial Conduct (discussed in Chapter 4) addresses these kinds of behaviors; Canon 3B(4) requires judges to be "patient, dignified, and courteous to litigants, jurors, witnesses, lawyers, and others with whom the judge deals in an official capacity" and requires judges to demand "similar conduct of lawyers, and of staff, court officials, and others subject to the judge's direction and control."[31] At a minimum, judges need to attempt to prevent such behavior and discipline offenders when it occurs. Among the means that judges have at their disposal to control errant counsel are attorney disqualifications, new trials, and reporting of attorneys to disciplinary boards.[32]

Judicial misconduct: inappropriate behavior by a judge.

Judges are responsible for regulating the behaviors of all courtroom participants and observers, including attorneys, defendants, witnesses, court personnel, jury members, and members of the public.

Judicial Misconduct

What types of judicial misconduct must the judiciary confront? Sometimes medications may affect a judge's cognitive process or emotional temperament, causing him or her to treat parties, witnesses, jurors, lawyers, and staff poorly. Some stay on the bench too long; such judges will ideally have colleagues who can approach them, suggest retirement, and explain why this would be to their benefit. And sometimes, according to one author, judicial arrogance (sometimes termed "black robe disease" or "robe-itis") is the primary problem. This is seen when judges "do not know when to close their mouths, do not treat people with dignity and compassion, do not arrive on time, or do not issue timely decisions."[33]

Some bar associations or judicial circuits perform an anonymous survey of a sample of local attorneys who have recently argued a case before a particular judge and then share the results with the judge. Sometimes these surveys are popularity contests, but a pattern of negative responses can have a sobering effect on the judge and encourage him or her to correct bad habits. Many judges will be reluctant to acknowledge they have such problems as those described here. In such cases, the chief judge may have to scold or correct a subordinate judge. Although difficult, it may be imperative to do so in order to maintain good relations with bar associations, individual lawyers, and the public. A single judge's blunders and behaviors can affect the reputation of the entire judiciary as well as the workloads of the other judges in his or her judicial district. Chief judges must therefore step forward to address such problems formally or informally.[34]

The Committee on Codes of Conduct of the Judicial Conference of the United States provides guidance to U.S. federal judges to help promote ethical behavior. In a recent attempt to curb judicial misconduct, the committee condemned the use of a wide variety of common social media behaviors. For example, they argue that judges must carefully word every personal social media comment, post, or blog in an effort to avoid any appearance of impropriety. They caution against using social media to engage in improper communications with lawyers or others (e.g., commenting on or "liking" posts that support particular people or causes); participating in activities that might adversely impact perceptions of impartiality (e.g., maintaining a blog that promotes particular political positions); using court email accounts for personal social activities (e.g., forwarding chain emails); or engaging in social media activities that could reveal any confidential, sensitive, or nonpublic information

The Model Code of Judicial Conduct requires judges to be "patient, dignified, and courteous" to all persons engaged in court business.

Going Global

Studying Law

In the United States, prospective law school students must first (in most cases) earn an undergraduate degree at an accredited college or university. Law schools use a competitive admission process, so potential students are judged based on their undergraduate grade point average, recommendation letters, personal statement, and Law School Admissions Test (LSAT) score. The LSAT was designed to measure student skills thought to be needed to successfully complete law school, including reading comprehension, analytical reasoning, and logical reasoning.

Other countries manage law school admissions very differently. One of the biggest differences is that many European countries do not require an undergraduate degree for law school admission. For example, German students are among those who do not need to complete an undergraduate degree before studying law. German law school admissions are based on high school grades—personal statements, recommendations, and additional tests are generally not required. Further, most German law students do not pay for their education, while U.S. law students usually pay more than $100,000 for their three-year degree (without scholarships). The German system may sound enticing, but in reality it typically takes seven years or more to complete a law degree in Germany. Germany uses a two-step system. First, students must obtain a university law degree (*Erste Juristische Prüfung*). Second, the candidate must complete a several-stage mandatory clerkship to learn necessary practical skills. After the clerkship, the candidate must pass a set of written and oral examinations (*Zweites Staatsexamen*).

Sources: "How to Qualify as a Lawyer in Germany," International Bar Association, https://www.ibanet.org/PPID/Constituent/Student_Committee/qualify_lawyer_Germany.asp; to learn more about law schools throughout the world, visit the International Bar Association and obtain a student membership at www.ibanet.org.

obtained through the court.[35] In 2017, an American Bar Association publication addressed similar ethical concerns associated with lawyers and judges using social media sites such as Facebook, Twitter, and YouTube.[36]

THE ATTORNEYS

Next we look at the roles and strategies of attorneys who serve on both sides of the courtroom aisle—as prosecutors and defense attorneys.

"Gatekeeper" of the Justice System: Prosecutor

The prosecutor may be fairly said to be the single most powerful person in the American criminal justice system—and to have tremendous discretion in what he or she does. As described by the Southern Poverty Law Center, "Prosecutorial discretion is a necessary and important part of our system of justice—it allocates sparse prosecutorial resources, provides the basis for plea-bargaining and allows for leniency and mercy in a criminal justice system that is frequently harsh and impersonal. They literally have unchecked power to decide who will stand trial for crimes."[37] Indeed, prosecutors have the authority and power to make all of the following decisions, at their sole discretion, all of which affect criminal defendants and the criminal justice system in general:

- The decision to charge
- Types of charges
- Whether to recommend granting or denying bail
- Plea agreements—whether to entertain such agreements and, if so, the terms
- Sentencing recommendations

Prosecutors represent the people, the victims in particular, and investigate crimes—often out in the field, having been called to the scene of a particularly heinous crime by the police. Still, remember that the primary role of the prosecuting attorney, as set forth by the U.S. Supreme Court (and as noted in Chapter 4), is "not that he shall win a case, but that justice shall be done."[38]

Prosecuting attorney: one who brings prosecutions, representing the people of the jurisdiction.

Once the police have completed a preliminary investigation, the prosecutor evaluates the arrest report and other documents to determine whether there is sufficient evidence to bring charges. Prosecutors also have the ability to rebuke officers who have not done their work properly—perhaps failing to have the requisite probable cause prior to making a search or an arrest—and can quash the arrest report. They have contact with the person suspected of the crime, the victim and witnesses, and the police. For them, the overarching question is, "Can I prove that a defendant committed a particular criminal act beyond a reasonable doubt?" If so, the prosecutor's office files charges and handles the case through pretrial negotiations (if any) and ultimately takes the case to trial. Other determining factors concerning how to handle a case are as follows:

- The type of crime charged (personal or property crime)
- The prior criminal record of the person accused
- The number of counts in the complaint (the more counts there are, the stiffer the sentence sought)
- Whether there are aggravating or mitigating circumstances in the case
- The victim's attitude—what he or she wants done with the case (this is particularly important in cases of violent crimes)

You Be the . . .

Victim Advocate

Michelle Cruz, the state of Connecticut's victim advocate, confers with Hakima Bey-Coon, an office attorney, during a hearing at New Britain Superior Court concerning grand jury testimony involving a missing person.

A relatively new member of the courtroom work group is the victim advocate. In our adversarial system of justice, the prosecutor represents the people of his or her state or county and seeks justice for them and the victim, but the prosecutor is not the victim's personal representative. Despite best efforts, victims can often feel lost in the dizzying process that is a criminal case. Victim advocates seek to remedy that problem, providing victims with information about the criminal justice process, resources for recovery and counseling (especially for victims of violent crimes), legal rights, and a host of other services to help the victim navigate the uncertainties of postvictimization life.

Not surprisingly, these advocates (both paid and volunteer) work in a variety of places along the criminal justice spectrum, often being called to crime scenes to comfort victims immediately after a crime. They also work at police stations and hospitals and are often in or around the court, to accompany victims who have been asked to testify, to work with prosecutors and defense attorneys as they negotiate plea deals or case outcomes, and to monitor the court process so that they can better inform the victim about what to expect. They also accompany victims' families to the morgue to claim personal effects.

If you were responsible for recruiting or hiring victim rights advocates in your jurisdiction:

1. What type of educational degree (e.g., field of study) and background experience would you want your candidates to possess?
2. How would you address burnout and psychological trauma that victim advocates (like many other first responders who assist victims) are likely to face?

To learn more about the role of victim advocates, visit the National Center for Victims of Crime at https://victimsofcrime.org.

Good prosecutors will also try to establish rapport with the victim prior to trial, to personalize the justice system. If possible, the prosecutor or a victim advocate might take the victim to the court and show him or her the courtroom and witness stand and where the offender will be seated, explaining the process along the way.

Prosecutorial Immunity and Misconduct

Not only do prosecutors have nearly unfettered discretion and power, but they are also immune from prosecution for actions taken in their official capacity. In other words, defendants cannot sue prosecutors for civil damages for how they handled a case.[39] This "civil immunity" is unique in our system of justice. In fact, it's unique in the professional realm in general. Doctors, other lawyers, and most professionals (except judges) are subject to civil prosecution if they fail to maintain standards of conduct and performance that apply to their field. Probably the most dramatic contrasting example is that of police officers, who are not granted such immunity and yet are tasked with making a multitude of professional decisions in the field, many of them in a split second and in dynamic and dangerous situations.

Some scholars and observers believe prosecutorial immunity goes too far and unfairly insulates the most powerful player in the criminal justice system.⁴⁰ Proponents of this long-standing immunity counter that prosecutors, in serving the people and in seeking to do justice on behalf of communities, cannot be looking over their shoulders or second-guessing their decisions because they fear civil suits. As the U.S. Supreme Court has put it, prosecutorial immunity represents a "balance of evils," and that it is better "to leave unredressed the wrongs done by dishonest officers than to subject those who try to do their duty to the constant dread of retaliation."⁴¹

"Guiding Hand of Counsel": Defense Attorney

In many countries, a person mired in some stage of a legal proceeding might also find himself or herself standing alone in the courtroom, overwhelmed by fear and befuddled by the activities swirling around him or her. Not so in the United States, where the fundamental principles of liberty and justice require that all Americans, even the poorest among us, will be given the "guiding hand of counsel" at all critical stages of a criminal proceeding.

Duties and Strategies

As noted in Chapter 8, many people believe that the Sixth Amendment's provision for effective counsel is the most important right we enjoy in a democracy. The law is complicated, and by requiring the state to prove its case and helping defendants understand their options in the criminal justice system, defense attorneys can try to ensure that the state does not commit innocent people to jail or prison. Furthermore, defendants have the right to counsel during all "critical stages" of the proceedings—those in which rights could be lost—which include interrogation, jury selection, arraignment, trial, sentencing, and first appeal of conviction (but not the initial appearance, where the judge simply informs the defendant of his or her charges and rights), as well as pretrial testing of fingerprints, blood samples, clothing, hair, and so on.⁴²

What does "ineffective" counsel mean in practice? Basically it means the attorney was deficient in his or her performance, and in being so, the resulting prejudice to the defendant was so serious as to bring the outcome of the proceeding into question.⁴³ This standard, often referred to as the Strickland test, was initially established by the U.S. Supreme Court in *Strickland v. Washington* (1984).⁴⁴ Examples would include one's failures to investigate an alibi defense, investigate prosecution witnesses, obtain experts to challenge the prosecution's physical evidence, or even attend or stay awake for hearings.⁴⁵ The burden of proving ineffective counsel is high, and is on the defendant to show that "a reasonable probability" exists that, but for counsel's unprofessional errors, the result of the proceeding would have been different.⁴⁶ But it is possible to do so: In one Texas case, a defense attorney claimed he did not believe he needed to go into "sleazy bars to look for witnesses." The appeals court essentially informed him that that's precisely what he would do, if doing so was required to locate witnesses for the defendant, persons to confirm the defendant's alibi, and so on.⁴⁷

When someone is charged with a crime, his or her defense lawyer, either hired or court-appointed, should do the following:

- Explain the offense the accused is charged with, including the possible punishments and probation options
- Advise the accused of his or her rights, ensure those rights are upheld, and inform the accused of what to expect during the different stages of the criminal process
- Investigate the facts of the case

Defense attorney: one whose responsibility it is to see that the rights of the accused are upheld prior to, during, and after trial; the Sixth Amendment provides for "effective" counsel, among other constitutionally enumerated rights that defense attorneys must see are upheld.

- Explain what is likely to happen if the case goes to trial
- If beneficial for the accused, attempt to negotiate a plea bargain with the prosecutor (bear in mind that more than 90 percent of criminal convictions come from negotiated pleas of guilty, which must be approved by the judge; therefore, less than 10 percent of criminal cases go to trial)[48]—this can involve arranging for reduced charges, a shorter sentence, sentences for different crimes to be served consecutively instead of concurrently, probation or a disposition that avoids certain imprisonment, and/or other consideration, in exchange for entering a plea of guilty

Priscilla Prendez speaks with Public Defender Joe Cress during her first court appearance on September 1, 2017, in Sacramento County Superior Court. Prendez faced charges for vehicle theft and felony evasion stemming from a car chase that led to the fatal shooting of a Sacramento sheriff's deputy.

- If the case goes to trial, cross-examine government witnesses, object to improper questions and evidence, and present applicable legal defenses,[49] as described later in this chapter

Other defense strategies might include the following:

- Trying to make the victim appear to be the aggressor, or someone who "deserved" what happened to him or her (the general rule is that the defense attorney wants to try to overlook the victim's story, while the victim wishes to punish the defendant, and will also try to engender sympathy; particularly if the victim appears to have precipitated or participated in the crime, the defense will attack his or her faults at trial, within legal bounds)
- Coming up with ways to compensate the victim (e.g., determining whether he or she will accept restitution or be satisfied if the defendant attends counseling)
- Getting continuances (which might mean that key witnesses move away, emotions and local publicity surrounding the crime diminish, and so forth)

Indigent Services

In *Griffin v. Illinois* (1956), the U.S. Supreme Court observed that "there can be no equal justice where the kind of trial a man gets depends on the amount of money he has."[50] There are basically three systems for providing legal representation to indigent persons in criminal prosecutions: the public defender system, the assigned counsel system, and the contract system.[51]

Public defenders, like prosecutors, are paid government employees—most commonly found in larger jurisdictions—whose sole function is to represent indigent defendants. Public defenders perform many of the duties of prosecutors, described earlier in this chapter. They provide representation to people who not only are indigent but also may be illiterate, uneducated, and uncooperative, while managing a large caseload. Public defenders might also represent juveniles charged with acts of delinquency (offenses that would be a felony if committed by an adult) as well as children in child abuse and neglect cases.

The assigned counsel system uses private attorneys appointed on an as-needed basis by the court. A primary problem with assigned counsel is that the attorney may have little

Public defender: an attorney whose full-time job is to represent indigent defendants.

or no experience handling the criminal matter at hand; indeed, it may have been long ago that the assigned counsel studied subjects such as criminal law, criminal procedure, rules of evidence, and so on, and such attorneys may have limited knowledge about their state's criminal statutes.

The contract system is one whereby an attorney, a law firm, or a nonprofit organization contracts for a certain dollar amount—often after engaging in competitive bidding—with a unit of government to represent its indigent defendants. Advantages of this system can include reduced and predictable costs, streamlining of the counsel appointment process,

Practitioner's Perspective

Court Administrator

Maxine Cortes
Court Administrator

Name: Maxine Cortes
Position: Court Administrator
Location: Reno, Nevada

What are the primary duties and responsibilities of a practitioner in this position? As a court administrator, I am responsible for facilitating policies, procedures, and operational needs of the courts. I report directly to the judges. So in that capacity, I write grants, handle the budget, am responsible for recruiting facilities, technology projects, and jury systems.

What are some challenges you face in this position? The biggest challenge is that you don't really have control of your day. So every day, you have things that you need to do, meetings that you need to attend. But at a moment's notice, whether it is a phone call, an email, somebody walking through the door, everything can change. Being able to pivot and be professional and positive, and continue to handle any task or issue, being solution-oriented, flexible, and patient—I think that is the biggest challenge that I have every day.

What role does diversity play in this position? Diversity is huge. We serve diverse individuals from all walks of life, all socioeconomic backgrounds, all different ethnicities. The people we work with are also very diverse. Working in the court system, I'll sometimes see people come in, and it looks like they're going to the dentist—they really don't want to be there. To be able to maneuver and help them understand that not everyone thinks alike and sees the world through the same lenses, and being able to take the opportunity with diversity to approach people in different manners that will help them maneuver through the court system, is a major part of the role.

Do you see any common trends in this position? The trends in the court system in the last 10 years have been very exciting. Technology has played a huge role. We used to hire court reporters every day, but we do everything pretty much now through audio-video systems. In the future, I think we will see more technology playing a role in the courts, bringing an opportunity to the public to have that access to the system easily, whether it's through an iPad or a mobile phone, or a PC at home.

What advice would you give to someone either wishing to study, or now studying, criminal justice and wanting to become a practitioner in this position? My advice for students who are looking for any career, whether it be the court system or anywhere else, is to shadow. Find someone who's willing to have them shadow for one to two weeks if they're amenable. Walk in their shoes, learn what they do. I think that is the best way to really determine if you want to spend your life in a career. I also think if you do choose a career in the court system, I highly recommend taking a few classes: leadership, conflict resolution, mediation, budgeting, and communication.

To learn more about Maxine Cortes' experiences as a court administrator, watch the Practitioner's Perspective video in SAGE vantage.

and greater expertise of the attorneys. A major disadvantage is that obtaining legal counsel from the "lowest bidder" may result in inadequate or ineffective legal services—which may, of course, interfere with the defendant's Sixth Amendment right to effective counsel and be the basis for appealing a conviction.

As with many things in life, it is said that with regard to legal representation, "You get what you pay for." Obviously, people with financial means to do so will typically "go to the marketplace" and hire the best-trained legal counsel they can afford to represent them for their particular criminal matter. At the opposite end of this continuum is the *pro se* defendant who chooses instead to represent himself or herself. In such cases, there is an old adage: "He who represents himself at trial has a fool for a client."

COURTROOM WORK GROUP

Like the police subculture you learned about in Chapter 6, courtroom actors are also part of a subculture. The courtroom subculture is influenced heavily by the need to process large numbers of cases. Although our trial courts are designed to promote adversarial processes, in which defense and prosecuting attorneys "battle" to win court cases, courtroom actors—including the prosecutor, defense attorney, and judge—must work together to keep cases moving as quickly as possible and prevent delays that could violate the accused's Sixth Amendment right to a speedy trial. Accordingly, interactions between courtroom actors, who make up the courtroom work group,[52] are more likely to be cooperative than combative in nature.

In addition to the judge, prosecutor, and defense attorney, there are three other key courtroom work group participants: the court reporter, the clerk, and the bailiff. The court reporter attends legal proceedings, including trials and depositions (in which witnesses answer attorneys' questions under oath prior to trial), in order to record what is said and create transcripts of the proceedings. According to the Bureau of Labor Statistics, the justice system employs almost 20,000 court reporters.[53] The clerk of the court performs a wide array of functions. In essence, the clerk organizes and catalogs all of the paperwork generated during a trial, including all exhibits introduced into evidence (e.g., photographs and transcripts). The clerk also manages the jury subpoena and selection processes, and administers oaths to witnesses and jurors. The bailiff is a law enforcement officer who is responsible for maintaining order and safety in the courtroom and the judge's chambers. Bailiffs assist with the movement of defendants and jury members in and out of the courtroom, and they remove any persons ordered out of the courtroom by the judge.

Courtroom work group: the criminal justice professionals who work together to move cases through the court system.

DEFENSES

As mentioned earlier in this chapter, defense attorneys present applicable legal defenses for defendants. In the U.S. system of justice, criminal defendants have the opportunity to defend their actions by asserting affirmative defenses, in which the defendant admits to the criminal conduct but offers his or her reasons for acting. Because the defendant asserts such defenses, he or she typically has the burden to prove them. These defenses fall into two categories: justifications and excuses. When using justification defenses, defendants argue they were justified in acting because, for example, they were defending themselves or others. A police officer who had to injure a fleeing felon could claim a justification defense. When using excuse defenses, defendants admit to the criminal act but claim they are not legally responsible—they are excused—because they are too young or are insane, for example.

Learning about defenses is another way to learn about the critically important element of *mens rea*. Most defenses are designed to negate or reduce criminal liability by showing that the accused did not act with the required criminal intent. The prosecution may be able

Affirmative defense: the response to a criminal charge in which the defendant admits to committing the act charged but argues that for some mitigating reason he or she should not be held criminally responsible under the law.

Defense: the response by a defendant to a criminal charge, to include denial of the criminal allegations in an attempt to negate or overcome the charges.

to easily show that the criminal act—the *actus reus*—was committed (e.g., the killing, the assault, the breaking and entering), but the defense can then defeat the criminal charges by showing that the required *mens rea* simply was not present (killing in self-defense is not the same as killing intentionally because you are trying to save yourself, and breaking and entering to save yourself from freezing to death is not the same as burglarizing a home to steal things). As a result, examining these defenses helps us understand how *mens rea* operates in real cases.

Justification Defenses
Self-Defense

Self-defense is a justification defense rooted in legal doctrine that permits the use of force against others who pose a threat to one's person or interests. Under early common law of England, people had a "duty to retreat," also known as "retreat to the wall," prior to using force to defend themselves. In effect, a person could not respond to an attacker until he or she was "cornered" and had no other retreat option available. Today, most state laws do not impose a duty to retreat and, in fact, provide in many situations that people may "stand their ground" (see discussion in the accompanying "Investigating Further" box). Under modern laws, one may use force, even deadly force, without first "retreating to the wall" against another person if he or she reasonably believes that an attack against him or her is imminent, but defensive actions must be proportionate to the threatened harm and not unreasonable for the circumstances. One cannot respond to an attack with a small tree branch by using a shotgun.

Necessity

If a criminal act is committed in the event of an emergency, and if the harm avoided outweighs the harm committed by the defendant, then a person might escape criminal liability by employing the necessity defense. For example, the necessity defense could be used by a person who trespassed on private property during a fire to save a child or unattended pet, someone who broke into a home to escape a life-threatening storm, or a person who drove at a reckless speed to transport a pregnant woman to the hospital. However, the necessity defense has not been successfully used by every defendant who has committed a crime with the intent to avoid a seemingly greater harm. For example, two people operated a needle-exchange program in Massachusetts to attempt to reduce the transmission of AIDS caused by contaminated hypodermic needles. They were charged with violating a state law prohibiting hypodermic needle distribution without a physician's prescription. Although the defendants were attempting to prevent harm, the court rejected the defendants' necessity defense on the grounds that the situation posed no clear and imminent danger.[54]

Duress

The duress defense involves defendants' claims that they committed the act only because they were not acting of their own free will. For example, the wife of a bank president calls her husband and informs him that someone has broken into their home and put a gun to her head, and if he does not bring money home immediately, she will be killed. The husband then removes the money from his bank to supply the ransom. The husband could argue that he acted under duress, only to save his wife. Other actual cases include a person who was forced by gangsters to commit certain criminal acts or be killed, a drug smuggler who argued that his family would have been killed if he did not do what he was told,[55] and a Texas prison inmate whose three cellmates planned an escape and threatened to slit his throat if he did not accompany them.[56] Again, the burden will be on the accused to convince the jury that he or she committed the act under duress. For the duress defense to be successful, a jury must conclude the following:

1. The threatening conduct was sufficient to create in the mind of a reasonable person the fear of death or serious bodily harm;
2. The conduct in fact caused such fear of death or serious bodily harm in the mind of the defendant;
3. The fear or duress was operating upon the mind of the defendant at the time of the alleged act; and
4. The defendant committed the act to avoid the threatened harm.[57]

Excuse Defenses
Age

The infancy defense excuses the acts of children ages 7 and under because they are too young to be criminally responsible for their actions—they are too young to form the requisite *mens rea*. Minors between ages 7 and 14 are presumed incapable of committing a crime, but prosecutors may challenge that assumption in certain cases. Minors over age 14 have no infancy defense, but those under 16 at the time of the crime are typically tried in juvenile court. Under some state statutes, however, serious felony cases are transferred

Investigating Further

"Stand Your Ground" Laws

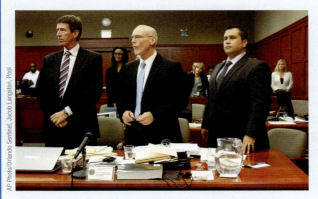

The fatal shooting of Trayvon Martin by George Zimmerman in Sanford, Florida, generated tremendous controversy because of its racial overtones and the state's "stand your ground" law. In July 2013, Zimmerman, right, was acquitted of second-degree murder.

When George Zimmerman shot and killed an unarmed teen named Trayvon Martin in February 2012, a major controversy erupted calling into question the entire criminal justice system and a controversial law that binds police and prosecutors. The "stand your ground" law essentially sets forth the common law "castle doctrine" that allows a homeowner to use deadly force against an intruder and then expands the right to defend beyond the home, to any place someone has a right to be. Under the law, an accused killer may argue he or she acted in self-defense because the killer believed he or she was facing the threat of seriously bodily injury or death. The burden then shifts to the prosecutor, who must prove *beyond a reasonable doubt* (discussed earlier) that the killer was not facing such a threat of serious bodily harm or death, and did not act in self-defense. The laws were originally intended to give citizens a presumption of innocence when defending themselves, while also generally banning police from detaining someone if they have evidence that the shooter was attacked "in a place he had a right to be." Prosecutors largely despise the law because of the aforementioned burden of proof, whereas defense attorneys have found it to be a means of defending people who claim they had a right to meet force with force. "Stand your ground" became law in Florida in 2005, and at least 25 states have since enacted some version.

Source: John Arnold, "The Law Heard Round the World," *Time,* April 9, 2012, http://www.time.com/time/magazine/article/0,9171,2110471,00.html; also see "Trayvon Martin Case (George Zimmerman)," *New York Times,* July 19, 2012, http://topics.nytimes.com/top/reference/timestopics/people/m/trayvon_martin/index.html.

automatically to adult court, or the prosecutor has the option to seek such a transfer if the juvenile is not a suitable candidate for the more lenient and protective philosophy and law of the juvenile court (see Chapter 15).

Entrapment

If the police induced a person to commit a crime that he or she would otherwise not have attempted, the defendant can claim the defense of entrapment.[58] But it is not always clear what constitutes entrapment. A state supreme court deemed that police officers posing as homeless persons with cash sticking out of their pockets was entrapment because it could tempt even honest persons who were not otherwise predisposed to committing theft. But the U.S. Supreme Court did not find entrapment where undercover drug agents provided an essential chemical to defendants who were already planning to manufacture illegal drugs.[59] Nor is it entrapment when a drug agent sells drugs to a suspected drug dealer, who then sells it to government agents. The defense of entrapment will fail where the government has merely set the scene for people to commit a crime they are predisposed to commit anyway, such as where a police officer positions himself on the route of a known working prostitute and offers her money for sex when she comes by.

Entrapment: police tactics that unduly encourage or induce an individual to commit a crime he or she typically would not commit.

Intoxication

The intoxication defense is rooted in the concept of *mens rea*, and defendants must show that they were operating under such "diminished capacity" that they could not know what they were doing and cannot be held responsible. The defense is not available in cases of voluntary intoxication (except in some cases of severe alcoholism where *mens rea* is impaired permanently) and is successful—albeit rarely—only in cases of involuntary intoxication (the spiked drink or slipped drug), where the intoxicant was ingested without awareness of its intoxicating nature or where the consumption was coerced. The burden on the defendant is high in these cases, and defense attorneys generally have a difficult time convincing juries that defendants should be excused (although diminished capacity can be useful for defense attorneys to seek reduced charges or punishment).

Double Jeopardy

The Fifth Amendment to the U.S. Constitution states that no person shall be "subject for the same offense to be twice put in jeopardy of life or limb," prohibiting the government from prosecuting someone for the same offense more than once (double jeopardy). Other than some specific exceptions (a mistrial, a reversal on appeal, or a situation in which the crime violates laws of separate jurisdictions such as civilian/military or federal/state), the government has only one attempt to obtain a conviction. If a defendant is acquitted, the prosecution may not appeal that conviction or retry the defendant.

Double jeopardy: the prosecution of an accused person twice for the same offense; prohibited by the Fifth Amendment except under certain circumstances.

Mental Illness/Insanity

The insanity defense is perhaps the most misunderstood area of the criminal law. Ask anyone on the street, and most people will say that the insanity defense is a way for criminals to "get off" by arguing that they were "crazy" at the time of the crime. Some crimes by their very nature seem to indicate that the perpetrator was indeed not thinking straight, and many people believe that those who commit especially gruesome crimes will, by default, plead insanity. These are just a few of the common misconceptions about this defense.

Several notorious trials have contributed to the confusion. Most notably, in 1981, John Hinckley Jr. attempted to assassinate President Ronald Reagan but was found not guilty by reason of insanity after he claimed he had done so in an effort to impress actress Jodie Foster and after psychiatrists testified at length about his childhood.[60] Then, in 1986, Steve Roth hired two men who slashed model Marla Hanson's face with razors after Hanson rejected Roth's sexual advances. Her injuries required more than 100 stitches. Roth's insanity defense—based on the psychiatric effects of his short stature—failed, and all three men were convicted.[61] The 2008 movie *Milk* recalled the so-called Twinkie defense from the trial of Dan White, who in 1978 murdered Harvey Milk, a San Francisco gay rights activist and politician. Although the defense never even mentioned Twinkies during White's trial, the media coined the term following psychiatric testimony that White had been depressed and consuming junk food and sugar-laden soft drinks—allegedly "blasting sugar through his arteries and driving him into a murderous frenzy."[62] Despite these high-profile cases, the insanity defense is raised in less than 1 percent of felony cases and is successful in only a fraction of those.[63] The defense is really quite simple if you think of it as another way of examining the critical element of *mens rea*: Defendants must prove that they have a recognized, diagnosable mental illness—a disease of the brain (e.g., schizophrenia, bipolar disorder, psychosis)—and that because of that mental illness, they cannot be held criminally responsible for their actions.

State laws set forth the applicable test for legal insanity. Most states use the M'Naghten Rule, also known as the right-wrong test. Under this test, it must be "proved that, at the time of the committing of the act, the defendant suffered from a mental illness and

Right-wrong test: the test of legal insanity, asking whether the defendant understood the nature and quality of his or her act and, if so, if he or she understood it was wrong.

Investigating Further

James Holmes—The "Batman" Shooter

When James Holmes made his first appearance in court, accused of turning a Colorado movie theater into a shooting gallery, killing 12 and injuring 70, many people assumed he must be "crazy," but the question of his guilt and mental state is much more complicated under the criminal law.

In July 2013, James Holmes went to the midnight viewing of the new Batman movie, *The Dark Knight Rises*. He had dyed his hair orange like the Joker character in the movie, but otherwise, Holmes seemed like any other Batman fan. While the movie got under way, Holmes slipped out an exit door, propped it open, went to his car and picked up SWAT gear, firearms, and ammunition, and then went back to the theater and opened fire, killing 12 and injuring 70. When law enforcement officers later caught Holmes outside the theater, he was quickly subdued and told officers he had booby-trapped his apartment with bombs and other weapons. There would seem to be no clearer case of someone acting with *mens rea* and premeditation, but questions quickly arose regarding Holmes's psychiatric condition in the months leading up to the shooting. His attorneys ultimately entered a plea of not guilty by reason of insanity, and the world watched to see if this apparently evil, plotting killer would be convicted and sentenced to death. But the insanity defense in Colorado requires that the prosecution—not the defense—show that Holmes understood right from wrong (the M'Naghten Rule) and that he was not acting on impulses he could not control (the irresistible impulse test). The defense countered with evidence of Holmes's mental illness to lay the foundation for a finding that he could not have fully understood or controlled what he was doing. In July 2015, a jury decided Holmes was not insane and convicted him of 24 counts of first-degree murder, 140 counts of attempted murder, and one explosives count. Despite the prosecution's arguments that Holmes deserved to die for his crimes, the jury sentenced him to life in prison without parole.

Source: Colo. Rev. Stats §16–8; see also Denver Post Editorial Board, "Shining a Light on Insanity Plea," *Denver Post*, June 9, 2013, http://www.denverpost.com/ci_23406862/shining-light-james-holmes-insanity-plea.

because of that disease of the mind, was laboring under such a defect of reason that he did not know the nature and quality of the act he was doing, or if he did know it, that he did not understand what he was doing was wrong."[64] Another test is the "irresistible impulse test," requiring a showing that the defendant, because of a mental illness, could not control his or her impulses or volition. Also known as "the policeman at your elbow" test, this standard for legal insanity requires a showing that the defendant would have committed the crime even if a police officer had been on the scene, literally at the accused's elbow, thereby evidencing that the defendant had no impulse control.[65]

Contrary to another popular misconception, a finding of legal insanity does not mean the defendant walks free. Instead, the defendant will be committed to a psychiatric facility. In some states, in reaction to the Hinckley verdict, the jury can reach a "guilty but mentally ill" verdict, allowing mentally ill defendants to be found guilty but to receive psychiatric treatment while incarcerated or to be placed in a mental hospital until well enough to be moved to a prison to serve their sentences.[66] After Hinckley's trial, many states shifted the burden of proving insanity to the defense, requiring them to show either clear and convincing evidence or a preponderance of the evidence that the defendant was legally insane at the time of the crime. Consider the following notorious post-Hinckley cases in which the insanity defense failed:

- Jeffrey L. Dahmer, the serial killer who claimed that necrophilia drove him to murder and dismember/cannibalize 15 men and boys, was convicted in 1992.[67]
- David Berkowitz, known as the Son of Sam killer (he reported receiving messages from the devil through a neighbor's dog, Sam), murdered six people in New York in the mid-1970s and was deemed fit to stand trial (despite a psychiatric report that found him paranoid and delusional).[68]
- John Wayne Gacy, the Chicago-area so-called Killer Clown who murdered more than 30 youths, pleaded not guilty by reason of insanity but was convicted and executed in 1994.[69]

/// IN A NUTSHELL

- The debate over how we select our judges has escalated in the 21st century. Adding fuel to the fire over judicial selection is the amount of money now being spent by judges to fund their elections; across the nation, states use five basic methods of judicial selection. One of the more common methods is the merit plan (or "Missouri Plan").
- Judges enjoy several distinct benefits of office, including life terms for federal positions and a high degree of respect and prestige. But problems can await new judges as well: mastering the breadth of law they must know and apply; administering the court and the docket; supervising court staff; and coping with the psychological discomfort and loneliness that accompany the new position.
- The prosecutor is probably the most powerful person in our criminal justice system, controlling the floodgates in determining whether or not to file charges (and these attorneys also have the ability to rebuke officers who fail to do their work properly). The prosecutor also interacts with the person suspected of the crime, the victim, and witnesses.

- Defense attorneys require the state to prove its case, help defendants understand their options in the criminal justice system, and attempt to ensure that the entire slate of rights owed to the defendant is upheld. Like prosecutors, defense attorneys have a number of strategies at their disposal.
- The courtroom work group consists of individuals who play key roles during the trial process. The six main courtroom work group actors employed by the criminal justice system are the judge, prosecutor, defense attorney, court reporter, clerk, and bailiff.
- Our system of justice allows for persons charged with crimes to offer defenses for their behavior; one can argue that his or her acts were justified (e.g., self-defense, necessity, duress); or the accused can admit wrongdoing but argue that he or she is not deserving of blame due to circumstances surrounding the offense (e.g., age, entrapment, intoxication, mental illness).

/// KEY TERMS & CONCEPTS

Review key terms with eFlashcards at **edge.sagepub.com/peak4e**.

Affirmative defense 253	Double jeopardy 256	Merit selection 241
Courtroom work group 253	Entrapment 256	Prosecuting attorney 248
Defense 253	Judicial misconduct 246	Public defender 251
Defense attorney 250	Judicial selection (methods of) 241	Right-wrong test 257

/// REVIEW QUESTIONS

Test your understanding of chapter content at **edge.sagepub.com/peak4e**.

1. What are the five methods by which judges are selected?
2. Why is the partisan election method of selecting judges currently under severe criticism?
3. What are the key points of the merit selection plan for selecting judges?
4. What is meant by "good judging," and why is courtroom civility so important?
5. Why is the prosecutor believed to occupy the most powerful position in the criminal justice system?
6. What is prosecutorial immunity, and why is it both important and potentially dangerous in our adversarial system?
7. What is a defense attorney's primary responsibility under the Sixth Amendment?
8. Which individuals play prominent roles in the courtroom work group?
9. What is double jeopardy, why does this constitutional protection from the Fifth Amendment exist, and what are some examples of exceptions to the rule? Many years after O. J. Simpson was acquitted of murdering his ex-wife and her friend, he finalized a contract to publish a book entitled *If I Did It*, which detailed how he "could have" committed the murders. Could prosecutors retry Simpson for the murders based on this new "evidence"?
10. How can age, entrapment, intoxication, and duress each be used as a criminal defense?

/// LEARN BY DOING

1. Your local League of Women Voters is establishing a new study group to better understand merit selection, or the so-called Missouri Plan for selecting judges, so as to be better informed when the matter comes up for a referendum. You are asked to explain this system of selecting judges, including its pros and cons when compared with, say, judges running for election on a partisan ticket. Develop your presentation.

2. You have been asked by your criminal justice department chairperson to participate in the annual "Career Day" program that the faculty conducts. The focus is on different careers in law enforcement, courts, and corrections. Because the faculty members know you recently completed an internship with your local prosecutor's office, they ask you to make a presentation on the functions and challenges that exist for a prosecutor. Develop and organize into a 10-minute speech what you will say in your comprehensive presentation.

3. Below is a case study grounded in actual case facts and chapter materials concerning self-defense. Answer the following questions yourself before reviewing answers and/or outcomes for the case in the Notes section. For purposes of discussion, however, approach all of the questions as if there are no absolute, totally correct answers.

   A woman is at home with her two children when her estranged husband arrives and begins threatening and assaulting her, following a pattern of alleged past conduct with this woman and prior women. Fearing for her and her children's safety, she flees to the garage but later claims she was unable to open the garage door. Instead, she gets a gun out of her car and returns to the house. Her husband tells her he will kill her, and their young son witnesses the threat. The woman fires a warning shot that hits the wall behind the husband and then deflects into the ceiling, injuring no one. The woman is charged with aggravated assault with a deadly weapon, but she lives in a "stand your ground" jurisdiction and argues that she acted in self-defense.

- How can the prosecutor argue that the woman had no right to "stand her ground" and exercise her self-defense rights? What other options did she have in the situation?
- How can the defense argue that this is precisely the type of case in which the wife should be able to argue self-defense? What other facts would you want to know about the husband-wife relationship?
- What are the dangers if the wife is successful at using this defense? What are the dangers if she fails and is convicted of attempted murder? Think about broader social policy issues.[70]

/// STUDY SITE

Get the tools you need to sharpen your study skills. SAGE edge offers a robust online environment featuring an impressive array of free tools and resources.

Access practice quizzes, eFlashcards, video, and multimedia at **edge.sagepub.com/peak4e**.

Introducing...

SAGE vantage™

Course tools done right.
Built to support teaching. Designed to ignite learning.

SAGE vantage is an intuitive digital platform that blends trusted SAGE content with auto-graded assignments, all carefully designed to ignite student engagement and drive critical thinking. Built with you and your students in mind, it offers easy course set-up and enables students to better prepare for class.

SAGE vantage enables students to **engage** with the material you choose, **learn** by applying knowledge, and **soar** with confidence by performing better in your course.

PEDAGOGICAL SCAFFOLDING

Builds on core concepts, moving students from basic understanding to mastery.

CONFIDENCE BUILDER

Offers frequent knowledge checks, applied-learning multimedia tools, and chapter tests with focused feedback.

TIME-SAVING FLEXIBILITY

Feeds auto-graded assignments to your gradebook, with real-time insight into student and class performance.

QUALITY CONTENT

Written by expert authors and teachers, content is not sacrificed for technical features.

HONEST VALUE

Affordable access to easy-to-use, quality learning tools students will appreciate.

To learn more about **SAGE vantage**, hover over this QR code with your smartphone camera or visit **sagepub.com/vantage**

CHAPTER 11

COURT METHODS AND CHALLENGES
Sentencing and Punishment

If you are going to punish a man retributively, you must injure him. If you are going to reform him, you must improve him. And men are not improved by injuries.

—George Bernard Shaw[1]

LEARNING OBJECTIVES

As a result of reading this chapter, you will be able to

1. Delineate the four goals of punishment and explain the factors that influence the type of punishment that a convicted person will receive
2. Describe the historical development of, and different philosophies regarding, crime and punishment from the colonial era to today, and how different types of prisons were built accordingly
3. Describe the differences between, and purposes of, both determinate and indeterminate sentences
4. Review federal and state-level sentencing guidelines
5. Explain the law and purposes surrounding the use of victim impact statements
6. Describe the fundamental arguments for and against capital punishment, including key Supreme Court decisions concerning its existence and application, methods of execution, and DNA exonerations from death sentences
7. Describe aggravating and mitigating circumstances as they apply to sentencing decisions
8. Explain the right to appeals by those who are convicted

ASSESS YOUR AWARENESS

Test your knowledge of criminal sentencing and punishment by responding to the following seven true-false items; check your answers after reading this chapter.

1. Historically, people have been punished for one purpose only: retribution.
2. A small number of offenders commit a disproportionately large number of offenses.
3. Today, U.S. society adheres to the rehabilitation model, which considers criminals to have been failed by society and emphasizes offender treatment.
4. Offenders' sentences can be served in determinate or indeterminate and concurrent or consecutive configurations.
5. Prosecutors and defense attorneys can influence judges' sentencing decisions.
6. Victims' families are not allowed to present impact statements in court at the time of sentencing.
7. Federal sentencing guidelines are to be merely advisory and not mandatory.

<< Answers can be found on page 419.

On November 30, 1983, Michael Conley shot and killed 21-year-old Marsy Nicholas, his neighbor and former girlfriend of three years, at his home. Nicholas was a model and award-winning equestrian. She was completing her last quarter at the University of California, Santa Barbara, and had plans to teach disabled children following graduation.

Conley became jealous after learning that Nicholas had been dating a mutual friend. Nicholas's mother said that Marsy went to see Conley because he had threatened suicide. Conley shot Nicholas in the head with a shotgun, later claiming that the gun went off on accident. Conley was eventually found guilty of second-degree murder.[2]

Nicholas's family became victim's rights advocates. Her brother said in an interview, "After [Marsy's] funeral service, we were driving home and stopped at a market so my mother could just run in and get a loaf of bread. And there in the checkout line was my sister's murderer, glowering at her."[3] Nicholas's family were key backers of a California Victims' Bill of Rights approved by voters in 2008. This proposition became known as "Marsy's Law" and called for increased protection and rights for victims. There are 17 Marsy's Rights, including victims' right to be heard at multiple stages of criminal proceedings (you

SAGE edge™
Master the content at edge.sagepub.com/peak4e

will learn more about victim impact statements later in this chapter). Like accused persons are read their *Miranda* rights, victims in California who are contacted by police are now informed of their Marsy's Rights and provided with a "Marsy's Card" that lists these rights.

Similar laws have been passed by multiple states throughout the country, but they remain controversial. At least two state supreme courts have ruled that the laws are unconstitutional.

California Attorney General's Office

Contact Name: _____

Phone No.: _____

Police Report / Case No.: _____

Notes: _____

Marsy's Card and Resources

The California Constitution, Article 1, Section 28(b), confers certain rights to victims of crime. Those rights include:

1. **Fairness and Respect** – To be treated with fairness and respect for his or her privacy and dignity, and to be free from intimidation, harassment, and abuse, throughout the criminal or juvenile justice process.
2. **Protection from the Defendant** – To be reasonably protected from the defendant and persons acting on behalf of the defendant.
3. **Victim Safety Considerations in Setting Bail and Release Conditions** – To have the safety of the victim and the victim's family considered in fixing the amount of bail and release conditions for the defendant.
4. **The Prevention of the Disclosure of Confidential Information** – To prevent the disclosure of confidential information or records to the defendant, the defendant's attorney, or any other person acting on behalf of the defendant, which could be used to locate or harass the victim or the victim's family or which disclose confidential communications made in the course of medical or counseling treatment, or which are otherwise privileged or confidential by law.
5. **Refusal to be Interviewed by the Defense** – To refuse an interview, deposition, or discovery request by the defendant, the defendant's attorney, or any other person acting on behalf of the defendant, and to set reasonable conditions on the conduct of any such interview to which the victim consents.
6. **Conference with the Prosecution and Notice of Pretrial Disposition** – To reasonable notice of and to reasonably confer with the prosecuting agency, upon request, regarding the arrest of the defendant if known by the prosecutor, the charges filed, the determination whether to extradite the defendant, and, upon request, to be notified of and informed before any pretrial disposition of the case.
7. **Notice of and Presence at Public Proceedings** – To reasonable notice of all public proceedings, including delinquency proceedings, upon request, at which the defendant and the prosecutor are entitled to be present and of all parole or other post-conviction release proceedings, and to be present at all such proceedings.
8. **Appearance at Court Proceedings and Expression of Views** – To be heard, upon request, at any proceeding, including any delinquency proceeding, involving a post-arrest release decision, plea, sentencing, post-conviction release decision, or any proceeding in which a right of the victim is at issue.
9. **Speedy Trial and Prompt Conclusion of the Case** – To a speedy trial and a prompt and final conclusion of the case and any related post-judgment proceedings.
10. **Provision of Information to the Probation Department** – To provide information to a probation department official conducting a pre-sentence investigation concerning the impact of the offense on the victim and the victim's family and any sentencing recommendations before the sentencing of the defendant.
11. **Receipt of Pre-Sentence Report** – To receive, upon request, the pre-sentence report when available to the defendant, except for those portions made confidential by law.
12. **Information About Conviction, Sentence, Incarceration, Release, and Escape** – To be informed, upon request, of the conviction, sentence, place and time of incarceration, or other disposition of the defendant, the scheduled release date of the defendant, and the release of or the escape by the defendant from custody.
13. **Restitution**
    A. It is the unequivocal intention of the People of the State of California that all persons who suffer losses as a result of criminal activity shall have the right to seek and secure restitution from the persons convicted of the crimes causing the losses they suffer.
    B. Restitution shall be ordered from the convicted wrongdoer in every case, regardless of the sentence or disposition imposed, in which a crime victim suffers a loss.
    C. All monetary payments, monies, and property collected from any person who has been ordered to make restitution shall be first applied to pay the amounts ordered as restitution to the victim.

14. **The Prompt Return of Property** – To the prompt return of property when no longer needed as evidence.
15. **Notice of Parole Procedures and Release on Parole** – To be informed of all parole procedures, to participate in the parole process, to provide information to the parole authority to be considered before the parole of the offender, and to be notified, upon request, of the parole or other release of the offender.
16. **Safety of Victim and Public are Factors in Parole Release** – To have the safety of the victim, the victim's family, and the general public considered before any parole or other post-judgment release decision is made.
17. **Information About These 16 Rights** – To be informed of the rights enumerated in paragraphs (1) through (16).

****

Additional Resources

The Attorney General does not endorse, have any responsibility for, or exercise control over these organizations' and agencies' views, services, and information.

Victim Compensation Board – Can help victims pay for: mental health counseling, funeral costs, loss of income, crime scene cleanup, relocation, medical and dental bills. **1-800-777-9229** *www.victims.ca.gov*

CA Dept. of Corrections and Rehabilitation, OVSRS – Provides information on offender release, restitution, parole conditions and parole hearings when the offender is incarcerated in prison. **1-877-256-6877** *www.cdcr.ca.gov/victim_services*

McGeorge School of Law – Victims of Crime Resource Center - Provides resources for victims by their geographic area along with information on victims' rights. **1-800-Victims (1-800-842-8467)** *www.1800victims.org*

National Domestic Violence Hotline – **1-800-799-7233** *www.thehotline.org*

Adult Protective Services County Information – (Elder abuse) 24 hour hotline numbers by county in California. *www.cdss.ca.gov/inforesources/County-APS-Offices*

National Child Abuse Hotline – Treatment and prevention of child abuse. **1-800-422-4453** *www.childhelp.org*

Rape, Abuse & Incest National Network – **1-800-656-4673** *www.rainn.org*

National Human Trafficking Resource Center Hotline – 24-hour hotline: **1-888-373-7888** *www.humantraffickinghotline.org*

The California Relay Service: For speech impaired, deaf or hard-of-hearing callers: Dial 711. TTY/HCO/VCO to Voice for English: 1-800-735-2929 and for Spanish: 1-800-855-3000. Voice to TTY/VCO/HCO for English: 1-800-735-2922 and for Spanish: 1-800-855-3000. Speech to Speech – English and Spanish: 1-800-854-7784.

Attorney General's Victims' Services Unit – Provides local victim/witness information, geographic resource information and appeal status to victims of crime. For more information, call **1-877-433-9069** or visit: *www.oag.ca.gov/victimservices* For local Human Trafficking information, visit: *www.oag.ca.gov/human-trafficking*

****

A 'victim' is defined under the California Constitution as "a person who suffers direct or threatened physical, psychological, or financial harm as a result of the commission or attempted commission of a crime or delinquent act. The term 'victim' also includes the person's spouse, parents, children, siblings, or guardian, and includes a lawful representative of a crime victim who is deceased, a minor, or physically or psychologically incapacitated. The term 'victim' does not include a person in custody for an offense, the accused, or a person whom the court finds would not act in the best interests of a minor victim." (Cal. Const., art. I, § 28(e).)

A victim, the retained attorney of a victim, a lawful representative of the victim, or the prosecuting attorney upon request of the victim, may enforce the above rights in any trial or appellate court with jurisdiction over the case as a matter of right. The court shall act promptly on such a request. (Cal. Const., art. I, § 28(c)(1).)

Funding is made possible through the United States Department of Justice, Victims of Crime Act, 2016-VA-GX-0057

VSU Rev 10/2017

As you read this chapter and learn about the history and theories of punishment and sentencing in the United States, think about the moment when a court hands down a sentence to a criminal offender. What are we trying to achieve through the process? How can we best offer redress to victims and communities, if at all, through punishment and sentencing? Should victims or their families be allowed to testify, or is such testimony too inflammatory to juries? Similarly, should defendants be allowed to make statements about their crime and punishment? Finally, how can we possibly find an appropriate punishment for every new offender, or for the thousands of repeat offenders moving through our criminal justice system every year?

INTRODUCTION

For what reasons and purposes are people punished? Do punishments always fit the crimes committed? Does capital punishment work? Punishing those who violate the right to life, liberty, and property of their fellow human beings is one of the primary functions of the American criminal justice system. However, many questions concerning the "how" and "how much" need to be addressed. As the chapter-opening quotation by George Bernard Shaw might indicate, an enigma for our time is what might best be done with people who must be punished for their transgressions. As will be seen in this chapter, sentencing and punishment are complicated issues, with both having financial and societal factors that must be included in these discussions.

Although violent crime rates have been declining in the new millennium, people are increasingly being victimized by intelligent white-collar criminals, identity thieves, and cybercriminals. How should our society deal with these new types of offenders? Into this complicated mix might also be included the adage that "it is better to let a hundred guilty people go free than to convict one innocent person." The federal and state sentencing guidelines discussed in this chapter indicate how much concern and effort have recently gone into sentencing and punishment. This chapter approaches sentencing and punishment from several perspectives, including their purposes, types, and methods, as well as the more recent influence of DNA evidence. Also examined are capital punishment and criminal appeals.

PURPOSES OF PUNISHMENT

The need to punish some of our fellow citizens has existed since the beginning of time—at least since biblical times, and likely much earlier. It would seem there have always been attempts—by a variety of methods and for a variety of reasons—to convince people that they should change their behavior and either obey the customs and laws of their society or suffer the consequences. Very often those attempts at changing behaviors meant that—by one means or another, such as imprisonment, banishment, or death—offenders would be removed from society in such a way that they were no longer in a position to do further harm to their fellow citizens. Here, we discuss the four goals of punishment—some or all of which are hoped to be achieved by all societies, even the most primitive. Furthermore, we will see that throughout history, crimes and criminals have been viewed and punished differently, depending on several factors. Some of those factors that determine punishment today were described in Chapter 1, in the discussions of the wedding cake, crime control, and due process models of crime.

Four Goals

Punishment (and its purposes): penalties imposed for committing criminal acts, to accomplish retribution, deterrence, incapacitation, and/or rehabilitation.

Retribution: punishment that fits the crime, that is "equitable" for the offense.

Following are the historical reasons and goals for punishment of our fellow citizens—what is hoped will be achieved (note that all of these goals and justifications may also be achieved by methods employed in community-based corrections, discussed in Chapter 14):

- *Retribution*: Retribution has its roots in Old Testament law where, in Exodus 21:24, the phrase "eye for eye, tooth for tooth, hand for hand, foot for foot" appears for the first time—labeled *lex talionis*, the law of equitable retribution. Death penalty supporters also quote this phrase often as justification for their position. However, neither the phrase "eye for eye" nor the verse itself is a complete sentence, and the death penalty is not mentioned. For many people, "eye for eye" dictates that offenders should be punished in a manner that reflects their crime: It is instinctive for people to want to get even when wronged by another, and it is deeply engrained within ourselves and our society that punishment should be meted out when someone breaks the law.

- *Deterrence:* **Deterrence** probably makes more sense than retribution in terms of betterment of society because it is not grounded on our primal human emotions and instincts. The concept of deterrence stems from the classical school of criminology (see Chapter 3). Since people will typically avoid unpleasant things, they are much less likely to commit a crime if they know that punishment will result if they are caught. Deterrence has two components: general and specific. By seeing others being punished for their crimes, the public experiences a *general* deterrent effect because they can see what will befall them should they engage in similar behavior. *Specific* deterrence involves using punishment against specific offenders for their criminal acts in order to discourage them from committing such acts again in the future.

Placing people in stocks was used internationally and during medieval, Renaissance, and colonial American times as a form of physical punishment as well as for public humiliation.

Deterrence: the effect of punishments and other actions to deter people from committing crimes.

Incapacitation: rendering someone as unable to act or move about, either through incarceration or by court order.

- *Incapacitation:* **Incapacitation**, by its very meaning, is beneficial in that it prevents criminals from victimizing others by placing them in a situation where they are physically unable to commit crimes. The best examples, of course, are incarceration in jails and prisons as well as execution. Bear in mind, however, that one can still commit crimes while in a state of incarceration. The methods of community corrections—probation and parole and other alternatives to incarceration—are forms of incapacitation that also aim to prevent offenders from committing new crimes.

- *Rehabilitation:* Almost since its beginning, the modern criminal justice system has had as a primary goal—indeed a responsibility—to change criminals so that they become law-abiding citizens, in other words, to rehabilitate them. In fact, for most of the 20th century, rehabilitation was the system's primary goal in terms of how it was to function and be organized. Since the mid-1960s, however, that ideology has been modified to the point that it is hardly recognizable.[4] The reasons for this ideological change are several, and include changing governmental priorities, other concerns of the public (as revealed in national polls), and institutional and political resistance to change.[5] Furthermore, politicians can point to the historical "nothing works" idea put forth by Robert Martinson, who studied prison programs and found no "appreciable effect" on recidivism. Still, a wide array of correctional programs (i.e., vocational, educational, counseling) continues to be offered in prisons and jails, and with marked success. One cost-benefit analysis of 14 correctional treatment programs found that, in all but one of the programs, program benefits outweighed program costs. Such programs can be crucial for assisting offenders to reenter society and not recidivate (commit more crimes).[6]

Rehabilitation: attempts to reform an offender through vocational and educational programming, counseling, and so forth, so that he or she is not a recidivist and does not return to crime and prison.

Sentencing and punishment must accomplish one or more of these goals if the public is to be supportive of them. If increases in prison and jail sentences do not provide effective means of preventing crime, then a more cost-effective strategy must be found that will target the offenders most likely to commit serious crimes at high rates. As a federal report noted:

It is frequently observed that a small number of offenders commit a disproportionately large number of offenses. If prison resources can be effectively targeted to high-rated offenders, it should be possible to achieve . . . levels of crime control. The key to such a policy rests on an ability to identify high-rate offenders . . . and at relatively early stages in their careers.[7]

Judges consider a variety of factors in sentencing criminal offenders. Despite competing arguments from defense attorneys and prosecutors, fundamental factors like a prior criminal record and the seriousness of the offense typically guide judges' discretion in handing down punishments.

Factors Influencing Punishment

As noted earlier, sentencing and punishment involve issues concerning their financial and societal benefit. On average it costs about $35,000 per year to house an inmate in prison,[8] but costs vary widely by jurisdiction. For example, the annual cost of imprisoning a single California inmate is greater than $81,000, exceeding the cost of attending Harvard with room and board by about $14,000.[9] For that amount of money, society expects to be able to accomplish one or more of the four goals described earlier. Regarding the cost-benefit effect of prisons, some researchers argue that prisons should be used to greater advantage, believing it is at least twice as costly to let a prisoner be loose in society than it is to lock him or her up. For example, comparing the cost of incarceration with the human and financial toll of crime, prison expert John DiIulio Jr. believes that prisons are a "real bargain."[10]

You Be the . . .

Judge

A habitual offender is essentially one who has been convicted of a crime several times (either a misdemeanor or a felony, and typically at least twice). Habitual offender laws usually impose additional punishments on such offenders. Such laws can even address traffic violations. For example, a first-time driving under the influence (DUI) offense is usually a misdemeanor that results in a fine and jail time of less than one year. However, upon being arrested for a second or third DUI, the offender may be charged with a felony (depending on state law). Being classified as a habitual offender can thus result in higher criminal fines, longer jail or prison sentences, and loss of various rights and privileges (e.g., the right to own a firearm or to possess a driver's license).

An example is a Florida law stating that if you receive three (3) or more convictions of serious offenses on separate occasions you will be deemed a habitual offender. Examples of serious traffic offense include voluntary manslaughter while driving, involuntary manslaughter while driving, [and] felony while driving. Other serious traffic offenses include not stopping at an accident with a personal injury or death, or driving with a suspended or revoked license. Three convictions of these offenses and you will be considered a habitual traffic offender.

1. Do you agree with the spirit and intent of habitual offender laws?
2. Are such laws too harsh or too lenient?

Sources: See LegalMatch, "What Is a Habitual Offender," http://www.legalmatch.com/law-library/article/what-is-a-habitual-offender.html; see also Florida Drivers Association, "How to Get a Hardship License for Habitual Offenders," http://www.123driving.com/habitual-offender.shtml.

In addition to victims making their wishes known early on to the prosecution concerning punishment, as well as victim impact statements and aggravating or mitigating circumstances involved in a crime (discussed briefly in Chapter 1 and later in this chapter), there are other factors that influence sentencing and punishment. First, the U.S. Constitution speaks briefly but forcefully regarding the use of punishment. The Eighth Amendment provides that incarceration will not involve "cruel and unusual punishment," and that fines will not be excessive. Furthermore, the Thirteenth Amendment states that U.S. citizens have a right against involuntary servitude.

Prosecutors can influence the sentencing decision by agreeing to engage in plea negotiation in terms of the number of charges filed or the maximum penalty the judge may impose, or by explaining to the sentencing judge that the offender was particularly cruel in his or her crime or, alternatively, was very cooperative with the police and/or remorseful about the crime. In many states, prosecutors can also make a specific sentencing recommendation to the court that has been agreed upon with the defense.

Defense attorneys probably have less influence than prosecutors over sentencing decisions. Nonetheless, they can seek to obtain the lightest sentence possible, including probation or other alternatives to sentencing, as well as emphasize prior to sentencing such things as the defendant's minor involvement in the crime, the victim's participation, and so on.

The seriousness of the offense is the most important factor in determining the sentencing received for an offense. For instance, a violent crime against a person warrants a harsher penalty than an offense against one's property, and the judge, jury, prosecutor, and defense attorney must take into account the victim's suffering when carrying out their roles in arriving at a proper punishment.

Where sentencing is concerned, next in importance is the defendant's prior criminal record. The existence of a lengthy criminal record—particularly a record of violence or even habitual crimes against property, such as home invasion—can weigh heavily in terms of sentencing and punishment. Many states have habitual offender laws, which are related to and often viewed as identical to three-strikes laws (discussed in Chapter 1). (See the accompanying "You Be the . . . Judge" box.) These laws vary widely from state to state but typically apply only to felonies and require third-time felons to serve a mandatory 25 years to life. Furthermore, many police departments have repeat offender units dedicated solely to surveilling known offenders.

Punishment Models, Methods, and Reforms

Philosophies of crime and punishment have changed significantly since the late 1700s, when the United States was relatively sparsely populated and predominantly rural. However, with the Industrial Revolution came a new concept of criminal punishment embracing various correctional methods (see timeline in Figure 11.1).[11]

- *The colonial model (1600s–1790s):* During the colonial period, most Americans lived under laws that were transferred from England. Puritans rigorously punished violations of religious laws, and banishment from the community, fines, death, and other punishments were the norm. Use of the death penalty was common.
- *The penitentiary model (1790s–1870s):* With the Industrial Revolution—and increasing populations—came a new concept of criminal punishment. Criminal offenders were to be isolated from the bad influences of society and from one another so that, while engaged in productive labor, they might reflect on their past misdeeds and be "penitent" or remorseful for their crimes. As a result, what has been termed "the first American penitentiary, if not the first one in the world," was established in Philadelphia, in 1790, in the Walnut Street Jail. This penitentiary introduced the institutional pattern of outside cells with a central corridor and the use of solitary confinement as the central

Figure 11.1 /// A Timeline of Correctional Models
1600s–1790s — The Colonial Model
1790s–1870s — The Penitentiary Model
1870s–1890s — The Reformatory Model
1890s–1930s — The Progressive Model
1930s–1960s — The Medical Model
1960s–1970s — The Community Model
1970s–2000s — The Crime Control Model

method of reforming inmates to "the good life." Inmates were also segregated according to "age, sex, and the type of the offenses charged against them."[12] Auburn Prison, built in New York in 1821, reflected this shift, emphasizing individual cell-block architecture to create an environment to rehabilitate and reform, separate criminals from all contact with corruption, and teach them moral habits, by means of severe discipline. Inmates worked as contract convict labor 10 hours per day, 6 days per week. The Auburn model influenced the emergence of reform schools and workhouses in the 1820s. Then, Eastern State Penitentiary, a huge fortress with thick walls near Philadelphia, was built in 1829, emphasizing complete solitary confinement rather than Auburn's contract labor. New inmates wore hoods when marched to their cells so that they would not see other prisoners. Regimentation included use of the lockstep (marching everywhere in single file), shuffling with the head turned right, practices that continued into the 1930s. No visitors, mail, or newspapers were allowed. The design of this prison became the most influential in U.S. history.

What is often termed the "first American penitentiary, if not the first in the world," was established in Philadelphia, in 1790: the Walnut Street Jail.

Built in 1829, Eastern State Penitentiary, a huge fortress near Philadelphia, emphasized complete solitary confinement.

- *The reformatory model (1870s–1890s):* By the middle of the 1800s, reformers became disillusioned with the results of the penitentiary movement, and soon a new generation of reform came to the fore, motivated by humanitarian concerns. This new approach to penology emphasized inmate change and indeterminate sentences. Fixed sentences, lockstep, silence, and isolation were seen as destructive to inmate initiative. This wave of prison reform began with the founding of today's American Correctional Association in 1879 and the building of Elmira Reformatory in 1876. At Elmira, Zebulon Brockway began classification and segregation of prisoners, as well as providing vocational training and rewards for good behavior—including early release for good behavior and parole. Brockway's "New Penology" included the creation of specialized institutions to care for the young, females, and the mentally impaired. The juvenile court system, created in Chicago in 1899, gave wide discretionary powers to judges, and Indiana's Female Prison and Reformatory Institution for Girls and Women was opened in Indianapolis in 1873. Inmates began producing license plates, constructing public highways, and working at prison farms and factories that produced food and items for internal consumption. In 1927, the first federal prison for women opened in Alderson, West Virginia; the minimum-security campus-like prison used residential cottages for inmates. Elsewhere, the camps that housed inmates working on roads became models for minimum-security prisons that emerged in the 1930s. Then, with Congress recognizing the need to build federal penitentiaries, the Three Prisons Act of 1891 authorized the first federal penitentiaries. The old army prison at Fort Leavenworth, Kansas, became the first U.S. penitentiary in 1895; the second opened in 1902 at Atlanta, Georgia; and the third was located at the old territorial prison on McNeil Island in Puget Sound, Washington.

- *The progressive model (1890s–1930s):* The first two decades of the 20th century saw the Progressives—activists seeking to address perceived social problems caused by corruption in government, urbanization, industrialization, and immigration—wanting to understand and cure crime; they sought, first, to improve social conditions that appeared to breed crime and, second, to treat criminals so that they would lead crime-free lives. Treatment would be focused on the individual and his or her specific problem. Probation was launched as an alternative to incarceration, allowing offenders to be treated in the community under supervision, and indeterminate sentences came into being.

- *The medical model (1930s–1960s):* Grounded in positivist criminology (see Chapter 3), this model generally included the idea that criminals are mentally ill, and the emphasis of corrections shifted to treatment. Criminals were seen as persons whose social, psychological, or biological deficiencies had caused them to engage in illegal activity and who should receive treatment. Rehabilitation took on national legitimacy and became the primary purpose of incarceration. The Federal Bureau of Prisons (discussed in Chapter 12) was established in 1930 to oversee the 11 federal prisons then in existence. In 1933, Alcatraz was acquired from the U.S. Army for a federal prison. The gangster era was in full swing, and national Prohibition wrought violent crime waves. Alcatraz was the ideal solution—serving the dual purpose of holding public enemies and being a visible icon to warn this new brand of criminal. Under Warden James A. Johnston, Alcatraz's rules of conduct were among the most rigid in the correctional system, and harsh punishments were delivered to inmates

In 1941, James V. Bennett, director of the Federal Bureau of Prisons, oversaw construction of the Federal Correctional Institution at Seagoville, Texas, a prison without walls.

Chapter 11: Court Methods and Challenges ■ 271

who defied prison regulations. More in keeping with the medical model was the appointment in 1937 of James V. Bennett as director of the Federal Bureau of Prisons. In 1941, he built the Federal Correctional Institution at Seagoville, Texas, a prison without walls. Similar prisons became widespread in the 1960s. Different treatment programs were offered to prisoners, and the Federal Prison Industries program, which began in 1934, allowed inmates to be furloughed out of prison for work and other purposes.

- *The community model (1960s–1970s):* Following the inmate riot and hostage taking at New York state's Attica Correctional Facility in 1971 (see Chapter 13), prisons were seen as artificial institutions that interfered with the offender's ability to develop a crime-free lifestyle. Community reintegration was the dominant idea until the 1970s, when it gave way to a new punitive stance in criminal justice.

- *The crime control model (1970s–2000s):* The pendulum swung again in the late 20th century—and continues today—with the public becoming concerned about rapidly rising crime rates and studies of inmate treatment programs challenging their success and worth. Critics attacked the indeterminate sentence and parole, calling for longer sentences for career criminals and violent offenders. Legislators, judges, and officials responded with determinate sentencing laws, three-strikes laws, mandatory sentencing laws (e.g., doubling one's sentence for a crime committed with a weapon), and so forth. (Regarding the accompanying changes in prisons, in 1961, Texas prison system director George Beto, in opposition to the medical model, had begun emphasizing strict discipline. In 1972, David Ruiz sued the Texas prison system, claiming that the system constituted "cruel and unusual punishment" prohibited by the Eighth Amendment to the U.S. Constitution. His class action suit was settled in 1980, the longest-running prisoners' lawsuit in U.S. history.)

Making Punishment Fit the Crime

We might consider punishment from this perspective: A report by Amnesty International discusses capital punishment around the world, including beheadings in Saudi Arabia; hangings in Japan, Iraq, Singapore, and Sudan; firing squads in Afghanistan, Belarus, and Vietnam; stonings in Iran; and "the only country in the Americas that regularly executes: the United States." Amnesty reports that in the 54 countries retaining the death penalty, at least 19,336 people are now under sentence of death, and at least 690 people were executed worldwide in 2018, excluding China (which does not release its figures).[13] This represents the lowest number of executions recorded in the past decade. The death penalty was administered to 25 people in 2018 in the United States (and that number has generally declined since 2000).[14]

The concept of "justice" and acts deserving of punishment vary across nations. Consider that in many other countries people are executed for their political thoughts, apostasy (improper religious beliefs), and "highway robbery"—or that people are flogged 80 times for possessing alcohol, or, as in Singapore, flogged with a rattan cane for vandalism.[15] Although the crime rates in these venues are likely to be relatively low, the question to be asked, related to classical theory (discussed in Chapter 3), is this: Are these punishments proportional to these crimes?

As you will learn in Chapter 12, for many offenders in the United States, being sentenced to prison is a "step up," partly because there they receive "three hots and a cot" without having to support a family, and they might even be surrounded by their family, friends, and affiliate gang members. If that sad commentary on American life is true, then one is left to wonder how our society can allow that to happen—or, perhaps, why we devote the time, effort, and money—at least $71 billion annually for state and local corrections expenditures alone[16]—to basically "warehouse" 1.5 million people.[17] Some observers

Practitioner's Perspective

Criminal Defense Attorney

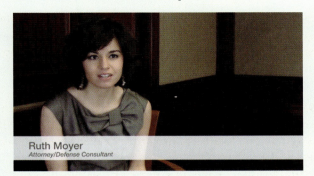

Name: Ruth Moyer
Position: Criminal Defense Attorney
Location: Philadelphia, Pennsylvania

How long have you been a practitioner in this criminal justice position? I've been practicing law for six years.

What is your career story? I received my bachelor's degree in history, and I attended Temple Law School. While I was in law school, I took many public law elective courses. I took a course on federal courts and jurisdiction, an elective course on posttrial review in criminal cases, and I also audited a course on the death penalty, which I found very interesting. While I was in law school, I also interned in the U.S. attorney's office, which gave me a more prosecutorial background. Now, I work at a criminal defense firm, which is very small. So I definitely have gotten a sense of both sides of the criminal justice system.

What are the primary duties and responsibilities of a practitioner in this position? I write many, many trial motions and trial memorandums. I've served as court-appointed counsel for defendants charged with misdemeanors who are unable to afford their own counsel. I've also done a lot of work at the appellate and collateral review stages of litigation in which, after a person has been convicted, either at trial or through a guilty plea, he has a right to challenge his conviction through what's called an appellate review or collateral review.

What are some challenges you face in this position? One of the greatest challenges of criminal defense attorneys is really twofold: first is ensuring that an innocent person isn't convicted, and second is ensuring to the extent possible that even when a person is guilty the government doesn't obtain the conviction in some violation of a person's rights. One very specific challenge I've encountered is with defendants who have no prior criminal record. And I've encountered this a lot with my court-appointed misdemeanor clients. One conviction for an otherwise law-abiding person with no criminal history could have very detrimental consequences on their life. It could result in a loss of employment and a whole range of collateral consequences.

What advice would you give to someone either wishing to study, or now studying, criminal justice and wanting to become a practitioner in this position? One skill I think is important is the ability to listen. And listening is important whether it's interviewing clients or a potential witness, or in court during cross-examination. Another very important skill is the ability to ask the right questions. That can be either researching a legal issue or, in a courtroom, asking a witness the right question. Another very important skill, of course, is oral advocacy. Good oral advocacy develops through lots and lots of practice. It's not something that most people are innately born with. The ability to analyze law and to write well are also very important skills. Unfortunately, sometimes those skills aren't emphasized as much as they should be for criminal defense attorneys. But so much of being an effective advocate for one's client requires the ability to really analyze a statute, or take five different cases and the holding from each of those cases and make it into one coherent rule, or to write a brief that's going to persuade a judge on a close legal issue.

To learn more about Ruth Moyer's experiences as a criminal defense attorney, watch the Practitioner's Perspective video in SAGE vantage.

might say we should abandon the warehousing approach and make every effort to try to identify those individuals for whom the prison experience can be beneficial. Then, while those individuals are a "captive audience" in prison, we should make all manner of rehabilitative educational and vocational programming available to them. But others might

You Be the...

Legislator

In June 2019, Alabama enacted a law that requires convicted child sex offenders (those who abused children under the age of 13) to undergo "chemical castration" as a condition of parole. Although one representative initially advocated a surgical approach to castration, the approved method involves administering drugs to reduce testosterone levels. The law is highly controversial, with some critics arguing that it violates basic human rights and others pointing to research findings that suggest a high libido is not linked to child sexual abuse. Think about this form of punishment from a lawmaker's standpoint:

1. Do you support this approach to managing sex offender recidivism? Would you alter your opinion if you were told that chemical castration was effective in only a very small number of cases? What if you were told it was not effective at all?
2. How do politics play a role in proposing new laws for heinous crimes?
3. Which, if any, of the four goals for punishment outlined at the beginning of the chapter does this punishment achieve?
4. Does it matter if lowering testosterone levels, even if only for a limited time, produces long-term health consequences?
5. Does this punishment violate the Eighth Amendment?

Source: James Hamblin, "Alabama Moves to State-Ordered Castration: A New Law for Child Sex Offenders Harkens Back to a Time When Much Less Was Known About Human Sexuality," *The Atlantic*, June 11, 2019, https://www.theatlantic.com/health/archive/2019/06/alabama-chemical-castration/591226/.

---

argue that those inmates for whom prison is a "step up" should be put to work at hard labor, to make prison life less attractive and thus discourage them from repeat offending. But which way should the pendulum swing?

The accompanying "You Be the... Legislator" box poses some thought-provoking questions regarding punishment. As you read them, consider the four goals of punishment discussed earlier, as well as your own philosophy concerning punishment.

TYPES OF SENTENCES TO BE SERVED

How offenders serve their sentences—in a determinate or indeterminate (defined in Chapter 1), as well as a concurrent or consecutive, fashion—is a crucial distinction, particularly in terms of how long an offender must remain in prison and where parole is concerned. Next we distinguish between these types.

Determinate and Indeterminate Sentences

Determinate sentencing is either legislatively determined or judicially determined. In states using a determinate sentencing structure, convicted offenders are sentenced for a fixed term, such as 10 years. There is no opportunity for a paroling authority to make adjustments in time served when making release decisions. Offenders are released at the expiration of their term, minus any good-time credits. Under a legislatively determined structure, the legislature fixes by law the penalty for specific offenses or offense categories. In a judicially determined system, the judge has broad discretion to choose a sanction, but once imposed, it is not subject to change.

Conversely, in an indeterminate sentencing format, the convicted individual will be sentenced for a set range of time, such as 5–10 years, so that his or her conduct inside the prison system, amenability to rehabilitative efforts (e.g., educational and vocational programs, counseling), apparent remorsefulness, and so forth can be taken into account in deciding a release date. The legislature sets a broad range of time, expressed as minimum and maximum sentences, for a particular offense or category of offenses, and the responsibility for determining the actual term of incarceration is divided between the judge and the parole board. The judge's sentence is also made in terms of a minimum and a maximum term.

Inmates often appear before their parole board to express remorse for their crimes, to explain how they have progressed while in prison, and to offer reasons they should be released and placed on parole.

The authority of a parole board to grant discretionary release to a prisoner before the expiration date of the maximum term varies from state to state. The parole board determines the actual release date, typically using a formula for determining earliest parole eligibility, which may occur after a percentage of the minimum, after a percentage of the maximum, or after the entire minimum has been served, depending on the state.[18] Those persons supporting the rehabilitative ideal for offenders will obviously be more in favor of indeterminate sentencing, which allows for the length of sentence to be adjusted in response to the offender's positive responses to treatment and programs.[19]

Concurrent and Consecutive Sentences

Assume that a man is convicted for committing three separate offenses as part of a night's crime spree: He unlawfully entered a couple's home (burglary), stole several valuable items (a felony theft), and violently assaulted the husband in making his escape. He is sentenced to 15 years, 3 years, and 20 years, respectively, for each of these crimes. Depending on the sentencing court's decision, the offender will serve his three sentences for those crimes either concurrently or consecutively.

A *concurrent* sentence means he will serve all three sentences *at the same time,* with each sentence running along the same timeline, along parallel tracks as follows:

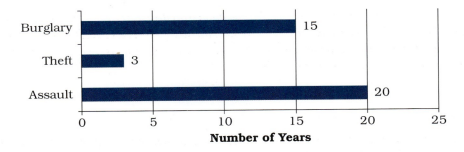

Because these sentences are running at the same time, the maximum amount of time the man will do is 20 years—his sentences of 3 and 15 years will have already run during the 20-year sentence.

If, instead, the offender is to serve the three sentences *consecutively,* each sentence will be served separately—in other words, when he finishes serving the sentence for the first crime, he immediately begins serving the sentence for the second crime, and so on. This approach is often referred to as "stacking" the sentences—one after the other—to maximize the sentence length, as follows:

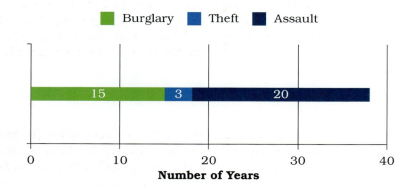

In this sentencing approach, the offender would serve a total of approximately 38 years (15 + 3 + 20), subject to reductions for good behavior and parole eligibility.

SENTENCING GUIDELINES

Sentencing guidelines: an instrument developed by the federal government that uses a grid system to chart seriousness of the offense, criminal history, and so forth and thus allows the court to arrive at a more consistent sentence for everyone.

The growing complexity and importance of the sentencing guidelines now found in criminal justice pose a bit of a dilemma for this introductory course textbook: On the one hand, they are too complicated to discuss comprehensively or in great detail; on the other hand, they are far too important to ignore. Therefore, this section strives to achieve an appropriate balance by looking at the guidelines in summary form.

Going Global

Sentencing Guidelines in Australia

Like the United States, Australia has introduced sentencing guidelines in an effort to promote more consistent and evidence-driven sentencing practices, as well as to improve public confidence in the justice system. Sentencing guidelines have been introduced in separate legislation aimed at Australia's six states, two mainland territories, and the federal jurisdiction. Legislation in all jurisdictions provides general guidance concerning the factors that should be considered during sentencing. The country continues to debate the potential need for mandatory minimum sentencing laws, but like U.S. sentencing guidelines, Australian guidelines simply provide guidance and are not mandatory in nature. Judges retain substantial sentencing discretion.

In an effort to provide greater transparency, the Judicial Conference of Australia created a booklet to answer questions that the public may have about how sentencing occurs, for example:

- What factors do judges consider?
- How much discretion does the judge have?
- Why are particular penalties chosen?
- Will the sentence be effective?

You can access the booklet by searching here: www.districtcourt.wa.gov.au.

Source: To learn more about sentencing guidelines used in common law countries throughout the world, visit the Library of Congress, Legal Reports—Sentencing Guidelines at www.loc.gov/law/help/sentencing-guidelines/index.php.

Background: Legislation and Court Decisions

In the mid- to late 1970s and early 1980s, many people were becoming discontented with the indeterminate sentencing process; they witnessed inmates often being released after serving only a fraction of their sentences (some jurisdictions even allowed 30 days of "good-time" reduction of a sentence for each 30 days served). That, coupled with renewed concern about the rising crime rate throughout the nation, resulted in wide experimentation with sentencing systems by many states and the creation of sentencing guidelines at the federal level.

Federal Sentencing Guidelines

After more than a decade of research and debate, Congress decided that (1) the sentencing discretion given federal trial judges needed to be structured; (2) the administration of punishment needed to be more certain; and (3) specific offenders (e.g., white collar and violent, repeat offenders) needed to be targeted for more serious penalties.[20] As a result, Congress abolished indeterminate sentencing at the federal level and created a determinate sentencing structure through the federal sentencing guidelines. The Sentencing Reform Act[21] was enacted in 1984 to ensure that similarly situated defendants were sentenced in a more uniform fashion rather than depending on the judge to which they happened to be assigned.[22] The federal sentencing system was thus reformed by

- Dropping rehabilitation as one of the goals of punishment
- Creating the U.S. Sentencing Commission and charging it with establishing sentencing guidelines
- Making all federal sentences determinate
- Authorizing appellate review of sentences[23]

A long line of legal challenges ensued involving these sentencing guidelines. The first such challenge came from the state of Washington, where the petitioner had pleaded guilty to kidnapping. Under Washington's law, the maximum penalty for that offense is 10 years. A separate range-of-sentence provision limited the maximum allowable sentence to 53 months, but it authorized an upward departure (i.e., longer sentences) for "exceptional" judge-determined factors. The trial judge increased the sentence to 90 months because the crime was committed with deliberate cruelty. Because the facts supporting the enhanced penalty were neither admitted by the petitioner nor found by a jury, the U.S. Supreme Court held in *Blakely v. Washington* (2004) that the sentence violated the petitioner's Sixth Amendment right to trial by jury.[24] This decision, however, applied only to Washington.

Then, six months later, the Supreme Court decided *United States v. Booker*, this time addressing sentencing guidelines nationally.[25] The defendant, Booker, was found guilty by a jury of possessing at least 50 grams of crack cocaine (he actually had 92.5 grams). Under those facts, the guidelines required a possible 210- to 262-month sentence. Although the jury never heard any such evidence, the judge, finding by a preponderance of the evidence that Booker possessed the much larger amount of cocaine, rendered a sentence that was almost 10 years longer than what the guidelines prescribed. By a vote of 5–4, the U.S. Supreme Court found that the U.S. sentencing guidelines violated the Sixth Amendment by allowing judicial, rather than jury, fact-finding to form the basis for the sentencing; in other words, letting in these judge-made facts is unconstitutional. The guidelines also allowed judges to make such determinations with a lesser standard of proof than the jury's "beyond a reasonable doubt" and to rely on hearsay evidence that would not be admissible at trial.[26] The Court did not discard the guidelines entirely. The guidelines, the Court said, are to be merely advisory and not mandatory. Thus, the guidelines are a resource a judge can look at but may choose to ignore. Although courts

Table 11.1 /// State of Washington Sentencing Grid

SERIOUSNESS LEVEL	OFFENDER SCORE									
	0	1	2	3	4	5	6	7	8	9+
LEVEL XVI				LIFE SENTENCE WITHOUT PAROLE/DEATH PENALTY						
LEVEL XV	180–240	187.5–249.75	195.75–260.25	203.25–270.75	210.75–280.5	218.25–291	234–312	253.5–337.5	277.5–369.75	308.25–411
LEVEL XIV	92.25–165	100.5–175.5	108–183	115.5–190.5	123.75–198.75	131.25–206.25	146.25–221.25	162–237	192.75–267.75	223.5–297.75
LEVEL XIII	92.25–123	100.5–133.5	108–144	115.5–153.75	123.75–164.25	131.25–174.75	146.25–195	162–216	192.75–256.5	223.5–297.75
LEVEL XII	69.75–92.25	76.5–102	83.25–110.25	90–120	96.75–128.25	103.5–138	121.5–162	133.5–177	156.75–207.75	180–238.5
LEVEL XI	58.5–76.5	64.5–85.5	71.25–93.75	76.5–102	83.25–110.25	90–118.5	109.5–145.5	119.25–158.25	138.75–183.75	157.5–210
LEVEL X	38.25–51	42.75–56.25	46.5–61.5	50.25–66.75	54–72	57.75–76.5	73.5–97.5	81–108	96.75–128.25	111.75–148.5
LEVEL IX	23.25–30.75	27–36	30.75–40.5	34.5–45.75	38.25–51	42.75–56.25	57.75–76.5	65.25–87	81–108	96.75–128.25
LEVEL VIII	15.75–20.25	19.5–25.5	23.25–30.75	27–36	30.75–40.5	34.54–5.75	50.25–66.75	57.75–76.5	65.25–87	81–108
LEVEL VII	11.25–15	15.75–20.25	19.5–25.5	23.25–30.75	27–36	30.75–40.5	42.75–56.25	50.25–66.75	57.75–76.5	65.25–87
LEVEL VI	9–10.5	11.25–15	15.75–20.25	19.5–25.5	23.25–30.75	27–36	34.5–45.75	42.75–56.25	50.25–66.75	57.75–76.5
LEVEL V	4.5–9	9–10.5	9.75–12.75	11.25–15	16.5–21.75	24.75–32.25	30.75–40.5	38.25–51	46.5–61.5	54–72
LEVEL IV	2.25–6.75	4.59	9–10.5	9.75–12.75	11.25–15	16.5–21.75	24.75–32.25	32.25–42.75	39.75–52.5	47.25–63
LEVEL III	0.75–2.25	2.25–6	3–9	6.75–9	9–12	12.75–16.5	16.5–21.75	24.75–32.25	32.25–42.75	38.25–51
LEVEL II	0–67.5 days	1.5–4.5	2.25–6.75	3–9	9–10.5	10.5–13.5	12.75–16.5	16.5–21.75	24.75–32.25	32.25–42.75
LEVEL I	0–45 days	0–67.5 days	1.5–3.75	1.5–4.5	2.25–6	3–9	9–10.5	10.5–13.5	12.75–16.5	16.5–21.75

Source: Reprinted with permission, copyright © 2012 State of Washington/John C. Steiger, PhD.

still must "consider" the guidelines, they need not follow them. In addition, sentences for federal crimes will become subject to appellate review for "unreasonableness," allowing appeals courts to clamp down on particular sentences that seem far too harsh.

In late 2007, the U.S. Supreme Court went further and explained what it meant in 2005 by "advisory" and "reasonableness," deciding two cases that together restored federal judges to their traditional central role in criminal sentencing. The Court found that district court judges do not have to justify their deviations from the federal sentencing guidelines and that they have broad discretion to disagree with the guidelines and to impose what they believe are reasonable sentences—even if the guidelines call for different sentences. Both cases—*Gall v. United States*[27] and *Kimbrough v. United States*[28]—were decided by the same 7–2 margin and chided federal appeals courts for failing to give district judges sufficient leeway. Further, in 2017, by a vote of 7–0, the U.S. Supreme Court struck down an argument that the federal sentencing guidelines are too vague, again noting that these are not strict guidelines, that they merely provide advice to judges who use their own discretion when determining appropriate sentences.[29]

State-Level Sentencing Guidelines

Several states have enacted sentencing guidelines. As an example, Table 11.1 shows the sentencing grid used by the state of Washington, which has developed a sophisticated and objective sentencing tool called *The Adult Sentencing Guidelines Manual*.[30] This manual provides comprehensive information on adult felony sentencing as set forth under state law, identifying the seriousness level of the offense and "scoring" the offender's criminal history. The seriousness of crimes listed on the vertical axis ranges from Level I (which includes offenses such as simple theft, malicious mischief, attempting to elude a pursuing police vehicle, and possessing stolen property) to Level XVI (aggravated murder, which includes first-degree murder with one or more of a number of aggravating circumstances). The offender score listed on the horizontal axis ranges from 0 to 9+, and it is determined based on five factors: (1) the number of prior convictions; (2) the relationship between any prior offense(s) and the current offense of conviction; (3) the presence of other current convictions; (4) the offender's custody status at the time the crime was committed; and (5) the length of time between offenses.

VICTIM IMPACT STATEMENTS

Victim impact statements are written or oral information provided in court—most commonly at sentencing—and at offenders' parole hearings concerning the impact of the crime on the victim and the victim's family. These statements generally inform the court of the crime's financial, emotional, psychological, and/or physical impact on their lives. They provide a means for the court to refocus its attention on the human cost of the crime, as well as for the victim to participate in the criminal justice process. The right to make an impact statement is generally available not only to the victim but also to survivors of homicide victims, the parent or guardian of a minor victim, and a person representing an incompetent or incapacitated victim. Victims can present oral or written impact statements, with some states allowing victims to submit video- or audio-taped statements. Some states allow child victims to present drawings to explain how the crime affected them.[31]

Victim impact statements were upheld in 1991 by the U.S. Supreme Court, in *Payne v. Tennessee*.[32] Payne was convicted of two counts of murder for stabbing to death a mother

Victim impact statements: information provided prior to sentencing by the victims of a crime (or, in cases of murder, the surviving family members) about the impact the crime had on their lives; allowed by the U.S. Supreme Court.

Victim impact statements are increasingly common in the sentencing phase of criminal cases, where the focus has traditionally been on the offender rather than the victims and their loved ones. These statements help judges and juries to more fully understand the impact of a crime and what punishment is appropriate.

Investigating Further

Victim Impact Statements

In June 2006, Brock Allen Turner, a champion swimmer at Stanford University, was found guilty of three counts of sexual assault. Facing a possible sentence of 14 years in state prison, the nation was shocked by the judge's lenient sentence: six months in county jail and probation. The other notable outcome of this case that captured national attention was the impact statement that his victim (referred to as "Emily Doe") read to Turner at his sentencing. She began by saying, "your Honor, if it is all right, for the majority of this statement I would like to address the defendant directly." Excerpts from her letter follow.

- "You don't know me, but you've been inside me, and that's why we're here today."
- "... all I was told was that I had been found behind a dumpster, potentially penetrated by a stranger, and that I should get retested for HIV because results don't always show up immediately."
- "After work, I would drive to a secluded place to scream. I didn't talk, I didn't eat, I didn't sleep, I didn't interact with anyone, and I became isolated from the ones I loved most."
- "One day, I was at work, scrolling through the news on my phone, and came across an article . . . This is how I learned what happened to me, sitting at my desk, reading the news at work."
- "To conclude, I want to say thank you . . . to the deputy who waited beside me, to the nurses who calmed me, to the detective who listened to me and never judged me, to my advocates who stood unwaveringly beside me . . . Thank you to girls across the nation that wrote cards to my DA to give to me, so many strangers who cared for me."

1. Should victim impact statements be allowed in court? Why or why not?
2. Should convicted offenders be allowed to offer statements during their sentencing phase? Why or why not?

Source: Katie J. M. Baker; "Here's the Powerful Letter the Stanford Victim Read to Her Attacker," *BuzzFeed News*, June 3, 2016, https://www.buzzfeednews.com/article/katiejmbaker/heres-the-powerful-letter-the-stanford-victim-read-to-her-ra.

---

and her 2-year-old daughter and also wounding her 3-year-old son. During the sentencing hearing, the boy's grandmother described how the killings affected the surviving grandson. On appeal, the Supreme Court held that the victim has a right to be heard, and quoted from a 1934 opinion by Justice Benjamin Cardozo: "Justice, though due to the accused, is due to the accuser also."[33] In 2016, the U.S. Supreme Court reiterated that victim impact statements concerning how the crime has impacted the individual are permissible, but that statements containing victims' opinions concerning the crime, defendant, or appropriate sentence violate the Eighth Amendment.[34] See the accompanying "Investigating Further" box for more discussion and an example from such a statement.

Marsy's Law: Given that Marsy's Law focuses on victim's rights, you might be surprised to learn that the American Civil Liberties Union's political director is against the national campaign to adopt these laws. Jeanne Hruska argues that the law is "poorly drafted and a threat to existing constitutional rights."[35] She notes that our constitutional rights (at both the national and state levels) protect individuals against government abuse, and that defendants' rights apply only when the state might harm an accused—not a victim. In her view, the law "pits victims' rights against defendants' rights" and strengthens the power of the state. Consider how victim impact statements might strengthen the state's power and increase the chance of an overly harsh sentence. Do you think this is a significant concern, or do the benefits of victim impact statements outweigh potential costs?

CAPITAL PUNISHMENT

Because of its finality, debate concerning the death penalty has always been emotionally charged. Strong arguments have been put forth by those who favor and those who oppose **capital punishment**.

Capital punishment: a sentence of death, or carrying out same via execution of the offender.

Arguments For and Against

For a politician or political entity to try to fashion a state or national policy on the death penalty that would definitively appeal to most Americans would be nearly impossible. The U.S. Supreme Court has halted death sentences and then approved them, and several states have done likewise (largely because many convicted murderers on death row have been found to be innocent). Some studies indicate that the death penalty works to prevent crimes of murder, and other studies show the opposite. Americans themselves seem fickle in their views of whether or not killers should be put to death.

Figure 11.2 shows the percentages of Americans who favor and oppose the death penalty. The percentages of people in favor of the death penalty rose steadily for the most part from about 1967 to 1995; from that point, however, there has been an overall decline in such support, dropping from about 80 percent to less than 60 percent. Meanwhile, the percentage of people saying they are in opposition to the death penalty is about the same today as it was in 1937, with 41 percent of the population reporting that they are not in favor, despite a significant drop to about 16 percent in the mid-1990s.

Arguments in Favor

People who support the death penalty often believe that it deters other people from committing murder, while others base their stand on theological grounds—the commandment "Thou shalt not kill." Others favor capital punishment because of the retribution it provides to family members and friends of the victim; "getting even" is a proper punishment in the eyes of many people, rather than some "rehabilitative" ideal. It is society's nod to *lex talionis*—"eye for an eye": "If you kill one of us, we will kill you." One thing the death penalty most certainly accomplishes, however, is the prevention of future murders by that particular offender. As James Q. Wilson noted, "Whatever else may be said about the death penalty, it is certain that it incapacitates."[36]

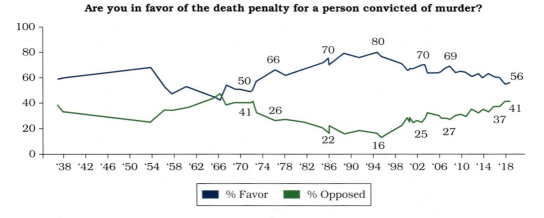

Figure 11.2 /// Percentage of Americans Favoring and Opposing the Death Penalty

Source: Copyright © 2018 Gallup, Inc. All rights reserved. The content is used with permission; however, Gallup retains all rights of republication.

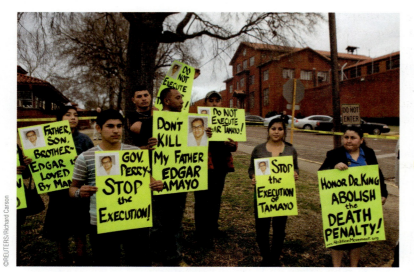

Many people oppose capital punishment and express their disapproval by protesting against it—especially when someone is about to be executed.

Does the existence of a death penalty deter individuals from committing murder? That is an important question, and one that is at the tip of the spear in this debate. The answer, unfortunately, is elusive, and it depends largely on which set of studies one looks at and gives credence to. Beginning in 2003, a number of studies were published that reportedly demonstrated the death penalty saves lives by acting as a deterrent to murder. One study that garnered a large amount of attention, conducted by Mocan and Gittings, analyzed 6,143 death sentences imposed in the United States between 1977 and 1997. Results indicated that each execution resulted in five fewer murders, and each commutation of a death sentence to a long or life prison term resulted in five additional homicides. Further, each additional removal from death row when one's sentence was vacated resulted in one additional homicide.[37] Another study, by professors at Emory University, using a panel data set of more than 3,000 counties from 1977 to 1996, found that each execution resulted in 18 fewer murders and that the implementation of state moratoria was associated with an increased incidence of murders.[38] Then, two studies by a Federal Communications Commission economist also supported the deterrent effect of capital punishment, finding that each additional execution, on average, resulted in 14 fewer murders[39] and that executions conducted by electrocution were the most effective at providing deterrence.[40] However, the findings of these studies were challenged by other criminologists.

Arguments in Opposition

Arguments against the death penalty include that it does not have any deterrent value, that it is discriminatory against minorities, that retribution is unfitting for a civilized society, and that it can (and does) claim the lives of innocent people.

At least two criminologists have identified serious flaws in the Mocan-Gittings study, which found that each execution resulted in five fewer murders. Richard Berk, using Mocan and Gittings's original data set, removed the Texas data, ran the model exactly as the original authors did for the other 49 states, and found that the deterrent effect disappeared.[41]

A second reexamination of the Mocan-Gittings study was conducted by Jeffrey Fagan, who, by modifying their measure of deterrence, also found that all the deterrent effects disappeared. Rather than prove that Mocan and Gittings erred in their assumptions, Fagan showed that small changes in their assumptions could produce wild fluctuations in their deterrence estimates.[42] Regarding the contention that the death penalty is discriminatory, many people would agree with a finding by the U.S. Government Accountability Office that there is "a pattern of evidence indicating racial disparities in the charging, sentencing, and imposition of the death penalty."[43] Amnesty International argues, furthermore, that "from initial charging decisions to plea bargaining to jury sentencing, African-Americans are treated more harshly when they are defendants, and their lives are accorded less value when they are victims. All-white or virtually all-white juries are still commonplace in many localities."[44] Following are other findings regarding the death penalty discrimination thesis:

- A report sponsored by the American Bar Association concluded that one-third of African American death row inmates in Philadelphia would have received sentences of life imprisonment if they had not been African American.
- A study of death sentences in Connecticut conducted by Yale University School of Law revealed that African American defendants receive the death penalty at three

times the rate of white defendants in cases where the victims are white. In addition, killers of white victims are treated more severely than people who kill minorities, when it comes to deciding what charges to bring.

- A study released by the University of Maryland concluded that race and geography are major factors in death penalty decisions. Specifically, in Maryland, depending on who is killed and where, prosecutors are more likely to seek a death sentence when the race of the victim is white and less likely to seek a death sentence when the victim is African American.[45]

Finally, of course, is the argument that innocent people can be—and have been—executed for crimes they never committed, which is discussed in the "Wrongful Convictions" section.

Key Supreme Court Decisions

In *Furman v. Georgia* (1972), by vote of 5–4, the U.S. Supreme Court, for the first time, struck down the death penalty under the cruel and unusual punishment clause of the Eighth Amendment. The decision involved not only Furman, convicted for murder, but also two other men (in Georgia and Texas) convicted for rape; juries at the trials of all three men had imposed the death penalty without any specific guides or limits on their discretion. The justices for the majority found this lack of guidelines or limits on jury discretion to be unconstitutional, as it resulted in a random pattern among those receiving the death penalty; one justice also felt that death was disproportionately applied to the poor and socially disadvantaged, and felt those groups were denied equal protection under the law.[46]

Four years after *Furman*, the Supreme Court rendered another major death penalty decision. A Georgia jury had found Troy Gregg guilty of armed robbery and murder and sentenced him to death. Gregg challenged his death sentence, claiming that it was, *per se*, a "cruel and unusual" punishment that violated the Eighth and Fourteenth Amendments. In a 7–2 decision, the Court held that a punishment of death did not violate the Constitution. Where a defendant has been convicted of deliberately killing another person, the careful and judicious use of the death penalty may be appropriate if employed carefully. The Court noted that Georgia's death penalty statute required a bifurcated proceeding (where the trial and sentencing are conducted separately), as well as specific jury findings as to the severity of the crime and the nature of the defendant and a comparison of aggravating and mitigating circumstances.[47] Another significant decision was rendered by the Supreme Court in 2005, in *Roper v. Simmons*, holding that the Eighth and Fourteenth Amendments forbid the execution of offenders who were under the age of 18 when their crimes were committed.[48] In addition, the Supreme Court has held that

- The Eighth Amendment prohibits the execution of persons who are mentally incompetent at the time of their execution.[49]
- The death penalty cannot be applied to adults who rape children (and, more broadly, that a state cannot impose the death penalty for a crime that did not result in the death of the victim, except for crimes committed against the state—i.e., espionage, treason).[50]
- To show their legal counsel was ineffective, defendants in capital cases must prove that the attorney's performance was less than reasonable (e.g., counsel did not present mitigating circumstances), and that there is a reasonable likelihood that this substandard performance changed the outcome of the trial.[51]
- People who are opposed to the death penalty cannot be automatically excluded from serving on juries in capital cases; however, people whose opposition is so strong as to "prevent or substantially impair the performance of their duties" (*Witherspoon v. Illinois*, 1968) may be removed from the jury pool during *voir dire* (preliminary examination).[52]

Methods of Execution

Here we discuss the methods of execution in use today in the United States. Figure 11.3 shows methods of execution, by state.

Although death by lethal injection has been widely thought to be much more humane than other methods, several challenges to this method of execution have been raised in the U.S. Supreme Court in recent years (and botched executions have ignited the out-of-court debate; see the accompanying "Investigating Further" box). Such challenges typically claim that the drugs used in the executions cause extreme and unnecessary pain, while masking the pain being experienced by the inmate, and thus violate the Eighth Amendment's ban on cruel and unusual punishment. In *Baze v. Rees* (2008), the U.S. Supreme Court held that the three-drug "cocktail" used by 35 states and the federal government did not violate the Eighth Amendment.[53] Chief Justice John Roberts observed that a method of execution would violate the Constitution only if it was "deliberately designed to inflict pain." Two years earlier, Clarence Hill, an inmate on Florida's death row, challenged the use of lethal injection, *per se*, as causing unnecessary pain contrary

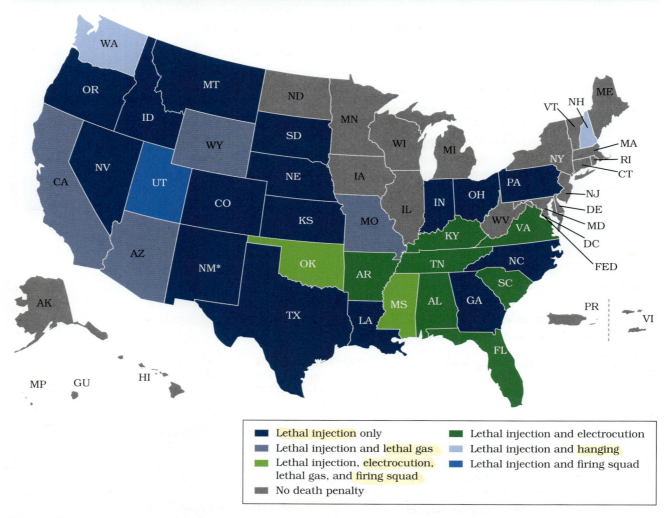

Figure 11.3 /// Method of Execution, by State, 2019

- Lethal injection only
- Lethal injection and lethal gas
- Lethal injection, electrocution, lethal gas, and firing squad
- No death penalty
- Lethal injection and electrocution
- Lethal injection and hanging
- Lethal injection and firing squad

*Although New Mexico abolished the death penalty, the act is not retroactive, leaving people on the state's death row.

Source: Death Penalty Information Center, "Methods of Execution," http://www.deathpenaltyinfo.org/executions/methods-of-execution.

Investigating Further

The Reality of Death by Lethal Injection

A series of botched executions in recent years has stirred the death penalty debate anew and refocused criticisms on the perceived "humane" method of lethal injection. In several cases since 2009, prison officials struggled for significant periods of time to find a suitable vein for the intravenous (IV) delivery of lethal drugs used in executions:

- Ohio (2009): Romell Broom: More than 2 hours to find a suitable vein in arms and legs; execution was stopped after Broom appeared to be in agonizing pain.

- Georgia (2010): Brandon Rhode: 40 minutes to find a vein; 14 minutes for Rhode to die.

- Arizona, Ohio, and Oklahoma (2014): Joseph R. Wood, Dennis McGuire, and Clayton D. Lockett: Took exceedingly long periods of time to die (24 minutes to 1 hour and 40 minutes), calling into further question the efficacy of the three-drug method and the death penalty in general.

- Georgia (2015): Brian Keith Terrell: More than 1 hour to properly insert an IV, eventually finding a suitable vein in Terrell's hand.

- Georgia (2016): Brandon Jones: After more than 30 minutes of unsuccessful attempts to insert an IV into Jones's arms, a physician was asked to violate several medical ethics codes and spent 13 minutes inserting and stitching the IV near Jones's groin to complete the execution.

- Alabama (2016): Ronald Bert Smith, Jr.: 34 minutes to die after drugs were administered; heaved, gasped, and coughed; clenched his fists and raised his head during the procedure.

- Ohio (2017): Alva Campbell: After officials spent 80 minutes trying to achieve successful needle insertion, the execution was called off.

- Alabama (2018): Doyle Lee Hamm: Execution called off after attempting to find a vein for 2.5 hours; leaving 10–12 puncture marks and piercing Hamm's bladder and femoral artery.

Source: Death Penalty Information Center, "Examples of Post-*Furman* Botched Executions," https://deathpenaltyinfo.org/executions/botched-executions.

to contemporary standards of decency; however, by a vote of 5–4, the U.S. Supreme Court denied a stay of execution (Justice Antonin Scalia noted that "lethal injection is much less painful than hanging"), and Hill was executed in September 2006.[54]

Wrongful Convictions: Rethinking the Death Penalty

Being convicted of a crime is no guarantee that one is actually guilty as charged. It means simply that a jury or judge was persuaded by the state's case against the defendant or, in the case of plea bargaining, the defendant was persuaded to plead guilty to avoid trial. Today, we know that many innocent people have nonetheless been

Lethal injection is the most commonly used method of execution in the United States. Shown here is the lethal execution chamber at San Quentin prison in California.

Chapter 11: Court Methods and Challenges

Investigating Further

DNA Exonerations

Henry James served nearly 30 years in Louisiana's infamous Angola prison for a sexual assault he did not commit. He was convicted in 1982 largely on the basis of an incorrect eyewitness identification—the cause of approximately 75 percent of all wrongful convictions. James was exonerated through DNA testing and finally released from Angola in 2011.

Henry James was 20 years old and poor when he was arrested and charged with aggravated sexual assault of his next-door neighbor's wife. His public defender failed to introduce key evidence that would have proved James innocent, and he was quickly convicted and sentenced to life without parole at arguably one of the toughest maximum-security prisons in the world—Louisiana's Angola State Prison. Thirteen years into James's sentence, the detective who worked his case was fired when an FBI task force discovered the detective had coached witnesses and destroyed evidence. Ten years later, the Innocence Project started searching for evidence in James's case. But the box on the police evidence shelf designated for his case was empty. Without the DNA evidence, James would die in Angola. Somewhat miraculously, five years later a lab technician stumbled on a DNA slide from James's case while working on evidence in another case. The sample was viable, and it proved James did not commit the sexual assault. Nearly 30 years after Angola's gates slammed shut on his life, Henry James walked out of prison a free man.

James's case is extraordinary because such chance circumstances led to the discovery of DNA evidence that proved his innocence. But the fact that he was wrongfully imprisoned in the first place is not so unique. His case is classic and highlights some of the issues that typically lead to wrongful convictions: faulty eyewitness identifications, ineffective assistance of counsel, and exclusion of exculpatory DNA evidence at trial.

James is one of more than 2,465 people who have been exonerated in the United States since 1989, and he is one of 484 people in that group who were exonerated using DNA evidence. Because of these cases, it is hoped that reforms in place or under way throughout the criminal justice system (regarding reformed lineup/eyewitness identification procedures, evidence collection and preservation, and videotaping of police interrogations, for example) will give professionals and offenders alike more confidence in the system.

Sources: The Innocence Project, May 2019, http://www.innocenceproject.org; National Registry of Exonerations, University of Michigan, May 2019, https://www.law.umich.edu/special/exoneration/Pages/about.aspx.

---

convicted and, in some cases, sentenced to death, until their names were cleared—they were exonerated—by DNA evidence (see the accompanying "Investigating Further" box). As of May 2019, the Death Penalty Information Center reports that 165 death row inmates in the United States have been exonerated since 1973, including at least 20 people previously facing death whose innocence was proved through DNA evidence.[55]

Exoneration: to absolve someone of criminal blame, or find someone not guilty.

These exonerations and problems with executions have not gone unnoticed. Since 2000, there has been an average of five death row exonerations a year.[56] Further, 40 states have not carried out an execution in the past five years, and 8 states have abolished the death penalty since 2004.[57] The U.S. Supreme Court held in 2002 that the execution of the intellectually disabled was unconstitutional[58] and that the finding of an aggravating factor justifying a death sentence must be made by a jury, not merely by the sentencing judge.[59] Then, in 2005, the Court limited the death penalty even further, ruling that executing offenders who were juveniles at the time of their crimes is cruel and unusual punishment.[60] In 2019, the U.S. Supreme Court agreed to hear a death penalty case involving mitigating factors in the case of Arizona prisoner James Erin McKinney.[61] The outcome of this case may have significant ramifications for the application of the death penalty across the United States.

Recent Trends in Federal Executions

In July 2019, U.S. Attorney General William Barr ordered the Bureau of Prisons to schedule executions for five federal death row inmates. All five of these inmates had been convicted of crimes involving the murder of children.[62] Barr's Justice Department directive followed a 16-year period in which the federal government had not carried out capital punishment sentences for those awaiting execution.

The U.S. federal government has executed only three inmates since 1988: two in 2001 and one in 2003.[63] All three were executed using lethal injection. The five inmates subject to Barr's order for capital punishment will likely be executed using a new protocol that requires the use of a single drug, pentobarbital, instead of the three-drug cocktail used in previous federal executions. In ordering the executions, Barr said, "Congress has expressly authorized the death penalty through legislation adopted by the people's representatives in both houses of Congress and signed by the President. . . . Under Administrations of both parties, the Department of Justice has sought the death penalty against the worst criminals, including these five murderers, each of whom was convicted by a jury of his peers after a full and fair proceeding. The Justice Department upholds the rule of law—and we owe it to the victims and their families to carry forward the sentence imposed by our justice system."[64]

AGGRAVATING AND MITIGATING CIRCUMSTANCES

In passing sentence, judges (and, in death penalty cases, the jury) will look at factors other than the crime itself. They consider the manner in which the crime was committed in order to determine whether or not they should increase or decrease the severity of the punishment. In other words, the judge or jury might "look behind" the crime to see if, for example, the victim was tortured prior to being killed or if the defendant played a minor role in the offense. These are termed aggravating and mitigating circumstances or factors.

Aggravating circumstances can include use of a weapon, an especially heinous or cruel crime, commission of murder for hire, or the offender's being a peace officer engaged in official duties.[65] *Mitigating circumstances* include little or no prior criminal history, the offender's acting under duress or under the influence of mental illness or extreme emotional disturbance, or the offender's being young.[66] Under the Supreme Court's decision in *Gregg v. Georgia,* discussed earlier, the judge will also instruct the jury members that they may not impose the death penalty unless they first determine the existence of one or more statutory aggravating circumstances beyond a reasonable doubt, as well as determine that the aggravating circumstances outweigh the mitigating circumstances beyond a reasonable doubt.

CRIMINAL APPEALS

In an appeal, one who has been convicted for a crime attempts to show that the trial court made a legal error that affected the decision in the case, or that he or she had ineffective counsel or that due process was violated in some other way. The defendant now asks a higher (appellate) court to review the transcript of the case for such errors—and possibly to have the conviction overturned or be granted a retrial. In addition, the defendant may contest the trial court's sentencing decision without challenging the underlying conviction. Then, if the appellate court grants the appeal, it may reverse the lower court's decision in whole or in part. However, if the appellate court denies the appeal, the lower court's decision stands.[67]

Article I, Section 9, of the Constitution speaks only briefly and indirectly to criminal appeals, saying that the privilege of the *writ of habeas corpus* (discussed in Chapter 9 in the case of *Kibbe v. Henderson*) shall not be suspended, "unless when in Cases of Rebellion or Invasion the public Safety may require it." The name of this writ, often referred to as "the great writ," is Latin for "you have the body." *Habeas corpus* is the inmate's means of asking a court to grant a hearing to determine whether or not he or she is being held illegally.

Convicted persons who are indigent (poor) are entitled to free legal counsel for their initial appeal[68] and a free copy of their trial transcript.[69] (However, the Supreme Court has held that prison inmates are not entitled to free legal counsel for subsequent "discretionary" appeals.[70]) Furthermore, as is noted in Chapter 12, prison inmates also have a right to access law libraries, and many law schools have defender clinics in which law students represent state and federal prisoners in appellate and postconviction litigation in state and federal courts. This is in addition to prison "writ-writers"—inmates who over time develop considerable expertise in constitutional law and means of filing writs and petitions.

Not only are inmates able to challenge their criminal conviction on a variety of grounds (the evidence introduced against them; the police arrest, search, and seizure of their person and property; the judge's instructions to the jury; and so on), but after being incarcerated they may attempt to obtain what are called postconviction remedies—making what are termed "collateral attacks." These lawsuits are civil in nature (unlike the original appeal of their conviction) and challenge, for example, the conditions of their confinement. Such cases often list the prison warden as the respondent and can involve the inmate's filing a *writ of habeas corpus*, typically in a federal court having jurisdiction over his or her place of incarceration.

/// IN A NUTSHELL

- Historically, we have punished people for the following reasons: retribution, deterrence, incapacitation, and rehabilitation. The U.S. Constitution speaks only briefly but forcefully regarding the use of punishment. The Eighth Amendment provides that incarceration will not involve "cruel and unusual punishment" and that fines will not be excessive.

- Prosecutors can influence the sentencing decision by agreeing to engage in plea negotiations concerning the number of charges filed or the maximum penalty the judge may impose, by explaining that the accused was very cooperative with the police and/or remorseful for the crime, and so on. Defense attorneys can seek to obtain the lightest possible sentence, or other alternatives to sentencing, or they can emphasize such things as the defendant's minor involvement in the crime.

- The seriousness of the offense is the most important factor in determining the sentencing received for an offense, followed by the defendant's prior criminal record.

- Philosophies of crime and punishment have changed significantly since the late 1700s; today people are calling for longer sentences for career criminals and violent offenders. Legislators, judges, and officials have responded with determinate sentencing laws, three-strikes laws, mandatory sentencing laws (e.g., doubling one's sentence for a crime committed with a weapon), and so forth.

- Under *determinate* sentencing, convicted offenders are sentenced for a fixed term, such as 10 years, with no opportunity for a paroling authority to make adjustments in time served. Conversely, in an *indeterminate* sentencing format, the convicted individual will be sentenced for a set range of time, such as 5–10 years, allowing for the length of sentence to be adjusted in response to the offender's positive responses to treatment and programs.

- Becoming discontented with the sentencing process and the rising crime rate throughout the nation, Congress abolished indeterminate sentencing at the federal level and created a determinate sentencing structure through the federal Sentencing Reform Act. The U.S. Supreme Court found that the guidelines violated the Constitution by allowing judicial, rather than jury, fact-finding to form the basis for the sentencing. The

Court said the guidelines are to be merely advisory and not mandatory. Thus, the guidelines are a resource a judge can look at but may choose to ignore.

- Victim impact statements are written or oral information provided in court—most commonly at sentencing—and at offenders' parole hearings, concerning the impact of the crime on the victim and the victim's family. These statements generally inform the court of the crime's financial, emotional, psychological, and/or physical impact on their lives.

- Supporters of the death penalty often believe that it deters other people from committing murder, while others base their stand on theological grounds. Others favor capital punishment because of the retribution it provides to family members and friends of the victim. Arguments against the death penalty include that it does not have any deterrent value, that it is discriminatory against minorities, that retribution is unfitting for a civilized society, and that it can (and does) claim the lives of innocent people. There is some, but not unanimous, research in support of the deterrence argument.

- In 1972, the U.S. Supreme Court struck down all death penalty laws as being cruel and unusual punishment, due to the manner in which the sanction was being administered. The Court later approved the death sentence in concept. Today, lethal injection is the method of execution authorized in a majority of the states.

- Since 1973, a total of 165 persons on death row in the United States have been exonerated. According to the Death Penalty Information Center, DNA evidence led to at least 20 of those death row exonerations.

- Convicted, indigent persons are entitled to free legal counsel for their initial appeal as well as a free copy of their trial transcript. However, the Supreme Court later held that prison inmates are not entitled to free legal counsel for subsequent "discretionary" appeals.

/// KEY TERMS & CONCEPTS

Review key terms with eFlashcards at **edge.sagepub.com/peak4e**.

Capital punishment 281
Deterrence 267
Exoneration 286
Incapacitation 267
Punishment (and its purposes) 266
Rehabilitation 267
Retribution 266
Sentencing guidelines 276
Victim impact statements 279

/// REVIEW QUESTIONS

Test your understanding of chapter content at **edge.sagepub.com/peak4e**.

1. How would you describe the four goals of punishment? Which one of them do you believe works the best? Which goal or function is now predominant in our society?

2. What are the factors that influence the degree—and harshness—of the punishment that a convicted person will receive?

3. How would you delineate the different philosophies regarding crime and punishment that evolved from the colonial era to today? How did prison construction change in accordance with those changes in punishment models?

4. What forms of punishment used around the world would you point to that are clearly excessive in terms of the offenses committed? Explain your answer.

5. What are the differences between, and purposes of, both determinate and indeterminate sentences? Which is likely used when the crime control model or due process model is more predominant in a community?

6. How would you explain the rationale for, and operation of, the federal sentencing guidelines?

7. What is the legal basis for victim impact statements? How do such statements work, and for what purpose?

8. What are the fundamental arguments for and against capital punishment? What did the Supreme Court say about capital punishment in *Furman* and *Gregg*?

9. What are the prevailing methods of execution in use today?

10. What changes have been brought by DNA with regard to the death penalty?

11. What are examples of both aggravating and mitigating circumstances, and how do they apply to sentencing decisions? To the death penalty?

12. What rights are possessed by a convicted person regarding access to legal counsel, trial transcripts, and law libraries?

/// LEARN BY DOING

1. Your state's governor is considering a moratorium on all executions because of DNA and death row exonerations. Knowing you are a criminal justice student, you are asked by a state senator to prepare a pro-con paper concerning the benefits and issues involved with doing so, and of DNA in general. How would you respond? Include in your response an assessment of the deterrent effects of capital punishment laws.

2. Assume your criminal justice professor has assigned you to read a journal article by Landy and Aronson titled "The Influence of the Character of the Criminal and His Victim on the Decisions of Simulated Jurors," published in the *Journal of Experimental Social Psychology* 5 (1969), pages 141–152. You find the article at https://www4.uwsp.edu/psych/s/389/landy69.pdf. Read Experiment II, including the instructions and case study (involving an incident with both an attractive victim and an unattractive victim) as given to university sophomores, as well as the experiment's results and discussion, on pages 146–151. Summarize and explain the above in written form.

3. Your criminal justice class is to debate the following: "RESOLVED: Deterrence is lost for the general public when an inmate remains on death row a dozen or more years." Plan how you would respond on both the pro and con sides of the debate.

/// STUDY SITE

Get the tools you need to sharpen your study skills. SAGE edge offers a robust online environment featuring an impressive array of free tools and resources.

Access practice quizzes, eFlashcards, video, and multimedia at **edge.sagepub.com/peak4e**.

Introducing...

SAGE vantage™

Course tools done right.
Built to support teaching. Designed to ignite learning.

SAGE vantage is an intuitive digital platform that blends trusted SAGE content with auto-graded assignments, all carefully designed to ignite student engagement and drive critical thinking. Built with you and your students in mind, it offers easy course set-up and enables students to better prepare for class.

SAGE vantage enables students to **engage** with the material you choose, **learn** by applying knowledge, and **soar** with confidence by performing better in your course.

PEDAGOGICAL SCAFFOLDING
Builds on core concepts, moving students from basic understanding to mastery.

CONFIDENCE BUILDER
Offers frequent knowledge checks, applied-learning multimedia tools, and chapter tests with focused feedback.

TIME-SAVING FLEXIBILITY
Feeds auto-graded assignments to your gradebook, with real-time insight into student and class performance.

QUALITY CONTENT
Written by expert authors and teachers, content is not sacrificed for technical features.

HONEST VALUE
Affordable access to easy-to-use, quality learning tools students will appreciate.

To learn more about **SAGE vantage**, hover over this QR code with your smartphone camera or visit **sagepub.com/vantage**

CORRECTIONS

PART 4

Chapter 12: Prisons and Jails: Structure and Function
Chapter 13: The Inmates' World: The "Keepers" and the "Kept"
Chapter 14: Corrections in the Community: Probation, Parole, and Other Alternatives to Incarceration

This part includes three chapters and examines many aspects of correctional organizations and operations.

Chapter 12 examines federal and state prisons and local jails in terms of their evolution and organization, inmate population trends (including mass incarceration) and classification, and some technologies.

Chapter 13 considers the "lives inside the walls" of both correctional personnel and inmates; included are selected court decisions concerning inmates' legal rights; administrative challenges with overseeing executions, inmate litigation, drugs, and gangs; and the work of personnel in local jails.

Chapter 14 reviews community corrections and alternatives to incarceration: probation, parole, and several other diversionary approaches. Included are discussions of the origins of probation and parole, functions of probation and parole officers, and several intermediate sanctions (e.g., house arrest, electronic monitoring).

CHAPTER 12

PRISONS AND JAILS
Structure and Function

Men who had been in prison as much as five years still knew next to nothing on the subject. It probably took a decade behind bars for any real perception on the matter to permeate your psychology and your flesh.

—Jack Henry Abbott, *In the Belly of the Beast: Letters From Prison*[1]

I can think of nothing, not even war, that has brought so much misery to the human race as prisons.

—Clarence Darrow, 1936

LEARNING OBJECTIVES

As a result of reading this chapter, you will be able to

1. Describe correctional populations, employment, expenditures, and institutional types
2. Review some of the factors that contribute to recent declines in prison and jail populations
3. Explain the basic structure and function of state prisons
4. Explain the basic structure and function of the federal prison system
5. Describe how supermax prisons function, how they differ from other prisons, and findings concerning their effects on inmates and constitutionality
6. Define and review the operation of private, for-profit prisons
7. Review how local jails are organized and constructed, including the new generation jail
8. Describe some of the technologies now in use in corrections, with particular emphasis on methods for halting drone and cell phone use by inmates

ASSESS YOUR AWARENESS

Test your basic knowledge of prisons and jails by responding to the following seven true-false items; check your answers after reading this chapter.

1. Factors influencing the recent (i.e., in the past decade, roughly) decline in prison and jail populations include reductions in violent crimes, greater use of alternatives to incarceration, and the early release of thousands of nonviolent offenders.
2. A person who is convicted of committing a murder will likely be forced to serve a lengthy sentence in a local jail.
3. The general mission of correctional institutions is to securely hold criminals while providing them with opportunities to become productive and law-abiding citizens.
4. There are basically two custody levels of prisons: maximum and minimum.
5. Supermax prisons are so named because they offer the maximum amount of freedom and programming permitted by the courts.
6. Today, very few prison inmates, and no jail inmates, are involved in productive work or treatment programs.
7. Owing to the latest technologies used by prison and jail personnel, inmate use of drones and cell phones has been eradicated.

<< Answers can be found on page 419.

There has probably never been a more pervasive, universal push for prison and jail reform than at the present time. The United Nations (UN), the U.S. Congress, and even a U.S. president's son-in-law (Jared Kushner) are involved in a growing movement to reform the manner in which our correctional institutions function. Because of the concerns that people and organizations have about the effects of incarceration on human rights, society in general (and persons living in poverty, in particular), the personal health of inmates, and governmental budgets, there is certainly ample room for concerted action. The UN Office on Drugs and Crime has delineated four specific "areas of work":

- Pretrial detention (e.g., Is it overused? Are detainees being abused?)
- Prison management (Is it in line with the rule of law with respect to individuals' human rights? Is imprisonment being used to prepare individuals for life outside prison following release?)
- Alternative measures and sanctions (Can more community-based sanctions be used?)
- Social reintegration (Are noncustodial sanctions—instead of isolation from society—and purposeful activities and programs in prisons, being considered and employed?)

Of course, the provision of adequate health care for detainees cuts across all of these four domains.[2]

As you read this chapter, consider if or where prison reform might or should be undertaken, as well as where more human and financial resources might be needed to bring about those reforms.

INTRODUCTION

What are the differences in definitions, missions, structures, and functions of prisons and jails and in the duties of persons working in them? How are decisions made concerning the type of institution to which one is sent? Are more people incarcerated when the economy takes a downturn? These are valid questions to ask, particularly given the expense associated with institutionalizing offenders rather than having them remain in the community.

In his classic 1961 book, *Asylums*, Erving Goffman described life inside what he termed "total institutions," or those places "organized to protect the community against what are felt to be intentional dangers to it: jail, penitentiaries, POW camps, and concentration camps."[3] Goffman said that total institutions share the following features:

- All aspects of life are conducted in the same place and under the same single authority.
- Each phase of the member's daily activity is carried on in the immediate company of a large batch of others.
- All phases of the day's activities are tightly scheduled.
- The various enforced activities are brought together in a single rational plan . . . to fulfill the official aims of the institution.[4]

Goffman appears to have captured the essence of our correctional organizations, which are typically viewed as the end result of one's movement through the criminal justice system (as described and illustrated in Chapter 1). However, it might well be argued that the correctional process begins at the point of one's *arrest*, when the individual is incarcerated in jail awaiting trial and official attempts are initiated to identify and change his or her criminal tendencies.

Inmates watch television in the recreational area of a county jail. Jails differ from prisons in that they are typically used as a short-term, temporary holding facility for persons recently arrested and awaiting trial.

In any case, corrections comprises agencies and programs that are responsible for carrying out the sentences and punishment that the courts have administered to those who have been accused, tried, and convicted for their criminal acts. Keep in mind that most of the work of corrections is accomplished not by locking people away but, rather, in the community, where offenders serve terms of probation or parole (see Chapter 14).

Unfortunately, most of what the public "knows" about prisons and jails is probably based on Hollywood's stylized (and often very unrealistic) portrayal in movies such as *The Shawshank Redemption, The Green Mile, Escape From Alcatraz, Cool Hand Luke, The Longest Yard,* and *The Great Escape*. These and other such portrayals of prison and jail life typically show the administrators and their staff being cruel, bigoted, corrupt, and morally base.

but not convicted, to spend weeks, months, or years in jail awaiting trial simply because they cannot afford to post bail.[15] This reform will have an impact on prison populations, as studies show that, for felony cases, the conviction rate increases from 50 percent to 85 percent for those defendants jailed pretrial who cannot make bail.[16] Indeed, it has been argued that what is termed mass incarceration (discussed in the next section) cannot end without reforming the money-bail system.[17] With respect to community-based supervision of offenders (as opposed to incarceration), about 4.6 million adults are now supervised in the community, with about 3.7 million of these adults being on probation and the remainder on parole.[18] In short, expanded use of several of the alternative-to-incarceration approaches to be discussed in Chapter 14 (e.g., probation and parole, house arrest, electronic monitoring, shock incarceration, and day reporting centers) are having a major impact.

Mass Incarceration in America: Time to Rethink and Reform?

Each year, a new crop of youths in their upper teens constitutes the majority of those arrested for serious crimes. As these offenders are arrested and removed from the crime scene, a new crop replaces them: "The justice system is eating its young. It imprisons them, paroles them, and rearrests them with no rehabilitation in between," according to prison researcher Dale Secrest.[19] Still, large-scale, long-term imprisonment unquestionably keeps truly serious offenders behind bars, preventing them from committing more crimes.

Although corrections populations have been declining for several years, many observers believe much work and analysis need to be done in terms of who is being incarcerated. David Garland, a sociologist at New York University, coined the term mass incarceration in 2001, to characterize the extraordinarily high incarceration rates (now at more than two million people) in the United States.[20] Together, the incarcerated population would constitute the fourth largest city in the nation (and if offenders on probation and parole were included, the population would be second only to New York City).

Michelle Alexander, Ohio State University law professor and civil rights advocate, wrote in *The New Jim Crow* (which spent 70 weeks on the *New York Times* best-seller list) that mass incarceration "emerged as a stunningly comprehensive and well-disguised system of racialized social control."[21] Alexander asserts that no other country imprisons as many of its racial or ethnic minorities. Alexander emphasizes that "nothing has contributed more to the systematic mass incarceration of people of color . . . than the War on Drugs." (*Note:* A prize-winning documentary film, *The House I Live In*, also explores the effects of U.S. drug policy on the nation's poor and minority communities.) Alexander predicts that, given current trends, one in three young African Americans will serve time in prison, and in some cities, more than half of all such men are currently under some form of correctional control.[22] In addition to the negative effects of one's coming out of prison with a felony record and typically few job skills, the additional effects of mass incarceration on such individuals include that for the rest of their lives, they can be denied the right to vote (in nearly half of the states, felons lose their voting rights during incarceration and for a period of time after), automatically excluded from juries, and legally discriminated against in employment, housing, and access to education and public benefits.[23] Furthermore, mass incarceration is said to cripple families (causing home instability and food insecurity) and communities, perpetuate poverty, and institutionalize a form of racial control.[24]

The Vera Institute of Justice has examined incarceration rates in *The New Dynamics of Mass Incarceration* and finds that the tendency to use state prison population figures (which, as noted earlier, have declined) as a sole indication of sentencing reform actually belies a more complex picture: In some states, the incarcerated population has shifted away from prisons and into local jails, so there has not been a reversal of mass incarceration. The report finds many jail populations are on the rise and that jails hold about 18 times as many people as state and federal prisons. Furthermore, while about a dozen states have increased their prison

Mass incarceration: a term generally referring to what is perceived as the United States's disproportionately high rates of imprisonment of young African American men; some believe it deters crime and incapacitates offenders, while others say that it weakens poor families and keeps them socially marginalized.

Many people believe that, rather than using punishment alone, it is also important to try to rehabilitate offenders—that is, providing treatment programs to help them to recover from a criminal lifestyle or personality disorders, from substance abuse or addiction, and so on, in order to become productive citizens.

populations, they have also increased their jail populations; at least eight states hold more people in jails than in prisons, and four states continue to lock up people in both prisons and jails at all-time high levels. In sum, Vera's view is that an urgent need exists to rethink our approach to ending mass incarceration.[25]

General Mission and Features

Correctional organizations are complex, hybrid organizations that utilize two distinct yet related management subsystems to achieve their goals: One is concerned primarily with managing correctional employees, and the other is concerned primarily with delivering correctional services to a designated offender population. The correctional organization, therefore, employs one group of people—correctional personnel—to work with and control another group: offenders.

The mission of correctional agencies has changed little over time. It is as follows: to protect the citizens from crime by safely and securely handling criminal offenders while providing offenders some opportunities for self-improvement and increasing the chance that they will become productive and law-abiding citizens.[26] An interesting feature of the correctional organization is that *every* correctional employee who exercises legal authority over offenders is a supervisor, even if the person is the lowest-ranking member in the agency or institution. Another feature of the correctional organization is that—as with the police—everything a correctional supervisor does may have civil or criminal ramifications, both for himself or herself and for the agency or institution. Therefore, the legal and ethical responsibility for the correctional (and police) supervisor is greater than it is for supervisors in other types of organizations.

Finally, it is probably fair to say there are two different philosophies concerning what a correctional organization should be: (1) a custodial organization, which emphasizes the caretaker functions of controlling and observing inmates, and (2) a treatment organization, which emphasizes rehabilitation of inmates. These different philosophies contain potential conflict for correctional personnel.

Punishment for Some, a "Step Up" for Others

Most Americans probably assume that sending offenders to prisons and jails—depriving them of their freedom of movement and many amenities while living under an oppressive set of rules—serves a useful purpose, will bring them to the "good life," and instills in them a desire to obey the laws and avoid returning to prison after their release. In fact, experts have said that such punishments will work only under the following two conditions: (1) if they injure the offender's "social standing by the punishment," and (2) if they make "the individual feel a danger of being excluded from the group."[27]

Unfortunately, however, this view overlooks two very important facts—facts that are perhaps a sad commentary on the kinds of lives being led by many people in the United States:

- Most serious offenders neither accept nor abide by those two conditions.
- Most incarcerated people today come from communities where conditions fall far below the living standards that most Americans would accept.[28] As stated by prison expert Joan Petersilia, the grim fact and national shame is that for many people who go to prison, the conditions inside are not all that different from (and might even

be better than) the conditions outside.[29] For some members of our society, going to prison or jail—and obtaining "three hots and a cot" (three meals and a bed)—may actually represent an *increased* standard of living. Obviously, for those individuals, the threat of imprisonment no longer represents a horrible punishment and therefore has lost much of its deterrent power. When such people go to prison, they seldom feel isolated but are likely to find friends, if not family, already there.[30]

Practitioner's Perspective

Jail Administrator

Name: Mitch Lucas
Position: Jail Administrator
Location: Charleston, South Carolina

What is your career story? I came to the Charleston County Sheriff's Office to be the public information officer (PIO). In my role as PIO, I had to deal with the folks at the jail, and I was absolutely astonished at how motivated and dedicated people could be in a very important role like that, but nobody outside the jail knew what they did. Most people have no idea what goes on in a jail—they only know what they see in the media. And the people at the jail were just so incredible when it came to helping me in my job and doing theirs. I told the sheriff that if I ever had the opportunity, I'd like to work at the jail in some capacity. A few years later, he made me the jail administrator. I served as the jail administrator for seven and a half years, absolutely the best job I ever had, mainly because of the people—both inside the jail and outside in the field—with whom I worked.

What are some challenges and misconceptions you face in this position? The biggest paradigm shift I had to make when I became the jail administrator was to realize that the jail is the common denominator of the criminal justice system. Everyone who is arrested, goes to court, whoever is indicted and ends up going to prison, all pass through the jail. The jail's main purpose is to maintain inmate behavior, and keep the community safe by keeping the jail running smoothly, and keeping the people that are in the jail safe. That was a bit of a shift for me. Because you have to sort of remove yourself from whether they're guilty or not guilty, and just deal with the situation at hand, and that's providing an environment that is safe for everyone.

There are two valleys of misconception. One is from law enforcement. Law enforcement officers believe that people work in jails because they can't be cops. I felt the same way at one point, but when I got to meet jail workers and work with them, I realized that's not the case. The other misconception comes from the media. All other public safety aspects—law enforcement, firefighters, dispatchers—all of them are portrayed as heroes in most of the stories. But the corrections officer, whether it's at a jail or in prison, is typically portrayed as cruel and vicious.

What characteristics and skills are most helpful to succeed in this position? There are two really important skills to be successful in law enforcement corrections. First are communication skills. The person should be able to communicate in a variety of ways, and they must be able to listen, analyze information, and act on it. The other one is writing. Probably the number one problem in all areas for criminal justice is poor report writing. You have to be able to write effectively, and I encourage anybody that talks to me about getting into law enforcement corrections to take as many English and public speaking courses as they can.

Do you see any common trends in this position? We're seeing more and more that education plays a greater role because of everything with the Freedom of Information Act. Everything that's done in the jail is no longer in a vacuum, at both the state and federal level. If a reporter or family member asks to see a video of a particular inmate or particular situation, they can get it. So the field is no longer just what we used to call a lockup, where you put someone in a cell, lock the door, and walk away.

To learn more about Mitch Lucas' experiences as a jail administrator, watch the Practitioner's Perspective video in SAGE vantage.

Furthermore, it appears that prison life is not perceived as being as difficult as it once was. Inmates' actions speak loudly in this respect: About two-thirds of today's parolees are rearrested within five years; evidently they believe the "benefits" of committing a new crime outweigh the costs of being in prison.[31] Finally, the stigma of having a prison record is not the same as in the past, because so many of the offenders' peers and family members also have done time. Imprisonment also confers status in some neighborhoods. To many people, serving a prison term is a badge of courage. It also is their source of food, clothing, and shelter.[32] Any discussion of jails and prisons should be prefaced with these facts concerning the inmates' world.

Classification of Inmates: A Cornerstone of Corrections

If the prison or jail experience is to carry any benefit, classifying inmates into the proper levels of housing, programming, and other aspects of their incarceration must be accomplished so as to have an influence on their behavior, treatment, and progress while in custody—as well as for the general safety of inmates and staff. Correctional staff must make classification decisions in at least two areas: the inmate's level of *physical restraint* or "security level," and the inmate's level of *supervision* or *custody grade*. These two concepts are not well understood and are often confused, but they significantly impact a prisoner's housing and program assignments,[33] as well as an institution's overall security level.

Classification (of inmates): an inmate security and treatment plan based on one's security, social, vocational, psychological, and educational needs while incarcerated.

The most recent development in classification is unit management, in which a large prison population is subdivided into several mini-institutions analogous to a city and its neighborhoods. Each unit has specified decision-making authority and is run by a staff of six, whose offices are on the living unit; this enables classification decisions to be made by personnel who are in daily contact with their inmates and know them fairly well.[34] Robert Levinson delineated four categories into which correctional officials classify new inmates:[35]

- *Security* needs are classified in terms of the number and types of architectural barriers that must be placed between the inmates and the outside world to ensure they will not escape and can be controlled. Most correctional systems have four security levels: supermax (highest), maximum (high), medium (low), and minimum (lowest).

- *Custody* assignments determine the level of supervision and types of privileges an inmate will have. A basic consideration is whether or not an inmate will be allowed to go outside the facility's secure perimeter, so some systems have adopted a four-fold array of custody grades—two inside the fence (one more restrictive than the other) and two outside the fence (one more closely supervised than the other).

- *Housing* needs were historically determined by an "assign to the next empty bed" system, which could place the new, weak inmate in the same cell with the most hardened inmate. A more sophisticated approach is known as internal classification, in which inmates are assigned to live with prisoners who are similar to themselves. This approach can involve the grouping of inmates into three broad categories: heavy—victimizers; light—victims; and moderate—neither intimidated by the first group nor abusers of the second.

- *Program* classification involves using interview and testing data to determine where the newly arrived inmate should be placed in work, training, and treatment programs. These programs are designed to help the prisoner make a successful return to society.

In the past, most prison systems used a highly subjective system of classifying inmates that involved a review of records pertaining to the inmate's prior social and criminal history, test scores, school and work performance, and staff impressions developed from interviews. Today, however, administrators employ a much-preferred objective system that is more rational, efficient, and equitable. Factors used in making classification decisions are measurable and valid, and are applied to all inmates in the same way. Criteria most often used are escape history, any detainers (requests filed with the institution holding an inmate asking that the jurisdiction hold the prisoner for that agency, or notify the agency when release of the prisoner is about to occur), prior commitments, criminal history, prior institutional adjustment, history of violence, and length of sentence.[36]

STATE PRISONS AS ORGANIZATIONS

Physical fitness and sports activities are popular among inmates, and jails and prisons at all levels typically offer a variety of such opportunities.

State prison: a correctional facility that houses convicted felons.

As noted earlier in this chapter, the mission of most prisons is to provide a safe and secure environment for staff and inmates, as well as programs for offenders that can assist them after release.[37] This section describes how state prisons are organized to accomplish this mission. First is a look at the larger picture—the typical organization of the central office within the state government that oversees *all* prisons within its jurisdiction—and then a look at the characteristic organization of an individual prison.

Prison organizational structures (see Figure 12.2) have changed considerably over time. Until the beginning of the 20th century, prisons were administered by state boards of

Figure 12.2 /// Organizational Structure for a Medium-Security Prison

Note: AA = administrative aide; C.E.R.T. = correctional emergency response team; PE & Rec. = physical education and recreation.

Chapter 12: Prisons and Jails 303

charities, boards composed of citizens, boards of inspectors, state prison commissions, or individual prison keepers. Most prisons were individual provinces; wardens, who were given absolute control over their domain, were appointed by governors through a system of political patronage. Individuals were attracted to the position of warden because it carried many fringe benefits, such as a lavish residence, unlimited inmate servants, food and supplies from institutional farms and warehouses, furnishings, and a personal automobile. Now most wardens or superintendents are civil service employees who have earned their position through seniority and merit.[38] We discuss the warden's position more later in this chapter.

Warden: the chief administrator of a federal penitentiary or state prison.

Reporting to the warden are deputy or associate wardens, each of whom supervises a department within the prison. The deputy warden for operations will typically oversee correctional security, unit management, the inmate disciplinary committee, and recreation. The deputy warden for special services will generally be responsible for the library, mental health services, drug and alcohol recovery services, education, prison job assignments, religious services, and prison industries. The deputy warden for administration will manage the business office, prison maintenance, laundry, food service, medical services, prison farms, and the issuance of clothing.[39]

We now discuss correctional security, unit management, education, and prison industries in greater detail:

- The correctional security department is usually the largest department in a prison, with 50 to 70 percent of all staff. It supervises all of the security activities within a prison, including any special housing units, inmate transportation, and the inmate disciplinary process. Security staff wears military-style uniforms; a captain typically runs each eight-hour shift, lieutenants often are responsible for an area of the prison, and sergeants oversee the rank-and-file correctional staff.

- The unit management concept was originated by the federal prison system in the 1970s and now is used in nearly every state to control prisons by providing a "small, self-contained, inmate living and staff office area that operates semi-autonomously within the larger institution."[40] The purpose of unit management is twofold: to decentralize the administration of the prison and to enhance communication among staff and between staff and inmates. Unit management breaks the prison into more manageable sections based on housing assignments; assignment of staff to a particular unit; and staff authority to make decisions, manage the unit, and deal directly with inmates. Units usually comprise 200–300 inmates; staff members are assigned to specific units, and their offices are located in the housing area, making them more accessible to inmates and better able to monitor inmate activities and behavior. Directly reporting to the unit manager are "case managers," or social workers, who develop the program of work and rehabilitation for each inmate and write progress reports for parole authorities, classification, or transfer to another prison. Correctional counselors also work with inmates in the units on daily issues, such as finding a prison job, working with their prison finances, and creating a visiting and telephone list.[41]

- Education departments operate the academic teaching, vocational training, library services, and sometimes recreation programs for inmates. An education department is managed in a fashion similar to that of a conventional elementary or high school, with certified teachers for all subjects that are required by the state department of education or are part of the General Educational Development (GED) test. Vocational training can include carpentry, landscaping or horticulture, food service, and office skills.

Prison industries: use of prison and jail inmates to produce goods or provide services for a public agency or private corporation.

- Prison industries are legislatively chartered as separate government corporations and report directly to the warden because there is often a requirement that the industry be self-supporting or operate from funds generated from the sale of products. Generally, no tax dollars are used to run the programs, and there is strict accountability of funds.

Do Prisons Rehabilitate?

As discussed in Chapter 11, the purposes of sentencing and punishment include rehabilitation—the goal of changing the offender so that he or she becomes a law-abiding citizen. Can and do prisons really rehabilitate? The data on recidivism (from the Latin word *recidivus*, which means "recurring"; an offender's committing new crimes) will address the question. Recidivism is one of the most important concepts in criminal justice, as it concerns a person's relapse into criminal behavior; recidivism is generally measured by one's criminal acts resulting in rearrest, reconviction, or return to prison within a three-year period after he or she was released from incarceration or placement on supervision for a previous criminal conviction.[42]

A study of state prisoners by the Bureau of Justice Statistics looked at recidivism beyond the aforementioned three-year threshold, with a nine-year follow-up of state prisoners; the study provides a dismal view of rearrest after release. In sum, five in six (83 percent) of released state prisoners committed a new offense for which they were rearrested. An estimated 68 percent were rearrested within three years; over the nine-year period, 82 percent of those persons arrested during the first three years were arrested during years four through nine, and almost half (47 percent) of those who did not have an arrest within three years were arrested during years four through nine.[43] Clearly, the longer one has been released from prison, the greater the likelihood of reoffending. More needs to be done to prepare inmates for reentry, providing educational opportunities, job training and counseling, and outreach and support services post-release.[44]

FEDERAL PRISONS

The Federal Bureau of Prisons (BOP) was established in 1930 to provide care for federal inmates. Today, the BOP has more than 36,000 employees and consists of 144 institutions of many types (including prisons, camps, medical centers, penitentiaries, transfer centers, and detention centers) and nearly 180,000 federal offenders.[45] Approximately 85 percent of these inmates are confined in BOP-operated facilities, while the remainder are confined in privately managed or community-based facilities and local jails.[46]

Prison Types and General Information

The BOP operates institutions at five different security levels in order to confine offenders in an appropriate manner.[47] The levels (and associated numbers of institutions) are discussed in the sections that follow; the federal supermax facility is discussed later in this chapter. Security levels are based on such features as the presence of external patrols, towers, security barriers, or detection devices; the type of housing within the institution; internal security features; and the staff-to-inmate ratio.

Minimum Security (7)

Minimum-security institutions, also known as federal prison camps, have dormitory housing, a relatively low staff-to-inmate ratio, and limited or no perimeter fencing. These institutions are work and program oriented, and many are located adjacent to larger institutions or on military bases, where inmates help serve the labor needs of the larger institution or base.

Low Security (42)

Low-security federal correctional institutions have double-fenced perimeters, mostly dormitory or cubicle housing, and strong work and program components. The staff-to-inmate ratio in these institutions is higher than in minimum-security facilities.

Prison housing units vary, but they usually consist of 200–300 inmates and place staff members in the housing area, to be more accessible to inmates and better able to monitor their activities and behavior.

Medium Security (47)

Medium-security correctional institutions and penitentiaries designated to house medium-security inmates have strengthened perimeters (often double fences with electronic detection systems), mostly cell-type housing, a wide variety of work and treatment programs, an even higher staff-to-inmate ratio than low-security federal correctional institutions, and even greater internal controls.

High Security (17)

High-security institutions, also known as U.S. penitentiaries, have highly secured perimeters (featuring walls or reinforced fences), multiple- and single-occupant cell housing, the highest staff-to-inmate ratio, and close control of inmate movement.

Administrative Security (20)

These are institutions with special missions, such as the detention of pretrial offenders; the treatment of inmates with serious or chronic medical problems; or the containment of extremely dangerous, violent, or escape-prone inmates (such as in the supermax prison, in Florence, Colorado).

In addition, a number of BOP institutions have a small, minimum-security camp adjacent to the main facility. These camps, often referred to as satellite camps, provide inmate labor to the main institution and to off-site work programs.

A Career With BOP

The General Schedule that is used for BOP position classification and pay has 15 grades—GS-1 (lowest) to GS-15 (highest). Agencies establish (classify) the grade of each position based on the level of difficulty, responsibility, and qualifications required. For example, individuals with a high school diploma and no additional experience typically qualify for GS-2 positions; those with a bachelor's degree, for GS-5 positions; and those with a master's degree, for GS-9 positions. Individuals who wish to investigate career opportunities with the BOP should visit the following websites:

1. Pay classification system: https://www.opm.gov/policy-data-oversight/pay-leave/pay-systems/general-schedule/
2. The hiring process: https://www.bop.gov/jobs/hiring_process.jsp
3. The correctional officer position: https://www.bop.gov/jobs/positions/index.jsp?p=Correctional%20Officer
4. Job benefits, which are exceptional: https://www.bop.gov/jobs/life_at_the_bop.jsp

Community Corrections in the Federal System

Parole was abolished in the federal prison system in 1987, when the federal sentencing guidelines went into effect (discussed in Chapter 11). Since then, inmates can have no more than 54 days a year subtracted from a federal sentence, commencing after the person has served 12 months; this policy was upheld in 2010 by the U.S. Supreme Court.[48] Nonetheless, the BOP is actively supporting and using community-corrections techniques.

SUPERMAX PRISONS

Super-maximum—or "supermax"—prisons represent the most secure form of incarceration now in existence in the United States and abroad (although they are given different names in other countries). They began to proliferate in the United States in the mid-1980s as a means of holding extremely disruptive or violent inmates. Such prisons have not been without controversy, however, and this section includes a brief history and description, some research findings on effects on inmates, and some constitutional questions that have been raised.

Origin

Supermax prisons exist in both state and federal prison systems and effectively originated in 1983 in Marion, Illinois, when two correctional officers were murdered by inmates on the same day and the warden put the prison in "permanent lockdown." Thus began 23-hour-a-day cell isolation and no communal yard time for inmates, who were also not permitted to work, attend educational programs, or eat in a cafeteria.[49]

Supermax prison: a penal institution that, for security purposes, affords inmates very few, if any, amenities and a great amount of isolation.

According to Amnesty International, today at least 40 states operate supermax prisons in the United States and house about 25,000 inmates.[50] To understand what supermax prisons are and how they operate, one can look at the federal "Administrative Maximum" prison, or ADX, located in Florence, Colorado, 90 miles south of Denver.

ADX is the only federal supermax facility in the country (the others are state prisons). It is home to a "who's who" of criminals: Boston Marathon bomber Dzhokhar Tsarnaev, "Unabomber" Ted Kaczynski; "Shoe Bomber" Richard Reid; Ramzi Yousef, who plotted the 1993 World Trade Center attack; Oklahoma City bomber Terry Nichols; and Olympic Park bomber Eric Rudolph—and, possibly soon, drug kingpin "El Chapo," discussed in Chapter 16. Ninety-five percent of the prisoners at ADX, known as the "Alcatraz of the Rockies," are the most violent, disruptive, and escape-prone inmates from other federal prisons.[51]

Two Key Components: Operation and Design

Upon viewing its external aspect for the first time, one immediately sees that this is not the usual prison: Large cables are strung above the basketball courts and track; they are helicopter deterrents.[52] Supermax inmates rarely leave their cells; in most such prisons, an hour a day of out-of-cell time is the norm. Inmates eat all of their meals alone in the cells, and typically no group or social activity of any kind is permitted. They are also typically denied access to vocational or educational training programs. Inmates can exist for many years separated from the natural world around them.[53]

The "Administrative Maximum" prison, or ADX, located in Florence, Colorado, is the only federal supermax in the nation.

Effects on Inmates

Given the high degree of isolation and lack of activities in supermax prisons, a major concern voiced by critics of these facilities is their "social pathology" and potential effect on inmates' mental health. Although there is very little research to date concerning the effects of supermax confinement,[54] some authors point to previous isolation research that shows greater levels of deprivation lead to psychological, emotional, and physical problems. For example, studies show that as inmates face greater restrictions and social deprivations, their levels of social withdrawal increase; limiting human contact, autonomy, goods, or services is detrimental to inmates' health and rehabilitative prognoses, and tends to result in depression, hostility, severe anger, sleep disturbances, and anxiety. Women living in a high-security unit have been found to experience claustrophobia, chronic rage reactions, depression, hallucinatory symptoms, withdrawal, and apathy.[55]

Some researchers argue that supermax facilities are not effective management tools for controlling violence and disturbances within prisons, nor are they effective in reducing violence or disturbances within the general population; they conclude that supermax prisons should not be used for their current purpose.[56]

Constitutionality

Because of the relatively recent origin of supermax prisons, their constitutionality has been tested in only a few cases. The first, *Madrid v. Gomez* (1995), addressed conditions of confinement in California's Pelican Bay Security Housing Unit.[57] The judge observed that its image was "hauntingly similar to that of caged felines pacing in a zoo"; however, the judge

---

Going Global

The World's Worst Prisons

Any attempt to set forth a list of the worst prisons in the world will be open to serious debate, and the list provided here of five such prisons is no exception. However, as will be seen, these are included (in no particular order) for very good reasons:

- *La Santé, France:* This institution, the last remaining prison in Paris, was established in 1867. Its mattresses are infested with lice; because prisoners can take only two cold showers per week, skin diseases are common. Overcrowded cells, infestation of vermin, and inmate rape are also common. Its rate of suicide attempts each year is estimated to be almost five times higher than that of California's prison system. Its conditions have been condemned by the UN Human Rights Committee and the country's own minister of justice.

- *Black Beach, Equatorial Guinea:* Amnesty International has described life in this prison as a slow, lingering death sentence. Torture, burning, beatings, and rape are systematic and brutal. Because food rations are minimal, with prisoners sometimes going up to six days without food, starving to death is common. Amnesty also reports that inmates are routinely denied access to medical treatment.

- *Vladimir Central Prison, Russia:* Constructed by Catherine the Great to house political prisoners, this prison during the Soviet era became synonymous with persecution of political dissidents. Today the prison also functions as a museum for the public. Visitors are not allowed into the penitentiary, where cells often contain six prisoners and reports of abuse by guards are common. HIV and tuberculosis are also rampant.

- *Camp 1391, Israel:* Officially, this prison does not exist, but descriptions of its conditions have been validated. Even the Red Cross is banned from visiting, and prisoners typically have no idea where they are being kept or when they might be released—a fact that former inmates say is the worst torture of all. Sexual humiliation and even rape are reportedly used as interrogation techniques.

- *The North Korean Gulag:* Up to 200,000 prisoners are held in these detention centers, and one houses more than 50,000 inmates. Entire families and even neighborhoods are sent here as punishment for the infraction of one member. In some camps, up to 25 percent of the prisoners die every year, only to be replaced by new inmates. Most of the camps are located along the North Korean border with China and Russia; thus, prisoners are forced to endure harsh weather conditions as well as inhumane treatment.

Again, any such list is debatable given harsh prison conditions in many places around the world; prisons and/or labor camps in China, Thailand, Cuba, Venezuela, Syria, Africa, and other venues could easily have been included.

Source: Adapted from "The List: The World's Most Notorious Prisons," *Foreign Policy*, https://foreignpolicy.com/2009/01/21/the-list-the-worlds-most-notorious-prisons/.

concluded that he lacked any constitutional basis to close the prison. In the most recent case, *Jones-El v. Berge* (2004), a federal district court in Wisconsin concluded that "extremely isolating conditions... cause SHU [Security Housing Unit] syndrome in relatively healthy prisoners.... Supermax is not appropriate for seriously mentally ill inmates."[58] The judge ordered several prisoners to be removed from the supermax facility.

PRIVATE PRISONS

Perhaps one of the most rapidly growing segments of corrections has been the outsourcing or privatization of prisons, a term that includes either the operation of existing prison facilities by a private company or the building and operation of a new prison by a for-profit company. At present, about 8.5 percent of state and federal prison inmates (128,000) and 73 percent of persons (34,900) held in immigration detention centers are in privately operated facilities.[59] The two largest private prison companies are CoreCivic (formerly the Corrections Corporation of America, or CCA) and the Geo Group, which together have annual revenues of more than $3.5 billion.[60]

Privatization: the operation of existing prison facilities, or the building and operation of new prisons, by for-profit companies.

Historically, strong arguments have been made, both pro and con, regarding the privatization of prisons. Proponents of the concept argue that private prisons provide an effective, cost-saving alternative for governments seeking to address significant capacity needs while taking pressure off of corrections budgets. Opponents maintain that there is no guarantee that standards will be upheld, no one will maintain security if employees go on strike, there will be different inmate disciplinary procedures, the company will be able to refuse certain inmates or could go bankrupt, and the company can increase its fees to the state.[61]

A legitimate question here is "which is better—public or private prisons?" The totality of both types of prisons has not often been studied, and it is known that custody level, size, crowding, age, and architecture can all have a strong influence on measures of quality. One comprehensive study, however, examined 1,129 institutions—105 of which were private. Only one significant difference was found: State prisons were much more likely than private prisons to be under a court order for the conditions of confinement. Given the negative effects of crowding, this is a significant finding.[62]

Prior to the 2016 presidential election, the U.S. Department of Justice announced it would discontinue the use of private prisons in the federal system, affecting 13 federal prisons. However, the Trump administration reversed that policy in 2017 and now houses about 34,000 inmates in such facilities, including halfway houses.[63] President Trump is known to support privatization and has claimed that private prisons work better than government-operated prisons.[64]

JAILS AS ORGANIZATIONS

Across the United States, approximately 3,283 jails are administered locally,[65] holding an average daily population of 727,000. As with state and federal prisons, the number of confined inmates in local jails has been declining since 2008.[66]

The primary purposes of local jails are (1) to hold accused law violators who cannot post bond so as to ensure their appearance at trial, and (2) to hold those persons convicted of lesser offenses until they complete their court-ordered sentences.

The incarceration of persons charged with crimes and awaiting trial, as well as some persons serving sentences for lesser offenses, distinguishes local jails from state and federal prisons. Whereas prisons house persons convicted of more serious offenses—usually felons with sentences of a year or more—jails generally hold persons charged with misdemeanors for up to a year.[67] Jail organization and hierarchical levels are determined by several factors: size, budget, level of crowding, local views toward punishment and treatment, and even the levels of training and education of the jail administrator. An organizational structure for a jail serving a population of about 250,000 is suggested in Figure 12.3.

Figure 12.3 /// Organization Structure for Jail Serving County of 250,000 Population

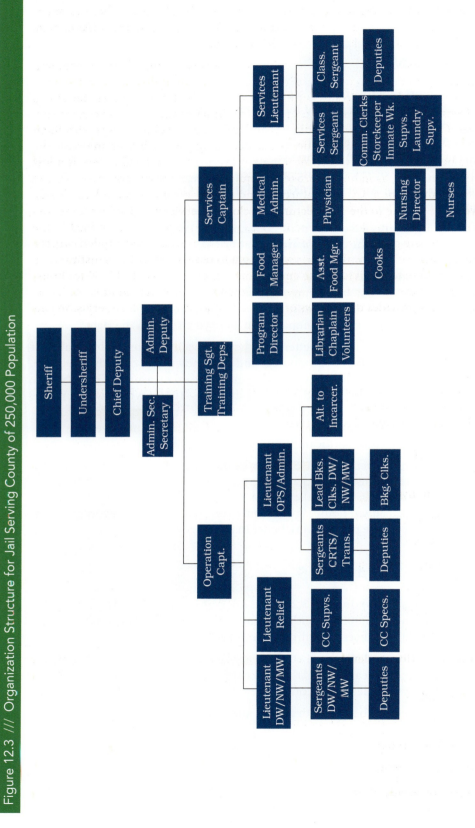

Note: DW = day watch; NW = night watch; MW = mid watch; CC = conservation camps; CRTS/Trans = court transportation; OPS/Admin = operation/administration; Comm. Clerks = commissary clerks.

The New Generation/Direct Supervision Jail

Federal courts have at times abandoned their traditional hands-off doctrine toward prison and jail administration, largely in response to the deplorable conditions and inappropriate treatment of inmates (discussed in more detail in Chapter 13). The courts became more willing to hear inmate allegations of constitutional violations ranging from inadequate heating, lighting, and ventilation to the censorship of mail.[68]

In response to lawsuits and to improve conditions, many local jurisdictions explored new ideas and designed new jail facilities. The first new generation/direct supervision jail opened in the 1970s in Contra Costa County, California. This facility quickly became a success, was deemed cost-effective to build and safer for inmates and staff, and carried several advantages: Officers "live" with the inmates and are encouraged to mingle with them and to provide them privileges and activities (thus increasing good behavior and reducing idleness) while being better able to control inmate movement. As a result, there is a low level of tension in the unit, as fights are broken up quickly, weapons are not involved, and sexual assaults are almost nonexistent. Bathroom and shower areas are monitored closely, and noise levels are low due to the architecture and close supervision.[69] To the extent possible, symbols of incarceration are removed in these new jails, which have no bars in the living units; windows are generally provided in every prisoner's room; and padded carpets, movable furniture, and colorful wall coverings are used to reduce the facility's institutional atmosphere. Inmates are to be divided into small groups of approximately 40–50 for housing purposes. All of these facility features were designed to reduce the "trauma" of incarceration.[70] Figure 12.4 provides three views of how new generation/direct supervision jails are configured.

New generation/direct supervision jail: a jail that, by its architecture and design, eliminates many of the traditional features of a jail, allowing staff members greater interaction and control.

Jail Treatment Programs

Rehabilitation and reintegration are considered secondary goals of local jails; however, many of them provide a wide array of programs for inmates, such as the following types as noted by the National Institute of Justice (NIJ):[71]

- Adult basic education (including computer and other desirable classes)
- Alcoholics Anonymous
- Behavior change programs
- Consumer education
- Criminal justice system programs
- Educational enrichment
- English as a Second Language
- Faith-based living skills
- General educational development (GED)
- Health education
- Mental and physical health programs
- Narcotics Anonymous
- Religious involvement
- Substance abuse education

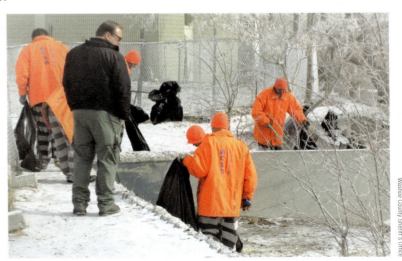

Many local jails have inmate work programs, such as graffiti removal, landscaping, snow removal for elderly citizens, and many others. Here, inmates clean up a municipal river's banks.

Washoe County Sheriff's Office

Figure 12.4 /// Direct Supervision Jails

Jails can have a combination of design styles—Jails that are not predominantly direct supervision in design or management can have an addition or section of inmate housing that uses direct supervision.

- **Podular/direct supervision jails—** Inmates' cells are arranged around a common area, usually called a "dayroom." An officer is stationed in the pod with the inmates. The officer moves about the pod and interacts with the inmates to manage their behavior. There is no secure control booth for the supervising officer, and there are no physical barriers between the officer and the inmates. The officer may have a desk or table for paperwork, but it is in the open dayroom area.

- **Linear/intermittent supervision jails—** Includes jails with cells arranged along the sides of a cell block. Officers come into the housing unit on scheduled rounds or as needed to interact with the inmates.

- **Podular/remote supervision jails—** Includes jails that have a podular design with cells around a dayroom, but no officer is permanently stationed inside the pod. Indirect supervision is provided through remote monitoring at a console.

Source: U.S. Department of Justice, National Institute of Corrections, *Direct Supervision Jails: 2006 Yearbook*, p. vii, http://nicic.org/Downloads/PDF/Library/021968.pdf.

According to the NIJ, which uses a seven-step review and evidence-rating process,[72] about 27 percent of such programs do not accomplish their goals, while about two-thirds are "promising," and 6 percent are "effective."[73]

Making Jails Productive Through Labor

The 1984 Justice Assistance Act removed some of the long-standing restrictions on interstate commerce of prisoner-made goods. By 1987, private-sector work programs were under way in 14 state correctional institutions and two county jails.[74] Today, many inmates in U.S.

jails are involved in productive work. Some simply work to earn privileges, and others earn wages applied to their custodial costs and compensation to crime victims. Some hone new job skills, improving their chances for success following release. At one end of the continuum is the "trusty" (an inmate requiring a low security level) who mows the grass in front of the jail and thereby earns privileges; at the other end are jail inmates working for private industry for real dollars.[75] Some jails have work programs involving training in dog grooming, auto detailing, food service, book mending, mailing service, painting, printing, carpet installation, and upholstering. In addition, some agencies have work programs that use inmates (who pass a review of their criminal history and disciplinary actions) for such activities as graffiti removal, landscaping, setup and teardown of special events, and snow removal for the elderly and/or disabled.[76]

TECHNOLOGIES IN CORRECTIONAL FACILITIES: GOING AFTER CONTRABAND

As with police and court systems, technologies are used in jails and prisons to provide a greater degree of safety for both officers and inmates and, thus, to improve efficiency and effectiveness of correctional practices. They employ video monitoring, GPS devices worn on wrists, biometric entry points that scan an inmate's iris or fingerprints, and remote medical tools so that inmates receive virtual checkups from doctors (discussed later in this section).

However, inmates have uses for technologies as well, including drones, for facilitating their unwavering attempts to bring contraband items into the facility and thus enhance their quality of life. Contraband—including drugs, cell phones, weapons, cigarettes, pornographic materials, and hacksaw blades—has been the bane of prisons and jails since the beginning of time. To obtain these items, inmates use the U.S. mail, visitors, staff members (correctional staff as well as outside persons, such as building contractors), people to throw items over the walls (such as tennis balls containing drugs), and drones. Some jail and prison officials try to control contraband by using a video visitation system, thereby reducing the amount of contact inmates have with family and friends, the need for inmate searches, and reductions in staff time. Short of that, however, several means are available for getting contraband and other such items inside the walls.

Next we focus on the twofold problem of drones and cell phones, and what prison officials are doing to try to stop these items from posing major security issues.

A Perilous Combination—Drones and Cell Phones

Today's drones have become cheap and thus more widespread; they can move quickly, hover, and be evasive when necessary. As noted, they can be used to deliver all manner of contraband items into correctional institutions, two highly sought-after items being drugs and cell phones. Regarding the former, drugs not only get inmates high, but they also create power struggles and disorder, thus threatening the lives of staff and inmates alike. Fentanyl, a synthetic opioid (see Chapter 16), can easily result in overdoses and pose a hazard to staff when exposed to the drug.

Regarding the latter, cell phones, their being smuggled into prisons and jails can cause all manner of problems, from directing gang activities and violent crimes inside and outside the facility to distributing child pornography and intimidating witnesses outside. This is not an insignificant issue, as the use of metal detectors, scanners, and security cameras have all failed to stop cell phones from being smuggled in. As an example, in a recent year California seized more than 13,000 cell phones in its prisons.[77]

What can be done? Regarding drones, federal laws and state statutes have been enacted in the United States to prevent drones from hovering over prison and jail airspace. In addition, private companies have developed technology that is essentially drone radar, to provide advance warning of an incoming drone, the direction it is coming from, and ultimately the identity of the package recipient and the location of the drone pilot.[78]

To combat the threat caused by cell phones, federal laws have stood in the way of "jamming" illicit calls by prisoners, as doing so can threaten the use of phones outside the prison and jail walls. However, the U.S. Department of Justice, the federal Bureau of Prisons, and researchers are testing technology that would disrupt wireless service for the thousands of cell phones inside the walls without posing such a threat to phones on the outside. Furthermore, judges in South Carolina and California have ordered wireless carriers to disable hundreds of contraband cell phones used by inmates.[79]

The Body Scanner

Another tool being used against contraband and adding another layer to the screening process is the body scanner, which functions the same as those used at airports. Penal facilities have long used metal detectors, but they cannot detect illegal drugs and nonmetallic objects. For about $125,000, body scanners can spare corrections officers the need to conduct traditional, unclothed searches of inmates requiring several minutes' time (these can be accomplished in 10 seconds). The devices pay for themselves by reducing the need for officer overtime and workplace injuries. Some institutions have even purchased scanners using funds from the prison canteen (a store where inmates buy snacks, hygiene items, and so on), which are normally used to buy items that benefit inmates; they justify this use by saying the device benefits inmates by sparing them the time and embarrassment of an unclothed search.

A county sheriff's office in Madison (Somerset County), Maine, averaged about eight incidents per year of smuggling of illicit materials into the jail's housing areas, but with the use of the body scanner, the jail has had no contraband instances, the deterrent effect was total, and the device paid for itself in personnel time savings.[80]

You Be the . . .

Warden

You are a prison warden in a city where three drone drops have occurred over the prison yard over the past month. This has led to an escalation in the institution's drug problems, particularly with synthetic opioids like fentanyl. You managed to capture one drone pilot, and suspect that the others, like this one, are not local but instead are experts who are hired by well-off inmates to fly in the illicit drugs and other items, which are then sold at exorbitant prices. While you are working on a solution, you learn from inside sources that more drops are planned in the near future.

You also hear of two possible means for intercepting the drones. One is the use of eagles, which police in the Netherlands have employed for grabbing and taking down rogue drones. Their sharp talons and keen eyesight make it possible for them to pinpoint and pluck a drone from the sky in a simple maneuver. The other means is the use of a laser weapons system that effectively blows drones out of the sky.

1. Assuming cost is not an issue, should your prison and others use one or both of these tools?
2. Can you foresee serious problems in the deployment of either method? If so, what are they?

See the Notes section at the end of the book for assistance in arriving at a decision.[81]

Offender Programming and Management

Technology is changing the methods of offender management through the use of web-based systems that provide educational programs to prisoners, treat prisoners who are addicted to drugs or are sex offenders, and provide vocational training. Prison administrators now keep accurate records of inmates' purchases for items in the prison store, payments to victims and their families, and other reasons for which money flows in and out of prisoners' bank accounts.[82] Automated systems also control access gates and doors, individual cell doors, and the climate in cells and other areas of the prison. Correctional agencies have also used computers to conduct presentence investigations, supervise offenders in the community, and train correctional personnel. With computer assistance, jail administrators receive daily reports on court schedules, inmate rosters, time served, statistical reports, maintenance costs, and other data.

"Virtual Visits" by Inmates and the Public

Prison and jail inmates make frequent visits to hospitals and courtrooms, which creates public safety concerns. In Ohio alone, 40,000 inmate trips to and from medical facilities were eliminated because videoconferencing technology—virtual visits—made medical consultations available from within the institution. An on-site prison physician or nurse assists with the physical part of the examination, taking cues from the offsite specialist via video and relaying information such as electrocardiogram and blood pressure data.[83]

/// IN A NUTSHELL

- Erving Goffman described the characteristics of "total institutions." His definition seems to capture the essence of correctional organizations. Unfortunately, most of what the public "knows" about prisons and jails is probably obtained through Hollywood's fictional versions.

- Sending people to prisons and jails is intended to serve a useful purpose. However, for many inmates, the conditions inside are not all that different from (and might even be better than) the conditions outside. Indeed, for some members of society, going to prison or jail may represent an increased standard of living.

- Several factors contribute to the recent decline in prison and jail populations; essentially, these are federal and state efforts to early-release nonviolent offenders. In addition, violent crimes are decreasing, and there is greater use of alternatives to incarceration.

- Mass incarceration is said to be a form of racialized social control, primarily affecting people of color, resulting in the imprisonment of large numbers of minorities for nonviolent drug offenses, and taking a huge toll on such individuals (in terms of rights lost) as well as minority families. Some researchers point to national increases in jail populations, which would override the belief that reductions in prison populations indicate that sentencing reform is occurring.

- Correctional organizations are complex, hybrid organizations that use two related management subsystems to achieve their goals: One is managing correctional employees, and the other is concerned primarily with delivering correctional services to a designated offender population.

- The mission of correctional agencies has changed little over time. It is to protect the citizens from crime by safely and securely handling criminal offenders while providing offenders some opportunities for self-improvement and increasing the chance that they will become productive and law-abiding citizens.

- The correctional security department is typically the largest department in a prison, with 50 to 70 percent of all staff. It supervises all of the security activities within a prison.

- The unit management concept was originated by the federal prison system in the 1970s, to control prisons by providing a "small, self-contained, inmate living and staff office area that operates semi-autonomously within the larger institution." Unit management breaks the prison into more manageable sections based on housing assignments.

- Education departments operate the academic teaching, vocational training, library services, and sometimes recreation programs for inmates.

- Prison industries are separate government corporations that provide meaningful, productive employment that helps reduce inmate idleness and supplies companies with a readily available and dependable source of labor.

- Correctional staff must make classification decisions in at least two areas: the inmate's level of physical restraint or "security level," and the inmate's level of supervision or custody grade.

- The Federal Bureau of Prisons operates institutions at five different security levels in order to confine offenders in an appropriate manner. Security levels are based on such features as the presence of external patrols, towers, security barriers, or detection devices; the type of housing within the institution; internal security features; and the staff-to-inmate ratio. Each facility is designated as minimum, low, medium, high, or administrative security.

- Supermax prison operations are quite different from traditional prisons. Inmates rarely leave their cells; they eat all of their meals alone in their cells, and typically no group or social activity of any kind is permitted; and they are typically denied access to vocational or educational training programs. Although little research has examined the effects of supermax confinement, some authors point to previous isolation research that shows greater levels of deprivation lead to psychological, emotional, and physical problems.

- A rapidly growing segment of corrections is the privatization of prisons, or operation by a for-profit company; proponents argue that they are an effective, cost-saving alternative; opponents say there is generally less accountability and that a private prison company might go bankrupt or increase its fees to the state.

- The primary purpose of jails is to hold accused law violators who cannot post bond to ensure their appearance at trial, and to hold those persons convicted of lesser offenses until they complete their court-ordered sentences.

- The term *new generation jail* refers to a style of architecture and inmate management that is totally new and unique to local detention facilities. There is a greater level of personal safety for both staff and inmates, greater staff satisfaction, more orderly and relaxed inmate housing areas, and a better maintained physical plant; these facilities are also cost-effective to construct and to operate.

- Today, many inmates in U.S. jails are involved in productive work and treatment programs. Some simply work to earn privileges, and others earn wages applied to their custodial costs and compensation to crime victims. Some hone new job skills, improving their chances for success following release.

- Technological developments have improved the operations and safety of correctional institutions, but inmate use of drones and cell phones has created serious security concerns.

/// KEY TERMS & CONCEPTS

Review key terms with eFlashcards at **edge.sagepub.com/peak4e**.

Classification (of inmates)   302
Jail   297
Mass incarceration   299
New generation/direct supervision jail   311
Prison   297
Prison industries   304
Privatization   309
State prison   303
Supermax prison   307
Warden   304

/// REVIEW QUESTIONS

Test your understanding of chapter content at **edge.sagepub.com/peak4e**.

1. What factors have been recognized as decreasing prison and jail populations?
2. What is meant by mass incarceration, and what are its causes?
3. What is the general mission of a correctional organization?
4. How is it that, for many members of our society, being incarcerated is not "punishment" but rather an improved lifestyle?
5. What is the basic purpose underlying prison inmate classification?
6. What are the basic elements of the federal prison system?
7. How would you describe supermax prisons and how they differ from conventional prisons?
8. How do private prisons differ in structure and function from traditional, government-operated institutions?
9. How do jails differ in structure and function from prisons, what programs are provided for inmate rehabilitation, and how does the new generation jail differ from the traditional model?
10. Describe some of the technologies now in use in corrections, with particular emphasis on methods for halting drone and cell phone use by inmates.

/// LEARN BY DOING

1. Assume you are on a high school recruiting trip for your university's criminal justice department, and a member of a large student group mentions that he wishes to major in criminal justice. He is motivated to do so by an uncle's criminal experiences, for which he is "serving a three- to five-year *supermax* sentence *in a private city jail* for *robbing* people's homes while they were away at work." Because he is overheard by the group in obviously misspeaking about several terms and concepts, you wish to tactfully correct his miscues. What will you say?

2. You are assigned as part of a "Current Correctional Practices" class project to explain the differences between supermax and traditional prisons as well as traditional and new generation jails. What will be your response?

3. Your criminal justice professor assigns the class to prepare a paper on the major differences between state prisons and local jails, including their structure and function. How will you delineate the differences between them?

/// STUDY SITE

Get the tools you need to sharpen your study skills. SAGE edge offers a robust online environment featuring an impressive array of free tools and resources.

Access practice quizzes, eFlashcards, video, and multimedia at **edge.sagepub.com/peak4e**.

CHAPTER 13

THE INMATES' WORLD
The "Keepers" and the "Kept"

The mood and temper of the public in regard to the treatment of crime and criminals is one of the most unfailing tests of the civilization of any country.

—Winston Churchill, to the House of Commons, 1910

Boredom is beautiful.

—Former Nevada prison warden

LEARNING OBJECTIVES

As a result of reading this chapter, you will be able to

1. Describe the differences between prisons and jails, including the nature of incarceration, its deprivations and effects, and the process of prisonization
2. Explain the conditions of regular and solitary confinement, particularly as found in supermax prisons
3. Review the general duties of correctional staff members, particularly wardens and correctional officers
4. Describe the unique challenges posed for prison governance by sexual violence, drugs, gangs, and riots, as well as by female, mentally ill, and elderly inmates
5. Describe several major federal court decisions that greatly expanded prisoners' rights
6. Describe some important measures that can be taken to assist with inmates' reentry and aftercare

ASSESS YOUR AWARENESS

Test your knowledge of prison inmates and employees by responding to the following seven true-false items; check your answers after reading this chapter.

1. Under our system of justice, it may be said that incarcerated persons generally are not to suffer pains beyond the deprivation of liberty; confinement itself is the punishment.
2. The warden's philosophies regarding security and treatment will have a major impact on prison inmates and staff.
3. Today, the courts generally follow a hands-off policy regarding prison and jail administration, allowing administrators to run their institutions as they see fit.
4. Supreme Court decisions support the notion that there exists an "iron curtain" between the U.S. Constitution and the prisons—that is, inmates have no rights.
5. Federal legislation exists to collect data concerning the incidence of sexual assault in correctional facilities and to develop national standards for preventing prison rape.
6. Prisonization, a process whereby an inmate takes on the value system of the prison and its culture, actually helps rehabilitate the offender.
7. Like the police, prisons and their personnel subscribe to the paramilitary system, having ranks, division of labor, and so on.

<< Answers can be found on page 419.

Shirley Schmitt was certainly no one's idea of a dangerous person, one who belonged in prison for a large chunk of her life. Living a meager existence on a farm in Iowa, she raised her horses and her daughter as a single mom after her husband died in 2006. Being depressed and suffering from chronic physical pain, she began using methamphetamine. Eventually, however, she became unable to afford her habit, and began (with some friends) to make the drug for her own personal use. She was arrested in 2012, underwent drug treatment, and by all accounts had remained drug-free after that. However, federal mandatory minimum sentencing rules, along with Schmitt's previous convictions for drug possession and livestock neglect, forced the judge to sentence her to 10 years in prison—at an annual cost to taxpayers of about $30,000.[1]

As you read this chapter, consider whether our prison sentences are working or are in need of reform. Is "more" always "better"? Are lengthy sentences for nonviolent offenders a crime deterrent, for both society in general and the individual offender in specific? Are such sentences cost-effective, and do they help to bring about rehabilitation?

INTRODUCTION

In 1971, Stanford University researcher Philip Zimbardo set up a mock prison experiment he hoped would explain the abusive behaviors that had been going on in prisons. He paid 24 undergraduate student volunteers to assume the roles of "prisoners" and "guards" and run the prison as they saw fit. The experiment lasted only six days; volunteers internalized their roles to the extent that the guards began using authoritarian measures and ultimately subjected some of the prisoners to psychological torture. Within 36 hours, prison revolts broke out.[2] More than four decades later, this study is still widely discussed in academia and the media and often cited as one of the most influential studies of human behavior. Indeed, in early 2015 a film based on the study had its world premiere at the Sundance Film Festival in Park City, Utah.[3]

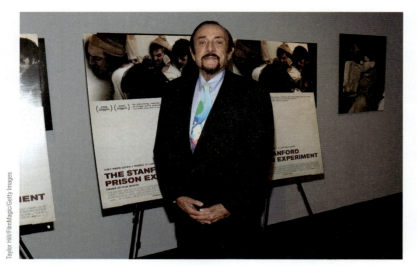

Dr. Philip Zimbardo's Stanford Prison Experiment examined the psychological effects of becoming a prison guard or inmate. Here, Dr. Zimbardo attends the New York premiere of the *The Stanford Prison Experiment* in New York City in July 2015.

As indicated in Chapter 12, prisons and jails, and the lives of their inhabitants, have always held a fascination for many of us. We wonder, what kinds of lives are led by those who are confined in and those who work in that environment? What are the challenges faced by female, elderly, or mentally ill inmates? How are gangs and drugs dealt with administratively? What constitutional rights do inmates possess? This chapter addresses those questions.

Presented first is a look at the general nature of incarceration, including its deprivations, effects, prisonization of inmates, and conditions of confinement (including solitary). Following that is a discussion of the roles of prison wardens, correctional officers, and jail personnel. Next are reviews of several issues of prison governance: inmate sexual violence, drug use, inmates with special needs (e.g., women, the mentally ill, the elderly), gangs, and riots. Finally, after examining prisoners' constitutional rights based on selected federal court decisions, we offer a brief discussion of how inmates are prepared for reentry and aftercare.

When examining what correctional personnel do, it would be good to remember two basic principles put forth by prison expert John DiIulio Jr.: First, incarcerated persons are not to suffer pains beyond the deprivation of liberty; as indicated earlier, confinement itself is the punishment. Second, regardless of the crime, even the most heinous offender is to be treated with respect and dignity.[4] The analysis of correctional institutions that follows is predicated of these two principles.

THE NATURE OF INCARCERATION

As noted in Chapter 12, about 1.5 million Americans are now incarcerated in U.S. federal and state prisons, and another 740,000 persons are held in local jails.[5] The United States has (with about 655 inmates per 100,000 population) the highest imprisonment rate in the world.[6] There are about 10.75 million prisoners worldwide.[7]

In this section, we briefly examine the deprivations and conditions of confinement, as well as some of the means (mostly illegitimate) employed by inmates to try to ease their discomfort. Included are findings on the effects of solitary confinement.

Deprivations and "Pains" of Imprisonment

Prisons vary in their environments and practices. Most prisons are said to "expose prisoners to severe levels of deprivation, degradation, and danger."[8] The extreme stress that can arise due to these circumstances can adversely affect inmates' physical and mental health. Emotional numbing, anxiety, isolation, and hypervigilance—not unlike what is experienced by military veterans with posttraumatic stress disorder (PTSD)—can occur in prisoners as much as 10 times more often than in the general population.[9] Furthermore, these pains of imprisonment can produce long-lasting effects that persist well after a prisoner is released.

Among the deprivations of incarceration are those involving goods and services; inmates do not have access to the wide array of food, entertainment, and services that free people enjoy.

Although many people—and certainly many crime victims—would argue that prison life today is too "soft" for inmates, Gresham Sykes described the following "pains of imprisonment":

- *Deprivation of liberty:* The inmate's loss of freedom is the most obvious aspect of incarceration; however, not only does this restriction of movement include living in a small space such as a prison cell, but it also includes doing so involuntarily. Friends and family are prohibited from visiting except at limited times, causing relationships to fray. Sykes said this pain of imprisonment is the most acute, because it represents a "deliberate, moral rejection of the criminal by free society."[10]

- *Deprivation of goods and services:* Inmates do not have access to the wide array of food, entertainment, and services that free people enjoy. For some inmates, this is a relative loss, because prison life is a "step up," and having room and board provided to them each day is an improvement in lifestyle (as discussed in Chapter 12). Sykes, however, felt that some inmates view this impoverishment as the prison's acting as a tyrant to deprive them of the kinds of goods and services they deserve.[11]

- *Deprivation of heterosexual relationships:* Inmates do not leave their sexuality at the front gate while incarcerated. This is certainly an area of prison life that represents a source of major stress and violence. In men's prisons, Sykes contended, where one's self-concept is tied to his sexuality, depriving men of female company means that their "self-image is in danger of becoming half complete, fractured," and, as described later, with often-violent results.[12]

- *Deprivation of autonomy:* Inmates cannot make decisions for themselves about the most basic tasks, such as walking from one room to another, when they will eat and sleep, and so forth, and they must ask for everything. Bureaucratic rules and staff control their lives, and finding ways to cope with this deprivation can lead to stress.

- *Deprivation of security:* Perhaps the most stressful pain of imprisonment, there are few places in the institution where the inmate can feel secure, and he or she is confined with people who are brutish and violent. Having to "watch one's back" and cope with people who continually test each other and seek out weaknesses in others will lead to internal power struggles, development of gangs, and other forms of "protection."

Becoming "Prisonized"

Prisoners differ in their ability to adapt, cope, and adjust to the pains of imprisonment. The process of socialization—legitimizing, adjusting to, and accommodating the prison subculture's norms and values—is termed prisonization. According to prison expert Jeanne Stinchcomb, inmates conform to the norms and values considered socially acceptable by other inmates—"for example, disdain for the system and those in authority, use of vulgar language, name calling, distrust of fellow prisoners and staff, and acceptance of the status quo."[13] Stinchcomb compares the institutional adaptation of an inmate to

> breaking the spirit of a wild horse to shape its response to the commands of the rider. Like horse and rider—who develop a working accommodation with each other—the subsequent relationship is characterized by routines of dominance, surrender, and behavior on cue. Among inmates, this conformity creates a façade of courtesy toward authority figures and promotes flat, noncommittal responses to others, which are devoid of any emotional investment.[14]

Furthermore, every correctional institution has informal and unwritten norms, the violation of which can quickly bring the wrath of other inmates, ranging from ostracism to physical violence or death. These informal rules, as originally set down by Gresham Sykes and Sheldon Messinger, are as follows:[15]

- *Don't interfere* with the interests of other inmates: This means that inmates "never rat on an inmate" or betray each other; don't be nosy, don't have loose lips, and never put an inmate on the spot. There is no justification for not complying with these rules.

- *Don't quarrel or feud* with fellow inmates: This is expressed in the directives "Play it cool" and "Do your own time."

- *Don't exploit* other inmates: In inmate culture, this means "Don't break your word," "Don't steal from other inmates," and "Don't go back on bets."

- *Don't weaken; withstand frustration or threat without complaint:* This means "Be tough," and "Be a man."

- *Don't trust the custodians* or the things they stand for: This translates to "Don't be a sucker" and "The officials are wrong and the prisoners are right."

Inmates living in a poorly run prison may face a stark choice: become either a victim or a victimizer. A study of a maximum-security prison in the South found that three-fourths of the inmates had been forced to "get tough" with other inmates to avoid victimization, and more than one-fourth kept a "shank" (some object fashioned into a makeshift knife) for self-defense.[16] Fear is equated with weakness, and weakness invites aggression.[17]

Overcrowding can exacerbate all of the other pains of imprisonment. Not only is crowding a major source of administrative problems, but it also can adversely affect inmates' health, behavior, and morale. Crowding has been shown to elevate inmates' blood pressure, lead to increased illness complaints, and cause high levels of stress.[18]

Conditions of Confinement

What constitutional requirements of confinement must be met with persons who are incarcerated? (Specific rights such as access to courts and legal materials, religion, and

Prisonization: the process whereby an inmate becomes socialized into the culture and social life of prison society so that adjusting to the norms of outside society becomes difficult.

In addition to obtaining drugs, tobacco products, and homemade alcohol, inmates also manage to obtain such contraband as cell phones—2,000 of which were confiscated from inmates in California's state prison in Solano.

due process are discussed later in this chapter.) To begin, in *Price v. Johnston* (1948), the Supreme Court observed that "lawful incarceration brings about the necessary withdrawal or limitation of many privileges and rights."[19] More recently, in 1981, the Court stated that routine discomfort is "part of the penalty that criminal offenders pay for their offenses against society"; therefore, only those deprivations that deny "the minimal civilized measure of life's necessities" are sufficient to be considered in violation of the Eighth Amendment (i.e., constitute cruel and unusual punishment).[20]

However, the courts have said that conditions in prison must not involve the wanton and unnecessary infliction of pain, nor be grossly disproportionate to the severity of the crime for which one is imprisoned. Even in the case of emergency actions or critical incidents, only malicious or sadistic acts by prison officials will be deemed unconstitutional. When an inmate alleges that excessive force was used, the standard involved is whether or not the force was applied in good faith so as to maintain or restore discipline.[21] Finally, in *Whitley v. Albers* (1986), the Court held that correctional staff in Oregon did not violate the Eighth Amendment when using potentially deadly force rather than tear gas to quell a prison riot (the plaintiff was shot in the knee during the riot).[22] The Court said that the use of such force to quell a disturbance is unconstitutional only if it is done "sadistically or maliciously." Thus, the court continued its trend of allowing prison officials broad discretion to preserve order and discipline, while restricting inmate rights where necessary.

Investigating Further

How a 7-Year Sentence Became 22 Years in Solitary Confinement

Sent to an Illinois prison in 1994 as a young man convicted of robbery, Rock Island native Anthony Gay endured 22 years (about 8,000 days) in solitary confinement as a result of fights with other inmates, a deteriorating mental state, and bizarre behavior. His original sentence: 7 years (which likely would have been reduced to 3.5 years). Soon after Gay was placed in isolation, the cutting and suicide attempts—and acute mental illness—began. Transferred to several facilities for his bizarre behavior, he gravitated further toward self-destruction. Observing that after fellow inmates injured themselves, nurses, therapists, and other staff members rushed to their aid, he began mimicking their behavior in order to obtain similar human contact. He sliced himself hundreds of times (on his neck, forearms, legs, and genitals) with contraband razor blades or an object from something he had broken, resulting in a trip to the hospital. Other forms of mutilation included inserting a fan motor inside a gaping leg wound, cutting open his scrotum and inserting a zipper, and removing a light switch and sticking the screw in his ear—again bringing human interaction. Gay's aberrant behaviors brought a series of 21 indictments over a five-year period; at trial, he typically acted as his own attorney. Ultimately, he would have another 97 years tacked on to his sentence. Looking at a lifetime of solitary confinement, Gay began writing lawyers and begging for assistance. He finally found one who would take up his cause and challenge how the sentences were structured. These efforts eventually got Gay out of prison.

Gay filed suit in U.S. district court claiming that his treatment amounted to torture and that he was denied proper mental health care. Released from prison in August 2018, he hopes his lawsuit will help to change the system. Already it has: In October 2018, a federal judge ordered the Illinois Department of Corrections to improve its mental health services.

Ironically, in 2016 the American Correctional Association had issued new standards that called for limits on restricted housing, including a statement that prisoners with mental illnesses should not be placed in solitary confinement for an extended period. At any given time, about 67,000 inmates nationwide are spending up to 22 hours a day alone in a cell, according to a study by Yale University.

Source: Adapted from Jeff Coen and Stacy St. Clair, "How Solitary Confinement Drove a Young Inmate to the Brink of Insanity," *Chicago Tribune*, January 2, 2019, https://www.chicagotribune.com/news/ct-met-anthony-gay-solitary-confinement-suit-20181206-story.html.

Practitioner's Perspective

Corrections Sergeant

Name: Ray Bynam
Position: Corrections Sergeant
Location: Pima County Sheriff's Department, Arizona

What is your career story? When I was young, I wanted to work for NASA, until they shut down the shuttle program. Instead I wound up going into criminal justice. I was a military police officer for a few years. I went to visit family in Missouri, and I went to the sheriff's department. They wanted to know if I'd work in a jail. I'd never thought about it, but I said sure. So I got hired and I started the next day. I worked at the jail for a while, worked in different parts of the sheriff's department. And then I went to visit a friend in Arizona, and I applied at the sheriff's department in Tucson, and I got hired six months later. I worked there for 28 years, and 26 as a sergeant.

What are some challenges and misconceptions you face in this position? One of the biggest misconceptions is that people don't like working in corrections. It's a challenge, it's not an easy job, but most people actually like their jobs. And the other misconception is that people in corrections aren't educated. In reality, corrections employees often have associate, bachelor's, and master's degrees. I even got a doctorate eventually.

In general, what does a *typical* day look like for a practitioner in this position? A typical day consists of coming in, getting briefed, going to the housing unit, and dealing with inmates all day. In the new type of facilities, this is called direct supervision, where the officers are actually in the area with the inmates. You interact with them, and your role is basically that of the town marshal—we're there to keep peace. You enforce the laws, you do investigations. If there are crime scenes, you deal with those. You protect the weaker inmates from the stronger inmates. And you get involved in a lot of different things that people don't even know we do.

What role does diversity play in this position? When I first started, we actually had a lot of diversity already. In the jail I worked in at Tucson, 52 percent of the staff was female. And Tucson is a predominantly Hispanic community, so a large portion of the corrections staff was Hispanic. In Tucson, especially at the University of Arizona, it's a fairly international community. We had people from different countries like Russia, England, and Israel. We also had to hire officers that reflected those communities, because they have different traditions, different customs. This also helped because we had officers who were fluent in different languages. We would arrest people from the Russian mafia, for example, and it was helpful to have somebody who could actually speak Russian. This made communication a lot easier.

Do you see any common trends in this position? Technology has changed a lot of things for the role. They use motion detectors, iris scans, and detectors to check cell phones that may be in the facility. Because of this, you need to have people from the younger generations who understand the technology, and these newer people are more open to different changes in the society and they usher in these changes.

What advice would you give to someone either wishing to study, or now studying, criminal justice and wanting to become a practitioner in this position? In the 1960s, one of the biggest recommendations for the criminal justice system was that all the police officers obtain at least a four-year-degree. The idea was, the higher education you had, the less chance you had of being prejudiced. Students studying correction need to develop skills like stress management, time management, how to write a report, and how to give a presentation. These are the skills we want you to come in with.

To learn more about Ray Bynam's experiences as a corrections sergeant watch the Practitioner's Perspective video in SAGE vantage.

Solitary Confinement: Use and Effects

As noted in the accompanying "Investigating Further" box, today an estimated 67,000 inmates nationwide are spending up to 22 hours a day alone in a cell. The number of inmates serving time in **solitary confinement** (also termed administrative segregation, restrictive housing, or the box) has grown tremendously, coinciding with the supermax prison concept (discussed in Chapter 12) that began to proliferate in the mid-1980s. The solitary cells typically have a toilet and a shower, a slot in the door large enough for an officer to slip a food tray through, and little else. Prisoners in solitary confinement are generally not allowed to make telephone calls or have contact visits, and their recreational regimen often involves being taken to another solitary area where they pace alone for an hour before being returned to their cell.[23]

Contrary to what the general public might believe, there is no limit on the length of time an inmate might serve in solitary confinement; the courts' primary concern is that the constitutional requirements for care and custody that apply to all inmates be met. Indeed, there have been cases where inmates have spent decades in such confinement. One case involved the so-called Angola Three, prison inmates Robert H. King, Albert Woodfox, and Herman Wallace, three Black Panthers who were put in solitary confinement in Louisiana's Angola Prison after the 1972 killing of a correctional officer. King spent 29 years in solitary confinement before his conviction was overturned and he was released. Wallace and Woodfox both spent 40 years in solitary confinement. The prisoners have been the subject of two documentary films and international attention.[24]

A large number of studies—dating back to the 19th century—have indicated that solitary confinement profoundly affects inmates' psychological and physical health.[25] As a result, many researchers and civil rights organizations have long called for it to be banned. Most of the damage done to an inmate is psychological and can include psychosis and paranoia; anxiety; depression, varying from low mood to clinical depression; anger; cognitive disturbances; and perceptual distortions. Physiological effects of solitary confinement, owing largely to lack of access to fresh air and sunlight and long periods of inactivity, include gastrointestinal, cardiovascular, and genitourinary problems; migraine headaches; and profound fatigue. Insomnia; back and other joint pains; deterioration of eyesight; and poor appetite and weight loss are often observed.[26] Although the U.S. Supreme Court has taken notice of such negative effects, for more than 125 years (see *In re Medley* [1890]),[27] the federal courts have generally not intervened unless the conditions of confinement were so inadequate as to be tantamount to cruel and unusual punishment.

In the summer of 2016, President Obama directed the Department of Justice (DOJ) to review the use of solitary confinement for the 100,000 persons then being held in federal prisons. Although finding certain circumstances in which such confinement is a necessary tool (e.g., to protect the inmates themselves, staff, and other inmates), the DOJ put forth a number of recommendations to reform the federal prison system, which the president adopted: banning solitary confinement for juveniles, expanding treatment for the mentally ill, and increasing the amount of time inmates in solitary can spend outside of their cells.[28]

Solitary confinement: a form of imprisonment in which an inmate is isolated from any human contact (except for members of prison staff).

PRISON AND JAIL AS WORK

As perilous as places of confinement are for inmates, so too are they perilous for prison correctional staff—all of whom are generally unarmed, and most of whom are outnumbered. It is probably a tribute and great credit to both prison and jail administrators and staff across the nation that so few institutional riots and other serious incidents occur in the United States, especially when one considers that staff is so outnumbered.

Even so, since the beginning of institutional confinement there has been a need for prison (and jail) administrators and **correctional officers** (COs) to develop tactics and equipment

Correctional officer: one who works in a prison or jail and supervises correctional inmates.

to handle outbreaks of violence among inmates. COs often train with such devices in full view of the inmates to demonstrate the kinds of tools that can be employed. According to one prison administrator, what separates prison professionals from inmates is constant training as well as measured, unflappable control.[29] In this section, we look at the work of wardens as well as front-line COs and other custodial staff.

The Warden: Profile and Role

Who are prison wardens? Succinctly, a national survey of 326 wardens in 43 states found they had been working in the corrections field for about 27 years; more than three-fourths (78 percent) were male, and their average age was 52 years. Most of them (51 percent) possessed a bachelor's degree, and another 21 percent had a higher degree. About three-fourths identified as Caucasian, 18 percent as African American, and 4 percent, Hispanic.[30]

Ultimately, all topics discussed in this chapter are the responsibility of those who govern the prisons—state directors of prisons and their individual prison wardens. The challenges these administrators face include such daunting responsibilities as addressing prison litigation, administering capital punishment, attempting to prevent institutional problems relating to drugs and gangs, and addressing all manner of staffing needs and problems.

Prison administration is now more challenging than ever—made much more so because of recent fiscal crises facing all states as well as the federal government. Two former prison wardens from a western state have provided solid advice for administering prisons in general and, specifically, in times of fiscal exigency.

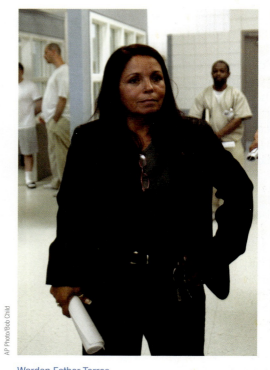

Warden Esther Torres walks through one of the dormitories at the Willard-Cybulski Correctional Institution in Connecticut. Torres oversees a staff of 234 people and 1,160 prisoners.

First, the wise prison warden will recognize that there is simply never enough money to accomplish all four goals of punishment: to *incapacitate* and *rehabilitate* offenders, and to provide *deterrence* to crime and *retribution*. Different states have different correctional philosophies, and that will affect how they budget and spend their prison monies. Choices need to be made—bearing in mind that the warden must, first and foremost, provide for incapacitation—while providing society, staff, and inmates a safe facility. Therefore, it is important to focus on operations, programs, and finances.[31] The warden's philosophies regarding security and treatment will have a major impact on both the prison inmates and staff. In addition to providing inmates with a variety of vocational training programs (including manufacturing items such as limousines and outdoor furniture, and training wild horses) and a wide variety of physical fitness equipment, some prisons have allowed inmates to ride and repair their motorcycles inside the walls;[32] have an inmate band; and engage in unlimited planting of gardens, sunflowers, and fruit trees to occupy their time.

Other wardens take a more hard-line approach and even discontinue those amenities that their predecessors initiated. For example, one warden recently halted the planting of sunflowers because inmates were planting them close to the fence line, and when the night breeze caused the sunflowers to stir from side to side, officers in the gun towers were lulled into a state of complacency—becoming conditioned to ignore the movement in the area, which posed a security risk. Another prison director recently disallowed inmate bands and the planting of gardens and flowers in the prison yard on grounds of institutional security (inmates were concealing weapons and other contraband in the gardens and flowers).[33] Note also that once such privileges are given to inmates, it is very difficult to take them away without generating considerable angst.

Today's prison wardens and other correctional staff members (and jail personnel as well) need to be as aware as possible of their surroundings and the general goings-on within the institution. As with police officers, whose academy training was discussed in Chapter 6, these correctional workers must also nurture a "sixth sense": a suspicion that something may be wrong.

A former western prison warden termed this ability JDLR—knowing when things "just don't look right."[34] To maintain a sense of what's going on with the inmates—"reading the yard"— some wardens recommend that they and their staff walk the yard at least two times each day. Following are some aspects of the yard that should be noted and may portend trouble:

- Inmates banding together in groups—in political associations (i.e., by race, ethnicity, gang affiliation, and so forth)
- Loud music playing (possibly to conceal conversations and activities from the staff)
- Unusually high canteen spending, with inmates purchasing long-term items, such as canned goods (which might indicate that a riot is being planned)[35]

JDLR: in prison jargon, the sense that things "just don't look right."

Other custodial staff members at most prisons are typically divided into the following ranks: captain, lieutenant, and sergeant. Captains typically work closely with the prison administration in policy making and disciplinary matters; lieutenants are even more closely involved with the security and disciplinary aspects of the institution; and sergeants oversee in their span of control a specified number of rank-and-file COs (discussed next) who work in their assigned cell blocks or workplaces.

Correctional Officers

Subordinate to the prison administrators, middle managers, and supervisors are the correctional staff members—those persons who ensure the care, custody, and control of inmates as per agency policies and procedures and, in the words of Gordon Hawkins, are "the other prisoners."[36] According to the Bureau of Labor Statistics, there are approximately 470,000 correctional officers in the United States, with a median annual salary of about $43,500.[37] Their primary role is to provide the front-line supervision and control of inmates and constitute the level from which correctional administrators may be chosen. They manage and communicate with inmates, peers, and supervisors; direct inmate movement; maintain key, tool, and equipment control; distribute authorized items to inmates; and maintain health, safety, and sanitation.

The term *correctional officer* was adopted during the 1970s (replacing *guard*) as the official occupational reference term used by the U.S. Department of Labor. The position of correctional officer became available to both men and women. Other changes included closer screening and hiring by civil service exams. Likewise, the entry-level salary, overtime and hazardous duty pay, pension plans, and recognition as public safety "peace officer" status by state law also served to enhance the recruitment pool and long-term retention of correctional personnel. Staff training programs were also improved, to include topics such as constitutional law and cultural awareness, inmate behavior, contraband control, custody and security procedures, fire and safety, inmate legal rights, written and oral communication, use of force, first aid including cardiopulmonary resuscitation (CPR), and physical fitness training.[38]

Although sharing some traits and duties in common with police officers—academy training, paramilitary nature (e.g., chain of command, wearing of uniforms, use of weapons, enforcement of laws), problem solving—the jobs of police officers and correctional officers are vastly different. First, whereas police officers typically deal with only a small segment of the general public who wish to do them harm, a CO works with hundreds of convicted felons who can easily become dangerous.

Furthermore, COs experience stimulus overload, assailed with the sounds of "doors clanging, inmates talking or shouting, radios and televisions playing, and food trays banging ... [and odors] representing an institutional blend of food, urine, paint, disinfectant, and sweat."[39] According to a federal report, sources of stress for COs include organization-related conditions, such as understaffing, overtime, shift work, and unreasonable supervisor demands; work-related sources of stress, including the threat of inmate violence, actual inmate violence, inmate demands and manipulation, and problems with coworkers; and a poor public image and low pay.[40] According to one Michigan study, all of this can lead to high levels of PTSD for the officer.[41] Furthermore, due process rights for prisoners and the constant threat of lawsuits have made corrections jobs even more difficult,[42] leading to what Richard Hawkins and Geoffrey Alpert referred to as "the big bitch" of correctional officers: They are losing power and influence while inmates are gaining them.[43] This frustration can be vented in physical ways.[44] Following is a more specific listing of duties of the correctional officers:

- *Cell block officers:* Officers supervise the daily activities and the general "well-being" of the inmates in the cell blocks, to ensure that inmates follow institutional rules and routines, to ensure that inmates do not harm themselves or others, and to assist inmates who are experiencing problems of a personal nature.

- *Work detail supervisors:* Many prisons have inmates working in various positions, such as the prison cafeteria, laundry, and other such locations; officers must supervise them during such activities.

- *Industrial shop and educational programs:* Prison industries have inmates producing everything from license plates and state-use paint to mattresses and computer parts; correctional officers ensure that inmates do not create any problems during their work day and do not misappropriate any related tools that may be fashioned into weapons.

- *Yard officers:* While inmates are outdoors and engaged in physical exercise and socialization, there is the potential for problems, such as fights between different racial or ethnic groups; officers must be alert for breaches of security and order.

- *Tower officers:* Officers observe inmates who are in the prison yard while encased in an isolated, silent post high above the prison property, being vigilant for any outbreaks of violence or attempts to escape while inmates are outdoors.

- *Administrative building assignments:* Officers are responsible for providing security at all prison gates, places where inmates' families come to visit, clerical work that involves inmate transfer, and so on.[45]

Jail Personnel

Succinctly stated, jail personnel have many of the same duties as described for their prison counterparts; and, like their counterparts, jail employees must conduct themselves in an exemplary manner at all times while ensuring the care, custody, and control of inmates as per agency policies and procedures. Indeed, many of their duties mirror those of prison COs.

Jail administrators and employees need to be thoroughly trained in all aspects of their jobs. Jail workers have been criticized for being untrained and apathetic, although most are highly effective and dedicated. One observer wrote that

> personnel is still the number one problem of jails. Start paying decent salaries and developing decent training and you can start to attract bright young people to jobs in jails. If you don't do this, you'll continue to see the issue of personnel as th number one problem for the next 100 years.[46]

Training should be provided on the booking process; inmate management and security; general liability issues; policies related to AIDS; problems of inmates addicted to alcohol and other drugs; communication and security technology; and issues concerning suicide, mental health problems, and medication.

ISSUES OF PRISON GOVERNANCE

Next are brief discussions of some issues and challenges that can confront prison (and, often, jail) staff: sexual violence; the needs of female, geriatric, or mentally ill inmates; drug use; gangs; and inmate riots.

Sexual Violence and Coercion

People who live and work in correctional institutions obviously do not leave their sex drive (libido) at the institution's front gate when they enter. Physical violence is a constant possibility, and sexual violence must also be addressed. Sexual violence is defined by the World Health Organization as

> any sexual act, attempt to obtain a sexual act, unwanted sexual comments or advances, or acts to traffic, or otherwise directed, against a person's sexuality using coercion, by any person regardless of their relationship to the victim, in any setting, including but not limited to home and work.[47]

Inmates express their sexuality in many forms, with solitary or mutual masturbation at one end of the continuum, consensual homosexual behavior in the middle, and gang rapes at the other end. Factors that appear to increase sexual coercion rates include large population size (more than 1,000 inmates), understaffed workforces, racial conflict, barracks-type housing, inadequate security, and a high percentage of inmates incarcerated for crimes against persons.[48]

A study by Wolff and Shi examined sexual victimizations that were reported by nearly 7,000 male inmates.[49] Their results were illuminating:

- On average, the victims were typically in their early 30s, African American, and had spent two years at their prison.
- The inmate's cell was the most likely place of occurrence, and inmates were at greatest risk of sexual assault by other inmates between 6 p.m. and midnight.
- Inmate-on-inmate sexual assault incidents most often involved attackers with a gang affiliation, the use of a weapon (typically a knife or homemade shank), and a repeat perpetrator.
- One-third of the sexual assaults resulted in medical attention.[50]

Several policy issues arise from these findings. First, an intervention plan should be employed that is targeted to high-risk prison areas and times of day, and to inmates who are most likely to be victimized (e.g., those with mental illness; mental disabilities; or bisexual, transsexual, or homosexual orientations). At-risk individuals should be placed in single cells or protective units. Furthermore, prison administrators must attempt to prevent and prosecute sexual assaults as well as increase surveillance in vulnerable areas such as transportation vans, holding tanks, shower rooms, stairways, and storage areas.[51]

The **Prison Rape Elimination Act of 2003** (P.L. 108-79) mandated a new national data collection effort concerning the incidence and prevalence of sexual assault in correctional facilities. A decade later, the U.S. Department of Justice required that detention facilities not only give inmates multiple ways to report sexual abuse, but also investigate every allegation. The latter regulation seems to be working: The number of reported sexual assaults in prisons skyrocketed, tripling in number from 2011 to 2015; this indicated to advocacy groups that more assaults were being reported, not actually occurring, because inmates trusted that the reporting and investigating systems work.[52]

Drug Interdiction and Treatment

Every adult in our society is aware of the problems wrought by drug abuse. That problem is reflected within prison populations, where nearly half (47 percent) of federal prison inmates and 15 percent of state prison inmates are incarcerated for drug crimes.[53] Furthermore, offenders still manage to obtain illicit drugs during their incarceration, threatening the safety of inmates and staff while undermining the authority of correctional administrators, contradicting rehabilitative goals, and reducing public confidence.[54]

What can be done about drug abuse in prisons and jails? The state of Pennsylvania realized that drug use was pervasive in several of its prisons. Six inmates had died from overdoses in a two-year period, and assaults on correctional officers and inmates had become more common. To combat the problem, the state first adopted a zero-tolerance drug policy, the so-called Pennsylvania plan: Inmates caught with drugs were to be criminally prosecuted, and those testing positive (using hair testing) were to serve disciplinary custody time. Highly sensitive drug detection equipment was employed to detect drugs that visitors might try to smuggle into the prison, to inspect packages arriving in the mail, and to detect drugs that correctional staff might try to bring in. New policies were issued for inmate movement and visitation, and a new phone system was installed to randomly monitor inmates' calls.[55] The results were impressive. The state's 24 prisons became 99 percent drug free, the number of drug finds during cell searches dropped 41 percent, assaults on staff decreased 57 percent, inmate-on-inmate assaults declined 70 percent, and the number of weapons seized during searches dropped from 220 to 76.[56]

Women in Prison: Selected Rights and Challenges

The numbers speak to the large role that women now occupy in the nation's crime picture: About 112,000 women are being held in U.S. prisons.[57] The major area of difference between male inmates and female inmates concerns their children, because child rearing tends to fall on a mother's shoulders. Added to the "pains" of imprisonment for women, therefore, are the further frustration, conflict, and guilt that arise when women are removed from their homes and are unable to care for their children.[58]

Only seven states allow women who are pregnant at the time of sentencing to keep their infants with them inside a correctional facility after the baby's birth, and in most prisons the length of the child's stay with the mother depends on the length of the mother's sentence.[59] About one-fourth (approximately 22,000 inmates of 89,000 total) of all women in state prisons are incarcerated for either possessing or trafficking drugs—a higher proportion than for males, and almost as high as the percentage of women serving time in state prisons for property crime.[60] Therefore, it is desirable for women incarcerated for such offenses to have access to drug treatment programs, to include detoxification, counseling, education, vocational courses, and group therapy.

Women held in state and federal prisons have other unique challenges—and constitutional rights, such as the following:

- Female prisoners have different, and often more severe, health problems than male prisoners. Many women prisoners suffer from chronic and complex health conditions resulting from lives of poverty, drug use, family violence, sexual assault, adolescent pregnancy, malnutrition, and poor health care.[61]

- About 6 percent of female prisoners report being pregnant at the time of their incarceration.[62] Many prisons thus assess the diet and nutrition, prenatal care, and work assignments for such inmates. In a related vein, although federal prisons and some state prisons prohibit the use of shackles or leg irons on pregnant women while being transported to the hospital or during labor, in some states it is still common to shackle women while on the way to the hospital, or even while they are in labor.[63]

- Women have the right to be free from unreasonable searches and seizures of their property. However, the Supreme Court has found that this right is severely limited in prison because of the security concerns of prison and incarceration. An exception, however, was found in *Jordan v. Gardner*,[64] where female prisoners protested the prison policy of random full-body pat-down searches by male officers (see the accompanying "You Be the . . . Judge" box and its corresponding endnote for the case and its outcome). Many of these female prisoners had been severely sexually and physically abused by men in the past, and experienced severe trauma and revictimization during these searches.

A conundrum has occurred where male correctional officers observe women inmates while in various states of undress: in bed, showering, or using toilet facilities. The U.S. Supreme Court stated in *Turner v. Safley* (1987) that prison regulations that restrict the rights of prisoners must be substantially related to some legitimate concern of the prison.[65] Beyond that, however, the lower federal courts differ on what expectation of privacy women enjoy in prison. Some courts have indicated that all prisoners have a right to be free from unnecessary viewing by correctional officers of the opposite sex while nude or performing private bodily functions in their cells, requiring that women thus be allowed to cover their windows as needed when undressing or using the toilet. Other courts, however, have merely suggested that prisons should allow women to cover their windows while dressing or using the toilet,[66] or have suggested that these prisoners be allowed to cover the window of their cells for privacy for brief time intervals.

You Be the . . .

Judge

"[U]se a flat hand and pushing motion across the [inmate's] crotch area. . . . [P]ush inward and upward when searching the crotch area and upper thighs of the inmate." All seams in the leg and the crotch area are to be "squeezed and kneaded." Using the back of the hand, the guard also is to search the breast area in a sweeping motion, so that the breasts will be "flattened."

Thus read the training instructions as given to male prison guards at the Washington Corrections Center for Women in 1989, when the superintendent of the women's correctional facility instituted a pat-frisk policy permitting male guards to randomly search the clothed bodies of female inmates.

1. When challenged by female inmates, will this policy be allowed to stand on the grounds of institutional security?
2. Alternatively, do you believe it will be struck down by the courts as too intrusive?

The facts of this case, and its outcome, are provided in the Notes section at the end of the book.[67]

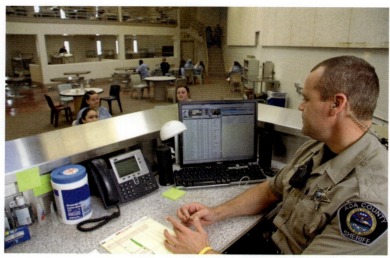

A correctional officer keeps watch on female inmates in an indoor room at the Maricopa County tent jail.

The U.S. Constitution guarantees the right to be free from unreasonable searches and seizures of one's property. However, the Supreme Court has found that this right is severely limited in prison, again, because of security concerns. Prisons may conduct a visual body cavity search (where the prisoner's ears, nose, mouth, anus, or vagina are inspected for contraband); the prison's interest in maintaining a secure facility is deemed to outweigh the prisoner's need for privacy. This interest includes body frisks, cell searches, and strip searches. However, the test for when a digital body cavity search may be performed is stricter because of its intrusive nature—a guard places his or her fingers into a prisoner's ears, nose, mouth, anus, or vagina. Here, prison officials must have a reasonable suspicion that is specific to the individual prisoner, such as a suspicion that a prisoner has a weapon.[68] Female prisoners also have a right to be free from unwanted sexual activity. Any unwanted sexual attention that a female inmate experiences, like leering, pinching, patting, verbal comments, and pressure to engage in sexual activity, can be considered sexual assault or harassment.[69]

Mentally Ill Inmates

The degree to which U.S. inmates suffer mental illness is indeed catastrophic (see, for example, the "Investigating Further" feature concerning Anthony Gay): The federal Bureau of Justice Statistics estimates that about one in seven state and federal prisoners and one in four jail inmates (26 percent of all female inmates, 20 percent of males) meet the threshold for serious psychological distress.[70] Many of them had been homeless in the year preceding their arrest, and about two-thirds of state prisoners with a mental health problem used drugs during the month prior to their arrest. Such individuals are often violent and may be serving long sentences; therefore, they require a high level of security and are housed with other offenders who have committed equally serious offenses and who are serving equally long sentences.[71] Indeed, prisons and jails have been referred to as America's "new asylums."[72]

Prison administrators often conduct surprise inspections (shakedowns) of inmates' cells to search for weapons and other contraband items.

Here's an example of such a condition: While in solitary confinement in a Massachusetts prison, an inmate cut his legs and arms, tried to hang himself with tubing from a breathing machine, smashed the machine to get a sharp fragment to slice his neck, and ate pieces of it, hoping to cause internal bleeding; he eventually hanged himself.[73]

The care and treatment of this group requires resources, trained staff, and appropriate facilities. Yet that is a daunting task for prison staff because, according to the Treatment Advocacy Center, prison and jail administrators are neither trained nor equipped to handle such inmates, often do not have the medications needed to treat their conditions, and sometimes rely on solitary confinement to cope with the problem. Among the solutions offered by the Treatment Advocacy Center are the following: (1) eliminate barriers to treatment in the community; (2) reform laws so that inmates can receive adequate mental health services while behind bars; (3) promote diversion programs such as mental health courts; and (4) develop release planning to increase the odds of recovery.[74]

Geriatric Inmates

Between 1995 and 2010, the number of inmates aged 55 and up (generally termed geriatric inmates) almost quadrupled, owing in part to the tough-on-crime sentencing laws of the 1980s and 1990s; by 2030, one-third of all inmates will be over 55. At the same time, it is widely accepted that prisoners age faster than the general population because they tend to arrive at prison with more health problems or develop them during incarceration.[75] Indeed, such inmates have chronic health problems (e.g., arthritis, diabetes, cardiovascular diseases, failing eyesight and hearing, and other problems), memory and cognitive problems, mental health issues, and substance abuse and other criminal histories.

A unique program at the Northern Nevada Correctional Center in Carson City, called the Senior Structured Living Program (SSLP), is designed to work with such inmates. The program provides physical fitness, diversion therapy (arts, crafts, games, reading, poetry), music (a choir and band), wellness and life skills training, individual and group therapy, and community involvement (involving area social services, veterans' groups, Alcoholics Anonymous, and other groups). Volunteers also provide psychological, spiritual, and social support to the men. To enter the program, inmates must be at least 60 years of age and not be engaged in a full-time job or educational program. The prison medical department has witnessed a significant reduction in the men's overall medical complaints, overutilization of medical care, and use of psychotropic medications.[76]

Geriatric inmates: inmates age 55 and up.

Prison Gangs

According to the National Institute of Justice, about 200,000 of the 1.5 million inmates in the United States are affiliated with gangs. An element of prisonization and a highly negative aspect of prison life is the widespread existence of prison gangs, which develop in prison for several reasons, including solidarity, protection, and power. They often continue their operations outside of the penal system.

Typically, a prison gang consists of a select group of inmates who have an organized hierarchy and who are governed by an established code of conduct. They vary from highly structured to loosely structured associations, generally have fewer members than street gangs, are structured along racial or ethnic lines, and typically are more powerful in state correctional facilities than in the federal penal system.[77]

Furthermore, gang members returning to the community from prison often adversely affect neighborhoods and foment notable increases in crime, violence, and drug trafficking.[78] Prison gangs have also made it more difficult for prison officials to maintain order and discipline[79] and have wrought a rapid increase in inmate violence—often related to increases in drug trafficking, extortion, prostitution, protection, gambling, and contract inmate murders.[80] One study of

A heavily tattooed inmate in California State Prison, Lancaster.

The aftermath of the inmate riot at the Attica Correctional Facility in September 1971, in which 10 hostages and 29 inmates were killed and 89 other persons were seriously injured.

prison gangs reported that they account for half or more of all prison problems.[81] Gang members have a belligerent attitude toward all authority and its institutions when they enter prison; members are preoccupied with status and gang rivalry. They plan boycotts, strikes, and even riots. Despite administrative attempts to accommodate gangs in some prisons, they continue to pursue "loot, sex, respect, revenge, [and] will attack any outsider."[82]

What can be done? Although controversial, there is growing interest around the country (about one-half to two-thirds of all jails and prisons) in the use of restrictive housing—administrative segregation and solitary confinement—to manage the threat posed by gangs. Removing such inmates from the general population is believed to incapacitate highly disruptive inmates, normalize prisons, soothe tensions, and deter both misbehaving inmates and the prison population at large from disruptive behavior. Such confinement has been challenged in state courts, and inmates have prevailed in some cases. For example, in California, inmates may no longer be placed in segregation simply for being a member of a gang;[83] however, inmates are typically placed in restrictive housing for disciplinary, protective, or administrative purposes, and gang members often fit one or more of those categories.[84]

Coping With Riots

It is probably a tribute to correctional institution staff members in the United States that there are not more riots and disturbances, given that the correctional officers are vastly outnumbered as a rule and the institutions essentially function with the consent and cooperation of the inmates. But institutions can go through cycles where the balance of power shifts, and inmates are dominant and staff is submissive, per studies by Lofgreen.[85] Consider the following examples of incidents in which inmates took over all or part of their institutions:

- Trouble had long been brewing at Delaware's Vaughn Correctional Center due to overcrowding, mismanagement, a cultural of negativity, and bad staff-inmate relations. In mid-2018, inmates took control of a building, killed one CO, and injured several others. An independent review found that prison administrators had long dismissed warnings of impending trouble. The two-day riot resulted in several criminal trials and a $7.55 million settlement on behalf of the slain officer and six staff members.[86]

- At the Morey Unit of the Lewis Prison Complex in Buckeye, Arizona, two inmates took two COs hostage and seized the unit's tower, triggering a 15-day standoff that remains the longest prison hostage situation in this nation's history.[87]

- Approximately 450 prisoners at the Southern Ohio Correctional Facility in Lucasville engaged in a riot, resulting in the deaths of nine inmates and one officer during the 10-day siege.[88]

- A sheriff's negotiator won the release of three employees before a SWAT team stormed the Bay County Jail in Florida. Inmates had threatened to rape and cut off the body parts of a fourth hostage, a nurse. They had taken over the jail's infirmary, and one was holding a scalpel to the nurse's neck when the SWAT team and armed COs ended the 11-hour standoff.[89]

- Permanently seared in the annals of corrections rioting are the horrific incidents at the Attica Correctional Facility in New York in 1971 (39 inmates and employees killed) and at the New Mexico State Prison in Santa Fe in 1980 (33 inmates dead).[90]

As may be seen with these tragic events, jail and prison rioting and hostage taking are potentially explosive and perilous situations from beginning to end. Hostages always are directly in harm's way, and their jeopardy is continuous and uninterrupted until they are released and safely in the hands of authorities.[91] Some inmate-involved riots and hostage situations come as a complete surprise, whereas others flow from a precipitating event or some type of a "spark."

Corrections hostage-taking events can involve any individuals, employees, visitors, or prisoners held against their will by an inmate seeking to escape, gain concessions, or achieve other goals, such as publicizing a particular cause. They can be planned or impulsive acts,[92] and they can involve one hostage or hundreds.[93] It is critical that both prisons and jails have a coordinated plan to address such incidents, not only to keep a small disturbance from escalating into a full-fledged riot but, more important, to prevent unnecessary deaths.[94]

Prisons and jails must have a coordinated plan to address riot and hostage incidents, not only to keep a small disturbance from escalating into a full-fledged riot but also to protect staff and inmates from harm. Here, correctional officers in full riot gear escort prisoners back to their quarters at Baker Community Correctional Facility in California after a riot sent several prisoners to the hospital.

PRISONERS' CONSTITUTIONAL RIGHTS

As will be seen in the following discussion, the rights and remedies available to prisoners have been expanded greatly over the past 150 years. Prison and jail administrators must know—and apply—the law in order to be in compliance with the Constitution and federal court decisions.

Demise of the Hands-Off Doctrine

Historically, the courts followed a hands-off doctrine regarding prison administration and prisoners' rights, deeming prisoners to be "slaves of the state." The judiciary, recognizing that it was not trained or knowledgeable in penology, allowed wardens the freedom and discretion to operate their institutions without outside interference, while being fearful of undermining the structure and discipline of the prison.

All that has changed, and the era of the hands-on doctrine, beginning in the mid-1960s, brought about a change of philosophy in the courts regarding prisoners' rights. Prison inmates now retain all the rights of free citizens except those restrictions necessary for their orderly confinement or to provide safety in the prison community.

Hands-off doctrine: the notion held by courts that prison administrators should be given free rein to run their prisons as they deem best.

Prisoners' rights: the collective body of rights given to inmates by the courts, in such areas as conditions of confinement, communications (mail and letters), access to law library and medical facilities, and so on.

Hands-on doctrine: the belief by courts that inmates have certain constitutional rights that the courts must see are upheld and that prison administrators must obey.

Selected Court Decisions

Following is a brief discussion of selected major U.S. Supreme Court decisions that spelled the demise of the hands-off era, while also vastly improving the everyday lives of prison and jail inmates and reforming correctional administration.

A "Slave of the State"

The 1871 case of Woody Ruffin serves as an excellent beginning point for an overview of significant court decisions concerning inmates' rights. Ruffin, an inmate in Virginia, killed a correctional officer while attempting to escape, and later challenged his conviction; the Virginia Supreme Court stated that Ruffin, like other prisoners, had "not only

"Slave of the state": an early philosophy toward prison inmates, essentially stating that inmates had no legal rights that had to be observed by prison administrators.

forfeited his liberty, but all his personal rights." The court added that inmates were "slaves of the state," losing all their citizenship rights, including the right to complain about living conditions (*Ruffin v. Commonwealth*, 1871).[95]

Legal Remedy and Access to the Courts

In *Cooper v. Pate* (1964), the Supreme Court first recognized the use of Title 42 of U.S. Code Section 1983 (discussed in Chapter 7) as a legal remedy for inmates.[96] An Illinois state penitentiary inmate sued prison officials claiming that he was unconstitutionally punished by being placed in solitary confinement and being denied permission to purchase certain religious materials. The Supreme Court decided that he was entitled to purchase the articles—and that he could use Section 1983 to sue the prison administration.

Another significant case involved the right of access to the courts. Here, a Tennessee prisoner was disciplined for assisting other prisoners in preparing their legal writs, which violated a prison regulation. The Court acknowledged that "writ writers" are sometimes a menace to prison discipline, and their petitions are often a burden on the courts. However, because the state provided no "reasonable alternative" for illiterate or poorly educated inmates to prepare appeals, the Supreme Court said inmates could not be prevented from giving such assistance to other prisoners (*Johnson v. Avery*, 1969).[97] In 1977, in another court-access decision, the Court said prisoners have a constitutional right to adequate law libraries or assistance from persons trained in the law. Alternative methods for providing such access included training inmates as paralegals; using paraprofessionals and law students to advise inmates; hiring lawyers on a part-time consultant basis; and having voluntary programs through bar associations, where lawyers make visits to the prisons to consult with inmates (*Bounds v. Smith*, 1977).[98]

Going Global

One of the World's Most Congested, Wretched Prisons

If Winston Churchill (see opening quote) were alive and could visit Haiti's National Penitentiary in Port-au-Prince, the world's most congested prison, he would be appalled. In effect this is a jail, as three-fourths of the inmates are awaiting trial. Many inmates are emaciated with sunken cheeks and protruding ribs, while living in cells made for 20 inmates that house 80 to 100 other men. Filthy conditions, malnutrition, and infectious diseases are rampant and have led to an upsurge of inmate deaths (as many as 20 per month). The corpse of an inmate who died of malnutrition might be found in a hallway shrouded beneath a plastic tarp, and some inmates must sleep in hammocks suspended from the ceiling or squeeze four to a bunk. About 80 percent of these men have not been convicted of a crime but are facing prolonged pretrial detention—some up to eight years—waiting for their chance to see a judge. Prison authorities say they try their best to meet inmates' needs but repeatedly receive insufficient funds from the state to buy food and cooking fuel, leading to deadly cases of malnutrition-related ailments such as beriberi and anemia. Inmates are fed twice a day but receive little or no protein on a diet of rice, oats, or cornmeal.[99] In sum, given the proportion of inmates held there for more than two years awaiting trial, and those who have not seen a magistrate in six months, it can be said that about 9 in 10 persons detained in Haiti's National Penitentiary are deprived of their liberty unlawfully or arbitrarily.[100]

In contrast, consider that cells in Norway's prisons have no bars on the windows and many are single occupancy. Inmates there can access vocational programs, including woodworking, assembly workshops, and even a recording studio. In Norway, removing people's freedom is considered enough of a punishment and the goal is to mimic the free world as much as possible; the recidivism rate there is 20 percent (Haiti's current rate is not available).

Source: Cristina Sterbenz, "Why Norway's Prison System Is So Successful," *Business Insider*, December 11, 2014, https://www.businessinsider.com/why-norways-prison-system-is-so-successful-2014-12.

First Amendment: Freedom of Religion and Mail Communications

A landmark 1972 case clarified the right of inmates to exercise their religious beliefs. The plaintiff, a Buddhist, was not allowed to use the prison chapel and was placed in solitary confinement on a diet of bread and water for sharing his religious material with other prisoners. The Supreme Court held that inmates with unconventional religious beliefs must be given a reasonable opportunity to exercise those beliefs (*Cruz v. Beto*, 1972).[101]

The Supreme Court has also looked at prison mail censorship regulations that permitted authorities to hold back or to censor mail to and from prisoners. The Court based its ruling not on the rights of the prisoner but, instead, on the *free-world* recipient's right to communicate with the prisoner, either by sending or by receiving mail. The court said mail censorship, if it is to be done, must be shown to enhance security, order, and rehabilitation; it must not be used simply to censor opinions or other expressions (*Procunier v. Martinez*, 1974).[102]

Eighth Amendment: Search and Seizure

Estelle v. Gamble (1976) was the first major prison medical treatment case decided by the Supreme Court.[103] Here, the Court coined the phrase "deliberate indifference," which is where the serious medical needs of prisoners involve the unnecessary and wanton infliction of pain. A Texas inmate claimed that he received cruel and unusual punishment due to inadequate treatment of a back injury sustained while he was engaged in prison work. The Court found that, because medical personnel saw him on 17 occasions during a three-month period and failed to treat his injury and related problems, such deliberate indifference to his medical needs constituted the "unnecessary and wanton infliction of pain."

Fourteenth Amendment: Due Process

The Supreme Court's decision in *Wolff v. McDonnell* (1974) is significant because, for the first time, the court acknowledged that inmates are entitled to certain due process rights during prison disciplinary proceedings.[104] McDonnell and other inmates at a Nebraska prison alleged, among other things, that disciplinary proceedings at the prison violated due process. The Court said that "there is no iron curtain drawn between the Constitution and the prisons of this country," that "a prisoner is not wholly stripped of constitutional protections." This statement has become known as the Court's "iron curtain" speech. Prisoners were given several due process rights:

- Advance written notice of charges
- A written statement as to the evidence being relied on for the disciplinary action
- Ability to call witnesses and to present documentary evidence in the inmate's defense
- Use of counsel substitutes (e.g., a friend or staff member) if the inmate is illiterate or when complex issues require such assistance
- An impartial prison disciplinary board

"Iron curtain" speech: in *Wolff v. McDonnell* (1973), the Supreme Court stated that there is no iron curtain between the Constitution and the prisons of the United States; in sum, inmates have rights.

The U.S. Supreme Court has required that inmates must be given a reasonable opportunity to exercise their religious beliefs.

You Be the...

Criminal Justice Policy Maker

For nearly a half century, multiple murderer Charles Manson, who died at age 83 in November 2017, personified a horrifying time in American culture, becoming notorious in 1969 when his followers killed seven people, including pregnant actress Sharon Tate. But even Manson had committed relationships and nearly got married while in prison.

Indeed, Manson was issued a marriage license in late 2014 to wed 26-year-old Afton Burton (nicknamed "Star"), who said she loved Manson and even left her Illinois home in order to live near Manson's place of incarceration, the California State Prison, Corcoron. (Manson later cancelled the wedding plans after learning that Star planned to put his corpse on display after his death and charge people money for the right to look at it.)

Criminologist James Alan Fox of Northeastern University characterizes such individuals as Star as "killer groupies," and notes that there is even a clinical label for them: hybristophilia, where someone is sexually aroused or attracted to a person who has committed a particularly violent crime. Some such groupies, Fox believes, are attracted to their idol's controlling, manipulative personalities, or attempt to prove that their lover is innocent or a victim of injustice. Others wish to break through their lover's vicious façade with warm feelings, while still others merely wish to acquire the glamour and celebrity status that killer groupies find exciting.

1. Should prison inmates such as Manson and others mentioned—incarcerated for heinous, capital crimes—be permitted to marry?
2. If you believe not, then should inmates convicted of nonviolent crimes (i.e., property or drug offenses) be allowed to do so?

Sources: Rogene Fisher, "What Draws People to Marry Prison Inmates?" ABC News, August 10, 2005, http://abcnews.go.com/GMA/US/story?id=889903&page=1; James Alan Fox, "Lovesick Over Charles Manson. Really?" *USA Today*, November 19, 2014, http://www.usatoday.com/story/opinion/2014/11/19/james-alan-fox-manson-nuptials/19279531/; Brad Reed, "Charles Manson Calls Off Wedding After Learning His Fiance Is Too Evil Even for Him," BGR Media, http://bgr.com/2015/02/10/charles-manson-wedding-called-off/.

PREPARATION FOR REENTRY AND AFTERCARE

Reentry and aftercare: providing services to, and supervision for, paroled inmates who are about to reintegrate into the community.

Like one who is returning home after a long hospital stay for serious illness, individuals who return to their homes after release from prison will be faced with many challenges. This process, known as reentry and aftercare, involves providing services to, and supervision for, paroled inmates who are about to reintegrate into the community. This population often has multiple deficiencies and problems: little education, poor work record and thus few job prospects, substance abuse or drug dependency, mental and physical health issues, few positive role models, and so on. It is no surprise, then, that reoffending rates upon release are high: As mentioned in Chapter 12, nearly two-thirds of all released prisoners will be rearrested within five years. Thus, it is imperative that prison be viewed as an opportunity to improve inmates' skills, treat their addictions, improve their job skills and education, and so on.[105] Evidence suggests that correctional programming should include adult drug courts, prison therapeutic communities, drug treatment, behavioral treatment, industry programs, basic adult education, and employment and vocational training.[106]

Then, as the parolee reenters the community, a comprehensive program should be in effect to monitor and assist the individual with finding housing and employment, reconnecting with family and friends, addressing any drug and alcohol problems, avoiding reoffending, and so on. Some halfway houses assist with these activities—as do reentry courts, which review the prisoner's plans and progress, oversee the prisoner's reentry, and see that he or she participates in the individualized array of transitional programs that are to be attended.[107] Studies have shown that parolees who have completed both the prison-based and the ensuing aftercare programs have fewer substance abuse problems and rearrests, compared with an untreated comparison group.[108]

/// IN A NUTSHELL

- Prison expert John DiIulio Jr. stated that incarcerated persons are not to suffer pains beyond the deprivation of liberty; confinement itself is the punishment. Furthermore, regardless of the crime, even the most heinous offender is to be treated with respect and dignity.
- Gresham Sykes described the "pains of imprisonment" as deprivations of liberty, goods and services, heterosexual relationships, autonomy, and security.
- Even with certain constitutional protections in place, there are a number of deprivations and ill effects of living in confinement, especially in solitary confinement. Prisoners use an underground economy to make their incarceration less unpleasant. In addition, inmates can become "prisonized," where they adopt the morals and values of the prison culture.
- Some wardens believe there is simply never enough money to accomplish all four goals of punishment: to *incapacitate* and *rehabilitate* offenders, and to provide *deterrence* to crime and *retribution*. Choices need to be made—bearing in mind that the warden must, first and foremost, provide for incapacitation.
- Astute prison leadership will develop a JDLR mentality—knowing when things "just don't look right." It refers to having a sense of what's going on with the inmates—"reading the yard"—and thus knowing when problems are about to erupt.
- Prison administrators and staff must have plans in place for dealing with potential (and often existing) problems such as inmates' sexual violence, drugs, gangs, and riots.
- Women who are in prison pose unique problems: They often are in poor health, they are likely to have substance abuse problems, and they have special needs in terms of the right to privacy and the Fourth Amendment (i.e., the need to be searched). The mentally ill inmate population poses special needs as well, given that many of them used drugs prior to their arrest, are violent, and require a high level of security.
- The proportion of geriatric inmates is expanding, and programs are being developed to address their needs and to keep them engaged.
- Prisons and jails are dangerous settings, and rioting and hostage taking are potentially explosive and perilous situations. It is critical that both prisons and jails have a coordinated plan to address such incidents.
- It is essential that correctional programs (e.g., drug and behavioral treatment, adult employment and education) exist to assist inmates prior to their reintegration into the community.
- Historically, the courts followed a hands-off policy regarding prisons and prisoners' rights; the hands-on era, beginning in the mid-1960s, brought about a change of philosophy in the courts regarding prisoners' rights. Prison inmates now retain all the rights of free citizens except those restrictions necessary for their orderly confinement or to provide safety in the prison community.
- Prison administrators must know and understand the constitutional rights and privileges that exist for inmates under the U.S. Constitution as well as those established by federal court decisions.

/// KEY TERMS & CONCEPTS

Review key terms with eFlashcards at **edge.sagepub.com/peak4e**.

Correctional officer 325	"Iron curtain" speech 337	Reentry and aftercare 338
Geriatric inmates 333	JDLR 327	"Slave of the state" 336
Hands-off doctrine 335	Prisoners' rights 335	Solitary confinement 325
Hands-on doctrine 335	Prisonization 322	

/// REVIEW QUESTIONS

Test your understanding of chapter content at **edge.sagepub.com/peak4e**.

1. What did Philip Zimbardo set out to prove in his mock prison experiment? What was the outcome?
2. What are the constitutional conditions of confinement, and what are the deprivations of prison life that are said to be the "pains" of imprisonment?
3. How does an inmate become "prisonized"?
4. What kinds of factors make prisons and jails dangerous in nature, and what indicators or conditions might foreshadow a riot or another type of major incident?
5. How do jails differ from prisons in terms of purpose and types of inmates?
6. What are the duties of wardens? Correctional officers?

7. What are some of the unique aspects of women being in prison in terms of their deprivations and adjustment? Of older (geriatric), mentally ill, drug-addicted, and gang-affiliated inmates?

8. What is the nature and extent of sexual violence in prisons? How is federal law attempting to reduce such victimization?

9. What kinds of correctional programming can assist with inmate reintegration into the community?

10. What major federal court decisions have been rendered concerning prisoners' rights?

/// LEARN BY DOING

1. Running a "take back the streets" anticrime campaign, a newly elected governor sends all prison wardens a letter stating in effect that prisons should not be a "Hotel Ritz" operation and that he is considering a new policy that would end all "useless educational programs beyond a GED," and "end all weight-lifting and such programs as Alcoholics Anonymous, the prison band, and gardening." The governor asks you as a warden for your viewpoint concerning these changes, particularly the following:

   a. Do such prison programs have positive benefits for the inmates? Negative aspects for the institution?

   b. Where might you try to negotiate with the governor?

2. The prison warden's associate director for security has been directed to prepare an immediate plan for dealing with the following situation:

   Inmates in the local prison are stocking up on long-term items (e.g., canned goods) in the commissary and banding together more than usual throughout the institution by racial groupings; furthermore, inmates tend to be seen standing in or near doorways, as if preparing for a quick exit. Over the past several months, the inmates have become increasingly unhappy with their conditions of confinement—not only concerning the food, but also with the increasing numbers of assaults and gang attacks. The staff members, for their part, have also become increasingly unhappy, particularly with their low salaries and benefits, perceived unsafe working conditions and attacks on officers, prison overcrowding, and a trend toward greater amounts of contraband being found in the cell blocks. They demand that the prison administration ask the parole board to grant more early releases and the courts to give more consideration to house arrest and electronic monitoring to ease the situation.

   What sort of plan should the associate warden prepare? Include in your response the critical issues that should be dealt with immediately, what steps you would take to defuse the potential for a riot, and measures that might be adopted later, in the long term, concerning staff morale and demands.

/// STUDY SITE

$SAGE edge™

Get the tools you need to sharpen your study skills. SAGE edge offers a robust online environment featuring an impressive array of free tools and resources.

Access practice quizzes, eFlashcards, video, and multimedia at **edge.sagepub.com/peak4e**.

Introducing…

SAGE vantage™

Course tools done right.

Built to support teaching. Designed to ignite learning.

SAGE vantage is an intuitive digital platform that blends trusted SAGE content with auto-graded assignments, all carefully designed to ignite student engagement and drive critical thinking. Built with you and your students in mind, it offers easy course set-up and enables students to better prepare for class.

SAGE vantage enables students to **engage** with the material you choose, **learn** by applying knowledge, and **soar** with confidence by performing better in your course.

PEDAGOGICAL SCAFFOLDING

Builds on core concepts, moving students from basic understanding to mastery.

CONFIDENCE BUILDER

Offers frequent knowledge checks, applied-learning multimedia tools, and chapter tests with focused feedback.

TIME-SAVING FLEXIBILITY

Feeds auto-graded assignments to your gradebook, with real-time insight into student and class performance.

QUALITY CONTENT

Written by expert authors and teachers, content is not sacrificed for technical features.

HONEST VALUE

Affordable access to easy-to-use, quality learning tools students will appreciate.

To learn more about **SAGE vantage**, hover over this QR code with your smartphone camera or visit **sagepub.com/vantage**

CHAPTER 14

CORRECTIONS IN THE COMMUNITY
Probation, Parole, and Other Alternatives to Incarceration

Everyone makes mistakes. It's how you respond to corrections that shows the level of your character.

—Unknown

LEARNING OBJECTIVES

As a result of reading this chapter, you will be able to

1. Describe what is meant by community corrections
2. Explain why the criminal justice system uses alternatives to incarceration
3. Describe the definitions and origins of probation and parole, as well as the differences between them
4. Identify the eligibility and rights accorded to people serving terms of probation or parole
5. Explain the functions of probation and parole officers—and the impact of high caseloads
6. List and explain the purposes and functions of several intermediate sanctions and alternatives to incarceration
7. Provide an overview of the risk-need-responsivity (RNR) model for addressing reoffending
8. Explain the rationale that underlies the use of restorative justice

ASSESS YOUR AWARENESS

Test your knowledge of probation and parole by responding to the following seven true-false items; check your answers after reading this chapter.

1. Probation began with the voluntary work of a simple Boston shoe cobbler.
2. Probation, because it is more costly than prison, is used sparingly in the United States.
3. An offender placed on parole does not serve any time in prison or jail and serves the entirety of his or her sentence in the community.
4. A person may have his or her probation revoked and then be sent to prison for behaviors such as using alcohol, violating curfew, and associating with other known criminals.
5. Persons whose probation or parole status might be revoked, and who thus might be sent to prison, enjoy no legal rights or benefits.
6. In addition to probation and parole, other alternatives to prison include house arrest, electronic monitoring, and boot camps.
7. Restorative justice places emphasis on giving victims a voice and placing greater accountability on the offender.

<< Answers can be found on page 419.

Carlos Eduardo Arevalo Carranza, 24, was arrested in March 2019, accused of stalking and then killing 59-year-old Bambi Larson of San Jose, California. When Larson did not show up for work, coworkers notified her son. He found his mother dead in her bedroom with multiple lacerations and stab wounds. Video surveillance in the area was not clear enough to provide a positive suspect identification, but police were able to trace the suspect's path and find a shirt containing both the victim's and the suspect's DNA. Police eventually arrested Carranza in connection with the murder, finding Larson's phone and e-reader in Carranza's possession at the time of arrest. The Santa Clara County District Attorney's Office charged Carranza with first-degree murder and two special circumstances of burglary and mayhem.

Carranza is a self-identified gang member and a transient, with an extensive criminal history. He had been previously charged with (and in several cases convicted of) a wide variety of crimes, including burglary, drug possession, entering and occupying a property, resisting arrest, and battery.

Although the media have given much attention to Carranza's illegal immigration status, it is also important to note that he was on probation at the time that he allegedly murdered Larson. When a person commits a crime while serving a sentence in the community (e.g., while under probation or parole supervision), we are naturally critical of the decisions made by the judge or parole board members

SAGE edge™
Master the content at edge.sagepub.com/peak4e

Authorities in Northern California are criticizing so-called sanctuary policies they say prevented federal authorities from detaining Carlos Eduardo Arevalo Carranza, who was in the country illegally before he allegedly killed a woman inside her home.

Community corrections: probation, parole, and a variety of other measures that offer convicted offenders an alternative(s) to incarceration.

involved in the case. If you had been the judge in any of Carranza's previous cases, would you have allowed this individual to serve his sentence on probation in the community? How much money should we spend to punish offenders, and what are our alternatives? As you read this chapter, think about how justice can be achieved (or not) when offenders are sentenced to corrections in the community.

INTRODUCTION

"I would like to use my college degree to help people who have gotten into trouble. Should I work in probation or parole? Should I work with adults or juveniles? And what kind of work would I be doing?" These questions have a ring of familiarity to most if not all criminal justice professors, as many students today seek to make their contributions to society by working with and trying to reform criminal offenders.

The word *probation* is probably familiar to most college and university students. If they don't "make the grades," they can be placed on academic probation; if their athletic programs fail to adhere to the rules of the National Collegiate Athletic Association (NCAA), the institution and its athletic program(s) can be placed on probationary status. The common thread here is that each group or individual is served warning that it had better change its behavior, or more severe penalties will follow. And so it is with criminal offenders—most of whom are sentenced to a *community-based* form of punishment, with probation being a commonly used form.

A majority of persons under correctional supervision are on probation or parole—together termed community corrections. Probation and parole alone represent a significant component of the U.S. criminal justice system, with about 4.5 million adults now being supervised in the community; about 3.7 million of these adults are on probation in lieu of incarceration, and the remainder are on early release from incarceration but under conditions as per terms of their parole.[1]

This chapter examines probation, parole, and a variety of other measures that constitute a broad array of alternatives to incarceration. It begins by looking at both philosophical and economic arguments for having alternatives to incarcerations, followed by discussions of the origins and contemporary aspects of probation and parole. Included are the rights that probationers and parolees have when the state wishes to remove their freedom and send them to prison, as well as the functions of probation and parole officers—including the impact of high caseloads and the debate concerning whether or not these officers should be armed. The chapter then discusses intermediate sanctions. These alternatives to incarceration may be lesser known but are still quite beneficial to offenders and help to decrease prison and jail populations; they include intensive supervision (of probation), house arrest, electronic monitoring, shock incarceration/boot camps, day reporting centers, halfway houses, and furloughs. Following a review of the risk-need-responsivity (RNR) model, which is used to assess what programs to use with offenders to stop the cycle of reoffending and reincarceration, is a discussion of a relatively new movement in criminal justice: restorative justice.

Several topics relating closely to this chapter—for example, issues facing offenders concerning release, reentry, and aftercare—were discussed in Chapter 13.

Probation: an alternative to incarceration in which the convict remains out of jail or prison and in the community and thus on the job, with family, and so on, while subject to conditions and supervision of the probation authority.

WHY ALTERNATIVES TO INCARCERATION?

The leading alternative to incarceration is probation, which was discussed briefly in Chapter 1 and is defined as the court's allowing a convicted person to remain at liberty

344 ■ Part 4: Corrections

in the community, while being subject to certain conditions and restrictions on his or her activities. The United States is not soft on crime, but there are several valid reasons for using **alternatives to incarceration**:

- It allows the offender to remain in the community, which has a greater rehabilitative effect than incarceration, thereby reducing recidivism (repeat offending).
- It allows the offender to take greater advantage of treatment or counseling options.
- It allows the offender to avoid the "pains" of imprisonment (as discussed in Chapter 13).
- It is far less expensive.
- It permits ongoing ties with family, employment, and other social networks.

Alternatives to incarceration: a sentence imposed by a judge other than incarceration, such as probation, parole, shock probation, or house arrest.

However, to be effective, a real alternative to incarceration needs to have three elements: It must incapacitate offenders enough so that it is possible to interfere with their lives and activities to make committing a new offense extremely difficult; it must be unpleasant enough to deter offenders from wanting to commit new crimes; and it has to provide real and credible protection for the community.[2]

More than a half century ago, the President's Commission on Law Enforcement and Administration of Justice (1967) endorsed community-based corrections—the use of probation and parole—as a humane, logical, and effective approach for working with and changing criminal offenders. According to the commission, that includes

> building or rebuilding solid ties between the offender and the community, obtaining employment and education, securing in the large sense a place for the offender in the routine functioning of society. This requires . . . efforts directed towards changing the individual offender (and) mobilization and change of the community and its institutions.[3]

The demand for prison space has created a reaction throughout corrections.[4] With the cost of prison construction now exceeding a quarter of a million dollars per cell in maximum-security institutions, cost-saving alternatives are becoming more attractive, if not essential.

The realities of prison construction and overcrowding have led to a search for intermediate punishments.[5] This in turn has brought about the emergence of a new generation of programs, making community-based corrections, according to Barry Nidorf, a "strong, full partner in the fight against crime and a leader in confronting the crowding crisis."[6] Economic reality dictates that cost-effective measures be developed, and this is motivating the development of intermediate sanctions.[7]

ORIGINS OF PROBATION AND PAROLE

The concepts of probation and parole have long and interesting histories.

Probation Begins: The Humble Shoe Cobbler

Although contemporary probation has roots dating to biblical times,[8] its history in the United States dates to the 19th century. "Judicial reprieve" was used in English courts to serve as a temporary suspension of sentence to allow the defendant to appeal to the Crown for a pardon. In the United States, the suspended sentence was used as early as 1830 in Boston and became widespread in American courts, even though there was no statutory provision for it. By the mid-19th century, though, many courts were using a judicial reprieve to suspend sentences.[9] This posed a legal question: Could judges suspend sentences wholesale, after trials that were scrupulously fair, simply to give the defendant a second chance?[10]

In 1916, the U.S. Supreme Court, in a decision affecting only the federal courts, held that judges did not have the discretionary authority to suspend sentences. However, the Court ruled that Congress could authorize the temporary or indefinite suspension of sentences; this led to the development of probation statutes.[11]

John Augustus, a Boston shoe cobbler, is credited as being the "father of probation." In 1841, Augustus appeared in court on behalf of a drunkard; as Augustus later explained, "I was in court one morning . . . in which the man was charged with being a common drunkard. He told me that if he could be saved from the House of Correction, he never again would taste intoxicating liquors; I bailed him, by permission of the court."[12] During his first year of service as an unpaid, volunteer probation officer, Augustus assisted 10 drunkards. By Augustus's own account, he eventually bailed "eleven hundred persons, both male and female."

Augustus performed several tasks that are reminiscent of modern probation. He investigated each case—inquiring into the offender's character, age, and influences—and kept careful records of each person's progress. His probation work soon caused him to fall into financial difficulties, however, requiring his friends' monetary assistance. Augustus died in 1859.

By 1869, the Massachusetts legislature had required that a state agent be present if court actions might result in the placement of a child in a reformatory (the forerunner of today's caseworkers). Then, in 1878, Massachusetts passed the first probation statute, mandating an official state probation system with salaried probation officers. Other states quickly followed suit:

- By 1900, Vermont, Rhode Island, New Jersey, New York, Minnesota, and Illinois passed probation laws.
- By 1910, 32 more states passed legislation establishing juvenile probation.
- By 1930, juvenile probation was legislated in every state except Wyoming.[13]

Parole Origins: Alexander Maconochie

The word *parole* stems from the French *parol*, or "word of honor," which was a means of releasing prisoners of war who promised not to resume arms in a current conflict.[14] One writer cited the year 1840 as one in which "one of the most remarkable experiments in the history of penology was initiated."[15]

In that year, Alexander Maconochie became superintendent of the British penal colony on Norfolk Island, about 930 miles northeast of Sydney, Australia. He began a philosophy of punishment based on reforming offenders: The convict was to be punished for the past while being trained for the future. Maconochie advocated open-ended ("indeterminate") sentences. His system worked, although it was harshly ridiculed by some Australians as "coddling criminals."

Returning to England in 1844, Maconochie began writing and speaking of his experiment. One of those impressed by Maconochie was Walter Crofton, who in 1854 became director of the renowned Irish system of penal management. Crofton implemented, among many other things, a "ticket of leave" system, allowing inmates to be conditionally released from prison, to be supervised by the police. Crofton recommended a similar system for the United States.

In 1876, when Zebulon Brockway was appointed superintendent of the Elmira Reformatory in New York, he drafted a statute providing for indeterminate sentences. Continued good behavior by inmates resulted in early release—America's first parole system. Paroled inmates remained under the jurisdiction of reformatory authorities for an additional 6 months, during which the parolee was required to report on the first day of every month to his appointed guardian and provide an account of his conduct and situation (a decade after Elmira began operations, New York opened three women's reformatories). This system was copied by other states; it was expanded further by the Great Depression, which abolished economic exploitation of convict labor.[16] Once introduced in the United States, parole spread fairly rapidly. In doing so, it survived an early series of constitutional challenges.[17] A 1939 survey reported that, by 1922, parole existed in 44 states, the federal system, and Hawaii.[18] Mississippi adopted a parole law in 1944, becoming the last state to do so.

Inmates on parade in Elmira's yard.

A few reasons have been offered for the relatively rapid spread of parole legislation:

- There was general dissatisfaction with the determinate sentencing provisions of the time, and parole was seen as a response to some of the criticisms: Parole would promote reformation of prisoners by providing an incentive to change; at the same time, it would serve as a means of equalizing disparate judicial sentences.[19]

- Release before sentence expiration was already an aspect of most prison systems—through "good-time" deductions, which began in New York in 1817, and through gubernatorial clemency, which was used far more extensively than today.

- Parole was believed useful for enforcing prison discipline and for controlling prison population levels.[20]

PROBATION AND PAROLE TODAY

Probation: Eligibility and Legal Rights

As noted earlier, today about 3.7 million adults are on probation in lieu of being incarcerated. As seen in Table 14.1, more than half (59 percent) of those persons were convicted for committing a felony; furthermore, about one-fourth of them committed a drug offense, while another 26 percent committed a property offense, and 20 percent committed a violent offense.[21]

Judges consider a number of factors when evaluating the eligibility of an offender for probation:

- The nature and seriousness of the current offense
- Whether a weapon was used and the degree of physical or emotional injury, if any, to the victim
- Whether the victim was an active or a passive participant in the crime
- The length and seriousness of the offender's prior record
- The offender's previous success or failure on probation
- The offender's prior incarcerations and success or failure on parole[22]

Chapter 14: Corrections in the Community ■ 347

Table 14.1 /// Characteristics of Adults on Probation, 2000, 2015, and 2016

Characteristic	2000	2015	2016
Sex	100%	100%	100%
Male	78	75	75
Female	22	25	25
Race/Hispanic origin*	100%	100%	100%
White	54	55	55
Black/African American	31	30	28
Hispanic/Latino	13	13	14
American Indian/Alaska Native	1	1	1
Asian/Native Hawaiian/other Pacific Islander	1	1	1
Two or more races	...	—	—
Status of supervision	100%	100%	100%
Active	76	76	75
Residential/other treatment program	...	1	1
Financial conditions remaining	...	2	2
Inactive	9	4	4
Absconder	9	7	7
Supervised out of jurisdiction	3	2	2
Warrant status	...	5	5
Other	3	4	4
Type of offense	100%	100%	100%
Felony	52	57	59
Misdemeanor	46	41	40
Other infractions	2	2	2
Most serious offense	100%	100%	100%
Violent	...	20	20
Domestic violence	...	4	4
Sex offense	...	4	4
Other violent offense	...	13	13
Property	...	28	26
Drug	24	25	24
Public order	24	15	17
DWI/DUI	18	13	14
Other traffic offense	6	2	2
Other**	52	12	13

Note: Detail may not sum to total due to rounding. Estimates are based on most recent data and may differ from previously published statistics. See *Methodology*. Characteristics are based on probationers with a known type of status.

—Less than 0.05%.

... Not available.

*Excludes persons of Hispanic or Latino origin, unless specified.

**Includes public order offenses.

Source: Bureau of Justice Statistics, *Probation and Parole in the United States*, April 2018, p. 17, https://www.bjs.gov/content/pub/pdf/ppus16.pdf.

Although a decision is made for the offender to remain free and avoid incarceration, the probationer must still abide by certain conditions that the court and probation officers will put in place to govern his or her behavior. If the probationer does not comply with those conditions, there are two possible types of violations that might be committed—**technical violations** or **substantive violations**:

- *Technical violations:* These may include failing to pay court costs or fines, missing a probation meeting, using alcohol, violating curfew, associating with other known criminals, failing to submit to a mandatory drug test, failing a drug test, failing to complete community service, or engaging in out-of-state travel or changing address without permission.

- *Substantive violations:* These occur when the probationer commits a new criminal offense.

Technical violation: in probation and parole, when one violates certain conditions that must be obeyed to remain out of prison, such as violating curfew, using drugs or alcohol, or not maintaining a job.

Substantive violation: an allegation that one was arrested for a new criminal offense while serving probation.

Following are several factors that the judge and prosecutor may take into account when considering a probation violation:

- The seriousness and nature of the probation violation
- The history of previous probation violations
- New criminal activity surrounding the probation violation

You Be the . . .

Judge

After 33 days of testimony from 60 witnesses and 400 pieces of evidence, a jury acquitted 25-year-old Casey Anthony in July 2011 on charges of first-degree murder in the June 2008 death of her 2-year-old daughter, Caylee. As you read in Chapter 9, after lying many times to detectives and appearing culpable under the evidence, Anthony was charged with killing Caylee by covering her mouth with duct tape (her body was found six months later in woods near Anthony's home). The defense maintained that Caylee had accidentally drowned while in her parents' care and that Anthony's father attempted to cover up the death.

After acquittal for murder (the actual cause of Caylee's death was never established, nor was Anthony's DNA found on her daughter's skeletal remains, among other evidentiary shortcomings), the only convictions that remained were for Anthony's lying to detectives about her actions and what happened to the child. The task then facing the judge was to determine whether and how to sentence Anthony. In the end, Anthony was given one year's probation for a 2010 check fraud conviction, which she served in an undisclosed Florida location. The judge who presided over the trial later stated that he believed Anthony did in fact kill Caylee, by accidentally administering too much chloroform in an effort to sedate her (during the trial, evidence showed that Anthony researched the use of chloroform, which was once used as an inhaled anesthetic during surgery).

1. Had you been the judge in this case, would you have granted probation to Anthony?
2. Why did this case, relative to most, receive and continue to receive such extraordinary public attention?
3. Do you believe Anthony would pose a danger to other children she might bear or with whom she might otherwise be associated in the future?
4. What elements might have contributed to Anthony's acquittal?

Sources: For more background and legal analysis of the case, see David Lat, "Trials and Error: The Casey Anthony Case," *Above the Law*, June 1, 2012, http://abovethelaw.com/2012/06/trials-and-error-the-casey-anthony-case/?rf=1.

- Aggravating and mitigating circumstances of the probation violation
- The probation officer's and/or probation department's view of the probation violation
- The probation violation with respect to the probation term (whether it occurred at the beginning, middle, or end of the probationary term)

About 18 percent of probationers exit probation supervision each year for some untoward reason, for example, they were incarcerated for a new crime, violated a condition of supervision, or absconded.[23] The violation of probation is a serious offense, can be a felony, and can result in a judge's revoking probation. As soon as a probation violation occurs, an arrest may soon follow, and the defendant may be ordered to appear in court for a

Investigating Further

Terms and Conditions of Probation

Rules of the Superior Court of the State of New Hampshire Applicable in Criminal Cases Filed in Superior Court

Sec. 107. The probationer shall:

(a) Report to the probation or parole officer at such times and places as directed, comply with the probation or parole officer's instructions, and respond truthfully to all inquiries from the probation or parole (P&P) officer;

(b) Comply with all orders, including orders for payment of money;

(c) Obtain permission before changing residence, employment, or traveling out of State;

(d) Notify the P&P officer immediately of any arrest or questioning by a law enforcement officer;

(e) Diligently seek and maintain lawful employment, notify employer of legal status, and support dependents to the best of your ability;

(f) Not receive, possess, control or transport any weapon, explosive or firearm, or simulated weapon, explosive, or firearm;

(g) Be of good conduct, obey all laws, and be arrest-free;

(h) Submit to reasonable searches of person, property and possessions as requested by the P&P officer and permit same to visit the residence at reasonable times, to examine and inspect conditions of probation or parole;

(i) Not associate with any person having a criminal record or with other individuals;

(j) Not indulge in the illegal use, sale, possession, distribution, or transportation, or be in the presence, of controlled drugs, or use alcoholic beverages to excess;

(k) Agree to waive extradition to the State from any State in the U.S. if directed by the P&P officer; and

(l) Comply with the following, or any other special conditions as may be imposed by the Court or the P&P board or officer:

  (1) Participate regularly in Alcoholics Anonymous;
  (2) Secure written permission prior to purchasing and/or operating a motor vehicle;
  (3) Participate in and satisfactorily complete a specific designated program;
  (4) Enroll and participate in mental health counseling on a regular basis;
  (5) Not be in the unsupervised company of minors of one or the other sex at any time;
  (6) Not leave the county without permission of the probation or parole officer;
  (7) Refrain totally from the use of alcoholic beverages;
  (8) Submit to breath, blood or urine testing for abuse substances as directed; and
  (9) Comply with designated house arrest provisions.

Source: For the purpose of brevity, this list is adapted and condensed from the original; for the complete listing of rules, see http://www.courts.state.nh.us/rules/sror/sror-h3–107.htm.

probation violation hearing. If a judge revokes probation, state laws often allow the judge to impose the maximum penalty for the charge.

Certain rights have been afforded probationers who are about to undergo a probation revocation hearing. First, in *Mempa v. Rhay* (1967), the U.S. Supreme Court held that such hearings are a "critical stage" where substantive rights could be lost, and that the Sixth Amendment therefore required the presence of counsel to help in "marshaling facts."[24] Later, in 1973, the Supreme Court decided *Gagnon v. Scarpelli*, in which a probationer had his probation revoked without a hearing; the court determined that probationers had certain due process rights, including the following:[25]

- Notice of the alleged violation
- A preliminary hearing to determine probable cause
- The right to present evidence
- The right to confront adverse witnesses
- A written report of the hearing
- A final revocation hearing

Revocation: the court's revoking probation or parole status for the purpose of returning an offender to prison (usually for not following the conditions of probation or parole, or for committing a new offense).

Parole: Eligibility and Legal Rights

Table 14.2 shows that about one-third of all parolees were incarcerated for a drug offense, one-third were incarcerated for a violent offense, and 21 percent had committed a property offense.[26]

Table 14.2 /// Characteristics of Adults on Parole, 2000, 2015, and 2016			
Characteristic	2000	2015	2016
Sex	100%	100%	100%
Male	88	87	87
Female	12	13	13
Race/Hispanic origin*	100%	100%	100%
White	38	44	45
Black/African American	40	38	38
Hispanic/Latino	21	16	15
American Indian/Alaska Native	1	1	1
Asian/Native Hawaiian/other Pacific Islander	—	1	1
Two or more races	...	—	—
Status of supervision	100%	100%	100%
Active	83	83	82
Inactive	4	5	5
Absconder	7	6	7
Supervised out of state	5	4	4
Financial conditions remaining	...	—	—
Other	1	3	2

(Continued)

Table 14.2 /// (Continued)			
Characteristic	2000	2015	2016
Maximum sentence to incarceration	100%	100%	100%
Less than one year	3	6	6
One year or more	97	94	94
Most serious offense	100%	100%	100%
Violent	. . .	32	30
. . . Sex offense	. . .	8	8
. . . Other violent offense	. . .	24	22
Property	. . .	21	21
Drug	. . .	31	31
Weapon	. . .	4	4
Other**	. . .	13	13

Note: Detail may not sum to total due to rounding. Estimates are based on most recent data and may differ from previously published statistics. Characteristics are based on probationers with a known type of status.

—Less than 0.05%.

. . . Not available.

*Excludes persons of Hispanic or Latino origin, unless specified.

**Includes public order offenses.

Source: Bureau of Justice Statistics, *Probation and Parole in the United States*, April 2018, https://www.bjs.gov/content/pub/pdf/ppus16.pdf, p. 24.

Similar to probation decision making, judges will take into account the following general criteria when considering whether or not an inmate should be granted parole:

- The nature and seriousness of the current offense, including aggravating and mitigating circumstances
- Statements made in court concerning the sentence
- The length and seriousness of the offender's prior record
- The inmate's attitude toward the offense, family members, the victim, and authority in general
- The attitude of the victim or victim's family regarding the inmate's release
- The inmate's insight into causes of past criminal conduct
- The inmate's adjustment to previous probation, parole, or incarceration
- The inmate's participation in institutional programs
- The adequacy of the inmate's parole plan, including residence and employment[27]

Like probationers, the parolee must still abide by certain conditions that the court and parole officers will put in place. As with probation, if the parolee does not comply with conditions of parole, there are two possible types of violations that might be committed:

- *Technical violations:* These may include failing to report regularly to the parole officer (PO), not keeping the PO advised of changes in address, not providing notice of change in employment, not reporting any new arrest, associating with other felons, traveling in violation of time or distance constraints, possessing weapons, using alcohol or drugs, wearing electronic monitoring device improperly, or contacting a partner who was victimized in a domestic violence case.
- *Substantive violations:* These occur when the parolee commits a new criminal offense.

One of the typical conditions placed on a probationer is that he or she submit to mandatory drug tests.

If either or a combination of these violations occurs, the parole officer may initiate charges of parole violation. The violation of parole conditions is viewed as a serious offense and can be a felony and result in a judge's revocation order. As soon as a parole violation occurs, an arrest may soon follow, and the defendant may be ordered to appear in court for a violation hearing (described more below). Over 25 percent of adult parolees exit that status each year due to some negative event; for example, they received a new sentence, parole was revoked because they committed a new crime, they violated a condition of supervision, or they absconded.[28]

Until 1972, decisions to revoke one's parole and return him or her to prison could be made arbitrarily by individual parole officers. However, the U.S. Supreme Court, in *Morrissey v. Brewer*, held in that year that parolees who faced the possibility of losing their freedom possessed certain rights under the Fourteenth Amendment:[29]

- Written notice of the alleged violation(s)
- A preliminary hearing to establish whether there is probable cause that the parolee violated the conditions of parole
- Disclosure of the evidence against the parolee
- The opportunity to be heard in person and to present witnesses and documentary evidence
- The right to confront and cross-examine adverse witnesses
- A neutral and detached body to hear the evidence
- A written statement by the fact finders concerning the evidence relied upon for any revocation decision

If the hearing officer (not necessarily a judge) finds that probable cause exists to believe that a violation has occurred, the hearing will move to the adjustment phase, which is where the information is introduced about why the individual should or should not be continued on supervision.

One of the most important groups of individuals that parole board members come in contact with is victims of crime. At one time, victims were not typically involved with the parole process in the United States, but that has changed. Through strong victim advocacy, crime victims have begun to be recognized as key stakeholders in the criminal justice process. Today, paroling authorities typically provide victims with information concerning any activity in

Chapter 14: Corrections in the Community   353

their offender's case, provide opportunities for input to the board—in person and/or in writing—and take into account the needs of and dangers to victims as part of their decision-making procedures. A number of states now appoint victims of crime or victim advocates as members of their paroling authorities.[30] Figure 14.1 shows the parole decision-making guidelines employed by the Pennsylvania Board of Probation and Parole.

Figure 14.1 /// Pennsylvania Board of Probation and Parole, Parole Decision-Making Guidelines

PENNSYLVANIA BOARD OF PROBATION AND PAROLE

PAROLE DECISION MAKING GUIDELINES

Name _____
Parole No. _____ SID No. _____ Institution No. _____
Date of Interview _____ Institution _____
Interview Type ___ Minimum ___ Review ___ Reparole Review ___ Parole Application

Violence Indicator

1. Instant Offense

   Violent ☐ +3
   Non-Violent ☐ +1

   (1) Murder, Voluntary Manslaughter, Aggravated Assault, Robbery, Arson, Burglary (Residential), Assault by Prisoner, Assault by Life Prisoner, Kidnapping, Extortion Accompanied by Threats of Violence, all Sex Crimes, and criminal attempt, criminal conspiracy, and/or criminal solicitation to commit any of the above-noted offenses.

Risk/Needs Assessment

2. Level of Service Inventory - Revised   Sex Offender Risk Assessment (Static 99)

   Raw Score: _____   Raw Score: _____

   High Risk   ☐ +3   High Risk   ☐ +3
   Medium Risk ☐ +2   Medium Risk ☐ +2
   Low Risk   ☐ +1   Low Risk   ☐ +1

   (All offenders considered for parole shall be assessed using the Level of Service Inventory - Revised ("LSI-R"). Offenders convicted of a sex offense shall be assessed using the LSI-R as well as the Sex Offender Risk Assessment Instrument. The higher level of risk shall be used for all sex offenders.

Institution Adjustment

3. Institutional Programming

   Unacceptable Program Compliance   ☐ +3
   Reasonable Efforts (2)   ☐ +2
   Currently Involved   ☐ +1
   Completion of Required Programs (3)   ☐ +0

   (2) No access or on waiting list.
   (3) Includes offenders who are currently involved and will complete prior to release

Source: Peggy B. Burke, *A Handbook for New Parole Board Members* (Washington, D.C.: U.S. Department of Justice, National Institute of Corrections, and Association of Paroling Authorities International, April 2003), pp. 41–42, http://www.apaintl.org/documents/CEPPParoleHandbook.pdf.

Note: The Level of Service Inventory—Revised (LSI-R) mentioned in the figure includes both criminal history items and measures of offender needs, such as substance abuse, employment, and special-needs accommodations. The tool is administered during a standardized, one-hour interview, and it evaluates indicators of program success (e.g., residence, family ties, employment) and predictors of program failure (e.g., prior convictions, prior failures to appear, prior violations of sentence). It includes 54 items, and responses are totaled to give a risk-needs score. *Source:* Joan Petersilia *When Prisoners Come Home* (New York: Oxford University Press, 2003), pp. 72–73.

You Be the . . .

Parole Board

Bernie Madoff's fraudulent Ponzi scheme bilked investors out of tens of billions of dollars, for which he was sentenced to 150 years in prison. Indeed, the former NASDAQ chairman victimized nearly 5,000 clients involving more than 20,000 individual investors, pension funds, corporations, universities, and celebrities; to date, several billion dollars in payouts to victims have begun. Meanwhile, as a federal prison inmate in Durham, North Carolina, Madoff, now nearly 79 years of age, is said to have an easy job selling commissary items to inmates. Reportedly, other inmates accord him great respect due to the scale of his crimes and for his refusal to implicate any of his employees in the scheme (while also providing other inmates stock tips and financial advice). He is also said to be experiencing heart problems and physical pain, having no family visitors (two sons have died since his arrest), and avoiding any responsibility or remorse for his crimes. Instead, he is said to be devoting a large amount of his time to attempting to rehabilitate his public image and shift blame to his investors—whom he argues expected unrealistic returns on their investments, which then led to his being set up for a fraud conviction. These claims have caused a former FBI profiler to deem Madoff a classic sociopath, someone who functions without a conscience and has an antisocial personality.

There appear to be two "faces" of Bernie Madoff. On the one hand, he appears to be an ailing, elderly inmate who is estranged from his family, had no prior record of violence, and is serving a lengthy sentence. On the other hand, he perpetrated the largest financial fraud in history, is apparently unwilling to accept responsibility or express remorse for his crimes, and caused devastating losses to tens of thousands of Americans. Given all that,

1. Would you vote to grant Madoff parole at the soonest possible time?
2. If not, are there rehabilitative or victim restitution programs or activities in which Madoff might participate that would help to support his being granted parole in the future?

Sources: Brian Ross, Rhonda Schwartz, and Megan Christie, "Bernie Madoff 'Doing Fine' in Prison Despite Heart Issues, Few Visitors," ABC News, February 2, 2016, http://abcnews.go.com/US/bernie-madoff-fine-prison-heart-issues-visitors/story?id=36552841.

DO PROBATION AND PAROLE WORK?

Do probation and parole work by reducing arrests? An ambitious study by California's Council of State Governments (CSG) Justice Center attempted to learn the answer, examining more than 2.5 million adult arrest, probation, and parole supervision records from 11 agencies in four cities—Los Angeles, Redlands, Sacramento, and San Francisco—over a 42-month period.[31] The CSG wanted to determine (1) the extent to which people on probation and parole contribute to crime, as measured by arrests, and (2) the types of crimes these people are most likely to commit.[32]

The findings were a bit surprising. First, people under probation or parole supervision accounted for 22 percent of total arrests—which means that nearly 8 of 10 arrestees were not supervised, certainly a respectable finding. However, one in three arrests for drug crimes involved someone who was on probation or parole—in fact, people under supervision were more likely to be arrested on drug offenses than for violent, property, or other types of crimes.[33] During the study period, the number of total arrests declined by 18 percent, while the number of arrests of people who were under supervision declined by 40 percent—61 percent for persons on parole and 26 percent for individuals under probation supervision.[34] It seems, therefore, that supervision generally works, but more work remains to be done in terms of keeping parolees and probationers from reoffending for drug abuse. Figure 14.2 displays some of the findings.

Figure 14.2 /// Do Probation and Parole Work?

RESEARCH FINDINGS

Approximately one in five arrests involved an individual under probation or parole supervision; the majority of total arrests involved people who were not under supervision.

A key objective of this study was to determine to what extent people under correctional supervision drove arrest activity. To make that determination, researchers matched arrest data with parole and probation supervision data.

Supervision Status Among All Adult Arrestees:

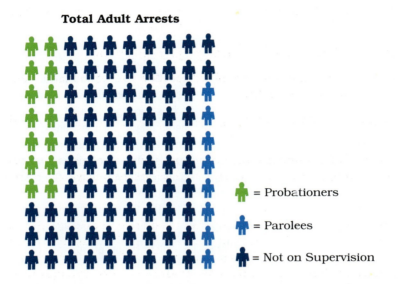

Designation	Adult arrests	% of total
Total	476,054	100%
Parolees	40,476	8.5%
Probationers	66,251	13.9%
Not Supervised	369,327	77.6%

Source: Council of State Governments Justice Center, *The Impact of Probation and Parole Populations on Arrests in Four California Cities,* January 2013, http://www.cdcr.ca.gov/Reports/docs/External-Reports/CAL-CHIEFS-REPORT.pdf, p. 14.

FUNCTIONS OF PROBATION AND PAROLE OFFICERS

Both probation and parole officers perform similar functions; in fact, in some states, the jobs of parole and probation officers are combined. Both must possess important skills, such as good interpersonal communication, decision-making, and writing skills. They operate independently, with less supervision than most prison staff experience. Both are trained in the techniques for supervising offenders and then assigned a caseload. They may be on call 24 hours a day to supervise and assist offenders at any time.[35]

Probation and "Front-End" Duties

Probation officer: one who supervises the activities of persons on probation.

Probation officers supervise offenders at the *front* end of the sentencing continuum—those offenders with a suspended prison sentence—monitoring their behavior in the community and their compliance with the conditions of probation. Probation officers usually work with either adults or juveniles exclusively. Only in small, usually rural, jurisdictions do probation officers counsel both adults and juveniles.

Probation officers have a number of duties, including

- Reporting to the court any violations of probation
- As officers of the courts, performing presentence investigations (as discussed in Chapter 9) and preparing reports concerning the clients on their caseload
- Enforcing court orders, such as arresting those who violate the terms of their probation
- Performing searches, seizing evidence, and arranging for drug testing
- Attending hearings to update the court on offenders' efforts at rehabilitation and compliance with the terms of their sentences
- Utilizing technologies as required, including electronic monitoring devices and drug screening
- Seeking the assistance of community organizations, such as religious institutions, neighborhood groups, and local residents, to monitor the behavior of many offenders[36]

Probation officers—as well as parole officers—often experience role conflict, which is brought about by what they perceive as a discrepancy between their two main functions: On the one hand, their job is to "enforce" lawful behavior of their clients, and sometimes revoke probation and parole, which is obviously more law enforcement oriented in nature; on the other hand, they must also be empathetic and understanding, and provide guidance and counseling to their clients, which is more of a social worker role.[37] These seemingly contradictory roles can contribute to job stress.

Parole and "Back-End" Duties

Parole officers perform *back-end* duties of the sentencing continuum, supervising offenders who have been released from prison. Parole officers are most often employed by the state department of corrections; the state criminal justice department; or a youth authority/juvenile corrections, county, or federal justice department. Like probation officers, parole officers supervise offenders through personal contact with the offenders and their families; this can be quite dangerous (and lead to role conflict, discussed previously), as parole officers work with paroled convicts, their friends, and their family. Like probationers, some parolees are required to wear an electronic device so that probation officers can monitor their location and movements. Parole officers' duties include

Parole officer: one who supervises those who are on parole.

- Helping parolees adjust back into society, as well as avert any actions that would jeopardize their parole status
- Developing a plan for the parolee before he or she is released from prison
- Planning employment, housing, health care, education, drug screening, and other activities that help the parolee's rehabilitation and functioning in a community environment
- Arranging for offenders to get substance abuse rehabilitation or job training
- Attending parole hearings and making recommendations based on their interviews with and surveillance of parolees[38]

Going Global

Probation Supervision

Mariel Alper, Alessandro Corda, and Kevin R. Reitz of the Robina Institute of Criminal Law and Criminal Justice compared community supervision rates in the United States with other countries throughout the world. These researchers argue that America suffers not only from "mass incarceration" but also from "mass probation." Although we commonly think of probation as an alternative to jail or prison sentences, they argue that our punitive approach to justice has led us to use all types of sanctions, including probation and incarceration, more than other countries across the world. They note that although the European countries they studied had roughly twice the population of the United States, the United States had more than 2.5 times the number of adults on probation when compared to these countries.

The United States reports an average adult probation supervision rate of 1,605 per 100,000 residents, while the other 38 countries examined report an average rate of 297 per 100,000 residents. The use of probation varies widely between U.S. states. For example, Ohio reports an average adult probation supervision rate of 2,802, whereas New Hampshire reports an average of 379. The country that comes closest to the U.S. average is Turkey, with an average adult probation supervision rate of 1,212. Including Turkey, only five other countries have rates higher than the state with the lowest average (New Hampshire): Latvia (837), Poland (554), Estonia (503), Hungary (399), and France (399).

Source: To review the data brief produced by the Robina Institute of Criminal Law and Criminal Justice, visit https://robinainstitute.umn.edu/publications/data-brief-american-exceptionalism-probation-supervision.

The Burden of Large Caseloads

Caseload: the number of cases awaiting disposition by a court, or the number of active cases or clients maintained by a probation or parole officer.

Caseload refers to the average number of cases supervised by a probation or parole officer in a given period. Each case represents an offender on probation or parole supervised by an individual officer. As John Conrad observed,

> There is much that a good probation/parole officer can do for the people on his or her caseload. A parole officer who makes it clear that, "fellow, if you don't watch your step I'm gonna run your ass right back to the joint," is not in a position to be helpful as a counselor or facilitator. With the best intentions, a[n] officer struggling with the standard unwieldy caseload of 100 or more will deal with emergencies only, and sometimes will not be able to do that very well.[39]

As noted earlier, about 4.5 million persons are on either probation or parole in the United States. Is there a precise number of offenders who can be supervised effectively by an officer? The answer is no, because the number of offenders an officer can supervise effectively is a function of the type of offenders being supervised by certain officers; all offenders and officers are unique and bring different knowledge, skills, capacities, and competencies. The American Probation and Parole Association (APPA) asks the question, rhetorically,

> How many patients can a surgeon operate on in a given day? How many cars can a mechanic fix each week? How many haircuts can a barber complete in a month? It does not take an expert in any of these fields to realize the answer normally is that *it depends*.[40]

Of course, caseload size can affect the quality of supervision that an officer is able to provide—and can also bring the glare of the media when something goes horribly wrong. For example, a newspaper in Detroit published an exposé titled "Felons on Probation Often Go Unwatched." The article reported that the county had roughly 30,000 probationers and approximately 250 officers to supervise them—an average of nearly 120 offenders per officer. In one case, an officer was fired after a probationer was arrested for attempted murder and engaging in a shootout with police. The probationer was a fugitive, missing several office visits, but he was never reported as an absconder, nor was he listed as a fugitive at the time of the shooting. According to the article, the probation officer "was so overworked that she failed to get an arrest warrant for [the probationer] when he became a fugitive for missing his monthly probation office appointment. [The officer] still hadn't done so by March 28 when he was arrested."[41]

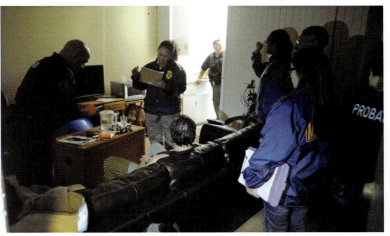

Probation officers monitor offenders' behavior in order to check their compliance with the conditions of their probation. These probation officers are performing a compliance sweep at a probationer's home.

The APPA points out that caseload sizes have long been too large, and for several identifiable reasons:

> For at least the past four decades it has been well-known to professional insiders that probation and parole officer workloads exceed realistic potential for accomplishing the numerous tasks required to supervise offenders. The point here is that many departments are increasing caseloads to well over 200 offenders per officer, making it virtually impossible for offenders to receive adequate attention and interaction from officers to have any substantial rehabilitative effect. Compounding these issues is the current trend of concentrating on sex offenders, the infusion of electronic monitoring technologies, and increasing the use of probation for higher-risk offenders as well as widening the justice net to low risk offenders.[42]

To Arm or Not to Arm

Whether probation and parole officers should be armed has also been debated. Traditionalists believe that carrying a firearm contributes to an atmosphere of distrust between the client and the officer; they argue that if officers carry weapons, they are perceived differently than as counselors or advisors, whose purpose is to guide offenders into treatment and self-help programs. Conversely, some people view a firearm for these officers as essential for protecting them from the risks associated with confronting violent, serious, or high-risk offenders.[43] Officers must visit homes and places of employment in the neighborhoods in which offenders live; some of these areas are not safe. Equally or more dangerous is when officers must revoke parole or probation, which could result in the offender's imprisonment.

There is no national or standard policy regarding weapons, and officers themselves are not in agreement about being armed. Some states classify probation and parole officers as peace officers and grant them the authority to carry a firearm both on and off duty.[44] In sum, it would seem that the prudent decision concerning arming should be based on the need, officer safety, and local laws and policies.

OTHER ALTERNATIVES: INTERMEDIATE SANCTIONS

Intermediate sanctions: forms of punishment that are between freedom and prison, such as home confinement and day reporting.

In addition to the diversionary (or problem-solving) drug, mental health, and other specialty courts discussed in Chapter 9 that are reducing jail and prison populations, there are corrections programs—intermediate sanctions—that are less restrictive than total confinement but more restrictive than probation and that reduce those populations as well. In fact, a survey by the federal Bureau of Justice Statistics found that in addition to the 745,200 persons who are confined in U.S. jails, approximately 55,900 are supervised outside the jail facility under electronic monitoring, home detention, day reporting, community service, treatment programs, and other pretrial and work programs.[45] These and other forms of supervision are discussed in the following sections.

Intensive Supervision Probation and Parole

Intensive supervision probation and parole: post-release supervision that usually includes much closer and stricter supervision, more contact with offenders, more frequent drug tests, and other such measures.

Since their beginning, intensive supervision probation and parole have been based on the premise that increased client contact would enhance rehabilitation while affording greater client control. Current programs are largely a means of easing the burden of prison overcrowding.[46]

Intensive supervision programs can be classified into two types: those stressing diversion and those stressing enhancement. A *diversion program* is commonly known as a "front door" program because its goal is to limit the number of generally low-risk offenders who enter prison. An *enhancement program* generally selects already-sentenced probationers and parolees and subjects them to closer supervision in the community than they receive under regular probation or parole.[47] As of 1990, jurisdictions in all 50 states had instituted *intensive supervision probation* (ISP). Persons placed on ISP are supposed to be those offenders who, in the absence of intensive supervision, would have been sentenced to imprisonment. Although ISP is invariably more costly than regular supervision, the costs "are compared not with the costs of normal supervision but rather with the costs of incarceration."[48]

ISP is demanding for probationers and parolees and does not represent freedom; in fact, it may stress and isolate repeat offenders more than imprisonment does. Given the option of serving prison terms or participating in ISPs, many offenders have chosen prison.[49] Consider the alternatives now facing offenders in one western state:

- *ISP:* The offender serves two years under this alternative. During that time, a probation officer visits the offender two or three times per week and phones on the other days. The offender is subject to unannounced searches of his or her home for drugs and has his or her urine tested regularly for alcohol and drugs. The offender must strictly abide by other conditions as set by the court: not carrying a weapon, not socializing with certain persons, performing community service, and being employed or participating in training or education. In addition, he or she will be strongly encouraged to attend counseling and/or other treatment, particularly if he or she is a drug offender.

- *Prison:* The alternative is a sentence of two to four years, of which the offender will serve only about three to six months. During this term, the offender is not required to work or to participate in any training or treatment but may do so voluntarily. Once released, the offender is placed on a two-year routine parole supervision and must visit his or her parole officer about once a month.[50] Although evidence of the effectiveness of this program is lacking, it has been deemed a public relations success.[51] Intensive supervision is usually accomplished by severely reducing caseload size per probation or parole officer, leading to increased contact between officers and clients or their significant others (such as spouse or parents).[52]

Practitioner's Perspective

Probation Officer

Name: Jessica Johnston
Position: Probation Officer
Denver, Colorado

What is your career story? I was always interested in the field of justice, but I never really had a strong concept of how that would look as a career. So I studied it in school. I got a bachelor's degree in sociology and psychology, and then went on to pursue a master's degree in criminology. It was then that I realized I really wanted to have direct service experience. So probation was just a really natural fit given the academic studies that I had pursued. I originally started in a municipal probation office, where I handled municipal violations, city ordinance violations, and other things like that. I ultimately moved into a state and county probation office. I think probation is this wonderful opportunity for intervention in people's lives, and it offers them a chance to stay connected in the community and really make the necessary changes in the least invasive way possible.

What misconceptions do you often hear about this position? I've encountered a couple common misconceptions about probation officers. The first one is that we're the tough guy, that we're really throwing the book at folks and all the emphasis is on accountability. But what you find when you start working in the field is that you wear many hats. Yes, you are a source of accountability for probationers, but you're also a resource for them. You help connect them to services they really need in order to make a meaningful change in their lives. That gets lost on a lot of people who don't work in the field, that the role is much more of a relationship where you build a rapport, and you really try to help people to take control of their circumstances. Another big misconception is that a lot of people who enter this field, including myself, really want to work with the highest risk people, the worst of the worst. But when you start out, you often start with the lower risk caseloads, so you can get your feet wet and learn the ropes. I actually came to enjoy working with low- and moderate-risk clients far more, because what I found was that on probation, most people are actually ordinary people that have made a mistake or have an unresolved problem or issue. It's really an exciting experience to be part of an intervention that helps them self-correct or get them the help they need.

What role does diversity play in this position? The front line of probation is dominated by women, which is different from how it was historically. I do think that management positions continue to be held by more males. That's slowly changing, but I still see that divide between men in management and women as front-line workers. In terms of the clientele, it's really contextualized by the jurisdiction you're in. There are a lot of rural places in Colorado that just don't have the diversity that urban Denver does, so we've had a lot of conversations about what our client population looks like and whether that's reflective of what it should look like. We're moving in the right direction, but we still see a lot of disproportionate representation of minorities, and we see them underrepresented in the specialized programs. Where I worked was an urban area, so we had officers of every race. We also had a number of officers who spoke Spanish, which was critical because we had a large Hispanic population in our area. We absolutely needed officers who came with the interpretation skills and were able to converse with clients and work with them just as we did with our English-speaking clients.

To learn more about Jessica Johnston's experiences as a probation officer watch the Practitioner's Perspective video in SAGE vantage.

Electronic monitoring systems are particularly useful for high-risk offenders, especially sex offenders for whom use of a global positioning system (GPS) is desirable.

House arrest/home confinement: detention of offenders in their own homes; compliance is often monitored electronically.

Electronic monitoring: use of electronic devices (bracelets or anklets) to emit signals when a convicted offender (usually on house arrest) leaves the environment in which he or she is to remain.

This point also can be illustrated with a case in Colorado, in which a felon convicted of sexual exploitation of a child asked the court to send him to prison, rather than serving out 20 years on ISP.[53] The court agreed to revoke his probation, and he was sentenced to 12 years in prison. At the hearing, the offender argued that he did not want to be in the "probation/treatment" trap any longer.[54]

House Arrest

Since the late 1980s, house arrest (also known as home confinement) has become increasingly common. With house arrest, offenders receive a "sentence" of detention in their own homes, and their compliance is often monitored electronically. The primary motivation for using this intermediate sanction is a financial one: the conservation of scarce resources. Note that house arrest is often used in tandem with electronic monitoring, discussed in the next section.

Many people apparently feel that house arrest is not effective or punitive enough for offenders. Indeed, one study reported that only about 20 percent of the public think prisoners could be safely released into the community, even if under supervision;[55] and nearly half (44 percent) of the public feel that house arrest is not very effective or not effective at all.[56] Does house arrest work? Looking at a sample of 528 adult felony offenders who had been released from house arrest, Jeffery Ulmer found that the sentence combination associated with the least likelihood of rearrest was house arrest/probation.[57] The combinations of house arrest/work release and house arrest/incarceration were also significantly associated with decreased chances of rearrest compared to traditional probation. Furthermore, whenever any other sentence option was paired with house arrest, that sentence combination significantly reduced the chances of rearrest and the severity of rearrest charges.[58] House arrest puts the offender in touch with opportunities and resources for rehabilitative services (substance abuse or sex offender counseling, anger management classes, and so on), which supports the contention that for intermediate sanctions of any type to reduce recidivism, they must include a rehabilitative emphasis.[59]

Electronic Monitoring

Electronic monitoring (EM) or supervision can be used for a variety of offenders, but it is particularly useful for high-risk offenders, especially sex offenders for whom use of a global positioning system (GPS) is desirable.[60] The Urban Institute, in conjunction with the District of Columbia Crime Policy Institute, reports that EM reduces arrests by 24 percent, on average, for program participants.[61] Estimates suggest that EM costs about $750 per day and saves society $5,300 per program participant.[62]

Some early forms of EM technology are still in use today. There are two basic types of EM devices: active and passive. Active forms are continuous signaling devices attached to the offender that monitor his or her presence at a particular location. A central computer accepts reports from the receiver-dialer over telephone lines, compares them with the offender's curfew schedule, and alerts correctional officials to unauthorized absences.[63] Simpler systems consist of only two basic components: a transmitter and a portable receiver. The transmitter, which is strapped to the offender's ankle or wrist or worn around the neck, emits a radio signal that travels about one city block. By driving past the offender's residence, his or her place of employment, or wherever he or she is supposed to be, the officer can verify the offender's presence with the handheld portable receiver.⁶⁴ The passive type of EM involves the use of programmed devices that contact the offender periodically to verify his or her presence. One system uses voice verification technology. Another system uses satellite technology; the subject wears an ankle bracelet and carries or wears a portable tracking device about the size of a small lunchbox and weighing 3.5 pounds. A GPS satellite constellation is able to establish an offender's whereabouts within 150 feet of his or her location 24 hours a day.⁶⁵ However, technology is evolving and offender tracking systems continue to improve. The National Institute of Justice recently released a report specifying national minimum performance requirements and testing methods for EM devices to enhance public safety.⁶⁶

Correctional boot camps, also called shock incarceration, have been used in jails and prisons to place offenders in a quasi-military program to instill discipline and thus reduce recidivism, prison and jail populations, and operating costs.

Shock Probation/Parole

Shock probation/parole is another less costly intermediate alternative to incarceration that is supported by many correctional administrators. Typically used for first-time or early-career lower-level offenders who are eligible (drug crimes, larceny/theft), this form of corrections combines a brief exposure to incarceration with subsequent release. It allows sentencing judges to reconsider the original sentence to prison and, upon motion, to recall the inmate after a few months in prison and place him or her on probation, under conditions deemed appropriate. The idea is that the "shock" of a short stay in prison will give the offender a taste of institutional life and will make such an indelible impression that he or she will be deterred from future crime and will avoid the negative effects of lengthy confinement.⁶⁷ Like other alternatives to incarceration, shock probation can result in a cost savings (compared to longer term incarceration) and can provide the offender with community resources once on supervised probation.

Shock probation/parole: a situation in which individuals are sentenced to jail or prison for a brief period, to give them a taste or "shock" of incarceration and, it is hoped, turn them into more law-abiding citizens.

Boot Camps/Shock Incarceration

Correctional boot camps, also called shock incarceration, were first implemented as an intermediate sanction in 1983.⁶⁸ Early versions of boot camps placed offenders in a quasi-military program of 36 months' duration similar to a military basic training program. The goal was to reduce recidivism, prison and jail populations, and operating costs. Offenders generally served a short institutional sentence and then were put through a rigorous regimen of drills, strenuous workouts, marching, and hard physical labor. To be eligible, inmates generally had to be young, nonviolent offenders.

Unfortunately, early evaluations of boot camps generally found that participants did no better than other offenders without this experience.⁶⁹ The National Institute of Justice, in an overview of correctional boot camp research, reports that boot camps are generally not effective in reducing recidivism.⁷⁰ Only boot camps that were carefully designed, targeted the right offenders, and provided rehabilitative services and aftercare were deemed likely to save the state money and reduce recidivism.⁷¹ As a result of these findings, the number of boot camps declined; by the year 2000, only 51 prison boot camps remained.⁷² So-called second-generation boot camps have evolved over time, however, and added

Boot camp: a short-term jail or prison program that puts offenders through a rigorous physical and mental regimen designed to instill discipline and respect for authority.

Investigating Further

Success for the Waukesha County, Wisconsin, Day Report Center

Begun in 2007, the Waukesha County, Wisconsin, Day Report Center has received praise from county officials for its contribution to public safety and prisoner rehabilitation. Officials have concluded that—at least for many offenders—jail is not necessary, offenders can be held accountable in other ways, and offenders should be given a chance and support to change their behavior.

A county circuit judge called the Day Report Center's establishment and success his proudest accomplishment in six years on the job. According to program statistics, the Day Report Center has experienced an 85 percent success rate with offenders who have successfully completed a regimen of drug and alcohol testing, electronic monitoring, job searches, community service, and regular meetings with case managers (who connect with, monitor, advise, encourage, and support the clients).

The program, established in an open hallway area of a jail, now has several offices and a group meeting room so that participants can meet with staff. The program has 50 participants, many of whom have been convicted of drunken driving but also including those convicted of other nonviolent misdemeanors and felonies.

Judges order Day Report Center reporting in addition to or as a condition of sentences, while the sheriff uses it as a supplement for some inmates who are released on electronic monitoring. Officials also say it has reduced crowding in jails and has changed clients' behavior.

Sources: Adapted from Laurel Walker, "Officials Laud Success of Waukesha County Day Report Center," http://www.jsonline.com/news/waukesha/waukesha-county-day-report-centers-success-lauded-0h40u0c-144731385.html; also see Court Services and Community Alternatives, "Waukesha Day Report Center," http://archive.jsonline.com/news/waukesha/waukesha-county-day-report-centers-success-lauded-0h40u0c-144731385.html.

---

components such as alcohol and drug treatment and social skills training (some even include postrelease electronic monitoring, house arrest, and random urine tests); some boot camps have also substituted an emphasis on educational and vocational skills for the military components.[73] As an example of the latter, Pennsylvania's Motivational Boot Camp—one that combined militaristic exercise with multilayered treatment—had disappointing results with recidivism when boot camp participants were compared to those released from prison; however, more encouraging results were found regarding recidivism for participants who were employed or were repeat offenders. On average, a boot camp sentence reduced a prison stay by one year.[74]

Day Reporting Centers

Another intermediate sanction that has recently gained popularity among correctional administrators and policy makers is the day reporting center (DRC). DRCs are places where offenders report with some frequency (usually once or twice a day); treatment services (job training and placement, counseling, and education) are usually provided at the DRCs, either by the agency running the program or by other human services agencies.[75]

The purposes of DRCs are to heighten control and surveillance of offenders placed on community supervision, increase offender access to treatment programs, give offenders more proportional and certain sanctions, and reduce prison or jail crowding. One study of the effect of DRCs on recidivism, however, found no significant reduction in the rate of rearrest.[76]

Day reporting center: a structured corrections program requiring offenders to check in at a community site on a regular basis for supervision, sanctions, and services.

Halfway Houses

Another approach to rehabilitation and incarceration is the halfway house (often called a community correctional center, a residential rehabilitation center, or, at the federal level, a residential reentry center). Here, convicted individuals who are serving alternative sentences or who have been released early from jail or prison live in a state-run or for-profit facility in hopes of transitioning to life outside. Like most reentry programs that attempt to transition offenders back into communities, the research on halfway house effectiveness is mixed. Some studies show declines in recidivism, while others show no effect on reoffending.[77] The idea of housing certain convicts in a less punitive setting was emphasized in 1961 by then–U.S. attorney general Robert Kennedy as a means of grooming young offenders for a law-abiding life.[78] Generally, such facilities are to provide a safe, structured, supervised environment, as well as employment counseling, job placement, financial management assistance, and other programs and services.[79]

Halfway house: a community center or home staffed by professionals or volunteers designed to provide counseling to ex-prisoners as they transition from prison to the community.

Furloughs

Another means by which a prison or jail inmate can leave a correctional facility is via furlough. For jail inmates, the purpose of furlough is commonly to allow—on a limited-time basis—them to obtain medical or mental health treatment, attend the birth of a child or a relative's funeral, and so on. For prison inmates, the release is also typically for a limited-time basis and for one of the following reasons: to transfer from one correctional facility to another or to home confinement, to attend to a family crisis or other urgent situation, or to engage in structured group programs (usually for vocational, medical, religious, educational, or recreational reasons) for a short period of time.[80]

CONFRONTING RECIDIVISTS: THE RISK-NEED-RESPONSIVITY (RNR) MODEL

How can the cycle of reoffending and reincarceration be stopped? Should an offender be confined in prison, placed on community supervision, or both? Several decades of research and experience have provided specific programs—practices and principles—that, when implemented, can answer this age-old question.

First, it is imperative that an offender's future risk for reoffending be assessed and that it be possible to do so. As an example, in 2009 the Washington state legislature required its department of corrections to develop and use an instrument that has the "highest degree of predictive accuracy" for assessing an offender's risk of reoffense. After considering a number of such instruments, five assessment tools were selected and used for this purpose.[81] Next, what kinds of programs should be used with these offenders who are in jails and prisons, and on probation and parole? Such approaches are known collectively as the risk-need-responsivity (RNR) model. In short, they operate on the assumption that using trained personnel to identify individual offenders' risks and needs—and then responding to those needs with the best combination of services and supervision—can lead to a significant reduction in recidivism.[82] Offenders' risk levels are determined by certain factors or characteristics that can be changed through intervention: one's antisocial behavior, close association with known offenders, poor family and/or marital relationships, bad school or work relationships, and substance abuse. Once these risks are identified, specific treatment interventions can be put in place to reduce offenders' likelihood of continuing criminality.[83] Screening and assessment instruments are used for these purposes within the corrections field. Dozens of studies have shown, unequivocally, that using RNR principles of offender

Figure 14.3 /// Center for Advancing Correctional Excellence Criminal Cognitions Scale, RNR Simulation Tool

Externalization of Blame

Statement	Strongly Disagree	Disagree	Agree	Strongly Agree
Bad childhood experiences are partly to blame for my current situation.	○	○	○	○
I feel like what happens in my life is mostly determined by powerful people.	○	○	○	○
Because of my history I get blamed for a lot of things I did not do.	○	○	○	○
Sometimes I cannot control myself.	○	○	○	○
I am just a "born criminal."	○	○	○	○

Notions of Entitlement

Statement	Strongly Disagree	Disagree	Agree	Strongly Agree
When I want something, I expect people to deliver.	○	○	○	○
I will never be satisfied until I get all that I deserve.	○	○	○	○
I expect people to treat me better than other people.	○	○	○	○
I insist on getting the respect that is due me.	○	○	○	○
I deserve more than other people.	○	○	○	○

Devaluing Authority

Statement	Strongly Disagree	Disagree	Agree	Strongly Agree
Most of the laws are good.	○	○	○	○
Most police officers/guards abuse their power.	○	○	○	○
People in authority are usually looking out for my best interest.	○	○	○	○
If a police officer/guard tells me to do something, there's usually a good reason for it.	○	○	○	○
People in positions of authority generally take advantage of others.	○	○	○	○

Immediate Gratification

Statement	Strongly Disagree	Disagree	Agree	Strongly Agree
The future is unpredictable and there is no point planning for it.	○	○	○	○
Even though I got caught, it was still worth the risk.	○	○	○	○
Why plan to save for something if you can have it now?	○	○	○	○
I think it is better to enjoy today than worry about tomorrow.	○	○	○	○
I do not like to be tied down to a regular work schedule.	○	○	○	○

Insensitivity to Impact of Crime

Statement	Strongly Disagree	Disagree	Agree	Strongly Agree
My crime(s) did not really harm anyone.	○	○	○	○
A theft is all right as long as the victim is not physically injured.	○	○	○	○
Victims of crime usually get over it with time.	○	○	○	○
When you commit a crime the only one affected is the victim.	○	○	○	○
Society makes too big of a deal about my crime(s).	○	○	○	○

Source: Adapted from Jeffrey Stuewig, Emi Furukawa, Sarah Kopelo, June Price Tangney, Sarah Kopelovich, Patrick J. Meyer, and Brandon Cosby, "Reliability, Validity, and Predictive Utility of the 25-Item Criminogenic Cognitions Scale (CCS)," *Criminal Justice and Behavior* 39 (October 2012): pp. 1340–1360.

rehabilitation significantly reduces recidivism.[84] Although a one-size-fits-all model has been used in the past, recent advancements in this field have suggested the need for culturally specific and gender-specific tools to enhance RNR effectiveness.[85] Figure 14.3 shows the kinds of questions used in an RNR assessment tool.

RESTORATIVE JUSTICE

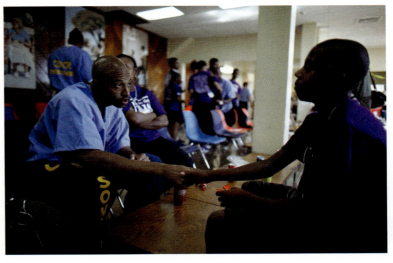

In the view of many American citizens, a major shortcoming in the criminal justice system is that it considers crime as an act against the *state*, rather than against *people*, and thus removes human victims and their voices from the entire process. They believe that, even though costs of prisons and jails have skyrocketed (now estimated at a minimum of $71 billion),[86] we are not safer. Meanwhile, most offenders while away their time in prisons and jails without any encouragement or incentive to take responsibility for their crimes and are not changed upon release, leaving their victims dissatisfied with the entire experience.

Restorative justice works to remove the barriers between victims and offenders, who many times have a strong desire to meet each other and to discuss the criminal event that brought them together. It is victim driven, emphasizing ways to transform offenders by learning of the harms they perpetrated against the victim and community and making them more accountable (and thus less likely to recidivate). It can involve victims and offenders having a dialogue by meeting face-to-face or merely exchanging letters, and any type of crime. Although difficult for offenders to do, it can be for them (and their victims) a very satisfying and rewarding experience that is critical to restoration and healing.

A national organization, Restorative Justice International, provides a wealth of information about restorative justice efforts both in the United States and abroad, as well as a short, informative video (see http://www.restorativejusticeinternational.com/about/).

Restorative justice maintains that crime affects not only the victim but the entire community as well, so it involves meetings including the offender, the victim, and members of the community in order to devise a rehabilitative plan to make them whole again.

Restorative justice: the view that crime affects the entire community, which must be healed and made whole again through the offender's remorse, community service, restitution to the victim, and other such activities.

/// IN A NUTSHELL

- Probation involves a court allowing a convicted person to remain at liberty in the community, subject to certain conditions and restrictions; similarly, parole is the conditional release of a prisoner but before the prisoner's full sentence has been served. Both allow the offender to remain in the community to take advantage of treatment or counseling, maintain family and employment ties, and so on.

- If one is allowed to be placed on probation, the probationer must still abide by certain conditions. A technical violation occurs when, for example, the probationer fails to pay court costs or fines, misses a probation meeting, uses alcohol, or violates curfew. A substantive violation occurs when the probationer commits a new crime.

- Because they may lose their freedom, probationers are allowed to have counsel present at the probation revocation hearing; other due process rights are afforded as well.

- Parolees must also abide by certain conditions that the court and parole officers put in place. If they do not comply, parole may be revoked and the parolee returned to prison. Parolees also have certain due process rights prior to revocation.

- Probation officers perform duties such as reporting to the court any violations of probation, performing presentence investigations, arresting those who violate the terms of their probation, performing searches, seizing evidence, and arranging for drug testing.

- Parole officers supervise offenders who have been released from prison through personal contact with offenders and their families. They help parolees adjust back into society, developing a plan for employment, housing, health care, education, drug screening, and other activities.
- Whether probation and parole officers should be armed has been a debated topic in corrections; there is no national or standard policy for these personnel regarding weapons, and officers themselves are not in agreement about being armed.
- A number of intermediate sanctions are used in attempting to further rehabilitative efforts and to reduce jail and prison populations. These include intensive supervision probation and parole, house arrest, electronic monitoring, shock probation/parole, boot camps/shock incarceration, day reporting centers, halfway houses, and furloughs.
- To avoid reincarceration, offenders' future risk for reoffending must be assessed; approaches used are known as the risk-need-responsivity (RNR) model.
- Restorative justice holds that the first priority of justice processes is to assist victims, whereas the second priority is to restore the community.

/// KEY TERMS & CONCEPTS

Review key terms with eFlashcards at **edge.sagepub.com/peak4e**.

Alternatives to incarceration   345
Boot camp   363
Caseload   358
Community corrections   344
Day reporting center   364
Electronic monitoring   362
Halfway house   365
Home arrest/home confinement   362
Intensive supervision probation and parole   360
Intermediate sanctions   360
Parole officer   357
Probation   344
Probation officer   356
Restorative justice   367
Revocation   351
Shock probation/parole   363
Substantive violation   349
Technical violation   349

/// REVIEW QUESTIONS

Test your understanding of chapter content at **edge.sagepub.com/peak4e**.

1. What is meant by the term *community corrections*?
2. What historical events led to modern-day probation? Parole?
3. What are the rights granted by the U.S. Supreme Court to people who are on probation and parole in general? When the state wishes to revoke their probation/parole status and send them to prison?
4. What are some examples of technical and substantive conditions that correctional agencies commonly apply to probationers and parolees?
5. Why does the criminal justice system use alternatives to incarceration?
6. How would you describe the primary functions of probation and parole officers, and the impact of high caseloads in terms of how these officers are able to achieve their goals?
7. How would you describe the arguments for and against arming probation and parole officers?
8. What are the purposes and functions of intermediate sanctions, including intensive supervision, house arrest, electronic monitoring, shock probation/parole, shock incarceration/boot camps, day reporting centers, halfway houses, and furloughs?
9. How does the risk-need-responsivity model work with offenders to stop the cycle of reoffending and reincarceration?
10. What is the meaning and purpose of the restorative justice concept, and how does it function?

/// LEARN BY DOING

1. You graduated recently with a criminal justice degree and are now employed as a state probation and parole officer. You are asked by a criminal justice professor at a nearby college to guest lecture in an introduction to criminal justice course concerning the primary challenges of working in probation and parole. Develop a presentation for the class.

2. Assume it is your first day working as a state probation and parole officer and your new training officer says the following:

    Hi, nice to meet you. I'm Chuck, the training advisor. Here's what I tell everyone on their first day. First, the real world is different from what you've been told in college classes. Politicians promise the public that they will get tough on crime, so first off they spend money for more police officers. No one gets elected by promising to build more courts, or add more probation and parole officers. Eventually having more police means the courts get backlogged, which in turn crowds the prisons and the jails, puts more people on probation, and forces the parole board to grant more early releases. Meanwhile, our average caseload increases by 50 percent. We also have more drug and sex offenders than we know what to do with. We spend too much time bailing water out of the boat, with no one steering, so we are just drifting in circles. To vent the frustrations, about once a week the gang and I hold "choir practice" at a bar down the street. After about five or six beers and some carousing and loud singing, then this job looks a lot better.

a. Should Chuck be retained as a training officer? Why or why not?
b. How would changes in politics affect the corrections system directly and indirectly?
c. Do you believe Chuck's comments are accurate concerning the police getting so much new funding—and the subsequent impacts on courts and corrections?
d. Why do crowded jails and prisons make the job of parole officers more difficult?
e. If you were Chuck's supervisor and heard others discussing their frequent "choir practices" at the bar, would you attempt to discontinue such gatherings or leave the situation alone?

3. Your criminal justice instructor has assigned a class debate concerning the use of incarceration versus alternatives to incarceration (e.g., probation and parole, electronic monitoring, house arrest, halfway houses). What will be your argument?

/// STUDY SITE

Get the tools you need to sharpen your study skills. SAGE edge offers a robust online environment featuring an impressive array of free tools and resources.

Access practice quizzes, eFlashcards, video, and multimedia at **edge.sagepub.com/peak4e**.

SPANNING THE SYSTEM
Methods and Issues

PART 5

Chapter 15: Juvenile Justice: Philosophy, Law, and Practices
Chapter 16: On the Crime Policy and Prevention Agenda: Drug Abuse, Sex Trafficking, Terrorism, and Immigration

This part contains two chapters. **Chapter 15** examines juvenile justice—an area in which the treatment of offenders is quite different from that of adults in terms of its overall philosophy, legal bases, and judicial process. Included are the history and extent of juvenile crime, risk assessment (of offending), the case flow of juvenile courts, labeling, whether there is a school-to-prison pipeline, youth gangs, and juveniles' legal rights.

Chapter 16 provides an in-depth view of four particularly challenging problems and policy issues confronting society and the criminal justice system today: drug abuse, sex trafficking, terrorism, and immigration.

REUTERS/Stringer Mexico

CHAPTER 15

JUVENILE JUSTICE
Philosophy, Law, and Practices

There are three ways of trying to win the young. You can preach at them, that is a hook without a worm. You can say, "You must volunteer," that is the devil; and you can tell them, "You are needed." That appeal hardly ever fails.

—Kurt Hahn

LEARNING OBJECTIVES

As a result of reading this chapter, you will be able to

1. Describe the early treatment of juveniles and history of our juvenile justice system, which includes houses of refuge, reformatories, and the first juvenile court, created in Illinois
2. Explain the unique philosophy, principles, goals, and legal protections underlying the treatment of and philosophy toward youthful offenders by the juvenile court system
3. Review the process and flow of cases through the juvenile justice system
4. Discuss whether or not there exists a school-to-prison pipeline and, if so, reasons for and possible solutions to it
5. Elaborate on the extent of—and possible solutions to—youth gangs
6. Review approaches to providing formal aftercare and reentry services for juveniles upon leaving physical custody
7. Delineate due process and other major rights of juveniles as set forth by the U.S. Supreme Court

ASSESS YOUR AWARENESS

Test your knowledge of juvenile rights and the justice system by responding to the following nine true-false items; check your answers after reading this chapter.

1. The prevailing philosophy toward all juveniles is that the state should have as much involvement as possible, through the juvenile justice system.
2. The overall justice philosophy, process, and terminology are essentially the same for juvenile offenders as for adult offenders.
3. It is generally best to place some type of label on juvenile offenders, to assist with their classification and treatment.
4. Paramilitary juvenile boot camps have been proven to be an ineffective means of treating delinquency.
5. A juvenile who commits a heinous crime, and is thus not felt to be suited to the philosophy of the juvenile court, may be transferred to the jurisdiction of an adult court.
6. Procedural safeguards in the juvenile court system include the right to counsel, the right to confront and cross-examine witnesses, and the privilege against self-incrimination.
7. Juvenile offenders who are under the age of 18 when they commit a murder may be executed.
8. Police do not need to read the *Miranda* warning to juveniles being questioned while in custody.
9. Juveniles may still be sentenced to life without parole.

<< Answers can be found on page 419.

Their faces were cherubic at the time of their crimes: the 17-year-old sniper with delicate features and a sad look who participated in a 2003 shooting spree that terrorized our nation's capital (Lee Malvo), and the chubby 12-year-old who stomped to death a 6-year-old girl in 1999. Both are serving life sentences, though Malvo was recently granted a new sentencing hearing.

Why these young boys committed these horrific crimes may never be fully understood, but, as is often stated by persons working in the juvenile justice arena, "All roads lead to home." Their cases also continued a debate that has been going on for decades: How do we prevent, understand, and address the crimes of children? In recent decades, our criminal justice system has sought to deal with juvenile offenders by treating them like adults who are responsible for their actions, to be isolated and punished for their crimes.

The result of that policy—as argued by scholars, psychologists, and lawyers—has been that high numbers of young people have been sentenced to juvenile detention facilities that increasingly house mentally disturbed youth. To compound the problem, these facilities have been essentially "dumping grounds" for poor, minority youth with mental disorders and learning disabilities; furthermore, many youths are remanded to adult court for trial.

SAGE edge™
Master the content at edge
.sagepub.com/peak4e

As you read this chapter, consider how the criminal justice system might devise remedies that fit both the crime and the juvenile offender. Should juvenile offenders be treated differently, as many argue, due to reduced brain development and given that they are more impulsive, less able to think through the consequences of their actions, more susceptible to coercion, and more likely to take risks? Or should those arguments be rejected, as some noted criminologists have long argued, because these youthful offenders are rational, know right from wrong, are a product of their environment more than their biological makeup, and thus warrant harsh treatment?[1]

INTRODUCTION

What is a "juvenile delinquent"? What rights does one possess as a juvenile? What are the differences in law and criminal justice treatment of juveniles? These are important questions, because as an old adage states, crime is primarily a "young person's game."

As indicated in Chapter 1, the criminal justice system's philosophy toward juveniles is very different from its philosophy toward adults. Consequently, police officers and others whose occupations put them in frequent contact with juvenile offenders must know and apply a different standard of treatment in these situations. The philosophical approach toward juvenile offenders overall is that society—through poor parenting, poverty, environment, and so forth—is primarily responsible for their criminal behavior.

As is also emphasized in this chapter, the juvenile justice system seeks to protect the child—to rehabilitate, not punish; therefore, the juvenile justice process is generally amiable, not adversarial. However, many of today's juvenile offenders are also quite violent. When a juvenile commits an act that is so heinous and violent that the juvenile court philosophy is not tenable in the matter, the protective shroud extended by the juvenile justice process can disappear. In such cases, the youthful offender may be transferred to the jurisdiction of the adult court to be processed as an adult. Conversely, as will be seen later in this chapter, there has been for many years a movement to expand the rights and privileges of juvenile offenders in many areas.

This chapter begins with a discussion of the origins of juvenile justice, including houses of refuge and the creation of the juvenile court. Next is a look at the unique philosophy, principles, goals, and legal protections that underlie today's juvenile justice system. Following a discussion of the recent shift in juvenile offender policy and treatment and a look at juvenile offending today, we review the general flow of juvenile cases through the juvenile justice process. Several related methods and challenges are then discussed: the problem of labeling offenders, the school-to-prison pipeline, youth gangs, and the need for aftercare and reentry services for juveniles returning home from custody. The chapter concludes with an examination of several major U.S. Supreme Court decisions granting juveniles legal rights.

HISTORY OF JUVENILE JUSTICE

Our society has long been concerned with its minors (usually defined as those persons between the ages of 10 and 18) who violate the law; such persons are commonly termed juvenile delinquents.[2] As a result of this concern, there has long been a U.S. juvenile justice system that functions quite differently from the one that addresses crimes committed by adults. The U.S. juvenile justice system has a rich and, at times, painful history. Here, we discuss the early treatment of juveniles, and how the system developed from one that was very harsh and dangerous to that of today, which is much more protective and rehabilitative in philosophy and practice.[3]

Early Treatment: Houses of Refuge, Reformatories

In the early part of the 19th century, to the chagrin of prosecutors and many citizens, juries were acquitting children who were charged with crimes—not wishing to see children incarcerated with adults in ramshackle facilities. Quakers in New York City sought to establish a balance between those two camps—people wanting to see justice done with child offenders, and those not wanting them to be incarcerated—and founded the first house of refuge in 1825 to "receive and take . . . all such children as shall be taken up or committed as vagrants, or convicted of criminal offenses." The children worked an eight-hour day at various trades in addition to attending school for another four hours. Many of them had not committed any criminal act, and a number were probably status offenders (breaking criminal laws that apply only to minors, described later in this chapter).[4]

At about the middle of the 19th century, the house of refuge movement evolved into the slightly more punitive reform school, or reformatory, approach,[5] which served to segregate young offenders from adult criminals; imprison the young and remove them from adverse home environments until the youths were reformed; help youth avoid idleness through military drills, physical exercise, and supervision; focus on education—preferably vocational and religious; and teach sobriety, thrift, industry, and prudence.

Later in the 19th century, an occasional legal attack on the incarceration of children in such youth prisons was successful. In an 1870 case, the Illinois Supreme Court held it unconstitutional to confine in a Chicago reform school a youth who had not been convicted of criminal conduct or afforded legal due process.[6] It was against this backdrop in the last quarter of the 19th century that the juvenile court movement began.

Houses of refuge: workhouses established in the early 1800s as a means of separating juvenile offenders from adult offenders.

Reformatory: a detention facility designed to reform individuals—historically juveniles.

A Movement Begins: Illinois Legislation

In 1899, the Illinois legislature enacted the Illinois Juvenile Court Act,[7] creating the first separate juvenile court. At that time in the United States, juveniles were tried along with adults in criminal courts and sometimes sentenced to prison and occasionally to death. Prior to 1900, at least 10 children were executed in the United States for crimes committed before their 14th birthdays.[8]

Illinois Juvenile Court Act (1899): legislation that established the first juvenile court in the United States.

Juvenile court: a court that has original jurisdiction to hear juvenile crime matters.

Other children died in adult prisons. Virginia penitentiary records from 1876 reflect that a 10-year-old prisoner died from being scalded accidentally in a tub of boiling coffee. These deaths shocked the public conscience. Accordingly, Americans in the 20th century sought more pervasive reform than the infancy defense (see Chapter 10) to address the distinctive nature of children and youth.[9]

Although the Illinois act did not fundamentally change procedures in the courts that were then sitting as juvenile courts to adjudicate cases involving children, it did emphasize the *parens patriae* philosophy (discussed later in this chapter) to govern such cases. In addition to giving the courts jurisdiction over children charged with crimes, the act gave them jurisdiction over a variety of behaviors and conditions, including

Quakers in New York City founded the House of Refuge in 1825 to provide an alternative to children being housed with adult offenders. This picture depicts some of the work- and school-related daily activities at the House.

> any child who for any reason is destitute or homeless or abandoned; or dependent on the public for support; or has not proper parental care or guardianship; or who habitually begs or receives alms; or who is living in any house of ill fame or with any vicious or disreputable person; or whose home, by reason of neglect, cruelty

or depravity on the part of its parents, guardian or other person in whose care it may be, is an unfit place for such a child; and any child under the age of 8 who is found peddling or selling any article or singing or playing a musical instrument upon the street or giving any public entertainment.[10]

The act was unique in that it created a special court for neglected, dependent, or delinquent children under age 16; defined a rehabilitative rather than punishment purpose for that court; established the confidentiality of juveniles' court records to minimize stigma; required that juveniles be separated from adults when placed in the same institution in addition to barring altogether the detention of children under age 12 in jails; and provided for the informality of procedures within the court.[11]

In 1909, Judge Julian Mack, one of the first judges to preside over the juvenile court, described the court's goals as follows:

> The child who must be brought into court should, of course, be made to know that he is face to face with the power of the state, but he should at the same time, and more emphatically, be made to feel that he is the object of its care and solicitude. The ordinary trappings of the courtroom are out of place in such hearings. The judge on a bench, looking down upon the boy standing at the bar, can never evoke a proper sympathetic spirit. Seated at a desk, with the child at his side, where he can on occasion put his arm around his shoulder and draw the lad to him, the judge, while losing none of his judicial dignity, will gain immensely in the effectiveness of his work.[12]

Status Offenses

Status offense: a crime committed by a juvenile that would not be a crime if committed by an adult; examples would be purchasing alcohol and tobacco products, truancy, and violating curfew.

PINS (persons in need of supervision): usually juveniles thought to be on the verge of becoming delinquent.

The post–World War II period witnessed further development, as the status offense became a separate category, covering acts that would not be criminal if committed by an adult (e.g., purchasing alcohol and tobacco products, truancy, and violating curfew). New York created a new jurisdictional category for persons in need of supervision (PINS): runaways, truants, and other youths who committed status offenses. Other states followed New York's lead. Then came the enactment of the powerful and far-reaching Juvenile Justice and Delinquency Prevention Act of 1974,[13] which removed status offenders from secure detention and correctional facilities and—more significant, perhaps—prevented the placement of any juveniles in any institutions where they would have regular contact with adults convicted of criminal charges.

UNIQUE PHILOSOPHY, PRINCIPLES, AND GOALS

This section examines the philosophical underpinnings of the juvenile justice system as well as a number of contrasts (in both terminology and court proceedings) between these and the adult criminal courts.

Parens patriae: a doctrine according to which the state is the ultimate parent of the child (and will step in to provide and care for the child if parents neglect those duties).

In loco parentis: a doctrine according to which the state will act in place of the parents if they fail in their duties to protect and provide for the child.

Parens Patriae and In Loco Parentis

The prevailing doctrine or philosophy guiding our treatment of juveniles is *parens patriae*, meaning that the "state is the ultimate parent" of the child. In effect, this means that as long as we as parents adequately care for and provide at least the basic amenities for our children as required under the law, they are ours to keep. But when our children are physically or emotionally neglected or abused, the juvenile court and police may intervene and remove the children from that environment. Then the doctrine of *in loco parentis* takes hold, meaning that the state will act in place of the parent.

For police and other criminal justice personnel, there is perhaps no greater or more somber duty than having to testify under subpoena in juvenile court that a parent is unfit (and that his or her parental ties should be legally severed). However, when a parent or guardian's actions indicate a pattern of neglect and/or abuse toward a child, it is clearly better that the state assume responsibility for the child's care and custody.

Table 15.1 shows the idealistic contrast between the juvenile court process and the adult criminal justice process. Note that this is the *ideal* process for juveniles, in keeping with the more nurturing and forgiving juvenile justice philosophy; however, that can easily go away when a juvenile commits a crime(s) that is so heinous that he or she is deemed not to be amenable to the more lenient philosophy and jurisdiction of the juvenile courts, and will thus be remanded to the custody of the appropriate adult court. Also note that much of the difference between the philosophies of juvenile and adult courts is found in the terminology used.

An 8-year-old boy charged with stealing a bicycle appears in juvenile court in 1910.

Idealistic contrast: the differences between juvenile and adult criminal justice processes, to include treatment and terminology.

Underlying Principles of the Juvenile Court

Most states' juvenile court decisions and legislation contain three underlying principles:[14]

- The presumption of innocence
- The presumption of the least amount of involvement with the system
- The presumption of the best interest of the minor

The decision maker—whether the police deciding to take a minor into custody, an intake worker deciding to detain a child, or a juvenile court judge presiding at a hearing—must apply these three principles unless evidence exists to the contrary. The amount of evidence may vary depending on the decision maker. For example, although police

Table 15.1 /// The Idealistic Contrast Between Juvenile and Adult Criminal Justice Processes

Adult	Juvenile
Adversarial procedure	Relatively amiable procedure
Individual responsibility for crime	Societal/family factors involved
Punishment is typically the goal	Rehabilitation is the goal
Arrest process	Petition
Trial—public	Hearing—private
Guilt or innocence	Guilt not the sole issue
Public record	Confidential record
Verdict	Decision
Sentence	Disposition

Children from poor, disadvantaged backgrounds are much more likely to engage in delinquent behavior.

Presumption of innocence: the premise that a defendant is assumed to be innocent until guilt is established beyond a reasonable doubt.

or detention intake may hold a minor if reasonable or probable cause exists to believe that the minor has committed an offense, a judge must be satisfied beyond a reasonable doubt that an offense has been committed.

Presumption of Innocence

The presumption of innocence is one of the hallmarks of our criminal justice system. It places the burden on the state to prove that the accused has committed an offense. The state cannot force accused persons to testify against themselves, cannot use illegally seized evidence, and must use a process consistent with due process standards to establish guilt.

Least Involvement With the System

The principle of least involvement assumes that minors, like adults, have liberty interests that include the right to be left alone or the right to live in a family situation without state interference. The state has the burden of showing that intervention is necessary for the protection of either the minor or society. Diversion should be considered before a formal petition is filed, and probation should be considered before commitment to an institution. In the detention situation, many states require that a child not be held unless a probable cause exists to believe that he or she has committed a crime and an immediate and urgent necessity exists to admit the child. Detention is discussed more later in this chapter.

Best Interest of the Child

The primary purpose of juvenile justice is to operate in the best interest of the child; this interest must be balanced against the interests of society. Society benefits from programs that help minors mature into law-abiding citizens, and children benefit by being held accountable and developing responsibility.

Goals of the Juvenile Justice System

The four primary goals of the juvenile justice system are as follows:

- *Separation from adults:* This is clearly the most important goal of the juvenile justice system. Reformers argued that children and families needed (1) a different form of justice, (2) separate courtrooms, (3) separate detention centers and institutions to avoid corruption of juveniles by adult criminals (the so-called "sight and sound separation"), and (4) separate sentencing guidelines to avoid the harsh penalties of adult sentencing. Furthermore, there is a separate group of professionals, judges, probation officers, and detention staff with specialized training who are dedicated to working with youths and their families.

- *Youth confidentiality:* Confidentiality of court proceedings and services for youths reinforces the belief that they will mature beyond a criminal lifestyle if given proper guidance and alternatives. Because of their immaturity, youths lack sound judgment and should not be held fully accountable. Consequently, no criminal record should hinder adult advancement. From a developmental standpoint, confidentiality minimizes stigma and labeling, and helps them to maintain a positive self-image, thereby reducing the likelihood that they will perceive themselves as criminals.

- *Community-based corrections:* Reformers strongly believed that young people should learn and grow in their own communities. Offering probation as a method for monitoring youth behavior in the community, while providing services that allow youths to grow to adulthood, is seen as the primary dispositional alternative.

- *Individualized justice of minors:* Each case is to be viewed separately. A social history explores the total social circumstances of the youth and his or her family, and a casework plan is developed that encourages appropriate development and reduced future criminality. Probation staff members are to look into the social situation early in the process and be involved in the decision to file a case. Whenever possible, the case is not filed formally, and an informal outcome is encouraged.[15]

Society benefits from programs that help young offenders to mature into law-abiding citizens, be accountable for their actions, and develop responsibility. These youths are attending a class while in juvenile corrections.

More Legal Protection: The Juvenile Justice Reform Act of 2018

The Juvenile Justice and Delinquency Prevention Act (JJDPA) was first authorized in 1974, to ensure that all states and territories met certain standards for how youth across the country were treated in the juvenile justice system. It established two principles: a prohibition on the incarceration of youth charged with status offenses (discussed earlier), and a requirement that youth have sight and sound separation from adult inmates. Later, in 2002, two additional protections were added: a prohibition against housing young people in adult facilities while awaiting trial as juveniles, and a requirement that states address disproportionate minority contact.

On December 13, 2018, Congress passed H.R. 6964, with a number of significant amendments. First, in an attempt to address racial and ethnic disparities (RED), the law requires that states collect and analyze data on RED, determine at which points RED occur, and establish a plan to address RED. Second, states are required to ensure sight and sound separation and jail removal for youth awaiting trial as adults (this protection previously applied only to youths being held on juvenile court charges). Third, youths who are found in violation of a valid court order may be held in detention, but for no longer than seven days, if the court finds that such detention is necessary and enters an order that specifies reasonable cause for such detention.[16] The legislation includes grants to fund delinquency prevention programs.

A Recent Shift in Policy, Principles, and Processes

To fully comprehend today's juvenile justice policy, principles, and processes in the United States, it is necessary to take a brief look back in time. Succinctly, after decades of a punitive, "adult time for adult crime," "tough-on-crime" view toward juvenile offenders, policy makers are now returning to the first principles of juvenile justice, discussed earlier: a belief that young people are still developing (as well as more impulsive, less able to think through the consequences of their actions, and more likely to take risks) and should be afforded opportunities for treatment, rehabilitation, and positive reinforcement.

Using child advocacy, legislation, and reallocation of resources (as noted in the accompanying "Investigating Further" feature), a majority of states are attempting to expand juvenile rights, study their offending, prevent delinquency, and develop community alternatives

Investigating Further

A Sampling of Recent Laws Enacted to Protect Juveniles

According to the Campaign for Youth Justice, 2017–2018 was "a legislative season that included 121 state-level bills related to juvenile justice." To get a sense of the aspects of juvenile justice considered important by the states to be committed to law, here, in no particular order, is a sampling of recently enacted statutes:

- Broadly speaking, every state has statutes or policies that allow youths accused of certain offenses (especially older teens) to be transferred from the juvenile justice system and tried as adults. But now only four states still set their "age of jurisdiction" below 18, meaning minors are considered as adults when it comes to the criminal justice system: Georgia, Michigan, Texas, and Wisconsin.

- *California:* Prosecutors can no longer recommend that 14- and 15-year-olds be tried as adults, including where one is charged with first-degree murder and other serious crimes; makes a person eligible for release or parole during the 25th year of incarceration if he or she was given a life sentence without the possibility of parole as a minor.

- *Utah:* Encourages state school districts to implement restorative justice in public schools (giving victims of juvenile crimes the opportunity to be heard, ask questions, and seek restoration).

- *North Carolina:* Allows a juvenile's criminal record to be expunged for nonviolent offenses; limits detention for certain offenses; requires a parent, a guardian, or an attorney to be present during police interrogations of any child under the age of 16; and ended a century-long practice of prosecuting teens as adults by raising the age of criminal responsibility to 18 (most 16- and 17-year-olds will be prosecuted in juvenile court).

- *Delaware:* Expands the use of civil citations instead of criminal charges, ends shackling of youths except where necessary for safety, provides free legal representation to all children charged with a crime, and makes it easier for juveniles to expunge their records.

- *North Dakota:* Funds a study of the juvenile justice process; alternative dispositions; and improvement of outcomes, probation, support services, and unwarranted institutional placements.

- *Illinois:* Directs a commission to review the current practice of restorative justice in juvenile justice systems.

- *Virginia:* Studies expungement of juvenile records.

- *Colorado:* Recommends that juvenile delinquency petitions be assigned to a single court so that those judges may develop expertise in the handling of juvenile cases.

- *Illinois:* Implements a study to develop policies and interventions to address juvenile justice disparities and disproportionate minority contact.

- *New Mexico:* Funds a strategy for educating children who have been suspended, expelled, or detained in the juvenile or criminal justice systems for misconduct.

Source: Campaign for Youth Justice, quoted in the *Chronicle of Social Change*, "In Another Big Year for 'Raise the Age' Laws, One State Now Considers All Teens as Juveniles," June 25, 2018, https://chronicleofsocialchange.org/youth-services-insider/juvenile-justice-raise-the-age-vermont-missouri-state-legislation; also see Samantha Solomon, "A Look at California's New Juvenile Justice Laws," ABC10, October 22, 2018, https://www.abc10.com/article/news/a-look-at-californias-new-juvenile-justice-laws/103-606868472; for state law changes generally, see the National Conference of State Legislatures, "Juvenile Justice Bills Tracking Database," http://www.ncsl.org/research/civil-and-criminal-justice/ncsls-juvenile-justice-bill-tracking-database.aspx.

Life without parole: a penalty or sentence imposed under which an inmate is to serve a life sentence without eligibility for parole.

to incarceration. Serious attempts are thus being made to reduce the "school-to-prison pipeline" (discussed later in this chapter) and to end excessive sentences and extreme punishments, juvenile life-without-parole (JLWOP) sentences, and the use of solitary confinement for incarcerated youth (both JLWOP and solitary confinement are discussed later in this chapter).[17] One side benefit of the demise of the punitive trend is that the juvenile justice system no longer represents a dumping ground for poor, minority youth with mental disorders and learning disabilities.

An area in which child advocates are particularly adamant about reform is the use of solitary confinement. According to both The Sentencing Project and the Juvenile Law Center, every day children in the justice system endure such confinement and the possibility of strip searches, shackling, pepper spray, restraints, and physical and sexual abuse. They may be housed in small cells 22–24 hours per day, with no personal belongings and no access to treatment services or peer interaction. Research shows that not only does such confinement not work, but it often makes things worse.[18]

They point to such cases as that of Kalief Browder, whose case was featured in Chapter 1. Accused of stealing a backpack at age 16, he was sent to New York City's Rikers Island jail to await trial. During the three years he spent there, he fought with other teenagers and correctional officers and was placed in the Central Punitive Segregation Unit (CPSU)—a euphemism for solitary confinement, with cells about 12 feet by 7 feet. He spent most of his last 17 months at Rikers, including 10 months straight, in the CPSU. After his release at age 20, he endured mental anguish from his incarceration, and after four failed suicide attempts, he took his own life.[19]

The United States is the only country in the world that permits its youth to be sentenced to life without parole. As noted in Chapter 11, in *Roper v. Simmons*, the Court banned the juvenile death penalty; also, in *Graham v. Florida* (2010), the Court banned life-without-parole sentences for youth convicted of nonhomicide crimes; and in *Miller v. Alabama* (2012), the Court banned mandatory sentences of life without parole for youths convicted of homicide crimes. However, in some states a youth may still be sentenced to discretionary life without parole in homicide cases if the sentencing court, after a hearing, determines that juvenile is permanently incorrigible and incapable of rehabilitation. Twenty-eight states still allow life without parole as a sentencing option for juveniles.[20]

Finally, many juvenile justice scholars believe that detention should be avoided altogether when possible, with a comprehensive approach used instead—working with the offender in his or her own home and with the youth's family, going to the home as often as possible; there, a therapist can get a feel for the family's strengths and problems, see who and where the youth's peer influences are, and thus provide the most appropriate services.[21]

JUVENILE OFFENDING TODAY: EXTENT AND POSSIBLE CAUSES

There is good news in terms of the numbers of juvenile arrests in the United States. As seen in Figure 15.1, the juvenile arrest rate for all offenses reached its highest level in 1996 and

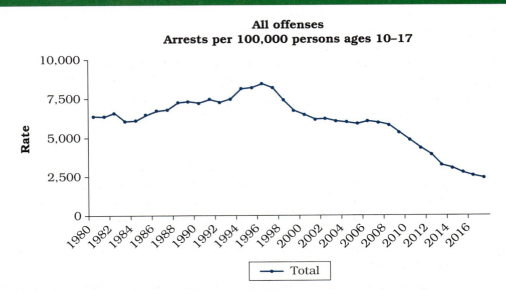

Figure 15.1 /// Juvenile Arrest Rates for All Crimes

Source: Office of Juvenile Justice Delinquency and Prevention, "Juvenile Arrest Rate Trends," https://www.ojjdp.gov/ojsTaTbb/crime/JAR_Display.asp?ID=qa05200.

Practitioner's Perspective

Juvenile Court Counselor

Name: Jennine Hall
Position: Juvenile Court Counselor
Location: Colorado

What is your career story? I currently work for the Division of Youth Corrections in the state of Colorado. I am what you call a clinical trainer. I train all of the clinical staff that are rehabilitating kids in the state of Colorado that are currently in custody. When I first started off, I was working with at-risk adults with underlying mental health issues. I had a friend that was working with kids in juvenile justice, and she suggested that I do it too. I was doubtful at first, but I decided to shadow her for a day and fell in love with the adolescent population, and more importantly, kids that have problematic behavior that inevitably end up with criminal prosecutions and things of that nature. So quickly thereafter, I applied and ended up getting an entry-level position. Although my experience really was more in the mental health field, the entry-level position allowed me to get my feet wet, so to speak, with this population. I literally fell in love, and I have been there over 16 years now. I never have a dull day. It's just been a wonderful career for me.

What are some challenges you face in this position? It's always challenging when you're working with an at-risk population, especially when it consists of children or adolescents. The community places people that work in juvenile justice in a very high level of trust. Not only trust with regards to how to effectively rehabilitate a criminal offender, but also really trusting us as professionals to take care of these kids while in custody, and understand their individualized needs as they go through the rehabilitative process. Think of a child that you love, and imagine walking into a secure facility with them and walking out without them. I think that really speaks to the level of trust that our taxpayers and stakeholders expect of people in this profession. It's a high level of authority and trust that they place on us.

Do you see any common trends in this position? The field has totally changed in my 15 years in it, especially in research. Evidence-based practice has completely transformed the juvenile justice system. When I first came into the system as a juvenile parole officer, we really didn't know what worked. There were state- and nationwide inconsistencies on how to rehabilitate the juvenile offender. But since then, there have been huge bodies of research that have given us a road map. Our system has really begun to integrate programs and principles into everything we do, and that has made a world of difference in the services we provide to kids and to families. It's definitely one of those jobs that if you expect one day to walk in and say, "I've got it, I know everything," the juvenile justice field might not be the right field for you because it's changing constantly.

What role does diversity play in this position? Diversity plays a huge role. I think there was a time when we would say the word *diversity* and people would think specifically in terms of race and gender. But now, diversity is much broader than that, and it needs to be. We need to be a system that has people from all walks of life, people with all different types of experience. You don't want a system where everybody thinks and talks and acts alike. You want to create bodies of employees that breed innovation and creativity. That's what diversity offers to organizations such as juvenile justice. It's critical, because we work with people from all walks of life. It's important for us to be open-minded and curious about the people we're working with and the world in which they live.

To learn more about Jennine Hall's experiences as a juvenile court counselor watch the Practitioner's Perspective video in SAGE vantage.

then declined 72 percent by 2017. Why this long-running reduction in juvenile arrests? Two reasons are commonly offered: First, the drop in juvenile violent crime arrests virtually coincides with the drop in juvenile commitments to residential facilities (studies show that juveniles who are kept in the community recidivate less often than previously detained youths). Second, states are increasingly using alternative forms of punishment over incarceration (discussed later in the chapter).[22] Other possible reasons are the increasing immigrant population—a group that tends to have lower crime rates—and the fact that marijuana laws are becoming more lax.[23]

However, ample room remains for concern with juvenile crime. According to arrest data from the Federal Bureau of Investigation's *Uniform Crime Reports*, about 620,000 juveniles (persons under age 18) are arrested for crimes each year.[24]

Many theories have been offered by experts to explain juvenile crime; however, no single theory has been universally accepted. Nevertheless, experts agree that a correlation exists between juvenile crime and the following factors:

- *Family dysfunction:* Family background is one of the most potent influences on juvenile development. Dysfunctional families transfer dysfunctional norms to their children. Juveniles who live in unstable homes and social environments are deemed to be *at-risk* children because of their vulnerability to detrimental influences. Such environments can contribute to antisocial behavior in children, often resulting in criminally deviant behavior later in life.

- *Drug use and deviance:* Alcohol and tobacco are the drugs of choice for many juveniles.

- *Socioeconomic class:* Children from poor and working-class backgrounds are much more likely than other children to engage in delinquent behavior. Studies of the inner-city underclass have found that large numbers of the urban poor are caught in a chronic generational cycle of poverty, low educational achievement, teenage parenthood, unemployment, and welfare dependence.

- *Educational experiences:* Academic achievement is considered to be one of the principal stepping stones toward success in American society. Ideally, opportunities for education, mentoring, and encouragement to excel would be equally available for all children. Unfortunately, that is not the situation. Socioeconomic and demographic factors can also have an impact on educational opportunities and performance. Poor children often experience a very different educational environment in comparison to middle-class children, such as in inner-city, underclass environments, where educational achievement is often not commonly encouraged—or achieved.[25]

Case Flow of the Juvenile Justice Process

This section describes the youthful offender's flow through the juvenile justice process, using as a guide the diagram shown in Figure 15.2.[26]

Note that each state's processing of law violators is unique, depending on local practice and tradition; therefore, any description of juvenile justice processing must be general, outlining a common series of decision points:

1. *Law enforcement diverts many juvenile offenders out of the justice system:* Young law violators generally enter the juvenile justice system through police contacts, but school officials, social services agencies, neighbors, and even parents provide information about a juvenile's crime that commences the process. At arrest, a decision is made either to send the matter further into the justice system or to divert the case out of the system, often into alternative programs. Usually the police make this decision after talking to the victim, the juvenile, and the parents and after reviewing the juvenile's prior contacts with the juvenile justice system. Examples of alternative programs include drug treatment, individual or group counseling, or referral to educational and recreational programs.

Figure 15.2 /// Case Flow Diagram of the Juvenile Justice Process

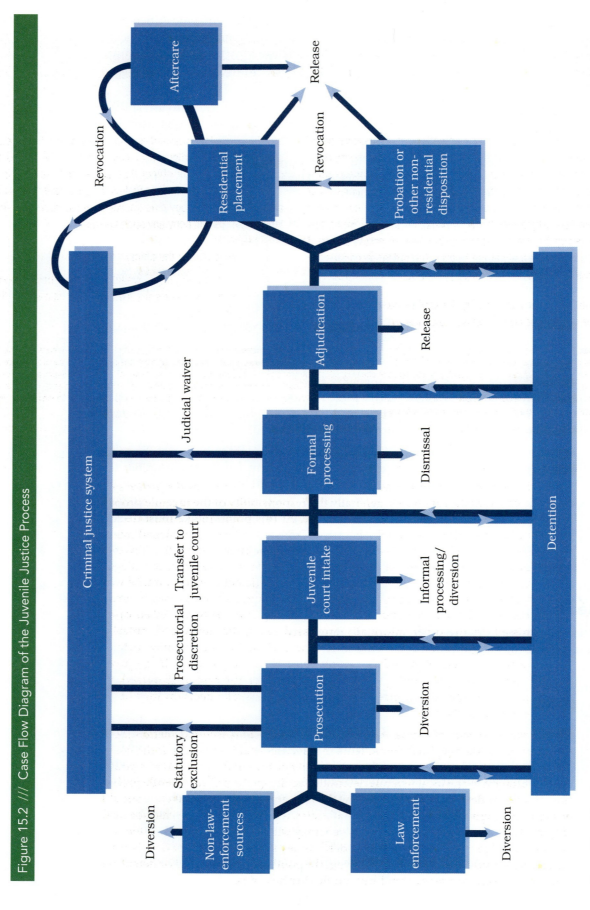

Source: Office of Juvenile Justice and Delinquency Prevention, https://www.ojjdp.gov/ojstatbb/structure_process/case.html.

You Be the . . .

Police Officer

It is about 10:00 on a warm summer's night. A municipal police officer is dispatched to a residence to take a theft report. Upon arrival, she is informed by the residents that a very expensive bicycle has been stolen from their front porch. The victims further inform the officer that earlier that afternoon they observed a juvenile—whom they know by name, because he lives a few blocks up the street—walking on the sidewalk across the street and looking furtively at the bicycle. The officer recognizes the youth's name by reputation (i.e., prior involvement with police).

She drives her patrol car by the youth's home and, through the open front door, observes that the living room is dark but the television is turned on. She goes to the front door, and the juvenile is alone watching television; he comes to the door and tells the officer that his parents are sleeping. The officer knows that if she wakes the parents and (in their presence) asks the boy if he knows anything about the stolen bicycle, he will deny any such knowledge.

1. How should the officer proceed?
2. Is there an option available that will have a positive outcome for the juvenile, the victims, and the police officer?

Note: This relatively simple case study represents police work as it often occurs on the streets, where there is a solitary officer with little or no opportunity to immediately seek a search warrant. It also involves the Fourth Amendment (probable cause, arrest, search and seizure); the police being aware of someone's history with and reputation for committing certain types of offenses; police policy and procedures (regarding treatment of juveniles); and, of course, police ethics. Also implicated are the informal nature of police work; use of discretion; and Wilson's "watchman," order maintenance role of police (see Chapter 6); and Packer's crime control/due process dichotomy (discussed in Chapter 1). In this actual case, the officer persuaded the youth to take her to where the bike was hidden (in a thick wooded area) and thus avoid involvement with the justice system.

---

2. *A non–law enforcement agency may divert juvenile offenders out of the justice system:* The court intake function is generally the responsibility of the juvenile probation department and/or the prosecutor's office. At this point, intake must decide whether to dismiss the case, handle the matter informally, or request formal intervention by the juvenile court. To make this decision, an intake officer first reviews the facts of the case to determine if there is sufficient evidence to prove the allegation. If there is not, the case is dismissed. If there is sufficient evidence, intake will then determine if formal intervention is necessary. About half of all cases referred to juvenile court intake are handled informally. Most informally processed cases are dismissed. In the other informally processed cases, the juvenile voluntarily agrees to specific conditions for a specific time period. Conditions may include victim restitution, school attendance, drug counseling, or a curfew. If the juvenile successfully complies with the informal disposition, the case is dismissed. If, however, the juvenile fails to meet the conditions, the intake decision may be to formally prosecute the case.

3. *During the processing of a case, a juvenile may be held in a secure detention facility:* Juvenile courts may hold delinquents in a secure detention facility if the court believes it is in the best interest of the community or the child. After arrest, a youth is often brought to the local juvenile detention facility by the police. Juvenile probation officers or detention workers review the case and decide if the juvenile should be held pending a hearing by a judge. In all states, a detention hearing must be held within a time period defined by statute, generally within 24 hours. At the detention hearing, a judge reviews the case and determines if continued detention is warranted. As a result of the detention hearing, the youth may be released or detention continued. Detention may extend beyond further hearings.

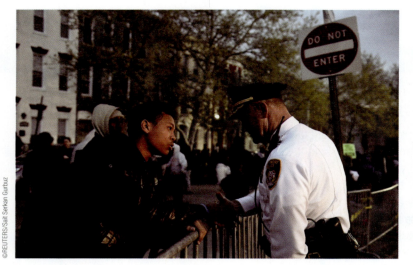

A youth shakes hands with a police captain in front of a Baltimore Police Department stationhouse on April 23, 2015, during a protest against the police-custody death of Freddie Gray in Baltimore.

Transfer (remand): the movement or assigning of a juvenile offender to an adult court, because the youth's behavior is such that he or she is not amenable to the juvenile court's rehabilitative philosophy.

Disposition: an outcome of a criminal or juvenile court process signifying that the matter is completed.

4. *Cases may be filed in either juvenile or criminal court*: In many states, the legislature excludes certain (usually serious) offenses from the jurisdiction of the juvenile court regardless of the age of the accused. In other states and at the federal level under certain circumstances, prosecutors have the discretion to either file criminal charges against juveniles directly in criminal courts or proceed through the juvenile justice process. The juvenile court's intake department or the prosecutor may petition the juvenile court to transfer (also termed remand) jurisdiction to criminal court. The juvenile court also may order referral to criminal court for trial as adults. In some jurisdictions, juveniles processed as adults may upon conviction be sentenced to either an adult or a juvenile facility.

5. *A disposition is reached in the case*: At the disposition hearing, recommendations are presented to the judge. The prosecutor and the youth (usually through his or her guardian *ad litem*—often an attorney or other trained professional appointed by a court to help protect the juvenile's rights and determine what solutions would be in his or her best interests) may also present dispositional recommendations. After considering options presented, the judge orders a disposition in the case. Most juvenile dispositions are multifaceted. In disposing of cases, juvenile courts usually have far more discretion than adult courts. In addition to such options as probation, commitment to a residential facility, restitution, and fines, state laws grant juvenile courts the power to order removal of children from their homes to foster homes or treatment facilities. Juvenile courts also may order participation in special programs aimed at shoplifting prevention, drug counseling, or driver education. Once a juvenile is under juvenile court disposition, the court may retain jurisdiction until the juvenile legally becomes an adult (at age 21 in most states). In some jurisdictions, juvenile offenders may be classified as youthful offenders, which can lead to extended sentences.

6. *The judge may order the juvenile committed to a residential placement*: Residential commitment may be for a specific or indeterminate time period. The facility may be publicly or privately operated and may have a secure prison-like environment or a more open, even home-like setting. In many states, when the judge commits a juvenile to the state department of juvenile corrections, the department determines where the juvenile will be placed and when the juvenile will be released. In other instances, the judge controls the type and length of stay. In these situations, review hearings are held to assess the juvenile's progress.

7. *The juvenile receives aftercare, similar to adult parole*: Following release from an institution, the juvenile is often ordered to a period of aftercare or parole. During this period, the juvenile is under supervision of the court or the juvenile corrections department. If the juvenile does not follow the conditions of aftercare, he or she may be recommitted to the same facility or to another facility.[27]

The Problem of Labeling

Looking at steps 1 through 7 in the previous section—after the youth has been apprehended, adjudicated, and placed—there is a concern that he or she will be officially labeled as deviant. A consequence of labeling in our society is that the individual may never be redeemed in the eyes of the community. Cox et al. stated that when labeling offenders, "John Q. Convict does not become John Q. Citizen. Instead, he becomes John Q. Ex-Convict."[28] Being labeled can thus make it extremely difficult for one who is a former "deviant" to find employment and succeed in society. Furthermore, labeling can change the delinquent's self-image to one that is negative. This "disintegrative shaming" (negative stigmatization) morally condemns and isolates the individual and does not attempt to reintegrate the youth into the larger society. Conversely, a better approach is to practice "reintegrative shaming," where there is an attempt to reconnect the stigmatized person to the larger society.[29]

Residential commitment may provide juveniles with either a secure prison-like environment or a more open, even home-like setting. This teen lives in a small, home-like setting that stresses personal development over isolation and punishment.

Is There a "School-to-Prison Pipeline"?

Some authors believe there is a school-to-prison pipeline—often perceived as grounded in racial discrimination—that is an epidemic plaguing our schools (black youths are twice as likely to be arrested as white youths, and although black youths represent only 14 percent of the youth population, they represent 40 percent of youths who are incarcerated).[30] In sum, students who are expelled from school for disruptive behavior are then compelled to live in the homes and neighborhoods of negative influences where their problems began, causing them to become stigmatized, more hardened and embittered, and often more engaged in criminality.

Regarding the possible link of racial discrimination with this "pipeline," according to Rocque and Paternoster, African American youth fare worse in schools than whites in several areas: They show less interest in school activities, have lower grades, are more likely to be held back and to be in special education, and have higher rates of incarceration.[31] Added to those factors is their lower socioeconomic status and their environment, in which the youth's peers may dismiss and ridicule academic success, as well as the increased likelihood that they will be singled out for punishment in school—and a school-to-prison pipeline trajectory for minorities is present.

School-to-prison pipeline: the notion that certain policies and practices push schoolchildren, particularly those who are most at risk, out of classrooms and into the juvenile and adult criminal justice and prison systems.

What can be done about this pipeline or trajectory? First, according to some educators, is the need to realize that suspensions do not really work—they merely get the individual out of the classroom. Next is the need to examine existing discipline structures to ensure that they help, rather than hurt, students. Examples of the need to reassess discipline policies include the youth who spent 21 days in a juvenile detention center for talking back in class, the 7-year-old who was suspended for chewing his Pop-Tart into the shape of a gun, the senior expelled for forgetting the pocketknife in her purse, and seven teenagers who were arrested and charged with disorderly conduct for an end-of-the-year water balloon fight.[32] Some school districts have signed "memorandums of understanding" with local law enforcement agencies that keep minor offenders out of criminal courts.[33] Others have attempted something called "restorative practices," which entails more adult involvement in letting youths know that their behavior is detrimental to the needs of the community and to themselves. It involves getting to the root cause of the problem so that it does not recur, through the use of restorative justice circles; in this way, adults show children that they care about them and do not wish to suspend them from the classroom.[34]

YOUTH GANGS: AN OVERVIEW

What Defines a Youth Gang and Its Members?

Although it is difficult to arrive at a common definition of a youth gang—because state and local jurisdictions often devise their own definitions—it is generally defined as a group or association of peers sharing a gang name, recognizable symbols, and identifiable leadership; having an identified geographic territory; holding regular meetings; and being collectively engaged in illegal activities. Second, the age range given for youth gang members is wide—about 12 to 24 years—with gang membership being more common at the top of the age range.[35]

Youth Gang Membership

A recent study estimated that there are more than one million juvenile gang members in the United States, more than three times the number estimated by law enforcement.[36] There is some good news in the study, however. Gangs have a high turnover rate (about 36 percent), with about 400,000 youth joining gangs and another 400,000 youth leaving gangs every year. The study belies a common misconception concerning gangs: that once a person joins, he or she stays in the gang for many years. Instead, researchers find that for

Going Global

Juvenile Torture in Iraq

By now it seems unlikely that humans will ever cease torturing other humans in their quest to obtain a confession for some alleged act(s), even though the accuracy of such confessions is questionable at best. But such has been the case in a juvenile facility in Kurdistan, northern Iraq, where interrogators attempt to ferret out and eradicate the Islamic State (ISIS) in part by torturing children, according to Human Rights Watch. Young boys were subjected to beatings, prolonged stress positions, and electric shock; they had no access to lawyers; and they were not allowed to read the confessions they allegedly wrote and were forced to sign.

Human Rights Watch interviewed 37 boys, ages 14 to 17, at a children's facility encircled by high walls and concertina wire—one of three such facilities in northern Iraq. The boys had been charged with or convicted of ISIS affiliation. Interrogators beat the children with plastic pipes, electric cables, or rods, and administered electric shocks. They threatened to break the boys' bones if a confession was not forthcoming. All but one youth interviewed said they eventually confessed in order to stop the torture—but when they later told the trial judge of the coerced confession, they were ignored. None of the boys were brought before a judge within 24 hours of their initial detention, as required by the Kurdistan penal code, and only a few had legal representation. None of them were allowed to communicate with their families while in custody, and most were denied phone calls until after sentencing.

Many of these children have already been scarred by conflict and ISIS abuses, according to Human Rights Watch. International human rights law prohibits torture and other ill treatment, and dictates that children should be detained only as a last resort and for the shortest appropriate period. The law also requires that assistance be provided to children illegally recruited by armed groups or forces, and that children charged with criminal offenses have the right to legal assistance and a prompt determination of their case; they also have the right not to be compelled to give testimony or confess guilt, and statements derived from torture cannot be used as evidence in court.

Source: Adapted from Human Rights Watch, "Kurdistan Region of Iraq: Detained Children Tortured," January 8, 2019, https://www.hrw.org/news/2019/01/08/kurdistan-region-iraq-detained-children-tortured.

young gang members, the money, cars, girls, and protection is more myth than reality.[37] Most youths who join a gang remain active members for only about 12 years. Another positive finding is that even in the most gang-ridden areas of the United States, most youths do not join a gang.[38]

What Works With Youth Gangs?

Targeted patrols or a dedicated gang unit (or officer) are the measures used most frequently to combat gangs, in addition to participation in a multiagency gang task force and coordinated probation searches. Less frequently used are civil gang ordinances or injunctions. A civil gang injunction is a court order issued in a civil case against a criminal street gang and its members to prohibit certain behavior within a defined safety zone—which may include associating together in public, and violating trespass and curfew laws.[39]

Finally, as with other crime and disorder problems, arrests alone do not solve problems in the long term. A comprehensive, multifaceted approach to the gang problem is needed. Such an approach would include fundamental changes in the way schools operate (acting as community centers involved in teaching, providing services, and serving as locations for activities before and after the school day); job skills development; a range of services provided to families (parental training, child care, health care, and crisis intervention); changes in the way the criminal justice system—particularly policing—responds generally to problems, by increasing their understanding of the communities they serve; and intervention and control of known gang members—either by diverting peripheral members from gang involvement and criminal activity or by arresting and incapacitating hard-core gang members, thus sending a message that the community will not tolerate intimidating, violent, and/or criminal gang activity.[40]

AFTERCARE AND REENTRY

Although no program evaluations have shown a conclusive means of doing so, as with adult offenders (discussed in Chapter 13), a youth who is about to reenter the community after being in a custodial facility sorely needs aftercare services. Given that up to two-thirds of all youths will be rearrested and one-third will be reincarcerated within a few years after release, it is imperative that support services be in place to facilitate this reentry. Services should include wraparound support services that are collaborations between family members and a transition specialist to ensure that the transition is successful. Because many of these youths have depression, schizophrenia, other mental disorders, or learning disabilities, it is important that aftercare includes helping them to develop skills for participating in the workforce, school, and/or independent living; interacting appropriately with others; and developing a positive self-image and the ability to set personal goals.[41]

SIGNIFICANT COURT DECISIONS

In the mid-1960s to the mid-1970s, several important decisions by the U.S. Supreme Court addressed and expanded the legal rights of juveniles. Then, from 2010 to 2016, there was another spate of decisions.

Right to Counsel

Kent v. United States (1966) involved a 16-year-old boy who was arrested in the District of Columbia for robbery, rape, and burglary.[42] The juvenile court, without conducting a formal hearing, transferred the matter to a criminal court, and Kent was tried and convicted as an adult. Kent appealed, arguing that the transfer to adult court without a hearing violated his right to due process. The Supreme Court agreed and also decided that there must be a meaningful right to representation by counsel—who must be given access to the documents being considered by the juvenile court in making its decision—and that the court must also provide reasons for transfer.[43]

The Centerpiece: *In Re Gault*

Gerald Gault, age 15, was accused of making an obscene call to a neighbor. The police picked up Gault and took him to the juvenile detention center while his parents were at work. His parents were told later that a hearing would be held the next day, but the charges against Gault were not explained. The complaining neighbor did not show up at the hearing; rather, a police officer testified to what the neighbor had said. Gault, who had no attorney present, denied making the obscene calls. No record was made of the court testimony, and there was no jury present; only a judge heard the case, who declared Gault to be a delinquent and ordered him to be sent to a state reform school—until he was released or turned 21 years old,[44] whichever came first. Ultimately, Gault filed a *writ of habeas corpus* (discussed in Chapter 9), claiming that he had been denied due process rights at his hearing. This writ was denied, and state courts offered him no relief. The case was eventually taken up by the U.S. Supreme

Investigating Further

Forty-Five Years After *Gault:* The Experience of Corey Bauer

Corey Bauer, at age 11, a diminutive (five feet five inches tall) youth who loved four-wheeling in the woods, became depressed upon the death of his grandmother. He was caught shoplifting a pack of cigarettes from a grocery store and was placed on probation. Soon he was caught again, this time for violating his probation by breaking school rules: smoking, skipping classes, and carrying scissors through a metal detector. He was then sent to a juvenile court and placed in detention in Louisiana. Neither he nor his mother was advised of his right to legal counsel. Instead, they were informed that police and court personnel would help get him "back on track" by providing counseling services instead of a defense lawyer who would just "slow things down."

After Corey's release from detention, his situation worsened when he was arrested for vehicle burglary and possession of illicit drugs. Back in court, Corey's probation officer recommended that he be placed in "state secure care," where he would supposedly receive mental health and substance abuse treatment and education. Again, with no attorney or advocate present, Corey accepted a plea bargain and agreed to enter this program.

In reality, Corey, then age 14, would be sent to what was effectively a maximum-security prison for youth in northwestern Louisiana—a compound of brick buildings with razor-wire fences, security checkpoints, and boys in orange jump suits. At her first visit, Corey's mother was shocked to find that Corey had a boot print on his rib cage, a black eye, and a knot on his forehead. He informed her that he had been locked up, beaten by guards, placed in solitary confinement, and sexually assaulted. He would spend the next six years, until he was 20 years old, in and out of adult and juvenile prisons. In addition to his horrific treatment, the lack of legal counsel stands out as a significant aspect of Corey's criminal and judicial affairs.

In some jurisdictions around the nation, as many as 80 to 90 percent of youth offenders waive their right to counsel, not realizing that doing so can later contribute to a loss of employment opportunities, access to student loans, and other benefits. Do you believe all youths should have a right to counsel at hearing or trial (whether requested or not)? Explain.

Source: James Swift, "A Mother's Mission," Juvenile Justice Information Exchange, July 29, 2013, https://jjie.org/2013/07/29/a-mothers-mission/; also see Lauren Pearle, "Broken Promises: The Challenge of Juvenile Justice," ABC News, https://abcnews.go.com/TheLaw/story?id=3183886&page=1.

Court in 1967.⁴⁵ The Court noted the historically different treatment of juveniles, including their often being committed to an institution for several years, where "his world is peopled by guards, custodians, state employees, and 'delinquents' confined with him for anything from waywardness to rape and homicide." Finding that the Fourteenth Amendment is not "for adults alone,"⁴⁶ the Court held that juveniles were entitled to the same basic procedural safeguards afforded therein, including advance notice of charges; right to counsel and to confront and cross-examine witnesses; and the privilege against self-incrimination.

Burden of Proof Standard

In 1970, *In re Winship* involved a 12-year-old boy convicted of larceny in New York.⁴⁷ At trial, the court relied on the "preponderance of the evidence" standard of proof against him rather than the more demanding "beyond a reasonable doubt" standard used in adult courts. The U.S. Supreme Court reversed Winship's conviction on grounds that the "beyond a reasonable doubt" standard had not been used.

Trial by Jury, Double Jeopardy, and Executions

In *McKeiver v. Pennsylvania* (1971), Joseph McKeiver and another juvenile were charged with robbery. Both were denied a request for a jury trial by the juvenile court; the state superior court, state supreme court, and a federal appeals court all upheld the lower court decision, finding no constitutional right to a jury trial for juveniles. The U.S. Supreme Court, however, said that juveniles do not have an absolute right to trial by jury; whether or not a juvenile receives a trial by jury is left to the discretion of state and local authorities.⁴⁸ Then, in *Breed v. Jones* (1975), the Court concluded that the Fifth Amendment protected juveniles from double jeopardy, or being tried twice for the same offense.⁴⁹ (Breed had been tried both in California Juvenile Court and later in Superior Court for the same offenses.) Finally, as noted in Chapter 11, the U.S. Supreme Court held in 2005 that the Eighth and Fourteenth Amendments forbid the execution of offenders who were under the age of 18 when their crimes were committed.⁵⁰

Right to the *Miranda* Warning

In 2011, the U.S. Supreme Court expanded the *Miranda* warning for suspects to include children questioned by police in school. In *J. D. B. v. North Carolina*, a 13-year-old North Carolina boy was taken from his classroom by a police officer and questioned, without an attorney or guardian present, in a conference room (where a police investigator and three school officials were present) concerning a string of burglaries. The boy eventually confessed, and his attorney lost his state appeal in trying to have the confession thrown out due to the boy's age and lack of *Miranda* warning (the state had argued that the boy should have felt free to leave the room and, therefore, was not in custody). The Supreme Court agreed with his attorney, saying for the first time that age must be considered in determining whether a suspect is aware of his or her rights.⁵¹ This decision tells police they cannot avoid giving a youth the *Miranda* warning simply by questioning the youth at school, away from his or her parents or guardians; it is thus expected to force police to adopt a "when in doubt, give the *Miranda* warnings" approach with juveniles.

The U.S. Supreme Court has decided that juveniles have the right to be represented by counsel as well as several other procedural rights prior to and during their involvement with the juvenile justice process. Pictured is Nathaniel Abraham; in 1999 he was tried as an adult and convicted of a murder he committed at age 11 in Michigan.

/// IN A NUTSHELL

- Quakers in New York City in 1825 sought to establish a balance between two camps—people wanting to see justice done with child offenders, and those not wanting them to be incarcerated; they founded the first house of refuge.

- At about the middle of the 19th century, the house of refuge movement evolved into the slightly more punitive reform school, or reformatory, approach, which involved segregating young offenders from adult criminals, removing the young from adverse home environments, minimizing court proceedings, and providing indeterminate sentences.

- In 1870, the Illinois Supreme Court held it unconstitutional to confine in a Chicago reform school a youth who had not been convicted of criminal conduct or afforded legal due process; thus, the juvenile court movement began.

- In 1899, the Illinois legislature enacted the Illinois Juvenile Court Act, creating the first separate juvenile court.

- In the post–World War II period, status offenses became a separate category, covering acts that would not be criminal if committed by an adult.

- Experts agree that a correlation exists between juvenile crime and family dysfunction, drug use and deviance, socioeconomic class, and educational experiences.

- The prevailing philosophy of the treatment of juveniles is *parens patriae*, meaning that the "state is the ultimate parent" of the child; the doctrine of *in loco parentis* means the state will act in place of the parent.

- An idealistic contrast exists between the juvenile court process and the criminal procedure for adults, involving different terminology and court processes.

- Most states' juvenile court decisions and legislation contain three underlying principles: the presumption of innocence, the presumption of the least amount of involvement with the system, and the presumption of the best interest of the minor.

- The primary goals of the juvenile justice system are separation from adults, youth confidentiality, community-based corrections, and individualized justice of minors.

- The newly enacted Juvenile Justice Reform Act of 2018 attempts to provide more protections for juvenile offenders, particularly concerning racial disparities and detention.

- The juvenile arrest rate for all offenses reached its highest level in 1996, and then declined 72 percent by 2017; however, more than 600,000 juveniles are arrested each year.

- A consequence of labeling juveniles is that they may never be redeemed in the eyes of the community.

- Some authors believe there is a school-to-prison pipeline, whereby students who are expelled from school become more engaged in criminality as a result of being in their neighborhoods with negative influences and becoming stigmatized and more hardened.

- Although the membership of youth in gangs now exceeds one million, the good news is that about as many youths leave gangs each year as join them; also youths do not remain in gangs forever, and there are successful programs that work to help get youths out of gangs.

- As with adult offenders, a youth who is about to reenter the community after being in a custodial facility sorely needs aftercare services, to reduce his or her chances of being rearrested and reincarcerated.

- Several important rights have been granted to juveniles by the courts in the areas of due process, representation by counsel, advance notice of charges, confronting and cross-examining witnesses, the privilege against self-incrimination, the burden of proof standard, and having *Miranda* warnings given.

- The U.S. Supreme Court has held that the Eighth Amendment's ban on cruel and unusual punishment prohibits mandatorily sentencing a juvenile offender who commits murder to serve a term of life without parole. Recently the Court expanded its original decision to make it retroactive.

/// KEY TERMS & CONCEPTS

Review key terms with eFlashcards at **edge.sagepub.com/peak4e**.

Disposition 386
Houses of refuge 375
Idealistic contrast 377
Illinois Juvenile Court Act (1899) 375
In loco parentis 376

Juvenile court 375
Life without parole 380
Parens patriae 376
PINS (person in need of supervision) 376

Presumption of innocence 378
Reformatory 375
School-to-prison pipeline 387
Status offense 376
Transfer (remand) 386

/// REVIEW QUESTIONS

Test your understanding of chapter content at **edge.sagepub.com/peak4e**

1. How would you describe the early treatment of juveniles, including houses of refuge and reformatories?
2. What contributions were made by the Illinois legislation that created the first juvenile justice/court system?
3. What are the major differences in philosophy and treatment (to include the "idealistic contrast") between juvenile and adult offenders?
4. What is the definition of a status offense?
5. What are the prevailing theories underlying juvenile criminality causation?
6. How would you describe the protections afforded under the Juvenile Justice Reform Act of 2018 and its previous versions?
7. How would you describe the recent shift in policy, principles, and processes as they now exist in the juvenile justice system? Legal protections (including the state of life-without-parole sentences across the United States)?
8. How would you explain the process and flow of cases through the juvenile justice system?
9. For what reason(s) might a juvenile offender be transferred to the jurisdiction of an adult criminal court?
10. What concerns exist with labeling of juvenile offenders?
11. Is there evidence that a school-to-prison pipeline exists? If so, what are some reasons for and possible solutions to it?
12. What is the current membership of juveniles in gangs? What approaches might be taken to keep or get them out of gangs?
13. What are some reasons for, and approaches to, providing formal aftercare and reentry services for juveniles as they leave custodial confinement and return to their homes and neighborhoods?
14. What due process rights were given to juveniles in *In re Gault*?
15. Aside from the rights secured in *Gault*, what other rights do juveniles now have in their justice system?

/// LEARN BY DOING

1. Your criminal justice class has been assigned a group project, with each group citing what it believes to be the major factors contributing to juvenile delinquency and related policy implications. Develop your argument using the following article: Terence P. Thornberry, David Huizinga, and Rolf Loeber, "The Causes and Correlates Studies: Findings and Policy Implications," *Juvenile Justice* 9, no. 1 (September 2004), www.ncjrs.gov/html/ojjdp/203555/jj2.html.

2. A number of potential interview topics are presented in this chapter regarding the treatment of juveniles in your area or region. As examples, you can inquire of area juvenile judges, facility staff, probation officers, and police officers concerning their work generally, as well as the use of secure and nonsecure confinement facilities in your area, whether or not they believe there exists a school-to-prison pipeline, how often juvenile offenders are transferred to the adult courts or placed in solitary confinement, and the aftercare/reentry services that are provided.

/// STUDY SITE

Get the tools you need to sharpen your study skills. SAGE edge offers a robust online environment featuring an impressive array of free tools and resources.

Access practice quizzes, eFlashcards, video, and multimedia at **edge.sagepub.com/peak4e**.

CHAPTER 16

ON THE CRIME POLICY AND PREVENTION AGENDA

Drug Abuse, Sex Trafficking, Terrorism, and Immigration

The human story does not always unfold like a mathematical calculation on the principle that two and two make four. Sometimes in life they make five or minus three; and sometimes the blackboard topples down in the middle of the sum and leaves the class in disorder.

—Winston Churchill

LEARNING OBJECTIVES

As a result of reading this chapter, you will be able to

1. Describe the current drug epidemic in the United States, particularly the status of opioid use and marijuana legislation, and what is being done by first responders, courts, and legislators toward dealing with illicit drug abuse

2. Define and explain major issues facing the United States and its criminal justice system relating to handling of sex trafficking, to include current legislation, programs, and proposals to address those challenges

3. Delineate the types of terrorism—including cyberterrorism, bioterrorism, school shootings, and gun violence in general—and some approaches for combating these issues

4. Explain the controversial nature and recent patterns of illegal immigration, what is known about the link between illegal immigration and crime, dealing with asylum seekers, and the debate surrounding construction of a border wall

ASSESS YOUR AWARENESS

Test your knowledge of selected criminal justice policy issues by responding to the following six true-false items; check your answers after reading this chapter.

1. Currently, the prescription drug problem (particularly involving opioids) in the United States has all but driven heroin and cocaine use out of existence.

2. Putting drug addicts in jail does little to stop prescription drug abuse, so many police agencies are cooperating with initiatives that put substance abusers into treatment programs.

3. At the federal level, the government has softened in its views of enforcement of marijuana laws, even while marijuana remains classified as a Schedule I substance under the Controlled Substances Act.

4. Victims of sex trafficking buy into the traffickers' promise of a better life in the United States, only to find they have been lied to, forced into servitude, or otherwise victimized.

5. Terrorist attacks have become increasingly focused on civilian targets, with terrorists using more traditional methods of violence such as employing guns and hostage-taking, rather than large-scale bombings.

6. The rates of crimes committed by illegal immigrants in the United States are extraordinarily high, driving the current fervor for closing the borders.

<< Answers can be found on page 419.

Now more than ever, Americans need to be able to rely on crime policies and practices that will guard against all types of crimes and vulnerabilities. Perhaps nowhere is that vulnerability more apparent than in Las Vegas, Nevada (indeed, the October 2017 shooting deaths of 58 people, and wounding of 422, by Stephen Paddock on the Las Vegas Strip would qualify as an act of domestic terrorism under 18 U.S. Code Sec. 2331). Each year more than 36 million people are drawn to this valley, the self-proclaimed "Entertainment Capital of the World," where they can enjoy 18 of the world's 25 largest hotels and countless entertainment acts and events. For those reasons, Las Vegas has long been viewed as a prime terrorist target and hotbed for all manner of crimes. Given that, under the veneer of Vegas's glitter and fun is an underlying layer of security that may be unprecedented, and it starts with what is termed a *fusion center*.

SAGE edge™
Master the content at edge.sagepub.com/peak4e

Las Vegas's status as a world destination, with more than 40 million visitors per year and about 40 casinos on its famed Strip, stands as a prime terrorist target.

Although there are more than 75 state and local fusion centers identified by the U.S. Department of Homeland Security,[1] the one in Las Vegas is unique. Inside its walls are 14 different federal, state, and local law enforcement agencies collaborating 24/7 to keep residents and tourists safe, focusing on all crimes and hazards, not just terrorism. Personnel in the center work in either an intelligence collections section or a crime analysis section to connect the dots between crimes that may look unrelated but could be precursors to a bigger event, collecting and sharing information about suspicious activities. The intelligence collections section follows up on suspicious activity reports, collects information in the field, and conducts surveillance. The crime analysis group looks at all types of crime occurring in the valley, from robberies to rapes and murders, to analyze trends. But the two sections often work together. For example, upon seeing a 700 percent increase in thefts of 20-pound propane tanks, the crime analysis section wasn't sure if the thefts were terrorism related (the tanks could be used to make bombs). The intelligence collections section began interviewing people who were caught stealing propane tanks and determined they were not terrorism related at all. Rather, people were selling them to recycling yards and using them to heat homes. Looking at police reports to identify trends or activities is obviously key to the center's success.[2]

Although fusion centers are often seen as dealing only with the specter of terrorism, they work with all types of real and potential problems that can and do plague the United States. This chapter explores some of those pressing issues.

INTRODUCTION

What can be done with the current opioid epidemic in the United States, and how might law enforcement and legislative enactments assist in addressing it? What does the future hold for recreational use of marijuana? How can we protect individuals from becoming victims of sex traffickers? What should be done about terrorists who now attack using little help and with inexpensive, widely available weapons and explosives made from everyday ingredients—and, increasingly, computers?[3] How should the United States resolve the tension between national security and protecting civil liberties for all? What is the answer to the long-standing debate surrounding immigration and border protection? There is no shortage of crime and policy challenges in America today—issues that affect and must be confronted by its criminal justice system.

This chapter briefly examines these four "hot-button" issues in terms of the problems and policy questions they pose. Each has deservedly received widespread attention and publicity, and been the subject of great concern, but they give no indication of abating in the foreseeable future.

AMERICA'S DRUG EPIDEMIC

Heroin, Cocaine, and Opioid "Pill Mills"

Opioids: a class of drugs that includes heroin, synthetic opioids such as fentanyl, and pain relievers available legally by prescription.

So-called pill mills run by physicians who are prescribing **opioids** (a class of drugs naturally found in the opium poppy plant) illegally and/or excessively, and residents who engage in "doctor shopping" to feed an addiction, have been garnering most of the nation's attention. For example, in Reno, Nevada, federal drug agents in 2016 raided a car dealership and arrested nine persons for operating an opioid distribution ring, including the prescribing physician, who was sentenced to 10 years in prison. More than $8 million in drugs were put on the streets in about two years' time.[4] At the same time, the levels of heroin and cocaine use in the United States remain significant: According to the National Survey on Drug Use and Health, about 948,000 Americans reported using heroin in the previous year, a number that has been on the rise since 2007. This trend appears to be driven largely by young adults, aged 18–25, among whom there have been the greatest increases.[5] Similarly, cocaine use in the United States gives no indication of slowing. Cocaine is the second most common cause of fatal drug overdose, nearly a million people try it for the first time each year, it can be mixed with potent opioids, and its use can easily undergo a resurgence in the United States at any time.[6]

Drug use in the United States, fueled by heroin, cocaine, and opioid "pill mills," has reached epidemic proportions.

The most alarming form of synthetic opioid is fentanyl, which is similar to morphine but 50–100 times more potent. Given its strength, fentanyl is now the drug most often involved in fatal overdoses. Its illegal form is made in labs and sold as a powder, on blotter paper, or put in eye droppers or nasal sprays or pills; mixing it with other drugs (such as heroin, cocaine, or meth) makes it a cheaper option for obtaining a high.[7]

This epidemic has reached staggering levels, with about 47,600 people dying from opioid overdoses in 2018[8] (on top of the 49,000 deaths in 2017 and the 64,000 in 2016). In a recent year, 11.4 million people misused opioid prescriptions, 2.1 million people had an opioid use disorder, and 28,500 deaths were attributed to synthetic opioids other than methadone (see Figure 16.1 for more statistics); indeed, in late 2017 the federal government declared

Figure 16.1 /// The Opioid Epidemic by the Numbers

 130+ People died every day from opioid-related drug overdoses[3] (estimated)

 11.4 m People misused prescription opioids[1]

 47,600 People dies from overdosing on opioids[2]

 2.1 million People had an opioid use disorder[1]

 886,000 People used heroin[1]

 81,000 People used heroin for the first time[1]

 2 million People misused prescription opioids for the first time[1]

 15,482 Deaths attributed to overdosing on heroin[2]

 28,466 Deaths attributed to overdosing on synthetic opioids other than methadone[2]

Source:
1. 2017 National Survey on Drug Use and Health. Mortality in the United States, 2016
2. NCHS Data Brief No. 293, December 2017
3. NCHS, National Vital Statistics System. Estimates for 2017 and 2018 are based on provisional data.

Investigating Further

Chasing "El Chapo"

Joaquin "El Chapo" (translating to "The Shorty") Guzman was extradited to the United States and put on federal trial in early 2019 in Brooklyn, New York. After more than two decades of eluding police and accomplishing several escapes from prison, the Mexican drug lord—who rose from working in the opium poppy fields at age 15 to being kingpin of the infamous Sinaloa cartel—finally saw his career brought to an end. Guzman led an organization that, over three decades, trafficked $14 billion in drugs to the United States, caused 119,000 murders (including thousands in the United States), and contributed to $1 trillion in U.S. spending on the war on drugs. So much cash is reaped in this trade that, as one author put it, "they don't even count it, they *weigh* it."

After 56 prosecution witnesses testified for more than 200 hours, Guzman was convicted in February 2019 of multiple counts of distributing large amounts of narcotics internationally. His conviction should be viewed as a hollow victory, though. Guzman will likely die in a U.S. supermax prison, but the Sinaloa cartel is still known to be operating as the most powerful cartel in Mexico. Indeed, two weeks prior to Guzman's conviction, enough fentanyl for 100 million lethal doses was seized at the Nogales port of entry.

Sources: Ioan Grillo, "Where the Legend of El Chapo Was Born, *Newsweek*, May 21, 2018, pp. 31–36; Don Winslow, quoted in George Will, "Worse Living Through Chemistry," *Reno Gazette Journal*, March 17, 2019, p. 5D; and Daniela Silva, "El Chapo's Conviction Is 'Great Moral Victory,' but Has 'Done Nothing' Against Sinaloa Cartel, Experts Say," NBC News, February 13, 2019, https://www.nbcnews.com/news/us-news/el-chapo-s-conviction-great-moral-victory-has-done-nothing-n971201.

---

this epidemic a public health emergency.[9] Moreover, for the first time, in early 2019 it was announced that Americans had greater odds of dying from an accidental opioid overdose than from a motor vehicle accident.[10]

What Can Be Done?

First, go after profits; in August 2019 an Oklahoma jury fined a major drug company $572 million for helping to fuel its epidemic (and more than 1,500 similar lawsuits have been filed).

Members of Congress are attempting to stem the tide of addiction in several ways: by encouraging research on new nonaddictive pain medications, electronically linking all nationwide efforts to fight the epidemic, stemming the influx of illicit drugs into the country, establishing grants to help fight addiction, directing the U.S. Food and Drug Administration to set up programs for the safe return of unused opioids, and ensuring that medical professionals have access to a consenting patient's complete health history when deciding how to treat a patient (to avoid overprescribing opioids).[11]

In addition, realizing that putting drug addicts in jail does little or nothing to stop drug use, many police agencies are cooperating with initiatives that put substance abusers into treatment rather than jail, while also supporting an "early warning system" of rapid testing of confiscated substances and directing aid to people who have overdosed on opioids. Regarding the latter, when encountering a fatal overdose, expediting the testing of the substance that was used can help public health agencies to more quickly identify any overdose clusters or new batches of particularly dangerous substances. Furthermore, often being first on the scene, officers and other first responders are being trained in the administration of medications such as **Narcan/naloxone** (though fentanyl, being much stronger than other opioids, might require multiple doses); a Police Executive Research Forum study found that this approach has already saved 3,500 lives in 276 agencies

Narcan/naloxone/suboxone: a medication that can be used to block the effects of opioids, particularly for overdoses.

surveyed.[12] Police can also provide drug treatment in jails; incarceration can provide an opportunity to help addicted persons undergo treatment. **Suboxone** can be administered in the jails to relieve withdrawal and cravings for opioids without causing the "high" of heroin or dangerous side effects.[13]

Finally, specialty problem-solving drug courts (discussed in Chapter 9) can assist persons who are addicted to opioids by providing medication-assisted treatment (MAT). However, many drug courts do not recommend (or even allow) the use of such treatment for opioid dependence. One survey of drug courts found that although 98 percent of their drug court participants were opioid dependent, only about half of the courts offered any form of MAT to participants.[14]

The Status of Medical and Recreational Marijuana Use

Although the number is subject to rapid change, 33 states and the District of Columbia currently have legalized marijuana in some form. The District of Columbia and 10 states—Alaska, California, Colorado, Maine, Massachusetts, Michigan, Nevada, Oregon, Vermont, and Washington—have adopted the most expansive laws legalizing marijuana for recreational use.[15] In addition, at least nine states all across the map are looking at legislation that would legalize marijuana in the near future.[16]

Note that **marijuana decriminalization** and **marijuana legalization** are two different concepts and approaches. Decriminalization involves a state repealing or amending its marijuana laws to make certain acts criminal (such as sales or trafficking), but some aspects are no longer subject to prosecution (e.g., individuals with small amounts of marijuana for personal consumption). Marijuana legalization typically means that one will not be arrested for marijuana use if he or she follows the state laws as to age, place, and amount for consumption (however, one might still be arrested for selling or trafficking if such are prohibited under the law).

At the federal level, the government has softened in its views of enforcement of marijuana laws, even while marijuana remains classified as a Schedule I substance under the Controlled Substances Act. In early 2019, U.S. Attorney General William Barr indicated that he favors a more lenient, albeit federalist, approach to marijuana laws, and for cannabis to be legalized nationwide rather than having states continue to go against the federal prohibition.[17]

Today it is estimated that 61 percent of Americans favor legalizing adult-use marijuana, while 88 percent favor legalizing medical marijuana nationwide. The police certainly stand to benefit from this trend, with an estimated $10 billion to $20 billion being spent each year on marijuana enforcement. Given that more than 600,000 marijuana arrests have been made during each of the past several years (about 9 in 10 for possession only), at an estimated cost of $750 per arrest, the police would surely have many resources to divert elsewhere.[18] Similarly, courts and corrections agencies would realize tremendous savings if not having to adjudicate and house such offenders.

Marijuana decriminalization: where a state has repealed or amended its marijuana laws to make certain acts criminal but no longer subject to prosecution (e.g., individuals caught with small amounts of marijuana for personal consumption may not be prosecuted and, thus, avoid a criminal record).

Marijuana legalization: typically, where one will not be arrested for marijuana use if he or she follows the state laws as to age, place, and amount for consumption (however, one might still be arrested for selling or trafficking if such are prohibited under the law).

SEX TRAFFICKING

Definition and Victimization

The U.S. Department of Justice defines **sex trafficking** as a commercial sex act that is "induced by force, fraud, or coercion, or in which the person induced to perform such act has not attained 18 years of age." It can also include "recruitment, harboring, transportation, provision, or obtaining of a person for labor or services, through the use of force, fraud, or coercion."[19] Today sex trafficking is a $99 billion annual industry that encompasses about 4.8 million victims around the world, mostly women and children.[20]

Sex trafficking: the use of humans for the purpose of sexual slavery or commercial sexual exploitation.

Investigating Further

How Some Sex Trafficking Victims Are Made

Often, stories of sex trafficking victims are buried beneath the statistics of the crime. It is important to remember that behind each statistic is a suffering and often physically and emotionally abused person whose entire life has been tragically affected. Although each case is certainly unique in its circumstances, the following two individuals are not atypical:

- Rosa, a young woman from Mexico, was brought to the United States at age 17 to work as a babysitter for a Mr. Lopez, who was also from Mexico but had been in the U.S. several years operating a furniture business. Lopez married an American woman, and they had two young children. He often traveled to Mexico and eventually met Rosa through her family's business. He offered her a job taking care of his two young children in the United States; her parents consented, and soon she was in the United States working as a nanny as well as cooking, cleaning, and doing laundry and yard work. Rosa did not have her own room and seldom was she given a day off to rest. She was not paid for her work, nor was she allowed to speak to anyone outside of Lopez's family. She was also drugged and raped on several occasions by Lopez. She eventually befriended a woman at church who helped her escape from her trafficker. Then, determined that Lopez should pay for his crimes, Rosa had him arrested and prosecuted for rape and sex trafficking. Lopez was sent to prison, ordered to forfeit property, and then was sentenced to be deported upon finishing his sentence.

- John was 16 years old when he ran away from his home in Nebraska, hoping to travel the country. Upon arriving in New York City, however, he ran out of money. Sleeping on the streets, he soon fell in with a group of older homeless youth who introduced him to heroin. Soon thereafter they also introduced him to older men who would pay John for sexual favors so that he could feed his heroin habit. John eventually met social workers who referred him to resources he needed to take care of himself, including shelter and addiction treatment. After weeks of counseling, John began to discuss his life on the streets and was able to get his GED, find a job, and move into a supportive housing program for young recovering drug users.

Source: Adapted from City of New York, "Example of Sex Trafficking," https://www1.nyc.gov/site/endhumantrafficking/about/example-of-human-trafficking.page.

The United States is known as a destination country for transnational trafficking networks that bring foreign nationals into the country for purposes of both sexual and labor exploitation. Trafficking victims in the United States are primarily from Asia, Latin America, Eastern Europe, and Africa.[21]

What Can Be Done?

No single agency can prevent sex trafficking or protect its victims while also prosecuting traffickers. First and foremost, relationships must be developed between law enforcement and social services agencies before sex trafficking can be addressed and victims assisted. In particular, the two agencies need to be able to delegate tasks and clearly define their respective roles.

Sex trafficking typically occurs behind the closed doors of private homes or under the radar of legitimate businesses; crime rings have also become quite astute in the methods of smuggling persons across borders and hiding victims of trafficking as they move them between cities. Victims believe the promise of traffickers of a better life in the United States, only to find they have been lied to, forced into servitude, or otherwise victimized. These victims need assistance and benefits, such as those provided by the Trafficking

Victims Protection Act of 2000 (TVPA), which specified severe punishment for traffickers and afforded qualifying victims shelter, rehabilitation programs, freedom from deportation, and other benefits.[22]

The T Visa

In conjunction with the aforementioned TVPA and other laws created to protect victims of trafficking, the T visa was also created in 2000. It allows some victims of sex trafficking and their immediate family members to remain and work temporarily in the United States if they agree to assist law enforcement in testifying against the perpetrators. Such legislation was necessary because victims of sex trafficking in the United States are usually undocumented and subject to deportation; therefore, while a criminal case is developing against the victim's trafficker(s), the victim may now be allowed to legally remain here to assist with the prosecution. Furthermore, three years after obtaining a T visa, victims may apply for permanent resident status and even file for immediate family members to join them legally in the United States.[23] In addition, such victims may qualify for federal and state benefits and programs, such as food stamps, Medicaid, and cash assistance.[24]

T visa: a type of visa that allow victims of human trafficking and their immediate family members to remain and work temporarily in the United States (provided certain conditions are met).

Additional Efforts: The Diagnostic Center

Notwithstanding all of the legislative and enforcement efforts now in place, effectively addressing sex trafficking can still be extremely challenging for communities that do not possess established practices for identifying and protecting sex trafficking victims and investigating and prosecuting cases. Now, however, the U.S. Department of Justice, Office of Justice Programs, provides assistance in what is termed a *diagnostic center*. Established in 2012, diagnostic centers employ data-driven strategies for combating sex trafficking.

With such efforts as those described here, and a variety of training programs and other resources in the police toolkit,[25] there have been some impressive results:

- In Los Angeles County, 510 people were arrested and 56 persons rescued in a crackdown on trafficking by regional task forces.[26]
- A state trooper, a pastor, and a convicted sex offender were among 1,000 people arrested in a national operation run by the National Johns Suppression Initiative and law enforcement agencies across the country.[27]
- A national operation resulted in 120 arrests and 84 children rescued as part of the Innocence Lost National Initiative; during this operation a three-month-old girl and her five-year-old sister were recovered after a family friend made a deal with an undercover officer to sell both children for sex for $600.[28]

POLICING TERRORISM

Definitions and Types

The FBI succinctly defines terrorism as an act "perpetrated by individuals and/or groups inspired by or associated with primarily U.S.-based movements that espouse extremist ideologies of a political, religious, social, racial, or environmental nature."[29] More broadly, terrorism as defined in the U.S. Code can be both domestic and international in nature and is any act that appears to be intended to intimidate or coerce a civilian population; to influence the policy of a government by intimidation or coercion; or to affect the conduct of a government by mass destruction, assassination, or kidnapping (see Figure 16.2). School shootings (often involving mass killings) fall within those parameters and thus are included in this discussion of terrorism.[30]

Figure 16.2 /// FBI Most Wanted Poster

IBRAHIM SALIH MOHAMMED AL-YACOUB

Conspiracy to Kill U.S. Nationals; Conspiracy to Murder U.S. Employees; Conspiracy to Use Weapons of Mass Destruction Against U.S. Nationals; Conspiracy to Destroy Property of the U.S.; Conspiracy to Attack National Defense Utilities; Bombing Resulting in Death; Use of Weapons of Mass Destruction Against U.S. Nationals; Murder While Using Destructive Device During a Crime of Violence; Murder of Federal Employees; Attempted Murder of Federal Employees

DESCRIPTION

Date(s) of Birth Used: October 16, 1966
Hair: Black
Height: 5'4"
Build: Unknown
Sex: Male
Languages: Arabic

Place of Birth: Tarut, Saudi Arabia
Eyes: Brown
Weight: 150 pounds
Complexion: Olive
Citizenship: Saudi Arabian
Scars and Marks: None known

REWARD
The Rewards For Justice Program, United States Department of State, is offering a reward of up to $5 million for information leading directly to the apprehension or conviction of Ibrahim Salih Mohammed Al-Yacoub.

REMARKS
Al-Yacoub is an alleged member of the terrorist organization, Saudi Hizballah.

CAUTION
Ibrahim Salih Mohammed Al-Yacoub has been indicted in the Eastern District of Virginia for the June 25, 1996, bombing of the Khobar Towers military housing complex in Dhahran, Kingdom of Saudi Arabia.

SHOULD BE CONSIDERED ARMED AND DANGEROUS

If you have any information concerning this person, please contact your local FBI office or the nearest American Embassy or Consulate.

Field Office: Washington D.C.

Terrorism, as defined previously, occurs around the world, as suicide bombings and shootings, kidnappings, assassinations, and beheadings each year will attest. International terrorist groups have become more adept at recruiting "foot soldiers" through the Internet and other means. These attacks have become increasingly focused on civilian targets, with terrorists using more traditional methods of violence such as deploying guns and hostage-taking, rather than large-scale bombings. **International terrorism** pointedly demonstrates the need for the international law enforcement community to become much more knowledgeable about terrorists' methods, how to predict and possibly prevent future attacks, and how to respond when terrorists do strike in the event of an attack.

International terrorism: acts of terrorism perpetrated in a foreign country by terrorists who are not native to that country.

These and other attacks similarly have called the nation's law enforcement agencies to action, to learn more about terrorists' methods here and abroad, as well as how to predict and possibly prevent future attacks. In addition, they have had to adopt a broader view of protecting the homeland (the organization and functions of the Department of Homeland Security were discussed in Chapter 5).

Right-Wing Extremists and Lone-Wolf Terrorists

In December 2015, a husband and wife wearing military-style clothing and black masks entered a Christmas party for employees of the San Bernardino, California, county health department and opened fire with two assault-style weapons, killing 14 people in what was the deadliest terrorist attack in the United States since 9/11. The couple were parents and college graduates, solidly middle class, with no criminal records, but they were also typical homegrown **extremists** wanting to defend or spread their beliefs.

Extremists: persons who hold extreme or fanatical political or religious views, which can lead to the commission or advocacy of extreme action.

Then, in October 2018, Robert Bowers, harboring anti-Semitic views, carried out a mass shooting at the Tree of Life Synagogue near Pittsburgh, Pennsylvania. Bowers was charged with 63 counts, including obstructing religious beliefs resulting in death as well as violations of the Matthew Shepard and James Byrd Jr. Hate Crimes Prevention Act.[31]

Also in October 2018, 56-year-old Cesar Sayoc, who drove a white van with stickers depicting some of President Trump's critics and targets over their images, was arrested for sending 14 pipe bombs through the mail to prominent Democrats around the nation (none of which detonated).[32] Officials admitted the difficulty of trying to detect dangerous items such as these, given that the U.S. Postal Service handles millions of packages each day.[33]

Although none of these individuals was known to be formally affiliated with a foreign terrorist group, they could easily turn to an extremist community online, for training, to espouse their views, and to try to incite others. Such extremists—**homegrown violent extremists** (HVEs)—warrant particular concern today. They are self-radicalized and "encourage, endorse, condone, justify, or support the commission of a violent criminal act" in order "to achieve political, ideological, religious, social, or economic goal." HVEs "can include U.S.-born citizens, naturalized citizens, green card holders or other long-term residents, foreign students, or illegal immigrants" wishing to commit terrorist acts inside Western countries or against Western interests abroad.[34] Some might have been inspired by calls by the Islamic State of Iraq and the Levant (ISIL) for individual jihadists in the West to retaliate for U.S.-led airstrikes on ISIL.[35]

Homegrown violent extremists: persons who are inspired by foreign terrorist organizations and radicalized in the countries in which they are born, raised, or reside.

A related concern is the **lone-wolf terrorist** who undergoes **radicalization** (see the accompanying "Investigating Further" box)—a single individual driven to hateful attacks based on a particular set of beliefs without a larger group's knowledge or support.

Lone-wolf terrorist: one who plans and commits acts of terrorism without the support of a larger terrorist group.

Cyberterrorism: The Asian Threat

Our foreign adversaries are very much aware that U.S. businesses, public agencies, citizens, and governments are so dependent on computer systems to run everything that hackers

Radicalization: a process whereby one adopts radical positions on political or social issues.

Investigating Further

The Radicalization of Zachary Chesser

Zachary Chesser, a U.S. citizen, used his computer and graphics skills to promote violent extremist messages and was ultimately arrested for attempting to provide material support to a terrorist organization.

Zachary Chesser was an average high school student in northern Virginia. He participated in his high school's gifted and talented program, joined his high school break-dancing team, was an avid soccer player with aspirations of getting a scholarship to play in college, and worked part time at a video rental store.

In the summer of 2008, the 18-year-old Chesser converted to Islam and quickly became radicalized, solely on the Internet. He began posting views that supported Islamist terrorist groups, watching sermons by Anwar al-Awlaki, and he exchanged emails with the cleric about joining Al-Shabab. Within weeks, he had quit his job because he "objected to working at a place that rented videos featuring naked women" and became increasingly hostile to his parents.

Soon Chesser had committed himself solely to using his computer and graphics skills to contribute to and promote violent extremist messages. He also attempted to travel to Somalia with his wife to join Al-Shabab but was unsuccessful when his mother-in-law hid his wife's passport. Next, he uploaded a video to YouTube in which he threatened the creators of the television show *South Park* after an episode depicted the Prophet Muhammad dressed in a bear costume. He then attempted to join Al-Shabab once again but was held for questioning at the airport. A few days after being questioned, Chesser was arrested for attempting to provide material support to a terrorist organization. He pleaded guilty to three federal felony charges—communicating threats, soliciting violent jihadists to desensitize law enforcement, and attempting to provide material support to a designated foreign terrorist organization—and was sentenced to 25 years in federal prison.

Source: See, generally, Senate Committee on Homeland Security and Governmental Affairs, *Zachary Chesser: A Case Study in Online Islamist Radicalization and Its Meaning for the Threat of Homegrown Terrorism*, February 2012, https://www.hsgac.senate.gov/imo/media/doc/CHESSER%20FINAL%20REPORT(1)2.pdf.

Cyberterrorism: a premeditated, politically motivated attack against computer systems, computer programs, or data.

Cybercrime: the use of computers to commit crimes, such as embezzlement, diversion of bank monies to other accounts, and hacking personal information.

who can infiltrate those systems can be as effective and damaging as a military effort using troops and weaponry. Which foreign power is now the biggest threat against the United States with respect to cyberattacks or **cyberterrorism**? Although Russia was recently at or near the top of the list for its suspected efforts to disrupt the 2016 U.S. presidential elections, the most challenging and potentially disastrous type of **cybercrime**—actually, cyberespionage—now being perpetrated against the United States is by China's state-supported cyber warfare. Its three categories of cyber warfare—involving specialized military forces, military-authorized cyber warfare specialists, and civilians—have over the past dozen years stolen data from the U.S. Navy (concerning submarine warfare), NASA, IBM, and other agencies and companies and compromised many of the nation's most sensitive advanced weapons systems, including missile defense technology and combat aircraft.[36] China's interests have shifted recently to stealing financial and tech-related secrets from corporations, universities, government departments, and biotech firms.[37] Not to be overlooked, however, is the rising threat from North Korea, where the economy has long struggled and a group of hackers is believed to be actively targeting U.S. businesses and "critical infrastructure." North Korean hackers have tried to infiltrate finance, telecommunications, energy, and defense sectors around the world.[38]

According to INTERPOL, cybercrime is one of the fastest growing areas of crime and includes attacks against computer hardware and software; financial crimes and corruption; and abuse, in the form of grooming or "sexploitation," especially crimes against children.[39]

Practitioner's Perspective

Director of IT and Electronic Security

Name: Dennis Bachman
Position: Director of IT and Electronic Security, Kansas Racing and Gaming Commission
Location: Kansas

What is your career story? I've been in law enforcement for 42 years now. I started with the Topeka Police Department as a patrol officer, progressed up through the ranks—detective, field sergeant—until I was injured and had to leave. Fortunately, I had obtained my degree while I was working. From there, I went to another role in the criminal justice system, as a probation officer, and started out doing presentence investigations. From that position, I went on to be chief of one of the regions in Kansas, to the Third Judicial District. I went back to the Third Judicial District and became a supervising probation officer. At this point, I had developed an expertise in handling high-risk offenders working with gang members. Because of that, the state parole board requested that I come over and handle high-risk offenders for them, so I went into the Department of Corrections. In that role, and because of my background of working as a law enforcement officer, I also worked on fugitive apprehension and was cross-deputized as a special deputy U.S. marshal in their Fugitive Apprehension Unit. After I'd been out in the field doing that, I realized I wanted to find work that was a little bit more subdued. I had the background in information technology [IT] and started using that specialty in the area of regulatory work and gaming. I started out working with tribal gaming and then worked in casino gaming with the state.

What are some challenges and misconceptions you face in this position? One of the misconceptions in my field is that people don't think my role is necessary because they think you can't cheat the slot machines. The fact is you can, and people try, and they do. We catch them. That's our specialty, figuring out how we catch them. There are a lot of ways of cheating slot machines. There are a lot of reasons that we work with the machines before they get put on the floor.

Do you see any common trends in this position? One of the ways that our field is going to change is how it's going to handle the Millennials. The way the game works now, they're actually set up more for people my age and older. The Millennials are more gaming oriented. They are going to change gaming to accommodate their expertise, but at the same time, to get a continuous flow of play that requires placing coins in the machine. Mobile gaming is also a new trend. People don't want to be tied to the machine. They like being able to move around and go from spot to spot while playing. We are going to see a rise in wireless gaming.

What advice would you give to someone either wishing to study, or now studying, criminal justice and wanting to become a practitioner in this position? One of the things I would say—and I would do this in any part of the criminal justice system—is to keep information technology in your training. When I was in probation and parole both, I used databases. I built them, they helped me a lot all the way through. When I was with the Topeka Police Department, I was in criminal intelligence—built databases, worked with different systems, so having that background helped me all the way through my career. And right now, I'm seeing a lot of people coming in, and they're having problems with some very basic IT work. So I would stress that you're going to need these skills, and having a good foundation for IT will help you.

To learn more about Dennis Bachman's experiences as a director of IT and electronic security watch the Practitioner's Perspective video in SAGE vantage.

Unquestionably, many people around the world are now working full time trying to hack into online data, and the threats Americans face have never been more real or severe. According to the Privacy Rights Clearinghouse, for the 9,100 data breaches that were made public since 2005, about 11.6 billion records were breached.[40] Furthermore, each breach is estimated to cost American businesses an average of nearly $8 million, and that figure is increasing.[41]

There are also concerns about threats posed to U.S. nuclear reactors, banks, subways, and pipeline companies. The specter of electricity going out for days and perhaps weeks, the gates of a major dam opening suddenly and flooding complete cities, or pipes in a chemical plant rupturing and releasing deadly gas are nightmare scenarios that keep homeland security professionals awake at night.

Bioterrorism

Bioterrorism: the use of biological material, such as anthrax or botulin, to commit an act of terrorism.

Another means of attack by terrorists involves the use of chemical/biological agents, or **bioterrorism**. Poisons have been used for several millennia; recent attacks using chemical/biological agents including toxins, viruses, or bacteria such as anthrax, ricin, and sarin have underscored their potential dangers and uses by terrorists today. Chemical weapons—including several types of gases—suffocate the victim immediately or cause massive burning. Biological weapons are slower acting, spreading a disease such as anthrax or smallpox through a population before the first signs are noticed. Many experts believe it is only a matter of time before chemical/biological weapons are used like explosives have been to date.[42] All that is required is for a toxin to be cultured and put into a spray form that can be weaponized and disseminated into the population. Fortunately, such bioterrorism agents are extremely difficult for all but specially trained individuals to make in large quantities and in the correct dosage; they are also difficult to transport because live organisms are delicate.

What Can Be Done?
Federal Efforts Against Terrorism and Cyber Warfare

Police have several possible means of attempting to prevent or address acts of terrorism. On a practical level, there is the federal Department of Homeland Security (DHS, discussed in Chapter 5), which has more than 240,000 employees in jobs that range from aviation and border security to emergency response, from cybersecurity analyst to chemical facility inspector.[43]

Furthermore, the Federal Emergency Management Administration (FEMA) administers a National Incident Management System (NIMS), which provides a framework for agencies of all levels to work effectively together to prepare for, prevent, respond to, and recover from domestic incidents.[44] With respect to cyber warfare, American governments, businesses, and citizens have long had a fortress mentality, putting faith in firewalls, patching software, guarding passwords—approaches that have failed, as we know from major hacks. Governments and businesses are now working harder to guard their systems from the inside rather than protecting against hacks from the outside, such as by creating information security departments, hiring "white-hat" consultants (hacking-savvy persons who can detect weak points), and hardening their systems.[45]

At the federal level is the U.S. Cyber Command, which protects U.S. Department of Defense networks and conducts "full spectrum military cyberspace operations."[46] At the state and local levels, three approaches have been undertaken: First, a growing number of state governments are using multiagency groups to tackle cybersecurity and to analyze real and emerging threats. Some such alliances include the FBI, the DHS, and academic institutions, in hopes of determining ways to speed up coordinated responses to cyberattack. Second, employees are being trained to make them more conscious of security overall and to reduce the kinds of mistakes that can bring about an intrusion, cause an attack, or allow certain types of fraud. Third, interestingly enough, is that both states and local governments can now purchase cyber insurance to help cover the cost of investigating an attack, notifying individuals impacted by the breach, and recovering the theft of government funds.[47]

From a local policing standpoint, the minimal approach is to have trained personnel gathering digital evidence; this has even been termed the "future of policing." Not only must these personnel know how to secure a computer's memory cache, activity logs, and Internet history, but they also must maximize speed in getting to and securing the crime scene. Every second a computer is left unattended, it loses data stored in its memory cache and crucial evidence is permanently lost. Police themselves must also know how to hack, from conducting information-gathering reconnaissance to covering their tracks by restoring the criminal's computer to its preattack state.[48]

Legislative Measures

Several types of federal legislation have been enacted to help criminal justice agencies in the nation's fight against terrorism. First, although the Posse Comitatus Act of 1878 prohibits using the military to execute the laws domestically, the military may be called on to provide personnel and equipment for special support activities, such as responding to domestic terrorism events involving weapons of mass destruction.[49]

Immediately following the 9/11 attacks, Congress passed the USA PATRIOT Act (Uniting and Strengthening America by Providing Appropriate Tools Required to Intercept and Obstruct Terrorism Act of 2001). The act dramatically expanded the federal government's ability to investigate Americans without establishing probable cause for "intelligence purposes" and to conduct searches if there are "reasonable grounds to believe" there may be national security threats. Federal agencies such as the FBI and others are given access to financial, mental health, medical, library, and other records. The act was reauthorized in March 2006, providing additional tools: the "roving wiretap" portion and the "sneak and peek" section. The first allows the government to get a wiretap on every phone a suspect uses, while the second allows federal investigators to access library, business, and medical records without a court order. In June 2015, Congress extended the act through 2019 but amended it to stop the National Security Agency from continuing its mass phone data collection program.[50]

Furthermore, in October 2006 President George W. Bush signed the Military Commissions Act (MCA).[51] Under the MCA, the president is authorized to establish military commissions to try unlawful enemy combatants. The commissions are authorized to sentence defendants to death, and defendants are prevented from invoking the Geneva Conventions as a source of rights during commission proceedings. The law also strips detainees of the right to file *habeas corpus* petitions in federal court and also allows hearsay evidence to be admitted during proceedings, so long as the presiding officer determines it to be reliable.[52]

Posse Comitatus Act of 1878: legislation that prohibits the federal government from using the armed forces for the purpose of law enforcement, except in cases authorized by the Constitution or an act of Congress.

Domestic terrorism: the commission of terrorist acts in the perpetrator's own country against his or her fellow citizens.

USA PATRIOT Act: broadly written legislation that affords law enforcement with new tools to detect and prevent terrorism.

Military Commissions Act: legislation authorizing trial by military commission for violations of the law of war, and for other purposes.

Related Issues: School Shootings and Gun Violence
Extent and Nature

As Daniel Victor wrote in the *New York Times* in May 2018, "It's never long until the next school shooting in America."[53] Sad but, unfortunately, true; according to the Center for Homeland Defense and Security, there have been more than 1,350 school shootings in the United States since 2000 (see Figure 16.3). Of those, a little more than half (51 percent) occurred outside, on school property, and about 44 percent were inside the school building. Incidents occurred about equally by day of week, being slightly higher in number on Fridays, and were more common in January/February and September/October. Finally, most shootings tend to be perpetrated by a small (.22 caliber) handgun.[54]

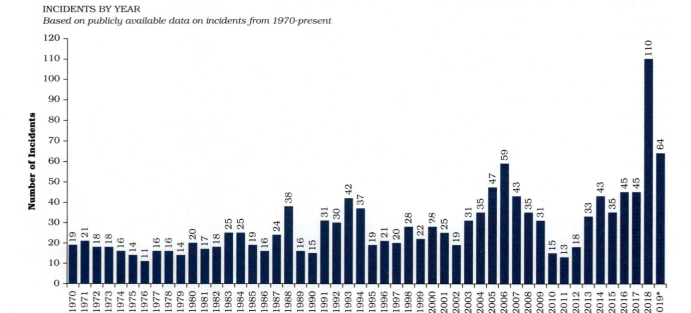

Figure 16.3 /// K–12 School Shooting Database, Incidents by Year

*As of October, 2019.

Active shooter: an individual seeking to kill or attempting to kill people in a confined and populated area.

With respect to police response to an active-shooter situation, much has changed in the decade since the April 1999 mass murders by two shooters at Columbine High School in Littleton, Colorado. Thirteen people were killed while on-scene officers waited 45 minutes for an elite SWAT team to arrive. Police have greatly modified their protocols for dealing with such critical incidents. The most immediate change in protocol calls for police across the country to react swiftly to an active-shooter situation; responding officers are being trained to rush toward gunfire and—if necessary—even step over victims in order to stop the **active shooter** before more lives are lost. Such training is grounded on the assumption that, in a mass shooting, a gunman kills a person every 15 seconds. (Prior to Columbine, the protocol was for police to take a contain-and-wait strategy, intended to prevent officers and bystanders from getting killed; first responders would establish a perimeter to contain the situation and then wait for the special-weapons team to go in and neutralize the shooters(s).) Finally, another change in tactics wrought by Columbine is that special-weapons teams now typically have armed medics and rescue teams trained to remove wounded persons under fire.

With respect to prevention, it is known that after school shootings occur, so-called red flags are always discovered concerning the shooter, so the key to prevention is to find those red flags before shootings occur. The key is information sharing: People who become concerned about a fellow student, a coworker, or a neighbor need to share information. K–12 schools and universities have student privacy laws, but every law has a safety provision that lets someone exchange information if it is a matter of public safety. Police, school personnel, parents, and other stakeholders must find all the flags, to include talking to the person's neighbors, coworkers, or whoever else might be able to reveal something.[55]

Closely related to the subject of school shootings is that of gun violence. For our Founding Fathers, the right to "keep and bear arms" with a "well-regulated militia" was "so central to the notion of liberty that it came second in the Bill of Rights only to the freedom to think and speak."[56] But they could not have foreseen a time when each year more than 42,000 people would die or be injured through firearms violence (including about 700 children)[57] and more than 300 mass shootings would occur.[58]

In the United States today, approximately 265 million guns are privately owned (although only 4 percent of Americans hunt); each day those guns are used to kill 97 persons, and guns are used in 97 percent of all homicides.[59] Yet—although two-thirds of Americans say they want stricter laws regarding firearms sales, nearly one-half support a ban on assault-style weapons, and more than 80 percent support requiring background checks for private sales and at gun shows[60]—there seems to be little appetite among lawmakers to attempt to enact stricter gun control laws.

Widely publicized, senseless mass shootings have prompted what may be a turning point in gun control laws and related violence. Signs of a growing gun control movement include protests by high school students, legislation by politicians, and boycotts of corporate America. In addition, for the first time, gun control advocates outspent the National Rifle Association during the 2018 midterm elections, and new gun control measures were enacted in several states (including increasing the minimum age for purchasing a firearm, requiring waiting periods, and allowing temporary confiscation of weapons from people deemed a safety risk). In early 2019, the U.S. House of Representatives held its first hearing on gun control in a decade, and some financial firms refused to do business with gun makers or companies that sell firearms and ammunition.[61]

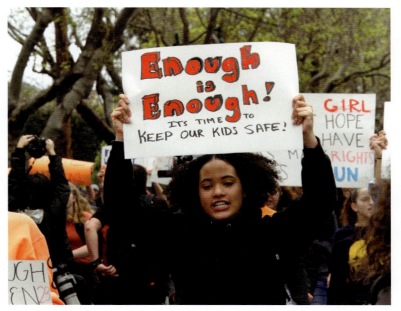

Approaches to gun violence include background checks, preventing mentally ill people from purchasing guns, tracking gun sales, banning assault-style weapons, and barring gun purchases by people on watch or no-fly lists.

Studies of prison inmates show that about 80 percent of these offenders used a handgun to commit their offenses. Nearly all (96 percent) who were legally prohibited from gun ownership acquired their guns from a supplier not required to conduct a background check.[62] The message is clear: (1) Stricter gun ownership laws would have made firearm possession illegal for many state prison inmates who used a gun to commit a crime; (2) guns in the hands of high-risk individuals present a serious threat to public safety (given that the United States has an extraordinarily high rate of firearm homicides); and (3) requiring all gun sales to be subject to a background check would make it more difficult for these offenders to obtain guns.[63]

What Can Be Done?

Several approaches can be taken toward mitigating the harms caused by firearms. First are legislative enactments: background checks, preventing people with mental illness from purchasing guns, creating a federal database to track gun sales, banning assault-style weapons (with bump stocks), and barring gun purchases by people on watch or no-fly lists.[64] In addition to watching for red flags and sharing information, as mentioned earlier, the following recommendations by the Police Executive Research Forum could be given due consideration:

- *Gun owners must secure their guns in their homes:* Doing so can dramatically decrease the risk of domestic violence homicide, suicide, and mass shootings. Child access protection statutes should be enacted for the safe storage of firearms in homes and vehicles, and laws enacted that allow family members or friends to petition the courts to order the temporary removal of firearms from individuals who may be at risk of harming themselves or others.

Whether or not public school teachers (and university professors) should be armed has become a flashpoint of controversy in the discussion of gun control.

- *Target the small number of offenders who are responsible for most gun violence:* Most gun crimes take place in a relatively small number of compact geographic areas; enforcement strategies should include identifying and deterring these small groups of gun criminals, and police should vigorously investigate nonfatal shootings and gun possession cases.
- *Ballistics technology should be fully utilized to connect guns to shooters:* The same weapon is frequently used in multiple gun crimes, and today's technology makes it easier and faster to connect weapons that are used in multiple crimes and to trace them to their original purchaser.[65]

Should School Teachers Be Armed?

An area of debate—especially in the aftermath of a school shooting—concerns whether or not public school teachers should be armed. On one side are those who support such a policy as a "last defense" against armed attackers; on the other are those who believe it would bring about more problems than it would solve. The Gun-Free School Zones Act, enacted in 1990 (later overturned, but reenacted by Congress in 1996), makes knowingly possessing a firearm in a school zone a federal offense (with certain exceptions); however, the law also allows states to authorize certain individuals to carry firearms on school grounds. At present, at least nine states have policies that specifically allow school employees—other than security personnel—to carry guns on school property, and the number is greater if including those states that grant school districts power to make their own decisions and do not limit carrying to school employees. Furthermore, half of the states have policies allowing schools or districts to give permission to "individuals" to carry guns.[66]

IMMIGRATION: WHO SHOULD BE COMING TO AMERICA?

Many Questions, Few Answers

Today, of the 326 million people in the United States, an estimated 11 million are undocumented immigrants, 5.9 million of whom are under age 18. Most (56 percent) have come from Mexico, while 11 percent arrived here from Guatemala and El Salvador. In four states—Texas, California, Nevada, and New Jersey—such persons make up more than five percent of the total population.[67] However, **immigration** is a national issue—with political, economic, and social elements—and not one that only impacts a few states.

What should be done with those **undocumented immigrants** who are already here? And in the future, should all such persons who wish to migrate to the United States be allowed to cross its borders? Or, rather, should all such persons be banned? Or, should only *some* be admitted onto our soil? Should the United States erect walls to separate it from its neighbors? Deny protection to victims of gang and domestic violence who are from other countries and seek asylum here?

Immigration: the act of relocating to and living permanently in a foreign country.

Undocumented immigrant: one who is foreign born and does not have a legal right to be or remain in the United States.

These are complex social, political, and humanitarian questions, each of them leading to dozens more issues and questions. At times it seems unlikely that one could find any two U.S. politicians who could agree on the answers to these policy questions. Indeed, immigration has become one of the most vexing and polarizing challenges of our time—and our law enforcement agencies are often caught in the middle while the political battles are being waged.

Making the issue even more complicated is that U.S. citizens themselves cannot seem to agree on whether immigration is good or bad. On the one hand, it is argued that the nation is richer in culture, diversity, and civilization as it is reshaped by people from around the world. Conversely, immigration also has illegal and dangerous aspects that threaten the nation's security (as illustrated in the earlier discussion of terrorism). Nor do we agree on whether immigration helps (through reduced labor costs) or hurts (via displaced U.S.-born workers and lower wages) the U.S. economy. The U.S. labor industry certainly has no problem with hiring undocumented immigrants, with an estimated 8 million undocumented immigrants now working in all sorts of occupations.[68]

Whether or not the United States should open its borders—and make it richer in culture, diversity, and civilization, while also possibly threatening the nation's security— has also, like gun control, become a flashpoint of controversy.

Not even police executives seem to support stricter immigration enforcement. For example, a 40-member task force of the National Immigration Forum has argued that immigration enforcement is primarily a federal responsibility. They believe that immigration enforcement at the local level diverts limited resources from already financially strapped agencies, hinders community policing efforts, and damages relationships with immigrant communities.[69]

Under the law, immigration enforcement is a duty of all federal, state, and local law enforcement officers and agents; in practice, however, immigration enforcement decisions are made from the top of our federal government, with the executive branch (i.e., the president) having much of the control. As examples, in past presidential administrations, law enforcement agencies had "prosecutorial discretion" in determining when and whether to enforce immigration laws and deport certain criminal groups. Under the recent Trump administration policy, however, nearly all such discretion was removed when a 2017 executive order directed the enforcement of immigration laws against "all removable aliens."[70]

The Wall Conundrum

The question of whether or not there should be a southwestern **border wall** (alternatively termed a fence or barrier) has been at the heart of a major political divide in the United States concerning immigration, and it has been so since the 2016 presidential campaign. After President Trump's election, U.S. Customs and Border Protection (CBP) proposed a plan for a wall to extend 316 miles (resulting in a total length of 970 miles) that would cost $18 billion (for construction as well as ongoing personnel, roads, towers, technology, and maintenance).[71] Later, the cost was downgraded to $5.7 billion for a 100-mile wall along the southern border.[72] Then, in February 2019—following a 35-day federal government

Border wall: some form of separation barrier that runs along an international border.

shutdown and a declaration of national emergency (resulting in several legal challenges[73])—another political compromise was reached: President Trump signed a bipartisan spending bill allocating $1.38 billion for 55 miles of border barriers—far less than the amounts CBP and the president had initially requested. In fact, over time eight different prototypes of walls were designed and proposed for this purpose.[74]

Although President George W. Bush performed what he called "the first step toward immigration reform" by signing the $35 billion Secure Fence Act into law in 2006, authorizing the construction of 700 miles of double-layer fencing along the southwestern border (and deploying National Guard troops there, as did President Barack Obama),[75] whether or not there will ever be a wall along the entire 2,000-mile southwestern border remains to be seen.

The Controversy Over Criminality

Another controversial and often-used argument for a strong border policy and hardening of immigration enforcement is that undocumented immigrants commit more crimes than U.S.-born citizens. Widely publicized murders committed by undocumented immigrants—such as the murders of four people in northern Nevada in early 2019,[76] an Iowa college student in mid-2018,[77] and a 32-year-old woman in San Francisco in 2015[78]—have fomented angst and ire among many Americans who believe, as one national news commentator put it, that "illegal immigration kills Americans."[79] Further, because the San Francisco woman was shot by a known criminal who had slipped into the United States illegally on multiple occasions, the killing prompted a national debate about sanctuary cities.

At the same time, a number of immigration experts and academic researchers have long held that immigrants commit fewer crimes. But what is the truth? The research is frustrated by the fact that local police do not list the immigration status of those persons arrested, meaning it is impossible to determine with certainty how many crimes are committed by legal immigrants, undocumented immigrants, and native-born citizens.

Attempts to learn the "truth" have compared incarceration rates for both native-born citizens and undocumented immigrants, violent crime rates both at times when national immigration trends were high and low, and numbers of persons removed from the United States after committing crimes or being identified as gang members. All of these attempts to research the question have flaws, according to the Center for Immigration Studies. The center argues that the crime rates of such persons don't matter. What *does* matter is what we do with those undocumented immigrants who are committing crimes and causing problems.[80]

Those Who Would Seek Asylum

We are a world of refugees; more than 40 million people across the globe have recently been forced to flee their homes as a result of war, famine, and political instability.[81] Another recent issue concerns **asylum seekers**—now ranging from about 2,000 to 10,000 applications per month (many are from Mexico and Central America, but the most are from China, as political and religious dissidents[82])—wishing to migrate to the United States to escape violence, poverty, political volatility, and persecution of all kinds in their home countries.[83] In late 2018 and early 2019, 7,000 active-duty troops were sent to southwestern border communities to guard fences, install razor wire, and halt asylum seekers' northward march toward the United States from Central America.[84] Meanwhile, the U.S. Department of Homeland Security offered support to its Mexican counterparts who were attempting to block the caravans of people heading north.

Asylum seekers: persons fleeing their home countries (often due to persecution on the basis of race, religion, nationality, political affiliation, and so on) in search of sanctuary in another country, where they hope to remain permanently.

Under laws enacted in 1948 for "displaced persons" who needed refuge following World War II, asylum could be granted for people seeking to enter the United States when certain criteria were met. Under current practice, people who meet with immigration authorities and express a fear of returning to their home country will be interviewed (to judge whether or not their fears are well grounded); however, it is when a person is *not* granted asylum that this issue becomes charged with controversy. With a current backlog of nearly 800,000 cases, there simply are not enough judicial and enforcement personnel to handle these numbers, so a "catch-and-release" system evolved where people can stay in the country while awaiting their court date.[85]

As with the other issues discussed in this chapter, refugee and asylum policy is driven largely by the nation's chief executive—who gets to decide whether to commit resources to working with asylum seekers or instead devote those resources to immigration enforcement.[86]

What Can Be Done?

In the foreseeable future, there will likely remain much turmoil concerning immigration issues as they relate to law, policy, and enforcement at the federal level. So what can state and local law enforcement agencies do?

First, state and local agencies should continue to cooperate with federal immigration officials in order to protect our national security. This network is of critical importance for dealing with crimes and threats involving lone-wolf, homegrown terrorists as well as gangs, sex trafficking, smuggling, illicit drug offenses, and other serious crimes that are often tied to illegal immigration. Furthermore, federal agencies rely on and benefit greatly from intelligence developed at the state and local levels; therefore, these agencies should never turn a blind eye to immigration violations, particularly those committed by persons who engage in other criminal activity while in the United States. Agencies operating intelligence units (often referred to as fusion centers) must continue to do their work.

Finally, as they will come into frequent contact with immigrants, police officers should receive adequate training and possess a working knowledge of immigration law and policy (see the accompanying "You Be the . . . Police Officer" box).[87]

You Be the . . .

Police Officer

U.S. Immigration and Customs Enforcement (ICE) is responsible for enforcing federal immigration laws as part of its homeland security mission. The so-called 287(g) program, contained in the Illegal Immigration Reform and Immigrant Responsibility Act of 1996,[88] is one of ICE's top partnership initiatives; it allows a state or local law enforcement entity to enter into a partnership with ICE immigration enforcement and allows certain selected and specially trained police officers to locate and apprehend undocumented immigrants in their communities.[89]

These deputized officers are allowed to interview individuals to ascertain their immigration status, check DHS databases for information or to enter information on individuals, issue detainers to hold individuals for ICE, file documents to begin the removal process, and make recommendations for detention and immigration bond.

Currently, ICE has 287(g) agreements with 78 law enforcement agencies in 20 states. ICE has trained and certified more than 1,500 state and local officers work in the program.[90]

/// IN A NUTSHELL

- International terrorist groups have become more adept at recruiting "foot soldiers" through the Internet and other means. These attacks have become increasingly targeted at civilians, and great concern now focuses on homegrown violent extremists (HVEs) as well as the lone offender who becomes radicalized.
- Cybercrime is one of the fastest growing areas of crime; the most challenging and potentially disastrous type of cybercrime now being perpetrated against the United States is China's state-supported cyber warfare.
- Many experts believe it is only a matter of time before chemical/biological weapons are used by terrorists; all that is required is for a toxin to be cultured and put into a spray form that can be weaponized and disseminated into the population.
- Police have several possible means of attempting to prevent or address acts of terrorism, including legislative measures such as the USA PATRIOT Act.
- There have been more than 1,350 school shootings in the United States since 2000; new policies and practices have been developed for responding to and preventing such acts in the future.
- Closely related to the subject of school shootings is that of gun violence; although the topic of gun control has long been controversial, it has received new attention due to mass shootings.
- Another long-standing issue is what should be done with undocumented individuals, including those wishing to come here and those who are already here. A tandem issue concerns what to do with those seeking asylum. The criminal justice system—and the police in particular—are caught in the middle of this political, economic, and social debate. Related to the question of immigration are questions concerning whether or not undocumented immigrants commit more crimes.

/// KEY TERMS & CONCEPTS

Review key terms with eFlashcards at **edge.sagepub.com/peak4e**.

Active shooter 408	Homegrown violent extremists 403	Opioids 396
Asylum seekers 412	Immigration 410	Posse Comitatus Act of 1878 407
Bioterrorism 406	International terrorism 403	Radicalization 403
Border wall 411	Lone-wolf terrorist 403	Sex trafficking 399
Cybercrime 404	Marijuana decriminalization 399	T visa 401
Cyberterrorism 404	Marijuana legalization 399	Undocumented immigrant 410
Domestic terrorism 407	Military Commissions Act 407	USA PATRIOT Act 407
Extremists 403	Narcan/naloxone/suboxone 398	

/// REVIEW QUESTIONS

Test your understanding of chapter content at **edge.sagepub.com/peak4e**.

1. What are today's most pressing issues concerning drug abuse, and what are some approaches that legislatures, police, and other agencies can take toward addressing them?
2. What is the legal status of medical and recreational marijuana use?
3. What are the major issues facing the United States and its criminal justice system with respect to handling of sex trafficking, to include current legislation, programs, and proposals to address those challenges?
4. What is a commonly accepted definition of terrorism?
5. Why are homegrown and lone-wolf extremists of concern today?
6. What kinds of measures might police employ against all types of terroristic acts?
7. What is cyberterrorism, and what are some of the kinds of activities cybercriminals engage in?
8. What is bioterrorism, and why have those who would employ it been largely unsuccessful?
9. What role is played by legislation (e.g., the USA PATRIOT Act, the Military Commissions Act, and the Posse Comitatus Act of 1878) in combatting terrorism?
10. What is the status of gun ownership and violence in our society? What are some methods police can use to control such

violence, and what kinds of policy issues might be in play to effect stronger gun control measures?

11. What is the extent and status of immigration to the United States today? The status of federal law? The building of a wall? The granting of asylum?

12. What is known about the link between illegal immigration and crime?

/// LEARN BY DOING

1. How would you determine whether or not an opioid epidemic exists in your community? Consider what resources—data, agencies, publications, interviews, Internet searches, and so on—you would employ in this endeavor.

2. Assume that you are assigned a class presentation in which you will investigate what measures police and social services agencies in your area are taking to combat sex trafficking (to include such approaches as the T visa). How will you approach these questions?

3. Assume that shortly after 8 p.m., a lone male throws a pipe bomb amongst moviegoers in a theater complex. The initial 911 call reported numerous injuries, and that the suspect had left the theater running toward another retail mall. What kinds of resources should the police and other first responders deploy to the scene and beyond?

4. Terrorists often seek out public gathering areas and critical infrastructures (such as dams, nuclear reactors, chemical plants, tourist attractions, water systems, public safety and emergency services). Therefore, first responders should develop advance plans for identifying and protecting these assets *as well as* an action plan in the event a terrorist attack or other significant event occurs. What such events and critical infrastructures in your community would warrant such careful pre- and post-planning?

5. To better grasp the methods used and problems confronted by federal, state, and local law enforcement agencies regarding the immigration issues discussed in this chapter, you could do no better than to interview individuals who work in this arena on a daily basis—in this case, a homeland security specialist or fusion center employee, a member of the Border Patrol or ICE, and so on.

/// STUDY SITE

SAGE edge™

Get the tools you need to sharpen your study skills. SAGE edge offers a robust online environment featuring an impressive array of free tools and resources.

Access practice quizzes, eFlashcards, video, and multimedia at **edge.sagepub.com/peak4e**.

BILL OF RIGHTS: THE FIRST 10 AMENDMENTS TO THE UNITED STATES CONSTITUTION[1]

According to the Library of Congress, "On September 25, 1789, the First Federal Congress of the United States proposed to the state legislatures twelve amendments to the Constitution. The first two, concerning the number of constituents for each Representative and the compensation of Congressmen, were not ratified. Articles three through twelve, known as the Bill of Rights, became the first ten amendments to the U.S. Constitution and contained guarantees of essential rights and liberties omitted in the crafting of the original document. The Bill of Rights was ratified on December 15, 1791. Because certain parts of those ten amendments contain essential rights and liberties and have major impact on the U.S. criminal justice system (and are in fact mentioned numerous times in this textbook), they are presented here.

Amendment I

Congress shall make no law respecting an establishment of religion, or prohibiting the free exercise thereof; or abridging the freedom of speech, or of the press; or the right of the people peaceably to assemble, and to petition the Government for a redress of grievances.

Amendment II

A well regulated Militia, being necessary to the security of a free State, the right of the people to keep and bear Arms, shall not be infringed.

Amendment III

No Soldier shall, in time of peace be quartered in any house, without the consent of the Owner, nor in time of war, but in a manner to be prescribed by law.

Amendment IV

The right of the people to be secure in their persons, houses, papers, and effects, against unreasonable searches and seizures, shall not be violated, and no Warrants shall issue, but upon probable cause, supported by Oath or affirmation, and particularly describing the place to be searched, and the persons or things to be seized.

Amendment V

No person shall be held to answer for a capital, or otherwise infamous crime, unless on a presentment or indictment of a Grand Jury, except in cases arising in the land or naval forces, or in the Militia, when in actual service in time of War or public danger; nor shall any person be subject for the same offence to be twice put in jeopardy of life or limb; nor shall be compelled in any criminal case to be a witness against himself, nor be deprived of life, liberty, or property, without due process of law; nor shall private property be taken for public use, without just compensation.

Amendment VI

In all criminal prosecutions, the accused shall enjoy the right to a speedy and public trial, by an impartial jury of the State and district wherein the crime shall have been committed, which district shall have been previously ascertained by law, and to be informed of the nature and cause of the accusation; to be confronted with the witnesses against him; to have compulsory process for obtaining witnesses in his favor, and to have the Assistance of Counsel for his defence.

Amendment VII

In Suits at common law, where the value in controversy shall exceed twenty dollars, the right of trial by jury shall be preserved, and no fact tried by a jury, shall be otherwise re-examined in any Court of the United States, than according to the rules of the common law.

Amendment VIII

Excessive bail shall not be required, nor excessive fines imposed, nor cruel and unusual punishments inflicted.

Amendment IX

The enumeration in the Constitution, of certain rights, shall not be construed to deny or disparage others retained by the people.

Amendment X

The powers not delegated to the United States by the Constitution, nor prohibited by it to the States, are reserved to the States respectively, or to the people.

ASSESS YOUR AWARENESS ANSWERS

Chapter 1: 1. True; 2. False; 3. False; 4. False; 5. True; 6. False

Chapter 2: 1. True; 2. False; 3. False; 4. True; 5. True; 6. False; 7. True; 8. True; 9. False

Chapter 3: 1. True; 2. False; 3. True; 4. False; 5. True; 6. False; 7. False

Chapter 4: 1. True; 2. False; 3. True; 4. False; 5. False; 6. False; 7. False

Chapter 5: 1. True; 2. False; 3. True; 4. False; 5. True; 6. False; 7. True; 8. True; 9. False

Chapter 6: 1. False; 2. False; 3. False; 4. False; 5. True; 6. False; 7. False

Chapter 7: 1. True; 2. False; 3. True; 4. False; 5. False; 6. False; 7. True; 8. False

Chapter 8: 1. True; 2. True; 3. True; 4. True; 5. False; 6. True; 7. True

Chapter 9: 1. True; 2. True; 3. True; 4. False; 5. False; 6. False

Chapter 10: 1. False; 2. True; 3. True; 4. False; 5. True; 6. True; 7. False

Chapter 11: 1. False; 2. True; 3. False; 4. True; 5. True; 6. False; 7. True

Chapter 12: 1. True; 2. False; 3. True; 4. False; 5. False; 6. False; 7. False

Chapter 13: 1. True; 2. True; 3. False; 4. False; 5. True; 6. False; 7. True

Chapter 14: 1. True; 2. False; 3. False; 4. True; 5. False; 6. True; 7. True

Chapter 15: 1. False; 2. False; 3. False; 4. True; 5. True; 6. True; 7. False; 8. False; 9. True

Chapter 16: 1. False; 2. True; 3. True; 4. True; 5. True; 6. False

/// GLOSSARY

Absolute ethics: the type of ethics where there are only two sides—good or bad, black or white; some examples would be unethical behaviors such as bribery, extortion, excessive force, and perjury, which nearly everyone would agree are unacceptable for criminal justice personnel.

Academy training: where police and corrections personnel are trained in the basic functions, laws, and skills required for their positions

Accepted lying: police activities intended to apprehend or entrap suspects. This type of lying is generally considered to be trickery.

Acquittal: a court or jury's judgment or verdict of not guilty of the offenses charged.

Active shooter: an individual seeking to kill or attempting to kill people in a confined and populated area.

Actus reus: Latin for "guilty deed"—an act that accompanies one's intent to commit a crime, such as pulling out a knife and then stabbing someone.

Adjudication: the legal resolution of a dispute—for example, when one is declared guilty or not guilty—by a judge or jury.

Adoption studies: criminological research that looks at whether adopted children share criminal tendencies with their biological or adoptive parents.

Adversarial system: a legal system wherein there is a contest between two opposing sides, with a judge (and possibly a jury) sitting as an impartial arbiter, seeking truth.

Affidavit: any written document in which the signer swears under oath that the statements in the document are true.

Affirmative defense: the response to a criminal charge in which the defendant admits to committing the act charged but argues that for some mitigating reason he or she should not be held criminally responsible under the law.

Aggravating circumstances: elements of a crime that enhance its seriousness, such as the infliction of torture, killing of a police or corrections officer, and so on.

Alternatives to incarceration: a sentence imposed by a judge other than incarceration, such as probation, parole, shock probation, or house arrest.

Arraignment: a criminal court proceeding during which a formally charged defendant is informed of the charges and asked to enter a plea of guilty or not guilty.

Arrest: the taking into custody or detaining of one who is suspected of committing a crime.

Asylum seekers: persons fleeing their home countries (often due to persecution on the basis of race, religion, nationality, political affiliation, and so on) in search of sanctuary in another country, where they hope to remain permanently.

Bail: surety (e.g., cash or paper bond) provided by a defendant to guarantee his or her return to court to answer to criminal charges.

Bioterrorism: the use of biological material, such as anthrax or botulin, to commit an act of terrorism.

Black Lives Matter: a movement that initiated national scrutiny of police shootings after an unarmed black teenager, Michael Brown, was shot by police and died in St. Louis in August 2014.

Blue Lives Matter: a movement formed in New York City after the killings of two officers, to publicize that dozens of police officers are murdered each year and that police work is increasingly dangerous.

Body-worn camera: an audio, video, or photographic recording system worn by police to record their interactions with the public or to gather video evidence at crime scenes.

Booking: the clerical procedure that occurs after an arrestee is taken to jail, during which a record is made of his or her name, address, charge(s), arresting officers, and time and place of arrest.

Boot camp: a short-term jail or prison program that puts offenders through a rigorous physical and mental regimen designed to instill discipline and respect for authority.

Border wall: some form of separation barrier that runs along an international border.

Burden of proof: the requirement that the state must meet to introduce evidence or establish facts.

Capital punishment: a sentence of death, or carrying out same via execution of the offender.

Caseload: the number of cases awaiting disposition by a court, or the number of active cases or clients maintained by a probation or parole officer.

Causation: a link between one's act and the injurious act or crime, such as one tossing a match in a forest and igniting a deadly fire.

Chain of command: vertical and horizontal power relations within an organization, showing how one position relates to others.

Circuit courts: originally courts wherein judges traveled a circuit to hear appeals, now courts with several counties or districts in their jurisdiction; the federal court system contains 11 circuit courts of appeals (plus the District of Columbia and territories), which hear appeals from district courts.

Civil law: a generic term for all noncriminal law, usually related to settling disputes between private citizens, governmental, and/or business entities.

Civil liability: in tort law, the basis for which a cause of action (e.g., fine) is made to recover damages; in criminal justice, where a police or corrections officer, for example, violates someone's civil rights.

Classical school (of criminology): a perspective indicating that people have free will to choose between criminal and lawful behavior, and that crime can be controlled by sanctions and should be proportionate to the offense.

Classification (of inmates): an inmate security and treatment plan based on one's security, social, vocational, psychological, and educational needs while incarcerated.

Clearance rate: the percentage of crimes that either resulted in an arrest or were cleared by some other means.

Cold case: no standard time-related definition of a "cold case" exists regarding when an investigation goes "cold"; rather, it is generally the point when all viable leads in an investigation have been exhausted and detectives cease their investigative efforts—to be reopened if further information or evidence becomes available.

Community corrections: probation, parole, and a variety of other measures that offer convicted offenders an alternative(s) to incarceration.

Community era: beginning in about 1980, a time when the police retrained to work with the community to solve problems by looking at their underlying causes and developing tailored responses to them.

Community policing and problem solving: a proactive management philosophy that involves police-community collaboration and a four-step process (scanning, analyzing, response, and assessment) to focus police activities and thus enable officers to respond more effectively to crime and disorder with arrests or other appropriate actions.

Conflict theory of justice: explains how powerful groups create laws to protect their values and interests in diverse societies.

Consensus theory of justice: explains how a society creates laws as a result of common interests and values, which develop largely because people experience similar socialization.

Consent decree: where police officers have violated citizens' civil rights, a tool used by the courts to compel an agency to generally perform within the dictates of the Constitution and make specific reforms.

Constable: in England, favored noblemen who were forerunners of modern-day U.S. criminal justice functionaries; largely disappeared in the United States by the 1970s.

Constitutional policing: policing practices that emphasize the protection of civilians' civil rights and equal protection under the law.

Contract services: a for-profit firm or individuals hired by an individual or company to provide security services.

Control theory: a theory that describes criminal behavior as a natural outcome of people's desire to seek pleasure in the absence of effective social controls.

Conviction: the legal finding, by a jury or judge, or through a guilty plea, that a criminal defendant is guilty.

Coroner: an early English court officer; today one (usually a physician) in the United States whose duty it is to determine cause of death.

Correctional officer: one who works in a prison or jail and supervises correctional inmates.

County sheriff's office: a unit of county government with a sheriff (normally elected) and deputies whose duties vary but typically include policing unincorporated areas, maintaining county jails, providing security to courts in the county, and serving warrants and court papers.

Court of last resort: the last court that may hear a case at the state or federal level.

Courtroom work group: the criminal justice professionals who work together to move cases through the court system.

Crime control model: a model by Packer that emphasizes law and order and argues that every effort must be made to suppress crime and to try, convict, and incarcerate offenders.

Crime rate: the number of reported crimes divided by the population of the jurisdiction, and multiplied by 100,000 persons; developed and used by the FBI *Uniform Crime Reports*.

Crime scene: any location where a crime occurred and that may contain forensic evidence relating to and supporting a criminal investigation.

Crimes against persons: violent crimes, to include homicide, sexual assault, robbery, and aggravated assault.

Crimes against property: crimes during which no violence is perpetrated against a person, such as burglary, theft, and arson.

Criminal justice flow and process: the movement of defendants and cases through the criminal justice process, beginning with the commission of a crime, and including stages that involve actions of criminal justice actors working within police, courts, and correctional agencies.

Criminal law: the body of law that defines criminal offenses and prescribes punishments for their infractions.

Criminalistics: the interdisciplinary study of physical evidence related to crime; drawing on mathematics, physics, chemistry, biology, anthropology, and many other scientific fields.

Cybercrime: the use of computers to commit crimes, such as embezzlement, diversion of bank monies to other accounts, and hacking personal information.

Cyberterrorism: a premeditated, politically motivated attack against computer systems, computer programs, or data.

Day reporting center: a structured corrections program requiring offenders to check in at a community site on a regular basis for supervision, sanctions, and services.

Defendant: a person against whom a criminal charge is pending; one charged with a crime.

Defense: the response by a defendant to a criminal charge, to include denial of the criminal allegations in an attempt to negate or overcome the charges.

Defense attorney: one whose responsibility it is to see that the rights of the accused are upheld prior to, during, and after trial; the Sixth Amendment provides for "effective" counsel, among other constitutionally enumerated rights that defense attorneys must see are upheld.

Delay (trial): an attempt (usually by defense counsel) to have a criminal trial continued until a later date.

Deontological ethics: one's duty to act.

Detective/criminal investigator: a police officer who is assigned to investigate reported crimes, to include gathering evidence, completing case reports, testifying in court, and so on.

Determinate sentence: a specific, fixed-period sentence ordered by a court.

Deterrence: the effect of punishments and other actions to deter people from committing crimes.

Deviant lying: occasions when officers commit perjury to convict suspects or are deceptive about some activity that is illegal or unacceptable to the department or public in general.

Discovery: a procedure wherein both the prosecution and the defense exchange and share information as to witnesses to be used, results of tests, recorded statements by defendants, or psychiatric reports, so that there are no major surprises at trial.

Discretion: authority to make decisions in enforcing the law based on one's observations and judgment ("spirit of the law") rather than the letter of the law.

Disposition: an outcome of a criminal or juvenile court process signifying that the matter is completed.

District courts: trial courts at the county, state, or federal level with general and original jurisdiction.

Diversion program: a sentencing alternative that removes a case from the criminal justice system, typically to move a defendant into another treatment program or modality.

DNA: deoxyribonucleic acid, which is found in all cells; used in forensics to match evidence (hair, semen) left at a crime scene with a particular perpetrator.

Domestic terrorism: the commission of terrorist acts in the perpetrator's own country against his or her fellow citizens.

Double jeopardy: the prosecution of an accused person twice for the same offense; prohibited by the Fifth Amendment except under certain circumstances.

Dual court system: the state and federal court systems of the United States.

Dual hazard prediction: the argument that people are most likely to engage in criminal behavior if they (1) have traits associated with crime and (2) are raised in environments conducive to criminal behavior.

Due process model: a model by Packer that advocates defendants' presumption of innocence, protection of suspects' rights, and limitations placed on police powers to avoid convicting innocent persons.

Duty of care: a legal obligation imposed on someone; in the case of the police, they have a legal responsibility to see that persons in their custody are free from harm, given necessary medical assistance when necessary, and treated humanely.

Eighth Amendment: in the Bill of Rights, it contains the protection against excessive bail and fines, as well as cruel and unusual punishment.

Electronic monitoring: use of electronic devices (bracelets or anklets) to emit signals when a convicted offender (usually on house arrest) leaves the environment in which he or she is to remain.

Entrapment: police tactics that unduly encourage or induce an individual to commit a crime he or she typically would not commit.

Ethics: a set of rules or values that spell out appropriate human conduct.

Evidence-based policing: an approach and tactical decision-making process that emphasizes statistical analysis, empirical research, and controlled field experiments.

Exclusionary rule: the rule (see *Mapp v. Ohio*, 1961) providing that evidence obtained improperly cannot be used against the accused at trial.

Exigent circumstance: an instance in which quick, emergency action is required to save lives, protect against serious property damage, or prevent suspect escape or evidence destruction; in such cases, officers can enter a structure without a search warrant.

Exoneration: to absolve someone of criminal blame, or find someone not guilty.

Extremists: persons who hold extreme or fanatical political or religious views, which can lead to the commission or advocacy of extreme action.

Failure to protect: a situation in which police place someone in jeopardy, such as by giving out the location of a battered spouse or names of victims or witnesses.

False arrest: unlawful physical restraint by a police officer, for no valid reason.

Federal court system: the four-tiered federal system that includes the Supreme Court, circuit courts of appeal, district courts, and magistrate courts.

Federal law enforcement agencies: federal organizations that, for example, are charged with protecting the homeland (DHS); investigating crimes (FBI) and enforcing particular laws, such as those pertaining to drugs (DEA) or alcohol/tobacco/firearms/explosives (ATF); and guarding the courts and transporting prisoners (USMS).

Federalism: a type of government that divides powers between a national (federal) government and governments of smaller geographic territories, including states, counties, and cities.

Felony: a serious offense with a possible sentence of more than a year in prison.

Felony-murder rule: the legal doctrine that says that, if a death occurs during the commission of a felony, the perpetrator of the crime may be charged with murder in the first degree, regardless of the absence of intent, premeditation and deliberation, or malice aforethought.

Feminist theory: a theory that explains how gender inequality affects female offending and justice system responses to crimes committed by females.

Field training officer (FTO): one who is to oversee and evaluate the new police officer's performance as he or she transitions from the training academy to patrolling the streets.

Fifth Amendment: in the Bill of Rights, among other protections, it guards against self-incrimination and double jeopardy.

Forensic science: the study of causes of crimes, deaths, and crime scenes.

Fourth Amendment: in the Bill of Rights, it contains the protection against unreasonable searches and seizures and protects people's homes, property, and effects.

Geriatric inmates: inmates age 55 and up.

Grand jury: a body that hears evidence and determines probable cause regarding crimes and can return formal charges against suspects; use, size, and functions vary among the states.

Gratuities: the receipt of some benefit (a meal, gift, or some other favor) either for free or for a reduced price.

Halfway house: a community center or home staffed by professionals or volunteers designed to provide counseling to ex-prisoners as they transition from prison to the community.

Hands-off doctrine: the notion held by courts that prison administrators should be given free rein to run their prisons as they deem best.

Hands-on doctrine: the belief by courts that inmates have certain constitutional rights that the courts must see are upheld and that prison administrators must obey.

Hierarchy rule: in the FBI *Uniform Crime Reports* reporting scheme, the practice whereby only the most serious offense of several that are committed during a criminal act is reported by the police.

Higher education (for police): education beyond high school, at a college or university, in particular.

Homegrown violent extremists: persons who are inspired by foreign terrorist organizations and radicalized in the countries in which they are born, raised, or reside.

House arrest/home confinement: detention of offenders in their own homes; compliance is often monitored electronically.

Houses of refuge: workhouses established in the early 1800s as a means of separating juvenile offenders from adult offenders.

Idealistic contrast: the differences between juvenile and adult criminal justice processes, to include treatment and terminology.

Illinois Juvenile Court Act (1899): legislation that established the first juvenile court in the United States.

Immigration: the act of relocating to and living permanently in a foreign country.

In loco parentis: a doctrine according to which the state will act in place of the parents if they fail in their duties to protect and provide for the child.

Incapacitation: rendering someone as unable to act or move about, either through incarceration or by court order.

Indeterminate sentence: a scheme whereby one is sentenced for a flexible time period (e.g., 5–10 years) so as to be released when rehabilitated or when the opportunity for rehabilitation is presented.

Informant: a person who covertly provides information about criminal activity to police, with some expectation of benefit in exchange—money, dropped or reduced charges, and so on. However, because such persons are often criminals themselves, their credibility and use are often questioned.

Initial appearance: a formal proceeding during which the accused is read his or her rights and informed of the charges and the amount of bail required to secure pretrial release.

Intensive supervision probation and parole: post-release supervision that usually includes much closer and stricter supervision, more contact with offenders, more frequent drug tests, and other such measures.

Intent, specific: a purposeful act or state of mind to commit a crime.

Intermediate court of appeals: a state court that stands between a trial court and a court of last resort; it typically has appellate jurisdiction only.

Intermediate sanctions: forms of punishment that are between freedom and prison, such as home confinement and day reporting.

International terrorism: acts of terrorism perpetrated in a foreign country by terrorists who are not native to that country.

INTERPOL: the only international crime-fighting organization; it collects intelligence information, issues alerts, and assists in capturing world criminals, and it has nearly 200 member countries.

Interrogation: in criminal law, the process whereby police question a person who is suspected of having knowledge of or having committed a crime; it typically involves informing the suspect of his or her rights under *Miranda*.

"Iron curtain" speech: in *Wolff v. McDonnell* (1973), the Supreme Court stated that there is no iron curtain between the Constitution and the prisons of the United States; in sum, inmates have rights.

Jail: a facility that holds persons who have been arrested for crimes and are awaiting trial, persons who have been convicted for misdemeanors and are serving a sentence (up to a year in jail), federal offenders, and others.

JDLR: in prison jargon, the sense that things "just don't look right."

Judicial misconduct: inappropriate behavior by a judge.

Judicial selection (methods of): means by which judges are selected for the bench, to include election, a nominating commission, or a hybrid of these methods.

Jurisdiction, court: the authority of a court to hear a particular type of case, based on geography (city, state, or federal) and subject matter (e.g., criminal, civil, probate).

Justice of the peace (JP): a minor justice official who oversees lesser criminal trials; one of the early English judicial functionaries.

Juvenile court: a court that has original jurisdiction to hear juvenile crime matters.

Kansas City Preventive Patrol Experiment: in the early 1970s, a study of the effects of different types of patrolling on crime—patrolling as usual in one area, saturated patrol in another, and very limited patrol in a third area; the results showed no significant differences.

Labeling theory: a theory contending that labeling a person as a deviant or criminal makes that person more likely to engage in future criminal behavior.

Learning theory: a theory asserting that criminal behaviors are learned from associating with others and from social interactions and social experiences.

Legal jurisdiction: the authority to make legal decisions and judgments, often based on geographic area (territory) or the type of case in question.

Legitimacy (of police): the extent to which the community believes that police actions are appropriate, proper, and just, and its willingness to recognize police authority.

Lex talionis: Latin for "an eye for an eye, a tooth for a tooth"; retaliation or revenge that dates back to the Bible and the Middle Ages.

Life without parole: a penalty or sentence imposed under which an inmate is to serve a life sentence without eligibility for parole.

Lineup: a procedure in which police ask suspects to submit to a viewing by witnesses to determine the guilty party, based on personal and physical characteristics; information obtained may be used later in court.

Locard's exchange principle: the notion that offenders both leave something at the crime scene and take something from it; the crime scene analyst or investigator's job is to locate that evidence and use it in the investigation.

Lone-wolf terrorist: one who plans and commits acts of terrorism without the support of a larger terrorist group.

Marijuana decriminalization: where a state has repealed or amended its marijuana laws to make certain acts criminal but no longer subject to prosecution (e.g., individuals caught with small amounts of marijuana for personal consumption may not be prosecuted and, thus, avoid a criminal record).

Marijuana legalization: typically, where one will not be arrested for marijuana use if he or she follows the state laws as to age, place, and amount for consumption (however, one might still be arrested for selling or trafficking if such are prohibited under the law).

Mass incarceration: a term generally referring to what is perceived as the United States's disproportionately high rates of imprisonment of young African American men; some believe it deters crime and incapacitates offenders, while others say that it weakens poor families and keeps them socially marginalized.

Mens rea: Latin for "guilty mind"—the purposeful intention to commit a criminal act.

Merit selection: a means of selecting judges whereby names of interested candidates are considered by a committee and recommendations are then made to the governor, who then makes the appointment; known also as the Missouri Plan.

Militarization (of the police): the idea that the increasing use (since 9/11) of military equipment and tactics by the police has made them pattern themselves around and adopt the military model.

Military Commissions Act: legislation authorizing trial by military commission for violations of the law of war, and for other purposes.

Misdemeanor: a lesser offense, typically punishable by a fine or up to one year in a local jail.

Mitigating circumstances: circumstances that would tend to lessen the severity of the sentence, such as one's youthfulness, mental instability, not having a prior criminal record, and so on.

Model Code of Judicial Conduct: adopted by the House of Delegates of the American Bar Association in 1990, it provides a set of ethical principles and guidelines for judges.

Motive: the reason for committing a crime.

Municipal police department: a police force that enforces laws and maintains peace within a specified city or municipality.

Narcan/naloxone/suboxone: a medication that can be used to block the effects of opioids, particularly for overdoses.

National Crime Victimization Survey: a random survey of U.S. households that measures crimes committed against victims; includes crimes not reported to police.

National Incident-Based Reporting System: a crime reporting system in which police describe each offense that occurs during a crime event as well as characteristics of the offender.

Negligence: failure to perform a duty owed.

Neoclassical criminology: an approach to crime that is grounded in the concept of rational choice but that views the accused as exempted from conviction if circumstances prevented the exercise of free will.

New generation/direct supervision jail: a jail that, by its architecture and design, eliminates many of the traditional features of a jail, allowing staff members greater interaction and control.

Noble cause corruption: a situation in which one commits an unethical act but for the greater good; for example, a police officer violates the Constitution in order to capture a serious offender.

Opioids: a class of drugs that includes heroin, synthetic opioids such as fentanyl, and pain relievers available legally by prescription.

Organization: an entity of two or more people who cooperate to achieve one or more objectives.

Organizational structure or chart: a diagram of the vertical and horizontal parts of an organization, showing its chain of command, lines of communication, division of labor, and so on.

Organized crime: crimes committed by members of illegal organizations.

Parens patriae: a doctrine according to which the state is the ultimate parent of the child (and will step in to provide and care for the child if parents neglect those duties).

Parole: early release from prison, with conditions attached and under supervision of a parole agency.

Parole officer: one who supervises those who are on parole.

PINS (person in need of supervision): usually a juvenile thought to be on the verge of becoming a delinquent.

Plaintiff: the party bringing a lawsuit or initiating a legal action against someone else.

Plea negotiation (or bargaining): a preconviction process between the prosecutor and the accused in which a plea of guilty is given by the defendant, with certain specified considerations in return—for example, having several charges or counts tossed out, and a plea by the prosecutor to the court for leniency or shorter sentence.

Police brutality: unnecessary use of force by police against citizens, resulting in injury.

Police corruption: misconduct by police officers that can involve but is not limited to illegal activities for economic gain, gratuities, favors, and so on.

Policing role: the function of the police in contemporary society.

Policing styles: James Q. Wilson argued that there are three styles of policing: watchman, legalistic, and service.

Policy making: the act of creating laws or setting standards to govern the activities of government; the U.S. Supreme Court, for example, has engaged in policy making in several areas, such as affirmative action, voting, and freedom of communication and expression.

Political era: from the 1840s to the 1930s, the period of time when police were tied closely to politics and politicians, dependent on them for being hired and promoted, and for assignments—all of which raised the potential for corruption.

Positivist school: a school of thought that argues science can be used to discover the true causes of crime, which include factors outside of offenders' control.

Posse Comitatus Act of 1878: legislation that prohibits the federal government from using the armed forces for the purpose of law enforcement, except in cases authorized by the Constitution or an act of Congress.

Preliminary hearing: a stage in the criminal process conducted by a magistrate to determine whether a person charged with a crime should be held for trial based on probable cause; does not determine guilt or innocence.

Presumption of innocence: the premise that a defendant is assumed to be innocent until guilt is established beyond a reasonable doubt.

Pretrial motions/processes: any number of motions filed by prosecutors and defense attorneys prior to trial, for instance, to quash evidence, change venue, conduct discovery, challenge a search or seizure, raise doubts about expert witnesses, or exclude a defendant's confession.

Prison: a state or federal facility housing long-term offenders, typically felons, for a period greater than one year.

Prison industries: use of prison and jail inmates to produce goods or provide services for a public agency or private corporation.

Prisoners' rights: the collective body of rights given to inmates by the courts, in such areas as conditions of confinement, communications (mail and letters), access to law library and medical facilities, and so on.

Prisonization: the process whereby an inmate becomes socialized into the culture and social life of prison society so that adjusting to the norms of outside society becomes difficult.

Private police/security officers: all nonpublic officers, including guards, watchmen, private detectives, and investigators; they have limited powers and only the same arrest powers as regular citizens.

Privatization: the operation of existing prison facilities, or the building and operation of new prisons, by for-profit companies.

Probable cause: a reasonable basis to believe that a crime has been, or is about to be, committed by a particular person.

Probation officer: one who supervises the activities of persons on probation.

Probation: an alternative to incarceration in which the convict remains out of jail or prison and in the community and thus on the job, with family, and so on, while subject to conditions and supervision of the probation authority.

Procedural justice: a philosophy meaning that the manner in which an individual regards the criminal justice system is tied closely to the perceived fairness of the *process* and how he or she was treated rather than to the perceived fairness of the *outcome.*

Procedural law: rules that set forth how substantive laws are to be enforced, such as those covering arrest, search, and seizure.

Proprietary services: in-house security services whose personnel are hired, trained, and supervised by the company or organization.

Prosecuting attorney: one who brings prosecutions, representing the people of the jurisdiction.

Prosecution: the bringing of charges against an individual, based on probable cause, so as to bring the matter before a court.

Proximate cause: a factor that contributed heavily to an event, such as an auto crash or death.

Public defender: an attorney whose full-time job is to represent indigent defendants.

Public order crimes: offenses that violate a society's shared norms.

Punishment (and its purposes): penalties imposed for committing criminal acts, to accomplish retribution, deterrence, incapacitation, and/or rehabilitation.

Radicalization: a process whereby one adopts radical positions on political or social issues.

Reasonable doubt: the standard used by jurors to arrive at a verdict—whether or not the government (prosecutor) has established guilt beyond a reasonable doubt.

Reasonable suspicion: suspicion that is less than probable cause but more than a mere hunch that a person may be involved in criminal activity.

Reentry and aftercare: providing services to, and supervision for, paroled inmates who are about to reintegrate into the community.

Reform era: also the professional era, from the 1930s to 1980s, when police sought to extricate themselves from the shackles of politicians, and leading to the crime-fighter era—with greater emphases being placed on *numbers*—arrests, citations, response times, and so on.

Reformatory: a detention facility designed to reform individuals—historically juveniles.

Rehabilitation: attempts to reform an offender through vocational and educational programming, counseling, and so forth, so that he or she is not a recidivist and does not return to crime and prison.

Relative ethics: the gray area of ethics that is not so clearcut, such as releasing a serious offender in order to use him later as an informant.

Respondeat superior: Latin for "let the master answer"—a doctrine in liability that establishes a duty of supervisors to control their employees and be considered liable for their actions.

Restorative justice: the view that crime affects the entire community, which must be healed and made whole again through the offender's remorse, community service, restitution to the victim, and other such activities.

Retribution: punishment that fits the crime, that is "equitable" for the offense.

Revocation: the court's revoking probation or parole status for the purpose of returning an offender to prison (usually for not following the conditions of probation or parole, or for committing a new offense).

Right-wrong test: the test of legal insanity, asking whether the defendant understood the nature and quality of his or her act and, if so, if he or she understood it was wrong.

Routine activity theory: a theory that explains the elements necessary for a crime to occur, as well as the types of controllers who can block criminal opportunities.

Sanction: a penalty or punishment.

School-to-prison pipeline: the notion that certain policies and practices push schoolchildren, particularly those who are most at risk, out of classrooms and into the juvenile and adult criminal justice and prison systems.

Search and seizure: in the Fourth Amendment, the term refers to an officer's searching for and taking away evidence of a crime.

Section 1983: a portion of the U.S. Code that allows a legal action to be brought against a police officer or other person in position of authority who, it is believed, used his or her position ("acted under color of law") to violate one's civil rights.

Sentencing guidelines: an instrument developed by the federal government that uses a grid system to chart seriousness of the offense, criminal history, and so forth and thus allows the court to arrive at a more consistent sentence for everyone.

Sex trafficking: the use of humans for the purpose of sexual slavery or commercial sexual exploitation.

Sheriff: the chief law enforcement officer of a county, typically elected and frequently operating the jail as well as law enforcement functions.

Shock probation/parole: a situation in which individuals are sentenced to jail or prison for a brief period, to give them a taste or "shock" of incarceration and, it is hoped, turn them into more law-abiding citizens.

Situational crime prevention: a theory maintaining that crimes will occur if they are easy to commit, carry low risk, provide large rewards, provoke people, and are excusable, as judged by a wide range of potential offenders.

Sixth Amendment: in the Bill of Rights, it guarantees the right to a speedy and public trial by an impartial jury, the right to effective counsel at trial, and other protections.

Sixth sense: in policing, the notion that an officer can "sense" or feel when something is not right, as in the way a person acts, talks, and so on.

"Slave of the state": an early philosophy toward prison inmates, essentially stating that inmates had no legal rights that had to be observed by prison administrators.

Slippery slope: the idea that a small first step can lead to more serious behaviors, such as the receipt of minor gratuities by police officers believed to eventually cause them to desire or demand receipt of items of greater value.

Social conflict theory: a theory that explains crime as an outcome of conflicting interests between groups in society and the dominant group's attempts to control and exploit groups with less power.

Social disorganization theory: a theory maintaining that neighborhood characteristics, including poverty, racial heterogeneity, and resident transiency, break down social controls and lead to criminal behavior.

Solitary confinement: a form of imprisonment in which an inmate is isolated from any human contact (except for members of prison staff).

Special-purpose state agencies: specially trained units for particular investigative needs, such as those for violations of alcoholic beverage laws, fish and game laws, organized crime, and so on.

Speedy Trial Act of 1974: later amended, a law originally enacted to ensure compliance with the Sixth Amendment's provision for a speedy trial by requiring that a federal case be brought to trial no more than 100 days following the arrest.

Standing: a legal doctrine requiring that one must not be a party to a lawsuit unless he or she has a personal stake in its outcome.

Stare decisis: Latin for "to stand by a decision"—a doctrine referring to court precedent, whereby lower courts must follow (and render the same) decisions of higher courts when the same legal issues and questions come before them, thereby not disturbing settled points of law.

State bureau of investigation: a state agency that is responsible for investigating crimes involving state statutes; they may also be called in to assist police agencies in serious criminal matters, and often publish state crime reports.

State court system: civil or criminal courts in which cases are decided through an adversarial process; typically including a court of last resort, an appellate court, trial courts, and lower courts.

State police: a state agency responsible for highway patrol and other duties as delineated in the state's statutes; some states require their police to investigate crimes against persons and property.

State prison: a correctional facility that houses convicted felons.

Status offense: a crime committed by a juvenile that would not be a crime if committed by an adult; examples would be purchasing alcohol and tobacco products, truancy, and violating curfew.

Strain theory: a theory that argues criminal behavior is caused by feelings of strain, which occur when people believe that legitimate means of achieving success are not accessible to them.

Stress: discomfort and distress caused by situations that officers face on the job.

Substantive law: the body of law that spells out the elements of criminal acts.

Substantive violation: an allegation that one was arrested for a new criminal offense while serving probation.

Supermax prison: a penal institution that, for security purposes, affords inmates very few, if any, amenities and a great amount of isolation.

T visa: a type of visa that allow victims of human trafficking and their immediate family members to remain and work temporarily in the United States (provided certain conditions are met).

Tasks of policing (four basic): enforce the law, perform welfare tasks, prevent crime, and protect the innocent.

Technical violation: in probation and parole, when one violates certain conditions that must be obeyed to remain out of prison, such as violating curfew, using drugs or alcohol, or not maintaining a job.

Terry Stop: also known as a "stop and frisk"; when a police officer briefly detains a person for questioning and then frisks ("pats down") the person if the officer reasonably believes he or she is carrying a weapon.

Theoretical paradigm: a framework consisting of a group of theories that propose similar explanations for a particular type of behavior or event (e.g., crime).

Three-strikes law: a crime control strategy whereby an offender who commits three or more violent offenses will be sentenced to a lengthy term in prison, usually 25 years to life.

Tort: a civil wrong or infraction; the remedy will be damages awarded in civil trial.

Transfer (remand): the movement or assigning of a juvenile offender to an adult court, because the youth's behavior is such that he or she is not amenable to the juvenile court's rehabilitative philosophy.

Trial process: all of the steps in the adjudicatory process, from indictment or charge to conviction or acquittal.

Undocumented immigrant: one who is foreign born and does not have a legal right to be or remain in the United States.

Uniform Crime Reports: published annually by the FBI, each report describes the nature of crime as reported by law enforcement agencies; includes analyses of Part I crimes.

U.S. Supreme Court: the court of last resort in the United States, also the highest appellate court; it consists of nine justices who are appointed for life.

USA PATRIOT Act: broadly written legislation that affords law enforcement with new tools to detect and prevent terrorism.

Use of force: the type and amount of effort required to compel compliance by an unwilling suspect.

Utilitarianism: in ethics, as articulated by John Stuart Mill, a belief that the proper course of action is that which maximizes utility—usually defined as that which maximizes happiness and minimizes suffering.

Vicarious liability: a legal doctrine whereby a person is responsible for the actions of another and is to exercise reasonable and prudent care in supervising that person.

Victim impact statements: information provided prior to sentencing by the victims of a crime (or, in cases of murder, the surviving family members) about the impact the crime had on their lives; allowed by the U.S. Supreme Court.

Warden: the chief administrator of a federal penitentiary or state prison.

Warrant, arrest: a document issued by a judge directing police to immediately arrest a person accused of a crime.

Warrant, search: a document issued by a judge, based on probable cause, directing police to immediately search a person, a premises, an automobile, or a building for the purpose of finding illegal contraband felt to be located therein and as stated in the warrant.

Wedding cake model of criminal justice: a model of the criminal justice process whereby a four-tiered hierarchy exists, with a few celebrated cases at the top, and lower tiers increasing in size as the seriousness of cases declines and informal processes (use of discretion) become more likely to occur.

Whistleblower Protection Act: a federal law prohibiting reprisal against employees who reveal information concerning a violation of law, rules, or regulations; gross mismanagement or waste of funds; an abuse of authority; and so on.

White-collar crime: crimes committed by wealthy or powerful individuals in the course of their professions or occupations.

XYY chromosome: the so-called criminal chromosome; criminal behavior is thought to be caused, in some offenders, by an extra Y chromosome—believed to cause agitation, aggression, and greater criminal tendencies.

/// NOTES

// CHAPTER 1

1. Jennifer Gonnerman, "Before the Law," *The New Yorker*, September 29, 2014, https://www.newyorker.com/magazine/2014/10/06/before-the-law.
2. Benjamin Weiser, "Kalief Browder's Suicide Brought Changes to Rikers. Now It Has Led to a $3 Million Settlement.," *New York Times*, January 24, 2019, https://www.nytimes.com/2019/01/24/nyregion/kalief-browder-settlement-lawsuit.html.
3. Federal Bureau of Investigation, "Table 2. Crime in the United States by Community Type, 2017," *Crime in the United States—2017* (Washington, D.C.: Uniform Crime Reporting Program), https://ucr.fbi.gov/crime-in-the-u.s/2017/crime-in-the-u.s.-2017/tables/table-2.
4. Jennifer Bronson, "Justice Expenditures and Employment Extracts, 2015—Preliminary," *Statistical Tables* (Washington, D.C.: U.S. Department of Justice, Office of Justice Systems, Bureau of Justice Statistics, June 2018), https://www.bjs.gov/index.cfm?ty=pbdetail&iid=6310.
5. YourDictionary, "Justice Quotes," *Webster's New World Dictionary of Quotations* (Hoboken, N.J.: Wiley, 2010), http://www.yourdictionary.com/quotes/justice.
6. James Austin, "'Three Strikes and You're Out': The Likely Consequences on the Courts, Prisons, and Crime in California and Washington State," *St. Louis University Public Law Review* 14, no. 1 (1994): 239–257.
7. See, for example, Joe Domanick, *Cruel Justice: Three Strikes and the Politics of Crime in America's Golden State* (Berkeley: University of California Press, 2004).
8. Austin, "'Three Strikes and You're Out,'" pp. 239–257.
9. Scott Ehlers, Vincent Schiraldi, and Jason Ziedenberg, *Still Striking Out: Ten Years of California's Three Strikes* (Washington, D.C.: Justice Policy Institute, 2004), http://www.justicepolicy.org/research/2028.
10. Brent Staples, "California Horror Stories and the 3-Strikes Law," *New York Times*, November 24, 2012, http://www.nytimes.com/2012/11/25/opinion/sunday/california-horror-stories-and-the-3-strikes-law.html.
11. Ehlers et al., *Still Striking Out*.
12. Ibid.
13. John J. Sloan III and Lynne M. Vieraitis, "'Striking Out' as Crime Reduction Policy: The Impact of 'Three Strikes' Laws on Crime Rates in U.S. Cities," *Justice Quarterly* 21, no. 2 (2004): 207–239.
14. Staples, "California Horror Stories and the 3-Strikes Law."
15. Ibid.
16. Alexander B. Smith and Harriet Pollack, *Criminal Justice: An Overview* (New York: Holt, Rinehart and Winston, 1980), p. 9.
17. Ibid., p. 10.
18. Ibid., p. 366.
19. Thomas J. Bernard, *The Consensus-Conflict Debate: Form and Content in Social Theories* (New York: Columbia University Press, 1983), p. 78.
20. Thomas Hobbes, *Leviathan* (New York: E. P. Dutton, 1950), pp. 290–291.
21. Laws that prohibit conducting certain types of business on Sundays, sometimes called "Blue Laws," are still in effect in some locations throughout the United States. For a historical overview of these laws, see David N. Laband and Deborah Hendry Heinbuch, *Blue Laws: The History, Economics, and Politics of Sunday Closing Laws* (New York: Free Press, 1987).
22. Justin McCarthy, "Two in Three Americans Now Support Legalizing Marijuana," Gallup News, October 22, 2018, https://news.gallup.com/poll/243908/two-three-americans-support-legalizing-marijuana.aspx.
23. Jean-Jacques Rousseau, "A Discourse on the Origin of Inequality," in G. D. H. Cole (ed.), *The Social Contract and Discourses* (New York: E. P. Dutton, 1946), p. 240.
24. Bernard, *Consensus-Conflict Debate*, pp. 83, 85.
25. *Roe v. Wade*, 410 U.S. 113 (1973).
26. See Gallup, "Abortion," http://www.gallup.com/poll/1576/abortion.aspx.
27. U.S. Sentencing Commission, *Special Report to the Congress: Cocaine and Federal Sentencing Policy* (Washington, D.C.: Richard P. Conaboy et al., February 1995), http://www.ussc.gov/sites/default/files/pdf/news/congressional-testimony-and-reports/drug-topics/199502-rtc-cocaine-sentencing-policy/EXECSUM.pdf.
28. Herbert L. Packer, *The Limits of the Criminal Sanction* (Stanford, Calif.: Stanford University Press, 1968).
29. Herbert L. Packer, *Two Models of the Criminal Process*, 113 U. PA. L. Rev. 1, 2 (1964).
30. The President's Commission on Law Enforcement and Administration of Justice, *The Challenge of Crime in a Free Society* (Washington, D.C.: U.S. Government Printing Office, 1967), p. 5.
31. See Office of Juvenile Justice and Delinquency Prevention, "Upper Age of Original Juvenile Court Jurisdiction," *Statistical Briefing Book: Juvenile Justice System Structure and Process* (Washington, D.C.: U.S. Department of Justice, 2012), http://www.ojjdp.gov/ojstatbb/structure_process/qa04101.asp.
32. Samuel Walker, *Sense and Nonsense About Crime and Drugs*, 4th ed. (Belmont, Calif.: Wadsworth, 1997), p. 15.
33. Adapted from Mike Broemmel, *The Wedding Cake Model Theory of Criminal Justice* (Bellevue, Wash.: eHow, n.d.), http://www.ehow.com/about_5143074_wedding-model-theory-criminal-justice.html.

34. Robert F. Kennedy, *The Enemy Within: The McClellan Committee's Crusade Against Jimmy Hoffa and Corrupt Labor Unions* (Jackson, Tenn.: Perseus Books, 1994), p. 324.
35. Benjamin S. Bloom (ed.), Max D. Englehart, Edward J. Furst, Walker H. Hill, and David R. Krathwohl, *Taxonomy of Educational Objectives: The Classification of Educational Goals. Handbook I: Cognitive Domain* (New York: Longman, 1956).

// CHAPTER 2

1. Brian P. Block and John Hostettler, *Famous Cases: Nine Trials That Changed the Law* (Hook, Hampshire, U.K.: Waterside Press, 2002), pp. 9–12.
2. Henry Campbell Black, *Black's Law Dictionary*, 4th ed. (St. Paul, Minn.: West, 1951).
3. Law Library of Congress, "Case Law (or Common Law)," *American Memory*, http://memory.loc.gov/ammem/awhhtml/awlaw3/common_law.html.
4. Texas Politics, "State Constitutions," *The Texas Constitution Today*, http://texaspolitics.laits.utexas.edu/7_3_1.html.
5. Carissa Byrne Hessick, "Motive's Role in Criminal Punishment," *Southern California Law Review 80*, no. 89 (2006): 89.
6. See Arizona Criminal Code, generally, at http://www.azleg.gov/arizonarevisedstatutes.asp?title=13.
7. Ibid.
8. See Nevada Revised Statutes, generally, at https://www.leg.state.nv.us/NRS/.
9. *People v. Anderson*, 70 Ca1.2d 15 (1968).
10. *U.S. v. Brown*, 518 F.2d 821 (1975).
11. See, for example, James R. Elkins, "Depraved Heart Murder," *West Virginia Homicide Jury Instructions Project* (Morgantown: West Virginia University College of Law, Spring 2006), http://myweb.wvnet.edu/~jelkins/adcrimlaw/depraved_heart_murder.html.
12. Federal Bureau of Investigation, "Rape," in *Crime in the United States—2017* (Washington, D.C.: Uniform Crime Reporting Program), https://ucr.fbi.gov/crime-in-the-u.s/2017/crime-in-the-u.s.-2017/topic-pages/rape.
13. Federal Bureau of Investigation, "Robbery," in *Crime in the United States—2017* (Washington, D.C.: Uniform Crime Reporting Program), https://ucr.fbi.gov/crime-in- https://ucr.fbi.gov/crime-in-the-u.s/2017/crime-in-the-u.s.-2017/topic-pages/robbery.
14. Federal Bureau of Investigation, "Aggravated Assault," in *Crime in the United States—2017* (Washington, D.C.: Uniform Crime Reporting Program), https://ucr.fbi.gov/crime-in-the-u.s/2017/crime-in-the-u.s.-2017/topic-pages/aggravated-assault.
15. Federal Bureau of Investigation, "Burglary," in *Crime in the United States—2017* (Washington, D.C.: Uniform Crime Reporting Program), https://ucr.fbi.gov/crime-in-the-u.s/2017/crime-in-the-u.s.-2017/topic-pages/burglary.
16. For Nevada's larceny-theft statute, see *Nevada Revised Statutes*, Chapter 205.220; for Iowa's larceny statutes, see *Iowa Code*, Chapter 714.2, "Degrees of Theft," http://law.justia.com/codes/iowa/2011/titlexvi/subtitle1/chapter714/714–2.
17. Federal Bureau of Investigation, "Larceny-Theft," in *Crime in the United States—2017* (Washington, D.C.: Uniform Crime Reporting Program), https://ucr.fbi.gov/crime-in-the-u.s/2017/crime-in-the-u.s.-2017/topic-pages/larceny-theft.
18. Federal Bureau of Investigation, "Vehicle Theft," in *Crime in the United States—2017* (Washington, D.C.: Uniform Crime Reporting Program), https://ucr.fbi.gov/crime-in-the-u.s/2017/crime-in-the-u.s.-2017/topic-pages/motor-vehicle-theft.
19. Federal Bureau of Investigation, "Arson," in *Crime in the United States—2017* (Washington, D.C.: Uniform Crime Reporting Program), https://ucr.fbi.gov/crime-in-the-u.s/2017/crime-in-the-u.s.-2017/topic-pages/arson.
20. United Nations Office on Drugs and Crime, *Global Report on Trafficking in Persons*, 2014, https://www.unodc.org/documents/data-and-analysis/glotip/GLOTIP_2014_full_report.pdf.
21. Edwin H. Sutherland, "White Collar Criminality," *American Sociological Review* 5 (February 1940): 1–12.
22. Frank E. Hagan, *Introduction to Criminology: Theories, Methods, and Criminal Behavior*, 8th ed. (Los Angeles, Calif.: Sage Publications, 2013), p. 281.
23. Ibid., p. 288.
24. Ibid., p. 320.
25. Robert Lenzner, "Bernie Madoff's $50 Billion Ponzi Scheme," *Forbes*, December 12, 2008, http://www.forbes.com/2008/12/12/madoff-ponzi-hedge-pf-ii-in_rl_1212croesus_inl.html.
26. "Martha Stewart's Conviction Upheld," CBS News, February 11, 2009, http://www.cbsnews.com/2100-207_162-1183526.html.
27. Charles B. Fleddermann, "The Ford Pinto Exploding Gas Tank," in *Engineering Ethics*, 2nd ed. (Upper Saddle River, N.J.: Prentice Hall, 2004), pp. 72–73.
28. Bureau of Justice Statistics, *Victims of Identity Theft, 2014* (September 2015), p. 1, https://www.bjs.gov/content/pub/pdf/vit14.pdf.
29. Herbert Edelhertz, *The Nature, Impact and Prosecution of White-Collar Crime*, Report No. ICR 70–1 (Washington, D.C.: U.S. Department of Justice, 1970).
30. Federal Bureau of Investigation, *What We Investigate*, "Organized Crime," https://www.fbi.gov/investigate/organized-crime.
31. See "Statistics," http://www.twainquotes.com/Statistics.html.

32. Federal Bureau of Investigation, "Incidents and Offenses," *Hate Crime Statistics—2017* (Washington, D.C.: U.S. Department of Justice), https://ucr.fbi.gov/hate-crime/2017/topic-pages/incidents-and-offenses.
33. Madeline Masucci, *Hate Crime Victimization, 2004–2015* (Washington, D.C.: U.S. Department of Justice, Office of Justice Programs, Bureau of Justice Statistics, February 2014), https://www.bjs.gov/content/pub/pdf/hcv0415.pdf.
34. For access to the publications, see Federal Bureau of Investigation, *Uniform Crime Reports*, https://www.fbi.gov/services/cjis/ucr/publications.
35. Federal Bureau of Investigation, "Table 1," *Crime in the United States—by Volume and Rate per 100,000 Inhabitants, 1998–2017* (Washington, D.C.: U.S. Department of Justice), https://ucr.fbi.gov/crime-in-the-u.s/2017/crime-in-the-u.s.-2017/topic-pages/tables/table-1.
36. Ibid.
37. Federal Bureau of Investigation, "Murder," *Crime in the United States—2017* (Washington, D.C.: Uniform Crime Reporting Program), https://ucr.fbi.gov/crime-in-the-u.s/2017/crime-in-the-u.s.-2017/topic-pages/murder.
38. Federal Bureau of Investigation, "Offense Definitions," *Crime in the United States—2017*, https://ucr.fbi.gov/crime-in-the-u.s/2017/crime-in-the-u.s.-2017/topic-pages/offense-definitions.
39. Federal Bureau of Investigation, "FBI Releases 2015 Crime Statistics," *Press Releases* (Washington, D.C.: U.S. Department of Justice), https://www.fbi.gov/news/pressrel/press-releases/fbi-releases-2015-crime-statistics.
40. See, for example, Nathan James and Logan Rishard Council, "How Crime in the United States Is Measured," *Congressional Research Service Report for Congress*, January 3, 2008, pp. 17–20, http://www.policyarchive.org/handle/10207/bitstreams/18912.pdf.
41. See Federal Bureau of Investigation, *Uniform Crime Reporting Handbook* (Washington, D.C.: U.S. Department of Justice), p. 10, http://www.fbi.gov/about-us/cjis/ucr/additional-ucr-publications/ucr_handbook.pdf/view.
42. Federal Bureau of Investigation, "FBI Releases 2015 Crime Statistics from the National Incident-Based Reporting System, Encourages Transition," *Press Releases* (Washington, D.C.: U.S. Department of Justice), https://www.fbi.gov/news/pressrel/press-releases/fbi-releases-2015-crime-statistics-from-the-national-incident-based-reporting-system-encourages-transition.
43. Federal Bureau of Investigation, "FBI Releases 2017 NIBRS Crime Data as Transition to NIBRS 2021 Continues," *Press Releases* (Washington, D.C.: U.S. Department of Justice), https://www.fbi.gov/news/pressrel/press-releases/fbi-releases-2017-nibrs-crime-data-as-transition-to-nibrs-2021-continues.
44. Bureau of Justice Statistics, "Data Collection: National Crime Victimization Survey (NCVS)," http://bjs.ojp.usdoj.gov/index.cfm?ty=dcdetail&iid=245.
45. National Archive of Criminal Justice Data, "National Crime Victimization Survey Resource Guide," http://www.icpsr.umich.edu/icpsrweb/NACJD/NCVS/.
46. National Archive of Criminal Justice Data, "Accuracy of NCVS Estimates," https://www.icpsr.umich.edu/icpsrweb/NACJD/NCVS/accuracy.jsp.
47. *See State v. Thompson*, 865 p.2d 1125 (Mont. 1993) and Mont. Code. Ann. §§45–501–1-3. The principal was acquitted of sexual assault because the statute did not contemplate purely psychological force. The Montana legislature later amended the statute to clarify this issue in anticipation of future cases.
48. Defendant Peterson was charged with manslaughter. At trial, the judge instructed the jury that self-defense is *not* available as a defense when someone acts as the aggressor, stands one's ground when other options are available, and actually provokes a conflict. Peterson was convicted; he appealed on the grounds that his shooting the driver should be excused because he acted in self-defense. The appellate court agreed with the trial judge: One cannot claim to have acted in "self-defense" by a *self-generated necessity to kill* another person. The evidence demonstrated that Peterson instigated the confrontation, and his failure to retreat was also a factor that the jury could take into account. *U.S. v. Peterson*, 483 F. 2d 1222 (D.C. Cir. 1973).

// CHAPTER 3

1. Meghan Hoyer and Brad Heath, "Mass Killings Occur in USA Once Every Two Weeks," *USA Today*, December 19, 2012, http://www.usatoday.com/story/news/nation/2012/12/18/mass-killings-common/1778303/.
2. Cesare Beccaria, *On Crimes and Punishments*, trans. H. Paolucci (Indianapolis, Ind.: Bobbs-Merrill, 1963; original work published 1764).
3. Frank E. Hagan, *Introduction to Criminology: Theories, Methods, and Criminal Behavior*, 8th ed. (Los Angeles, Calif.: Sage, 2013), p. 115.
4. Adapted from George F. Cole and Christopher E. Smith, *Criminal Justice in America*, 6th ed. (Belmont, Calif.: Wadsworth, 2011), p. 56.
5. Hagan, *Introduction to Criminology*, p. 129.
6. Ibid.
7. Ibid.
8. Mary Gibson, *Born to Crime: Cesare Lombroso and the Origins of Biological Criminology* (Westport, Conn.: Praeger, 2002); David G. Horn, *The Criminal Body: Lombroso and the Anatomy of Deviance* (New York: Routledge, 2003).
9. Ibid.
10. William H. Sheldon, *Varieties of Delinquent Youth: An Introduction to Constitutional Psychiatry* (New York: Harper, 1949); William H. Sheldon, *The Varieties of Human*

Physique: An Introduction to Constitutional Psychology (New York: Harper, 1940).
11. See Sheldon Glueck and Eleanor Glueck, *Unraveling Juvenile Delinquency* (New York: Commonwealth Fund, 1950).
12. R. G. Fox, "The XYY Offender: A Modern Myth?" *Journal of Criminal Law, Criminology, and Police Science* 62 (March 1971): 59–73.
13. Melissa Peskin, Yu Gao, Andrea L. Glenn, Anna Rudo-Hutt, Yaling Yang, and Adrian Raine, "Biology and Crime," in Francis T. Cullen and Pamela Wilcox (Eds.), *The Oxford Handbook of Criminological Theory* (New York: Oxford University Press, 2013), pp. 22–39.
14. John Glatt, *Evil Twins: Chilling True Stories of Twins, Killing and Insanity* (New York: St. Martin's, 1999).
15. Adrian Raine, *The Psychopathology of Crime* (San Diego: Academic Press, 1993).
16. Francis T. Cullen, Robert Agnew, and Pamela Wilcox, *Criminological Theory: Past to Present* (New York: Oxford University Press, 2014).
17. David P. Farrington (Ed.), *Integrated Developmental and Life-Course Theories of Offending*, vol. 1 (New Brunswick, N.J.: Transaction Publishers, 2011).
18. See *Skinner v. State of Oklahoma, ex. rel. Williamson*, 316 U.S. 535 (1942).
19. Policy implications that flow from studies showing that criminals are biologically inferior include *selective incapacitation*—either imprisoning or executing people who have been adopted and whose natural fathers had a criminal record—which is of course repugnant to our sense of justice and values unless one has in fact committed a heinous crime. Some people may argue instead that neurological defects may be identified through diagnostic imaging and that medications can suppress violent tendencies. There may be help in the future in this regard, however, as scientists come closer to being able to identify and remove or alter defective genes through genetic engineering. Furthermore, one could argue that persons with learning disabilities may be helped by receiving special education and counseling.
20. Jason Fletcher and Barbara Wolfe, "Long Term Consequences of Childhood ADHD on Criminal Activities," *Journal of Mental Health Policy Economics*, 12, no. 3 (September 2009), 119–138.
21. Clifford R. Shaw and Henry D. McKay, *Juvenile Delinquency and Urban Areas* (Chicago: University of Chicago Press, 1942).
22. Ibid.
23. Robert J. Sampson, Stephen W. Raudenbush, and Felton Earls, "Neighborhoods and Violent Crime: A Multilevel Study of Collective Efficacy," *Science* 277, no. 5328 (August 15, 1997): 918–924.
24. Robert K. Merton, "Social Structure and Anomie," *American Sociological Review* 3, no. 5 (October 1938): 672–682.
25. Ibid.
26. Robert Agnew, *Pressured Into Crime: An Overview of General Strain Theory* (New York: Oxford University Press, 2005).
27. Robert Agnew, "General Strain Theory: Current Status and Directions for Further Research," in Francis T. Cullen, John Paul Wright, and Kristie R. Blevins (Eds.), *Taking Stock: The Status of Criminological Theory* (vol. 15): *Advances in Criminological Theory* (New Brunswick, N.J.: Transaction Publishers, 2006), pp. 101–123.
28. Jeffrey R. Kling, Jens Ludwig, and Lawrence F. Katz, "Neighborhood Effects on Crime for Female and Male Youth: Evidence From a Randomized Housing Voucher Experiment," *Quarterly Journal of Economics* 120, no. 1 (February 2005): 87–130.
29. E. D. Sutherland, D. Cressey, and D. Luckenbill, *Principles of Criminology* (Lanham, Md.: Rowman & Littlefield, 1992).
30. Ronald L. Akers and Gary F. Jensen, "The Empirical Status of Social Learning Theory of Crime and Deviance: The Past, Present, and Future," in Francis T. Cullen, John Paul Wright, and Kristie R. Blevins (Eds.), *Taking Stock: The Status of Criminological Theory* (vol. 15): *Advances in Criminological Theory* (New Brunswick, N.J.: Transaction Publishers, 2006), pp. 37–76.
31. Travis Hirschi, *Causes of Delinquency* (Berkeley: University of California Press, 1969).
32. Michael R. Gottfredson and Travis Hirschi, *A General Theory of Crime* (Stanford, Calif.: Stanford University Press, 1990).
33. Mark M. Lanier, Stuart Henry, and Desiré J. M. Anastasia, *Essential Criminology* (Boulder, Colo.: Westview Press, 2014).
34. Bald Eagle Protection Act of 1940, as amended, Public Law 95–616 (92 Stat. 3114), November 8, 1978.
35. Edwin Lemert, *Social Pathology: A Systematic Approach to the Theory of Sociopathic Behaviour* (New York: McGraw-Hill, 1951).
36. Howard S. Becker, *Outsiders: Studies in the Sociology of Deviance* (New York: Free Press, 1963), p. 9.
37. Jon Gunnar Bernburg, Marvin D. Krohn, and Craig J. Rivera, "Official Labeling, Criminal Embeddedness, and Subsequent Delinquency: A Longitudinal Test of Labeling Theory," *Journal of Research in Crime and Delinquency* 43, no. 1 (February 2006): 67–88.
38. David P. Farrington and Joseph Murray (Eds.), *Labeling Theory: Empirical Tests*, vol. 1. (New Brunswick, N.J.: Transaction Publishers, 2013).
39. Social process theory is obviously broad in its reach and includes a number of possible explanations for crime. Policy makers need to focus on the various means by which crime is learned, and address the aforementioned problems of control, association, and labeling by striving to provide programs that have positive role models and will reinforce the proper value system and norms. See A.

Matz, "Do Youth Mentoring Programs Work? A Review of the Empirical Literature," *Journal of Juvenile Justice* (Spring 2014), http://www.journalofjuvjustice.org/JOJJ0302/article06.htm.
40. Otwin Marenin, "Parking Tickets and Class Repression: The Concept of Policing in Critical Theories of Criminal Justice," *Contemporary Crises* 6 (1982): 241–266.
41. George Vold, *Theoretical Criminology* (New York: Oxford University Press, 1958).
42. Thorsten Sellin, *Culture and Conflict in Crime* (New York: Social Science Research Council, 1938); Austin Turk, *Criminality and Legal Order* (Chicago: Rand McNally, 1969); also see Vold, *Theoretical Criminology.*
43. Elliott Currie, "Market, Crime and Community: Toward a Mid-Range Theory of Post-Industrial Violence," *Theoretical Criminology* 1, no. 2 (May 1997): 147–172.
44. See Stephen B. Bright and Sia M. Sanneh, "Fifty Years of Defiance and Resistance After *Gideon v. Wainwright,*" *Yale Law Journal* 122, no. 8 (2013): 2150.
45. See The Sentencing Project, "It's Not Fair, It's Not Working," http://www.sentencingproject.org/crackreform/. Policy implications for the critical theory of crime—where the system itself foments crime—are certainly challenging. Decision makers must attempt to provide minorities with programs that will lessen or alleviate the injustices of the criminal justice system that might be found at the hands of the police, courts, or corrections system—while also making the system more equitable by meting out punishment more equally among upper-class as well as lower-class offenders.
46. See, for example, Mark Kleiman, "Smart on Crime," *Democracy: A Journal of Ideas* 28 (Spring 2013), http://www.democracyjournal.org/28/smart-on-crime.php?page=all.
47. Freda Adler, *Sisters in Crime: The Rise of the New Female Criminal* (New York: McGraw-Hill, 1975), p. 12.
48. Equal Employment Opportunity Act, Public Law 92–261.
49. Pregnancy Discrimination Act of 1978, 42 U.S.C. Sec. 2000e (k).
50. Family and Medical Leave Act (FMLA), Public Law 103–3, 5 U.S.C. 6381–6387, 5 CFR part 630.
51. Robert Witt and Ann Dryden Witte, "Crime, Imprisonment, and Female Labor Force Participation: A Time-Series Approach," *Social Science Research Network*, November 1998, http://papers.ssrn.com/s013/papers.cfm?abstract_id=226386.
52. Rita Simon, *Women and Crime* (Lexington, Mass.: Lexington Books, 1975).
53. M. Chesney-Lind and L. Pasko, *The Female Offender*, 3rd ed. (Thousand Oaks, Calif.: Sage, 2013).
54. B. Brown, "Women and Crime: The Dark Figures of Criminology," *Economy and Society* 15, no. 3 (1986): 355.
55. Meda Chesney-Lind, "Girls' Crime and Women's Place: Toward a Feminist Model of Female Delinquency," *Crime & Delinquency* 35, no. 1 (January 1989): 5–29.
56. Lawrence E. Cohen and Marcus Felson, "Social Change and Crime Rate Trends: A Routine Activity Approach," *American Sociological Review* 44 (August 1979): 588–608.
57. Ronald V. Clarke and John E. Eck, *Crime Analysis for Problem Solvers in 60 Small Steps* (Washington, D.C.: Center for Problem Oriented Policing, 2005).
58. Travis C. Pratt, Kristy Holtfreter, and Michael D. Reisig, "Routine Online Activity and Internet Fraud Targeting: Extending the Generality of Routine Activity Theory," *Journal of Research in Crime and Delinquency* 47, no. 3 (August 2010): 267–296.
59. Ronald V. Clarke, *Situational Crime Prevention: Successful Case Studies*, 2nd ed. (Monsey, N.Y.: Criminal Justice Press, 1997).
60. Richard T. Wright and Scott H. Decker, "Creating the Illusion of Impending Death," in Paul Cromwell, *In Their Own Words: Criminals on Crime*, 5th ed. (Cary, N.C.: Oxford University Press, 2009), pp. 159–164.
61. Ibid., pp. 161–162.
62. Ibid., p. 162.
63. Ibid., p. 164.
64. Richard T. Wright and Scott H. Decker, "Deciding to Commit a Burglary," in ibid., pp. 90–101.
65. Ibid., p. 100.
66. Volkan Topalli and Richard T. Wright, "Dubs and Dees, Beats and Rims," in ibid., pp. 129–141.
67. See the Anti Car Theft Act of 1992, Public Law 102–519; the full text of the act may be viewed at http://www.ojp.usdoj.gov/BJA/pdf/Anti_Car_Theft_Act.pdf.
68. Topalli and Wright, "Dubs and Dees, Beats and Rims," p. 129.
69. Ibid., pp. 131, 140.

// CHAPTER 4

1. Stewart was an associate justice of the U.S. Supreme Court from 1958 to 1981.
2. Adapted from Pamela Manson, "Utah Nurse Reaches $500,000 Settlement in Dispute Over Her Arrest for Blocking Cop From Drawing Blood From Patient," *Salt Lake Tribune*, November 1, 2017, https://www.sltrib.com/news/2017/10/31/utah-nurse-arrested-for-blocking-cop-from-drawing-blood-from-patient-receives-500000-settlement/.
3. Jodi S. Cohen, "Chicago Cop Under Investigation Again Over Social Media Posts," ProPublica Illinois, January 25, 2018, https://www.propublica.org/article/chicago-police-officer-john-catanzara-investigation.
4. This scenario is based loosely on David Gelman, Susan Miller, and Bob Cohn, "The Strange Case of Judge Wachtler," *Newsweek*, November 23, 1992, pp. 34–35. Wachtler was later arraigned on charges of attempting to extort money from the woman and threatening her

14-year-old daughter (it was later determined that the judge had been having an affair with the woman, who had recently ended the relationship). After being placed under house arrest with an electronic monitoring bracelet, the judge resigned from the court, which he had served with distinction for two decades.

5. ACLU/Florida, "Civil Rights Groups Call for Federal Investigation Into Solitary Confinement Abuse in Florida Prisons," March 11, 2016, https://www.aclufl.org/en/press-releases/civil-rights-groups-call-federal-investigation-solitary-confinement-abuse-florida a copy of the letter is available at: http://aclufl.org/resources/letter-to-doj-calling-for-investigation-into-abuse-of-solitary-in-florida-prisons/.
6. Immanuel Kant, "Foundations of the Metaphysics of Morals," *The German Library 13* (New York: Continuum, 2006).
7. Richard Kania, "Police Acceptance of Gratuities," *Criminal Justice Ethics* 7 (1988): 37–49.
8. John Kleinig, *The Ethics of Policing* (New York: Cambridge University Press, 1996).
9. T. J. O'Malley, "Managing for Ethics: A Mandate for Administrators," *FBI Law Enforcement Bulletin* (April 1997): 20–25.
10. Thomas J. Martinelli, "Unconstitutional Policing: The Ethical Challenges in Dealing With Noble Cause Corruption," *The Police Chief* (October 2006): 150.
11. John P. Crank and Michael A. Caldero, *Police Ethics: The Corruption of Noble Cause* (Cincinnati, Ohio: Anderson, 2000), p. 75.
12. U.S. Department of Justice, National Institute of Justice, Office of Community Oriented Policing Services, *Police Integrity: Public Service With Honor* (Washington, D.C.: U.S. Government Printing Office, 1997), p. 62.
13. Ibid.
14. Lawrence W. Sherman, ed., *Police Corruption: A Sociological Perspective* (Garden City, N.Y.: Anchor, 1974), p. 1.
15. Herman Goldstein, *Policing a Free Society* (Cambridge, Mass.: Ballinger, 1977), p. 188.
16. Ibid.
17. William A. Westley, *Violence and the Police* (Cambridge, Mass.: MIT Press, 1970), pp. 113–114.
18. International Association of Chiefs of Police, "Law Enforcement Oath of Honor," https://www.theiacp.org/sites/default/files/all/i-j/IACP_Oath_of_Honor_En_8.5x11_Web.pdf.
19. Ibid.
20. David Carter, "Theoretical Dimensions in the Abuse of Authority," in Thomas Barker and David Carter (Eds.), *Police Deviance* (Cincinnati, Ohio: Anderson, 1994), pp. 269–290; also see Thomas Barker and David Carter, "Fluffing Up the Evidence and 'Covering Your Ass': Some Conceptual Notes on Police Lying," *Deviant Behavior* 11 (1990): 61–73.
21. Gary T. Marx, "Who Really Gets Stung? Some Issues Raised by the New Police Undercover Work," *Crime & Delinquency* (1982): 165–193.
22. *Illinois v. Perkins*, 110 S. Ct. 2394 (1990).
23. Barker and Carter, *Police Deviance*.
24. Thomas Barker, "An Empirical Study of Police Deviance Other than Corruption," in Barker and Carter, *Police Deviance*, pp. 123–138.
25. For an excellent analysis of how the acceptance of gratuities can become endemic to an organization and pose ethical dilemmas for new officers within, see Jim Ruiz and Christine Bono, "At What Price a 'Freebie'? The Real Cost of Police Gratuities," *Criminal Justice Ethics* (Winter/Spring 2004): 44–54. The authors also demonstrate through detailed calculations how the amount of gratuities accepted can reach up to 40 percent of an annual officer's income—and is therefore no minor or inconsequential infraction of rules that can be left ignored or unenforced.
26. Quoted in David Burnham, "Police Aides Told to Rid Commands of All Dishonesty," *New York Times*, October 29, 1970, p. 1.
27. From the Washoe County Sheriff's Office, Reno, Nevada.
28. Edward Tully, "Misconduct, Corruption, Abuse of Power: What Can the Chief Do?" http://www.neiassociates.org/mis2.htm (Part I) and http://www.neiassociates.org/misconductII.htm (Part II).
29. See "Officer Caught on Camera Buying Shoes for Homeless Man," USA Today, December 3, 2015, https://www.usatoday.com/story/news/humankind/2015/12/03/officer-caught-camera-buying-homeless-man-shoes/76727994/; Anthony de Stefano, "Larry DePrimo, NYPD Cop, Buys Homeless Man Boots," *Huffington Post*, November 2017, https://www.huffingtonpost.com/2012/11/29/larry-deprimo-nypd-cop-gives-homeless-boots_n_2209178.html.
30. See "NY Police Apologize to Victim With Food, Favors," PoliceOne.com, May 14, 2014, https://www.policeone.com/police-heroes/articles/6999864-NY-police-apologize-to-victim-with-food-favors/.
31. "Arizona Cop Praised for Giving Bike, Riding Lessons to Teen," PoliceOne.com, May 13, 2013, https://www.youtube.com/watch?v=DcQ8M3hCeWc; "Teen Who Walked 2 Hours to Work Surprised by Cop Who Buys Him Bike," KTVU News, September 21, 2016, http://www.ktvu.com/news/mobile-app-ktvu/teen-who-walked-2-miles-to-work-surprised-by-cop-who-buys-him-bike.
32. See this and other such instances in Lorraine Burger, "5 Cases That Fight the Stigma of 'Unethical' Policing, PoliceOne.com, April 10, 2014, https://www.policeone.com/police-jobs-and-careers/articles/7063313-5-cases-that-fight-the-stigma-of-unethical-policing/.
33. Roscoe Pound, "The Causes of Popular Dissatisfaction With the Administration of Justice," address before the

annual convention of the American Bar Association, August 29, 1906. *American Lawyer* 14 (1906): 445.
34. John P. MacKenzie, *The Appearance of Justice* (New York: Scribner, 1974).
35. Pierro Calamandrei, quoted in Frank Greenberg, "The Task of Judging the Judges," *Judicature* 59 (May 1976): 464.
36. For thorough discussions and examples of these areas of potential ethical shortcomings, see Jeffrey M. Shaman, Steven Lubet, and James J. Alfini, *Judicial Conduct and Ethics*, 3rd ed. (San Francisco: Matthew Bender, 2000).
37. Ibid.
38. Ibid., p. vi.
39. Tim Murphy, "Test Your Ethical Acumen," *Judges' Journal* 8 (1998): 34.
40. American Judicature Society, *Judicial Conduct Reporter* 16 (1994): 2–3.
41. Shaman, Lubet, and Alfini, *Judicial Conduct and Ethics*, p. viii.
42. *Berger v. U.S.*, 295 U.S. 78 (1935).
43. See *Dunlop v. U.S.*, 165 U.S. 486 (1897), involving a prosecutor's inflammatory statements to the jury.
44. 386 U.S. 1 (1967). In this case, the Supreme Court overturned the defendant's conviction after determining that the prosecutor "deliberately misrepresented the truth."
45. Elliot D. Cohen, "Pure Legal Advocates and Moral Agents: Two Concepts of a Lawyer in an Adversary System," in Michael C. Braswell, Belinda R. McCarthy, and Bernard J. McCarthy (Eds.), *Justice, Crime and Ethics*, 2nd ed. (Cincinnati, Ohio: Anderson, 1996), p. 168.
46. Ibid.
47. Ibid., pp. 131–167.
48. Cynthia Kelly Conlon and Lisa L. Milord, *The Ethics Fieldbook: Tools for Trainers* (Chicago: American Judicature Society, n.d.), pp. 23–25.
49. Administrative Office of the United States Courts, *Code of Conduct for United States Judges*, http://www.uscourts.gov/RulesAndPolicies/CodesOfConduct/CodeConductUnitedStatesJudges.aspx; further guidance appears in Federal Judicial Center, *Guide to Judiciary Policies and Procedures* (vol. 2): *Maintaining the Public Trust: Ethics for Federal Judicial Law Clerks* (Washington, D.C.: Author, 2002).
50. Criminal Justice Research, "Correctional Ethics," http://criminal-justice.iresearchnet.com/criminal-justice-ethics/correctional-ethics/
51. Ibid., p. 28.
52. Elizabeth L. Grossi and Bruce L. Berg, "Stress and Job Dissatisfaction Among Correctional Officers: An Unexpected Finding," *International Journal of Offender Therapy and Comparative Criminology* 35 (1991): 79.
53. Irving L. Janis, "Group Dynamics Under Conditions of External Danger," in Darwin Cartwright and Alvin Zander (Eds.), *Group Dynamics: Research and Theory* (New York: Harper & Row, 1968).
54. Ibid.
55. American Correctional Association, "Code of Ethics," http://www.aca.org/ACA_Prod_IMIS/ACA_Member/About_Us/Code_of_Ethics/ACA_Member/AboutUs/Code_of_Ethics.aspx?hkey=61577ed2-c0c3-4529-bc01-36a248f79eba.
56. CBS News, March 30, 1977; see John R. Jones and Daniel P. Carlson, *Reputable Conduct: Ethical Issues in Policing and Corrections*, 2nd ed. (Upper Saddle River, N.J.: Prentice Hall, 2001), p. 76.
57. Adapted from Florida Regional Community Policing Institute, *Ethical Issues and Decisions in Law Enforcement* (March 2005): 37–39, http://cop.spcollege.edu/Training/Ethics/EN/ethicsInstructorMarch2005.pdf.
58. Kleinig, *The Ethics of Policing*.
59. Adapted from Gail Diane Cox, "Judges Behaving Badly (Again)," *National Law Journal* 21 (May 3, 1999): 1–5.

// CHAPTER 5

1. A number of articles focus on "federalizing" the local police, meaning granting them more authority (to enforce federal immigration laws and so on); here, however, we consider whether or not there should be a single, national police agency. But see Glenn Harlan Reynolds, "Want a Lawless Police Force? Federalize It." *USA Today*, May 3, 2015, https://www.usatoday.com/story/opinion/2015/05/03/baltimore-federal-drugs-evidence-fbi-column/26830873/; Lance Eldridge, "The Federalization of Local Law Enforcement," PoliceOne.com, January 3, 2011, https://www.policeone.com/patrol-issues/articles/3139476-The-federalization-of-local-law-enforcement/.
2. Bruce Smith, *Rural Crime Control* (New York: Columbia University, 1933), p. 40.
3. Ibid.
4. Ibid.
5. Ibid., pp. 182–184.
6. Ibid., pp. 188–189.
7. Ibid., pp. 218–222.
8. Ibid., pp. 245–246.
9. David R. Johnson, *American Law Enforcement History* (St. Louis, Mo.: Forum Press, 1981), pp. 18–19.
10. Leon Radzinowicz, *A History of English Criminal Law and Its Administration From 1750* (vol. IV): *Grappling for Control* (London: Stevens and Son, 1968), pp. 20–21.
11. C. Germann, Frank D. Day, and Robert R. J. Gallati, *Introduction to Law Enforcement and Criminal Justice* (Springfield, Ill.: Charles C Thomas, 1962), p. 63.
12. Johnson, *American Law Enforcement History*, p. 26.
13. James F. Richardson, *Urban Police in the United States* (London: Kennikat Press, 1974), pp. 47–48.
14. Johnson, *American Law Enforcement History*, p. 26.
15. Herman Goldstein, *Policing a Free Society* (Cambridge, Mass.: Ballinger, 1977).

16. August Vollmer, "Police Progress in the Past Twenty-Five Years," *Journal of Criminal Law and Criminology* 24 (1933): 161–175.
17. Alfred E. Parker, *Crime Fighter: August Vollmer* (New York: Macmillan, 1961).
18. Nathan Douthit, "August Vollmer," in Carl B. Klockars (Ed.), *Thinking About Police: Contemporary Readings* (New York: McGraw-Hill, 1983), p. 102.
19. Ibid.
20. Ibid.
21. Richardson, *Urban Police in the United States*, pp. 139–143.
22. Goldstein, *Policing a Free Society*.
23. Kenneth J. Peak and Ronald W. Glensor, *Community Policing and Problem Solving: Effectively Addressing Crime and Disorder*, 7th ed. (New York: Pearson, 2016), pp. 10–11.
24. Elaine Cumming, Ian Cumming, and Laura Edell, "Policeman as Philosopher, Guide, and Friend," *Social Problems* 12 (1965): 285; T. Bercal, "Calls for Police Assistance," *American Behavioral Scientist* 13 (1970): 682; Albert J. Reiss Jr., *The Police and the Public* (New Haven, Conn.: Yale University Press, 1971).
25. Bureau of Justice Statistics, "Federal Law Enforcement Statistics, 2015–2016: Summary," January 2019, pp. 1, 3. https://www.bjs.gov/content/pub/pdf/fjs1516_sum.pdf.
26. U.S. Department of Homeland Security, "Creation of the Department of Homeland Security," http://www.dhs.gov/creation-department-homeland-security.
27. National Priorities Project, "U.S. Security Spending Since 9/11," February 28, 2013, https://www.nationalpriorities.org/analysis/2013/homeland-security-spending-since-911/.
28. U.S. Department of Homeland Security, "The Lifesaving Missions of CBP," August 20, 2018, https://www.dhs.gov/news/2018/08/20/life-saving-missions-cbp.
29. Department of Homeland Security, "On a Typical Day in Fiscal Year 2018, CBP . . . ," March 7, 2019, https://www.cbp.gov/newsroom/stats/typical-day-fy2018.
30. U.S. Immigration and Customs Enforcement, "Who We Aren't," https://www.ice.gov/about.
31. Ibid., "ICE: Enforcement and Removal Operations," http://www.ice.gov/about/offices/enforcement-removal-operations/.
32. Ibid., "Homeland Security Investigations," http://www.ice.gov/hsi; also see ICE, "Become a Criminal Investigator," http://www.ice.gov/careers/occupation/investigator.
33. Transportation Security Administration, "Jobs at TSA," https://www.tsa.gov/about/jobs-at-tsa.
34. See "Are TSA Screeners Really Law Enforcement 'Officers'?" KDVR, November 4, 2013, http://kdvr.com/2013/11/04/are-tsa-screeners-really-law-enforcement-officers/.
35. See U.S. Coast Guard, "Missions," https://www.work.uscg.mil/Missions/.
36. U.S. Secret Service, "Careers Built on Integrity," https://www.secretservice.gov/join/careers/
37. U.S. Secret Service, "About," https://www.secretservice.gov/about/history/; also see https://www.secretservice.gov/about/faqs/.
38. Federal Protective Service, *Annual Report, Fiscal Year 2015*, p. 20, https://www.dhs.gov/sites/default/files/publications/Federal%20Protective%20Service%20Annual%20Report%20508%20Compliant%20FY2015.pdf. This report is the latest available.
39. U.S. Department of Justice, Federal Bureau of Investigation, "A Brief History," https://www.fbi.gov/history/brief-history.
40. U.S. Department of Justice, Federal Bureau of Investigation, "Special Agent Selection Process All You Need to Know to Apply," https://www.fbijobs.gov/sites/default/files/how-to-apply.pdf.
41. U.S. Department of Justice, Federal Bureau of Investigation, "About," https://www.fbi.gov/about.
42. "FBI Seeks Sweeping New Powers," *The Nation*, August 22, 2008, www.thenation.com/article/fbi-seeks-sweeping-new-powers.
43. Bureau of Alcohol, Tobacco, Firearms and Explosives, "ATF's History," http://www.atf.gov/about/history/.
44. Bureau of Alcohol, Tobacco, Firearms and Explosives, "Fact Sheet—Facts and Figures for Fiscal Year 2017," https://www.atf.gov/resource-center/fact-sheet/fact-sheet-facts-and-figures-fiscal-year-2017.
45. U.S. Department of Justice, Drug Enforcement Administration, "DEA History," http://www.justice.gov/dea/about/history.shtml.
46. U.S. Department of Justice, Drug Enforcement Administration, "DEA Mission Statement," http://www.dea.gov/about/mission.
47. Bureau of Justice Statistics, "Federal Law Enforcement Statistics, 2015–2016: Summary," January 2019, https://www.bjs.gov/content/pub/pdf/fjs1516_sum.pdf.
48. See U.S. Marshals Service, "Facts and Figures," https://www.usmarshals.gov/duties/factsheets/facts.pdf.
49. U.S. Marshals Service, *The FY 1993 Report to the U.S. Marshals* (Washington, D.C.: U.S. Department of Justice, 1994), pp. 188–189; also see U.S. Marshals Service, "Fact Sheets: Facts and Figures," Office of Public Affairs, April 15, 2011, http://www.usmarshals.gov/duties/factsheets/facts-2011.html.
50. Central Intelligence Agency, "CIA Vision, Mission, & Values," https://www.cia.gov/about-cia/cia-vision-mission-values/index.html; also see CIA, "About CIA," https://www.cia.gov/about-cia/index.html.
51. Central Intelligence Agency, "Careers & Internships," https://www.cia.gov/careers/opportunities/cia-jobs/index.html.
52. Internal Revenue Service, "Financial Investigations: Criminal Investigation (CI)," http://www.irs.gov/uac/Financial-Investigations—Criminal-Investigation-(CI).

53. Ibid.; also see IRS, *Criminal Investigation: Annual Report, 2018*, p. 31, https://www.irs.gov/pub/irs-utl/2018_irs_criminal_investigation_annual_report.pdf.
54. Brian A. Reaves, *Census of State and Local Law Enforcement Agencies, 2013*, Bureau of Justice Statistics, May 2015, http://www.bjs.gov/content/pub/pdf/lpd13ppp.pdf. This is the most recent report available.
55. Missouri State Highway Patrol, Career Recruitment Division, "Duties of a Trooper," http://www.mshp.dps.missouri.gov/MSHPWeb/PatrolDivisions/HRD/Trooper/troopCareer.html.
56. State of Hawaii Department of Public Safety, http://dps.hawaii.gov/about/.
57. National Association of Attorneys General, http://www.naag.org/naag/about_naag/faq/what_does_an_attorney_general_do.php.
58. Bureau of Justice Statistics, *National Sources of Law Enforcement Employment Data*, October 4, 2016, p. 1, https://www.bjs.gov/content/pub/pdf/nsleed.pdf.
59. Reaves, *Census of State and Local Law Enforcement Agencies, 2013*, p. 2, Table 1, http://www.bjs.gov/content/pub/pdf/lpd13ppp.pdf.
60. Ibid.
61. Ibid.; see also Brian Reaves, *Local Police Departments, 2013: Equipment and Technology*. U.S. Department of Justice, Bureau of Justice Statistics, July 2015, http://www.bjs.gov/content/pub/pdf/lpd13et.pdf.
62. Andrea Burch, *Sheriffs' Offices, 2007*. U.S. Department of Justice, Bureau of Justice Statistics, December 2012, http://www.bjs.gov/content/pub/pdf/s007st.pdf.
63. Clemens Bartollas, Stuart J. Miller, and Paul B. Wice, *Participants in American Criminal Justice: The Promise and the Performance* (Englewood Cliffs, N.J.: Prentice Hall, 1983), pp. 51–52.
64. Gregory M. White, Resident Agent in Charge, U.S. Department of Homeland Security, U.S. Immigration and Customs Enforcement, personal communication, October 29, 2009.
65. Ibid.
66. Ibid.
67. See, for example, Lisa Riordan Seville, Hannah Rappleye and Andrew W. Lehren, "22 Immigrants Died in ICE Detention Centers During the Past 2 Years," NBC News, January 6, 2019, https://www.nbcnews.com/politics/immigration/22-immigrants-died-ice-detention-centers-during-past-2-years-n954781; Cristobal Ramon and Raven Quesenberry, "Police, Jails, and Immigrants: How Do Immigrants and the Immigration Enforcement System Interact With Local Law Enforcement?" Bipartisan Policy Center, February 23, 2018, https://bipartisanpolicy.org/library/police-jails-and-immigrants-how-do-immigrants-and-the-immigration-enforcement-system-interact-with-local-law-enforcement/; Tal Kopan, "States Taking More of a Lead on Immigration, Citing Federal Inaction," CNN, August 17, 2017, https://www.cnn.com/2017/08/07/politics/states-immigration-policies/index.html.
68. Saul D. Astor, "A Nation of Thieves," *Security World* 15 (September 1978).
69. Bureau of Justice Statistics, *Criminal Victimization—2017*, December 2018, pp. 1, 5, https://www.bjs.gov/content/pub/pdf/cv17.pdf.
70. Bureau of Labor Statistics, "Occupational Employment Statistics, July 2018," https://www.bls.gov/ooh/protective-service/security-guards.htm.
71. Niall McCarthy, "Private Security Outnumbers the Police in Most Countries Worldwide," *Forbes*, August 31, 2017, https://www.forbes.com/sites/niallmccarthy/2017/08/31/private-security-outnumbers-the-police-in-most-countries-worldwide-infographic/#6358df2a210f.
72. "10 Things You May Not Know About the Pinkertons," History Channel, October 23, 2015, https://www.history.com/news/10-things-you-may-not-know-about-the-pinkertons.
73. George F. Cole and Christopher E. Smith, *The American System of Criminal Justice*, 11th ed. (Belmont, Calif.: Thomson Wadsworth, 2007), p. 253.
74. Law Enforcement—Private Security Consortium, *Operation Partnership Trends and Practices in Law Enforcement and Private Security Collaborations*, August 2009, pp. 34–40, https://www.nationalpublicsafetypartnership.org/clearinghouse/Content/ResourceDocuments/OperationPartnership-TrendsandPracticesinLawEnforcementandPrivateSecurityCollaborations.pdf.
75. Shoshana Walter and Ryan Gabrielson, "America's Gun-Toting Guards Armed With Poor Training, Little Oversight," Center for Investigative Reporting, December 9, 2014, https://www.revealnews.org/article/americas-gun-toting-security-guards-may-not-be-fit-for-duty/; also see Byard Duncan, "5 Ways the Armed-Guard Industry Is Out of Control," Reveal, May 4, 2015, https://www.revealnews.org/article/heres-whats-wrong-with-the-us-armed-security-industry/; First Security, "Should Your Security Guards Be Armed or Not?" https://www.firstsecurityservices.com/should-your-security-guards-be-armed-or-not/.

// CHAPTER 6

1. Justin Jouvenal, "To Find Alleged Golden State Killer, Investigators First Found His Great-Great-Great-Grandparents," *Washington Post*, April 30, 2018, https://www.washingtonpost.com/local/public-safety/to-find-alleged-golden-state-killer-investigators-first-found-his-great-great-great-grandparents/2018/04/30/3c865fe7-dfcc-4a0e-b6b2-0bec548d501f_story.html; also see Joseph Serna and Benjamin Oreskes, "Why Did It Take So Long to Arrest the Golden State Killer Suspect?

Interagency Rivalries, Old Technology, Errors and Bad Luck," *Los Angeles Times*, May 25, 2018, http://www.latimes.com/local/lanow/la-me-ln-golden-state-killer-case-20180525-story.html.
2. William A. Westley, *Violence and the Police* (Cambridge, Mass.: MIT Press, 1970).
3. Quoted in V. A. Leonard and Harry W. More, *Police Organization and Management*, 3rd ed. (Mineola, N.Y.: Foundation Press, 1971), p. 128.
4. U.S. Department of Justice, Bureau of Justice Statistics, *Local Police Departments, 2013: Personnel, Policies, and Practices* (May 2015), p. 7.
5. National Advisory Commission on Criminal Justice Standards and Goals, *Police* (Washington, D.C.: U.S. Government Printing Office, 1973), p. 369.
6. Gerald W. Lynch, "Why Officers Need a College Education," *Higher Education and National Affairs* (September 20, 1986): 11.
7. Victor E. Kappeler, Allen D. Sapp, and David L. Carter, "Police Officer Higher Education, Citizen Complaints and Departmental Rule Violations," *American Journal of Police* 11 (1992): 37–54.
8. Charles L. Weirman, "Variances of Ability Measurement Scores Obtained by College and Non-College Educated Troopers," *The Police Chief* 45 (August 1978): 34–36.
9. Ibid.
10. Robert Trojanowicz and T. Nicholson, "A Comparison of Behavioral Styles of College Graduate Police Officers v. Noncollege-Going Police Officers," *The Police Chief* 43 (August 1976): 56–59.
11. A. F. Dalley, "University and Non-University Graduated Policemen: A Study of Police Attitudes," *Journal of Police Science and Administration* 3 (1975): 458–468.
12. Wayne F. Cascio, "Formal Education and Police Officer Performance," *Journal of Police Science and Administration* 5 (1977): 89–96; Bernard Cohen and Jan M. Chaiken, *Police Background Characteristics and Performance* (New York: RAND, 1972); B. E. Sanderson, "Police Officers: The Relationship of College Education to Job Performance," *The Police Chief* (August 1977): 62–63.
13. James W. Sterling, "The College Level Entry Requirement: A Real or Imagined Cure-all?" *The Police Chief* 41 (April 1974): 28–31.
14. Gerald W. Lynch, "Cops and College," *America* (April 4, 1987): 274–275.
15. *Davis v. City of Dallas*, 777 F.2d 205 (5th Cir. 1985).
16. Norm Stamper, *Breaking Rank: A Top Cop's Exposé of the Dark Side of American Policing* (New York: Nation Books, 2005, p. 178.
17. Roger G. Dunham and Geoffrey P. Alpert, *Critical Issues in Policing: Contemporary Readings*, 5th ed. (Long Grove, Ill.: Waveland, 2005), p. 12.
18. Ibid., p. 111.
19. Steven M. Cox, *Police: Practices, Perspectives, Problems* (Boston: Allyn and Bacon, 1996), p. 61.
20. See Albert Reiss, *The Police and the Public* (New Haven, Conn.: Yale University Press, 1971), p. 96.
21. Jerome H. Skolnick and David H. Bayley, *The New Blue Line: Police Innovation in Six American Cities* (New York: Free Press, 1986), p. 4.
22. Jerome Skolnick, "A Sketch of the Policeman's Working Personality," quoted in Jack Goldsmith and Sharon S. Goldsmith (Eds.), *The Police Community* (Pacific Palisades, Calif.: Palisades, 1974), p. 106.
23. James Q. Wilson, *Varieties of Police Behavior* (Cambridge, Mass.: Harvard University Press, 1968), pp. 140–226.
24. Michael B. Sauter and Charles Stockdale, "The Most Dangerous Jobs in the US Include Electricians, Firefighters and Police Officers," *USA Today*, January 8, 2019, https://www.usatoday.com/story/money/2019/01/08/most-dangerous-jobs-us-where-fatal-injuries-happen-most-ofter/38832907/.
25. National Law Enforcement Officers Memorial Fund, "Deaths, Assaults and Injuries," 2019, https://nleomf.org/facts-figures/deaths-assaults-and-injuries.
26. Officer Down Memorial Page, "Honoring Officers Killed in 2019," https://www.odmp.org/search/year/2019.
27. Quoted in Kevin Krajick, "Does Patrol Prevent Crime?" *Police Magazine* 1 (September 1978): 4–16.
28. Quoted in J. Bartlett, ed., *Familiar Quotations*, 16th ed. (Boston: Little, Brown, 1992).
29. Merry Morash and Robin Haarr, "Gender, Workplace Problems, and Stress in Policing," paper presented at the annual meeting of the Academy of Criminal Justice Sciences, Nashville, Tennessee (March 12, 1991).
30. Herman Goldstein, "Police Discretion: The Ideal Versus the Real," *Public Administration Review* 23, no. 3 (1963): 140–148.
31. Carl B. Klockars and Stephen D. Mastrofski, "Police Discretion: The Case of Selective Enforcement," in Carl B. Klockars and Stephen D. Mastrofski (Eds.), *Thinking About Police: Contemporary Readings*, 2nd ed. (Boston: McGraw-Hill, 1991), p. 330.
32. David H. Bayley and Egon Bittner, "Learning the Skills of Policing," in Roger G. Dunham and Geoffrey P. Alpert (Eds.), *Critical Issues in Policing: Contemporary Readings* (Prospect Heights, Ill.: Waveland, 1989), pp. 87–110.
33. Kenneth Culp Davis, *Police Discretion* (St. Paul, Minn.: West, 1975), p. 73.
34. Kenneth Culp Davis, *Discretionary Justice* (Urbana: University of Illinois Press, 1969), p. 222.
35. Klockars and Mastrofski, "Police Discretion," p. 331.
36. Lawrence Sherman, "Ideas in America Policing: Evidence-Based Policing," Police Foundation, p. 2, https://www.cebma.org/wp-content/uploads/Sherman-Evidence-Based-Policing.pdf.
37. Pat Marshall Training, "The History of the Tourniquet," http://www.patmarshall.co.uk/first_aid/tourniquet-history.htm
38. Laura Clark, "The Doctor Who Introduced the Virtues of Hand Washing Died of an Infection,"

39. Cynthia Lum and Christopher S. Koper, "Evidence-Based Policing," in Kenneth J. Peak (Ed.), *Encyclopedia of Community Policing and Problem Solving* (Los Angeles: SAGE, 2013), pp. 154–159.
40. Adapted from George Mason University, Center for Evidence-Based Policing, "Evidence-Based Policing Tools—The Matrix Demonstrations," https://cebcp.org/evidence-based-policing/the-matrix/matrix-demonstration-project/.
41. Peter R. DeForest, R. E. Gaensslen, and Henry C. Lee, *Forensic Science: An Introduction to Criminalistics* (New York: McGraw-Hill, 1983), p. 29.
42. Quoted in Leonard Roy Frank, ed., *Random House Webster's Quotationary* (New York: Random House, 1999), p. 761.
43. Solomon Moore, "Progress Is Minimal in Clearing DNA Cases," *New York Times*, October 24, 2008, http://www.nytimes.com/2008/10/25/us/25dna.html.
44. Marc H. Caplan and Joe Holt Anderson, *Forensic: When Science Bears Witness* (Washington, D.C.: U.S. Government Printing Office, 1984), p. 2.
45. Charles R. Swanson, Neil C. Chamelin, Leonard Territo, and Robert W. Taylor, *Criminal Investigation*, 9th ed. (Boston: McGraw-Hill, 2006), p. 10.
46. DeForest, et al., *Forensic Science*, p. 29.
47. W. Jerry Chisum and Brent E. Turvey, "Evidence Dynamics: Locard's Exchange Principle & Crime Reconstruction," *Journal of Behavioral Profiling* 2, no. 1 (2000): 3.
48. President's Commission on Law Enforcement and the Administration of Justice, *Task Force Report: Science and Technology* (Washington, D.C.: U.S. Government Printing Office, 1967), pp. 7–18.
49. Paul B. Weston and Kenneth M. Wells, *Criminal Investigation: Basic Perspectives*, 4th ed. (Englewood Cliffs, N.J.: Prentice Hall, 1986), pp. 5–10.
50. U.S. Department of Justice, National Institute of Justice, *Crime Scene Investigation: A Reference for Law Enforcement Training* (Washington, D.C.: Author, 2004).
51. Alexandra Natapoff, "Snitching and Use of Criminal Informants," *Oxford Bibliographies*, http://www.oxfordbibliographies.com/view/document/obo-9780195396607/obo-9780195396607-0044.xml.
52. See, for example, Clayton Browne, "Police Interview Techniques," *Chron* (2013), http://work.chron.com/police-interview-techniques-11580.html; Ronald P. Fisher and R. Edward Geiselman, "The Cognitive Interview Method of Conducting Police Interviews: Eliciting Extensive Information and Promoting Therapeutic Jurisprudence," *International Journal of Law and Psychiatry* 23, no. 5 (November–December 2010): 321–328, http://www.sciencedirect.com/science/article/pii/S0160252710000762; Steve Finney, "Interview & Interrogation," University of Texas at Dallas, http://www.learningace.com/doc/2638370/4822684bc121a8f797316ce9c5fe573a/interview-interrogation.
53. U.S. Department of Justice, Federal Bureau of Investigation, "Clearances," in *Crime in the United States*, https://ucr.fbi.gov/crime-in-the-u.s/2017/crime-in-the-u.s.-2017/topic-pages/clearances.
54. Aamer Madhani, "Unsolved Murders: Chicago, Other Big Cities Struggle; Murder Rate a 'National Disaster,'" *USA Today*, August 10, 2018, https://www.usatoday.com/story/news/2018/08/10/u-s-homicide-clearance-rate-crisis/951681002/.
55. Ibid.
56. DeForest et al., *Forensic Science*, p. 11.
57. John S. Dempsey and Linda S. Forst, *An Introduction to Policing*, 6th ed. (Independence, Ky.: Cengage, 2012), p. 470.
58. University of Michigan Law School, The National Registry of Exonerations, "Exonerations by State," http://www.law.umich.edu/special/exoneration/Pages/Exonerations-in-the-United-States-Map.aspx.

// CHAPTER 7

1. Ray Inoue, "New Bill Would Limit Police Firearm Use," City on a Hill Press, http://www.cityonahillpress.com/2018/04/12/new-bill-would-limit-police-firearm-use/.
2. AP 931 was killed in the assembly in August 2018; see Christopher Damien, "California Police Unions Defeat Use-of-Deadly-Force Bill; Supporters Vow to Keep Fighting Shootings," *Desert Sun*, August 30, 2018, https://www.desertsun.com/story/news/politics/2018/08/30/california-police-unions-defeat-use-deadly-force-bill/1146185002/.
3. *Graham v. Connor*, 490 U.S. 386 (1989), at p. 397.
4. President's Task Force on 21st Century Policing, 2015, *Interim Report of the President's Task Force on 21st Century Policing* (Washington, D.C.: Office of Community Oriented Policing Services, April 2015), http://www.cops.usdoj.gov/pdf/taskforce/Interim_TF_Report.pdf, p. 1.
5. James Baldwin, *Nobody Knows My Name: More Notes of a Native Son* (New York: Dial Press, 1962), p. 98.
6. See https://www.law.miami.edu/about/interdisciplinary-programs/courses/black-lives-matter-course; https://newsone.com/3740503/black-lives-matter-college-course-slammed-san-diego-state-university/; and Jessica Dickerson, "'Black Lives Matter' Course to Be Offered at Dartmouth College," *Huffington Post*, February 7, 2015, http://www.huffingtonpost.com/2015/02/06/black-lives-matter-dartmouth-class_n_6632570.html.
7. Courtland Milloy, "A Mentality of Brutality That Knows No Color," *Washington Post*, February 13, 2000, https://www.washingtonpost.com/archive/

8. Human Rights Watch, *Shielded From Justice: Police Brutality and Accountability in the United States* (New York: Author, 1998).
9. Black Lives Matter, "About," https://blacklivesmatter.com/about/.
10. Adia Robinson, "After 5 years, Black Lives Matter inspires new protest movements," ABC News, July 21, 2018, https://abcnews.go.com/Politics/years-black-lives-matter-inspires-protest-movements/story?id=56702439.
11. Julia Craven, "32 Blue Lives Matter Bills Have Been Introduced Across 14 States This Year, *Huffington Post*, December 17, 2017, https://www.huffingtonpost.com/entry/blue-black-lives-matter-police-bills-states_us_58b61488e4b0780bac2e31b8; also see "US Senate Bill Would Liken Violence Against Police to Hate Crimes," *The Guardian*, May 18, 2018, https://www.theguardian.com/us-news/2018/may/08/police-violence-hate-crimes-us-senate-bill.
12. Quoted in President's Task Force on 21st Century Policing, *Interim Report of the President's Task Force on 21st Century Policing*, p. 9.
13. Quoted in ibid., p. 10.
14. Quoted in Police Executive Research Forum, *Constitutional Policing as a Cornerstone of Community Policing* (Washington, D.C., April 2015), p. 18.
15. Quoted in ibid., p. 2.
16. President's Task Force on 21st Century Policing, *Interim Report of the President's Task Force on 21st Century Policing*, p. 1.
17. Adapted from ibid., pp. 5–10.
18. Quoted in President's Task Force on 21st Century Policing, 2015, *Interim Report of the President's Task Force on 21st Century Policing*, p. 9.
19. Kevin Johnson, "Panel to Consider Tracking of Civilians Killed by Police," *USA Today*, December 12, 2014, http://www.usatoday.com/story/news/nation/2014/12/11/tracking-cop-deaths/20104193/.
20. Police Executive Research Forum, *Civil Rights Investigations of Local Police: Lessons Learned* (July 2013), p. 1, http://www.policeforum.org/assets/docs/Critical_Issues_Series/civil%20rights%20investigations%20of%2010cal%20police%20-%201essons%201earned%202013.pdf
21. Ibid.
22. Ibid.
23. Police Executive Research Forum, *Civil Rights Investigations of Local Police*, p. 31.
24. See Bureau of Justice Statistics, *Local Police Departments, 2013: Personnel, Policies, and Practices* (May 2015), pp. 4–5, https://www.bjs.gov/content/pub/pdf/lpd13ppp.pdf.
25. National Center for Women & Policing, *Hiring & Retaining More Women: The Advantages to Law Enforcement Agencies* (Spring 2003), http://womenandpolicing.com/pdf/NewAdvantagesReport.pdf.
26. Kenneth J. Peak, *Policing America: Challenges and Best Practices*, 6th ed. (Upper Saddle River, N.J.: Prentice Hall, 2009), p. 263.
27. C. Germann, Frank D. Day, and Robert R. J. Gallati, *Introduction to Law Enforcement and Criminal Justice* (Springfield, Ill.: Charles C Thomas, 1976), p. 225.
28. See Urban Institute, "Current Laws Applicable to Body-Worn Cameras," October 29, 2018, https://apps.urban.org/features/body-camera-update/.
29. Richard N. Holden, "The Technology Cycle and Contemporary Policing," paper presented at the annual meeting of the Academy of Criminal Justice Sciences, March 5, 2015, Orlando, Florida.
30. John Surico, "A Lawyer Explains Where Police Shooting Settlement Cash Actually Goes," *Vice*, April 27, 2016, https://www.vice.com/en_us/article/a-lawyer-explains-where-police-shooting-settlement-cash-actually-goes.
31. Jerome Skolnick, "A Sketch of the Policeman's Working Personality," quoted in *The Police Community*, eds. Jack Goldsmith and Sharon S. Goldsmith (Pacific Palisades, Calif.: Palisades, 1974), p. 106.
32. See, for example, Rod Brunson and Jody Miller, "Young Black Men and Urban Policing in the United States," *British Journal of Criminology* 46 (2006), 613–640; Jeannine Bell, Bell, Jeannine, The Symbolic Assailant Revisited (April 2017). Indiana Legal Studies Research Paper No. 371; Akwasi Owusu-Bempah, "Race and policing in historical context: Dehumanization and the policing of Black people in the 21st century," *Theoretical Criminology* 21(1) (2017), pp. 23–34.
33. Greg Botelho and Sonia Moghe, "North Charleston Reaches $6.5 Million Settlement With Family of Walter Scott," CNN, October 9, 2015, http://www.cnn.com/2015/10/08/us/walter-scott-north-charleston-settlement/index.html.
34. Don E. Woods, "Family of Man Who Died in Police Custody File $10M Lawsuit," NJ.com, November 8, 2016, http://www.nj.com/cumberland/index.ssf/2016/11/family_files_10m_lawsuit_against_police_for_in-cus.html; also see Catherine Shoichet, Alina Machado, and Javier De Diego, "Did Police Use Excessive Force? 3 Cases in the Spotlight," CNN, April 10, 2015, http://www.cnn.com/2015/04/09/us/police-use-of-force-cases/.
35. Jeffrey Collins, "Ex-SC Cop Gets Probation for Fatal Shooting of Black Man in His Driveway," *Talking Points Memo*, April 12, 2016, https://talkingpointsmemo.com/news/justin-craven-probation-ernest-satterwhite.
36. "Family Files Suit in Deadly Miami Gardens Police Shooting," CBS Miami, March 2, 2015, http://miami.cbslocal.com/2015/03/02/family-files-suit-in-deadly-miami-gardens-police-shooting/; also see David Ovalle, "No Charges for Miami Gardens Officer Who Fatally Shot Mentally Ill Man," *Miami Herald*, http://www.miamiherald

.com/news/local/community/miami-dade/miami-gardens/article58513108.html.
37. Juliet Linderman, "Baltimore Police, City Officials Get Ready for 2nd Pretrial Hearing in Freddie Gray Case," *U.S. News & World Report*, September 9, 2015, https://www.usnews.com/news/us/articles/2015/09/09/experts-say-settlement-in-gray-case-could-affect-hearing.
38. Eric Heisig, "Cleveland's $6 Million Settlement in Tamir Rice Case Likely City's Largest for a Police Shooting, Cleveland.com, April 15, 2016, http://www.cleveland.com/court-justice/index.ssf/2016/04/clevelands_6_million_settlemen_1.html.
39. See, for example, City of New York, "Annual Claims Report," February 20, 2018, https://comptroller.nyc.gov/reports/annual-claims-report/; Crain's Chicago Business, "How Chicago Racked Up a $662 Million Police Misconduct Bill," March 20, 2016, *Crain's Chicago Business*, https://www.chicagobusiness.com/article/20160320/NEWS07/160319758/how-chicago-racked-up-a-662-million-police-misconduct-bill.
40. H. E. Barrineau III, *Civil Liability in Criminal Justice* (Cincinnati, Ohio: Pilgrimage, 1987), p. 58.
41. Ibid., p. 5.
42. See, for example, *Black v. Stephens*, 662 F.2d 181 (1991).
43. *Fielder v. Jenkins* (N.J. Super. A.D. 1993833 A.2d 906).
44. Kenneth J. Peak, Larry K. Gaines, and Ronald W. Glensor, *Police Supervision and Management: In an Era of Community Policing*, 3rd ed. (Upper Saddle River, N.J.: Prentice Hall, 2010).
45. *Thomas v. Williams*, 124 S.E.2d 409 (Ga. App. 1962).
46. *Guice v. Enfinger*, 389 S0.2d 270 (Fla. App. 1980).
47. *Davis v. City of Detroit*, 386 N.W.2d 169 (Mich. App. 1986).
48. Ronald Palmer, chief of police, *Procedure Manual* (Tulsa, Okla.: Police Department, June 10, 1998), p. 1.
49. See *County of Sacramento v. Lewis*, 118 S.Ct. 1708 (1998).
50. *Scott v. Harris*, 550 U.S. 372 (2007), at p. 13.
51. The U.S. Supreme Court said, in a 7–2 decision, that Gonzales could not sue the city and claim the police had violated her rights to due process. Furthermore, it held she had no constitutionally protected interest in the enforcement of the restraining order. The opinion also established that the holder of a restraining order is not entitled to any specific mandatory action by the police; rather, restraining orders only provide grounds for *arresting* the person restrained by order. See *Castle Rock v. Gonzales*, 545 U.S. 748 (2005).
52. Brad Heath, "New Police Radars Can 'See' Inside Homes," *USA Today*, January 19, 2015, http://www.usatoday.com/story/news/2015/01/19/police-radar-see-through-walls/22007615/.
53. Daniel Castro, "Collateral Damage," *Government Technology*, July/August 2018, p. 10, https://archives.erepublic.com/GT/GT_Mag_July2018.pdf.
54. Taylor Hatmaker, "What We Know About Maryland's Controversial Facial Recognition Database, *TechCrunch*, June 29, 2018, https://techcrunch.com/2018/06/29/capital-gazette-maryland-face-recognition-mirs-law-enforcement/.
55. Marco della Cava and Elizabeth Weis, "*Capital Gazette* Gunman Was Identified Using Facial Recognition Technology That's Been Controversial," *USA Today*, June 29, 2018, https://www.usatoday.com/story/tech/talkingtech/2018/06/29/capital-gazette-gunman-identified-using-facial-recognition-technology/744344002/.
56. Kevin Davis, "Preparing for a Future With Autonomous Vehicles," *The Police Chief* 83 (July 2016), http://www.policechiefmagazine.org/preparing-for-a-future-with-autonomous-vehicles/.
57. "Autonomous Vehicles: Coming to a Road Near You (If They're Not There Already)," *Government Technology*, July/August 2018, http://www.govtech.com/transportation/Autonomous-Vehicles-Coming-to-a-Road-Near-You.html.
58. Ibid.
59. Ibid.; also see Thomas J. Cowper and Bernard H. Levin, "Autonomous Vehicles: How Will They Challenge Law Enforcement?" *FBI Law Enforcement Bulletin*, February 13, 2018, https://leb.fbi.gov/articles/featured-articles/autonomous-vehicles-how-will-they-challenge-law-enforcement.
60. Ibid.
61. Jim Strickland, "Texting and Driving? Cops Could Have a New Tool on Their Side: A Textalyzer," WSB-TV Atlanta, November 1, 2017, https://www.wsbtv.com/news/local/textalyzer-for-texting-drivers-new-tech-aims-to-cut-down-on-distracted-drivers/630926836.
62. Ibid.
63. American Safety Council, "'Textalyzer' May Come to New York," April 25, 2017, https://blog.americansafetycouncil.com/textalyzer-may-come-to-new-york-2/.
64. Ibid.
65. Julie Planchet, "Why Handheld Narcotics Analyzers Are Worth the Investment," PoliceOne.com, May 16, 2017, https://www.policeone.com/emerging-tech-guide/articles/342076006-Why-handheld-narcotics-analyzers-are-worth-the-investment/.
66. Ibid.
67. Ibid.
68. Ibid.
69. Ibid.

// CHAPTER 8

1. *McCulloch v. Maryland*, 17 U.S. 316 (1819).
2. John Adams, "Novanglus Papers," in *The Works of John Adams*, ed. Charles Francis Adams (Boston: Little Brown and Company, 1851), p. 106.
3. David Neubauer, *America's Courts and the Criminal Justice System*, 9th ed. (Belmont, Calif.: Wadsworth, 2008), pp. 294–300.

4. *Draper v. United States*, 358 U.S. 307 (1959).
5. *Illinois v. Gates*, 462 U.S. 213 (1983).
6. *U.S. v. Sokolow*, 109 S.Ct. 1581 (1989).
7. *People v. Defore*, 242 N.Y. 214, 150 N.E. 585 (1926).
8. *Weeks v. United States*, 232 U.S. 383 (1914).
9. *Mapp v. Ohio*, 367 U.S. 643 (1961).
10. Ibid.
11. *Utah v. Strieff*, 579 U.S. ___, 136 S.Ct. 2056 (2016).
12. *Payton v. New York*, 445 U.S. 573 (1980).
13. *United States v. Reed*, 935 F. 2d 641 (4th Cir.), cert. denied, 502 U.S. 960 (1991).
14. *Delaware v. Prouse*, 440 U.S. 648 (1979).
15. *Michigan Department of State Police v. Sitz*, 110 S.Ct. 2481, 110 L.Ed.2d 412 (1990).
16. *Pennsylvania v. Muniz*, 110 S.Ct. 2638, 110 L.Ed.2d 528 (1990).
17. *Maryland v. Pringle*, 124 S.Ct. 795 (2004).
18. *Illinois v. Lidster*, 124 S.Ct. 885 (2004).
19. *Kentucky v. King*, 131 S.Ct. 1849 (2011).
20. *California v. Greenwood*, 486 U.S. 35 (1988).
21. *Florida v. Bostick*, 59 LW 4708 (June 20, 1991).
22. *California v. Hodari D.*, 59 LW 4335 (April 23, 1991).
23. *Chimel v. California*, 395 U.S. 752 (1969).
24. *Maryland v. Buie*, 58 LW 4281 (1990).
25. *Arizona v. Gant*, 07–542 (2009).
26. *Maryland v. King*, 569 U.S. 12 (2013).
27. *Riley v. California*, 573 U.S. ___ (2014).
28. *Terry v. Ohio*, 319 U.S. 1 (1968).
29. *Minnesota v. Dickerson*, 113 S.Ct. 2130 (1993).
30. *Maryland v. Wilson*, 117 S.Ct. 882 (1997).
31. *Missouri v. McNeely*, 569 U.S. ___ (2013).
32. *Birchfield v. North Dakota*, 579 U.S. ___ (2016).
33. *Carroll v. United States*, 267 U.S. 132 (1925).
34. *Harris v. United States*, 390 U.S. 234 (1968).
35. *Florida v. Jimeno*, 59 LW 4471 (May 23, 1991).
36. *Wyoming v. Houghton*, 119 S.Ct. 1297 (1999).
37. *Illinois v. Caballes*, 543 U.S. 405 (2005); *Florida v. Harris*, 568 U.S. 237 (2013): In a unanimous decision, the Supreme Court gave police authority to use dogs to uncover illegal drugs at traffic stops, upholding a police Labrador retriever's search of a truck that uncovered methamphetamine ingredients inside.
38. *Rodriguez v. United States*, 135 S.Ct. 1609 (2015).
39. *U.S. v. Jones*, 565 U.S. ___, 132 S.Ct. 945 (2012).
40. *Byrd n. United States*, 584 U.S. ___ (2018).
41. Read excerpts from foreign constitutions at: https://www.constituteproject.org/search?lang=en&key=privacy.
42. *New York v. Class*, 54 LW 4178 (1986).
43. *Oliver v. United States*, 466 U.S. 170 (1984).
44. *California v. Ciraolo*, 476 U.S. 207 (1986).
45. *Collins v. Virginia*, 584 U.S. ___ (2018).
46. *Florida v. Jardines*, 569 U.S. ___, 133 S. Ct. 1409 (2013): Justice Antonin Scalia's opinion stated that "to find a visitor knocking on the door is routine (even if sometimes unwelcome); to spot that same visitor exploring the front path with a metal detector, or marching his bloodhound into the garden before saying hello and asking permission, would inspire most of us to—well, call the police." Scalia said using the dog was no different from using thermal imaging technology from afar to peer inside homes without a warrant.
47. *Bumper v. North Carolina*, 391 U.S. 543 (1968).
48. *Stoner v. California*, 376 U.S. 483 (1964).
49. *City of Los Angeles v. Patel*, 576 U.S. ___ (2015).
50. *Georgia v. Randolph*, 126 S.Ct. 1515 (2006).
51. *Fernandez v. California*, 571 U.S. ___ (2014).
52. *Katz v. United States*, 389 U.S. 347 (1967).
53. *Berger v. New York*, 388 U.S. 41 (1967).
54. *Lee v. United States*, 343 U.S. 747 (1952).
55. John Kaplan, Jerome H. Skolnick, and Malcolm M. Feeley, *Criminal Justice: Introductory Cases and Materials*, 5th ed. (Westbury, N.Y.: Foundation Press, 1991), pp. 220–221.
56. *Miranda v. Arizona*, 384 U.S. 436 (1966)
57. *Edwards v. Arizona*, 451 U.S. 477 (1981).
58. *Arizona v. Roberson*, 486 U.S. 675 (1988).
59. *Berkemer v. McCarty*, 468 U.S. 420 (1984).
60. *Quarles v. New York*, 467 U.S. 649 (1984).
61. Adam Goodman, "How the Media Have Misunderstood Dzhokhar Tsarnaev's *Miranda* Rights," *The Atlantic*, April 22, 2013, http://www.theatlantic.com/national/archive/2013/04/how-the-media-have-misunderstood-dzhokhar-tsarnaevs-i-miranda-i-rights/275189/.
62. *Michigan v. Mosley*, 423 U.S. 93 (1975).
63. *Colorado v. Spring*, 479 U.S. 564 (1987).
64. *Connecticut v. Barrett*, 479 U.S. 523 (1987).
65. *Duckworth v. Eagan*, 109 S.Ct. 2875 (1989).
66. *Berghuis v. Thompkins*, 560 U.S. 370 (2010).
67. *Salinas v. Texas*, 133 S.Ct. 2174 (2013). In a narrow 5–4 decision, the Court concluded that the Fifth Amendment's privilege against self-incrimination does not extend to defendants who decide to remain silent during questioning. A witness (someone who is being questioned but is not yet in custody as a suspect) must explicitly claim that protection if he or she wants to guard against self-incrimination.
68. *U.S. v. Wade*, 388 U.S. 218 (1967).
69. *Kirby v. Illinois*, 406 U.S. 682 (1972).
70. *Foster v. California*, 394 U.S. 440 (1969).
71. E. F. Loftus, J. M. Doyle, and J. Dysert, *Eyewitness Testimony: Civil & Criminal*, 4th ed. (Charlottesville, Va: Lexis Law Publishing, 2008); E. F. Loftus, "The Malleability of Human Memory," *American Scientist* 67 (1979): 312–320; Gary L. Wells et al., "Eyewitness Identification Procedures: Recommendations for Lineups and Photospreads," *Law and Human Behavior* 22, no. 6 (1998): 603–647; Gary L. Wells, "Eyewitness Identifications: Systemic Reforms," *Wisconsin Law Review* 615 (2006): 628–629.
72. *State v. Henderson*, 27 A.3d 872 (2011).
73. *Powell v. Alabama*, 287 U.S. 45 (1932).
74. *Gideon v. Wainwright*, 372 U.S. 335 (1963).

75. *Argersinger v. Hamlin*, 407 U.S. 25 (1973).
76. *Luis v. United States*, 136 S.Ct. 1083 (2016).
77. *Escobedo v. Illinois*, 378 U.S. 478 (1964).

// CHAPTER 9

1. Erwin C. Surrency, "The Courts in the American Colonies," *American Journal of Legal History* 11 (1967): 258.
2. Kermit Hall, *The Magic Mirror: Law in American History* (New York: Oxford University Press, 1989).
3. Surrency, "The Courts in the American Colonies," p. 258.
4. Freda Adler, Gerhard O. W. Mueller, and William S. Laufer, *Criminal Justice: An Introduction* (Boston: McGraw-Hill, 2006), pp. 325–326.
5. Stephen Whicher and R. Spiller, eds., *The Early Lectures of Ralph Waldo Emerson* (Philadelphia: University of Pennsylvania Press, 1953), p. 112.
6. *Tehan v. U.S. ex rel. Shott*, 382 U.S. 406 (1966), p. 416.
7. Howard Abadinsky, *Law and Justice: An Introduction to the American Legal System*, 4th ed. (Chicago: Nelson-Hall, 1999), p. 174.
8. Ibid., p. 170.
9. For the last compiled database on prisoner petitions, see U.S. Department of Justice, "Table 5.65: Petitions Filed in U.S. District Courts by Federal and State Prisoners," *Sourcebook of Criminal Justice Statistics Online*, https://www.albany.edu/sourcebook/pdf/t5652012.pdf.
10. Malcolm M. Feeley and Edward L. Rubin, *Judicial Policy Making and the Modern State: How the Courts Reformed America's Prisons* (New York: Cambridge University Press, 1998).
11. *Brown v. Plata*, 131 S.Ct. 1910 (2011).
12. Stephen L. Wasby, *The Supreme Court in the Federal System*, 3rd ed. (Chicago: Nelson-Hall, 1989), p. 5.
13. Abadinsky, *Law and Justice*, p. 171.
14. Ibid., p. 166.
15. Cassie Spohn and Craig Hemmens, *Courts: A Text/Reader* (Thousand Oaks, Calif.: Sage, 2008), p. 10.
16. National Center for State Courts, Conference of State Court Administrators, *Courts Statistics Project, CSP DataViewer, 2016 Trial Court Data*, http://www.courtstatistics.org/.
17. David W. Neubauer, *America's Courts and the Criminal Justice System*, 8th ed. (Belmont, Calif.: Thomson Wadsworth, 2005), pp. 402–403.
18. Ibid., p. 82.
19. Ibid., pp. 81, 83.
20. Nevada Appellate Courts, http://nvcourts.gov/CourtOfAppeals.aspx.
21. R. Schauffler, R. LaFountain, S. Strickland, K. Holt, & K. Genthon, *Examining the Work of State Courts: An Overview of 2015 State Court Caseloads* (Williamsburg, Va.: National Center for State Courts, 2016).
22. Neubauer, *America's Courts and the Criminal Justice System*, 8th ed., p. 85.
23. Ibid.
24. Ibid., p. 87
25. The U.S. Supreme Court reversed the decision of the lower court (i.e., the circuit court), saying the lack of an instruction on causation by itself in this case was not a violation of due process rights. The Court also said, notably, that "a person who is aware of, and consciously disregards a risk, must foresee the ultimate harm involved." See *Kibbe v. Henderson*, 534 F.2d 493 (1976). Kibbe's adversary (the appellee) in this case, Henderson, was the superintendent at Auburn Correctional Facility in New York. The phrase "exhausting all possible state remedies" is a legal doctrine meaning that the *state*'s appeals courts are to be given the opportunity to correct any defects that occurred at trial before a party may pursue a case in federal court. This is basically the rule of comity, or courtesy—the federal courts defer to state courts to correct any defects prior to those claims being raised in a federal court. *Habeas corpus* (sometimes termed "the great writ") is a Latin term for "you have the body," and it is the inmate's means of asking a court to grant a hearing to determine whether or not he or she is being held illegally.
26. U.S. Courts, "Federal Judicial Caseload Statistics 2016" https://www.uscourts.gov/report-names/federal-judicial-caseload-statistics.
27. Federal Judicial Center, "Federal Judicial History," http://www.fjc.gov/history/home.nsf.
28. U.S. Courts, "Federal Judicial Caseload Statistics 2016."
29. Federal Judicial Center, "Federal Judicial History."
30. Supreme Court of the United States, "A Brief Overview of the Supreme Court," http://www.supremecourt.gov/about/briefoverview.aspx.
31. David W. Neubauer, *America's Courts and the Criminal Justice System*, 9th ed. (Belmont, Calif.: Thomson Wadsworth, 2008), p. 63.
32. Supreme Court of the United States, "Instructions for Admission to the Bar," http://www.supremecourtus.gov/bar/barinstructions.pdf.
33. See U.S. Courts, "U.S. Supreme Court Procedures," http://www.uscourts.gov/EducationalResources/ConstitutionResources/SeparationOfPowers/USSupremeCourtProcedures.aspx.
34. Ibid.
35. Supreme Court of the United States, "The Justices' Caseload," http://www.supremecourt.gov/about/justicecaseload.aspx; also see, as examples of written opinions, Supreme Court of the United States, "Opinions of the Court—2017," https://www.supremecourt.gov/opinions/slipopinion/17.
36. Ibid.; see the *Rules of the Supreme Court of the United States*, generally, at http://www.supremecourt.gov/ctrules/2010RulesoftheCourt.pdf.
37. Ram Subramanian et al., *Incarceration's Front Door: The Misuse of Jail in America* (New York: Vera Institute of Justice, 2015); Aimee Picchi, "Are America's Jails

37. ... Used to Punish Poor People?" CBS News, February 11, 2015, http://www.cbsnews.com/news/how-jails-are-warehousing-those-too-poor-to-make-bail/.
38. Bureau of Justice Statistics, "Jail Inmates in 2016," February 2018, https://www.bjs.gov/content/pub/pdf/ji16_sum.pdf.
39. American Bar Association, "FAQs About the Grand Jury System," http://www.abanow.org/2010/03/faqs-about-the-grand-jury-system/.
40. Larry Buchanan et al., "What Happened in Ferguson?" *New York Times*, November 25, 2014, http://www.nytimes.com/interactive/2014/08/13/us/ferguson-missouri-town-under-siege-after-police-shooting.html.
41. For more information, search "grand jury" at https://www.americanbar.org/.
42. Arlen Specter, book review, 76 *Yale Law Journal* 604 (1967): 606–607.
43. John Nisbet, *Burma Under British Rule—and Before*, Vol. I (London: Archibald Constable, 1901), p. 177.
44. Cora L. Daniels and C. M. Stevans (Eds.), *Encyclopedia of Superstitions, Folklore, and the Occult Sciences of the World*, Vol. III (Milwaukee: J. H. Yewdale, 1903), p. 1243.
45. "Trial by Ordeal," http://www.absoluteastronomy.com/topics/Trial_by_ordeal.
46. *Williams v. Florida*, 399 U.S. 78, 86 (1970).
47. *Apodaca v. Oregon*, 406 U.S. 404 (1972).
48. Vick and his attorneys bargained with federal prosecutors to avoid a trial. During this time, Vick tested positive for marijuana, in violation of his bail conditions, so the federal judge ordered stricter home-confinement conditions. Vick ultimately pleaded guilty to a variety of charges and was sentenced to, among other penalties, 21 months in federal prison at Leavenworth, Kansas, and extensive community service in the interest of stopping animal cruelty. While Vick was serving time at Leavenworth, Virginia authorities moved forward with their case, using Vick's guilty pleas in the federal case to bolster the state's evidence. Again, Vick pleaded guilty and struck a bargain for a suspended sentence conditioned on the successful serving of his federal sentence. Vick was released from prison in 2009 and ultimately returned to play in the NFL while devoting significant time to speaking out against animal cruelty.
49. See *Brady v. Maryland*, 373 U.S. 83 (1963).
50. Neubauer, *America's Courts and the Criminal Justice System*, 9th ed., p. 263.
51. National Association of Drug Court Professionals, "Did You Know?" https://www.nadcp.org/treatment-courts-work/; see also Douglas B. Marlowe, Carolyn D. Hardin, and Carson L. Fox, *Painting the Picture: A National Report on Drug Courts and Other Problem-Solving Court Programs in the United States*, June 2016, National Drug Court Institute, http://www.nadcp.org/sites/default/files/2014/Painting%20the%20Current%20Picture%202016.pdf.
52. Council of State Governments Justice Center, "Mental Health Courts," May 2015, http://csgjusticecenter.org/mental-health-court-project/.
53. Marlowe, Hardin, and Fox, *Painting the Picture: A National Report on Drug Courts and Other Problem-Solving Court Programs in the United States*.
54. Ibid.; see also National Association of Drug Court Professionals, "Problem Solving Courts" http://www.nadcp.org/learn/what-are-drug-courts/models/problem-solving-courts.
55. See Thomas Alexander Fyfe, *Charles Dickens and the Law* (London: Chapman and Hall, 1910), pp. 28–29.
56. Charles Dickens, *Bleak House* (London: Penguin Book, 1971; first published in 1853).
57. William Shakespeare, *Hamlet*, Act 3, Scene 1.
58. *Strunk v. U.S.*, 412 U.S. 434 (1973).
59. Speedy Trial Act of 1974, 18 U.S.C.S. §§ 3161–3174 (as amended, 1979).
60. *Barker v. Wingo*, 407 U.S. 514 (1972).
61. Ibid.
62. Ibid., p. 522.
63. "Casey Anthony Trial: Timeline of Key Events in the Murder Trial of the Florida Mother," ABC News, July 6, 2011, https://abcnews.go.com/US/casey-anthony-trial-timeline-key-events/story?id=13990853.
64. American Prosecutors Research Institute, *Basic Trial Techniques for Prosecutors*, May 2005, http://www.ndaa.org/pdf/basic_trial_techniques_05.pdf.
65. Justia, "Criminal Appeals Overview," http://www.justia.com/criminal/criminal-appeals/.
66. *Douglas v. California*, 372 U.S. 353 (1963).
67. *Ross v. Moffitt*, 417 U.S. 600 (1974).
68. Federal Judicial Center, *Annual Report*, 2015, https://www.fjc.gov/sites/default/files/2016/Annual%20Report%202015.pdf.
69. See U.S. Courts, "Chambers Online Automation Training (COAT)," http://uscourts.webapponline.com/.
70. Dwane Brown, "San Diego County Prosecutors Use App to Present Evidence," KPBS Public Broadcasting, May 29, 2015, http://www.kpbs.org/news/2015/may/29/san-diego-county-prosecutors-using-app-present-evi/.
71. Judge Herbert B. Dixon, Jr., "The Basics of a Technology-Enhanced Classroom," American Bar Association, November 1, 2017, https://www.americanbar.org/groups/judicial/publications/judges_journal/2017/fall/basics-technologyenhanced-courtroom/.
72. National Judicial College, "The Model Courtroom," http://www.judges.org/about/the-njc-experience/model-courtroom/.

// CHAPTER 10

1. Kevin Grasha, "After More Than 3 Years, Here's Where the Tracie Hunter Case Stands," *Cincinnati Enquirer*, April 8, 2018, https://www.cincinnati.com/story/news/2018/04/08/after-more-than-3-years-heres-where-tracie-hunter-case-stands/493333002/.
2. Kara Foxx, "Judge Nadel Sentences Tracie Hunter to 6 Months in Jail," Fox 19 News (Cincinnati, Ohio), December

5, 2014, https://www.fox19.com/story/27557626/judge-nadel-sentences-tracie-hunter-to-6-months-in-jail/.
3. Hollie Silverman, "A Former Ohio Judge Was Dragged From Court After Her Sentencing," CNN, July 23, 2019, https://www.cnn.com/2019/07/23/us/ohio-judge-dragged-from-court/index.html.
4. Jong Son, "Top 5 List of Real-Life Judicial Misconduct," Ballotpedia, September 26, 2014, https://ballotpedia.org/Top_5_List_of_Real-Life_Judicial_Misconduct.
5. Samuel J. Brakel and Alexander D. Brooks, *Law and Psychiatry in the Criminal Justice System* (Buffalo, N.Y.: William S. Hein, 2001), p. 130.
6. Quoted in David Landy and Elliott Aronson, "The Influence of the Character of the Criminal and His Victims on the Decisions of Simulated Jurors," *Journal of Experimental Social Psychology* 5 (1969), pp. 141–142.
7. Abraham Blumberg, *Criminal Justice* (Chicago: Quadrangle Books, 1967), p. 120.
8. See, for example, Pennsylvanians for Modern Courts, "Choosing Judges," http://www.pmconline.org/node/25.
9. U.S. Department of Justice, Bureau of Justice Statistics, *State Court Organization, 2004* (Washington, D.C.: Author, October 2006), p. 23.
10. American Judicature Society, *Judicial Selection in the States: How It Works, Why It Matters* (Des Moines, Iowa: Author, 2008), p. 4.
11. Ibid.
12. James Podgers, "O'Connor on Judicial Elections: 'They're Awful. I Hate Them,'" *ABA Journal*, May 9, 2009, http://www.abajournal.com/news/oconnor_chemerinsky_sound_warnings_at_aba_conference_about_the_dangers_of_s/.
13. Ibid.
14. "O'Connor Says Judges Shouldn't Be Elected," Law.com, November 8, 2007, http://www.law.com/jsp/law/LawArticleFriendly.jsp?id=1194429842107.
15. Martha Neil, "Top Court Hears Judicial Influence Case, Leans Toward Stricter Recusal Standard," *ABA Journal*, March 3, 2009, http://www.abajournal.com/news/top_court_hears_judicial_influence_case_leans_toward_stricter_recusal_stand.
16. *Caperton v. A.T. Massey Coal Co., Inc.*, 556 U.S. 868 (2009).
17. Jeff Cranson, "The Price of Justice: High Court Wrestles With a Case That Should Spark Discussion in Michigan," *The Grand Rapids Press*, March 3, 2009, http://blog.mlive.com/talkingpolitics/2009/03/the_price_of_justice_high_cour.html.
18. *Williams v. Pennsylvania*, 136 S.Ct. 28 (2015). In a 5–3 ruling, the U.S. Supreme Court ruled that Judge Castille should have recused himself from the case. Justice Anthony Kennedy wrote in the majority opinion that "where a judge has had an earlier significant, personal involvement as a prosecutor in a critical decision in the defendant's case, the risk of actual bias in the judicial proceeding rises to an unconstitutional level." The court ruled that Castille's failure to recuse himself violated the defendant's Fourteenth Amendment due process protections.
19. Alice Bannon, Cathleen Lisk, and Peter Hardin, "Who Pays for Judicial Races," Brennan Center for Justice, 2017, https://www.brennancenter.org/publication/politics-judicial-elections.
20. Ibid.
21. Blumberg, *Criminal Justice*, p. 120.
22. Russell R. Wheeler and Howard R. Whitcomb, *Judicial Administration: Text and Readings* (Englewood Cliffs, N.J.: Prentice Hall, 1977), p. 370.
23. Ibid., p. 372.
24. Ibid.
25. Ibid.
26. Ibid., p. 373.
27. William A. Batlitch, "Reflections on the Art and Craft of Judging," *The Judges' Journal* 43, no. 4 (Fall 2003), pp. 7–8.
28. Charles E. Patterson, "The Good Judge: A Trial Lawyer's Perspective," *The Judges' Journal* 43, no. 4 (Fall 2003), pp. 14–15.
29. See, for example, Allen K. Harris, "The Professionalism Crisis—The 'Z' Words and Other Rambo Tactics: The Conference of Chief Justices' Solution," 53 S.C. L. Rev. 549, 589 (2002).
30. *In re First City Bancorp of Tex., Inc.*, 282 F.3d 864 (5th Cir. 2002).
31. Marla N. Greenstein, "The Craft of Ethics," *The Judges Journal* 43, no. 4 (Fall 2003), p. 42.
32. Ty Tasker, "Sticks and Stones: Judicial Handling of Invective in Advocacy," *The Judges' Journal* 43, no. 4 (Fall 2003), pp. 17–18.
33. Collins T. Fitzpatrick, "Building a Better Bench: Informally Addressing Instances of Judicial Misconduct," *The Judges' Journal* 45, no. 2 (Winter 2005), pp. 16–20.
34. Ibid.
35. U.S. Courts, "Guide to Judiciary Policy," http://www.uscourts.gov/sites/default/files/v0102b-ch02.pdf.
36. Jan L. Jacobowitz and John G. Browning, *Legal Ethics and Social Media: A Practitioner's Handbook* (Chicago: ABA Book Publishing, 2017).
37. Southern Poverty Law Center, "Are There Limits to Prosecutorial Discretion?" http://www.splcenter.org/get-informed/intelligence-report/browse-all-issues/2007/summer/legal-brief#.UafrguDn_cs.
38. *Berger v. United States*, 295 U.S. 78 (1935).
39. *Connick v. Thompson*, 563 U.S. 51 (2011).
40. Radley Balko, "The Untouchables: America's Misbehaving Prosecutors, and the System that Protects Them," *Huffington Post*, August 1, 2013, http://www.huffingtonpost.com/2013/08/01/prosecutorial-misconduct-new-orleans-louisiana_n_3529891.html.
41. *Van De Kamp v. Goldstein*, 555 U.S. 335 (2009), quoting *Gregoire v. Biddle*, 177 F. 2d 579, 581 (2 Cir. 1949).
42. *Maine v. Moulton*, 474 U.S. 159 (1985).

43. Legal Information Institute, "Effective Assistance of Counsel," http://www.law.cornell.edu/anncon/html/amdt6frag9_user.html.
44. *Strickland v. Washington*, 104 S.Ct. 3562 (1984).
45. See California Innocence Project, "Ineffective Assistance of Counsel," http://californiainnocenceproject.org/issues-we-face/ineffective-assistance-of-counsel.
46. Ibid.; also see *Strickland v. Washington*, 466 U.S. 668 (1984).
47. William A. Mintz, "Lawyer Wouldn't Go to 'Sleazy Bar,' Client Wins Freedom From Life Term," *National Law Journal*, November 24, 1980, p. 7.
48. FindLaw, "Plea Bargaining Pros and Cons," http://criminal.findlaw.com/criminal-procedure/plea-bargain-pros-and-cons.html.
49. See, for example, Texas Fair Defense Project, "What Defense Lawyers Do," http://www.texasfairdefenseproject.org/info/right_to_counsel/defense_lawyers.
50. *Griffin v. Illinois*, 351 U.S. 12 (1956).
51. For more information about defense attorneys in general and indigent services specifically, see Cassia Spohn and Craig Hemmens, *Courts: A Text/Reader*, 2nd ed. (Los Angeles, Calif.: Sage, 2012), pp. 218–223.
52. James Eisenstein and Herbert Jacob, *Felony Justice: An Organizational Analysis of Criminal Courts* (Boston: Little, Brown, 1977).
53. U.S. Department of Labor, "Court Reporters," *Occupational Outlook Handbook, Legal*, https://www.bls.gov/ooh/legal/court-reporters.htm.
54. *Massachusetts v. Leno*, 415 Mass. 835, 616 N.E.2d 453 (1993).
55. Leo Katz, "Excuse: Duress—The Nature of the Threat, the Nature of the Crime, the Mistaken Defendant, the Semiculpable Defendant—Superior Orders: Husbands and Wives," *Law Library: American Law and Legal Information—Crime and Criminal Law*, http://law.jrank.org/pages/1128/Excuse-Duress.html.
56. *Spakes v. State*, 913 S.W.2d 597 (Tex. Crim. App. 1996).
57. *People v. Luther*, 394 Mich. 619, 232 N.W.2d 184 (1975).
58. *Sherman v. U.S.*, 356 U.S. 369 (1958).
59. *U.S. v. Russell*, 411 U.S. 423 (1973).
60. PBS, "Biography: John Hinckley, Jr.," *American Experience*, http://www.pbs.org/wgbh/americanexperience/features/biography/reagan-hinckley/.
61. David Gates, "Everybody Has Scars," *Newsweek*, October 13, 1986, p. 10; also see "Man Given 5-to-15-Year Term in Model's Slashing," *New York Times*, May 12, 1987, http://www.nytimes.com/1987/05/12/nyregion/man-given-5-to-15-year-term-in-model-s-slashing.html.
62. Carol Pogash, "Myth of the 'Twinkie Defense': The Verdict in the Dan White Case Wasn't Based on His Ingestion of Junk Food," *San Francisco Chronicle*, November 23, 2003, http://www.sfgate.com/health/article/Myth-of-the-Twinkie-defense-The-verdict-in-2511152.php.
63. Michael Perlin, *The Jurisprudence of the Insanity Defense* (Durham, N.C.: Carolina Academic Press, 1994), p. 108.
64. *M'Naghten's Case*, 8 Eng. Rep. 718 (H.L. 1843).
65. *Parsons v. State*, 2 So. 854 (Ala. 1887).
66. See, generally, James F. Hooper and Alix M. McLearen, "Does the Insanity Defense Have a Legitimate Role?" *Psychiatric Times*, April 1, 2002, http://www.psychiatrictimes.com/display/article/10168/54196.
67. Dirk Johnson, "Milwaukee Jury Says Dahmer Was Sane," *New York Times*, February 16, 1992, http://www.nytimes.com/1992/02/16/us/milwaukee-jury-says-dahmer-was-sane.html.
68. PBS, "Other Notorious Insanity Cases," *Frontline*, http://www.pbs.org/wgbh/pages/frontline/shows/crime/trial/other.html.
69. Ibid.
70. This is the Florida case of Marissa Alexander from 2010. Her defense failed because she took the time to go to the garage and get the gun, which the prosecution successfully argued meant she also had time to call the police and escape the "immediate" danger she feared. The state argued that she acted/fired out of anger and not fear, imperiling both her husband and children. She was convicted and sentenced to 20 years in prison (under a mandatory sentencing scheme triggered in part by her use of the gun). In the wake of the George Zimmerman acquittal, Alexander's case garnered renewed attention. In 2013, she won a new trial based on an error at her original trial: The burden of proving the self-defense issue had been improperly shifted to Alexander and not to the prosecution. She was released from prison in November 2013 and ordered to remain on house arrest. The Florida prosecutor—the same prosecutor from the Zimmerman trial—vowed she would retry Alexander and seek 60 years (the maximum sentence allowed on such a retrial). In November 2014, Alexander pleaded guilty in exchange for time served, to avoid retrial and the potential 60-year sentence. She was sentenced in January 2015 to two years of house arrest. See Irin Carmon, "Marissa Alexander Released From Jail," MSNBC, January 27, 2015, http://www.msnbc.com/msnbc/marissa-alexander-may-be-released.

// CHAPTER 11

1. Quoted in Louis P. Carney, *Probation and Parole: Legal and Social Dimensions* (New York: McGraw-Hill, 1977), p. 75.
2. Lyndon Stambler, "Point Dume Man Found Guilty of Murdering His Former Girlfriend," *Los Angeles Times*, April 18, 1985, https://www.latimes.com/archives/la-xpm-1985-04-18-we-23880-story.html.
3. David Colker, "Marcella Leach Dies at 85; Advocate for Marsy's Law on Victims' Rights," *Los Angeles Times*, March 27, 2015, https://www.latimes.com/local/obituaries/la-me-marcella-leach-20150328-story.html.

4. Francis T. Cullen and Paul Gendreau, "Assessing Correctional Rehabilitation: Policy, Practice, and Prospects," *Criminal Justice 2000*, p. 111, https://www.ncjrs.gov/criminal_justice2000/vol_3/03d.pdf.
5. Brandon C. Welsh, "Monetary Costs and Benefits of Correctional Treatment Programs: Implications for Offender Reentry," *Federal Probation* (September 2004), p. 12, http://bcotn.org/subcommittees/csct/monetary_costs_and_benefits_of_correctional_treatment.pdf.
6. Ibid., pp. 9–12.
7. Jacqueline Cohen, *Incapacitating Criminals: Recent Research Findings I* (Washington, D.C.: National Institute of Justice, Research in Brief, 1983), p. 2.
8. Bureau of Prisons, "Annual Determination of Average Cost of Incarceration," *Federal Register*, April 30, 2018, https://www.federalregister.gov/documents/2018/04/30/2018-09062/annual-determination-of-average-cost-of-incarceration.
9. "California's Annual Costs to Incarcerate an Inmate in Prison," *Legislative Analyst's Office*, 2018–2019, https://lao.ca.gov/PolicyAreas/CJ/6_cj_inmatecost.
10. John J. Dilulio Jr., "Prisons Are a Bargain, by Any Measure," *New York Times*, January 16, 1996, p. A17.
11. The discussion of the corrections models is adapted from Todd R. Clear, George F. Cole, and Michael D. Reisig, *American Corrections*, 8th ed. (Belmont, Calif.: Thomson Wadsworth, 2009), pp. 40–64; the discussion of the accompanying prison design and operation is adapted from Steven E. Schoenherr, "Prison Reforms in American History," http://history.sandiego.edu/gen/soc/prison.html.
12. Quotes taken from the *Handbook of Correctional Institution Design and Construction* (U.S. Bureau of Prisons, 1949).
13. Amnesty International Global Report, "Death Sentences and Executions 2018," https://www.amnesty.org/download/Documents/ACT5098702019ENGLISH.PDF.
14. Ibid.
15. Saudi Arabian International Schools, "An Introduction to the Kingdom of Saudi Arabia," Spring 1992, p. 11; "U.S. Student Tells of Pain of His Caning in Singapore," *New York Times*, June 26, 1994, http://www.nytimes.com/1994/06/26/us/us-student-tells-of-pain-of-his-caning-in-singapore.html.
16. Stephanie Stullich, Ivy Morgan, and Oliver Schak, *State and Local Expenditures on Corrections and Education* (U.S. Department of Education, Policy and Program Studies Service, July 2016), https://www2.ed.gov/rschstat/eval/other/expenditures-corrections-education/brief.pdf.
17. E. Ann Carson, *Prisoners in 2016* (U.S. Department of Justice, Bureau of Justice Statistics, January 2018), https://www.bjs.gov/content/pub/pdf/p16.pdf.
18. Adapted from U.S. Department of Justice, National Institute of Corrections, and Association of Paroling Authorities International, *A Handbook for New Parole Board Members* (April 2003), p. 3, http://www.apaintl.org/documents/CEPPParoleHandbook.pdf.
19. Quoted by Sheldon G. Glueck in his "Foreword" to John V. Barry, *Alexander Maconochie of Norfolk Island* (Melbourne: Oxford University Press, 1958).
20. Mark Allenbaugh, "The Supreme Court's New Blockbuster U.S. Sentencing Guidelines Decision," January 14, 2005, http://writ.news.findlaw.com/allenbaugh/20050114.html.
21. At 18 U.S.C. Secs. 3551–3626 and 28 U.S.C. Secs. 991–998 (October 12, 1984).
22. Allenbaugh, "The Supreme Court's New Blockbuster U.S. Sentencing Guidelines Decision."
23. Lisa M. Seghetti and Alison M. Smith, *Federal Sentencing Guidelines: Background, Legal Analysis, and Policy Options* (Congressional Research Service Report for Congress, June 30, 2007), http://www.fas.org/sgp/crs/misc/RL32766.pdf.
24. *Blakely v. Washington*, 542 U.S. (2004).
25. *United States v. Booker*, 543 U.S. 125 (2005).
26. Allenbaugh, "The Supreme Court's New Blockbuster U.S. Sentencing Guidelines Decision," p. 2.
27. *Gall v. United States*, 552 U.S. 38 (2007).
28. *Kimbrough v. United States*, 552 U.S. 85 (2007).
29. *Beckles v. United States*, 580 U.S. ___ (2017).
30. *2018 Washington State Adult Sentencing Guidelines Manual*, http://www.cfc.wa.gov/PublicationSentencing/SentencingManual/Adult_Sentencing_Manual_2018.pdf.
31. The National Center for Victims of Crime, "Victim Impact Statements," http://www.victimsofcrime.org/help-for-crime-victims/get-help-bulletins-for-crime-victims/victim-impact-statements.
32. *Payne v. Tennessee*, 501 U.S. 808 (1991).
33. *Snyder v. Massachusetts*, 291 U.S. 97 (1934), at 122.
34. *Bosse v. Oklahoma*, 580 U.S. ___ (2016).
35. Jeanne Hruska, "'Victims' Rights' Proposals Like Marsy's Law Undermine Due Process," American Civil Liberties Union, May 3, 2018, https://www.aclu.org/blog/criminal-law-reform/victims-rights-proposals-marsys-law-undermine-due-process.
36. James Q. Wilson, *Thinking About Crime* (New York: Vintage Books, 1985), p. 260.
37. H. Naci Mocan and R. Kaj Gittings, "Getting Off Death Row: Commuted Sentences and the Deterrent Effect of Capital Punishment," *Journal of Law and Economics* 46 (October 2003), pp. 453–478.
38. Hashem Dezhbakhsh, Paul H. Rubin, and Joanna M. Shepherd, "Does Capital Punishment Have a Deterrent Effect? New Evidence From Postmoratorium Panel Data," *American Law and Economics Review* 5, no. 2 (2003), pp. 344–376.
39. Paul R. Zimmerman, "State Executions, Deterrence, and the Incidence of Murder," *Journal of Applied Economics* 7, no. 1 (May 2004), pp. 163–193.
40. Paul R. Zimmerman, "Estimates of the Deterrent Effect of Alternative Execution Methods in the United States:

1978–2000," *American Journal of Economics and Sociology* 65, no. 4 (October 2006), pp. 909–941.
41. Richard Berk, "New Claims About Executions and General Deterrence: Déjà Vu All Over Again?" *Journal of Empirical Legal Studies* 2 (2005), pp. 303–330.
42. Jeffrey Fagan, "Death and Deterrence Redux: Science, Law and Causal Reasoning on Capital Punishment," *Ohio State Journal of Criminal Law* 4 (2006), pp. 255–320.
43. Quoted in Amnesty International, "Death Penalty and Race," https://www.amnestyusa.org/issues/death-penalty/death-penalty-facts/death-penalty-and-race/.
44. Ibid.
45. Ibid.
46. *Furman v. Georgia*, 408 U.S. 238 (1972).
47. *Gregg v. Georgia*, 428 U.S. 153 (1976).
48. *Roper v. Simmons*, 543 U.S. 551 (2005).
49. *Ford v. Wainwright*, 477 U.S. 399 (1986).
50. *Kennedy v. Louisiana*, 554 U.S. 407 (2008).
51. *Strickland v. Washington*, 466 U.S. 668 (1984).
52. *Witherspoon v. Illinois*, 391 U.S. 510 (1968).
53. *Baze v. Rees*, 553 U.S. 35 (2008).
54. *Hill v. Florida*, No. SC06–2 (2006).
55. Death Penalty Information Center, "Innocence," https://deathpenaltyinfo.org/policy-issues/innocence.
56. Death Penalty Information Center: "Facts about the Death Penalty," May 2019, https://files.deathpenaltyinfo.org/legacy/documents/FactSheet.pdf.
57. National Coalition to Abolish the Death Penalty, "State by State Stats," May 2019, http://www.ncadp.org/map.
58. *Atkins v. Virginia*, 536 U.S. 304 (2002).
59. *Ring v. Arizona*, 536 U.S. 584 (2002).
60. *Roper v. Simmons*, 125 S.Ct. 1183 (2005).
61. *McKinney v. Arizona*, https://www.supremecourt.gov/docket/docketfiles/html/public/18–1109.html.
62. Devlin Barrett, "Justice Department Plans to Restart Capital Punishment After Long Hiatus," *Washington Post*, July 25, 2019, https://www.washingtonpost.com/national-security/justice-department-plans-to-restart-capital-punishment-after-long-hiatus/2019/07/25/f2cc6402-aee5-11e9-bc5c-e73b603e7f38_story.html.
63. Death Penalty Information Center, "Executions Under the Federal Death Penalty," https://deathpenaltyinfo.org/state-and-federal-info/federal-death-penalty/executions-under-the-federal-death-penalty.
64. U.S. Department of Justice, "Federal Government to Resume Capital Punishment After Nearly Two Decade Lapse," *Justice News*, July 25, 2019, https://www.justice.gov/opa/pr/federal-government-resume-capital-punishment-after-nearly-two-decade-lapse.
65. Adapted from *Nevada Revised Statutes* 200.033.
66. Adapted from *Nevada Revised Statutes* 200.035.
67. "Criminal Appeals," http://www.justia.com/criminal/criminal-appeals/.
68. *Douglas v. California*, 372 U.S. 353 (1963).
69. *Griffin v. Illinois*, 351 U.S. 12 (1956).
70. *Ross v. Moffitt*, 417 U.S. 600 (1974).

// CHAPTER 12

1. Jack Henry Abbott, *In the Belly of the Beast: Letters From Prison* (New York: Vintage Books, 1981), p. x.
2. See, generally, UN Office on Drugs and Crime, "Why Promote Prison Reform?" https://www.unodc.org/unodc/en/justice-and-prison-reform/prison-reform-and-alternatives-to-imprisonment.html; also see Seung Min Kim and Anne Gearan, "Jared Kushner Ramps Up Push for Criminal Justice Reform," *Washington Post*, August 30, 2018, https://www.washingtonpost.com/politics/jared-kushner-ramps-up-push-for-criminal-justice-reform/2018/08/30/449e2d02-acb1–11e8–8f4b-aee063e14538_story.html.
3. Erving Goffman, *Asylums* (Garden City, N.Y.: Anchor Books, 1961), p. 5.
4. Ibid., p. 6.
5. Bureau of Justice Statistics, *Correctional Populations in the United States, 2016*, April 2018, p. 1, https://www.bjs.gov/content/pub/pdf/cpus16.pdf.
6. See, for example, Deanne Katz, "What's the Difference Between Jail and Prison?" *FindLaw*, December 10, 2012, http://blogs.findlaw.com/blotter/2012/12/whats-the-difference-between-jail-and-prison.html.
7. Bureau of Justice Statistics, *Correctional Populations in the United States, 2016*, p. 1.
8. Ibid., p. 16
9. "Death Penalty Fast Facts, CNN, March 22, 2019, https://www.cnn.com/2013/07/19/us/death-penalty-fast-facts/index.html
10. See Bureau of Justice Statistics, "Justice Expenditure and Employment Extracts, 2015—Preliminary," data table jeee15t01.csv, June 29, 2018, https://www.bjs.gov/index.cfm?ty=pbdetail&iid=6310.
11. See Bureau of Labor Statistics "Correctional Officers and Bailiffs," n.d., https://www.bls.gov/ooh/protective-service/correctional-officers.htm.
12. Timothy Williams, "U.S. Correctional Population at Lowest Level in Over a Decade," *New York Times*, December 29, 2016, https://www.nytimes.com/2016/12/29/us/us-prison-population.html.
13. John Gramlich, "5 Facts About Crime in the U.S.," Pew Research Center, January 3, 2019, https://www.pewresearch.org/fact-tank/2019/01/03/5-facts-about-crime-in-the-u-s/.
14. Rhonda McMillion, "Boosting Bail Reform: ABA Urges Congress to Limit Use of Cash Bail," *ABA Journal*, November 2017, http://www.abajournal.com/magazine/article/ABA_urges_Congress_to_limit_use_of_cash_bail.
15. See the Marshall Project, "New York City's Bail Success Story," March 14, 2019, https://www.themarshallproject.org/2019/03/14/new-york-city-s-bail-success-story; Stephanie Wykstra, "Bail Reform, Which Could Save Millions of Unconvicted People From Jail, Explained," *Vox*, October 17, 2018, https://www.vox.com/

future-perfect/2018/10/17/17955306/bail-reform-criminal-justice-inequality; Udi Ofer, "We Can't End Mass Incarceration Without Ending Money Bail," American Civil Liberties Union, December 11, 2017, https://www.aclu.org/blog/smart-justice/we-cant-end-mass-incarceration-without-ending-money-bail.
16. Ibid.
17. Ofer, "We Can't End Mass Incarceration Without Ending Money Bail."
18. Bureau of Justice Statistics, *Correctional Populations in the United States, 2016*, p. 2.
19. Quoted in D. A. Andrews, "Program Structure and Effective Correctional Practices: A Summary of the CAVIC Research," in Robert R. Ross and Paul Gendreau (eds.), *Effective Correctional Treatment* (Toronto, Canada: Butterworth, 1980), p. 42.
20. See David Garland, *Mass Imprisonment: Social Causes and Consequences* (Thousand Oaks, Calif.: SAGE), 2001; Bureau of Justice Statistics, *Correctional Populations in the United States*, 2016, p. 2.
21. Michelle Alexander, *The New Jim Crow* (New York: New Press, 2012).
22. Ibid.
23. Mark Karlin, "Michelle Alexander on the Irrational Race Bias of the Criminal Justice and Prison Systems," Truthout, http://truth-out.org/opinion/item/10629-truthout-interviews-michelle-alexander-on-the-irrational-race-bias-of-the-criminal-justice-and-prison-systems#.
24. Stephen Lurie, "The Only Man Who Can Fix Mass Incarceration Is Barack Obama," *The Atlantic*, November 12, 2014, http://www.theatlantic.com/politics/archive/2014/11/the-only-man-who-can-fix-mass-incarceration-is-barack-obama/382314/.
25. Jacob Kang-Brown, Oliver Hinds, Jasmine Heiss, and Olive Lu, *The New Dynamics of Mass Incarceration*, Vera Institute of Justice (June 2018), p. 14, https://www.documentcloud.org/documents/4516234-The-New-Dynamics-of-Mass-Incarceration-Report.html; also see Whittney Evans, "Are Prison Populations Decreasing? Depends on Where You Look," NPR, June 14, 2018, https://www.npr.org/2018/06/14/619827057/are-prison-populations-decreasing-depends-on-where-you-look.
26. Richard P. Seiter, *Correctional Administration: Integrating Theory and Practice* (Upper Saddle River, N.J.: Prentice Hall, 2002), p. 11.
27. Franklin E. Zimring and Gordon J. Hawkins, *Deterrence: The Legal Threat in Crime Control* (Chicago: University of Chicago Press, 1973).
28. Joan Petersilia, "When Probation Becomes More Dreaded Than Prison," *Federal Probation* 54 (March 1990), pp. 27.
29. Ibid.
30. Ibid.
31. Ibid., p. 25.
32. Ibid.
33. Robert B. Levinson, "Classification: The Cornerstone of Corrections," in Peter M. Carlson and Judith Simon Garrett (eds.), *Prison and Jail Administration: Practice and Theory* (Boston: Jones and Bartlett, 2006), pp. 261–267.
34. Ibid., p. 262.
35. Ibid., pp. 262–263.
36. James Austin and Patricia L. Hardyman, *Objective Prison Classification: A Guide for Correctional Agencies* (Washington, D.C.: National Institute of Corrections, July 2004); also see R. Buchanan, "National Evaluation of Objective Prison Classification Systems: The Current State of the Art," *Crime & Delinquency* 32, no. 3 (1986), pp. 272–290.
37. Ibid., p. 192.
38. James A. Inciardi, *Criminal Justice*, 7th ed. (Fort Worth, Texas: Harcourt Brace, 2001), p. 454.
39. Ibid., p. 194.
40. U.S. Bureau of Prisons, *Unit Management Manual* (Washington, D.C.: Author, 1977), p. 6.
41. Seiter, *Correctional Administration*, p. 196.
42. See National Institute of Justice, "Recidivism," https://www.nij.gov/topics/corrections/recidivism/pages/welcome.aspx.
43. Bureau of Justice Statistics, *2018 Update on Prisoner Recidivism: A 9-Year Follow-up Period (2005–2014)*, May 2018, p. 1, https://www.bjs.gov/content/pub/pdf/18upr9yfup0514.pdf.
44. See "Recidivism: What It Is and How to Prevent It," Florida Tech, https://www.floridatechonline.com/blog/criminal-justice/recidivism-what-it-is-and-how-to-prevent-it/.
45. Federal Bureau of Prisons, "About Our Agency," https://www.bop.gov/about/agency/; also see ibid., "Our Locations," https://www.bop.gov/locations/list.jsp.
46. Ibid., "Statistics," https://www.bop.gov/about/statistics/population_statistics.jsp.
47. Ibid., "Our Locations," https://www.bop.gov/locations/list.jsp.
48. *Barber v. Thomas*, No. 09–5201 (9th Cir., 2010); also see U.S. Department of Justice, United States Parole Commission, *History of the Federal Parole System*, http://www.usdoj.gov/uspc/history.pdf.
49. Laura Sullivan, "Timeline: Solitary Confinement in U.S. Prisons," NPR, July 26, 2006, http://www.npr.org/templates/story/story.php?storyId=5579901.
50. Amnesty International, "Entombed: Isolation in the US Federal Prison System," 2017, http://www.amnestyusa.org/research/reports/entombed-isolation-in-the-us-federal-prison-system.
51. Ashley May, "'El Chapo' Heading to Supermax Prison? Who Else Is Inside the Hellish 'Alcatraz of the Rockies,'" *USA Today*, February 14, 2019, https://www.usatoday.com/story/news/nation/2019/02/14/el-chapo-supermax-prison-joaquin-guzman-may-face/2868219002/.
52. Terry Frieden, "Reporters Get First Look Inside Mysterious Supermax Prison," CNN, September 14, 2007, http://www.cnn.com/2007/US/09/13/supermax.btsc/index.html?_s=PM:US.

53. Craig Haney, "Mental Health Issues in Long-Term Solitary and 'Supermax' Confinement," *Crime & Delinquency* 49, no. 1 (January 2003), pp. 124–156.
54. Ibid.
55. Jesenia Pizarro and Vanja M. K. Stenius, "Supermax Prisons: Their Rise, Current Practices, and Effect on Inmates," *The Prison Journal* 84, no. 2 (June 2004), pp. 248–264.
56. Ibid., p. 260.
57. *Madrid v. Gomez*, 889 F. Supp. 1146 (1995), at p. 1229.
58. *Jones-El v. Berge*, 374 F.3d 541 (7th Cir. 2004), at p. 1118.
59. The Sentencing Project, "Capitalizing on Mass Incarceration: U.S. Growth in Private Prisons," August 2, 2018, https://www.sentencingproject.org/publications/capitalizing-on-mass-incarceration-u-s-growth-in-private-prisons/.
60. Ibid.
61. Thomas R. O'Connor, "The Debate Over Prison Privatization," North Carolina Wesleyan College, http://faculty.ncwc.edu/TOConnor/417/4171ect14.htm, p. 1.
62. Matthew D. Makarios and Jeff Maahs, "Is Private Time Quality Time?" *Prison Journal* 92, no. 3 (September 2012), p. 336.
63. The Sentencing Project, "Capitalizing on Mass Incarceration: U.S. Growth in Private Prisons."
64. Chico Harlan, "The Private Prison Industry Was Crashing—Until Donald Trump's Victory," *Washington Post*, November 10, 2016, https://www.washingtonpost.com/news/wonk/wp/2016/11/10/the-private-prison-industry-was-crashing-until-donald-trumps-victory/.
65. Bureau of Justice Statistics, *Correctional Populations in the United States, 2016*, p. 2.
66. Bureau of Justice Statistics, *Jail Inmates in 2015*, December 2016, p. 3, https://www.bjs.gov/content/pub/pdf/ji15.pdf.
67. National Institute of Corrections, *Jail Resource Issues: What Every Funding Authority Needs to Know*, February 2012, https://s3.amazonaws.com/static.nicic.gov/Library/017372.pdf.
68. National Sheriffs' Association, *The State of Our Nation's Jails, 1982* (Washington, D.C.: Author, 1982), p. 55.
69. See a description of such a jail in use and its benefits, by the Corrections Center of Northwest Ohio, "The New Generation Direct Supervision Jail," http://www.ccnoregionaljail.org/newgenerationjail.htm.
70. Linda L. Zupan, *Jails: Reform and the New Generation Philosophy* (Cincinnati, Ohio: Anderson, 1991), p. 67.
71. National Institute of Justice, *Programs and Activities: Tools for Managing Inmate Behavior* (June 2010), pp. 103–105, http://www.bscc.ca.gov/downloads/Programs_and_Activities_Tools_for_Managing_Inmate_Behavior_NIC_024368.pdf.
72. National Institute of Justice, "How We Review and Rate a Practice From Start to Finish," https://www.crimesolutions.gov/about_practicereview.aspx.
73. Ibid., "Corrections & Reentry: Inmate Programs & Treatment," https://www.crimesolutions.gov/TopicDetails.aspx?ID=31.
74. U.S. Department of Justice, National Institute of Justice Research in Brief, *Making Jails Productive* (Washington, D.C.: Author, 1987), p. 1.
75. Ibid., p. 16.
76. Courtesy Sheriff Darin Balaam, Washoe County (Nevada) Sheriff's Office, "Inmate Work Programs," https://www.washoesheriff.com/sub.php?page=inmate-work-programs.
77. Susan Miller, "Prisons Fighting Contraband Phones Get Help From Courts," GCN, July 24, 2018, https://gcn.com/articles/2018/07/24/prison-cellphone-court-disable.aspx.
78. DroneShield, "How Prisons Can Combat Drone Threats," https://www.droneshield.com/blog-content/2017/1/14/how-prisons-can-combat-drone-threats.
79. Miller, "Prisons Fighting Contraband Phones Get Help From Courts."
80. Yoona Ha, "Case Study: How a Maine Correctional Facility Reduced Contraband Instances to Zero," October 26, 2018, https://www.correctionsone.com/products/facility-products/body-scanners/articles/481700187-Case-study-How-a-Maine-correctional-facility-reduced-contraband-instances-to-zero/.
81. See Luke Dormehl, "Watch Lockheed Martin Burn Drones Out of the Sky With a New Laser," *Digital Trends*, September 22, 1917, https://www.digitaltrends.com/cool-tech/athena-laser-drone/; Trevor Mogg, "Drone-Catching Eagles Aren't Such a Good Idea After All," *Digital Trends*, December 11, 2017, https://www.digitaltrends.com/cool-tech/drone-catching-eagles-retired/.
82. Shane Peterson, "The Internet Moves Behind Bars," *Government Technology* (Supplement: *Crime and the Tech Effect*) (April 2001), p. 18.
83. Jim McKay, "Virtual Visits," *Government Technology* (October 2001), p. 46.

// CHAPTER 13

1. "America's Prisons Are Failing. Here's How to Make Them Work," *The Economist*, May 27, 2017, https://www.economist.com/leaders/2017/05/27/americas-prisons-are-failing-heres-how-to-make-them-work.
2. Diana Le, "The Legacy of the Stanford Prison Experiment Lives on at Sundance," *The Stanford Daily*, February 6, 2015, http://www.stanforddaily.com/2015/02/06/legacy-of-the-stanford-prison-experiment-lives-on-at-sundance/.
3. Justin Chang, "The Stanford Prison Experiment," *Variety*, January 26, 2015, http://variety.com/2015/film/reviews/sundance-film-review-the-stanford-prison-experiment-1201415952/.

4. John J. DiIulio Jr., *Governing Prisons: A Comparative Study of Correctional Management* (New York: Free Press, 1987), p. 167.
5. Bureau of Justice Statistics, *Correctional Populations in the United States, 2016*, April 2018, https://www.bjs.gov/content/pub/pdf/cpus16.pdf, p. 1.
6. World Prison Brief, "United States of America," http://www.prisonstudies.org/country/united-states-america.
7. World Prison Brief, "World Prison Populations List," http://www.prisonstudies.org/sites/default/files/resources/downloads/wppl_12.pdf.
8. Craig Haney, "Prison Effects in the Age of Mass Incarceration," *Prison Journal* 20, no. 10 (2012): 3.
9. A. Goff, E. Rose, S. Rose, and D. Purves, "Does PTSD Occur in Sentenced Prison Populations? A Systematic Literature Review, *Criminal Behavior and Mental Health* 17 (2007): 152–162; C. Heckman, K. Cropsey, and T. Olds-Davis, "Traumatic Stress Disorder Treatment in Correctional Settings: A Brief Review of the Empirical Literature and Suggestions for Future Research," *Psychotherapy: Theory, Research Practice, Training* 44 (2007): 46–53.
10. Gresham Sykes, *The Society of Captives: A Study of Maximum Security Prison* (Princeton, N.J.: Princeton University Press, 1974), p. 65.
11. John Randolph Fuller, *Criminal Justice: Mainstream and Crosscurrents*, 2nd ed. (Upper Saddle River, N.J.: Prentice Hall, 2010), p. 396.
12. Sykes, *The Society of Captives*, p. 12.
13. Jeanne B. Stinchcomb, *Corrections: Past, Present, and Future* (Lanham, Md.: American Correctional Association, 2005), p. 307.
14. Ibid.
15. Gresham Sykes and Sheldon Messinger, "The Inmate Social Code," in Normal Johnston, Leonard Savitz, and Marvin Wolfgang (eds.), *The Sociology of Punishment and Corrections* (New York: Wiley, 1970), pp. 401–408.
16. Haney, "Prison Effects in the Age of Mass Incarceration," p. 56.
17. H. Toch and K. Adams, *Acting Out: Maladaptive Behavior in Confinement* (Washington, D.C.: American Psychological Association, 2002).
18. P. Paulus, V. Cox, G. McCain, and J. Chandler, "Some Effects of Crowding in a Prison Environment," *Journal of Applied Social Psychology* 5 (1975): 86–91; G. McCain, V. Cox, and P. Paulus, "The Relationship Between Illness Complaints and Degree of Crowding in a Prison Environment," *Environment and Behavior* 8 (1976): 283–290; D. D'Atri, "Psychophysiological Responses to Crowding," *Environment and Behavior* 7 (1975): 237–252.
19. *Price v. Johnston*, 334 U.S. 266, 144 F.2d 260 (1948).
20. *Rhodes v. Chapman*, 52 U.S. 347 (1981).
21. FindLaw for Legal Professionals, "Annotation 8: Eighth Amendment," http://constitution.findlaw.com/amendment8/annotation08.html#f173.
22. *Whitley v. Albers*, 475 U.S. 312 (1986).
23. The Center for Constitutional Rights, "Torture: The Use of Solitary Confinement in U.S. Prisons," http://ccrjustice.org/solitary-factsheet.
24. Ed Pilkington, "Angola Three Inmate in Longest Solitary Confinement Seeking Damages in Court," *The Guardian*, September 4, 2014, http://www.theguardian.com/world/2014/sep/04/angola-three-albert-woodfox-lawsuit-louisiana-prison.
25. See, for example, Sharon Shalev, "Solitary Confinement and Supermax Prisons: A Human Rights and Ethical Analysis," *Journal of Forensic Psychology Practice* 11, no. 2/3 (2011): 151–183; American Public Health Association, "Solitary Confinement as a Public Health Issue," http://www.apha.org/policies-and-advocacy/public-health-policy-statements/policy-database/2014/07/14/13/30/solitary-confinement-as-a-public-health-issue; Stuart Grassian, "The Psychiatric Effects of Solitary Confinement," *Washington University Journal of Law and Policy* 22 (2006): 325, 330.
26. Shalev, "Solitary Confinement as a Public Health Issue" (see section entitled "From Re: Medley To Madrid: A Brief History of Legal Challenges to Solitary Confinement in the American Courts").
27. *In re Medley*, 134 U.S. 160 (1890).
28. See U.S. Department of Justice Archives, *Report and Recommendations Concerning the Use of Restrictive Housing*, March 13, 2017, https://www.justice.gov/archives/dag/report-and-recommendations-concerning-use-restrictive-housing.
29. Thomas Hayden, "Putting Down a Riot," *U.S. News and World Report*, June 14, 2004, pp. 72–73.
30. Center for Innovative Public Policies, "Methodology and Results: 2013 National Survey of Prison Wardens, conducted in Conjunction With Updating the Resource Guide for Newly Appointed Wardens," http://www.cipp.org/uploads/3/7/5/7/37578255/attachment_2_nic_survey_summary__for_web.pdf.
31. Robert Bayer, personal communication, November 12, 2009.
32. John J. DiIulio Jr., *Governing Prisons: A Comparative Study of Correctional Management* (New York: Free Press, 1987), p. 37.
33. Bayer, personal communication.
34. John Slansky, personal communication, October 28, 1993.
35. Ibid.
36. Gordon Hawkins, *The Prison: Policy and Practice* (Chicago: University of Chicago Press, 1976).
37. Bureau of Labor Statistics, "Correctional Officers and Bailiffs," https://www.bls.gov/ooh/protective-service/correctional-officers.htm#tab-1.
38. Hawkins, *The Prison*, Chapter 4, generally.
39. Ben M. Crouch, *The Keepers: Prison Guards and Contemporary Corrections* (Springfield, Ill.: Charles C Thomas, 1980), p. 73.

40. Peter Finn, *Addressing Correctional Officer Stress: Programs and Strategies* (Washington, D.C.: U.S. Department of Justice, National Institute of Justice, December 2000), p. 2, https://www.ncjrs.gov/pdffiles1/nij/183474.pdf.
41. Anita Loyd, "Study: PTSD, depression common among Michigan corrections and forensic officers," http://www.mco-seiu.org/2016/05/25/press-release-study-ptsd-depression-common-among-michigan-corrections-and-forensic-officers/.
42. Richard Hawkins and Geoffrey P. Alpert, *American Prison Systems: Punishment and Justice* (Upper Saddle River, N.J.: Prentice Hall, 1989), p. 340.
43. Ibid., p. 345.
44. See Lee H. Bowker, *Prison Victimization* (New York: Elsevier, 1980), Chapter 7.
45. Adapted from Lucien X. Lombardo, *Guards Imprisoned: Correctional Officers at Work* (Cincinnati, Ohio: Anderson, 1989), pp. 51–71.
46. Quoted in Advisory Commission on Intergovernmental Relations, *Jails: Intergovernmental Dimensions of a Local Problem* (Washington, D.C.: Author, 1984), p. 1.
47. World Health Organization, *World Report on Violence and Health, 2002*, p. 149, http://www.who.int/violence_injury_prevention/violence/world_report/chapters/en/.
48. Cindy Struckman-Johnson and David Struckman-Johnson, "Sexual Coercion Rates in Seven Midwestern Prison Facilities for Men," *Prison Journal* 80 (December 2000): 379–390; see also Christopher Hensley, Robert W. Dumond, Richard Tewksbury, and Doris A. Dumond, "Possible Solutions for Preventing Inmate Sexual Assault: Examining Wardens' Beliefs," *American Journal of Criminal Justice* 27, no. 1 (2002): 19–33.
49. N. Wolff and J. Shi, "Contextualization of Physical and Sexual Assault in Male Prisons: Incidents and Their Aftermath," *Journal of Correctional Health Care* 15, no. 1 (2009), http://www.ncbi.nlm.nih.gov/pmc/articles/PMC2811042/.
50. Ibid.
51. Ibid.; also see Leanne Fiftal Alarid, "Sexual Assault and Coercion Among Incarcerated Women Prisoners: Excerpts From Prison Letters," *Prison Journal* 80 (December 2000): 391–406.
52. Alyssia Santo, "Prison Rape Allegations Are on the Rise," The Marshall Project, July 25, 2018, https://www.themarshallproject.org/2018/07/25/prison-rape-allegations-are-on-the-rise.
53. Bureau of Justice Statistics, *Prisoners in 2016*, January 2018, https://www.bjs.gov/content/pub/pdf/p16.pdf, pp. 1, 13.
54. Thomas E. Feucht and Andrew Keyser, *Reducing Drug Use in Prisons: Pennsylvania's Approach* (Washington, D.C.: National Institute of Justice Journal, October 1999), p. 11.
55. Ibid., pp. 11–12.
56. Ibid., pp. 14–15.
57. Bureau of Justice Statistics, *Prisoners in 2016*, p. 3.
58. Sandra Enos, *Mothering From the Inside: Parenting in a Women's Prison* (Albany: State University of New York Press, 2001).
59. Institute on Women and Criminal Justice, "Mothers, Infants and Imprisonment: A National Look at Prison Nurseries and Community-Based Alternatives," Women's Prison Association, May 2009, http://www.wpaonline.org/pdf/Mothers%20Infants%20and%20Imprisonment%202009.pdf, p. 9.
60. Bureau of Justice Statistics, *Prisoners in 2013*, September 2014, https://www.bjs.gov/index.cfm?ty=pbdetail&iid=5109, pp. 1516.
61. See World Health Organization Europe, *Women's Health in Prison: Correcting Gender Inequities in Prison Health*, 2009, http://www.euro.who.int/__data/assets/pdf_file/0004/76513/E92347.pdf.
62. Barbara A. Hotelling, "Perinatal Needs of Pregnant, Incarcerated Women," National Center for Biotechnology Information, Spring 2008, http://www.ncbi.nlm.nih.gov/pmc/articles/PMC2409166/.
63. ACLU Briefing Paper, "The Shackling of Pregnant Women & Girls in U.S. Prisons, Jails & Youth Detention Centers," https://www.aclu.org/files/assets/anti-shackling_briefing_paper_stand_alone.pdf.
64. *Jordan v. Gardner*, 986 F.2d 1521 (1993).
65. *Turner v. Safley*, 482 U.S. 78, 89 (1987).
66. *Forts v. Ward*, 621 F.2d 1210, 1214 16 (2d Cir. 1980).
67. In *Jordan v. Gardner*, 986 F.2d 1521, 1523 (9th Cir. 1993), a male guard at the WCCW conducted (as per the policy) such a random, full-body, clothed search of a female prisoner. He squeezed her breasts and probed her crotch as well as the seams in her crotch area. While being searched, the female inmate, being distressed and shocked, grabbed hold of nearby cell bars to the extent that later, her fingers had to be pried loose from them. The federal district court concluded that the cross-gender clothed body search policy constituted cruel and unusual punishment in violation of the Eighth Amendment.
68. For an excellent overview of incarcerated women's rights, see "A Jailhouse Lawyer's Manual, Chapter 41, Special Issues of Women Prisoners," *Columbia Human Rights Law Review* (9th ed., 2011), http://www3.law.columbia.edu/hrlr/jlm/chapter-41.pdf.
69. Ibid.
70. Jennifer Bronson and Marcus Berzofsky, "Indicators of Mental Health Problems Reported by Prisoners and Jail Inmates, 2011–12," Bureau of Justice Statistics, June 2017, https://www.bjs.gov/content/pub/pdf/imhprpji1112.pdf, p. 1.
71. Bureau of Justice Statistics, *Mental Health Problems of Prison and Jail Inmates*, Special Report, September 2006, https://www.bjs.gov/content/pub/pdf/mhppji.pdf, p. 1.

72. Treatment Advocacy Center, *The Treatment of Persons with Mental Illness in Prisons and Jails: A State Survey*, April 8, 2014, p. 6, http://www.treatmentadvocacycenter.org/storage/documents/treatment-behind-bars/treatment-behind-bars.pdf.
73. Pam Belluck, "Mentally Ill Inmates Are at Risk Isolated, Suit Says," *New York Times*, March 9, 2007, p. A10.
74. Treatment Advocacy Center, *The Treatment of Persons With Mental Illness in Prisons and Jails*, p. 8.
75. Maura Ewing, "When Prisons Need to Be More Like Nursing Homes," The Marshall Project, August 27, 2015, https://www.themarshallproject.org/2015/08/27/when-prisons-need-to-be-more-like-nursing-homes.
76. Mary Harrison, *True Grit Notes* 5, no. 3 (Summer 2009); Terence P. Hubert, Mary T. Harrison, and William O. Harrison, *"True Grit": An Innovative Humanistic Living Program for a Geriatric Population* (Carson City, Nev.: Nevada Department of Corrections, n.d.).
77. U.S. Department of Justice, "About Violent Gangs," http://www.justice.gov/criminal/ocgs/gangs/.
78. National Gang Intelligence Center, *National Gang Threat Assessment 2011* (Washington, D.C.: U.S. Department of Justice), http://www.fbi.gov/stats-services/publications/2011-national-gang-threat-assessment/2011-national-gang-threat-assessment-emerging-trends, p. 11.
79. Joel Samaha, *Criminal Justice* (St. Paul, Minn.: West, 1988), p. 558.
80. James Jacobs, *Stateville: The Penitentiary in Mass Society* (Chicago: University of Chicago Press, 1977).
81. John Irwin, *Prisons in Turmoil* (Boston: Little, Brown, 1980).
82. George M. Camp and Camille G. Camp, *The Correctional Year Book* (South Salem, N.Y.: Criminal Justice Institute, 1987).
83. See *Ashker v. Governor or California*, Civil Action No. 4:09-cv-05796-CW (N.D. California, 2012)
84. See David Pyrooz, *Using Restrictive Housing to Manage Gangs in U.S. Prisons*, National Institute of Justice, July 1, 2018, https://www.nij.gov/topics/corrections/institutional/Pages/using-restrictive-housing-to-manange-gangs-in-us-prisons.aspx; also see ibid., "Restrictive Housing," https://www.nij.gov/topics/corrections/institutional/Pages/restrictive-housing.aspx.
85. Victor D. Lofgreen, "A Model of the Dynamic Power Relationship Between Staff and Inmates in a Secure Correctional Facility," paper presented at the annual meeting of the Western Social Science Association, Reno, Nevada, 1991, p. 6.
86. Randall Chase, "Vaughn Prison Riot Survivor Says Officials Responsible: 'There's Blood Everywhere'," Associated Press, July 16, 2018, https://www.delawareonline.com/story/news/2018/07/16/vaughn-prison-riot-survivor-says-officials-responsible/790721002/.
87. State of Arizona, Office of the Governor, *The Morey Unit Hostage Incident: Preliminary Findings and Recommendations* (Phoenix, Ariz.: Author), p. 1.
88. Ohio History Central, "Lucasville Prison Riot," http://www.ohiohistorycentral.org/entry.php?rec=1634.
89. Associated Press, "Officials: Inmates Talked of Killing Jail Hostage," *St. Petersburg Times*, September 8, 2004, http://www.sptimes.com/2004/09/08/State/Officials__Inmates_ta.shtml.
90. For an examination and comparison of these two extremely violent prison riots, see Sue Mahan, "An Orgy of Brutality at Attica and the Killing Ground at Santa Fe: A Comparison of Prison Riots," in Michael C. Braswell, Reid H. Montgomery Jr., and Lucien X. Lombardo (eds.), *Prison Violence in America*, 2nd ed. (Cincinnati, Ohio: Anderson, 1994), pp. 253–264.
91. Thomas A. Zlaket, personal communication to Hon. Janet Napolitano, Governor of Arizona, October 25, 2004.
92. Kelly Taylor and Jilian Flight, *Hostage-Taking Incidents Involving Women Inmates: A Profile and Exploratory Investigation* (Ottawa, Ontario, Canada: Correctional Service of Canada, 2003), p. 5.
93. David Ensor, "U.S. Captures Mastermind of Achille Lauro Hijacking," CNN, April 15, 2003, http://www.cnn.com/2003/WORLD/meast/04/15/sprj.irq.abbas.arrested.
94. See, for example, Kenneth J. Peak, Eric Radli, Cecil Pearson, and Darin Balaam, "Hostage Situations in Detention Settings: Planning and Tactical Considerations," *FBI Law Enforcement Bulletin* 77, no. 10 (2008): 1–14.
95. *Ruffin v. Commonwealth*, 62 Va. 790 (1871).
96. *Cooper v. Pate*, 378 U.S. 546, 384 S.Ct 1733 (1964).
97. *Johnson v. Avery*, 393 U.S. 483, 89 S.Ct. 747 (1969).
98. *Bounds v. Smith*, 430 U.S. 817, 97 S.Ct. 1491 (1977).
99. Kelly McLaughlin, "Inside Haitian jail where prisoners starve to death and defecate on floors of overcrowded cells while waiting up to eight years for a trial," DailyMail.com, February 20, 2017, https://www.dailymail.co.uk/news/article-4241466/Haitian-prison-inmates-live-filthy-conditions.html.
100. Haiti ranked worst country for most overcrowded prisons in the world," *Jamaica Observer*, February 5, 2018, http://www.jamaicaobserver.com/latestnews/Haiti_ranked_worst_country_for_most_overcrowded_prisons_in_the_world?profile=1228.
101. *Cruz v. Beto*, 405 U.S. 319, 92 S.Ct. 1079 (1972).
102. *Procunier v. Martinez*, 416 U.S. 396, 94 S.Ct. 1800 (1974).
103. *Estelle v. Gamble*, 429 U.S. 974, 97 S.Ct. 285 (1976).
104. *Wolff v. McDonnell*, 418 U.S. 539, 394 S.Ct. 296 (1974).
105. Jeremy Travis, Amy L. Solomon, and Michelle Waul, *From Prison to Home—The Dimensions and Consequences of Prisoner Reentry* (Washington, D.C.: The Urban Institute, 2001), pp. 6, 9.
106. Pamela K. Lattimore, "The Challenges of Reentry," *Corrections Today* 69, no. 2 (April 2007), p. 90.

107. Richard P. Seiter, *Correctional Administration: Integrating Theory and Practice*, 2nd ed. (Upper Saddle River, N.J.: Prentice Hall, 2012), pp. 451–452.
108. Ibid.

// CHAPTER 14

1. Bureau of Justice Statistics, *Probation and Parole in the United States, 2016*, April 2018, https://www.bjs.gov/content/pub/pdf/ppus16_sum.pdf.
2. Peter J. Benekos, "Beyond Reintegration: Community Corrections in a Retributive Era," *Federal Probation* 54 (March 1990), p. 53.
3. See the President's Commission on Law Enforcement and Administration of Justice, *Task Force Report: Corrections* (Washington, D.C.: U.S. Government Printing Office, 1967), p. 7.
4. Benekos, "Beyond Reintegration," p. 53.
5. Belinda R. McCarthy, *Intermediate Punishments: Intensive Supervision, Home Confinement, and Electronic Surveillance* (Monsey, N.Y.: Criminal Justice Press, 1987), p. 3.
6. Barry J. Nidorf, "Community Corrections: Turning the Crowding Crisis Into Opportunities," *Corrections Today* (October 1989), p. 85.
7. Benekos, "Beyond Reintegration," p. 54.
8. Although neither the word *probation* nor today's definition of it appear in the Bible, it was historically assumed that all mankind was under the sentence of eternal death—an endless life in misery during this life. However, humans could escape this sentence through repentance and faith in Christ; this was man's "probation," an opportunity to escape hell and secure heaven. If he failed to improve this opportunity, and died impenitent, the sentence was irrevocably executed and the man was eternally lost. See Tentmaker, "Probation," http://www.tentmaker.org/books/SpiritOfTheWord/014Probation.htm.
9. Howard Abadinsky, *Probation and Parole: Theory and Practice*, 3rd ed. (Englewood Cliffs, N.J.: Prentice Hall, 1987), p. 18.
10. Lawrence M. Friedman, *A History of American Law* (New York: Simon and Schuster, 1973), p. 518.
11. Paul F. Cromwell Jr., George C. Killinger, Hazel B. Kerper, and Charles Walker, *Probation and Parole in the Criminal Justice System*, 2nd ed. (St. Paul, Minn.: West, 1985).
12. John Augustus, *John Augustus, First Probation Officer* (Montclair, N.J.: Patterson Smith, 1972), pp. 4–5.
13. John Augustus, *A Report of the Labors of John Augustus* (Boston: Wright & Hasty, 1852), republished in 1984 by the American Probation and Parole Association, Lexington, Ky., pp. 96–97.
14. Abadinsky, *Probation and Parole*, p. 143.
15. Torsten Eriksson, *The Reformers: An Historical Survey of Pioneer Experiments in the Treatment of Criminals* (New York: Elsevier, 1976), p. 81.
16. Abadinsky, *Probation and Parole*, pp. 146–147.
17. The issues concerned whether parole (1) infringed on the power of the judiciary to sentence, the governor to pardon, or the legislature to determine penalty levels; (2) denied prisoners due process; or (3) constituted cruel and unusual punishment.
18. U.S. Attorney General's Survey of Release Procedures, *Parole*, Vol. 4 (New York: Arno Press, 1974), p. 20.
19. Sheldon L. Messinger, "Introduction," in Andrew von Hirsch and Kathleen J. Hanrahan (eds.), *The Question of Parole: Retention, Reform, or Abolition?* (Cambridge, Mass.: Ballinger, 1970), pp. xviii–xix.
20. U.S. Attorney General's Survey of Release Procedures, *Parole*, p. 20.
21. Bureau of Justice Statistics, *Probation and Parole in the United States, 2016*.
22. Robert M. Regoli and John D. Hewitt, *Exploring Criminal Justice: The Essentials* (Sudbury, Mass.: Jones and Bartlett, 2010), p. 316.
23. Bureau of Justice Statistics, *Probation and Parole in the United States, 2016*, p. 17.
24. *Mempa v. Rhay*, 389 U.S. 128 (1967).
25. *Gagnon v. Scarpelli*, 411 U.S. 778 (1973).
26. Bureau of Justice Statistics, *Probation and Parole in the United States*, 2016.
27. Park Dietz, "Hypothetical Criteria for the Prediction of Individual Criminality," in Christopher Webster, Mark Ben-Aron, and Stephen Hucker (eds.), *Dangerousness: Probability and Prediction, Psychiatry, and Public Policy* (Cambridge, U.K.: Cambridge University Press, 1985), p. 32.
28. Bureau of Justice Statistics, *Probation and Parole in the United States, 2016*.
29. *Morrissey v. Brewer*, 92 S.Ct. 2593 (1972).
30. Ibid.
31. Council of State Governments Justice Center, *The Impact of Probation and Parole Populations on Arrests in Four California Cities*, January 2013, http://www.cdcr.ca.gov/Reports/docs/External-Reports/CAL-CHIEFS-REPORT.pdf, p. 4.
32. Ibid., p. 1.
33. Ibid., p. 17.
34. Ibid., p. 6.
35. U.S. Bureau of Labor Statistics, "Occupational Outlook Handbook: Probation Officers and Correctional Treatment Specialists," http://www.bls.gov/ooh/Community-and-Social-Service/Probation-officers-and-correctional-treatment-specialists.htm#tab-2.
36. Ibid.
37. H. S. Ntuli, V. I. Khoza, J. M. Ras, and P. J. Potgieter, "Role Conflict in Correctional Supervision," *Acta Criminologica* 20, no. 4 (2007), pp. 85–95.
38. Ibid.
39. John Conrad, "The Pessimistic Reflections of a Chronic Optimist," *Federal Probation* 55 (June 1991), pp. 4–9.

40. Matthew T. DeMichele, *Probation and Parole's Growing Caseloads and Workload Allocation: Strategies for Managerial Decision Making* (Lexington, Ky.: American Probation and Parole Association), http://www.appa-net.org/eweb/docs/appa/pubs/SMDM.pdf, pp. 14–15.
41. M. Claxton, N. Sinclair, and R. Hanson, "Felons on Probation Often Go Unwatched," *Detroit News*, December 10, 2002, p. 2.
42. DeMichele, *Probation and Parole's Growing Caseloads and Workload Allocation*, pp. 13, 33.
43. Shawn E. Small and Sam Torres, "Arming Probation Officers: Enhancing Public Confidence and Officer Safety," *Federal Probation* 65, no. 3 (2001), pp. 24–28.
44. Richard P. Seiter, *Correctional Administration: Integrating Theory and Practice* (Upper Saddle River, N.J.: Prentice Hall, 2002), p. 387.
45. U.S. Department of Justice, Bureau of Justice Statistics, *Jail Inmates in 2017*, April 2019, https://www.bjs.gov/content/pub/pdf/ji17.pdf.
46. Howard Abadinsky, *Probation and Parole: Theory and Practice*, 7th ed. (Upper Saddle River, N.J.: Prentice Hall, 2000), p. 410.
47. Joan Petersilia and Susan Turner, *Evaluating Intensive Supervision Probation/Parole: Results of a Nationwide Experiment* (Washington, D.C.: National Institute of Justice, 1993).
48. Lawrence A. Bennett, "Practice in Search of a Theory: The Case of Intensive Supervision—An Extension of an Old Practice," *American Journal of Criminal Justice* 12 (1988), pp. 293–310.
49. Ibid., p. 293.
50. This information was compiled from ISP brochures and information from the Oregon Department of Corrections by Joan Petersilia.
51. Todd R. Clear and Patricia R. Hardyman, "The New Intensive Supervision Movement," *Crime & Delinquency* 36 (January 1990), pp. 42–60.
52. Ibid., p. 44.
53. Brittany Anas, "Boulder Sex Offender Balks at 'Intensive,' Asks to Be Sent to Prison," *Daily Camera*, August 19, 2012, http://www.dailycamera.com/ci_20891466/boulder-sex-offender-balks-at-intensive-probation-asks.
54. Ibid.
55. Pew Research Center, "Public Opinion on Sentencing and Corrections Policy in America," March 2012, https://www.prisonpolicy.org/scans/PEW_NationalSurveyResearchPaper_FINAL.pdf.
56. Barbara A. Sims, "Questions of Corrections: Public Attitudes Toward Prison and Community-Based Programs," *Corrections Management Quarterly* 1, no. 1 (1997), p. 54.
57. Jeffery T. Ulmer, "Intermediate Sanctions: A Comparative Analysis of the Probability and Severity of Recidivism," *Sociological Inquiry* 71, no. 2 (Spring 2001), pp. 164–193.
58. Ibid., p. 184.
59. Ibid., p. 185.
60. Bureau of Justice Assistance, *Offender Supervision With Electronic Technology: Community Corrections Resource*, 2nd ed. (Washington, D.C.: U.S. Department of Justice, 2009), p. 16, http://www.appa-net.org/eweb/docs/APPA/pubs/OSET_2.pdf.
61. John K. Roman, Akiva M. Lieberman, Samuel Taxy, and P. Mitchell Downey, "The Costs and Benefits of Electronic Monitoring for Washington, D.C.," Urban Institute, September 2012, https://www.urban.org/sites/default/files/alfresco/publication-pdfs/412678-The-Costs-and-Benefits-of-Electronic-Monitoring-for-Washington-D-C-.PDF.
62. Ibid.
63. Annesley K. Schmidt, "Electronic Monitors: Realistically, What Can Be Expected?" *Federal Probation* 59 (June 1991), pp. 47–53.
64. Abadinsky, *Probation and Parole*, 7th ed., p. 428.
65. David Brauer, "Satellite 'Big Brother' Tracks Ex-Inmates," *Chicago Tribune*, December 18, 1998, p. 31.
66. National Institute of Justice, "Standard Offender Tracking Systems," U.S. Department of Justice, July 2016, https://www.ncjrs.gov/pdffiles1/nij/249810.pdf.
67. Jeanne B. Stinchcomb and Vernon B. Fox, *Introduction to Corrections*, 5th ed. (Upper Saddle River, N.J.: Prentice Hall, 1999), p. 165.
68. Gaylene Styve Armstrong, Angela R. Gover, and Doris Layton MacKenzie, "The Development and Diversity of Correctional Boot Camps," *Turnstile Justice: Issues in American Corrections*, ed. Rosemary L. Gido and Ted Alleman (Upper Saddle River, N.J.: Prentice Hall, 2002), pp. 115–130.
69. Doris Layton MacKenzie, "Boot Camp Prisons and Recidivism in Eight States," *Criminology* 33, no. 3 (1995), pp. 327–358.
70. National Institute of Justice, crimesolutions.gov.
71. Doris Layton MacKenzie and Alex Piquero, "The Impact of Shock Incarceration Programs on Prison Crowding," *Crime & Delinquency* 40, no. 2 (April 1994), pp. 222–249.
72. John Ashcroft, Deborah J. Daniels, and Sarah V. Hart, *Correctional Boot Camps: Lessons from a Decade of Research* (Washington, D.C.: U.S. Department of Justice, Office of Justice Programs, June 2003), p. 2. Note: A comprehensive list of correctional boot camps in operation is not currently available.
73. Ibid.
74. Joshua A. Jones, "A Multi-State Analysis of Correctional Boot Camp Outcomes: Identifying Vocational Rehabilitation as a Complement to Shock Incarceration," *Inquiries* 4, no. 9 (2012), pp. 1–3.
75. Dale G. Parent, "Day Reporting Centers: An Evolving Intermediate Sanction," *Federal Probation* 60 (December 1996), pp. 51–54.
76. Liz Marie Marciniak, "The Addition of Day Reporting to Intensive Supervision Probation: A Comparison of

Recidivism Rates," *Federal Probation* 64 (June 2000), pp. 34–39.

77. Nathan James, *Offender Reentry: Correctional Statistics, Reintegration Into the Community, and Recidivism*, Congressional Research Service, January 2015, https://fas.org/sgp/crs/misc/RL34287.pdf.

78. Janet Portman, "When Is a Prisoner Released to a Halfway House?" Lawyers.com, 2017, http://criminal.lawyers.com/criminal-law-basics/when-is-a-prisoner-released-to-a-halfway-house.html.

79. Federal Bureau of Prisons, "Completing the Transition: Reentry Assistance Reduces Recidivism," https://www.bop.gov/about/facilities/residential_reentry_management_centers.jsp.

80. See, for example, Federal Bureau of Prisons, "Inmate Furloughs," January 11, 2011, http://www.prisonology.com/files/1914/1514/8069/BOP_Inmate_Furloughs.pdf.

81. See Washington State Institute for Public Policy, *Predicting Criminal Recidivism: A Systematic Review of Offender Risk Assessments in Washington State*, February 2014, http://www.wsipp.wa.gov/ReportFile/1554/Wsipp_Predicting-Criminal-Recidivism-A-Systematic-Review-of-Offender-Risk-Assessments-in-Washington-State_Final-Report.pdf.

82. Bureau of Justice Assistance and the Council of State Governments, *Integrated Reentry and Employment Strategies: Reducing Recidivism and Promoting Job Readiness*, September 2013, https://www.bja.gov/Publications/CSG-Reentry-and-Employment.pdf, p. 10.

83. Ibid., p. 12.

84. Jan Looman and Jeffrey Abracen, "The Risk Need Responsivity Model of Offender Rehabilitation: Is There Really a Need for a Paradigm Shift?" *International Journal of Behavioral Consultation and Therapy* 8 (34) (2013), p. 32.

85. See Guy Bourgon and James Bonta, "Reconsidering the Responsivity Principle: A Way to Move Forward," *Federal Probation* 78(2), September 2014, https://www.uscourts.gov/sites/default/files/78_2_1_0.pdf

86. Stephanie Stullich, Ivy Morgan, and Oliver Schak, *State and Local Expenditures on Corrections and Education* (U.S. Department of Education, Policy and Program Studies Service, July 2016), https://www2.ed.gov/rschstat/eval/other/expenditures-corrections-education/brief.pdf. .

// CHAPTER 15

1. Adapted from Rob Waters, "Detention Facilities Have Become Warehouses for Mentally Disturbed Youth," Psychotherapy Networker, September 6, 2017, https://www.psychotherapynetworker.org/blog/details/1293/confronting-a-broken-juvenile-justice-system; also see "Leniency for Lionel Tate?" ABC News, March 7, 2018, https://abcnews.go.com/2020/story?id=123746&page=1.

2. FindLaw, "Juvenile Delinquents," http://criminal.findlaw.com/juvenile-justice/juvenile-delinquents.html.

3. For an excellent overview of both historical and contemporary juvenile justice processes, see the National Council of Juvenile and Family Court Judges, *Enhanced Juvenile Justice Guidelines: Improving Court Practice in Juvenile Cases*, 2018, https://www.ncjfcj.org/sites/default/files/NCJFCJ_Enhanced_Juvenile_Justice_Guidelines_Final.pdf.

4. Robert S. Pickett, *House of Refuge: Origins of Juvenile Reform in New York State 1815–1857* (Syracuse, N.Y.: Syracuse University Press, 1969), p. 21.

5. M. Platt, *The Child Savers: The Invention of Delinquency*, 2nd ed. (Chicago, Ill.: University of Chicago Press, 1977).

6. *People ex rel O'Connell* v. *Turner*, 55 Ill. 280, 283–84, 287 (1870).

7. 1899 Ill. Laws 132 *et seq.*

8. Victor L. Streib, *Death Penalty for Juveniles* (Bloomington: Indiana University Press, 1987).

9. Robert E. Shepherd Jr., "The Juvenile Court at 100 Years: A Look Back," *Juvenile Justice* 6, no. 2 (December 1999), http://www.ncjrs.gov/html/ojjdp/jjjourna11299/2.html.

10. Ibid.

11. Ibid.

12. Julian Mack, "The Juvenile Court," *Harvard Law Review* 23 (1909), pp. 104–122.

13. P.L. 93–415, 42 U.S.C. 5601 *et seq.*

14. David W. Roush, *A Desktop Guide to Good Juvenile Detention Practice* (Washington, D.C.: Office of Juvenile Justice and Delinquency Prevention, 1996), pp. 26–27.

15. Ibid., pp. 23–24.

16. See Annie E. Casey Foundation, "Five Things to Know About the New Juvenile Justice Act," February 8, 2019, https://www.aecf.org/blog/five-things-to-know-about-the-new-juvenile-justice-act/; also see John Kelly, "A Complete Breakdown of America's New Juvenile Justice Law," *Chronicle of Social Change*, January 8, 2019, https://chronicleofsocialchange.org/featured/a-complete-breakdown-of-americas-new-juvenile-justice-law.

17. See American Civil Liberties Union, "Juvenile Justice," 2019, https://www.aclu.org/issues/juvenile-justice.

18. Juvenile Law Center, "Youth in the Justice System," 2018, https://jlc.org/youth-justice.

19. Josh Rovner,"Solitary Confinement Is Widespread and Ineffective," The Sentencing Project, June 1, 2017, https://www.sentencingproject.org/news/opinion-solitary-confinement-widespread-ineffective/.

20. See Josh Rovner,"Juvenile Life Without Parole: An Overview," The Sentencing Project, October 22, 2018, https://www.sentencingproject.org/publications/juvenile-life-without-parole/.

21. Rob Waters, "Confronting a Broken Juvenile Justice System," Psychotherapy Networker, n.d., https://www

.psychotherapynetworker.org/blog/details/1293/confronting-a-broken-juvenile-justice-system.
22. Justice Policy Institute, "Juvenile Incarceration Rate Has Dropped in Half. Is Trend Sustainable?" November 10, 2015, http://www.justicepolicy.org/news/9854.
23. Manny Araujo, "Study: Number of Juvenile Arrests Declining," *Eureka Times-Standard*, November 7, 2016, http://www.times-standard.com/article/NJ/20161007/NEWS/161009838.
24. Federal Bureau of Investigation, *Crime in the United States, 2017*, Table 36, https://ucr.fbi.gov/crime-in-the-u.s/2017/crime-in-the-u.s.-2017/topic-pages/tables/table-36.
25. Adapted from Gus Martin, *Juvenile Justice: Process and Systems* (Thousand Oaks, Calif.: Sage, 2005), pp. 64–67.
26. Both the text and the diagram are from U.S. Department of Justice, Office of Juvenile Justice and Delinquency Prevention Programs, *Juvenile Justice Structure and Process: Case Flow Diagram*, http://www.ojjdp.gov/ojstatbb/structure_process/case.html.
27. Adapted from U.S. Department of Justice, Bureau of Justice Statistics, "The Juvenile Justice System," http://www.ojp.usdoj.gov/bjs/justsys.htm#sentencing.
28. Steven M. Cox, Jennifer M. Allen, Robert D. Hanser, and John J. Conrad, *Juvenile Justice: A Guide to Theory, Policy, and Practice* (Boston: Pearson, 2014), p. 104.
29. See John Braithwaite, *Crime, Shame and Reintegration* (Cambridge, U.K.: Cambridge University Press, 1989).
30. Molly Kneffel, "Trying to Fix America's Broken Juvenile Justice System," *Rolling Stone*, January 22, 2015, https://www.rollingstone.com/politics/politics-news/trying-to-fix-americas-broken-juvenile-justice-system-241177/.
31. Michael Rocque and Raymond Paternoster, "Understanding the Antecedents of the 'School-to-Jail' Link: The Relationship Between Race and School Discipline," *Journal of Criminal Law & Criminology* 101, no. 2 (2011), pp. 633–643; see also Carla Amurao, "Fact Sheet: How Bad Is the School-to-Prison Pipeline?" *Tavis Smiley Reports*, http://www.pbs.org/wnet/tavissmiley/tsr/education-under-arrest/school-to-prison-pipeline-fact-sheet/.
32. Mary Ellen Flannery, "The School-to-Prison Pipeline: Time to Shut It Down," *NEA Today*, January 5, 2015, http://neatoday.org/2015/01/05/school-prison-pipeline-time-shut/.
33. Ibid.
34. Stephanie Francis Ward, "How Do We Fix the School-to-Prison Pipeline?" *American Bar Association Journal*, August 4, 2014, http://www.abajournal.com/news/article/podcast_monthly_episode_53.
35. James C. Howell, *Youth Gangs*, U.S. Department of Justice, Office of Juvenile Justice and Delinquency Prevention (December 1997), https://www.ncjrs.gov/pdffiles/fs-9772.pdf, p. 1.
36. National Gang Center, "Frequently Asked Questions About Gangs," http://www.nationalgangcenter.gov/About/FAQ#q1.
37. See David Pyrooz and Gary Sweeten, "Gang Membership Between Ages 5 and 17 Years in the United States," *Journal of Adolescent Health* 56(4) (April 2015), pp. 414–419; also see Sam Houston State University, "New Study Finds U.S. Juvenile Gang Membership Tops 1 Million," February 16, 2014, https://www.shsu.edu/pin_www/T@S/2015/gangstudy.html
38. National Gang Center, "Frequently Asked Questions About Gangs."
39. See U.S. Department of Justice, Office of Juvenile Justice and Delinquency Prevention, *NGC Newsletter* (Winter 2013), p. 1.
40. Catherine H. Conly, Patricia Kelly, Paul Mahanna, and Lynn Warner, *Street Gangs: Current Knowledge and Strategies* (Washington, D.C.: U.S. Department of Justice, National Institute of Justice, 1993).
41. Daniel P. Mears and Jeremy Travis, "Youth Development and Reentry," *Youth Violence and Juvenile Justice* 2, no. 1 (January 2004), pp. 3–20; also see David Altschuler and Shay Bilchik, "Critical Elements of Juvenile Reentry in Research and Practice," April 21, 2014, http://csgjusticecenter.org/youth/posts/critical-elements-of-juvenile-reentry-in-research-and-practice/.
42. *Kent v. United States*, 383 U.S. 541 (1966).
43. American Bar Association, "Still Seeking the Promise of *Gault*: Juveniles and the Right to Counsel," http://www.abanet.org/crimjust/juvjus/cjmag/18-2shep.html.
44. American Bar Association, "For Schools: Lessons," http://www.abanet.org/publiced/lawday/schools/lessons/handout_gault.html.
45. *Gault v. Arizona*, 387 US 1 (1967).
46. Ibid., p. 14.
47. *In Re Winship*, 397 U.S. 358 (1970).
48. *McKeiver v. Pennsylvania*, 403 U.S. 528 (1971).
49. *Breed v. Jones*, 421 U.S. 519 (1975).
50. *Roper v. Simmons*, 543 U.S. 551 (2005).
51. *J. D. B. v. North Carolina*, No. 09–11121 (2011).

// CHAPTER 16

1. U.S. Department of Homeland Security, "Fusion Center Locations and Contact Information," https://www.dhs.gov/fusion-center-locations-and-contact-information.
2. Elaine Pittman, Jim McKay, "Las Vegas Fusion Center Is a Model for Public-Private Collaboration," Government Technology, May 24, 2011, https://www.govtech.com/em/safety/Las-Vegas-Fusion-Center-Public-Private-Collaboration-052411.html.
3. See, for example, a discussion of the "lone-wolf model" of terrorism now in use here and abroad—and discussed

in al-Qaeda publications—in Lori Hinnant, "Intel Dilemma in Boston, London, Paris Attacks," Associated Press, May 31, 2013, http://abcnews.go.com/International/wireStory/intel-dilemma-boston-london-paris-attacks-19294987#.UazbZuDn_cs.

4. See Marcella Corona, "'Pill-Mill' Case: Where Are the Defendants Now?" *Reno Gazette-Journal*, April 27, 2017, https://www.rgj.com/story/news/crime/2017/04/28/pill-mill-case-where-defendants-now/307384001/.

5. National Institute on Drug Abuse, "What Is the Scope of Heroin Use in the United States?" June 2018, https://www.drugabuse.gov/publications/research-reports/heroin/scope-heroin-use-in-united-states.

6. Francis Diep, "Some Officials Worry a Cocaine Epidemic Is About to Hit the U.S.," *Pacific Standard*, May 9, 2018, https://psmag.com/news/some-officials-worry-a-cocaine-epidemic-is-about-to-hit-the-u-s.

7. See National Institute on Drug Abuse, "What Is Fentanyl," February 2019, https://www.drugabuse.gov/publications/drugfacts/fentanyl; also see Meilan Solly, "Fentanyl Has Outpaced Heroin as Drug Implicated Most Often in Fatal Overdoses," *Smithsonian Magazine*, December 17, 2018, https://www.smithsonianmag.com/smart-news/fentanyl-has-outpaced-heroin-drug-implicated-most-often-fatal-overdoses-180971050/.

8. Abby Goodnough, Josh Katz, and Margot Sanger-Katz, "Drug Overdose Deaths Drop in U.S. for First Time Since 1990," *New York Times*, July 17, 2019, https://www.nytimes.com/interactive/2019/07/17/upshot/drug-overdose-deaths-fall.html.

9. U.S. Department of Health and Human Services, "What Is the U.S. Opioid Epidemic?" https://www.hhs.gov/opioids/about-the-epidemic/index.html.

10. Brett Molina, "Odds of Opioids Death Higher Than Car Crash," *USA Today*, January 15, 2019, https://epaper.daytondailynews.com/popovers/dynamic_article_popover.aspx?guid=1eaed9bc-711e-4ed2-bac0-70e9822e0c42&pbid=66ab59ea-5cfc-438d-83e4-dc9e4a34f79d&utm_source=app.pagesuite&utm_medium=app-interaction&utm_campaign=pagesuite-epaper-htm15_share-article.

11. Jerry Mitchell, "Is There a Solution to the Opioid Epidemic?" *USA Today*, January 30, 2018, https://www.usatoday.com/story/news/nation-now/2018/01/29/175-americans-dying-day-what-solutions-opioid-epidemic/1074336001/.

12. Police Executive Research Forum, *The Unprecedented Opioid Epidemic: As Overdoses Become a Leading Cause of Death, Police, Sheriffs, and Health Agencies Must Step Up Their Response*, September 2017, http://www.policeforum.org/assets/opioids2017.pdf, p. 14; Mitchell, "Is There a Solution to the Opioid Epidemic?"; also see U.S. Department of Health and Human Services Secretary Thomas E. Price's recommendations, https://www.hhs.gov/about/leadership/secretary/speeches/2017-speeches/secretary-price-announces-hhs-strategy-for-fighting-opioid-crisis/index.html.

13. Ibid.

14. Substance Abuse and Mental Health Services Administration, *Adult Drug Courts and Medication-Assisted Treatment for Opioid Dependence*, Summer 2014, https://store.samhsa.gov/system/files/sma14-4852.pdf.

15. "State Marijuana Laws in 2018 Map," *Governing*, http://www.governing.com/gov-data/safety-justice/state-marijuana-laws-map-medical-recreational.html.

16. Tom Angell, "These States Are Most Likely to Legalize Marijuana in 2019," *Forbes*, December 26, 2018, https://www.forbes.com/sites/tomangell/2018/12/26/these-states-are-most-likely-to-legalize-marijuana-in-2019/#20af12555add.

17. Sara Brittany Somerset, "Attorney General Barr Favors a More Lenient Approach to Cannabis Prohibition," *Forbes*, April 15, 2019, https://www.forbes.com/sites/sarabrittanysomerset/2019/04/15/attorney-general-barr-favors-a-more-lenient-approach-to-cannabis-legalization/#46e92297c4c8.

18. "Estimating Enforcement Costs in Legal States and Correlation to Marijuana Policy: Whack-a-Mole Cannabis Enforcement," WM Policy, August 14, 2017, http://www.wmpolicy.com/wp-content/uploads/sites/17/2017/11/11Estimating-Enforcement-Costs.pdf.

19. U.S. Department of Justice, "Sex Trafficking Defined," https://www.justice.gov/sextrafficking.

20. Aryn Barker, "The Survivor," *Time*, January 28, 2019, p. 38.

21. Ibid.

22. See U.S. Department of Health and Human Services, "Trafficking Victims Protection Act of 2000: Fact Sheet," http://www.markwynn.com/trafficking/trafficking-victims-protection-act-of-2000-fact-sheet.pdf.

23. U.S. Citizenship and Immigration Services, "Victims of Sex Trafficking: T Nonimmigrant Status," https://www.uscis.gov/humanitarian/victims-human-trafficking-other-crimes/victims-human-trafficking-t-nonimmigrant-status.

24. U.S. Department of Health & Human Services, Office of Refugee Resettlement, "Fact Sheet: Certification for Adult Victims of Trafficking," https://www.acf.hhs.gov/orr/resource/fact-sheet-certification-for-adult-victims-of-trafficking.

25. See, for example, International Association of Chiefs of Police, "Toolkit: Child Sex Trafficking: A Training Series for Frontline Officers," https://www.theiacp.org/resources/document/toolkit-child-sex-trafficking-a-training-series-for-frontline-officers.

26. Jovana Lara, "Sex-Trafficking Crackdown: 510 Arrested, 56 Rescued in California," ABC News, January 30, 2018, http://abc7news.com/hundreds-arrested-in-sex-trafficking-crackdown-in-california/3008362/.

27. Nicole Chavez, "More Than 1,000 Arrests in Sex Trafficking Operation," CNN, August 4, 2017, https://www.cnn.com/2017/08/04/us/sex-trafficking-sting/index.html.
28. Erin Calabrese, Todd Miyazawa, and Andrew Kozak, "84 Children Rescued, 120 Sex Traffickers Arrested Across U.S., FBI Says," *U.S. News*, October 18, 2017, https://www.nbcnews.com/news/us-news/84-children-rescued-120-sex-traffickers-arrested-across-u-s-n812156.
29. Federal Bureau of Investigations, "Terrorism," https://www.fbi.gov/investigate/terrorism.
30. 18 U.S.C. § 2331, states that international terrorism involves: violent acts or acts dangerous to human life that violate federal or state law; that appear to be intended (i) to intimidate or coerce a civilian population; (ii) to influence the policy of a government by intimidation or coercion; or (iii) to affect the conduct of a government by mass destruction, assassination, or kidnapping; and occur primarily outside the territorial jurisdiction of the U.S., or transcend national boundaries in terms of the means by which they are accomplished, the persons they appear intended to intimidate or coerce, or the locale in which their perpetrators operate or seek asylum.
31. Christal Hayes, Kevin Johnson, and Candy Woodall, "Who is Robert Bowers? Accused Pittsburgh Synagogue Shooter Left Anti-Semitic Trail," *USA TODAY*, https://www.cnn.com/2018/10/27/us/synagogue-attack-suspect-robert-bowers-profile/index.htmlhttps://www.cnn.com/2018/10/27/us/synagogue-attack-suspect-robert-bowers-profile/index.html.
32. Nicole Chavez, "Cesar Sayoc was a DJ, bodybuilder and pizza delivery man before he became a bomb suspect," CNN, October 27, 2018, https://www.cnn.com/2018/10/27/politics/cesar-sayoc-mail-bomb-suspect/index.html.
33. Nathan Bomey, "Suspect Devices Hard for Delivery Services to Detect," *USA Today*, October 27, 2018, https://www.usatoday.com/story/money/2018/10/25/suspicious-package-handling-ups-fedex-usps/1763186002/.
34. International Association of Chiefs of Police, "Homegrown Violent Extremism Awareness Brief," January 1, 2014, https://www.theiacp.org/resources/document/homegrown-violent-extremism-awareness-brief.
35. Peter Bergen, "Can We Stop Homegrown Terrorists?" *Wall Street Journal*, January 23–24, 2016, pp. C1–C2.
36. Sam O'Kane, "Chinese hackers charged with stealing data from NASA, IBM, and others," The Verge, December 18, 2018, https://www.theverge.com/2018/12/20/18150275/chinese-hackers-stealing-data-nasa-ibm-charged; also see Sam Bocette, "Chinese State Sponsored Hacking," The Bridge, November 23, 2017, https://www.realcleardefense.com/articles/2017/11/23/chinese_state_sponsored_hacking_112675.html.
37. "China overtakes Russia as world's biggest state hacker," The Week, October 10, 2018, https://www.theweek.co.uk/96999/china-overtakes-russia-as-world-s-biggest-state-hacker.
38. Donie O'Sullivan and Joshua Berlinger, "North Korea Hackers Targeting US 'Critical Infrastructure,' Cybersecurity Firm," CNN, March 5, 2019, https://www.cnn.com/2019/03/04/politics/north-korea-hackers-intl/index.htmlsayshttps://www.cnn.com/2019/03/04/politics/north-korea-hackers-intl/index.html.
39. Interpol, "Cybercrime," https://www.interpol.int/en/Crimes/Cybercrime.
40. Privacy Rights Clearinghouse, "Data Breaches," https://www.privacyrights.org/data-breaches.
41. Rob Marvin, "How Much Does a Data Breach Cost?" *PC Magazine*, July 19, 2018, https://www.pcmag.com/news/362543/how-much-does-a-data-breach-cost.
42. Dana A. Shea and Frank Gottron, *Small-Scale Terrorist Attacks Using Chemical and Biological Agents: An Assessment Framework and Preliminary Comparisons*, Congressional Research Service, Report for Congress, May 20, 2004, http://www.fas.org/irp/crs/RL32391.pdf.
43. See Department of Homeland Security, "About DHS," https://www.dhs.gov/about-dhs.
44. See FEMA, "National Incident Management System," https://www.fema.gov/national-incident-management-system.
45. Billy Max, "How to Prevent Hackers in a Company," *AZ Central*, April 13, 2018, https://yourbusiness.azcentral.com/prevent-hackers-company-23336.html.
46. Steve Ranger, "What Is Cyberwar? Everything You Need to Know About the Frightening Future of Digital Conflict," ZDNet, December 4, 2018, https://www.zdnet.com/article/cyberwar-a-guide-to-the-frightening-future-of-online-conflict/.
47. Tod Newcombe, "3 Ways Governments Are Fighting Hackers," *Governing*, September 2016, https://www.governing.com/columns/tech-talk/gov-cybersecurity-hackers-government.html.
48. Alex Bennett, "Teaching Our Police Force How to Hack Like the Pros," *Wired*, June 12, 2017, https://www.wired.co.uk/article/teaching-police-hacking.
49. D. G. Bolgiano, "Military Support of Domestic Law Enforcement Operations: Working Within Posse Comitatus," *FBI Law Enforcement Bulletin* (December 2001), pp. 16–24.
50. Erin Kelly, "Senate Approves USA Freedom Act," *USA Today*, June 2, 2015, http://www.usatoday.com/story/news/politics/2015/06/02/patriot-act-usa-freedom-act-senate-vote/28345747/.
51. Jurist: Legal News and Research, "Bush Signs Military Commissions Act," http://jurist.law.pitt.edu/paperchase/2006/10/bush-signs-military-commissions-act.php.

52. Ibid.
53. Daniel Victor, "School Shootings Have Already Killed Dozens in 2018," *New York Times*, May 18, 2018, https://www.nytimes.com/2018/05/18/us/school-shootings-2018.html.
54. For more information, see, generally, Center for Homeland Defense and Security, "K-12 School Shooting Database," https://www.chds.us/ssdb/incidents-by-month/.
55. Sue Riseling, quoted in *The Police Response to Active Shooter Incidents*, Police Executive Research Forum, March 2014, https://www.policeforum.org/assets/docs/Critical_Issues_Series/the%20police%20response%20to%20active%20shooter%20incidents%202014.pdf, p. 30.
56. Abigail Abrams and Melissa Chan, "Special Report: Guns in America," *Time*, November 5, 2018, p. 28.
57. Ibid., p. 29.
58. Gun Violence Archive, "Past Summary Ledgers," https://www.gunviolencearchive.org/past-tolls.
59. Sean Gregory, Chris Wilson, Alice Park, and Aric Jenkins, "Guns in America," *Time*, November 5, 2018, p. 32.
60. Ibid.
61. Lisa Marie Pane, "Parkland Attack Fueled Big Shift in America's Gun Politics," Associated Press, February 7, 2019, http://www.startribune.com/parkland-attack-fueled-big-shift-in-america-s-gun-politics/505504142/.
62. Katherine A. Vittes, Jon S. Vernick, and Daniel W. Webster, "Legal Status and Source of Offenders' Firearms in States With the Least Stringent Criteria for Gun Ownership," Center for Gun Policy and Research, Johns Hopkins Bloomberg School of Public Health, Baltimore, Maryland.
63. Ibid.
64. Abrams and Chan, "Special Report: Guns in America," p. 30.
65. Adapted from Police Executive Research Forum, *Key Findings and Actions That Will Have the Largest Impact in Reducing Gun Violence*, https://www.policeforum.org/assets/GunViolenceActionPlan.pdf.
66. Kayla Dwyer, "Guns in School? Here's a List of States That Allow Armed Teachers," *Morning Call*, February 14, 2019, https://www.mcall.com/news/education/mc-nws-guns-in-schools-list-20181108-story.html.
67. "U.S. unauthorized immigrant population estimates by state, 2016," Pew Research Center, February 5, 2019, https://www.pewresearch.org/hispanic/interactives/u-s-unauthorized-immigrants-by-state/.
68. Miriam Jordan, "8 Million People Are Working Illegally in the U.S. Here's Why That's Unlikely to Change," *New York Times*, December 11, 2018, https://www.nytimes.com/2018/12/11/us/undocumented-immigrant-workers.html.
69. National Immigration Forum, "Chiefs and Sheriffs Oppose Immigration Enforcement Policies Undermining Community Policing," July 20, 2015, https://immigrationforum.org/blog/chiefs-and-sheriffs-oppose-immigration-enforcement-policies-undermining-community-policing/.
70. Edwards, "Bye Dad, I Love You," p. 39.
71. Mike James, "Trump Seeks $18 Billion to Extend Border Wall Over 10 Years," *USA Today*, January 6, 2018, https://www.usatoday.com/story/news/2018/01/05/trump-border-wall-proposal/1009584001/.
72. Christal Hayes, "Not a 2,000-Mile Concrete Structure From Sea to Sea': Is Trump Scaling Back Border Wall Plan?" *USA Today*, January 19, 2019, https://www.usatoday.com/story/news/politics/2019/01/19/trump-wall-wont-2-000-mile-concrete-structure-sea-sea/2627378002/.
73. See Nina Totenberg, "Trump's National Emergency Sets Up Legal Fight Over Spending Authority," NPR, February 16, 2019, https://www.npr.org/2019/02/16/695321387/trumps-national-emergency-sets-up-legal-fight-over-spending-authority.
74. See Jackson Rollings, "Eight Border Wall Prototypes Are Unveiled Along the U.S.-Mexico Border," *The Architect's Newspaper*, October 25, 2017, https://archpaper.com/2017/10/eight-border-wall-prototypes-unveiled/#gallery-0-slide-0.
75. See Migration Policy Institute, "President Signs DHS Appropriations and Secure Fence Act, New Detainee Bill Has Repercussions for Noncitizens," https://www.migrationpolicy.org/article/president-signs-dhs-appropriations-and-secure-fence-act-new-detainee-bill-has-repercussions.
76. "Suspect in Four Northern Nevada Murders Arrested," KOLO TV, January 24, 2019, https://www.kolotv.com/content/news/Two-people-found-dead-in-south-Reno-home-504465091.html.
77. Alan Gomez, "Mollie Tibbetts Murder Case: Here Are the Facts on Immigrants Committing Crimes in US," *USA Today*, August 18, 2018, https://www.usatoday.com/story/news/nation/2018/08/22/mollie-tibbitts-murder-reignites-debate-over-immigrant-crime/1060792002/.
78. Kaitlyn Schallhorn, "Sanctuary Cities: What Are They?" Fox News, March 22, 2018, http://www.foxnews.com/politics/2018/03/22/sanctuary-cities-what-are.html.
79. Ibid.
80. Ibid.
81. "U.S. System for Refugee, Asylum Seekers Explained," NBC News, http://www.nbcnews.com/id/43442030/ns/us_news-life/t/us-system-refugee-asylum-seekers-explained/#.XGsJz_ZFzcs.
82. "Which Countries Do Most People Granted Asylum in the U.S. Come From?" NOLO, 2018, https://www.nolo.com/legal-encyclopedia/which-countries-do-most-people-granted-asylum-the-us-come-from.html.
83. See Sofia Martinez, "Today's Migrant Flow Is Different," *The Atlantic*, June 26, 2018, https://www.theatlantic.com/international/archive/2018/06/central-america-border-immigration/563744/.

84. W. J. Hennigan, "The Long Wait," *Time*, November 26/December 3, 2018, pp. 44–45.
85. Ibid.
86. Ibid.
87. For a fuller discussion of this topic, see Federation for American Immigration Reform, "The Role of State & Local Law Enforcement in Immigration Matters and Reasons to Resist Sanctuary Policies," January 2016, https://www.fairus.org/issue/illegal-immigration/role-state-local-law-enforcement-immigration-matters-and-reasons-resist .
88. See Division C of Public Law 104–208, 110 Stat. 3009–546, enacted September 30, 1996.
89. Alan Gomez, "Trump May Empower Local Police to Round Up Immigrants," *USA Today*, November 25, 2016.
90. See U.S. Immigration and Customs Enforcement, "Delegation of Immigration Authority Section 287(g) Immigration and Nationality Act," https://www.ice.gov/287g.

// APPENDIX

1. See Library of Congress, "Primary Documents in American History: The Bill of Rights," http://www.loc.gov/rr//program/bib/ourdocs/billofrights.html.

/// INDEX

Page numbers followed by f, t and b indicate figures, tables and boxes, respectively

Abbott, Jack Henry, 294
Abortion, 9
Absolute ethics, 80
Academy training, 133, 133–134t, 134f
Accepted lying, 84–86
Acquittal, 17
Active shooter, 408
Actus reus, 33, 254
Adams, John, 26, 183
Adjudication, 13f, 16–17
Adler, Freda, 66–68
Administrative building assignments, 328
Administrative law, 28
Administrative security prisons, 306
Adoption studies, 60
Adult Sentencing Guidelines Manual, 279
Adversarial system, 208, 209b
ADX Prison, 307
Affidavit, 186
African Americans
   capital punishment and, 282
   mass incarceration of, 299
   police use of force and, 157–158, 159–160
Aftercare and reentry, 338, 389
Age defense, 255
Aggravated assault, 38
Aggravating circumstances, 17, 287
Agnew, Robert, 61
Alcatraz Island, 271
Alexander, Michelle, 299
Alper, Mariel, 358b
Alpert, Geoffrey, 328
Alternatives to incarceration, 344–345
American Bar Association (ABA), 93–94, 282
American Civil liberties Union (ACLU), 280
American Correctional Association (ACA) Code of Ethics, 95
American Judicature Society, 91
American Probation and Parole Association (APPA), 358, 359
Amnesty International, 307, 308b
Annotation monitors, 234
Anthony, Casey, 207–208, 223, 229, 232
   acquittal of, 349b
Anthony, Caylee, 207, 349b
Appeals
   criminal, 287–288
   grounds for, 231
Appeals courts, 214–215, 214f
   circuit courts, 217
   stare decisis and, 27
Appellate review, 17–18
Apps, 233
Argersinger v. Hamlin, 200–201
Arizona v. Gant, 188

Armed robbery, 71–72
Arraignment, 16–17, 223
Arrest, 13f, 14, 182
   booking and, 220
   exclusionary rule and, 184
   false, 168
   house, 362
   probable cause for, 183–184
   rates of juvenile, 381f
   searches incident to lawful, 188
   warrants for, 183
   with and without a warrant, 186–187
Arson, 40
Assault
   aggravated, 38
   sexual, 37–38
Astor, Saul, 124
Asylums, 296
Asylum seekers, 412
Attica Correctional Facility, 272, 334f, 335
Attorneys
   courtroom work group and, 253
   defense (*See* Defense attorneys)
   practitioner perspective of, 210b
   prosecuting (*See* Prosecutors)
Augustus, John, 346
Australia, sentencing guidelines in, 276b
Automobiles. *See* Vehicles
Autonomous vehicles (AV), 175

Bachman, Dennis, 405b
Back-end duties of parole officers, 357
Bacon, Francis, 206
Bail, 221–222, 221f
Bailiffs, 253
Baldwin, James, 159
Barr, William, 287
Barrow, Clyde, 115
Bauer, Corey, 390b
Bay County Jail riot, 334
Bayley, David, 135, 141
Baze v. Rees, 284
Beccaria, Cesare, 57, 57f
Becker, Howard, 64
Benford, Angela, 148b
Benjamin, Brent, 243
Bennett, James V., 272
Berger v. United States, 91
Berk, Richard, 282
Berkeley Police Department, 108f, 109
Berkowitz, David, 258
Berry, Amanda, 59b
Best interest of the child principle, 378

Beto, George, 272
Bey-Coon, Hakima, 249b
Bill of Rights, 183. *See also* Constitution of the United States
Biological theories of criminal behavior, 58–60, 60f
Biometrics, 174
Bioterrorism, 406
Birchfield v. North Dakota, 194
Bittner, Egon, 141
Black Beach, Equatorial Guinea, prison, 308b
Black Lives Matter, 159, 160
Black Panthers, 325
Black's Law Dictionary, 27
Blakely v. Washington, 277
Blue Lives Matter, 160
Blumberg, Abraham, 240
Body scanners, 314
Body-worn cameras, 166
Booking, 220
Boot camps, 363–364, 363f
Border wall, 411–412
Boston marathon bombing, 19
Boston Strangler, 153
Bounds v. Smith, 336
Bowers, Robert, 403
Breed v. Jones, 391
British Crime Survey (BCS), 48b
Brockway, Zebulon, 346
Broom, Romell, 285b
Browder, Kalief, 3–4, 6, 11, 12
Brown, Michael, 158, 159–160, 222, 224f
Brown v. Plata, 211f
Brutality, police, 165–166
Building and construction standards, 29
Burden of proof, 29, 391
Bureau of Alcohol, Tobacco, Firearms and Explosives (ATF), 115–116
Burglary, 39
    motive for, 72–73
Burke, Dan, 191b
Burton, Afton, 338b
Bush, George W., 110, 407, 412
Business licenses, 29
Bynam, Ray, 324b
Byrd v. United States, 195

Cameras, body-worn, 166
Camp 1391, Israel, 308b
Campaign for Youth Justice, 380b
Campbell, Alva, 285b
Cannabis. *See* Marijuana
Capital punishment, 17, 281f, 282f
    aggravating and mitigating circumstances in, 287
    arguments for and against, 281–283
    automatic appellate review of, 17–18
    exonerations and, 286–287, 286b
    by lethal injection, 285b, 285f
    methods of execution, 284–285, 284f
    recent trends in, 287
    wrongful convictions and, 285–287
Cardozo, Benjamin, 184, 280
Careers. *See* Law enforcement careers

Carjacking, 73
Carpenter, Timothy, 181–182, 185
Carranza, Carlos Eduardo Arevalo, 343–344, 344f
Carroll v. United States, 194
Carter, David, 84
Carter, Michelle, 231f
Caseloads, probation and parole, 358–359
Castille, Ronald, 243b
Castro, Ariel, 59b
Causation, 215b
Celebrated cases, 18–20, 19f
Cell block officers, 328
Cell phones, 181–182, 192
    as contraband in correctional organizations, 313–314
    driving while texting using, 175–176
Center for Advancing Correctional Excellence Criminal Cognitions Scale, 366f
Central Intelligence Agency (CIA), 116–117
Chain of command, 122
Chambers Online Automation Training (COAT), 233
Chandler, Raymond, 128
Chemical castration of child sex offenders, 274b
Chemical weapons, 406
Chesser, Zachary, 404b
Chief justice, Supreme Court, 220
Chief of police, 169b
Chimel v. California, 188
Churchill, Winston, 318, 336b, 342, 395
Cicero, Marcus Tullius, 54
Circuit courts, 217, 219b
Citizen's attitude as determinant of discretionary action, 142
City/county law, 29
Civility, courtroom, 246
Civil law, 29–30, 30t, 32
Civil liability, police
    defined, 167
    potential areas of, 170–171
    process and personality in, 166–168
    Section 1983 and, 168
    torts and negligence in, 168
Civil rights and antidiscrimination laws, 29
Clark, Stephon, 157–158
Classical school of criminology, 57
Classical theory of criminal behavior, 57
Classification of inmates, 302–303
Clay, Henry, 24
Clearance rates, 151
Clerks, court, 253
Cleveland "Monster," 59b
Closing arguments, 230
Coast Guard, 112
Cocaine, 396
Code of Conduct for United States Judges, 93
Code of Hammurabi, 26f, 27
Code of silence, 81, 82–83
Codes, 27–28
Cohen, Elliot, 91
Cohen, Lawrence, 69
Cold cases, 153

Collins, Ryan Austin, 196
Collins v. Virginia, 196
Colonial era
    courts in, 208
    model of punishment in, 269
    roots of policing in, 104–107
Colorado theater shooting, 19, 257b
Commission-based appointment of judges, 241
Common law, 27
    federal, 28
    state, 28
Community corrections
    defined, 344
    in federal system, 306
    intermediate sanctions, 360–365
    juveniles and, 379
    parole (*See* Parole)
    probation (*See* Probation)
Community era in policing, 1980s-present, 109–110
Community model of punishment, 272
Community policing and problem solving, 143–145, 143f, 144f
Comte, Auguste, 58
Concurrent sentences, 275–276
Conferences, Supreme Court, 218–220
Confidentiality, youth, 378
Confinement
    conditions of, 322–323
    home, 362
    solitary, 325
Conflict theory of justice, 9
Conley, Michael, 263–264
Conrad, John, 358
Consecutive sentences, 275–276
Consensus theory of justice, 7–8
Consensus-versus-conflict debate, 6–9
Consent degree, 164–165
Consent to search, 188, 196–197
Constable, 105
Constitutional policing, 161–162
Constitution of the United States, 29f
    Eighth Amendment, 211, 269, 272, 280, 284, 337
    Fifth Amendment, 197–200, 391
    First Amendment, 337
    Fourteenth Amendment, 283, 337
    Fourth Amendment, 183–197
    introduction to rights under, 182–183
    rights of prisoners under, 335–338
    Sixth Amendment, 200–201, 225, 277
    supermax prisons and, 308–309
    as supreme law of the land, 28
Continuing investigation, 147
Contraband, 313, 322f
Contract services, 125
Control theory, 63–64
Conviction, 17
Conyers, Howard, 206
Cooper v. Pate, 336
Coping with stress, 139–140
Corda, Alessandro, 358b
CoreCivic, 309

Coroner, 105
Corpus delicti, 146
Correctional officers (COs), 325, 327–328, 332f
    discretion used by, 12
    ethics of, 79, 94–95
    number of, 297
Correctional organizations
    classification of inmates in, 302–303
    correctional facilities as, 297–303
    in criminal justice process, 18
    federal prisons, 305–306
    general mission and features of, 300
    inmates, employment, and expenditures in, 297–298, 298f
    jails, 297, 309–313, 310f, 312f
    jails vs. prisons as, 297
    as punishment for some, a "step up" for others, 300–302
    push to reform, 295–296
    reasons for decline in populations of, 298–299
    state prisons, 303–305, 303f
    supermax prisons, 307–309, 307f
    technologies in, 313–315
Corrections sergeant, 324b
Corruption, 115. *See also* Ethics
    noble cause, 81
    police, 82, 83b
Cortes, Maxine, 252b
County of Sacramento v. Lewis, 171
County sheriff's offices, 120
Court administrator
    practitioner perspective of, 252b
Court employees, ethics of, 92
Court of last resort, 214–215
Court reporters, 253
Courtroom work group, 253
Court system
    as adversarial system, 208–209, 209b
    appeals (*See* Appeals courts)
    attorneys and (*See* Defense attorneys; Prosecutors)
    colonial era, 208
    courtroom work group in, 253
    defenses in, 253–258
    diversion programs/problem-solving courts, 227–228
    dual, 208, 211–212, 212t
    ethics in, 78–79, 90–92
    federal (*See* Federal court system)
    influence in policy making, 209–211
    introduction to, 208–211
    judges in (*See* Judges)
    jury trials in, 225–227, 225f, 226f
    pretrial processes in, 220–228
    sentencing decisions and, 276
    state (*See* State court system)
    technologies in, 233–234, 233f
    three-tier, 27, 28f
    trial process in, 228–232
Crime
    aggravated assault, 38
    arson, 40
    burglary, 39

clearance rates for, 151
computerized mapping of, 174f
cyber-, 115, 149–150, 403–406
felonies and misdemeanors as broad categories of, 33
fetal abduction, 55–56, 63
homicide, 34–37, 35t
intent versus motive to commit, 25–26, 31–33, 33f
investigation of, 147, 147f
larceny-theft, 39
linking persons to scene of, 146
making punishment fit the, 272–274
measuring victimization and, 42–50, 43f, 45f, 45t, 46t
motor vehicle theft, 40
offense definitions and categories, 34–42
organized, 20–21, 42
against persons, 34–38
prevention of, by law enforcement, 137
against property, 39–40
public order, 40
robbery, 38, 38f
sexual assault, 37–38
in Venezuela, 118b
in wedding cake model of criminal justice, 18–20, 19f
white-collar, 40–42, 355b
Crime analysts, 62b, 65b
Crime Clock, 44, 45f
Crime control, 10–11, 11t
Crime control model of punishment, 272
Crime in the United States, 45
Crime policies, 395–396
 drug epidemic, 396–399, 397f
 immigration, 410–413
 school shootings and gun violence, 10b, 407–410, 408f, 410f
 sex trafficking, 399–401
 terrorism (*See* Terrorism)
Crime prevention through environmental design (CPTED), 145
Crime rate, 44
Crime Scene Investigation: A Reference for Law Enforcement Training, 148
Crime scene investigators, 148b
Crime scenes, 148
Crime Survey for England and Wales (CSEW), 48b
Criminal appeals, 287–288
Criminal behavior, theories of
 application of, 72b
 biological, trait, and developmental, 58–60, 60f
 classical and positivist, 56–58
 environmental criminology, 69–71, 69f, 70t, 71b
 feminist, 66–68, 67–68t
 introduction to, 56
 neoclassical criminology and, 57–58
 positivist criminology and, 58, 58f
 social conflict, 65–66
 social process, 62–64
 social structure, 60–62
Criminal investigators. *See* Detectives/criminal investigators
Criminalistics, 146
Criminal justice process
 adjudication in, 13f, 16–17
 appellate review in, 17–18
 corrections in, 18

juvenile justice system, 18, 383–386, 384f
 law enforcement in, 12, 13f, 14
 offender's pathway through, 13f, 14
 overview of flow and functions in, 12–18
 prosecution and pretrial activities in, 13f, 14–16
 sentencing and sanctions in, 17
 wedding cake model of, 18–20, 19f
Criminal justice program director, 49b
Criminal justice students, ethics tests for, 95–96
Criminal justice system
 changing laws and, 5–6
 consensus-versus-conflict debate in, 6–9
 crime control and due process in, 10–11, 11t
 discretion in, 11–12
 ethics in, 20–21
 introduction to 4
 legal and historical bases of, 4–9
 as source of stress, 139
Criminal law, 5–6, 29–30, 30t
Criminologists, 73b
Criminology, 56
 environmental, 69–71, 69f, 70t, 71b
 neoclassical, 57–58
 positivist, 58, 58f
Crisis intervention training or team (CIT) approaches, 172
Crofton, Walter, 346
Croswell, Scott, 240
Crowding, inmate 322
Cruz, Michelle, 249b
Cruz v. Beto, 337
Currie, Elliott, 66
Custody assignments and classification of inmates, 302
Customs and Border Protection (CBP), 110t, 112
Cybercrime, 115, 149–150, 403–406
 federal efforts against, 406–407
Cyberterrorism, 403–406

Dahmer, Jeffrey L., 258
Darrow, Clarence, 294
Davis, Kenneth Culp, 141
Davis, Richard Allen, 5, 7
Day, Frank, 166
Day reporting centers (DRC), 364
DeAngelo, Joseph James, 130
Death in Custody Reporting Act of 2014, 163
Death penalty. *See* Capital punishment
Declaration of Independence, 7
Decriminalization of marijuana, 8f, 9b, 399
Defendants, 29. *See also* Offenders
 adjudication of, 13f, 16–17
 arraignment of, 16–17, 223
 arrest of, 13f, 14
 burden of proof and, 29–30
 initial appearance of, 13f, 14–16
 justification, 254–255
Defense attorneys, 226b
 defenses presented by, 253–258
 duties and strategies of, 250–251
 ethics of, 92
 as guiding hand of counsel, 250–253
 practitioner perspective of, 273b

Defense case presentation, 230
Defenses
   affirmative, 253
   defined, 253
   excuse, 255–258
   justification, 254–255
DeJesus, Gina, 59b
Dekraal, Scott, 14f
Delay (trial), 228–229
Denmark, search and seizure in, 195b
Deontological ethics, 79
Department of Homeland Security (DHS), 110–113, 110t, 111f, 113f, 396, 406
Department of Justice (DOJ), 110, 110t, 113–116, 114f, 115f, 325
Deprivations of imprisonment, 321, 321f
DeSalvo, Albert, 153
Detectives/criminal investigators, 146. *See also* Forensic science
   attributes of, 146
   cybercrimes, 150b
   investigative stages and activities of, 147, 147f
Determinate sentences, 18, 274–275
Deterrence, 267, 326
Developmental theories of criminal behavior, 58–60, 60f
Deviant lying, 84–86
Diagnostic center, 401
Digital recording, 233
Dillinger, John, 115
Dillon, Mark, 214f
Dinkelacker, Patrick, 240
Director of IT and electronic security, 405b
Discovery, 227
Discretion, 11–12
   attempts to define, 141
   determinants of discretionary actions and, 141–142
   myth of full enforcement and, 140
   in policing, 140–143
   pros and cons of, 142–143
Disposition hearing, 386
Disraeli, Benjamin, 159
Distracted driving, 175
District courts, 213, 213f, 216–217, 216f
Diversion programs, 227–228
DNA analysis, 147, 151–152, 151f
   exonerations through, 286b
Double jeopardy, 256
Driving, texting while, 175–176
Driving statutes, 34b
Drones, 313–314
Drug abuse in prisons, 330
Drug Enforcement Administration (DEA), 116
Drug epidemic, 396–399, 397f
Drug-testing devices, handheld, 176
Dual court system, 208, 211–212, 212t
Dual hazard prediction, 60
Due process, 10–11, 11t, 337, 351
Duress defense, 254–255
Durkheim, Emile, 61
Duty of care, 170

Eastern State Penitentiary, 270f
Eck, John, 69

Edelhertz, Herbert, 41
Eighth Amendment, 211, 269, 272, 280, 284, 337
El Chapo, 398b
Electronic monitoring (EM), 362–363, 362f
Electronic surveillance, 197
Elmira Reformatory, 271, 346, 347f
Emerson, Ralph Waldo, 208
Enemy Within: The McClellan Committee's Crusade Against Jimmy Hoffa and Corrupt Labor Unions, The, 20–21
English and colonial roots of policing, 104–107
Entrapment defense, 256
Environmental criminology theories, 69–71, 69f, 70t, 71b
Equal Employment Opportunity Act, 67
Escobedo, Danny, 201
Escobedo v. Illinois, 201
Espionage, 115
Essays on Crime and Punishments, 57
Esserman, Dean, 162
Estelle v. Gamble, 337
Ethics
   absolute, 80
   in corrections, 79, 94–95
   of court employees, 92
   in the courts, 78, 90–92
   in the criminal justice system, 20–21
   of defense attorneys, 92
   deontological, 79
   examples of, 78–79
   of federal employees, 93–94
   introduction to, 78
   of judges, 90–91, 93–94
   philosophical foundations of, 79–81
   in policing, 78, 81–90
   of prosecutors, 91
   relative, 80
   tests for the criminal justice student, 95–96
   types of, 80–81
Ethics in Government Act of 1978, 93
Ethics Reform Act of 1989, 90, 93
Etzioni, Amitai, 102
Evans, William, 161
Evidence, 147
   cameras for, 234
   in plain view, 188
Evidence-based policing, 144–145, 144f
Exclusionary rule, 184–185, 185f
Excusable homicide, 34
Excuse defenses, 255–258
Exigent circumstances, 186
Exonerations, 286–287, 286b

Facial recognition, 174–175
Fackrell, Douglas, 185
Failure to act, 33
Failure to protect, 170
Fairness to all, 162
False arrest, 168
Family and Medical Leave Act, 67
Federal Bureau of Investigation (FBI), 39
   creation of, 113
   on crime prevalence, 4

definition of rape, 37
priority areas of, 115
Racketeer Influenced and Corrupt Organizations (RICO) statute and, 42
on terrorism, 401, 402f
Uniform Crime Reports (UCR), 42–46, 43f, 45f, 383
Federal Bureau of Prisons (BOP), 272, 305
  careers with, 306
Federal common law, 28
Federal court system, 208, 212t. *See also* Supreme Court, the
  circuit courts, 217, 219b
  district courts, 213, 213f, 216–217, 216f
  ethical conduct in, 93–94
  search and seizure warrant form for, 189–190f
  three-tier structure of, 27, 28f
Federal Emergency Management Administration (FEMA), 406
Federal employees, ethics of, 93–94
Federalism, 27
Federal law, 28
  other agencies in, 116–117
Federal law enforcement, 110–117, 110t
  Department of Homeland Security (DHS), 110–113, 110t, 111f, 113f
  Department of Justice (DOJ), 110, 110t, 113–116, 114f, 115f
Federal prisons, 305–306
Federal Protective Service, 112
Federal sentencing guidelines, 277–279
Felonies, 33
  lesser, 19f, 20
  serious, 19–20, 19f
Felony murder, 35t
Felony-murder rule, 36
Felson, Marcus, 69
Female offenders, 67, 67–68t
Female police officers, 165, 165f
Feminist theories, 67–68, 67–68t
Fentanyl, 176, 396, 397
Ferdinand I, Emperor, 239
Fetal abduction, 55–56, 63
Field interrogation searches, 188
Field training officer (FTO), 134–135
Fifth Amendment, 391
  application of, 197–199
  lineups and, 199f, 200, 200f
Figueroa, Clarisa, 55–56, 63
Fines, 17
First Amendment, 337
First-degree murder, 35–36, 35t
Fitch, Brian D., 106b
Florida v. Jardines, 196
Flow and functions, criminal justice, 12–18
Focusing the investigation, 147
Forcible rape, 37
Foreman, Percy, 240
Forensic science, 146–147. *See also* Detectives/criminal investigators
  DNA analysis in, 147, 151–152, 151f
  investigative stages and activities in, 147, 147f
  terminology of, 146
Foster, Jodie, 256
Fourteenth Amendment, 283, 337

Fourth Amendment
  arrests with and without a warrant and, 186–187
  electronic surveillance and, 197
  exclusionary rule, 184–185, 185f
  probable cause and, 183–184
  search and seizure in general and, 187
  searches and seizures with and without a warrant and, 188–197
Fox, James Allen, 338b
Freedom of Information Act (FOIA), 166
Front-end, back-end issues in mental health, 172
Front-end duties of probation officers, 356–357
Fuller, Mark, 92b
Furloughs, 365
Furman v. Georgia, 283

Gacy, John Wayne, 258
Gagnon v. Scarpelli, 351
Gallati, Robert, 166
Gall v. United States, 279
Gangs
  prison, 333–334, 333f
  youth, 388–389
Garner, Eric, 214f
Gault, Gerald, 390
Gay, Anthony, 323b
General jurisdiction, 213
General theory of crime, 64
Geneva Conventions, 407
Geo Group, 309
Geriatric inmates, 333
Germann, A. C., 166
Gideon v. Wainwright, 200
Gilbert, W. S., 138
Goffman, Erving, 296
Golden State Killer, 129–130
Gonzales, Jessica, 171b
Google, 174
Gottfredson, Michael, 64
Graham v. Connor, 77, 159
Graham v. Florida, 381
Grand jury, 16, 222–223
Gratuities, 86
Gray, Freddie, 168
Gray, William, 77
Greed and temptation, 87
Green River serial killing cases, 16f
Gregg v. Georgia, 287
Griffin v. Illinois, 251
Guardian vs. soldier distinction of police, 161, 163
Gubernatorial appointment of judges, 242
Guiding hand of counsel, 250–253
Guilty plea, 17
Gun-Free School Zones Act, 410
Gun violence, 10b, 407–410, 408f, 410f
Guzman, Joaquin "El Chapo," 398b

Habeas corpus, 288, 390, 407
Hagan, Frank, 41

Hahn, Kurt, 372
Haiti National Penitentiary, 336b
Halfway houses, 365
Hall, Jennine, 382b
Hamm, Doyle Lee, 285b
Handheld drug-testing devices, 176
Hands-off doctrine, 335
Hands-on doctrine, 335
Hardy, David A., 2
Hate Crime Statistics, 44
Hawkins, Richard, 327
Henry II, 27
Hernandez, Aaron, 19
Heroin, 396
Hierarchy rule, 46, 47
Higgins, Kevin, 232b
Higher education, 132
High security prisons, 306
High-speed pursuits, 170
Hill, Clarence, 284
Hinckley, John, Jr., 256
Hirschi, Travis, 63–64
Hobbes, Thomas, 6f, 7
Holes, Paul, 129
Holmes, James, 19, 257b
Home confinement, 362
Homegrown violent extremists (HVEs), 403
Homicide, 34–37, 35t
    clearance rates for, 151
Honduras, search and seizure in, 195b
Hoover, J. Edgar, 115, 115f
House arrest, 362
House I Live In, The, 299
House of refuge, 374–375
Housing needs and classification of inmates, 302, 306f
Hruska, Jeanne, 280
Human Rights Watch, 160, 164b, 388b
Hunter, Tracie, 239–240

Idealistic contrast, 377, 377t
Illinois Juvenile Court Act, 375
Illinois v. Perkins, 84
Immigration, 410–413, 411f
    asylum and, 412
    border wall and, 411–412
    crime and, 412
Immigration and Customs Enforcement (ICE), 110t, 112, 413b
Impartiality and unbiased decision making, 162
Incapacitation, 267
Incarceration, 17, 20f, 296, 296f. *See also* Correctional organizations; Inmates
    classification of inmates in, 302–303
    conditions of confinement and, 322–323
    deprivations and "pains" of, 321, 321f
    mass, 299–300
    nature of, 320–325
    number of people in, 297, 298f
    probation as alternative to, 344–345
    reasons for decline in, 298–299
    shock, 363–364, 363f

Indeterminate sentences, 17, 274–275
India, police in, 164b
Indigent services, 251–253
Individualized justice of minors, 379
Industrial shop and educational programs, 328
Informants, 149
Initial appearance, 14–16, 220
In loco parentis, 376–377
Inmates. *See also* Correctional organizations; Incarceration
    classification of, 302–303
    Constitutional rights of, 335–338
    crowding of, 322
    female, 330–332
    geriatric, 333
    mentally ill, 332–333
    number of, 297, 298f
    prisonization of, 322
    reentry and aftercare of, 338
    solitary confinement of, 325
Innocence Lost National Initiative, 401
Inquisitorial justice systems, 209b
In re Gault, 390
In re Medley, 325
In re Winship, 391
Intensive supervision probation and parole, 360–362
Intent, 25–26, 31–33, 33f
Intermediate court of appeals (ICA), 214–215
Intermediate sanctions, 360
    boot camps/shock incarceration, 363–364, 363f
    day reporting centers (DRC), 364
    electronic monitoring, 362–363, 362f
    furloughs, 365
    halfway houses, 365
    house arrest, 360–362
    intensive supervision probation and parole, 360
    shock probation/parole, 363
Internal affairs investigator, 88b
International Association of Chiefs of Police (IACP), 43, 83, 125
International terrorism, 403
INTERPOL (International Criminal Police Organization), 112, 113, 113b, 404
Interrogations, 149
In the Belly of the Beast: Letters from Prison, 294
Intoxication defense, 256
Investigations
    clearance rates and, 151
    of cold cases, 153
    crime scenes and, 148–149
    of cybercrimes, 115, 149–150
    DNA analysis in, 147, 151–152, 151f
    stages and activities in, 147, 147f
    uses of informants and interrogations in, 149
Involuntary manslaughter, 35t, 37
IPads, 233
Iraq, juvenile torture in, 388b
"Iron curtain" speech, 337
Islamic law, 140b
Islamic State (ISIS), 388b, 403
Italy, search and seizure in, 195b

Jail administrator, 301b
Jail personnel, 328–329
Jails, 297, 309–313, 310f, 312f
    employment in, 325–329, 326f
    new generation/direct supervision, 311, 312f
    treatment programs in, 311–312
    virtual visits in, 315
    work programs in, 312–313
James, Henry, 286b
J.D.B. v. North Carolina, 391
JDLR, 327
Jefferson, Thomas, 7
Johnson, Barbara Ann, 198
Johnson v. Avery, 336
Johnston, James A., 271
Johnston, Jessica, 361b
Jones, Antoine, 219b
Jones, Brandon, 285b
Jones-El v. Berge, 309
Judges, 21b, 331b
    benefits, training and challenges for, 244–245
    civil liability of, 171b
    courtroom civility and, 246
    discretion used by, 12
    ethics of, 90–91, 93–94
    "good judging" by, 245–246
    introduction to, 240–241
    "investing" in, 244
    misconduct by, 246–248
    politics and, 242–243
    selection of, 241–244, 242f
    Supreme Court, 217–218
Judicial misconduct, 246–248
Jurisdiction
    court, 211
    legal, 31
Jury deliberations and verdict, 230–231
Jury trials, 225–227, 225f, 226f
    jury instructions in, 230
    for juveniles, 391
Justice, procedural, 162
Justice Assistance Act, 312
Justice of the peace (JP), 105
Justifiable homicide, 34
Justification defenses, 254–255
Juvenile court, 375
    recent shift in policy, principles, and processes related to, 379–381
    underlying principles of, 377–378, 377t
Juvenile court counselor, 382b
Juvenile justice, 18, 373–374
    case flow in process of, 383–386, 384f
    goals of, 378–379
    history of, 374–376, 375f, 377f
    introduction to, 374
    judges in, 21b
    new laws related to, 378–379, 380b
    significant court decisions affecting, 389–391
    unique philosophy, principles, and goals in, 376–381, 377t
Juvenile Justice and Delinquency Prevention Act of 1974, 376
Juvenile Justice Reform Act of 2018, 379

Juvenile Law Center, 380
Juvenile life-without-parole (JLWOP) sentences, 380
Juveniles
    aftercare and reentry of, 389
    arrest rates of, 381f
    ban on solitary confinement of, 11, 12
    early laws on justice for, 374–375
    extent and possible causes of offending by, 381–387
    problem of labeling of, 386–387
    school-to-prison pipeline and, 387
    sentences of life without parole for, 380
    status offenses by, 376
    in youth gangs, 388–389

Kania, Richard, 80
Kansas City Preventive Patrol Experiment, 137, 138f
Kant, Immanuel, 79
Katz v. United States, 197
Kelly, R., 19
Kennedy, Robert F., 20–21, 365
Kentucky v. King, 187
Kent v. United States, 389
Kibbe, Barry, 208, 215b
Kibbe v. Henderson, 288
Killer Clown, 258
Killer groupies, 338b
Kimbrough v. United States, 279
King, Robert H., 325
King, Rodney, 170f
Klaas, Polly, 5, 6
Kleinig, John, 80
Knight, Michelle, 59b
Knock and announce cases, 187
Ku Klux Klan, 168
Kushner, Jared, 295

Labeling, problem of, 386–387
Labeling theory, 64
Landis, Kenesaw Mountain, 90
Larceny-theft, 39
Larson, Bambi, 343
La Santé, France, prison, 308b
Las Vegas, 395–396, 396f
Law
    administrative, 28
    antiterrorism, 407
    changes to, 5–6
    city/county, 29
    common, 27
    consensus-versus-conflict debate over, 6–9
    criminal vs. civil, 29–30, 30t
    as determinant of discretionary action, 141–142
    discretion in making and applying, 11–12
    ethics, 90–91
    federal, 28
    gun control, 10b
    immigration, 410–413
    introduction to, 26–27
    juvenile justice, 380, 380b
    marijuana, 8f, 9b, 399
    mens rea and, 31–33

modern-day sources and hierarchy of, 27–29
police enforcement of, 117
Section 1983, 168
sentencing, 276
sex trafficking, 401
"stand your ground," 255b
state, 28
substantive and procedural, 31
three-strikes, 5–6
Law enforcement, 136
Law enforcement careers. *See also* Policing
Central Intelligence Agency (CIA), 116–117
chief of police, 169b
corrections sergeant, 324b
crime analyst, 62b, 65b
crime scene investigator, 148b
in criminal justice flow and process, 12, 13f, 14
criminal justice program director, 49b
discretion used in, 12
FBI Special Agent, 115, 116f
general considerations in considering, 122–124
jail administrator, 301b
juvenile court counselor, 382b
police internal affairs investigator, 88b
police lieutenant, 106b
police officer, 15b, 385b
in prisons and jails, 325–329, 326f
probation and parole officers, 356–359, 359f, 361b
special agent, 191b
warden, 314b, 326–327, 326f
Law Enforcement Code of Ethics (LECE), 83
Law Enforcement Officers Killed and Assaulted, 44
Law schools, 247b
Learning theory, 62–63
Least involvement with the system principle, 378
Legalistic style of policing, 136
Legal jurisdiction, 31
Legislative appointment/election of judges, 242
Legislators, 10b
discretion used by, 11–12
Legitimacy, police, 162
Lemert, Edwin, 64
Lesser felonies, 19f, 20
Lethal injection, 285b, 285f
Leventhal, John, 214f
Levinson, Robert, 302
Lewis Prison Complex riot, 334
Lex talionis, 26f, 27, 266
Liability. *See* Civil liability, police
Life without parole sentences, 380
Lineups, 199f, 200, 200f
Local law enforcement agencies, 119–122, 120f, 121f
basic operations of, 119–120
organization of, 120–122, 120f, 121f
Locard's exchange principle, 147
Locke, John, 6f, 7
Lockett, Clayton D., 285b
Lombroso, Cesare, 58–59, 60f
Lone-wolf terrorists, 403
Low security prisons, 305

Lucas, Mitch, 301b
Luis, Sila, 201
Luis v. United States, 201
Lying, accepted and deviant, 84–86

Mack, Julian, 376
Maconochie, Alexander, 346–347
Madoff, Bernie, 41, 42f, 355b
Madrid v. Gomez, 308–309
Malice aforethought, 35
Manslaughter, 35t, 36–37
involuntary, 37
vehicular, 34b, 36f
voluntary, 36–37
Manson, Charles, 338b
Mapp, Dollree, 185
Mapping, computerized crime, 174f
Mapp v. Ohio, 185
Marijuana
medical and recreational use of, 399
U.S. laws regarding, 8f
worldwide laws on, 9b
Marshall, John, 180
Marsy's Law, 263, 280
Martin, Trayvon, 255b
Martinelli, Thomas, 81
Martinson, Robert, 267
Maryland v. King, 192
Maryland v. Wilson, 193
Mason, Jeff, 210b
Mass incarceration, 299–300
McCulloch v. Maryland, 180
McGuire, Dennis, 285b
McKay, Henry, 61
McKeiver, Joseph, 391
McKeiver v. Pennsylvania, 391
McKinney, James Erin, 287
McNeely, Tyler, 194
Measurement of crime and victimization
crime rate, 44
in England and Wales, 48b
hierarchy rule, 46
National Crime Victimization Survey (NCVS), 42, 47–50
National Incident-Based Reporting System (NIBRS), 47
Uniform Crime Reports (UCR), 42–46, 43f, 45f, 46t
variety of sources for, 42–43
Medical model of punishment, 271–272
Medication-assisted treatment (MAT), 399
Medium security prisons, 306
Mempa v. Rhay, 351
Mens rea, 31–33, 59b, 254, 256, 257b
ladder of homicide and, 35t
Mental illness/insanity defense, 256–258
Mentally ill population, 172–174, 173f
in prisons, 332–333
Merit selection, 241
Methuen fentanyl case, 25–26, 37
Mexican police, 83b
Militarization of police, 163
Military Commissions Act (MCA), 407
Milk, Harvey, 257

Miller v. Alabama, 381
Miller v. Pate, 91
Minimum security prisons, 305
Minnesota v. Dickerson, 193
Minorities in policing, 165, 165f
Minow, Newton N., 54
Miranda, Ernesto, 197–198
Miranda rights, 84, 125, 197f, 199b
   case origin of, 198–199
   decisions eroding, 199
   interrogations and, 149
   of juveniles, 391
Misdemeanors, 19f, 20, 33
Missouri v. McNeely, 194
Mitigating circumstances, 17, 287
M'Naghten Rule, 257
Model Code of Judicial Conduct, 90, 246, 246f
Modus operandi, 146
Morrissey v. Brewer, 353
Mosaic Code, 27
Motion to dismiss, 230
Motive, 31–33
   offenders on, 71–73
Motor vehicle theft, 40
Moyer, Ruth, 273b
Municipal police departments, 119
Murder, 35–36, 35t
   clearance rates for, 151
Murphy, Patrick V., 86
Myth of full enforcement, 140

Nadel, Norbert, 240
Nagel, Amanda, 228f
Narcan/naloxone, 398
National Advisory Commission on Criminal Justice Standards and Goals, 132
National Alliance on Mental Illness, 172
National Crime Information Center (NCIC), 115
National Crime Victimization Survey (NCVS), 42, 47–50
National Drug Court Institute, 227
National Guard, 160
National Incident-Based Reporting System (NIBRS), 47
National Incident Management System (NIMS), 406
National Institute of Justice (NIJ), 149, 311, 333
National Johns Suppression Initiative, 401
National Judicial College, 234
National Security Act of 1947, 116
National Sheriffs' Association, 125
Necessity defense, 254
Negligence, 168
Neoclassical criminology, 57–58
New Dynamics of Mass Incarceration, The, 299
New generation/direct supervision jail, 311, 312f
New Jim Crow, The, 299
New York Police Department (NYPD), 193b
Nicholas, Marsy, 263–264
Noble cause corruption, 81
Noise and nuisance standards, 29
Nolo contendere plea, 16, 223
Nonpartisan election of judges, 242

Northern Nevada Correctional Center, 333
North Korean Gulag, 308b
Norwood, Amos, 243b

Obama, Barack, 11
Ochoa-Lopez, Marlen, 55
O'Connor, Sandra Day, 242
Offenders. *See also* Defendant; Suspect
   adjudication of, 13f, 16–17
   aftercare and reentry of, 338, 389
   arrest of, 13f, 14
   female, 67, 67–68t
   field-research using, 71–73
   habitual, 268b
   incarceration of (*See* Incarceration)
   juvenile, 381–387, 381f
   and pathway through the criminal justice process, 13f, 14
   programming and management technologies for, 315
   restorative justice and, 367, 367f
   risk-need-responsivity (RNR) model and, 366, 366f
   sentencing of, 17
   in supermax prisons, 307–308
Officer's attitude as determinant of discretionary action, 141–142
Olive, Thomas, 208
Omission, 33
Open-field searches, 196
Opening statements, 230
Opioids, 396–399, 397f
Oral job interviews, 81–82
Ordinances, 27–28
   city/county, 29
Organization, definition of, 104
Organizational structure or charts, 120, 120f, 121f
Organized crime, 20–21, 42

Packer, Herbert, 10–11
Paddock, Stephen, 395
Paper on demand (POD), 233
Parens patriae, 375, 376–377
Parker, Bonnie, 115
Parole, 17, 300–302. *See also* Probation
   characteristics of adults on, 351–352t
   effectiveness of, 355, 356f
   eligibility and legal rights in, 351–354
   intensive supervision, 360
   origins of, 346–347
   parole officers and, 356–359, 359f
   shock, 363
Parole officers, 356–359, 359f
Partisan election of judges, 241
Patrol
   effectiveness of, 137, 138f
   evidence-based policing for proactive, 144–145, 144f
   perils of, 137
   state organizations and, 117–118, 117f
Payne v. Tennessee, 279–280
Peel, Robert, 106, 107f, 119, 143, 162
Penitentiary model of punishment, 269–270, 270f
Pennsylvania Board of Probation and Parole decision-making guidelines, 354f

Perils of patrol, 137
Perry, Belvin, Jr., 207
Persons in need of supervision (PINS), 376
Petersilia, Joan, 300
Pinkerton, Allan, 124
Plaintiff, 29, 211
Plain-view searches, 196, 196f
Plato, 9
Plea bargaining, 17, 223–225
Police careers. *See* Law enforcement careers
Police internal affairs investigator, 88b
Police legitimacy, 162
Police lieutenant, 106b
Police recruits
    characteristics of potential, 131
    college education of, 132–133
    field training officer (FTO) and, 134–135
    hiring process for, 131, 132f
    introduction to, 130
    oral job interviews of, 81–82
    screening methods for, 131, 131f
    training of, 133, 133–134t, 134f
Police use of force, 157–158, 170f
    Black Lives Matter and, 160
    brutality and, 165–166
    civil liability in (*See* Civil liability, police)
    defined, 158–159
    introduction to, 158
    police as "guardians" or "soldiers" question in, 161
    as a sacred trust, 158–166
Policing, 103
    accepted and deviant lying in, 84–86
    accepting gratuities in, 86
    body-worn cameras in, 166
    careers in (*See* Law enforcement careers)
    civil liability in, 166–174
    code of silence in, 82–83
    community, 143–145, 143f, 144f
    consent decree and, 164–165
    constitutional, 161–162
    corruption in, 82, 83b
    defining the role in, 135–138
    developing harmony, justice, and policy with, 163
    development of, in the United States, 107–110
    English and colonial roots of, 104–107
    ethics in, 78, 81–90
    evidence-based, 144–145, 144f
    by federal agencies, 110–117
    four basic tasks of, 136–137
    future of, 407
    greed and temptation in, 87
    as "guardians" or "soldiers," 161, 163
    Hippocratic Oath for, 89b
    introduction to, 104
    Law Enforcement Code of Ethics (LECE) and, 83–84
    by local agencies, 119–122, 120f, 121f
    mentally ill population and, 172–174, 173f
    militarization of, 163
    more women and minorities in, 165
    perils of, 137
    policies regarding conduct in, 85
    private, 124–126, 125f
    procedural justice in, 162
    random acts of kindness in, 87–90
    reforms to, 107
    by state agencies, 117–118
    stressors in, 138–140, 139f
    technologies in, 174–176
    three distinctive styles of, 136
    use of discretion in, 140–143
    working personality in, 135, 166
    work of forensics and detectives in, 145–153
Policing role, 135–138
Policing styles, 135–136
Policy making influence of courts, 209–211
Political era in policing, 1840s–1930s, 107
Politics and judges, 242–243
Polling the jury, 231
Positivist criminology, 58, 58f
Positivist school, 58
Posse Comitatus Act of 1878, 407
Posttrial motions, 231
Pound, Roscoe, 90
Powell v. Alabama, 200
Practitioner's perspective. *See* Law enforcement careers
Pregnancy Discrimination Act, 67
Preliminary hearing, 16, 222
Preliminary investigation, 147
Premeditation and deliberation, 35
Prendez, Priscilla, 251f
President's Commission on Law Enforcement and Administration of Justice, 12, 345
President's Task Force on 21st Century Policing, 156, 159
Presumption of innocence, 378
Pretrial motions, 227
Pretrial processes, 14–16
    arraignment in, 16–17, 223
    bail in, 221–222, 221f
    booking in, 220
    discovery, 227
    diversion programs/problem-solving courts, 227–228
    initial appearance in, 14–16, 220
    jury selection, 225, 226f
    plea bargaining in, 17, 223–225
    preliminary hearing or grand jury in, 16, 222
    pretrial motions, 227
Price v. Johnston, 323
Principle of double effect, 81
Prison gangs, 333–334, 333f
Prison industries, 304
Prisonization, 322
Prison Rape Elimination Act of 2003, 329–330
Prisons, 297
    drug interdiction and treatment in, 330
    employment in, 325–329, 326f
    federal, 305–306
    gangs in, 333–334, 333f
    geriatric inmates in, 332

governance of, 329–335
mentally ill inmates in, 332–333
private, 309
rehabilitation in, 305
riots in, 334–335, 334f
sexual violence and coercion in, 329
state, 303–305, 303f
supermax, 307–309, 307f
virtual visits in, 315
wardens in, 314b
women in, 330–332
world's worst, 308b
Privacy, 196
  electronic surveillance and, 197
Private police, 124–126, 125f
Private prisons, 309
Privatization of corrections, 309
Probable cause, 183–184
Probation, 17. *See also* Parole
  as alternative to incarceration, 344–345
  defined, 344
  effectiveness of, 355, 356f
  eligibility and legal rights in, 347–351
  intensive supervision, 360
  number of adults on, 347, 348t
  origins of, 345–346
  Pennsylvania Board of Probation and Parole decision-making guidelines, 354f
  probation officers and, 356–359, 359f
  revocation of, 351
  shock, 363
  terms and conditions of, 350b
Probation officers, 356–359, 359f, 361b
Problem analysis triangle, 69, 69f, 144f
Problem-solving courts, 227–228
Procedural justice, 162
Procedural law, 31
Procunier v. Martinez, 337
Program classification of inmates, 302
Progressive model of punishment, 271
Prohibition, 271
Property crime, 39–40
Proposition 47, California, 298
Proprietary services, 125
Prosecution, 14–16
  case presentation by, 230
  initial appearance and, 14–16
  preliminary hearing or grand jury in, 16
Prosecution rebuttal, 230
Prosecutorial immunity and misconduct, 249
Prosecutors, 39
  discretion used by, 12
  ethics of, 91
  as gatekeeper of justice system, 248–249
  prosecutorial immunity and misconduct and, 249
Protection of the innocent by law enforcement, 137
Proximate cause, 170
Public defenders, 251
Public health and safety laws, 29
Public order crimes, 40

Punishment, 231. *See also* Correctional organizations; Sentencing
  factors influencing, 268–269
  introduction to, 266
  models, methods, and reforms in, 269–272, 270f
  purposes of, 266–274
  reentry and aftercare after, 338
  that fits the crime, 272–274

Quakers, 375, 375f
Quintero, Richard Lee, 172

Racketeer Influenced and Corrupt Organizations (RICO) statute, 42
Radicalization, 403, 404b
Rahr, Susan, 161
Random acts of kindness in policing, 87–90
Rape, 37
Reagan, Ronald, 256
Reasonable doubt, 30
Reasonable suspicion, 192–193
Recidivism, 18, 305
  probation and parole effectiveness and, 355, 356f
  risk-need-responsivity (RNR) model and, 366, 366f
Reckless driving, 34b
Reconstructing the crime, 147
Reentry and aftercare, 338, 389
Reformatories (juvenile), 375
Reformatory model of punishment, 270–271
Reform era in policing, 1930s–1980s, 107–109
Reforms, police, 107
Rehabilitation, 267, 300f, 326
  in jails, 311–312
  in prisons, 305
Reintegrative shaming, 387
Reitz, Kevin R., 358b
Relative ethics, 80
Religious beliefs and First Amendment rights, 337, 337f
Rent control, 29
Respondeat superior, 168
Restitution, 17
Restorative justice, 366f, 367
Retribution, 266, 326
Revocation of probation, 351
Rhode, Brandon, 285b
Rhodes, David, 196
Rice, Tamir, 168
Ridgway, Gary Leon, 16f
Right to counsel, 200–201
Right-wrong test, 257
Riley, David, 181–182, 185, 192
Riots, prison, 334–335, 334f
Risk-need-responsivity (RNR) model, 365–367, 366f
Robbery, 38, 38f
  motive for, 71–72
Roberts, John, 192
Robina Institute of Criminal Law and Criminal Justice, 358b
Roe v. Wade, 9
Rogers, D. J., 65b
Roper v. Simmons, 381
Roth, Steve, 256
Rousseau, Jean-Jacques, 7f, 9

Routine activity theory, 69
Ruffin, Woody, 335–336
Ruiz, David, 272
Rule of four, 219
Russo, Michael, 59b

Salinas v. Texas, 199b
Sanctions, 17
Sanders, Scott, 14f
Saudi Arabia, police patrol in, 140b
Sayoc, Cesar, 403
Schmitt, Shirley, 319
School shootings, 407–410, 408f, 410f
School-to-prison pipeline, 387
Search and seizure, 182
   around the world, 195b
   of automobiles, 194–195
   consent to search and, 188, 196–197
   in general, 187
   incident to lawful arrest, 188
   plain-view and open-field, 196, 196f
   in prisons, 331, 332f
   probable cause for, 183–184
   stop-and-frisk, 192–194, 192f
   warrants for, 183
   with and without a warrant, 188–197
Second-degree murder, 35t, 36
Second Treatise on Civil Government, 7
Secret Service, 112
Section 1983, 168
Security needs and classification of inmates, 302
Security officers, private, 125, 125f
Self-defense, 254
Senior Structured Living Program (SSLP), 333
Sentencing, 231. *See also* Punishment
   aggravating or mitigating circumstances and, 17
   in Australia, 276b
   capital punishment (*See* Capital punishment)
   concurrent and consecutive, 275–276
   criminal appeals and, 287–288
   federal guidelines on, 277–279
   guidelines for, 276–279, 278t
   of habitual offenders, 268b
   indeterminate vs. determinate, 18
   of juveniles, 380
   state-level guidelines on, 278t, 279
   types of sentences and, 274–275
   victim impact statements and, 279–280, 280b
Sentencing Project, The, 380
September 11, 2001, terrorist attack, 110
Serious felonies, 19–20, 19f
Service style of policing, 136
Sex trafficking, 399–401
Sexual assault, 37–38
   and coercion in prisons, 329
Sgroi, Sandra, 214f
Shakespeare, William, 128
Shaw, Clifford, 61
Shaw, George Bernard, 262
Sheldon, William, 59, 61f

Sheriffs
   county offices of, 119–120
   English history of, 104–105
Sherman, Lawrence, 144
Sherman Antitrust Act, 40
Shock incarceration, 363–364, 363f
Shock probation/parole, 363
Simon, Rita, 67
Simple Art of Murder, The, 128
Simpson, O. J., 19, 30, 32
Sine qua non, 78
Situational action theory, 71b
Situational crime prevention, 70, 70t
Sixth Amendment, 200–201, 225, 277
Sixth sense, 133
Skolnick, Jerome, 135, 166
"Slave of the state," 335–336
Slippery slope, 84
Smith, Ronald Bert, Jr., 285b
Smollett, Jussie, 82f
Sobriety checkpoints, 187, 187f, 188f
Social conflict theories, 65–66
Social disorganization theory, 61
Social process theories of criminal behavior, 62–64
Social structure theories of criminal behavior, 60–62
Socrates, 239
Solitary confinement, 325
Son of Sam killer, 258
South Africa, search and seizure in, 195b
Southern Ohio Correctional Facility riot, 334
Southern Poverty Law Center, 248
Special agent, 191b
Special-purpose state agencies, 119
Speedy Trial Act of 1974, 229
Stamper, Norm, 133
Standing, 220
"Stand your ground" laws, 255b
Stare decisis, 27
State bureaus of investigation (SBIs), 118
State common law, 28
State constitutional law, 28
State court system, 208, 212–215, 212t, 214f
   incoming caseloads 2007–2016, 214f
   judge selection in, 241–242, 242f
State law, 28
State law enforcement agencies, 117–118
State-level sentencing guidelines, 278t, 279
State police, 117, 117f
State prisons, 303–305, 303f
State statutes, 28
State v. Kibbe, 215b
Status offenses, 376
Statutes, 27
   driving, 34b
   federal, 28
   state, 28
Statutory law, 27
Stewart, Martha, 41
Stewart, Potter, 76
Stop-and-frisk searches, 188, 192–194, 192f

Stored Communications Act, 181
Strain theory, 61–62, 63f
Stress in police work, 138–139, 139f
    coping with, 139
    criminal justice system as source of, 139
    intrinsic, 139
    organizational and administrative practices as source of, 138–139
    the public as source of, 139
Strickland v. Washington, 250
Strieff, Edward Joseph, Jr., 185
Suboxone, 399
Substantive law, 31
Substantive violations, 349, 353
Supermax prisons, 307–309, 307f
Supreme Court, the, 29f, 219f. *See also* Federal court system
    on abortion, 9
    administration of, 220
    on capital punishment, 283
    conferences and workload, 218–220
    on electronic surveillance, 197
    on exigent circumstances, 186
    judges and advocacy, 217–218
    on juvenile justice, 389–391
    on lawful incarceration, 323
    on *Miranda* warnings, 198
    on prisoners' rights, 335–338
    on privacy and searches, 196
    on probable cause, 184
    on reasonable suspicion, 192
    on right to counsel, 200
    on sobriety checkpoints, 187, 187f
    on speedy trial, 229
    stare decisis and, 27
    on use of force, 158–159
    on vehicle searches, 194–195
Suspects. *See also* Defendants; Offenders
    arrest of, 13f, 14
    booking of, 220
    DNA identification of, 147
    duty of care for, 170
    initial appearance of, 14–16, 220
    linking victims to, 146
    preliminary hearing or grand jury and, 16
Sutherland, Edwin, 62–63
Swift justice, 228
Sykes, Gresham, 321, 322

Tablets, 233
Tasks of policing, 136–137
Tate, Sharon, 338b
Technical violations, 349, 353
Technologies
    in correctional organizations, 313–315
    in the courts, 233–234, 233f
    cybercrime and, 115, 149–150, 403–406
    electronic monitoring (EM), 362–363, 362f
    policing and, 174–176
Tehan v. U.S. ex rel. Shott, 209
Temporary protection order (TPO), 30
Temptation and greed, 87
Tensing, Ray, 227f

Terrell, Brian Keith, 285b
Terrorism, 110, 115, 395–396, 396f
    bio-, 406
    cyber, 403–406
    definition and types of, 401–403
    federal efforts against, 406–407
    international, 402f, 403
    laws addressing, 407
    radicalization and, 403, 404b
    right-wing extremists and lone-wolf, 403
Terry Stop, 193
Testimony, witness, 147
Test of common sense, 95
Test of foresight, 96
Test of hurting someone else, 96
Test of one's best self, 95
Test of one's most admired personality, 96
Test of publicity, 95
Textalyzer, 176
Texting while driving, 175–176
Theft, 39
Theoretical paradigms of criminality, 56
Thew, Zack, 88b
Three Prisons Act of 1891, 271
Three-strike law, 5–6
Torres, Esther, 325f
Torts, 168
Total institutions, 296
Tower officers, 328
Trafficking Victims Protection Act of 2000 (TVPA), 400–401
Training, police
    academy, 133, 133–134t
    field training officer (FTO) and, 134–135
Trait theories of criminal behavior, 58–60, 60f
Transparency and openness of process, 162
Transportation Security Administration (TSA), 112
Trial, 17
    basic purpose of, 208
    burden of proof in, 29–30
    defenses in, 253–258
    delay of, 228–229
    discovery and, 227
    jury, 225–227, 225f, 226f, 391
    of juveniles, 391
    pretrial motions and, 227
    protocols of, 230–231
    reasonable doubt in, 30
    right to speedy, 228–229
Trial courts
    major, 213
    state, 212
Trump, Donald, 309, 403, 412
Tsarnaev, Dzhokhar, 19
Tully, Edward, 87
Turner, Brock Allen 280b
Turner v. Safley, 331
T visa, 401

Unbiased decision making, 162
Undocumented immigrants, 410

Uniform Crime Reports (UCR), 42–46, 43f, 383
   limitations of, 46t
United States Constitution, 417–418
United States v. Booker, 277
UN Office on Drugs and Crime, 295–296
Urban Institute, 362
Uruguay, 9b
USA PATRIOT Act, 407
Use of force. *See* Police use of force
U.S. Marshals Service (USMS), 116
U.S. v. Jones, 194
Utilitarianism, 80

Vaughn Correctional Center riot, 334
Vehicle pursuits, 170–171
Vehicles
   autonomous, 175
   searches of, 194–195, 194f
Vehicular manslaughter, 34b, 36f
Venezuela, crime in, 118b
Vera Institute of Justice, 299
Verro, Michael, 49b
Vicarious liability, 168
Vick, Michael, 218f, 226b
Victim advocates, 249b
Victim impact statements, 279–280, 280b
Victor, Daniel, 407
Videoconferencing, 233, 233f, 315
Virtual visit technologies, 315
Vladimir Central Prison, Russia, 308b
Voice, 162
Vold, George B., 66
Vollmer, August, 108–109, 108f, 109f, 131
Voltaire, 26
Voluntary manslaughter, 35t, 36–37

Walker, Samuel, 18
Wallace, Herman, 325
Walnut Street Jail, 270f
Wardens, 314b, 326–327, 326f
Warrants, 183
   arrests with and without, 186–187
   form for federal court search and seizure, 189–190f
   search and seizure with and without, 188–197

Watchman style of policing, 136
Waukesha County, Wisconsin, day reporting center, 364b
Weapons and probation/parole officers, 359
Wedding cake model of criminal justice, 18–20, 19f
Weeks v. United States, 185
Welfare tasks of police, 136–137
Westley, William, 130, 135
Whistleblower Protection Act, 93
White, Dan, 257
White-collar crime, 40–42, 355b
Wikström, Olof H., 71b
Williams, Alexander, 165
Williams, Jeri, 169b
Williams, Terrance, 243b
Williams v. Florida, 225
Wilmott, Kevin, 15b
Wilson, Darren, 222, 223f
Wilson, James Q., 136, 281
Witness testimony, 147
Wolff v. McDonnell, 337
Women
   in policing, 165, 165f
   in prison, 330–332
Women and Crime, 67
Wood, Joseph R., 285b
Woodfox, Albert, 325
Work detail supervisors, 328
Working personality of police, 135, 166
Work in jails, 312–313
Workload, Supreme Court, 218–220
World Health Organization, 329
Writ of certiorari, 215
Writ of habeas corpus, 288, 390, 407
Wrongful convictions, 285–287
Wubbels, Alex, 77

XYY chromosome, 59–60

Yard officers, 328
Youth gangs, 388–389

Zeigler, Terry, 161
Zimbardo, Philip, 320, 320f
Zimmerman, George, 255b

POLICING | COURTS

CRIME OBSERVED AND REPORTED → **INVESTIGATION**

INVESTIGATION → **ARREST** or **UNSOLVED/NO ARREST**

ARREST → **BOOKING** → Released (or) → **CHARGES FILED** → Prosecutor rejects case

CHARGES FILED → **INITIAL APPEARANCE** → Charges Dismissed

INITIAL APPEARANCE → Preliminary Hearing / Grand Jury → Charges Dismissed (or) → Bail/Detention Hearing → **INFORMATION OR INDICTMENT** → **ARRAIGNMENT** → Charges Dismissed / Diversion Program

ARRAIGNMENT → Pleads Not Guilty / Pleads Guilty

Pleads Not Guilty → **PLEA BARGAIN** → **TRIAL** → Jury Selection → Acquitted / Convicted → Victim/Witness Impact Statement

Police Agencies

FEDERAL AGENCIES
- Department of Homeland Security
- Department of Justice
- Other Federal Agencies With Law Enforcement Authority

STATE AGENCIES
- State Bureaus of Investigation
- State Police and Highway Patrol Agencies
- Special-Purpose (e.g., Campus-, Wildlife-, and Alcohol-Related) Agencies

LOCAL AGENCIES
- County Police Departments
- Municipal Police Departments

PRIVATE POLICE

NOTE: This chart gives a simplified view of caseflow through the criminal justice system. Procedures vary among jurisdictions.